FLORIDA STATE
UNIVERSITY LIBRARIES

JUL 0 3 2001

TALLAHASSEE, FLORIDA

Advances in
Self-Organization

Published by Economica Ltd.
9 Wimpole Street
London W1M 8LB

© *Economica Ltd., 1998*

All rights reserved

First published 1998

Printed in France

Jacques Lesourne & André Orléan, Editors

Advances in Self-Organization
and
Evolutionary Economics

ISBN 1-902282-00-0

Advances in Self-Organization and Evolutionary Economics

edited by

Jacques Lesourne

*Laboratoire d'Économétrie,
Conservatoire National des Arts et Métiers, France*

and

André Orléan

CREA, Ecole Polytechnique and CNRS, France

ECONOMICA
London • Paris • Genève

ACKNOWLEDGEMENTS

Financial support from the CNRS (program on "Innovation Management, Public Policies on Science and Technology and Knowledge Appropriation") and from the Conservatoire National des Arts et Métiers is greatly appreciated.

We thank Marie-France Hanseler for her administrative support, Sophie Bernier, Jeannine Daste and Christine Leite for their secretarial and organizational assistance and Gilbert Laffond and François Moreau for their editorial supervision.

Finally, we thank all the participants at the conference whose presentations and discussions made this volume possible.

Jacques Lesourne

André Orléan

CONTRIBUTORS

Paul Bourgine	CREA, Ecole Polytechnique, France
Uwe Cantner	Department of Economics, University of Augsburg, Germany
Olivier Chenevez	Laboratoire de Physique Statistique, Ecole Normale Supérieure, France
Patrick Cohendet	BETA, University Louis Pasteur, Strasbourg, France
Jean-Michel Dalle	IEPE-CNRS and Ecole Normale Supérieure de Cachan, France
Giovanni Dosi	Department of Economics, University of Rome "la Sapienza", Italy, and IIASA, Austria
Gunnar Eliasson	Royal Institute of Technology, Stockholm, Sweden
Giorgo Fagiolo	European University Institute, Florence, Italy
Emmanuelle Fauchart	Laboratoire d'Econométrie, Conservatoire National des Arts et Métiers, France
Dominique Foray	IRIS, IMRI, CNRS, University of Paris-Dauphine, France
Horst Hanusch	Department of Economics, University of Augsburg, Germany
Dorothea Herreiner	University of Bonn, Germany
Francis Kern	BETA, University Louis Pasteur, Strasbourg, France
Karim Kilani	Laboratoire d'Econométrie, Conservatoire National des Arts et Métiers, France
Alan Kirman	GREQAM EHESS and University of Aix-Marseille III, France
Gilbert Laffond	Laboratoire d'Econométrie, Conservatoire National des Arts et Métiers, France
Jean-François Laslier	CNRS and THEMA, University of Cergy-Pontoise, France
Jacques Lesourne	Laboratoire d'Econométrie, Conservatoire National des Arts et Métiers, France
Babak Mehmanpazir	BETA, University Louis Pasteur, Strasbourg, France
Francis Munier	BETA, University Louis Pasteur, Strasbourg, France
Jean-Pierre Nadal	Laboratoire de Physique Statistique, Ecole Normale Supérieure, France
André Orléan	CREA, Ecole Polytechnique and CNRS, France
André de Palma	THEMA, University of Cergy-Pontoise, France
Andreas Pyka	Department of Economics, University of Augsburg, Germany
Pier-Paolo Saviotti	INRA-SERD, University Pierre-Mendes-France, Grenoble, France
Gerald Silverberg	MERIT, University of Maastricht, The Netherlands

Richard Topol	*CNRS and Observatoire Français des Conjonctures Economiques, France*
Hélène Tordjman	*CREA, Ecole Polytechnique and CREI, University of Paris-Nord, France*
Gisèle Umbhauer	*BETA, University Louis Pasteur, Strasbourg, France*
Bart Verspagen	*MERIT, University of Maastricht, The Netherlands*
Bernard Walliser	*CERAS, Ecole Nationale des Ponts et Chaussées, and CREA, Ecole Polytechnique, France*
Gérard Weisbuch	*Laboratoire de Physique Statistique, Ecole Normale Supérieure, France*

CONTENTS

	Acknowledgements	IV
	Contributors	V
	Introduction	1
	Jacques Lesourne and André Orléan	
1	Evolution: History, Change and Progress	9
	Hélène Tordjman	

Part 1 Consumers and Firms Behaviors: from Heterogeneity to Mimetism

2	Informational Influences and the Ambivalence of Imitation	39
	André Orléan	
3	How Network Externalities Affect Product Variety	57
	André de Palma, Karim Kilani and Jacques Lesourne	
4	Routines, Structures of Governance and Knowledge-Creating Processes	77
	Patrick Cohendet, Francis Kern, Babak Mehmanpazir and Francis Munier	
5	Technological Evolution and Firm Behavior	92
	Pier Paolo Saviotti	
6	Pushing Technological Progress Forward: a Comparison of Firm Strategies	114
	Uwe Cantner, Horst Hanusch and Andreas Pyka	

Part 2 Markets' Self-Organization

7	A Formal Approach to Market Organization: Choice Functions, Mean Field Approximation and Maximum Entropy Principle	149
	Jean-Pierre Nadal, Gerard Weisbuch, Olivier Chenevez and Alan Kirman	
8	Market Organization	160
	Gerard Weisbuch, Alan Kirman and Dorothea Herreiner	
9	Risk Aversion and Emergence of a Wholesale Market	183
	Gilbert Laffond and Jacques Lesourne	

Part 3 Dynamics of Technological Systems

10 Survival and Exit in Markets: Assessing the Respective Role of Supply and Demand Effects 197
Emmanuelle Fauchart

11 Errors and Mistakes in Technological Systems: from Potential Regret to Path Dependent Inefficiency 217
Dominique Foray

12 Local Interaction Stuctures, Heterogeneity and the Diffusion of Technological Innovations 240
Jean-Michel Dalle

Part 4 Evolutionary Approaches to Economic Growth

13 Economic Growth as an Evolutionary Process 265
Gerald Silverberg and Bart Verspagen

14 On the Micro Foundations of Economic Growth 296
Gunnar Eliasson

15 Exploring the Unknown. On Entrepreneurship, Coordination and Innovation-Driven Growth 308
Giovanni Dosi and Giorgio Fagiolo

Part 5 Evolutionary Game Theory

16 Discrete Evolutionary Processes: Stationary Probabilities, Strategic Asymmetries and Learning Schemes 353
Gisèle Umbauher

17 Behavioral Learning 379
Jean-François Laslier, Richard Topol and Bernard Walliser

18 The Compromise between Exploration and Exploitation: from Decision Theory to Game Theory 397
Paul Bourgine

INTRODUCTION

by Jacques LESOURNE and André ORLÉAN

A revolution in the field of microeconomic theory is on its way. This movement relies on two complementary concepts: self-organisation and evolution.

These two concepts share 3 concerns:

1. They focus on economic systems which evolve autonomously in the course of time and are essentially concerned with the dynamics of these systems.

2. They consider agents who have imperfect knowledge of the environment and adopt rules of conduct of limited or procedural rationality.

3. They recognize the role of uncertainty which affect the environment, the information and the decisions of agents.

Thus a perspective of analysis which deeply renews the field and the tools of traditional microeconomics is emerging. While microeconomics is mainly concerned with the way fully rational agents reach an equilibrium, the approach supported in this book sets the dynamics of interaction between heterogeneous and partially ignorant agents as its central subject. From this viewpoint, whether it relies on evolutionism or self-organization, economic interaction is understood as an open relationship through which agents and society evolve. For that reason, our models are fundamentally dynamic, not only because they analyze evolutions and temporal movements, but also because they consider that these evolutions lead to qualitative transformations which modify individuals and social structures. This appears in the emphasis laid on learning.

Three points are strategically at stake in our modelling: to understand how information is produced and conveyed; how individuals acquire knowledge; and how beliefs and collective representations are formed. Knowledge is not an exogenous datum that individuals could freely dispose of. Instead, the matter is to analyze its accumulation as a result of interactions. To deal with this fundamental dimension of coordination, this book puts forward various formalisms. The abundance of hypotheses which are offered must thereby be underlined. The interest lies in imitation, routines, innovative behaviours, the exploration/exploitation dilemma, the role of beliefs, the distribution of knowledge... The analysis is always dynamic: the emergence of a stable system of coordination is the result of a collective learning process which provides agents and groups with necessary information and suitable beliefs.

This dynamic dimension is also applied to social forms: interactions studied in this book lead to qualitative transformations of interaction structures. This is actually a decisive point. According to us, economic dynamics cannot be reduced to a dynamics of prices and quantities, even if one should not underestimate their importance. Imagining economic evolution is also making intelligible the deep changes market or firm organizations face every day. One will find in this book a lot of examples about such a preoccupation. Thus, interest is shown in market structures (endogenous evolution of the variety of products and qualities, establishing preferential links between some buyers and some sellers) as well as in the organization of firms (technological choices, forms of management...). Such microfoundations lead to an approach to macroeconomic growth stressing the existence of various growth regimes characterized by distinct forms of competition and innovation.

At a purely formal level, the models developed here widely resorts to stochastic processes. The notion of unknown factors has indeed a central role in our understanding of evolution, whether through innovation, brutal changes of strategies or mistakes. This hypothesis, combined with the existence of non linear relations, opens into a catalogue which contains a great deal of possible dynamics: the latter can lead to path-dependent states, to convergence (or not) towards one or several stable states, to innumerable endogenous fluctuations, to chaotic attractors, to transitions of phase, to non-ergodicity, etc.

This constitutes the presentation of the wide field of common preoccupations federating evolutionary and self-organizational approaches. Yet, these two concepts differ in the importance given to these various preoccupations:

– Self-organization is mainly concerned with the emergence in the course of time of "structures" (in the most general sense of the word) which were not existing before: a price, a new market, a union,...

– Evolutionism tackles in a more general way changes likely to occur (the elimination of one technology by another, the appearance of new behaviours,...).

It is then possible to consider that self-organization processes constitute a subset of evolutionary processes.

The Centre de Recherche en Epistémologie Appliquée (CREA) at the Ecole Polytechnique and the Laboratoire d'Econométrie du Conservatoire National des Arts et Métiers (CNAM) which have been working together on these themes for several years organized an international conference on these topics in Paris on September 30th and October 1st 1996. It is from the papers which were given on that occasion that this collective book was compiled.

Articles have been logically grouped together in five parts which we are going to present, but we have put at the head of the book the text by Helene Tordjman (*Evolution in Economics: History, Change and Progress*) which examines modern evolutionary economic theories from the viewpoint of selection and variation. After underlining, following Nelson and Winter (1982), that evolution in economics is more Lamarckian than Darwinian, she recalls that complex processes of selection and interaction lead to unpredictable aggregate outcomes; the "chosen" path results from a combination between the inertial trends given by different kinds of collective and socially constructed norms and institutions on one hand and the novelty characterizing learning on the other hand. Two questions then seem to be extremely important for her: the first one is the open-endedness of the dynamics, i.e. its fundamentally contingent nature. The second is about the fact of hierarchical selection and its consequences on the definition of individuality and autonomy.

Then the first part opens: it deals with the behaviours of consumers and firms and consists of six chapters.

The text by André Orléan (*Informational Influences and the Ambivalence of Imitation*) emphasizes the role played by imitation in decentralized collective learning. Imitation is often thought of as an irrational behaviour which is responsible for pathological dynamics such as financial bubbles. A. Orléan shows that such a statement is not always true. Indeed, when private information is noisy, individuals can improve their performance in taking into account the way others behave, but imitation is ambivalent because it can improve collective performance only if the propension to imitate is not too strong: obviously, if everybody is imitating everybody, imitation becomes unproductive.

The following chapter by Andre de Palma, Karim Kilani and Jacques Lesourne (*How Network Externalities Affect Product Variety*) develops a dynamic model in order to see how network externalities affect market performance, when products are horizontally differentiated. Two parameters are introduced to represent respectively consumer heterogeneity and externality effects. The model points out that, with constant prices, a unique equilibrium is reached where diversity prevails, as soon as the heterogeneity parameter is greater than the externality parameter. Otherwise, the dynamics of adoption leads to a natural monopoly but, in this case, history matters since the selected product is not known in advance. However, when the price dynamics is taken into account, price reaction tends to sustain diversity instead of standardization.

In the article by Patrick Cohendet, Francis Kern, Babak Mehmanpazir and Francis Munier (*Routines, Structures of Governance and Knowledge-creating Processes*) analysis moves towards firms and their resort to routines to master the tension that exists between centralization and decentralization in learning processes. To that extent, routines are used to link individual autonomy which is the source of disorder, ambiguity, but also of creativity with incentives and constraints which insure the coherence of the set and which at the same time can cause sclerosis. They constitute governing mechanisms of the distribution of knowledge within the organization.

The part ends with a text by Uwe Cantner, Horst Hanusch and Andreas Pyka (*Pushing Technological Progress forward, a Comparison of Firm Strategies*).

4 | Introduction

Authors intend to establish comparisons between the performances of firms which adopt three different routines of innovative behaviour: an absorptive strategy where the ability to use technological spillovers plays the central role, a conservative strategy which relies only on firms own research efforts, and an imitative strategy which tries to catch up by imitating best-practice technologies. Firms take part in dynamic oligopolistic competition where they influence each other. One of the robust results of the simulations carried out is that the absorptive strategy dominates in the medium and long-run with respect to technological as well as economic performance.

The second part of the book no longer lays the emphasis on actors but on markets and phenomena of self-organisation.

Chapter 7 (*A Formal Approach to Market Organisation: Choice Functions, Mean Field Approximation and Maximum Entropy Principle*) written by Jean Pierre Nadal, Olivier Chenevez, Alan Kirman and Gerard Weisbuch is concerned with the way preferential links between a buyer and a seller can be established in a market composed of several buyers and sellers. It is supposed that these buyers only learn from their personal experience, and the influence of choice functions adopted by buyers are studied. In particular circumstances, two categories of buyers come out: those who select the visited seller at random and those who have a marked preference for particular sellers.

The following article by Gérard Weisbuch, Alan Kirman and Dorothea Herreiner (*Market Organisation*) is closely linked to the preceding one. This article models the emergence of an organization on a market of perishable goods. The model introduces preferential choices of sellers by buyers, according to fidelity parameters specific to buyer and seller pairs depending upon the previous history of transactions between partners. The article shows that buyers become either faithful partners or searchers. These results are compared to empirical data from the Marseille wholesale fish market.

Then comes an article by Gilbert Laffond and Jacques Lesourne (*Risk Aversion and Emergence of a Wholesale Market*). The chapter studies the dynamics of a self-organizing market on which the producers have the possibility to sell exclusively to the final consumers or to sell also to other producers at a reduced price. The producers with a low risk aversion may find convenient to buy the production of other producers and to sell it on the retail market while producers with a high risk aversion may decide to propose their supply to producers only. Of course, the risk aversion parameter of a producer is not given, but adapts to past experiments. Under the assumptions introduced, it is shown that the retail market always converges to the same price while a wholesale market emerges on which a unique price prevails depending on history. Links on this market may be interpreted as giving birth to firms.

The third part of the book tackles a theme dear to evolutionary economics: the dynamics of technological systems.

The first text by Emmanuelle Fauchart (*Survival and Exit in Markets: Assessing the Perspective Role of Supply and Demand Effects*) tackles the problem of the conditions of survival of firms, conditions which are the consequence of interaction between supply and demand. These conditions can give birth to logics of selection based either on differential abilities and strategies of firms in providing good and innovative products and services or on interdependence of customer choices in valuing the utility and performance of the competing options. These logics of selection give birth to two categories of market dynamics; one is driven by supply, the other by demand. Mixed dynamics can naturally exist.

Dominique Foray (*Errors and Mistakes in Technological Systems: from Potential Regret to Path Dependent Inefficiency*) addresses the issue of path-dependent selection and inefficiency. His message is that the theoretical argument to prove path-dependence inefficiency is relatively straightforward while empirical demonstrations, as well as the analysis of welfare implications are much more difficult. He synthesizes the most interesting historical studies which get "potential regret" results and asks whether these results suggest a large welfare loss.

In the last paper of this part, Jean-Michel Dalle (*Local Interaction Structures, Heterogeneity and the Diffusion of Technological Innovations*) analyzes diffusion processes with a stochastic aggregation model in which both the heterogeneity of agents and the existence of a local interaction structure are taken into account in a framework compatible with imperfect information and bounded rationality. Simulation experiments are presented, the results of which fit with the main facts described in the empirical literature on technological diffusion. It is shown that technological niches and enclaves always appear during diffusion processes and play a crucial role in shaping diffusion paths of technologies.

The fourth part is at the limit of microeconomics and macroeconomics, by grouping together three articles on the theme of evolutionary approaches to economic growth.

Gerald Silverberg and Bart Verspagen (*Economic Growth: an Evolutionary Perspective*) aim at elaborating an evolutionary theory of economic growth. To that end, they build a model including the formalization of selection, technical change and behavioural learning. This model is made up of three blocks: the first describes the evolution of the economy for a given group of technologies and firms (the selection being produced at both levels); the second introduces the rules which control the entry of technologies and firms in the economy; the third specifies the probability – for an individual firm – to achieve innovation. According to the authors, the model demonstrates that a bounded rationality approach to the theory of the firm coupled with an evolutionary framework for analyzing market selection and collective learning, does yield dividends in terms of explaining how identifiable patterns emerge from *profit-seeking* (and

6 | Introduction

not *profit-maximizing*) and how market structures and growth regimes may be simultaneously endogenized.

Gunnar Eliasson (*On the Micro-Foundations of the Economic Growth, Human Capital, Firm Organization and Competitive Selection*) explore a micro-based behavioural foundation of economic growth by slightly modifying the standard assumptions of the neowalrasian model such that "there is room for live actors in dynamic markets". In the resulting conceptualization of the economic system, – which he calls the *Experimentally Organized Economy* (EOE) – economic growth becomes truly endogenized and occurs through competitive selection in markets by way of innovative entry, reorganization and rationalization of incumbent firms and through forced exit, the latter freeing resources for new production.

Chapter 15 is by Giovanni Dosi and Giorgio Fagiolo (*Exploring the Unknown on Entrepreneurship, Coordination and Innovation-driven Growth*). They consider an economy made up by agents set in islands where they extract a resource – their knowledge can be locally spread – and then their procedures can be imitated. But these agents can also become explorers and go in search of unknown islands. Authors show that without geographic borders, the economy displays, for a wide range of parameters, patterns of self-sustaining growth. In this model, incremental knowledge accumulation, diffusion and random discoveries of new technologies interact as to yield persistent – and persistently – fluctuating growth.

This fourth part clearly shows that a new formulation of microeconomic theory is likely to influence economic science completely and in particular macroeconomic theory on growth.

Eventually the last part of the book tackles the theory of evolutionary games. The underlying question can be expressed in this way: what happens in game situations when agents have behaviours of limited rationality? The possibility to integrate game situations in processes of evolution or of self-organization depends on the answers likely to be given on that issue.

Chapter 16 by Gisèle Umbhauer (*Discrete Evolutionary Processes: Stationary Probabilities, Strategic Asymmetries and Learning Schemes*) is concerned, as regards game theory, in the dynamic and ambiguous context of the principle of backward induction and on weakly dominated strategies. In this article, each player is made up of a finite group of identical operators, an operator is selected at random at each period. A pure strategy and beliefs about the actions of other players are associated to an operator. He can learn, with a certain probability, and adapt his beliefs in a suitable way. He can be evolving as well, which gives him another stategy and other beliefs.

In the following article (*Behavioural Learning*), Jean-François Laslier, Richard Topol and Bernard Walliser think about repeated game situations in which each player adopts a behaviour according to the results of his past acts.

They compare in particular, within the scope of a 2 by 2 repeated game, the Relative Reinforcement Randomized rule and the Fictitious Play rule and give an account of results which were obtained as regards to the possible convergence of the players' strategies towards those of a Nash equilibrium.

Finally, in chapter 18 (*The Compromise between Exploration and Exploitation: from Decision Theory to Game Theory*), Paul Bourgine studies the strategy to be followed by an individual confronted with a k-armed bandit, each arm being pulled in any order and one at a time and each pull resulting in a random reward. In a decision theory context, it is in the interest of the individual, under specific hypotheses, to investigate and then choose the best decision resulting from his experiments, without being certain that his choice is the best. In a context of repeated games, it can also be interesting to adopt a behaviour of exploration and then of exploitation, but there is no sure convergence towards a Nash equilibrium of the complete information game.

Through this set of articles, it is interesting to observe the mixing of order and disorder in this active field of research. On the side of order, authors obviously share the same paradigm and the essential concepts which constitute it. They also discover in different ways similar properties, kinds of islands of knowledge (i.e. the possibility, of changing the phase between competing and monopolistic markets, according to the values of parameters, with relationships either stable or unstable between buyers and sellers, together with the phenomena of imitation either regulating or not...) On the side of disorder, the extreme variety of formalisms and studied objects can be remarked. It then appears that the consolidation of this new theoretical approach entail to work out an integrate general framework. This elaboration first implies a unification of conceptual definitions. Let us stress as well the sea which remains to be explored, in particular game theory.

We hope that this book will be a modest contribution to a revolution which is on its way and to which we eagerly look forward.

CHAPTER 1
EVOLUTION: HISTORY, CHANGE AND PROGRESS

Hélène TORDJMAN

1. Introduction

Evolutionary ideas in economics have a long and complicated history: from the first insights of Malthus to the Marshallian "Mecca", Friedman's "natural selection", and, more recently, neo-Schumpeterian approaches and Evolutionary Game Theory, evolutionary concepts have often been used by economists. However, these borrowings were not all made in the same spirit, and the theories which are now labelled "evolutionary" consequently encompass a great array of differing approaches. This is particularly true about the vision of time and economic dynamics embodied in different evolutionary models. To take a quite extreme example, compare Friedmanian natural selection, where the latter is used as a mechanism of convergence to equilibrium, to the "quasi open-ended" technological or financial dynamics engendered by self-organizing processes in e.g. neo-Schumpeterian models.

The purpose of this paper is to analyse modern evolutionary economic theories (by this term, we mean Evolutionary Game Theory – from now on EGT –; neo-Schumpeterian approaches à la Nelson and Winter; and more cognitive approaches modelled such as Artificial Economic Life) from the point of view of time and dynamics [1]. What vision of history and progress is embedded in EGT, and how does it differ from neo-Schumpeterian dynamics? This very general issue can be tackled in a more analytical way by examining the characteristics of the aggregate dynamics implied by these theories. Can we reasonably predict the outcome of such evolutionary processes? In order to answer these questions, we will need to go through the mechanisms by which a) different outcomes are selected and b) novelty is introduced in these models. Indeed, selection mechanisms and variation mechanisms are at the heart of evolutionary theories, as the latter is determining the possible worlds and the former is selecting among them. Hence, the precise specification of those two mechanisms are fundamental in shaping the dynamics of evolutionary processes.

Even if these approaches to economic evolution make different use of the biological metaphor, they all share some basic building blocks. First, they are

---

[1]. A rather technical survey of EGT can be found in Weibull (1996); classic texts on neo-Schumpeterian approaches are Nelson & Winter (1982), Dosi *et al.* (Eds.) (1988) ; on Artificial Life methodology, see Langton *et al.* (Eds.) (1991).

all populational: they study the evolution of the distribution of some interacting entities (agents, strategies, firms). The respective performances of those entities are evaluated on a unidimensional scale, e.g. profit, utility, fitness. Second, the mechanism governing the evolution of the population is a selection mechanism akin to Darwinian natural selection: the best entities (the higher on the scale just mentioned) survive and possibly reproduce themselves, and the worse disappear. Third, all of these approaches embody, one way or another and at different degrees, some kind of bounded rationality, which make them more adequate from a descriptive point of view than standard economic theory.

However, in most cases, evolutionary approaches still offer only gross representations of economic and social change. Indeed, if some categories of evolutionary biology are actually powerful in explaining some aspects of social change, the evolution of human societies have distinctive features which call for fundamental amendements of the biological metaphor. Among these features, one can mention that a) selection may not be a "neutral" mechanism, b) variations on which selection operates may not be random but generated by specific processes of change facing their own constraints (e.g. technological innovation, learning...), and c) the mechanisms of transmission of traits may be very different in social and cultural contexts from what they are in nature: as forcefully argued by Nelson and Winter (1982), transmission in social life is more Lamarckian than Darwinian. For all these reasons, it seems reasonable to consider that the domain of possible worlds in evolutionary theories of economic and social change is more restrained than what it is in biological evolution. In other words, it seems that the notion of history embodied in theories of social evolution presents, at different degrees, a complicated mix of indeterminacy and constraints. However, as we will see, the mixes between "chance and necessity" (Monod, 1970) differ from one approach to another. In what follows, the biological metaphor will thus be considered as a heuristic framework for analysing social evolution and not as a model to which social scientists should strictly conform.

A last remark about the method of investigation adopted here. We will not enter into the details of evolutionary models: the argument developed here belongs to a general epistemological reflexion. It discusses the issue of history and change by analysing different approaches to evolutionary economics, and how they compare with the biological theory of evolution. It tries to clarify what vision of history is entailed by each of them. Indeed, it will be argued here that their main differences can be understood from the point of view of how these theories characterize economic dynamics, i.e. what standpoint they take on history, change and progress. As noted by Hodgson (1993), these differences go back to debates in biology about the same topics which oppose, to put it grossly, pure neo-Darwinians, i.e. adaptationists on one hand, and authors like Gould, Eldredge, Lewontin, who emphasize contingency and historicity of biological evolution on the other.

Along the way, we will be lead to question the way the biological metaphor is used by economists and social scientists, and plead for some amendements in this use. Indeed, as just evoked, evolutionary theory in biology is not totally unified, and many questions are still open and unsettled. Interestingly, most of these unsettled issues resonate with economic debates; it is the case for instance for the important question of path-dependence and the place of contingency in the selection of economic equilibria or trajectories. Hence, those issues should be of guidance for an elaboration of an evolutionary theory in economics, and not be simply dismissed by considering that everything is solved (as is the tendency of a branch of evolutionary economics following sociobiological approaches – see Hodgson (1993) for a critical analysis).

The paper is organized as follows. First, some market selection mechanisms are discussed and compared with Darwinian natural selection (section II). Second, different sources of variation are considered and the means by which these variations are transmitted are analysed from the point of view of their dynamical properties (section III). Finally, section IV concludes by discussing the implications of the different specifications of these mechanisms on the aggregate economic dynamics, and more generally on the vision of history they embody.

2. Selection

Unless other evolutionary mechanisms, natural selection has a quite straight-forward translation in economics. Indeed, the functioning of a market offers many similarities with natural selection: the market is a locus where agents, through interaction, get the monetary result of the decisions they have previously taken, and more generally the payoff of their activity (which can be monetary or else -utility for instance). Hence, agents who do well receive positive payoffs and grow, and the ones who cumulate losses tend to disappear.

However, precise specifications of this selection mechanism and their associated hypotheses have some important implications on what has to be postulated about the variation mechanism (see section III), as well as on the resulting aggregate dynamics. That is why it is important to sketch the different standpoints which are taken by economists on the question of market selection and to raise some of the issues (like the one about levels of selection) which are of consequence on aggregate dynamics.

2.1. Population homogeneity and equilibrium

The parallel between market selection and Darwinian selection has first been drawn by Friedman (1953) to show that the normal functioning of a market leads to rational behaviour and equilibrium. As he puts it, "under a wide range of circumstances individuals [...] behave *as if* they were seeking rationally to maximize their expected returns [...] and had full knowledge of the data needed to succeed in this attempt. [...] The process of 'natural selection' thus helps to validate the hypothesis – or rather, given natural selection, acceptance of the hypothesis can be based largely on the judgement that it summarizes appropriately the conditions of survival" (pp. 21-22). In other terms, rational behaviour is the outcome of a process of "natural" selection which results in market equilibrium. Such a mechanism engenders a perfect homogeneity of a majority of agents: most of them must share the same "model of the world". If it were not the case, "deviant" individuals would have some opportunities of profit and thus would not be eliminated from the market (e.g. De Long *et al.* (1990)). This requirement of homogeneity is at odds with Darwinian selection. Indeed, natural selection is a process which selects, at a given moment of time, the individuals of a population who have characteristics which give them an advantage in survival and reproduction in a given environment. The underlying assumption is the Malthusian one: population increases geometrically whereas resources only grow arithmetically; hence the competition. But natural selection presupposes a variability of characteristics among the individuals of a population: selection operates on an heterogeneous population by winnowing on random variations. As noted by Darwin (1859), "individual variations are for us of the outmost importance, because they give the materials on which natural selection can work and accumulate...[specific features]" [1]. To put it differently, competition – what Darwin called "struggle for life" – has an evolutionary meaning only insofar there is variability within the population. Only in this case can selection be considered as the main mechanism of adaptation.

If, as in the Friedmanian case, the population is quasi homogeneous, once the deviants are eliminated, agents are all rational and the market is at an equilibrium. In this perspective, natural selection is not an evolutionary mechanism of adaptation but one of convergence to an equilibrium. This is so because no mechanism producing novelty (i.e. variability) is added to the selection mechanism: there is a given heterogeneity at the beginning of time, and it is slowly eliminated by market selection. When everybody is identically rational, the market is at an equilibrium; it is the "end of time" and no adaptation is required anymore. As put forward by Hodgson (1993, p. 27), "the natural selection ideas of Friedman [...] are a case of the importing of ill-formed ideas from biology to bolster rather than replace a fundamental mechanistic paradigm".

Indeed, the pseudo-evolutionary Friedmanian argument belongs to equilibrium theory, as it presents a mechanism of convergence to equilibrium, by which "everything is for the better in the best possible world". It conveys a finalist approach to evolution: rationality exists because it is optimal for individuals, as it is optimal it is selected and when it is selected the system is in equilibrium. Hence, everything which exists is optimal and the only possible dynamics comes from the reaction of the economic system to shocks and external perturbations temporarily moving it from equilibrium. The logical

---

1. P. 92 of the french translation published in 1992 by Flammarion, Paris.

fallacy of such finalist view has often been emphasized (e.g. Gould & Lewontin (1979)), as it amounts in a way to postulate that the future determines the present.

Other models of selection are developed by Evolutionary Game Theory, initiated by Maynard-Smith (1982), where some populations replicate through interaction (two-by-two matching). In economics, such models have been applied to different issues, among other the emergence of co-operative behaviour and market selection [1]. These models of "replicator dynamics" are defined on sets of given strategies, but random mutation are sometimes added. However, these mutations are generally modelled as white noises and do not really modify strategies as such. Some specific processes of mutation will be discussed in section III.

It should be emphasized that here, like in the Friedmanian perspective, variability is given: to borrow the term coined by Dosi *et al.* (1996), these are "fixed-menus" models where there is no true novelty. Hence, convergence to an equilibrium is possible and indeed has a meaning. This is not the case of approaches stressing the continuous novelty characterizing behaviours or technologies: because of learning for instance, heterogeneity of behaviours may well never disappear or even stabilize itself like what happens in EGT when strategies are evolutionary stable ones. In such cases, mainly studied by neo-Schumpeterian and "Artificial Life" approaches, the adaptation process never ends and evolutionary dynamics is open-ended. Nobody knows precisely what kind of innovation may arise and what will be its consequences: the set of possible worlds is not defined *ex ante*. In the latter view, the concept of equilibrium does not help to grasp the dynamical properties of the evolutionary process, as those properties are only transient ones. However, one can still "say something" about these properties, at least qualitatively, by examining some features of selection and variation mechanisms. Let us first go on with the selection mechanism.

2.2. *What is selected?*

In the original Darwinian formulation of natural selection, hereditary individual differences are the mean by which individuals within a population are selected. However, these differences and peculiarities, which at some instant give a reproductive and/or a survival advantage to the individual who display them, are not selected "for the good" of the population. The latter will evolve through the gradual accumulation of traits which are "good" at some point and in some environments, but selection operates at the level of the individual: the population (or variety) evolves as a result of such an "individualistic" selection process. Hence, aggregate outcomes of evolutionary processes have no reason

---

1. For an overview, see Banerjee & Weibull (1991).

to be optimal at the level of the population. Gould (1980, 1983) gives many examples of this non-optimality, many living forms displaying perennial but ill-adapted features. The giant panda for instance leaves on bamboo but has not evolved the right stomach for such food: it thus has to spend 16 hours a day eating just in order to survive, which does not look like an optimal design of the specie.

Part of this individualistic view has been challenged recently by different authors highlighting that selection also occurs at the level of genes, as well as at a more macro level, e.g. the varieties or the species. The debates concerning units and levels of selection are numerous and unsettled [1]. It is not the purpose of this paper to enter into them; let us just set up the scene by noticing the centrality of this issue. Indeed, the specification of units and levels of selection conditions the kind of entities which are deemed relevant in the evolutionary process. In other terms, and this is crucial for social sciences, the definition of individuality rests on that specification, as it sets the type of autonomous entities which may be envisioned.

What is the adequate level of description of economic phenomena? Of course, there is no unique answer to such a question. In neo-Schumpeterian models of industrial dynamics, the selected entities are generally firms, and countries in growth models, whereas the units of selection are organizational routines or technologies. For instance, Nelson & Winter (1982, ch. 12) develop a model of Schumpeterian competition where the population is one of firms; these firms expand or shrink (and may possibly disappear while new ones enter the market) depending on their respective profitability (fitness) which in turn is determined by their ability to innovate, i.e. to discover new and better techniques of production. Thus, individual differences here concerns technologies and the level at which selection operates is the one of individual firms. More precisely, individual differences (phenotypical level) concern technologies but the units of selection are the routines allowing a firm to innovate (the genotype). Note that Nelson & Winter provide the beginning of a theory of the links between phenotypic and genotypic levels, *via* the notions of skills and competences, but in general, these links are not so clear, neither in economics nor in biology (e.g. Gould (1991), Lewontin (1991)). Note also that in this model, the transmission process (inheritance) is not Darwinian but Lamarckian: firms acquire new techniques as a result of their activity and the choices they make, they are not "born" with them (we will come back to this important point in the next section) [2].

In EGT, selection mainly works on strategies: choices in simple contexts such as Prisoner Dilemma (e.g. Boyer & Orléan (1995), decision rules in more

---

1. On hierarchical selection, see Gould (1989, 1991) and Eldredge (1995). For an extreme individualistic perspective on the unicity of the selection level, see Dawkins (1976).
2. For a survey of this literature, see Dosi & Nelson (1994) and Nelson (1995).

complicated ones (for instance Blume & Easley (1989)). As mentioned before, EGT models in economics are pure selection models, as there is no variation modifying the existing set of strategies. The latter is pre-specified, i.e. the heterogeneity of the population is given, and the selection mechanism consists in replicating the individual strategies bringing highest payoffs to agents. Because there is no true variability, the distinction between individual differences giving advantages or disadvantages in terms of survival (unit of selection) and the entities who are selected is not relevant here. A strategy is selected when it brings high payoffs and such a property derives from the strategy itself, not from some peculiarities it may present. Hence, strategies are identified by some initial differences which do not evolve through time, and selection solely provides a mechanism by which the respective weight of these strategies within the population are modified [1].

The third approach to economic evolution this paper discusses is Artificial Economic Life (AEL). It is a modelling approach developed at the intersection of evolutionary biology, cognitive and computer sciences. Instead of being represented by a set of strategies, like in EGT, agents are modelled by connexionist networks such as neural networks or classifiers systems. Such systems have the great advantage to allow for an evolution of the strategies or decision rules used by agents. In other terms, these systems can learn and adapt to changing environments. Their application to economics thus open new perspectives in the modelling of evolving microbehaviours [2]. We shall illustrate this wide class of models by the classifiers systems developed by Holland (1975, 1986). Classifiers systems are systems of condition/action rules ("if then..." rules) which can be seen as some kind of routines (e.g. "If I observe A, I choose action X"). Agents are represented by a population of such rules evolving through selection ("bucket brigade algorithm"), mutation and crossover mechanisms ("genetic algorithm"). In this kind of models, the selected entities are generally the rules, while the differences and peculiarities which selection accumulates can be seen as "bits and pieces" of knowledge, i.e. categories and concepts. It should be noted that in these models, and even more so in the theories underlying such modelling approaches, the "bits and pieces" of knowledge are not considered independently one from the other, but in their articulation, the whole structure they form (Holland *et al.* (1986)). Hence, selection works on individual rules but also on groups of rules, i.e. mental models (see below for a definition), which is a case quite similar to the hierarchical selection perspective proposed by Gould and Eldredge.

---

1. As already said, some EGT models consider random mutations, but, as will be shown in section III, these mutations do not entail a true variability of strategies.
2. Applications to economics can be found in Palmer *et al.* (1994), Dosi *et al.* (1994), Marengo & Tordjman (1996). Methodological discussions about Artificial Life in economics are Arthur (1992), Holland & Miller (1991) and Lane (1993a and 1993b). Dosi *et al.* (1996) present a survey of learning processes in evolutionary environments. These tools have also been used in a rather different spirit to give an account of adaptive convergence to Rational Expectations Equilibria, i.e. as optimization algorithms (Sargent (1993)).

16 | Evolution: History, change and progress

This (non exhaustive) enumeration of possible selection levels in evolutionary approaches in economics points to what seems to be an important difference between biological and social evolution. Indeed, in biology, selection works at the level of individual bodies (Darwinian selection), and also at a more micro-level (DNA) and a more macro one (species). But even if it is shown that there exists more than one level of selection in biological life, the latter is a matter of the scale of the problem which is analysed and does not really depend on the problem itself. This is not the case in economics where the choice of units of selection and selected entities closely depends on the issue which is studied, and in what perspective it is studied; this choice is part of the formulation of the problem itself. To put it differently, take an issue in molecular biology: it will be studied at the genetic level, and no concurrent level of explanation exists for the same phenomenon. In social sciences on the contrary, it seems that one can find different levels of explanation for the same problem; the selection level thus has to be chosen by the modeller.

An example of such dependence can be found in the analysis of the functioning of financial, speculative markets. It is well known that on these markets, individual and collective opinions and beliefs play a central role in price dynamics. Since a decade, the Keynesian analysis of speculation has benefited from a renewed interest, and many models of contagion and epidemic-like effects have been drawn from Keynes' intuitions, most of them with an evolutionary flavour. In these models, agents have to choose between given strategies or opinions (see for instance Blume & Easley (1989), Orléan (1990), Kirman (1993)). They can change their opinion after meeting somebody with a different one – contagion –, or spontaneously – "learning", modelled as random mutations –, but these changes are discrete: individuals switch from one pre-specified opinion to another but cannot modify them or construct new ones. Like EGT, of which these models are very close, they are fixed-menus, pure selection models.

However, the functioning of financial markets displays more complex phenomena occurring at the level of individual representations: empirical studies of expectations (e.g. Frankel & Froot (1987), Shiller (1989)) show that agents do more than choosing among a portfolio of pre-specified opinions or strategies. Indeed, they construct and evolve "models of the world" in order to interpret information and form an opinion. A brief look at the foreign exchange market since 20 years illustrates this point. First, the variables which are judged important in exchange rates determination (the so-called fundamentals) change over time: from current imbalances and interest rates at the beginning of the 80's, the Forex successively focused on unemployement, growth, fiscal deficits and inflation. Hence, representations of exchange rate dynamics appear to change over time. Second, the same information may be interpreted in contradictory ways. For instance, two or three years ago, a rise in unemployement was a signal of an economic slowdown, and as such was provoking bearish pressures on the market. Now, in the US at least, unemployement decreases and it also generates bearish pressures on the market because it is believed to be an inflationary signal.

It thus seems that evolutionary approaches to financial markets should be designed in such a way as to take into account not only opinions, but more importantly representations, as the latter entail some interpretative process. A representation is a "model of the world" build by an agent in order to make sense of the complexity and diversity of his environment [1]. It is a "mental model" (Johnson-Laird (1983), Holland *et al.* (1986), Lakoff (1987)) of a phenomenon which organises the knowledge about this phenomenon along lines perceived by the individual to be important [2]. Building blocks of mental models are categories and prototypes, generally inductively constructed and modified, and articulated such as to reproduce the perceived structure of the world. It is through these representations that information is processed and beliefs and opinions are formed; hence the necessity, in order to analyse speculative markets, to envision the selection mechanism at the level of individual representations.

Indeed, on financial markets, there is no intrinsic winning strategy; the winners are those who have a good understanding of the functioning of the market, i.e. a "good" representation of it (e.g. Soros (1994)). An interesting example of this point is furnished by a study made by Shiller (1989). Just after the October 1987 crash, he sent a questionnaire to investors in order to identify the main factors at the origin of their massive selling behaviour. One reason frequently invoked was the similarity of the actual market configuration with the one just preceding the 1929 crisis. As Shiller puts it (p. 399): "Investors had expectations before the 1987 crash that something like a 1929 crash was a possibility, and comparisons with 1929 were an integral part of the phenomenon". In other words, the accuracy of general representations about market functioning and financial crisis was fundamental in the ability to understand the situation, time the crash and thus get out of the market before loosing too much.

However, fitness in such a context is very difficult to define unambiguously: it has to do with the "accuracy" of individual representations, the ability of agents to understand their environment and recognize familiar patterns (as the premises of a financial crisis), and their capability of expecting the expectations of others. Of course, it can be spotted *ex post* by tracking the monetary payoffs of each agent, but this is a mere tautology: we do not have yet a theory of how and why precisely some individuals survive and other do not. Moreover, fitness

---

1. The idea of a "model of the world" through which agents form their beliefs and take their decisions was first introduced by the Rational Expectations Hypothesis; however, as the latter postulates the possibility of a perfect knowledge, there is no room for diverging or evolving interpretations.
2. What is perceived to be important is not unambiguously defined, and usually depends on the social context and the personal history of the agent (e.g. Lakoff, and for a discussion of this issue on financial markets, Tordjman (1996)).

criteria on these markets may vary across periods and "regimes" of market. For instance, the abilities required to make profit on the forex market under fixed exchange rates and floating exchange rates may differ, because exchange rates determination has been modified, thus implying a change in expectations formation. The notion of fitness in such cases looses some of its explanatory power. The same remark also holds for the genotype/phenotype distinction: if differences in individual representations and learning abilities are, as just proposed, the material on which selection works, what would be the equivalent of the genotype? How far should we push the analogy with the biological model?

To conclude on the issue of levels of selection, let us emphasize two points. First, as shown by the example of financial markets, the same problem can be formulated in different ways: one can decide that selection operates directly on strategies or opinions, or one can instead adopt an approach where individual representations are the selected entities, strategies, opinions and beliefs being a result of those representations. Similarily, when studying industrial competition, firm profitability can be the outcome of an ability to innovate, or derive from good managerial skills, or from an efficient organization (and from many other factors as well). This multiplicity of possible selection units and levels in evolutionary approaches to economic change contrasts with biological evolution. The corollary of such multiple levels of selection is the difficulty encountered in defining fitness unambiguously: as there is no general theory of fitness in economic or social life (except for sociobiological approaches), selected entities and units of selection in a specific domain have to be defined together with fitness conditions.

Second, from the point of view of time and dynamics, there is a crucial difference between evolving entities such as representations and fixed ones (e.g. pre-specified opinions or technologies). In fixed-menus models like EGT or contagion models on financial markets, it is possible to specify the set of equilibria, even if we do not know which equilibrium will be reached because there may be positive feedbacks engendering path-dependent dynamics (see for instance Polya urns models, e.g. Arthur *et al.* (1987)). In most neo-Schumpeterian as well as in AEL approaches, the set of possible worlds is not fixed: technologies or representations evolve *via* learning processes, thus continuously introducing novelty into the system. When the selected entities evolve, there is a fundamental indeterminacy of where the system will go and what region of space will be explored: the dynamics is open-ended [1]. We will see below however that open-ended dynamics do not entail total indeterminacy, unlike evolution in biology, because diverse kind of constraints exist in social life which partly orient the aggregate dynamics.

---

1. Of course, this is true at a conceptual level, but things are much less clear-cut on a formal point of view. It is always possible to argue that the trillions of possibilities in e.g. classifiers systems models are also pre-specified, and that the only difference with, say, EGT, stems from the number of dimensions. Indeed, we still lack formalisms able to give an account of the emergence of novelty.

2.3. Is selection neutral?

In biology, it is usual to distinguish between natural and artificial selection, the latter corresponding for instance to what a breeder does when he selects particular traits he wants his animals to display. If natural selection is in this sense a "neutral" mechanism, depending only on the state of the environment at some instant, it is certainly not the case of artificial selection, which is an oriented process. "Nature furnishes the successive variations, man accumulates them in some useful directions" (Darwin (1859, p. 75)) [1]. Artificial or directed selection thus entails two steps: the first one consists in choosing what features have to be selected, the second one concerns the mechanisms by which these features are accumulated. Such a process engenders, at least in nature, some kind of well-defined "quality norms", e.g. a cocker spaniel has big and falling ears, which have nothing to do with environmental pressure.

What about selection in economics? Is it reasonable to consider it a neutral mechanism or is it, in some ways, oriented? To put it more precisely, are the peculiarities and differences characterizing firms and technologies, strategies and representations, accumulated along lines which are defined somewhere by whatever mechanism, or is this accumulation random, depending only on environmental pressures? Intuitively, one feels that selection in economic and social environments has different features from this point of view than selection in natural life. Indeed, the environmental pressure in the latter case is determined randomly, by climatic conditions or else, whereas social environments are the results of human actions and interactions. Even if they have unintended effects, those actions and interactions are motivated by specific goals, influenced by collective representations and ideologies, and constrained by norms and formal rules stemming from the social organization at large. Those are perennial factors of influence: hence, one should observe some orientation or direction of selection in social life.

Take for instance the selection process on the labour market. Let us suppose that -as it is traditionally the case in France- academic degree is the key characteristic for evaluating the quality of a worker, i.e. it is the fitness criterion on this market. Employers would then choose individuals with good diplomas instead of considering those having unusual profiles or practising a team sport. Is the fact that fitness results from a choice instead of environmental pressure enough to qualify such a selection process as oriented? It seems that deliberately chosen fitness criteria are not enough to qualify selection as oriented, because there is no accumulation, through the selection mechanism, of the particular traits which are deemed having a high adaptive value. The employer

---

1. I will not enter here into the debate opposing "traditionalists" like Mayr to "neutralists" such as Kimura concerning the possibility of random selection (for an account of this debate, see for instance Blanc (1990)). The qualificative "neutral" as it is used here does not deny that fitness plays a role in natural selection, but stresses the opposition between environmental or reproductive fitness vs. man defined fitness.

can choose a particular fitness criterion and thus punctually orient local selection, but the choice of which traits should be accumulated at a social level is certainly beyond his control -and beyond the control of any individual for that matter. The breeder of chickens or dogs controls the reproductive process which leads to a higher frequency of the desired traits, whereas the employer can only pray that the educational system will "produce" individuals with the required characteristics.

There are however at least two ways by which selection in social environments can be considered as oriented. Let us first go back to our employer. He chooses his employees by, say, their academic achievements. But, as a manager of a firm, he has to face other selection processes: his products have to be sold on the product market, and he has got to have access to some sources of financing. If his firm is successful, he may continue to hire people using the academic criterion he was using before; but if not, he may as well reconsider his hiring policy and modify his selection methods. Hence, the selection on the labour market partially depends on the selection on product and financial markets, and one can say that selection on the labour market is oriented by selection at other levels of economic activity. This is a case of hierarchical or nested selection, but with a fundamental difference with biology: here, fitness is more or less consciously chosen, it depends on human actions and their determinants. Hence, some socially chosen features can be accumulated through such a nested selection mechanism.

A second way by which selection in economics can be oriented has to do with the effect of social norms, traditions and institutions. We have just seen that deliberate choice of a particular fitness criterion does not suffice to direct selection, because, for the latter to be really oriented, it has to have lasting effects, i.e. to partially shape the evolutionary dynamics. It seems not too farfetched to assume that a large class of collective mechanisms such as norms and institutions plays a central role in the process of accumulation of specific traits that are, or were sometimes ago, socially desired. Indeed, collective representations, norms, traditions and institutions, by diverse means, assure the transmission of these social desires and obligations and imprint selection. Mechanisms of transmission will be detailed below; let us simply give an illustration of how institutions may orient selection.

To remain with our example of the labour market, the definition of fitness is more or less clearly announced by human resources directors and managers, but the role of the educational system in defining those criteria is crucial as it allows them to last long enough for an accumulation of some desired features to happen. Thus, the precise organization of schools and universities greatly matters in defining fitness and shaping selection.

For instance, on the higher segment of the labour market in France, an old tradition values mostly intellectual work and capacity for abstraction. Symmetrically, manual work is considered as quite pejorative and manual workers occupy the lower levels of the "social scale" – which is for instance not the case in Germany. Thus, through the dichotomic French educational system – "grandes écoles" teaching mainly mathematics and physics, universities occupying a sort of middle ground, and technical formation being reserved to people not having completed high school –, values shaping the selection mechanism on the labour market are reproduced and diffused.

In this example, the accumulation of "good" traits does not occur directly at the first level of selection on the labour market; it is the result of a complicated interaction between selection at school and on the labour market and is sustained by a) a whole array of norms and collective representations about work qualification, intelligence, social usefulness and individuals' abilities for abstraction, and b) formal institutions like school, university, and recruitment agencies. This complicated process of selection, occurring at different levels and in interaction with some institutional forms, deserves thorough empirical studies which would help isolating the precise role of those institutional forms in orienting and constraining selection. It should be emphasized that in this perspective, the economic efficiency of the selected features is ambiguous to establish. It may well be that they are indeed efficient, but in the absence of a general theory of fitness it is difficult to make such an assertion. The inertia entailed by collective representations and institutional forms could also be invoked as an alternative explanation for the perennity of non-efficient features, as it has been highlighted for instance in the case of some technologies (e.g. the well-known example of QWERTY studied by David (1985)).

A last argument favouring the thesis of some kind of oriented selection stems from the ambiguity of defining fitness independently from a) the considered activity, and b) the environment. The difficulties in defining fitness regardless of the issue at hand have been evoked in the last section. Concerning the dependence of fitness on the environment, many examples can be found. A highlighting one is once more provided by the labour market, and shows the dependence of the definition of fitness on collective representations and social norms and values. To caricature a little, good workers in France are those who have some ideas about Plato and Descartes, whereas in Germany, individuals who are looking for a job must be able to prove they master specific technical skills, and applicants in the US must display various experiences which shows their adaptability and entrepreneurship. One thus finds different fitness criteria on the same market – i.e. the labour market –, each of them being an emanation of more general values about work and social usefulness, and collective representations of what a "good" worker is. An important body of work about Japanese transplants in the US and in Europe has shown that such differences in social values and collective representations deeply shape the functioning of the labour market and the selection of the workforce (e.g. Dore (1987)).

This variability of fitness criteria only reflects the diversity of collective representations and social norms among different countries, cultures and societies. Such important contextual effects emphasize something which may seem trivial but is not: many of the characteristics on which selection operates are socially constructed traits, which in turn makes selection in economics a culturally and socially embedded mechanism (Granovetter (1985)). Selection is thus oriented by the specificities of the social organization in which it takes place and cannot be considered as neutral. Its social dimension should be studied more precisely in order to isolate a) the dependence of fitness on the social context and b) the mechanisms by which the accumulation of traits is influenced and constrained in specific situations (e.g. on the labour market, on financial markets).

3. Variation

The mechanisms producing variations are of the outmost importance in any theory of evolution, whether about nature or society. As selection works on the variations within a population, the kind of variations which are available at a given period constrains the existence of possible worlds. Interestingly, the only figure in Darwin's Origin of species shows the history of evolution as a branching process, where each possible world depends on the previous random variations. In other terms, effective variations decide of the new directions which may be taken, i.e. the dynamics is path-dependent, and the properties of the system's aggregate dynamics are to a great extent determined by the properties of the mechanisms generating those variations.

One of the main source of variability in economic and social life lies in human behaviour, and more precisely in learning. Individuals learn to appreciate things they did not before, they learn about their changing environment, they learn to perform new tasks in a firm or elsewhere and to modify the way they are performing old tasks; they learn to solve problems and to construct methods in order to learn better; they learn to interact with others in specific situations, to expect the way others may behave or sometimes to conform to what others expect from them. All these learning processes result in an evolution of individual representations, preferences, beliefs and decision rules [1].

These learning processes may also be analysed at a more aggregate level. In organizations (for instance firms), individuals' learning occurs in close interaction with others, and within explicit and implicit constraints stemming from

---

1. Learning here is viewed as a very general process which leads to a change in individual and/or collective behaviours. Such changes can be provoked by a modification of environmental conditions which call for an adaptation, or generated endogenously by the process of knowledge accumulation itself. One does not have yet a general theory of knowledge and many questions are still unsolved (Lakoff (1987)). Learning the way it is meant here concerns any change in representations, preferences, beliefs or decision rules, whatever the "direction" of this change. It may not lead to an increased performance, but as long as there is a modification in the state of knowledge of an individual or a group, we will talk about learning.

the necessities of the organization. Learning in organizations produces shared representations and "ways of doing things", i.e. routines, in which, as highlighted by the literature on organizational learning, the collective knowledge of the organization is crystallized [1]. Firms' behaviours, strategies and organizations evolve through such mechanisms of learning. Individual and collective learning is also at the origin of technological innovation, another main source of variation in the economy. Technical change is a process in which many different agents are involved: universities, firms and R & D labs, individual scientists and engineers, and political actors as well, whose interaction leads to changes in products and processes of production (for an overview, see Dosi (1988)). Hence, learning, be it individual or collective, organizational or technological, can be considered as one of the main source of novelty in the economic system, and learning properties doubtless greatly influence aggregate dynamical properties of economic change.

From an analytical point of view, the way biology addresses the problem of variation is fruitful, eventhough biological and social answers to the problem are very different. Let us use a standard distinction and differentiate between two issues. Both are stemming from the old debate opposing Darwinism to Lamarckianism; the first one concerns the randomness of variations and the second is about inheritance, i.e. the mechanisms of transmission of traits.

3.1. Random vs. directional variations

One of the most lively debate in 19th century's biology opposed Lamarckianists to Darwinists. Among the consequences of Lamarckianism was the claim that new variations appeared in order to answer environmental pressures: the long neck of the giraffe was evolved to help them eating leaves higher in the trees. The usefulness of a feature was deemed to guide the emergence of variation. Such a functionalist vision was challenged by Darwin, who claimed that variations were randomly produced (by exactly what mechanism he did not know) and that selection was winnowing on these random variations. This debate could only be settled with Weismann and Mendel works on the mechanisms of genetic transmission, which showed that basically Darwin was right. If the Darwinian atomistic perspective of variation (one gene/one feature) seems today too simple to account for the complexity of genetic recombination and transmission (e.g. Lewontin (1991)), the fundamental randomness of genetic variation on which Darwin built his theory still holds.

What about social evolution? Is it reasonable to consider that new routines, new strategies or new categories and concepts are randomly generated? I do not believe this to be a reasonable proposition, because learning processes are themselves constrained and oriented eventhough they do no always lead to a

---

1. See for instance Nelson & Winter (1982), March (1991), March & Simon (1993).

better understanding or a better action. Before developing this point, let us have a closer look at the treatment of variations in evolutionary approaches to economics.

In EGT and affiliates, one can distinguish between two classes of models: in the first one, developed by Maynard Smith (1982), strategies are given and what is studied is their evolutionary stability, i.e. their capacity to resist invasion from a mutant population. But the considered mutation is small and happens once for all. In such a framework, the evolution of the population is determined by a replication equation, namely by selection only, and, as noted by Orléan (1996), such an approach is fundamentally deterministic. The second class of approaches are still fixed-menus models but a mechanism of mutation is added to the system. Instead of a once for all mutation, continuous mutations are introduced [1]. The question of the convergence to an equilibrium becomes more complex, but that is not our direct interest here. What is of interest is how these mutations are modelled, and their meaning in terms of microeconomic behaviours.

Following Orléan's discussion (1996), one can distinguish between different ways of introducing mutations. One is to posit a given mutation rate which is simply added to the replicator dynamics. An example of such model is Kirman (1993) about changes in opinions on financial markets, where agents have a given probability to imitate each others (replication) and another given probability to spontaneously change their opinion. The latter mutation is sometimes interpreted as "learning", but nothing is said about the process which leads an agent to change his opinion. A second way was adopted by Foster & Young (1990), who add a Wiener process to the replication equation. However, in their modelling, this process does not depend on the relative proportion of each strategy; it is a general noise affecting the whole system which may come from a change in macroeconomic conditions or else: again, there is no explicit account of the microbehaviours leading to the mutations. Moreover, the added noise, a Wiener process, has an expectation equal to zero: the effects of mutation on the aggregate dynamics are thus neutralized. Other specifications can be found, which may affect the dynamics of the system and the selection of equilibria. However, as EGT does not jointly propose a theory of microbehaviours able to specify more precisely mutation processes (are all mutations possible? Do they occur at a constant rate? Are they independent from the environment?), the choice between different modelling is quite *ad hoc*; it does not reflect the reality of the sources of economic and social variability.

A last remark about EGT approaches to economics: mutations, whatever the manner they are modelled, represent at best the switching that an agent may operate between two known strategies. The fact that strategies are pre-specified

---

1. The term of mutation may not convey the right idea about variation in social life. However, its use is pervasive and I will thus keep it.

precludes any of their modification or adaptation. Hence, in all of these fixed-menus models, there is no novelty and no surprises; contingency does not have consequences on the possible worlds, defined *ex ante*, but only on the selection among them. Concerning microbehaviours, the implicit learning process leading to mutation is quite awkward: agents have a repertoire of strategies and when one of it does not bring payoffs high enough, they try another one. The way they choose the new one is unclear. Moreover, there are no links between the strategy which is dropped and the new one which has been chosen, as if individuals had the cognitive capabilities to use sometimes sophisticated strategies without being able to elaborate them: agents do not have an history. From the perfect rationality displayed by economic agents in general equilibrium and standard game theory, one thus directly go to the other end of the spectrum, modelling agents who do not understand their environment more than Skinner's rats do, randomly trying different behaviours until their reward is satisfycing.

Variability in neo-Schumpeterian and AEL approaches is taken care of in a very different manner [1]. Instead of being random, variations are directional, oriented by the specificities of learning processes. Depending on the chosen level of selection (representations, technologies, firms), three main sources of variation are considered: individual learning, technological learning and organizational learning, all grounded on a theory of adaptive and imperfect rationality. It is not the purpose of this paper to make a survey of learning in these approaches (see Dosi *et al.* (1996)); let us simply make a few remarks about some of the mechanisms orienting variations and their qualitative implications on the aggregate dynamics.

Unlike in EGT, novelty is not only allowed but emphasized as being a fundamental characteristic of evolutionary processes. Learning provides an explanation as to why the selected entities continuously evolve in new and possibly unexpected forms. Indeed, the theory of adaptive learning which microfounds neo-Schumpeterian and AEL approaches, even if it is not completed and perfectly consistent yet, allows nonetheless to sketch out some important mechanisms of learning which may give fundamental clues about the way variations can be oriented.

The first clue is given by the fact, now well-documented (see Johnson-Laird (1983, 1991), Holland *et al.* (1986) and Arthur (1992)), that most inferences are done inductively and not deductively. Formal analyses of induction (e.g. along

---

1. What follows concerns theoretical approaches: models developed along those theoretical lines unfortunately do not always embody the same richness, they may be limited by the available formal tools which are up to now not appropriate to modelling the emergence of novelty. Progress on the modelling side especially thanks to simulation methods is hopefully under way... Evolutionary models belonging to the neo-Schumpeterian and AEL approaches nonetheless retain, for most of them, the flavour of theoretical developments ; see Dosi & Nelson (1994), Nelson (1995) and Dosi *et al.* (1996).

a Bayesian approach to probability theory) have to face a main problem, which is the following: why do people not make all the possible inferences that may be done? Why do they not explore all the space of possible inferences? Indeed, if it was the case, random mutations on representations, routines or technologies would well fit the phenomenon. But it is not: knowledge accumulation through induction has properties which constrain and orient its dynamics. People do not make randomly all possible inferences because it has no meaning, it is not relevant and they would be starving before understanding they need food. In making inferences, we are guided by the knowledge we have already accumulated, by our history, and oriented by the goal we pursue, the task we have to perform or the problem we have to solve [1]. One does not develop the same routines of understanding and acting for driving a car, to manufacture a television or speculate on the forex market. The representations and decision rules used by agents in such diverse activities are oriented by the specificities of these activities.

Hence, inductive learning is both path-dependent and context-dependent. First, what one learns depends on what one already knows; second, what one learns is influenced by the purpose for which one has to learn, and more generally by the social context in which one is embedded. Variability of representations cannot thus be modelled as a purely random process: variations are directional, not all mutations are possible, and the orientation is given both by history and by the social context. Note that in such a perspective, "small historical events" can have a lasting effect on the dynamics of representations or technologies (this has been highlighted, in the case of technologies, by the QWERTY example studied by David (1985), as well as by Arthur (1989)).

Another property of inductive learning, often studied in the case of individual and organizational learning, is known as the exploitation/exploration dilemma. Because it is impossible to explore all of the possible inferences which could be made, individuals (and organizations as well, see March (1991)) tend to stick to a small number of representations and behaviours they know well (exploitation), while keeping some of their resources to explore new hypotheses and possibilities. As Holland (1986, p. 594) puts it: "because of the uncertainty of any induction, the process must be carried out in such a way that the system can absorb new, tentative rules without destroying capabilities in well-practised situations". These holds for technological innovation as well: think of the frequent choices which have to be made in e.g. R & D labs between ameliorating an existing technology or finding new domains of application for it on one hand, and investing in fundamental research in order to perhaps be able one day to elaborate a new technique on the other. In the terminology of EGT, mutations do not occur at a constant rate, and the latter differs across the population.

---

1. For an account of such approaches, emphasizing the orientation of inductive inferences, see Johnson-Laird (1983, 1991), Holland *et al.* (1986) and Lakoff (1987).

Such a pervasive dilemma also shape the processes engendering variability in the economy, and through variability, the aggregate dynamics. Intuitively, when an individual or a firm puts a high value on exploration and discovery, its behaviour may be quite unstable compared to what would be achieved with a high degree of exploitation of the existing knowledge base. More generally, the comparison between mutation scale and rate on one hand and selection on the other hand is crucial in the regularity, if not the stability, of the system behaviour (Sperber (1995)). However, even a high premium given to exploration relatively to exploitation does not lead to purely random variability. Exploration of new domains also obeys the historical inertia of knowledge accumulation and the contextual influences evoked above: hence, any representation of the sources of economic and social variations should highlight the precise mechanisms by which variations are oriented [1].

To summarize, let us emphasize a few points. First, one needs an approach to variation which is directional and not purely random. Precising the mechanisms that are sketched out above should certainly be on the agenda. Second, the envisioned variations must allow novelty to emerge, i.e. the selected entities have to be defined as evolving entities. Third, as one of the main source of variation is learning, one needs a theory of microbehaviours able to ground what is postulated about the form of variations: the possible domain of mutations, their rate, their dependence on contextual factors and so on.

A key issue which has not been raised up to now concerns another important source of variability, namely institutional and cultural change. The emphasis on learning, even if it is collective as in organizational learning, amounts to consider that the origin of variation exclusively stems from human actions and interactions. In this perspective, autonomous entities are individuals or organizations like firms, but no autonomy is conceded to higher levels of organization such as institutional forms, which are simply the result of "lower-levels" interactions. This issue is a complex one and has to be explored more precisely, but one should nonetheless consider that some autonomy has to be given to institutional forms. As put forward by Dosi & Nelson (1994, p. 156), "it happens in biology and even more so in social dynamics that the objects of selection are not single elementary traits but structures of much higher dimensions in which they are nested", like markets, science and technological systems and the education system (a survey about evolutionary perspectives on institutional and cultural change is in Nelson (1995)).

---

1. Such an inquiry has been started concerning the evolution of representations on financial markets (Tordjman (1996)). However, the identification of the mechanisms orienting the evolution of collective representations on these markets requires conceptual tools not available in economics; an anthropological and sociological perspective should help.

3.2. Inheritance or the transmission of traits

After having seen some of the sources of variability, let us now turn to the other part of the mechanism of variation. Evolutionary change goes on by selecting entities who present interesting peculiarities, the latter being transmitted to next generations. The notion of generation is a central one in biology, as traits are transmitted by reproduction. It is certainly one of the points where a theory of social evolution has to depart from the biological metaphor as unlike what is postulated by sociobiological approaches, genetic recombination does not play a fundamental role in the inheritance of social features. Indeed, social traits are acquired before being transmitted, and to my knowledge, no works in biology has positively shown that genes could code representations, routines, technologies or other socially constructed objects. As noted by Lewontin (1991, p. 32) about the old debate of nature and nurture and studies of family resemblance inspired by sociobiological approaches, "the two social traits that have the highest resemblance between parents and children in North America are religious sect and political party. Yet even the most ardent biological determinist would not seriously argue that there is a gene for Episcopalianism or voting Social Credit". Hence, to consider the transmission of traits in society, one has to start somewhere else, evolution in biology being only a loose metaphor for processes of social inheritance.

One first has to ask the question of what traits are transmitted in social evolution, and through what kind of process. About the transmitted features, many candidates instantaneously come to mind: language, traditions, beliefs, tastes, representations, ways of thinking and of doing things, values, technologies, institutions, social structures... These categories however have a different status: some doubtless concern the phenotypic level, like language, social values and institutions (but should they be considered as individuals or populations?). Others, like representations or technologies could be considered either as phenotypes or as genotypes, depending on the chosen level of selection. This ambiguity points again to the problematic nature of the phenotype/genotype distinction in its use in social sciences. Let us depart from it, and simply consider some of the traits that are transmitted in economic and social life, and some of the mechanisms by which they are transmitted.

In most neo-Schumpeterian models, the transmitted traits are routines or technologies. Such traits are socially constructed by diverse processes of learning evoked above; as such, they are not immovable but evolve. Indeed, the transmission of traits is usually associated with what lasts, with the "strong inertial tendencies preserving what has survived the selection process" (Nelson (1995, p. 54)). However, inertial tendencies do not preclude novelty, and the latter can arise either from an endogenous evolution of the considered features or because the transmitted traits are modified by the very process of transmission.

An illustration of endogenous evolution due to learning by doing is provided by routines as "operating procedures". For instance, routines embodying the necessary knowledge about how to manufacture the wheels of an automobile evolve through the experience of the workers using these routines. When a worker X, after 20 years of manufacturing wheels, teaches a newly arrived worker Y his know-how, the routines which will be transmitted from X to Y will be different from the one X learned when he started 20 years ago. This is so because they will embody all the cumulated experience X has acquired during these 20 years, as well as some possible technological and organizational innovations which may have changed the ways of doing things. Similar processes happen for technologies embedded in machine-tools or in final products: new "generations" of hybrid corn seeds embody progress made in genetic engineering and new cars, even if still exploiting the technology of the gas-powered engine, have more powerfull and less polluting engines. Hence, the transmitted traits can evolve with experience, organizational innovations, technological and scientific discoveries, which make the inheritance process more Lamarckian than Darwinian.

Transmitted features can also evolve because of the transmission mechanism itself. Before illustrating this point, let us briefly evoke some possible transmission processes.

Mechanisms of social inheritance are not yet much studied as such by economists, but the growing interest about the emergence of institutional forms could be interpreted in this light. Actually, from the New Institutional economics à la North to socio-economic and evolutionary approaches (e.g. Lesourne (1991) on self-organizing market processes; Granovetter & Swedberg (Eds.) (1992); Nelson (Ed.) (1993) on National Systems of Innovation), the analysis of institutions reflects a preoccupation with the origin of regularity and inertia in the economy. Institutions certainly participate to the transmission of traits. An unambiguous example is the one of the education system; its main purpose is to transmit knowledge across generations of individuals. This knowledge entails collective representations and myths about the history of the country, its arts and philosophy, as well as normative prescriptions about ways of thinking and of doing things. These collective views and norms help shaping individual representations and values, and as such, are mechanisms producing regularity and inertia in beliefs and behaviours across the population and over generations. It should be noted that many formal and less formal institutions like religion, traditions and conventions also produce collective norms and values shaping individual representations and behaviours. Indeed, there is a wide array of such collective mechanisms, the role of which just starts to be studied in economic contexts (e.g. Dosi *et al.* (1994), Orléan (Eds.) (1994)). The role of incentives, power and hierarchical relationships in the functioning of these institutions, and their links with more cognitive aspects of transmission are starting to be explored too (see Coriat & Dosi (1995)).

Another class of transmission mechanisms uses the channels of interpersonal communication. Under this heading, one may consider personal and professional relationships, the latter being possibly mediated by instances stemming from networks and organizations. Interpersonal communication may take different forms: it can be a quite egalitarian exchange (friendship) or a hierarchical one (employer/employee, teacher/student or familial relationships). The communication may lead to an exchange of representations, beliefs and routines, or to a modification of the latter. For instance, an employer showing an employee how to perform his task will transmit him more or less explicitly a representation about the task and the environment in which it takes place, as well as precise ways of doing things. Note that the latter takes place in a hierarchical relation where enforcement is a fundamental part of the process.

Another case of interpersonal transmission of traits is through the general mechanism of imitation. Some firms may imitate other more profitable ones, for instance by adopting their technology (technological diffusion); agents on financial markets may imitate the strategies of the more successful among them, gurus or else; consumers may imitate each other in their consumption choices because of a conformist behaviour. Imitation seems in fact to be quite pervasive in economic and social life and certainly is one important mechanism by which beliefs, tastes, opinions and technologies are transmitted from one agent to another.

However, unlike what is postulated by sociobiology, representations and beliefs are not replicators ("memes" or "culturgenes"). Instead, "representations transform themselves through a constructive cognitive process" (Sperber (1995, p. 141). In an epidemiological approach to representations, Sperber forcefully argues that transmitted traits are not exactly replicated because social transmission in many cases is not neutral but transforms what is transmitted. This is especially true for interpersonal communication: what one communicates to someone is generally not exactly what is received. This is so because of the constructive nature of representations; as already mentioned, the latter are not given and immovable but evolve with new information, experience, and interaction with others. Hence, representations and beliefs can be modified through encounters and discussions with others. The phenomenon of rumours, as extreme as it may be, represents a good example of how a belief can be transformed by the process of its diffusion, a detail or an exaggeration being added to the story at each step of the diffusion process. More generally, the kind of learning mechanisms sketched out above highlights the interpretative dimension of representations. This feature of representations could give an account for the transformation of traits through interpersonal communication. Such transformations are another source of novelty in economic and social systems.

As just seen, quite many different mechanisms can modify the transmitted features, from the endogenous dynamics of knowledge accumulation to institutional and interpersonal transmission like imitation. The reason why representations, routines or technologies can be modified is because they are socially constructed traits. As such, they are permeable to social influences and general mechanisms of social change. More fundamentally, their nature is constructive and they are evolving entities: they cannot be described as atomistic and fixed features like Dawkins' memes. In the perspective developed here, it is quite straightforward to see why the transmitted traits can be changed by the very processes of transmission.

4. Concluding remarks: history and progress

This paper has tried to highlight some main sources of change and regularity in social evolution and the way they are dealt with in evolutionary economic approaches. Among sources of change, one has emphasized learning mechanisms, be it individual, organizational or technological learning; on the side of regularity and inertia, one finds collective representations, norms, institutions and other collective objects shaping selection processes and mechanisms of inheritance. Both of those aspects of evolutionary dynamics are intimately intertwined, they continuously interact; hence, one should envision representations, organizations, technologies and institutions as co-evolving through numerous and complicated processes of interaction. As a result, aggregate economic and social dynamics obey to multiple and hierarchized determinants where contingency nonetheless plays a fundamental role. Prediction in such a perspective is an impossible exercise, which does not mean that nothing can be said on the dynamical properties of evolutionary economic systems.

Indeed, two issues raised along this paper are of the outmost importance for qualifying social evolutionary dynamics and thus allowing to grasp the notions of history and progress which are at stake here. To put it quite generally, the first issue concerns the open-endedness of the dynamics, i.e. its fundamentally contingent nature. The second issue is about the fact of hierarchical selection and its consequences on the definition of individuality and autonomy. Both issues raise, in a different but complementary manner, the question of how a society "chooses" a specific path instead another one, namely "chooses" an history.

The question of the open-endedness of the dynamics refers to the specificities of the mechanisms engendering variation as well as to the opposition between fixed and evolving entities. When variation consists in switching from one pre-specified representation or technology to another one, all the possible worlds are given *ex ante*. In this case, evolution is solely a matter of recombination where novelty and surprises have no place. History does not affect the very definition of possible paths but only the selection among them. Instead, when variation continuously modifies the selected entities, new and unexpected forms may appear which cannot be thought of before they come to existence: entities are constructed and evolve through contingency and necessity. Such an open-endedness has been highlighted in biology. However, evolution in social life presents a radical difference from what it is in nature because variations are not random but directional. To put it grossly, the opposition is between random mutations on fixed entities and directional variations on evolving ones. Indeed, processes of economic and social change like technological innovation or learning do not lead to totally indeterminate outcomes: even if it is difficult to analyse them in terms of amelioration, these processes are rather inertial and constrained enough to narrow the scope of novelty. An important challenge for any theory of social evolution is to identify such constraints more precisely and to develop formal tools, unfortunately not available yet, to give an account of such an "oriented novelty".

A second key issue concerns the levels at which one defines evolutionary dynamics and the kind of autonomous entities which are considered. We have seen that selection in social environments operates simultaneously at different levels with many feedbacks between those levels (remember the example of labour market and product market, or the interaction between rules and models of the world in classifier systems models). Such hierarchical selection oblige to rethink about some categories of evolutionary approaches to economic change in order to posit levels of explanation which are meaningfull to social dynamics. In other words, and to make a last reference to biology, one has to clearly sort out the kind of evolving entities which may ground a fruitful reformulation of microeconomic behaviours. We claimed that individual and collective representations are one of those, along with routines and technologies.

These complex processes of selection and interaction lead to unpredictable aggregate outcomes; the "chosen" path results from a combination between the inertial trends given by different kinds of collective and socially constructed norms and institutions on one hand and the novelty characterizing learning on the other hand. Hence, in such environments, criteria for social choices are of limited effect as a) their very definition is problematic, and b) the channels through which they may work are not straightforward and rather unclear. In this perspective, it is a puzzle that our Western societies give so much weight to economic efficiency as a selection criterion whereas at the same time, the perennial influences of social norms and institutional forms imprint their dynamics on a much pervasive scale than the explicit search for efficiency they seem to hold as a foundation (the QWERTY example of David (1985) as well as Arthur (1989) are illuminating on this point). A general theory of fitness in social life should certainly help, but is it only possible to design such theory when facing the multiple constraints stemming from the role of institutions without loosing the richness of such hierarchical approach?

REFERENCES

Arthur, W. B. (1989), "Competing Technologies, Increasing Returns and Lock-in by Historical Events", *The Economic Journal,* 99 (394), pp. 116-31.

Arthur, W. B. (1992), "On Learning and Adaptation in the Economy", *Santa Fe Institute Working Paper* # 92-07-038.

Arthur, W. B., Y. M. Ermoliev & Y. M. Kaniovski (1987), "Path-Dependent Processes and the Emergence of Macro-Structure", *European Journal of Operational Research*, 30, pp. 294-304.

Banerjee, A. & J. W. Weibull (1991), "Evolutionary Selection and Rational Behavior", mimeo.

Blanc, M. (1990), *Les héritiers de Darwin. L'évolution en mutation*, Paris, Seuil.

Blume, L. E. & D. Easley (1989), "Wealth Dynamics and the Market Selection Hypothesis", Cornell University, mimeo.

Boyer, R. & A. Orléan (1995), "Stabilité de la coopération dans les jeux évolutionnistes stochastiques", *Revue Economique*, 46 (3), pp. 797-806.

Coriat, B. & G. Dosi (1995), "Learning How to Govern and Learning How to Solve Problems: On the Co-Evolution of Competences, Conflicts and Organizational Routines", Laxenburg, Austria, *IIASA Working Paper* # 95-06.

Darwin, C. (1859), *On the Origin of Species*, french translation (1992), Paris, Flammarion.

David, P. A. (1985), "Clio and the Economics of QWERTY", *American Economic Review*, 75 (2), pp. 332-37.

Dawkins, R. (1976), *The Selfish Gene*, New-York, Oxford University Press.

De Long, J. B., A. Shleifer, L. H. Summers & R. J. Waldmann (1990), "Noise Trader Risk in Financial Markets", *Journal of Political Economy*, 98 (4), pp. 703-38.

Dore, R. (1987), *Taking Japan Seriously*, Stanford CA., Stanford University Press.

Dosi, G. & R. R. Nelson (1994), "An Introduction to Evolutionary Theories in Economics", *Journal of Evolutionary Economics*, 4, pp. 153-72.

Dosi, G. (1988), "Sources, Procedures and Microeconomic Effects of Innovation", *Journal of Economic Literature*, 26 (3), pp. 1120-71.

Dosi, G., C. Freeman, R. Nelson, G. Silverberg & L. Soete (Eds.), (1988), *Technical Change and Economic Theory*, London, Pinter Publishers.

Dosi, G., L. Marengo & G. Fagiolo (1996), "Learning in Evolutionary Environments", Trento, Italy, *CEEL Working Paper* # 1996-05.

Dosi, G., L. Marengo, A. Bassanini & M. Valente (1994), "Norm as Emergent Properties of Adaptive Learning", Laxenburg, Austria, *IIASA Working Paper* # 94-73.

Eldredge, N. (1995), *Reinventing Darwin. The Great Evolutionary Debate*, London, Weidenfeld and Nicolson.

Foster, D. & H. P. Young (1990), "Stochastic Evolutionary Game Dynamics", *Theoretical Population Biology*, 38, pp. 219-32.

Frankel, J. A. & K. A. Froot (1987), "Using Survey Data to Test Standard Propositions Regarding Exchange Rate Expectations", *American Economic Review*, 77 (1), pp. 133-53.

Friedman, M. (1953), *Essays in Positive Economics*, Chicago, The University of Chicago Press.

Gayon, J. (1992), *Darwin et l'après-Darwin*, Paris, Editions Kimé.

Gould, S. J. & R. C. Lewontin (1979), "The Spandrels of San Marco and the Panglossian Paradigm: a Critique of the Adaptationist Programme", *Proceedings of the Royal Society*, London, 205, pp. 581-98.

Gould, S. J. (1980), *The Panda's Thumb*, New York, W. W. Norton & Co.

Gould, S. J. (1983), *Hen's Teeth and Horse's Toes*, New-York, W. W. Norton & Co.

Gould, S. J. (1991), *The Individual in Darwin's World*, The Second Edinburgh Medal Address, London, Weidenfeld & Nicolson.

Granovetter, M. (1985), "Economic Action and Social Structure: The Problem of Embeddedness", *American Journal of Sociology*, 91 (3), pp. 481-510.

Granovetter, M. & R. Swedberg (Eds.) (1992), *The Sociology of Economic Life*, Boulder CO., Westview Press.

Hodgson, G. M. (1993), *Economics and Evolution*, Cambridge UK, Polity Press.

Holland, J. H. & J. H. Miller (1991), "Artificial Adaptive Agents in Economic Theory", *American Economic Review*, 81 (2), pp. 365-70.

Holland, J. H. (1975), *Adaptation in Natural and Artificial Systems*, Ann Arbor, University of Michigan Press.

Holland, J. H. (1986), "Escaping Brittleness: The Possibilities of General-Purpose Learning Algorithms Applied to Parallel Rule-Based Systems", in R. S. Michalski, J. G. Carbonell & T. M. Mitchell (Eds.), *Machine Learning II*, Los Altos CA., Morgan Kaufmann, pp. 593-623.

Holland, J. H., K. J. Holyoak, R. E. Nisbett & P. R. Thagard (1986), *Induction: Processes of Inference, Learning, and Discovery*, Cambridge MA., The MIT Press.

Johnson-Laird, P. N. (1983), *Mental Models*, Cambridge MA., Harvard University Press.

Johnson-Laird, P. N. (1991), "A Model Theory of Induction", *Journal of Technology and Social Studies on Society and Technology*.

Keynes, J. M. (1936), *The General Theory of Employment, Interest and Money*, New-York, Harcourt Brace & World.

Kirman, A. P. (1993), "Ants, Rationality and Recruitment", *Quarterly Journal of Economics*, 108, pp. 137-56.

Lakoff, G. (1987), *Women, Fire, and Dangerous Things. What Categories Reveal about the Mind*, Chicago, The University of Chicago Press.

Lane, D. A. (1993a), "Artificial Worlds in Economics: Part I", *Journal of Evolutionary Economics*, vol. 3, pp. 89-107.

Lane, D. A. (1993b), "Artificial Worlds in Economics: Part II", *Journal of Evolutionary Economics*, vol. 3, pp. 177-97.

Langton, C. G., C. Taylor, J. D. Farmer & S. Rasmussen (Eds.) (1991), *Artificial Life II*, Redwood City CA., Addison-Wesley.

Lesourne, J. (1991), *Economie de l'ordre et du désordre*, Paris, Economica.

Lewontin, R. C. (1991), *The Doctrine of DNA. Biology as an Ideology*, Penguin Books.

March, J. G. & H. A. Simon (1993), "Introduction to the Second Edition of *Organizations*", *Organizations*, Oxford, Blackwell Publishers.

March, J. G. (1991), "Exploration and Exploitation in Organizational Learning", *Organization Science*, 2 (1), pp. 71-87.

Marengo, L. & H. Tordjman (1996), "Speculation, Heterogeneity and Learning: A Simulation Model of Exchange Rates Dynamics", *Kyklos*, 49 (3), pp. 407-38.

Maynard-Smith, J. (1982), *Evolution and the Theory of Games*, Cambridge UK, Cambridge University Press.

Monod, J. (1970), *Le hasard et la nécessité*, Paris, Editions du Seuil.

Nelson, R. R. & S. G. Winter (1982), *An Evolutionary Theory of Economic Change*, Cambridge MA., The Belknap Press of Harvard University Press.

Nelson, R. R. (1995), "Recent Evolutionary Theorizing About Economic Change", *Journal of Economic Literature*, 33 (1), pp. 48-90.

Nelson, R. R. (Ed.) (1993), *National Innovation Systems: A Comparative Study*, Oxford, Oxford University Press.

Orléan, A. (1990), "Contagion mimétique et bulles spéculatives", in J. Cartelier (Ed.), *La formation des grandeurs économiques*, Paris, Presses Universitaires de France, pp. 285-321.

Orléan, A. (1996), "De la stabilité évolutionniste à la stabilité stochastique", *Revue Economique*, 47 (3), pp. 589-600.

Orléan, A. (Ed.) (1994), *Analyse économique des conventions*, Paris, Presses Universitaires de France.

Palmer, R.G., W. B. Arthur, J. H. Holland, B. LeBaron & P. Tayler (1994), "Artificial Economic Life: A Simple Model of a Stockmarket", *Physica D*, 75, pp. 264-74.

Sargent, T. (1993), *Bounded Rationality in Economics*, Oxford, Clarendon Press of Oxford University Press.

Shiller, R. J. (1989), *Market Volatility*, Cambridge MA., MIT Press, 3ᵉ édition (1991).

Soros, G. (1994), "A Theory of Reflexivity", MIT, mimeo.

Sperber, D. (1995), *La contagion des idées*, Paris, Odile Jacob.

Tordjman, H. (1996), "The Formation of Beliefs on Financial Markets: Representativeness and Prototypes", Laxenburg, Austria, *IIASA Working Paper* # 96-87.

Weibull, J. W. (1996), *Evolutionary Game Theory,* Cambridge MA., The MIT Press.

PART 1

Consumers and Firms Behaviors: from Heterogeneity to Mimetism

CHAPTER 2
INFORMATIONAL INFLUENCES AND THE AMBIVALENCE OF IMITATION

André ORLÉAN

1. Introduction

Imitation is a complex phenomenon that has been studied by economists and other social scientists for a long time. An individual can choose to imitate another individual or a group for a wide array of different reasons: because he is convinced by the other individual's argument; because of peer group pressure as in Leibenstein's (1982) situation where workers within a firm have to conform to the prevailing "effort convention"; because of manias and fads as in Kindleberger's (1978) or Shiller's (1989) analysis of financial instability; because of social sanctions as in Akerlof's (1980) interpretation of social customs; because of coordination externalities as in Arthur's (1989) or Young's (1993) models; to discover a better strategy as in Nelson and Winter (1982) or Axelrod (1984); because of tradition as in Boyd and Richerson's (1985; 1993) study of cultural transmission; for the sake of conformity as in Asch's (1951) experiment; and the list is not exhaustive [1].

The present paper is devoted to "informational influences" [2]. It considers a group situation where agents have no access to others' private information, but can only observe their actions. Since these actions reflect part of their private information, it is rational for each agent to take them into account. Informational influences can give rise to imitative behaviors. Imagine that a sudden fire breaks out in a room, that there are two doors, one being a dead end, the other one being the right exit, and that I do not know which is which. If I see one person leaving the room, it is rational for me to imitate him. If this person has no information and has formed his choice by pure chance, to follow him will not decrease my performance because he is exactly in the same situation than I am. But if this agent has some knowledge about the true distribution of doors, I will improve my performance by imitating him. My ability to evaluate the quality of the information on the basis of which the other has acted is clearly a central parameter in that reasoning. It should be noted that informational influences are

---

1. Let us remark that these different mechanisms can overlap. A more systematic presentation will be found in Bikhchandani, Hirshleifer, and Welch (1992).
2. The concept of "informational social influence" has been introduced by the social psychologists Deutsch and Gerard (1955). The economical notion of "informational influences" is akin to this concept.

very common in finance because traders usually have no access to others' information but can nevertheless observe prices which are generated by others' actions. The possibility for prices to reveal part or all of the private information is at the core of the notion of informational efficiency (Grossman 1976; Grossman and Stiglitz 1980).

A body of recent work have analyzed informational influences within a dynamical framework. These works have shown that pure informational influences can lead to imitative decision processes such as "herd behavior" (Banerjee 1992; Scharfstein and Stein 1990), "informational cascade" (Bikchandani, Hirshleifer and Welch 1992), or contagion (Arthur and Lane 1993; Kirman 1993). It has been demonstrated that optimizing agents can decide rationally to follow what previous agents have chosen rather than to use their own private information. Such a process leads to a general conformity on a certain behavior or opinion. These results have been obtained in models which assume a sequential decision process: individuals enter the market one by one, observe their predecessors and take a unique and irreversible decision (Banerjee 1992; Bikchandani, Hirshleifer and Welch 1992). The assumption of sequentiality is crucial. It allows the agent entering the market in $(t+1)$ to calculate the true probability $P(\mathbf{a}_t|\sigma_t, \theta)$ of previous choices $\mathbf{a}_t$ conditionally to σ_t, the set of the t first agents' private information, and θ the state of nature that has been drawn at the beginning of the process at time ($t=0$). Then, using Bayes' rule, the individual can infer $P(\theta|\mathbf{a}_t)$ and then compute his expected utility.

The aim of this paper is to extend these results to a non sequential framework where agents interact simultaneously with each other, modifying their action at each period of time without knowing when "the process has begun". In other words, agents do not know when θ is changing. Such a decision structure is better suited for the modeling of market situations. For instance in Bikchandani et al., "the order of individuals is exogenous and is known to all" (p. 999): the first individual chooses either H or L, according to the value of his private information + or − ; thus, the second individual is able to infer the first agent's private information from his decision. In our model, this is no longer possible. Because agents do not know when θ has changed, they do not know who is the first of the "new round" nor who is the second. We assume that at each period t, an agent' set of information is strictly reduced to his private information σ_t and a publicly available information expressing the group behavior in $(t-1)$, named $f(t-1)$. $f(t-1)$ can be considered in our model as equivalent to a price. In such a framework, a specific problem appears. In order to determine the relative weight μ they will give to their two informations, σ_t and $f(t-1)$, agents have to evaluate the quality of the signal f. But this quality is not exogenous; it depends on the way other agents have weighted the two informations. For instance, if previous agents have mainly relied on their private information, the signal f is very informative and posterior agents should increase the weight of f in their decision. But, because such a behavior will make f less informative, it may lead to an opposite change in μ. In such a context, we have to examine the existence of an equilibrium value of μ.

To handle this problem, we first begin, in section 2, by assuming that all the agents follow a constant rule of decision defined by μ. In our model, μ expresses the propensity to choose according to the majority side of the group rather than to use one's own information; it measures agents' propensity to imitate. Section 3 presents our basic model. It shows that, when μ is small, the individual and collective performance is low because agents neglect the important quantity of information contained in f. When the propensity to imitate increases, the collective and individual performance increases; the average error decreases. The role of imitation is clearly positive here because it allows agents to take into account part of the collective information. Hence, imitation can be viewed as the specific mechanism through which collective information is made available to individual agents within a decentralized information structure. Then we show that imitation improves individual and collective performance *only if the propensity to imitate is not too high*: when imitation gets to a certain threshold, self-validating processes appear which converge on wrong choices. Because agents insufficiently rely on their private information, the collective outcome f is no more informative and imitation becomes counter-productive. The fact that imitation can be either positive or negative according to its intensity is what we refer to as "the ambivalence of imitation". This ambivalence is a very intuitive result: it is efficient for me to imitate the others as long as they are better informed than I am; it becomes inefficient if they are also imitators. Such a situation has been described by Kindleberger (1978): "The action of each individual is rational -or would be, were it not for the fact that others are behaving in the same way" (p. 34). Nevertheless, as far as we know, the fact that imitation can be ambivalent has never been demonstrated.

In section 4, we calculate the optimal degree of imitation μ^* and consider the game where each agent i has to determine his strategy $\mu(i)$. We show that a situation where all the agents choose the same value μ^* is a very implausible Nash equilibrium as soon as the number of agents is large. It is always better to be a deviant. This paradoxical structure is quite similar to the one analyzed by Grossman-Stiglitz (1980) and highlights the complex role played by imitation on financial markets. Nevertheless, it should be emphasized that in finance "herding externalities" are only a part of the story because imitation has a cost (the stock market price) which is depending on the number of imitators [1]. Section 5 concludes by showing that our result on the ambivalence of imitation remains true for a very large set of decision rules.

2. The problem

Let us consider an economy composed of N agents noted i, $i \in \{1,2, ..., N\}$. The state of the world, named θ, is either $\{H\}$ or $\{L\}$ with equal

---

1. This point is discussed in Bikchandani *et al.* (1992, pp. 1012-3).

42 | Consumers and firms behaviors

prior probability. The agents cannot observe directly θ. In order to discover it, each individual independently observes a signal σ defined as follows: σ can be either $\{+\}$ or $\{-\}$, and its value is linked to the state of the economy through the following conditional probabilities:

$$\begin{cases} P(\sigma = + \,|H) = P(\sigma = - \,|L) = p > 0.5 \\ P(\sigma = - \,|H) = P(\sigma = + \,|L) = 1 - p < 0.5 \end{cases} \quad (2.1)$$

σ_i, the value of the independent observation made by agent i, is called his private information. Using Bayes' rule, a rational agent can easily evaluate the probability of being in state $\{H\}$ accordingly to his private information. He obtains:

$$P(H|\sigma_i = +) = P(H|\,+\,) = \frac{P(+\,|H) \cdot P(H)}{P(+)} = p_i$$

and

$$P(H|\sigma_i = -) = P(H|\,-\,) = \frac{P(-\,|H) \cdot P(H)}{P(-)} = 1 - p_i \quad (2.2)$$

where p_i is agent i's estimation of p. We will assume that agents do not know the exact value of p, but make no mistake about the "direction of the correlation"; i.e. $\forall i, p_i > 0.5$. Then, it follows from equations (2.2) that every agent i will choose $\{H\}$ if he has observed $\{\sigma_i = +\}$ and $\{L\}$ if $\{\sigma_i = -\}$. Thus the probability of making the wrong choice is equal to $(1 - p)$. The greater is the accuracy of the signal σ, the smaller is the probability of making the wrong choice. This general framework is the one proposed by Bikchandani *et al.* (1992).

Let us now consider the whole population. Let us note n, the number of individuals having chosen $\{H\}$ and f equal to n/N, the proportion of such individuals. If every individual is forming his choice on the sole basis of his private and independent information σ_i, the probability of choosing $\{H\}$ will be either p or $(1 - p)$ depending upon θ, the value of the state of the economy. Thus f is a realization of the binomial law $\tilde{A}(\theta)$ defined as follows:

$$\begin{cases} E[\tilde{A}(\theta)] = a(\theta) \\ Var[\tilde{A}(\theta)] = \frac{p \cdot (1-p)}{N} \end{cases} \text{with} \begin{cases} a(H) = p \\ a(L) = 1 - p \end{cases} \quad (2.3)$$

It follows that when agents make their choice on the sole basis of their private information, the average frequency of people having made the wrong choice is equal to $(1 - p)$. It is identical to the average mistake made by an individual

Informational influences and the ambivalence of imitation | 43

i drawn randomly within the population. Because the rule of choice that has been considered does not take into account the collective information collected by the group, the average collective performance is equal to the one of an isolated agent. Can the use of the collective information improve this result?

It is not difficult to see that the quantity of information contained within the whole group is much richer than the information possessed by an individual. To illustrate this point, let us assume the existence of a center than collects all the private information. Let us note f_+ the proportion of $\{+\}$ that have been observed within the whole population. This value is calculated by the center and then communicated to every agent. Obviously f_+ follows the binomial law $\tilde{A}(\theta)$. Let us assume that all the members of the group adopt the following rule of decision: "if $\{f_+ > 0.5\}$, they choose $\{H\}$; if $\{f_+ < 0.5\}$, they choose $\{L\}$; if $\{f_+ = 0.5\}$, they choose either $\{H\}$ or $\{L\}$ with probabilities equal to 0.5". This rule of choice will lead to a much better performance than the preceding one. Indeed the probability of error is equal to the following probability:

$$P(f_+ < 0.5|H) + 0.5 \cdot P(f_+ = 0.5|H) = P(f_+ > 0.5|L) + 0.5 \cdot P(f_+ = 0.5|L)$$

If N is great, this probability is very small. For instance, if $N = 51$ and $p = 0.7$, it is equal to 0.0013, to be compared to 0.30 in the former case. This rule is very efficient, but it needs a center which collects all the private information to be implemented. In this paper we will consider institutional settings where such a centralization of information is impossible or too costly. We will analyze a decentralized structure of interactions, i.e. a structure where agents have no direct access to other agents' private information, but can only observe their choices. More precisely, we will assume that only f, the collective choice, can be observed. This notion of decentralization has been considered because it is close to the way a market functions. In a market, at each date t, every agent only knows his private information and the value of the price in $(t-1)$ which aggregates individual choices. The question we wish to address is how these decentralized interactions can work. To begin with, we have to analyze the way individuals take their decisions.

We define a decentralized rule of decision as a couple of functions $q(f, \sigma_i)$, where σ_i is either $\{+\}$ or $\{-\}$, which gives the probability of choosing $\{H\}$ when the values σ_i and f have been observed. A first rule of decision is the one considered previously where the agent does not take into account the others. He chooses on the sole basis of his private information. We will note this rule q_0. It is defined as follows:

$$\begin{cases} q_0(f, +) = 1 \\ q_0(f, -) = 0 \end{cases} \quad (2.4)$$

This rule does not depend on f. We have seen that it leads to a situation where the average proportion of people having made the right choice, i.e. either

{H} if {θ = H} or {L} if {θ = L}, is equal to p. Our intuition is that taking care of f will improve this result.

The general rule that will be considered is determined as follows. When $\{\sigma_i = +\}$ and $\{f \geq 0.5\}$, both informations lead to the same decision $\{H\}$: they are consistant. The situation is different when $\{\sigma_i = +\}$ and $\{f < 0.5\}$ because then, the two signals are contradictory. If we note $\mu \in [0,1]$, the probability to choose according to f, the majority side, we obtain q_μ the following general rule of decision:

$$\begin{cases} \text{if } f \geq 0.5 & q_\mu(f, +) = 1 \\ \text{if } f < 0.5 & q_\mu(f, +) = 1 - \mu \end{cases} \text{ and } \begin{cases} \text{if } f > 0.5 & q_\mu(f, -) = \mu \\ \text{if } f \leq 0.5 & q_\mu(f, -) = 0 \end{cases}$$

Then we have the relation:

$$q_\mu(f, -) = 1 - q_\mu(1 - f, +)$$

which expresses the symmetry between $\{-\}$ and $\{+\}$. $(1 - \mu)$ measures the propensity to choose according to one's own private information.

When μ equals 0, i.e. when agents strictly follow their private information, the average error of the group is $(1 - p)$. Our central question is: what happens when every agent follows the rule q_μ with $\mu > 0$? In such a situation, agents' choices are no longer independent: the way agent i chooses depends upon previous agents' choices. It follows that in order to understand how f is determined, we have to be more precise about the definition of the dynamical process of interactions.

3. The basic model

Let us consider the following process. In $(t = 0)$, the state of the economy θ is drawn according to the probabilities $P(H) = P(L) = 0.5$ and will remain constant till date T. Because the sequence $[0,T]$ can be understood as a specific round amid a global process which began before time 0 and will continue after time T, $f(0)$ is depending on what has happened before $(t = 0)$ [1]. Within our model, it will be considered as an arbitrary given parameter. At time $(t > 0)$, one individual i is randomly drawn. He observes $f(t - 1)$ and the signal σ. Then he revises his last choice according to the rule $q_\mu(f, \sigma_i)$.

---

1. For instance θ_t can be viewed as a markovian process defined for $t \in Z$ by the following transition matrix:

$$\begin{bmatrix} 1 - \varepsilon & \varepsilon \\ \varepsilon & 1 - \varepsilon \end{bmatrix}$$

with ε being as small as wanted.

Let us emphasize that agent i does not take into account in t the information he could have observed before. This simplifying hypothesis can be justified because of the short memory of agents, and/or by the fact that agents do not know when θ is changing and, consequently, do not know if their past information is still relevant. We have also assumed that only one agent is drawn at each instant. We could have assumed that L agents are drawn randomly, with L smaller than N, without qualitatively modifying our results.

This set of hypotheses define a Markovian stochastic process. The variable we are interested in is the probability law $P(f; t)$ followed by $f(t)$. To what does it converge? To answer this question, we first have to determine the probability to choose $\{H\}$ at $(t+1)$ when $f(t) = f$. Because the probability to draw $\{+\}$ is equal to $a(\theta)$, we obtain:

$$J(f, \mu, \theta) = a(\theta) \cdot q_\mu(f, +) + [1 - a(\theta)] \cdot q_\mu(f, -) \qquad (3.1)$$

Let us emphasize that $J(f, \mu, \theta)$ depends on θ through the value of a, i.e. the average number of $\{+\}$ that agents have observed. Knowing the probability J, we can calculate:

$$\begin{cases} P[f(t+1) = f(t) + 1/N] = P(f \to f + 1/N) = (1-f) \cdot J(f, \mu, \theta) = W_+(f, \mu, \theta) \\ P[f(t+1) = f(t) - 1/N] = P(f \to f - 1/N) = f \cdot [1 - J(f, \mu, \theta)] = W_-(f, \mu, \theta) \end{cases}$$

These equations completely determined the stochastic process followed by $f(t)$, i.e. the way $P(f; t)$ varies through time. (When there is no possible confusion, θ and μ will be omitted for the sake of simplicity). The exact description of this process in terms of discrete numbers n is called the master equation (Weidlich and Haag 1983, chapter 2). To simplify the notations, it is more convenient to use an approximate description in terms of continuous variables. Because the exact form of the stationary distribution can be calculated in both cases, we have been able to verify that the continuous description constitutes a reliable approximation when N is large. The continuous stochastic process is a diffusion process defined by the standard form of a Fokker-Planck equation in one dimension:

$$\frac{\partial P(f; t)}{\partial t} = -\frac{\partial}{\partial f}[K(f) P(f; t)] + \frac{1}{2N} \frac{\partial^2}{\partial f^2}[Q(f) P(f; t)]$$

with:

$$\begin{cases} K(f) = W_+(f) - W_-(f) \\ Q(f) = W_+(f) + W_-(f) \end{cases}$$

46 | Consumers and firms behaviors

For $0 \leq \mu < 1$, it can be shown that the process is ergodic: whatever $P(f;0)$ [1], $P(f;t)$ converges to a unique stationary distribution $P_{st}(f,\mu,\theta)$. K, the drift function, is central to understand the dynamics:

$$K(f,\mu,\theta) = W_+(f,\mu,\theta) - W_-(f,\mu,\theta) = -f + J(f,\mu,\theta) \quad (3.2)$$

When K is positive, the probability that f increases is greater than the probability f decreases. More precisely one can associate to our stochastic process the following deterministic system:

$$\frac{df}{dt} = K(f,\mu,\theta) \quad (3.3)$$

This equation describes the deterministic path that would be observed if the fluctuations could be neglected. It is such that its fixed points are the extrema of the stationary distribution $P_{st}(f,\mu,\theta)$. A maximum (resp. minimum) corresponds to a stable (resp. unstable) fixed points. As $K(f,\mu,\theta)$ is equal to $-f + J(f,\mu,\theta)$ (equation 3.2), it is easy to find the extrema of $P_{st}(f,\mu,\theta)$. They are the solutions of the following system:

$$\begin{cases} 0 \leq f < 0.5 & J(f,\mu,\theta) = a(\theta)(1-\mu) = f \\ f = 0.5 & J(f,\mu,\theta) = a(\theta) = f \\ 0.5 < f \leq 1 & J(f,\mu,\theta) = a(\theta) + [1-a(\theta)]\mu = f \end{cases} \quad (3.4)$$

Because $J(f,\mu,L) = 1 - J(1-f,\mu,H)$, we know that:

$$P_{st}(f,\mu,L) = 1 - P_{st}(1-f,\mu,H)$$

and then, from now on, we will concentrate our attention on the case $\{\theta = H\}$.

When $p(1-\mu)$ is greater than $(0.5 - 1/N)$, i.e. if

$$\mu \leq \mu^* = 1 - \frac{0.5 - \frac{1}{N}}{p} \simeq \frac{2p-1}{2p} \quad (3.5)$$

$P_{st}(f)$ is a unimodal distribution (see Fig. 1.1). Its peak (I) is defined by $f_I(\mu,H) = p + (1-p)\mu$ and $f_I(\mu,L) = 1 - f_I(\mu,H)$. If we term "error" the proportion of agents who make the wrong choice, we can calculate the average

---

[1]. We have assumed that $P(f;0) = \delta(f - f(0))$, a Dirac distribution in $f(0)$, but our result holds for any distribution.

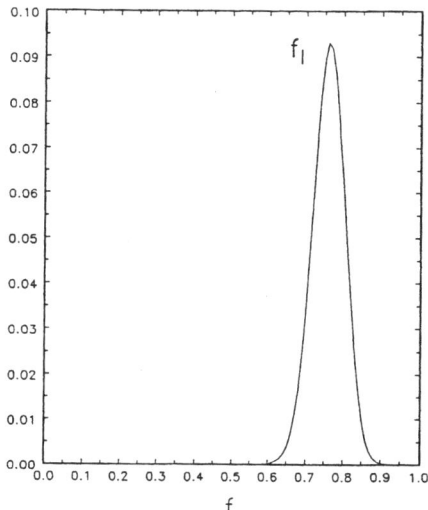

Figure 1.1: Stationary distribution $P_{st}(f)$ with $\mu = 0.2$ and $p = 0.7$

error, $\overline{E}(\mu)$. It is approximately equal to $E_I(\mu)$, the value of the error when f is equal to $f_I(\mu, \theta)$ [1]:

$$\overline{E}(\mu) = E_I(\mu) = 1 - f_I(\mu, H) = f_I(\mu, L) = (1 - \mu)(1 - p) \quad (3.6)$$

In other words, the average proportion of individuals having made the wrong choice is equal to $(1 - \mu)(1 - p)$: the greater μ, the better the performance of the group. Being imitative is efficient: it leads to better performances than following the independent rule q_0. This result is easy to understand: through imitation, an unlucky individual who has observed $\{-\}$ when the state of the world was $\{H\}$, can nevertheless make the right choice $\{H\}$ because in making his choice he takes into account not only his private "false" information $\{\sigma_i = -\}$, but also the fact that $\{f > 0.5\}$. Imitation can be viewed as the specific manner through which global information is disseminated within decentralized information structures.

When μ becomes greater than μ^* but remains strictly inferior to 1, the shape of the stationary distribution is qualitatively affected. This corresponds to a bifurcation of the equation 3.3. A new peak (M) appears, $f_M(\mu, H) = (1 - \mu)p$. The stationary distribution becomes bimodal (see Fig. 1.2). We can calculate the error in the state f_M:

$$E_M(\mu) = [1 - p(1 - \mu)] \quad (3.7)$$

---

1. When $N \to +\infty$, the variance of the stationary distribution is converging toward 0. It follows that, for N large, the stationary distribution is almost concentrated in $f_I(\mu, \theta)$.

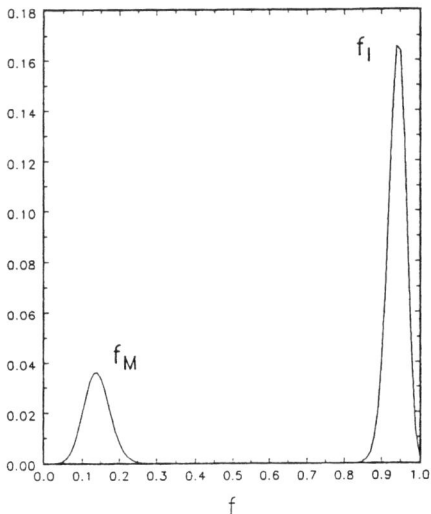

Figure 1.2: Stationary distribution $P_{st}(f)$ with $\mu = 0.8$ and $p = 0.7$

It is always greater than the average error $(1 - p)$ that would have prevailed if there was no imitation at all. The state $f_M(\mu, \theta)$ is the result of a self-validating process: because the propensity to imitate is large, the power of conformism dominates the role of the information, i.e. a large propensity of agents having observed $\{+\}$ will choose $\{L\}$ when $\{f(t) < 0.5\}$. This propensity to conform to the majority can lead the collective opinion toward a configuration where almost everybody has chosen the wrong opinion. For μ close to 0 and $\{\theta = H\}$, we can observe a quasi unanimity on $\{L\}$!

To have an accurate understanding of the way our system behaves when μ is greater than μ^*, note that the probability of transition from one peak to the other is very very small when N is great. The transition time is proportional to e^N. It follows that the process is "quasi" non ergodic for large N: $f(t)$ remains either in the vicinity of $f_I(\mu, \theta)$ or in the vicinity of $f_M(\mu, \theta)$. For a plausible time of observation T, we shall not observe transition from one peak to the other.

Figures 2 and 3 show two simulations of our process where p is equal to 0.7 and N is equal to 100. 5 000 periods are calculated. In $(t = 0)$, $f(0)$ is supposed to be equal to 0.5, and the state $\{\theta = H\}$ is drawn. Then every 1 000 periods, the state θ is changing. In figure 2, we assume that μ is equal to 0.2 which is inferior to $\mu^* = 0.28$. In that case, the stationary distribution is unimodal: $f_I(\mu, H) = 0.76$ and $f_I(\mu, L) = 0.24$. When θ changes from $\{H\}$ to $\{L\}$, the proportion of choices $\{H\}$ is moving from the neighborhood of the mode $f_I(\mu, H)$ to the neighborhood of the mode $f_I(\mu, L)$.

In Figure 3, μ is assumed to be equal to 0.8. The stationary distribution becomes bimodal and the dynamics is then very different. In the first round

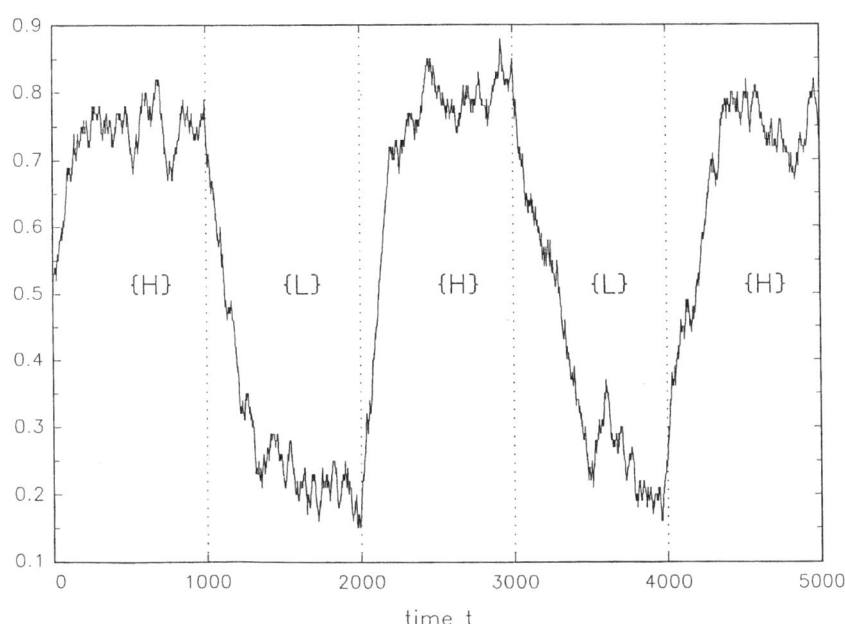

Figure 2: $f_I(0.2, H) = 0.76$ and $f_I(0.2, L) = 0.24$

$(t < 1\,000)$, $f(t)$ is converging to the neighborhood of the right mode $f_I(\mu, H)$. Its value is equal to 0.94 [1]. Almost every agent has found the right value of the state θ. The average error is inferior to the one prevailing in the previous case. But when θ changes from $\{H\}$ to $\{L\}$, $f(t)$ does not converge anymore to $f_I(\mu, L)$, but to the wrong mode $f_M(\mu, L) = 0.86$. In that state, only 14% of the population makes the right choice $\{L\}$. When the propensity to imitate is large, the changes in the state of the world have only a small impact on the collective choice because agents give an insufficient weight to their private information relatively to f. The majority side of the population remains unchanged.

When $\mu = 1$, the process is strictly non ergodic: $\{f = 0\}$ and $\{f = 1\}$ are absorbing states. There are two stationary distributions: δ_0 and δ_1, the Dirac distributions in $\{f = 0\}$ and $\{f = 1\}$.

4. The ambivalence of imitation

Imitation is ambivalent: to imitate is efficient only if the average propensity to imitate is small; it is getting counter-productive otherwise. This result is quite

---

1. Of course, we could have observed the convergence of $f(t)$ to the neighborhood of the other mode $f_M(\mu, H)$. In that case, when θ changes from $\{H\}$ to $\{L\}$, $f(t)$ goes to $f_I(\mu, L)$.

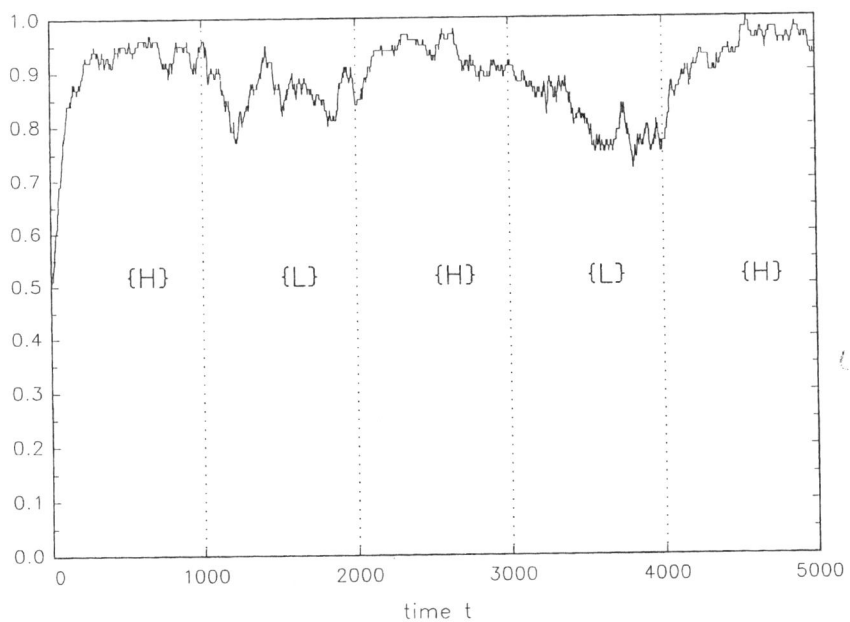

Figure 3: $f_I(0.8, H) = 0.94$ and $f_M(0.8, L) = 0.86$

intuitive: imitation is efficient if the individual I imitate is well-informed; it is not if the individual I imitate is himself an imitator. More precisely, we have shown that, when the propensity to imitate μ is smaller than μ^*, being imitative increases the accuracy of individual opinions: through imitation individuals have access to the global information which allows the agents having observed the "wrong" information to correct their error. Nevertheless, imitation is efficient only if the collective opinion embodies enough information. If μ is getting greater than μ^*, imitation gives rise to a self-validating dynamics where collective opinion becomes deconnected from fundamental information. This result is summarized in Figure 4[1]. It shows that there are two types of imitative processes, a positive one associated with $f_I(\mu, \theta)$ in which the error $E_I(\mu)$ is a decreasing function of μ; and a negative one associated with $f_M(\mu, \theta)$ where the error $E_M(\mu)$ is an increasing function of μ.

---

1. Figure 4 is also the bifurcation diagram of the equation 3.3.

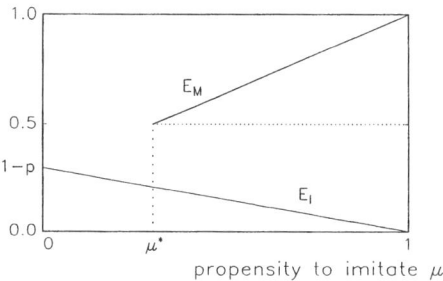

Figure 4: E_I and E_M

We have already seen that, for N large and $\mu \leq \mu^*$, the expected average error $\overline{E}(\mu)$ is close to $E_I(\mu)$ (equation 3.6). When $1 > \mu > \mu^*$ and N is large, it is more difficult to evaluate $\overline{E}(\mu)$ because the mathematical expectation:

$$\begin{cases} \int (1-f) \cdot dP_{st}(f, \mu, H) & \text{if } \{\theta = H\} \\ \int f \cdot dP_{st}(f, \mu, L) & \text{if } \{\theta = L\} \end{cases}$$

would be a good evaluation only if the dynamics could be observed during an infinite length of time in order to observe a great number of transitions from one peak to the other. For a plausible time T of observation, the following quantity will be a "satisfying" approximation:

$$\overline{E}(\mu) = \frac{E_M(\mu) + E_I(\mu)}{2} = (1-p) + \frac{(2p-1)\mu}{2} \geq (1-p)$$

because, in the situation under consideration, $f(t)$ oscillates only between neighborhoods of $f_I(\mu, H)$ and $f_M(\mu, L)$, (respectively between $f_I(\mu, L)$ and $f_M(\mu, H)$), as it has been illustrated by figure 3, with $\{H\}$ and $\{L\}$ being equiprobable. This measure is better suited to our problem because the probability to observe a transition from $f_I(\mu, \theta)$ to $f_M(\mu, \theta)$ for the given time T is negligible. In other words, the probability for the majority to be on the right side, either $\{f > \frac{1}{2}\}$ if $\{H\}$ or $\{f < \frac{1}{2}\}$ if $\{L\}$, is close to 1/2.

It follows that the minimum value for the average error $\overline{E}(\mu)$ is obtained for $\mu = \mu^*$. If the agents were acting cooperatively, they would decide collectively to choose the decision rule q_{μ^*}. In that situation, the average collective error would be:

$$E_{min}(p) = \overline{E}(\mu^*) = \frac{1-p}{2p}$$

52 | Consumers and firms behaviors

which is a decreasing function in p. The more the signal σ is accurate, the smaller is the average collective error.

What happens if each agent i can choose independently his degree $\mu(i)$ of imitation? Let us now consider the non-cooperative game defined as follows: (i) the N agents are the N players; (ii) each agent i has to choose a strategy $\mu(i)$ with $\mu(i)$ belonging to $[0, 1]$; (iii) the payoff for playing the strategy $\mu(i)$ is given by the probability of making the right choice when the stationary distribution is obtained. Let us examine if there exists a Nash equilibrium for this game. Before addressing this question, it should be noted that if every agent chooses a propensity $\mu(i)$ to imitate, the global process which is obtained is the one defined by $J(f, \mu_m, \theta)$ (equation 3.1), with μ_m being the average value of the distribution $\{\mu(i)\}_{i=1,\ldots,N}$. This result is easy to prove if one remarks that:

$$\sum_{i=1}^{i=N} \frac{1}{N} \cdot q_{\mu(i)}(f, \sigma_i) = q_{\mu_m}(f, \sigma_i) \quad \text{with} \quad \mu_m = \frac{1}{N} \sum_{i=1}^{i=N} \mu(i)$$

with $1/N$ being the probability to draw agent i at time t.

Let us consider agent N's choice. He is facing a set of strategies $\{\mu(i)\}_{i=1,\ldots,N-1}$ such that:

$$\mu_{-N} = \frac{1}{N-1} \sum_{i=1}^{i=N-1} \mu(i) \tag{4.1}$$

It follows that:

$$\mu_m = \frac{N-1}{N} \cdot \mu_{-N} + \frac{1}{N} \cdot \mu(N) \tag{4.2}$$

Agent N's optimal choice depends on the value of μ_{-N}. The central intuition is the following: if other individuals are mostly relying on their private information, i.e. μ_{-N} is "small", agent N's best choice is to be a full imitator, i.e. $\mu(N) = 1$, because the collective signal f is more precise that his private signal σ; whereas if other individuals are mostly imitators, i.e. μ_{-N} is "large", agent N's best choice is to ignore f, i.e. $\mu(N) = 0$, because the collective signal is then less precise than σ. If $\mu_{-N} = \mu^*$, then agent N's best choice is $\mu(N) = \mu^*$. $\{\mu(i) = \mu^*, \forall i\}$ is the only Nash equilibrium. To prove this statement, we have to take into account the fact that the value of μ_m is depending on agent N's choice, $\mu(N)$ (equation 4.2).

First let us consider small values of μ_{-N}, i.e. values such that:

$$\frac{N-1}{N} \cdot \mu_{-N} + \frac{1}{N} \leq \mu^* \quad \text{which is equivalent to} \quad \mu_{-N} \leq \frac{N\mu^* - 1}{N-1} \tag{4.3}$$

In that case, agent N's best choice is $\mu(N) = 1$. The proof of this result goes as follows. Because of inequality 4.3, μ_m will remain inferior or equal to μ^*, whatever the value of $\mu(N)$ chosen by agent N. This implies that the stationary distribution $P_{st}(f, \mu_m, \theta)$ will always be unimodal. Then it is easy to calculate the payoff of the strategy μ, i.e. the probability of making the right choice. When $\theta = \{H\}$, the right choice is made with probability 1 when $\{+\} \cup \{f_{st} \geq 0.5\}$ is observed; with probability $(1-\mu)$ when $\{+\} \cup \{f_{st} < 0.5\}$ is observed; and with probability μ when $\{-\} \cup \{f_{st} > 0.5\}$ is observed. Then the payoff m is equal to:

$$m(\mu|H) = pB + (1-\mu)pA + \mu(1-p)C \simeq p + \mu(C-p) \quad (4.4)$$

with:

$$A = \text{Prob}(f_{st} < 0.5), B = \text{Prob}(f_{st} \geq 0.5) \text{ and } C = \text{Prob}(f_{st} > 0.5) \simeq 1 - A$$

when $\theta = \{H\}$. Because $C > p$, this payoff is an increasing function in μ. Agent N's optimal choice is then $\mu(N) = 1$. When f is revealing an important part of the collective information, imitation is the best strategy.

Secondly, let us consider large values of μ_{-N}, i.e. values such that:

$$\frac{N-1}{N} \cdot \mu_{-N} > \mu^* \quad \text{which is equivalent to} \quad \mu_{-N} > \frac{N\mu^*}{N-1} \quad (4.5)$$

Whatever the value of $\mu(N)$, μ_m will remain superior to μ^*. The payoff is still given by equation 4.4. Because of the quasi non ergodicity of the stochastic process, for "plausible" values of T, the quantity C is now depending on $f(0)$. As it has been emphasized previously, a rough estimation of C is 1/2 [1]. It follows that agent N's best strategy is $\mu(N) = 0$. Because the collective signal has become a "bubble", the private information σ is more reliable and should be privileged.

If $\frac{N\mu^* - 1}{N-1} < \mu_{-N} \leq \frac{N\mu^*}{N-1}$, agent N's best choice is such that μ_m is equal to μ^*:

$$\mu(N) = N\mu^* - (N-1)\mu_{-N}$$

Thus $\{\mu(i) = \mu^*, \forall i\}$ is the only Nash equilibrium of our game. For N large, the ability for the group to converge on this equilibrium seems very implau-

---

1. Another way to justify this approximation is to consider the drift term $K(f)$ and the equation 3.3. For $\mu > \mu^*$, this deterministic equation has two stable fixed points: f_I and f_M. It converges to f_I if $f(0) < 0.5$; it converges to f_M if $f(0) > 0.5$. For N large, the drift term dominates the process. The greater μ, the more this approximation holds. For $\mu = 1$, the process is non ergodic and our evaluation of C is exact.

sible [1] but for the special case where agents know the exact value μ^*. More probably, we will observe cycles. At the beginning of the cycle, agents mostly rely on their private information, μ_m is close to 0. Because agents learn that the collective signal reveal an important part of the information, they will give a larger weight to f in their decision. μ_m will then increase. The agents who have chosen a large μ obtain better performances than others (equation 4.4). This situation generates a strong incentive to become more imitative. In a first step, this process is collectively positive because it improves the collective efficiency. But when μ goes beyond the threshold μ^*, the collective efficiency suddenly decreases. This new situation is not immediately perceived by the agents. But after a while they understand that the collective signal has become a "bubble": it does not reveal fundamental information anymore, but is the consequence of collective imitation. Then μ will decrease rapidly. This kind of cyclical process can explained certain features of financial dynamics where a succession of "normal" and "pathological" periods can be observed.

5. Conclusion

The decision rule $q_\mu(f, \sigma_i)$ we have considered until now is particular. It seems plausible that the propensity to imitate is an increasing function of f. If f is close to 0, the probability to choose $\{L\}$ can be greater than when f is equal to 0.45. We can even assume that when $\{+\}$ and $\{f > 0.5\}$ are observed some agents can choose $\{L\}$ because they wrongly interpret the signal σ. Will our result on the ambivalence of imitation remain true for a different family of decision rules? To answer this question, we have to determined the properties that rational private decision rules must satisfy. If we note s the degree of confidence in f, and $q(f, \sigma_i, s)$, the probability to choose $\{H\}$, the general family of decision rules $q(f, \sigma_i, s)$ must verify the following properties:

$$\begin{cases} \text{if } f \in \,]\frac{1}{2},1[& q(f, \sigma_i, s) \text{ is a decreasing function in } s \\ \text{if } f \in \,]\frac{1}{2},1] & q(f, \sigma_i, s) \text{ is an increasing function in } s \end{cases} \quad (5.1)$$

Thus the family of decision rules $q(f, \sigma_i, s)$ indexed by s will verify:

$$\begin{cases} q(f, \sigma_i, s) \text{ satisfies the condition } (5.1) \\ q(f, \sigma_i, s) \text{ is an increasing function in } f \\ q(f, \sigma_i, 0) = q_0(\sigma_i) \quad (\text{equation } 2.4) \\ q(f, -, s) = 1 - q[(1-f), +, s] \quad (\text{Symmetry}) \end{cases} \quad (5.2)$$

---

1. A more suggesting and intuitive argument can be proposed. If agent N believes that his action has no effect on μ_m (agents are price-takers), the preceeding analysis leads him to choose $\mu(N) = 1$, if $\mu \leq \mu^*$ and $\mu(N) = 0$ if $\mu > \mu^*$. In such a situation, there is no Nash equilibrium at all.

$q(f, \sigma_i, s)$ corresponds to $q_\mu(f, \sigma_i)$ within our model. Then we can show that if this family of rules verifies:

$$\exists \epsilon \text{ such that } \forall f \in [0, \epsilon[, \quad \lim_{s \to +\infty} q(f, \sigma_i, s) = 0$$

imitation remains ambivalent. In others words, the stationary distribution has always a good peak, whatever the value of s; and a new peak will appear on the wrong side for large values of s. Depending on the form of q, more than two peaks may exist.

REFERENCES

[1] Akerlof George A., "A Theory of Social Custom, of Which Unemployment May Be One Consequence", *Quarterly Journal of Economics* 94 (June 1980): 599-617.

[2] Arthur W. Brian, "Competing Technologies, Increasing Returns, and Lock-in by Historical Events", *Economic Journal* 99 (March 1989): 116-31.

[3] Arthur W. Brian, and Lane D. A., "Information Contagion", *Structural Change and Economic Dynamics* 4 (1993): 81-104.

[4] Asch Solomon E., "Effects of Group Pressure upon Modification and Distorsion of Judgment". In *Groups, Leadership, and, Men*, edited by H. Guetzkow, Pittsburgh: Varnegie Press, 1951.

[5] Axelrod Robert, *The Evolution of Cooperation*, New York: Basic Books, 1984.

[6] Banerjee Abhijit V., "A Simple Model of Herd Behavior", *Quarterly Journal of Economics* 107 (August 1992): 797-817.

[7] Bikhchandani Sushil; Hirshleifer David and Welch Ivo, "A Theory of Fads, Fashion, Custom, and Cultural Change as Informational Cascades", *Journal of Political Economy* 100, no. 5 (1992): 992-1026.

[8] Boyd Robert and Richerson Peter J., *Culture and the Evolutionary Process*, Chicago: Chicago University Press, 1985.

[9] —, "Rationality, Imitation, and Tradition". In *Nonlinear Dynamics and Evolutionary Economics*, edited by Richard H. Day and Ping Chen, New York, Oxford: Oxford University Press, 1993.

[10] Deutsch Morton and Gerard Harold B., "A Study of Normative and Social Influences upon Individual Judgment", *Journal of Abnormal and Social Psychology* 51 (1955): 629-36.

[11] Grossman Sanford J., "On the Efficiency of Competitive Stock Markets Where Traders Have Diverse Information", *Journal of Finance* 31 (May 1976): 573-85.

[12] Grossman Sanford J. and Stiglitz Joseph E., "On the Impossibility of Informationally Efficient Markets", *The American Economic Review* 70, no. 3 (June 1980): 393-408.

[13] Kindleberger Charles P., *Manias, Panics and Crashes*, New York: Basic Books, 1978.

[14] Leibenstein Harvey, "The Prisoners' Dilemma in the Invisible Hand: an Analysis of Intrafirm Productivity", *The American Economic Review* 72 (May 1982): 92-97.

[15] Kirman Alan, "Ants, Rationality and Recruitment", *Quarterly Journal of Economics* 108 (February 1993): 137-56.

[16] Nelson Richard R. and Winter Sidney G., *An Evolutionary Theory of Economic Change*, Cambridge (Mass.) and London: Belknap Press of Harvard University Press, 1982.

[17] Scharfstein David S. and Stein Jeremy C., "Herd Behavior and Investment", *The American Economic Review* 80 (June 1990): 465-79.

[18] Shiller Robert J., *Market Volatility*, Cambridge (Mass.) and London: The M.I.T. Press, 1989.

[19] Weidlich W. and Haag G., *Concepts and Models of a Quantitative Sociology*, Berlin, Heidelberg, New York: Springer-Verlag, 1983.

[20] Young Peyton H., "The Evolution of Conventions", *Econometrica* 61, no. 1 (January 1993): 57-84.

CHAPTER 3
HOW NETWORK EXTERNALITIES AFFECT PRODUCT VARIETY *

André de PALMA, Karim KILANI and Jacques LESOURNE

1. Introduction

Since many decades, economists (e.g. Chamberlin [20], Hotelling [8]) have recognized the fact that goods are not homogeneous but differentiated. That is, the choice of a good is not only based on its price but also on its quality. Goods are either vertically (unanimous ranking of the goods sold at the marginal cost price) or horizontally differentiated (no unanimous ranking). In this last case, it is generally assumed that the quality of the good corresponds to its intrinsic characteristics, that is to characteristics which are not affected by the number of individuals who have purchased each of them.

There are however many situations where this hypothesis is not satisfied. In this case, the quality of the goods (not intrinsic) depends upon the number of customers who have purchased them. This is the situation which will be treated in this paper. There are two extreme cases. Positive externalities occur when the quality of each good increases with the number of customers selecting it. But the reverse may also prevail, that is the quality of the good may decrease with the number of customers (negative externalities) purchasing it. The former case corresponds to faxes, telephone, computers, credit cards, etc., since their use is easier when more people have joined the network (externality can be direct – as in the case of the telephone – or indirect – as in the case of a credit card. See Katz and Shapiro [22]). The latter case arises basically when congestion appears, as in the road or recreational areas.

In their pioneer articles, Katz and Shapiro [21], Farrell and Saloner [18] analyze the way these network externalities modify oligopolistic competition. Several questions concerning standardization were studied by Farrell and Saloner [19]. Finally, compatibility and the use of an adapter were studied, among others, by Matutes and Regibeau [25].

Only few papers (see Church and Gandal [9] and de Palma and Leruth [13]) have analyzed the joined impact of product differentiation and network externalities. A basic problem in this formulation is that, with positive externalities, a demand system may not be uniquely defined (the demand may

---

* We thank Simon P. Anderson and participants to a seminar at CREA, Ecole Polytechnique, for their helpful comments.

be a correspondence rather than a function). For example, consider a duopoly model with two firms selling (intrinsically) homogenous goods with positive externalities. Clearly, competition between these two firms admit two equilibrium states: one where all customers purchase from firm 1 and the other where they purchase from firm 2. Therefore, the purchase of one of the good by an individual depends on some variable that he cannot observe, the expected number of customers that will purchase each good.

One way to solve this problem has been proposed by Katz and Shapiro who introduced the concept of fulfilling expectations. However, casual observation shows that matters are not so simple. For example, the outcome of the competition between the Mini Disc (Sony) and the Digital Cassette (Philips) has been fairly unpredictable for a long time (and it is still so for the time being), since the decision to purchase a technology depends on an important but an unknown factor (that is which system will be selected by the market). The agreement between the two companies suggests that Philips and Sony themselves were uncertain about the outcome of this competition. A similar example could be found in the case of the diffusion of the Ecu where it has been suggested that the slow diffusion of this innovation is due to the fact that no agent knows when the other agents will join the club.

Another way to solve this problem is to consider the dynamic evolution of the number of adopters as a function of time. In this paper, we assume that, each moment, a new potential user enters the market and has to select one of the goods according to the information he has, that is the price of the goods and the cumulative number of previous adopters. Moreover, we explicitly recognize that the goods are intrinsically differentiated. The intrinsic characteristics are observable by the individual but not observable by the modeler who describes choice behavior as random. For simplicity, the well known logit formulation (see Anderson, de Palma and Thisse [2]) is used to describe the consumer choice behavior. We show that this process is formally equivalent to a Polya process. Using recent results in probability, applied in the economic field by Arthur [6], we are able to derive a tractable model, using the fact that when the number of adopters become large enough, this stochastic process could be approximated by a deterministic process (also called the macroscopic process associated to the stochastic process).

The paper is organized as follows. In section 2, we cast the standard logit model within a dynamic setting. In section 3, we introduce network externalities of the Polya-type. In section 4, we compute the equilibrium of a pricing game and analyze the welfare benchmark. Finally, in section 5, we provide brief conclusions.

2. The Logit Model of Demand

Consider consumers facing the choice among n differentiated products. We suppose that they enter the market sequentially. That is, at the beginning of each

How Network Externalities Affect Product Variety | 59

time period, labelled by $t \in \mathbb{N}$, a consumer (indexed hereafter by t) is drawn from a large population and selects one of the n products [1].

A stochastic utility model is used in order to represent the consumer preferences. The utility derived by consumer t from buying one unit of product i is given by:

$$u_{i,t} = y_t + a_{i,t} - p_{i,t} + \mu \varepsilon_{i,t} \tag{1}$$

where y_t is consumer income, $a_{i,t}$ the quality and $p_{i,t}$ the price of product i at time t. The random element $\varepsilon_{i,t}$ takes into account the idiosyncratic taste heterogeneity among consumers. The positive scale parameter μ measures the intensity of taste dispersion in the population. In this interpretation, the value of the term $\varepsilon_{i,t}$ is known by the individual but not observable by the modeler (who describes individual specific preferences as random terms) [2].

Assume that consumers choose the product which yields the largest value of the utility (1). Moreover, suppose that the random components are independently and identically distributed according to the double exponential distribution with zero means [3] (See McFadden [26]). The probability that a consumer t randomly drawn from the population selects product i has an explicit analytical form given by:

$$\mathbb{P}_{i,t} \equiv \text{prob}\,[u_{i,t} > u_{j,t}, j \neq i] = \frac{\exp[(a_{i,t} - p_{i,t})/\mu]}{\sum_{j=1}^{n} \exp[(a_{j,t} - p_{j,t})/\mu]} \tag{2}$$

Let $N_{i,t}$ be the cumulative number of consumers who have selected product i before or at time t. We focus here on the situation where the parameters $a_{i,t}$ and $p_{i,t}$ are independent of time: $a_{i,t} = a_i$ and $p_{i,t} = p_i$. The strong law of large

---

1. The size of the time period is immaterial. In other words, we focus here on the sequence of events instead of their exact occurrence.
2. A second polar interpretation of these random elements is that they might reflect the consumer imperfect knoweldge about the true utility given by the deterministic parts of (1). In that case, the parameter μ measures the degree of imperfection in consumers' perception.
3. The double exponential distribution: $F(x) = \exp - [\exp - (x + \gamma)]$ ($\gamma \approx 0.5772$ being the Euler's constant) belongs to the family of extreme value distributions (see Anderson et al. [2] for more details).

numbers implies that the market shares $s_{i,t} \equiv N_{i,t} / \sum_{j=1}^{n} N_{j,t}$ converge with probability 1 to:

$$\lim_{t \to \infty} s_{i,t} \stackrel{a.s.}{=} \frac{\exp[(a_i - p_i)/\mu]}{\sum_{j=1}^{n} \exp[(a_j - p_j)/\mu]} \equiv \mathbb{P}_i \qquad (3)$$

which is the standard logit-type demand model.

The logit model has been primarily derived as a disaggregated model by Holman and Marley (see McFadden [26]). It has been used as a model of product differentiation by Anderson and de Palma [1] and Besanko, Perry and Spady [7]. The logit model and more generally the LRUMs (for linear random utility models) can also be derived using the standard representative consumer approach of Dixit and Stiglitz [15] and Spence [31]. More precisely, Anderson, de Palma and Thisse (see [2]) have shown that the logit demand system can be derived from the constrained maximization of a neoclassical utility function (which has an entropy form).

Finally, the logit system of probabilities might be derived by applying concepts that stem from statistical physics and information theory, instead of microeconomics. Consider the following generalized entropy function [1]:

$$\left[\bar{y} + \sum_{i=1}^{n} (a_i - p_i) \mathbb{X}_i \right] - \mu \sum_{i=1}^{n} \mathbb{X}_i \ln \mathbb{X}_i, \quad \mathbb{X}_i > 0 \qquad (4)$$

$$\sum_{i=1}^{n} \mathbb{X}_i = 1 \qquad (5)$$

where $\bar{y}$ is the average income of the consumers in the population. The term in brackets may be interpreted as the average systematic consumer benefit (observed by the modeler), while the second term is an entropic function which expresses the level of the uncertainty, from the modeler point of view, about consumer's preferences. The variable $\mathbb{X}_i$ is interpreted as the fraction of individuals selecting good i. Maximizing (4) with respect to $\mathbb{X}_i$ with constraint (5) yields the choice probabilities (3).

---

1. See Williams [32].

When $\mu \to 0$, almost all consumers select the product with the largest deterministic part $(a_i - p_i)$, since in this case, tastes tend to be perfectly homogeneous [1]. Conversely, when $\mu \to \infty$, the idiosyncratic elements will mask the information contained in product qualities and prices, consumer behavior being purely random from the modeler perspective. In this case, market shares are asymptotically divided among the products. Thus, a greater value of μ leads to a greater perceived *disorder* in consumer behavior.

Now, applying the strong law of large numbers to the *i.i.d.* variables $\max_{i=1...n} u_{i,i'}$ we deduce that the average consumer surplus converges almost surely towards:

$$V = \bar{y} + \mu \ln \left[\sum_{i=1}^{n} \exp[(a_i - p_i)/\mu] \right] \quad (6)$$

Note that it could be shown that this expression is the indirect utility function associated with the representative consumer utility. Moreover, (6) can be found by substituting the choice probabilities given by (3) into the entropy expression (4). It is worth to derive expression (6) in the symmetric case, that is when all the products have equal qualities, a, and equal prices, p, (in this case, market shares are equal at a stationary state):

$$V = \bar{y} + a - p + \mu \ln(n) \quad (7)$$

Hence, consumer surplus logarithmically increases with the number of products. Surplus does not increase linearly as a function of the number of products since the product space becomes crowded as more products are offered [2]. That is, when a consumer is already facing a large number of alternatives, there is a low probability that an additional product will offer him a highest utility (since only consumers who switch will increase welfare) [3].

3. The Logit with Network Polya Externalities

Now, assume that the utility (1) depends on the cumulative number of consumers who have chosen the same product during the previous periods. For

---

1. When more than one product have the largest value of $(a_i - p_i)$, the consumption is equally divided among those brands.
2. It is intuitively true that the benefit derived by a consumer facing an extra restaurant in a small town will be larger if the number of available restaurants is 2 rather than 100.
3. More generally, it could be shown that the welfare is an increasing and concave function of n (in the symmetric case), for *i.i.d.* random terms in the utility function (1).

this, we suppose that product i quality parameter $a_{i,t}$ is endogenously determined according to the following relationship:

$$a_{i,t} = a_i + \gamma \ln N_{i,t-1} \tag{8}$$

where a_i is an intrinsic product quality parameter and γ is a real parameter. There is no compatibility among products since the quality of good i only depends on the number of users of product i [1].

If $\gamma > 0$, adopters of good i induce a higher utility for product i. For example, the utility of using a specific computer, a credit card, a mobile phone, internet, etc. increases with the number of users of such goods. Conversely, if $\gamma < 0$, the consumption of the good decreases its value. For example, the utility of visiting a museum, a recreational area, of using a public transport decreases with the cumulative number of previous users (who tend to deteriorate the quality of the environment, of the air, etc.).

Positive and negative externalities correspond to the concepts of bandwagon and snob effects well used in economics. The parameter γ serves as a measure of the intensity and type of the network externalities (see Katz and Shapiro [21] and Farrell and Saloner [19]). Although the individual decisions are still based on the standard theory of individual choice behavior, decisions are now interdependent.

The justification of the logarithmic specification is as follows. First, according to Fechner [2], it is well known that the perception is a logarithmic function of the physical stimulus ("the sensation grows as the logarithm of the excitation"). Here the stimulus is the number of individuals linked to a specific network. In the case of positive externalities, it means that to get link to twice as much individuals less than double the benefit from interaction. Another theoretical justification of the logarithmic form is provided by (6), which shows that the expected benefit to have access to N_i goods (here users) is a logarithm function of the number of goods (users). Conversely, a more crowded place reduces visitors benefit, but additional visitors are likely to bother you less and less (which implies a concave perception function).

Note that we have assumed here that individuals are myopic, *i.e.* are unable to perfectly forecast the subsequent number of users of the network they decide to get linked to. The other polar case is considered by Katz and Shapiro [21] who assume that consumers have perfect foresight. However, recent examples concerning technologies such that the Mini-Disc and the Digital Tape systems

---

1. This assumption is also made in Miyao and Shapiro [27]. Our model may be extended in order to take into account a partial compatibility among different products.
2. See Falmagne [17] for a mathematical account of Fechnerian theory.

seem to confirm that, at least in some instances, consumers [1] are unable to forecast future market shares. The same myopic hypothesis was used by de Palma [14] who studied the diffusion of the European Currency Unit.

Substituting (8) into (2) yields the probability that consumer t selects product i sold at a given price p_i:

$$\mathbb{P}_{i,t}(\bar{s}_{t-1}) = \frac{s_{i,t-1}^{\gamma/\mu} \exp[(a_i - p_i)/\mu]}{\sum_{j=1}^{n} s_{j,t-1}^{\gamma/\mu} \exp[(a_j - p_j)/\mu]}, \quad i = 1...n \qquad (9)$$

where $\bar{s}_t = (s_{1,t}, ..., s_{n,t})$ is the vector of market shares. In this case, the standard strong law of large numbers no longer applies since the choice probabilities are now non-stationary. However, with the logarithmic specification adopted in (8), the choice probabilities are *extensive*, that is depend on the distribution of the consumers through their frequency of choice $\{s_{i,t-1}\}$ rather than through the absolute numbers $\{N_{i,t-1}\}$. The dynamics corresponding to the evolution of users of each product is then described by a Polya-type urn process. In this case, a theorem due to Arthur et al. [5] (see Theorem 1, p. 299) allows the computation of the long-run demand behavior ($t \to \infty$). This theorem provides sufficient conditions which guarantee that the stochastic trajectories of the Polya process could be approximated when t is large enough by an equivalent deterministic system [2]. A theorem in Appendix proves that this could be applied in our case and that the stochastic Polya process could be approximated (for t large enough) by the following system of differential equations:

$$\frac{ds_{i,t}}{dt} = \mathbb{P}_{i,t}(\bar{s}_t) - s_{i,t}, \quad i = 1...n$$

An equilibrium (stationary state) is such that the choice probabilities (9) exactly match the market shares. It is then a solution of the following fixed point problem:

$$\mathbb{P}_i^*(\bar{s}^*) = s_i^*, \quad i = 1...n \qquad (10)$$

Equilibria could be stable or unstable [3]. Obviously, stability conditions depend upon the values of parameters μ and γ. Equilibrium state and their stability are given by the following proposition (see Appendix).

---

1. As well as firms, since Sony and Philips signed an agreement to provide themselves against the failure of their systems.
2. In a similar vein, Lehosky [24] has shown that when the transition probabilities are extensive, interactive Markov random chains (introduced by Conlisk [10]) can be approximated by deterministic systems, as the population size tends to infinity.
3. An equilibrium will be unstable if small fluctuations around this state grow over time.

64 | Consumers and firms behaviors

Proposition 1 *Consider a dynamic Polya process with the choice probabilities given by (9). If $\gamma < \mu$, there is a unique globally stable equilibrium given by:*

$$\lim_{t \to \infty} s_i \stackrel{a.s.}{=} \frac{\exp[(a_i - p_i)/(\mu - \gamma)]}{\sum_{j=1}^{n} \exp[(a_j - p_j)/(\mu - \gamma)]} \equiv \mathbb{P}_i^*, \quad i = 1...n \quad (11)$$

If $\gamma = \mu$, there is one (globally) or several (locally) stable equilibria characterized by:

$$\mathbb{P}_i^* = \begin{cases} > 0 \text{ if } a_i - p_i = \max_{j=1...n}(a_j - p_j) \\ 0 \text{ otherwise} \end{cases}, \quad i = 1...n$$

If $\gamma > \mu$, all corner solutions, $\mathbb{P}_i = 1$, $i = 1...n$, are locally stable.

Proof: see appendix.

Comments.

• If $\gamma < \mu$, the long-run demand are still of the logit-type given by (11), but the heterogeneity parameter μ is replaced by $\mu - \gamma$ (note that this case necessarily occurs when $\gamma < 0$). When $\gamma \to -\infty$, congestion effect is very high and consumer choices are evenly spread among alternatives (since $\mu - \gamma \to +\infty$).

• As $\gamma \to \mu$, the positive externality effect exactly counteracts the heterogeneity component so that the solution is the same as that of the standard logit model with zero heterogeneity (products are perfect substitutes). Note that when more than one good have the highest value of $(a_i - p_i)$, the stable solution is no more unique.

• As $\gamma > \mu$, at a stable equilibrium, all consumers will select the same product (there are n stable solutions).

A long-run equilibrium involving several active products occurs when the degree of consumer heterogeneity is sufficiently large compared with the externality parameter. Therefore, $\gamma = \mu$ may be seen as a bifurcation point *(phase transition)* between two regimes qualitatively different. Note finally that the fixed point problem is explicitly solved here (see equation 10). If we had use a linear specification for the utility function (see equation 8), no explicit solution could have been found (see de Palma and Leruth [13]).

For $\gamma < \mu$, substituting (11) into (1), one can show [1] that the average consumer utility converges asymptotically to (up to an additive term [2]):

$$V = \bar{y} + (\mu - \gamma) \ln \left[\sum_{i=1}^{n} \exp[(a_i - p_i)/(\mu - \gamma)] \right] \qquad (12)$$

In the same way, one can show that for $\mu = \gamma$, the average consumer utility is given by [3]:

$$V = \bar{y} + \max_{i=1...n} (a_i - p_i) \qquad (13)$$

4. Market Competition and Welfare

Now, we consider a market with n competing firms. Each firm produces one good at the same marginal production cost c. Each time period t, one new customer enters the market and purchases one unit of product i with a probability given by (9). We assume that product qualities are the same and set w.l.o.g. equal to 0 ($a_i = 0$, $i = 1...n$). The expected profit function of firm i for time period t is:

$$\pi_{i,t} = (p_{i,t} - c) \, \mathbb{P}_{i,t}(\bar{s}_{t-1}) - F \qquad (14)$$

where F is the fixed cost per unit of time.

Firms are competing in prices and we restrict our analysis to symmetric equilibria. We focus on a simple pricing strategy assuming that prices are the result of two competing objectives: a myopic objective and a target objective. This corresponds to pricing strategies often discussed in the business literature [4]. More precisely, we assume that the price $p_{i,t}$ set by firm i in period t is a linear combination of a myopic price $p_{i,t}$ and of a target price $\tilde{p}_{i,t}$:

$$p_{i,t} = (1 - \delta) p_{i,t} + \delta \tilde{p}_{i,t}, \quad 0 \leq \delta \leq 1 \qquad (15)$$

---

1. Using a simple continuity argument.
2. This term is equal to $\gamma \ln T$, where T is the total number of individuals in the market.
3. This expression can also be obtained by taking the limit $\gamma \to \mu$ in expression (12).
4. See the review paper of Rao [29].

When $\delta = 0$, firms use a myopic pricing strategy. When $\delta = 1$, firms select a price to reach a given target objective [1]. It is not our purpose here to study whether or not this type of pricing policy is consistent with firms and consumers perfect foresight strategies.

Let $p_{i,t}$ be the myopic price, that is the price that maximizes firm i's profit in period t. We consider the monopolistic competition limit, à la Chamberlin, in which firms do not recognize their impact on market variables. More specifically, it is assumed that firms do not consider the impact of their price changes on the term $\sum_{i=1}^{n} s_{i,t-1}^{\gamma/\mu} \exp(-p_i/\mu) = \Phi_{t-1}$ appearing in (9) (see Besanko et al. [17]). Deriving profit (14) leads:

$$p_{i,t} = c + \mu \qquad (16)$$

Let $\tilde{p}_{i,t}$ be the target price. According to several studies in business and economics (see Dosi et al. [16]), firms try to reach specific market share targets. For example, a firm may be willing to increase its market share in order to preempt the market, decrease its cost (learning by doing), maximize the manager private benefits, etc.

Assume that each firm has a market share target denoted by $\mathbb{T}$. In order to reach this target, firm i should set a price $\tilde{p}_{i,t}$ which satisfies:

$$\frac{s_{i,t-1}^{\gamma/\mu} \exp(-p_i/\mu)}{\Phi_{t-1}} = \mathbb{T}$$

Obviously, this equation has always a unique solution given by:

$$\tilde{p}_{i,t} = \gamma \ln s_{i,t-1} - \mu(\ln \mathbb{T} + \ln \Phi_{t-1}) \qquad (17)$$

Substituting the expressions (16) and (17) into (15) yields:

$$p_{i,t} = (1-\delta)(c+\mu) + \delta[\gamma \ln s_{i,t-1} - \mu(\ln \mathbb{T} + \ln \Phi_{t-1})] \qquad (18)$$

The choice probabilities at time t (see 9), once firms have determined their pricing according to (18), are:

$$\mathbb{P}_{i,t} = \frac{s_{i,t-1}^{\gamma(1-\delta)/\mu}}{\sum_{j=1}^{n} s_{j,t-1}^{\gamma(1-\delta)/\mu}} \qquad (19)$$

---

[1]. The intertemporal optimisation for consumers and firms formally corresponds to a closed loop equilibrium. Unfortunately, this problem is hard to deal with and has been shown to have no solution in a similar context (see Deneckere and De Palma [12]).

Since the choice probabilities at time t only depend on market shares at time $t-1$, and have the same functional form as in (9), theorem 3 in appendix applies and we have:

Proposition 2 *Consider purchasing probabilities given by a Polya process defined by (19). The dynamic market shares converge to $1/n$ if $(1-\delta)\gamma < \mu$. They are given by any combination of market shares if $(1-\delta)\gamma = \mu$. They lead to a natural monopoly if $(1-\delta)\gamma > \mu$. Moreover, the equilibrium price is given by:*

$$p^* = (c+\mu) - \mu\frac{\delta}{1-\delta}\ln\left[\frac{\mathbb{T}}{(1/n)}\right] \qquad (20)$$

Proof: The proof of the stability criteria and the equilibrium market shares can be computed directly from propostion 1. The symmetric price equilibrium (20) is computed by substituting Φ_{t-1} by $n^{(\mu-\gamma)/\mu}\exp(-p/\mu)$ into (18) and solving this equation in p. ∎

Comments. If $\delta = 0$, firms are myopic and as expected, the stability conditions are the same as in the constant price case (see section 2). If $\delta \to 1$, the symmetric equilibrium $1/n$ is always stable. When firms have a consistent foresight $\mathbb{T} = 1/n$, then prices reduce to:

$$p^* = c + \mu$$

and consequently, profits are:

$$\pi^* = \frac{\mu}{n} - F \qquad (21)$$

Note that, once the convergence criterion is satisfied, the externality parameter γ does not influence the outcome of the equilibrium (since at equilibrium, the externality of each firm is the same and firms are basically myopic). However, the dynamic evolution towards the stationary state does depend on the value of γ.

We now examine market performance for $(1-\delta)\gamma < \mu$. At the free entry equilibrium, the zero-profit condition, $\pi^* = (\mu/n) - F = 0$, yields the number of firms entering the market:

$$n^* = \frac{\mu}{F} \qquad (22)$$

Welfare is measured by total consumer surplus plus total profits:

$$W = \bar{y} + (\mu - \gamma)\ln\left[\sum_{i=1}^{n}\exp[-p_i/(\mu-\gamma)]\right] + \sum_{i=1}^{n}\pi_i \qquad (23)$$

It is straightforward to show that prices are equal to c at the first-best optimum [1]. Therefore, the welfare function at the first-best is symmetric and equal to:

$$W = \bar{y} + (\mu - \gamma) \ln(n) - c - nF \qquad (24)$$

Maximizing this function with respect to n yields with an obvious notation (for the first and second best):

$$n^f = n^s = \frac{(\mu - \gamma)}{F} \qquad (25)$$

The second-best involves a zero-profit constraint. It is satisfied with a price equal to:

$$p^s = c + \mu - \gamma$$

The comparison between the free entry equilibrium and first-best and second-best optimum is provided below.

	Market solution	First best	Second best
Prices	$c + \mu$	c	$c + \mu - \gamma$
Number of firms	$\frac{\mu}{F}$	$\text{Max}\left[\frac{(\mu-\gamma)}{F}, 1\right]$	$\text{Max}\left[\frac{(\mu-\gamma)}{F}, 1\right]$

Comments.

- If $\gamma < 0$, that is when there are negative externalities, the market underprovides variety.

- If $\gamma = 0$, without externalities, the numbers of firms at equilibrium or in an optimum coincide.

- If $\gamma > 0$, that is in the presence of positive externalities, there are too many firms at the free entry equilibrium.

This last result is in accordance with the standard findings that overprovision is the norm in the case of oligopoly competition with horizontally differentiated goods (Anderson et al. [2]). However, when $\gamma < 0$, the result is overturned.

With network externalities, a new effect influences the market. With negative externalities, when a firm enters the market, it decreases the value of network externalities for all other firms since it induces consumers to switch from

---

1. Using arguments of concavity.

incumbent firms. This entry contributes to increase welfare (since the negative externalities are reduced). However, the new firm does not value this benefit. Since the equilibrium and the number of firms are close in the logit model (one firm difference), it should not be a surprise that this additional force can itself reverse the ranking between the equilibrium and the optimum number of firms.

5. Conclusion

We have developed a dynamic model in order to see how network externalities affect market performance, when products are horizontally differentiated. Two parameters have been introduced to represent respectively consumer heterogeneity and externality effects. It points out that, with constant prices, a unique equilibrium is reached where diversity prevails, as soon as the heterogeneity parameter is greater than the externality parameter. Otherwise, the dynamics of adoption leads to a natural monopoly but, in this case, history matters since the selected product is not known in advance. However, when the price dynamics is taken into account, it appears that price reaction tends to sustain diversity instead of standardization.

Moreover we have compared, in case of monopolistic competition, the market result with the social optimum. We found out that the market overprovides variety with positive externalities, and conversely, there are too few firms with negative externalities. However, to test the accuracy of these conclusions, the model must be extended in different ways: a no-purchase alternative which allows the consumer to leave the market must be added; the oligopolistically competitive case where firms take into account their impact on the market variables must be examined.

Appendix: Proof of propositions 1 and 2

These propositions are corollary of the following theorem:

Theorem 3 *Given a generalized urn process of the Polya-type with urn functions such that:*

$$q_i(\bar{s}) = \frac{(\lambda_i s_i)^{\gamma}}{\sum_k (\lambda_k s_k)^{\gamma}}, \quad \lambda_i > 0, \gamma \in \mathbb{R}, \quad i = 1...n \tag{26}$$

where $\bar{s}$ represents the vector of proportion of balls. Its asymptotic behavior is as follows:

70 | Consumers and firms behaviors

If $\gamma < 1$, the process converges to a unique equilibrium given by:

$$s_i^* = \frac{\lambda_i^{\gamma/(1-\gamma)}}{\sum_k \lambda_k^{\gamma/(1-\gamma)}}, \quad i = 1...n \qquad (27)$$

If $\gamma = 1$, the process converges to a point of the set:

$$\left\{ \bar{s} \in \mathbb{R}_+^n / \sum_i s_i = 1, s_i \neq 0 \Leftrightarrow \lambda_i = \max_{k=1...n} \lambda_k \right\} \qquad (28)$$

If $\gamma > 1$, the process converges to a corner solution characterized by:

$$\left\{ \bar{s} \in \mathbb{R}_+^n : \sum_i s_i = 1, \exists i \text{ such that } s_i = 1 \right\}$$

Proof: Following Arthur *et al* [5], it is sufficient to study the behavior of the *equivalent deterministic process*:

$$s_{i,t+1} = s_{i,t} + (1/t)[q_i(\bar{s}_t) - s_{i,t}], \quad i = 1...n \qquad (29)$$

A.1. Case $\gamma < 1$

For $0 < \gamma < 1$, it is easy to see that the unique interior equilibrium is given by (27). Define $\beta_{i,t} = s_{i,t}/s_i^*$ and let $\hat{\beta}_t = \max_{i=1...n} \beta_{i,t}$ and $\check{\beta}_t = \min_i \beta_{i,t}$. We will need the following lemma:

Lemma 4 *If $0 < \gamma < 1$, we have:*

i) $\beta_{i,t} < \beta_{j,t} \Rightarrow \beta_{i,t+1} < \beta_{j,t+1}$.

ii) $\hat{\beta}_{t+1} - \beta_{i,t+1} \leq \hat{\beta}_t - \beta_{i,t}$ and $\hat{\beta}_{t+1} < \hat{\beta}_t$.

iii) $\check{\beta}_{t+1} - \beta_{i,t+1} \geq \check{\beta}_t - \beta_{i,t}$ and $\check{\beta}_{t+1} > \check{\beta}_t$.

Proof: Property i) is obtained by dividing each equation of (29) by s_i^*:

$$\beta_{i,t+1} = (1/t)\left[(t-1)\beta_{i,t} + \left(\beta_{i,t}^\gamma / \sum_k s_k^* \beta_{k,t}^\gamma\right)\right] <$$

$$(1/t)\left[(t-1)\beta_{j,t} + \left(\beta_{j,t}^\gamma / \sum_k s_k^* \beta_{k,t}^\gamma\right)\right] = \beta_{j,t+1}$$

To proof ii), let j the component such that: $\hat{\beta}_t = \beta_{j,t}$ $\forall t$. We have:

$$\beta_{j,t+1} - \beta_{i,t+1} - (\beta_{j,t} - \beta_{i,t}) = (1/t)\left[\left((\beta_{j,t}^\gamma - \beta_{i,t}^\gamma)/\sum_k s_k^* \beta_{k,t}^\gamma\right) - (\beta_{j,t} - \beta_{i,t})\right]$$

$$\Rightarrow sgn[\beta_{j,t+1} - \beta_{i,t+1} - (\beta_{j,t} - \beta_{i,t})] = sgn\left[\beta_{j,t}^\gamma - \beta_{i,t}^\gamma - \sum_k s_k^* \beta_{k,t}^\gamma (\beta_{j,t} - \beta_{i,t})\right]$$

The r.h.s. of the previous equation can be rewritten:

$$\sum_k s_k^* \beta_{k,t}^{\gamma+1}[(\beta_{j,t}/\beta_{k,t})^\gamma - (\beta_{i,t}/\beta_{k,t})^\gamma - ((\beta_{j,t}/\beta_{k,t}) - (\beta_{i,t}/\beta_{k,t}))]$$

Clearly enough, the terms in brackets are negative. Therefore: $\hat{\beta}_{t+1} - \beta_{i,t+1} < \hat{\beta}_t - \beta_{i,t}$.

Now, write:

$$\hat{\beta}_{t+1} - \hat{\beta}_t = (1/t)\left[\left(\hat{\beta}_t^\gamma / \sum_k s_k^* \beta_{k,t}^\gamma\right) - \hat{\beta}_t\right] \Rightarrow sgn[\hat{\beta}_{t+1} - \hat{\beta}_t] = sgn\left[\hat{\beta}_t^\gamma - \sum_k s_k^* \beta_{k,t}^\gamma \hat{\beta}_t\right]$$

Rewrite the r.h.s. as follows:

$$\sum_k s_k^* \beta_{k,t}^\gamma \hat{\beta}_t[1 - (\beta_{k,t}^{\gamma-1}/\hat{\beta}_t^{\gamma-1})]$$

which is negative since the terms in brackets are negative.

Finally, iii) can be obtained with similar arguments as those used for property ii). ∎

From lemma 4, we conclude that all the components $\beta_{i,t}$ converge. Thus, the vector $\bar{s}_t$ converges towards a limit $\bar{s}$ which is necessarily an equilibrium. Otherwise, we could find a component j, a real $\varepsilon > 0$ and an integer T such that:

$$\forall t \geq T, q_i(\bar{s}_t) - s_{i,t} > \varepsilon$$

Using equation (29), we deduce that:

$$s_{i,T+t} - s_{i,t} > \varepsilon \sum_{t+1}^{T+t} \tau^{-1}$$

72 | Consumers and firms behaviors

which is absurd since the l.h.s. diverges.

Now, we study the stability of the equilibria. Thanks to lemma 4, the minimal component $\tilde{\beta}_{t+1}$ is strictly increasing. Therefore, for $0 < \gamma < 1$, the interior equilibrium is the sole stable equilibrium.

For $\gamma = 0$, the urn function is such that: $q_i(\bar{s}) = 1/n$, $i = 1...n$. Using the strong law of large numbers, we deduce that:

$$\lim_{t \to \infty} s_{i,t} \stackrel{a.s.}{=} 1/n$$

For $\gamma < 0$, consider the following lyapounov function defined on the n-dimensional unit simplex:

$$v(\bar{s}) = \frac{1}{2} \sum_i [(s_i - s_i^*)^2 s_i^*)]$$

Obviously, we have: $v(\bar{s}) > 0 \; \forall \bar{s} \neq \vec{s}^*$ and $v(\vec{s}^*) = 0$.

Furthermore, following Arthur et al. [4] (theorem 3.1, p. 291), we have to proof the following condition:

$$\langle \bar{q}(\bar{s}) - \bar{s}(\nabla v(\bar{s})) \rangle < 0, \quad \forall \bar{s} \in U(\vec{s}^*)$$

where $\bar{q}(\bar{s})$ is the vector $(q_1(\bar{s}), ..., q_n(\bar{s}))$ and $\nabla v(\bar{s})$ is the gradient vector of the function v and $U(\vec{s}^*)$ is an open neighborhood of $\vec{s}^*$. We have:

$$\langle \bar{q}(\bar{s}) - \bar{s}(\nabla v(\bar{s})) \rangle = \left(\sum_i s_i^* \beta_i^{\gamma+1} / \sum_i s_i^* \beta_i^\gamma \right) - \left(\sum_i s_i^* \beta_i^2 / \sum_i s_i^* \beta_i \right)$$

In order to show that this expression is negative, it is sufficient to show that:

$$\left(\sum_i s_i^* \beta_i^{\gamma+1} \right)\left(\sum_i s_i^* \beta_i \right) - \left(\sum_i s_i^* \beta_i^\gamma \right)\left(\sum_i s_i^* \beta_i^2 \right)$$

is negative.

This expression can be rewritten: $\sum_{i<k} s_i^* s_k^* (\beta_i^\gamma \beta_k - \beta_i \beta_k^\gamma)(\beta_i - \beta_k)$.

Clearly, this expression is negative. Therefore:

$$\lim_{t \to \infty} s_{i,t} \stackrel{a.s.}{=} s_i^*$$

A.2. Case $\gamma = 1$

We will use the following lemma:

Lemma 5 *Let* $\hat{\lambda} = \max_{i=1...n} \lambda_i$ *and* $A = \{i \in \mathbb{N}: 1 \leq i \leq n, \lambda_i = \hat{\lambda}\}$.

$$|A| < n \Rightarrow \forall i \in A, \quad s_{i,t+1} > s_{i,t}$$

Proof: Define: $\hat{\lambda} = \max_{i=1...n} \lambda_i$. Using equation (29), one obtains:

$$s_{i,t+1} - s_{i,t} = (s_{i,t}/t) \left[\left(\hat{\lambda} / \sum_k \lambda_k s_{k,t} \right) - 1 \right] \tag{30}$$

which is strictly negative if $|A| < n$. ∎

Now, if $|A| = n$, that is if the parameters λ_i are identical, the urn function is given by:

$$q_i(\bar{s}) = s_i$$

In this case, the whole unit simplex consists of solutions and in the limit, one gets a Dirichlet distribution.

If $|A| < n$, following lemma 5, one can conclude that $\sum_{i \in A} s_{i,t}$ converges. Moreover, in order to prove that the urn process converges toward the set given by (28), it is sufficient to show that: $\sum_{i \in A} s_{i,t} \to 1$. Suppose on the contrary that: $\sum_{i \in A} s_{i,t} \to l < 1$. Using equation (30), we have:

$$\sum_{i \in A} s_{i,t+1} - \sum_{i \in A} s_{i,t} - (1/t) \sum_{i \in A} s_{i,t} \left[\left(\hat{\lambda} / \sum_k \lambda_k s_{k,t} \right) - 1 \right] >$$

$$(1/t) \sum_{i \in A} s_{i,t} [((\hat{\lambda} - \hat{b})(1-l) + \hat{b})/(\hat{\lambda} - \hat{b})(l + \hat{b})]$$

where $\hat{b} = \max_{i \notin A} \lambda_i$. It is impossible since the serie $\sum \tau^{-1}$ diverges. ∎

A.3. Case $\gamma > 1$

The proof is omitted since one can use similar arguments as those previously used in A.2. with $0 < \gamma < 1$, and the following lemma:

Lemma 6 *If $\gamma > 1$, we have:*

i) $\beta_{i,t} < \beta_{j,t} \Rightarrow \beta_{i,t+1} < \beta_{j,t+1}.$

ii) $\hat{\beta}_{t+1} - \beta_{i,t+1} \geq \hat{\beta}_t - \beta_{i,t}$ and $\hat{\beta}_{t+1} > \hat{\beta}_t.$

iii) $\tilde{\beta}_{t+1} - \beta_{i,t+1} \leq \tilde{\beta}_t - \beta_{i,t}$ and $\tilde{\beta}_{t+1} < \tilde{\beta}_t.$ ∎

REFERENCES

[1] Anderson S.P. and A. de Palma, 1992, "The Logit as a Model of Product Differentiation", *Oxford Economic Papers*, 44, 51-67.

[2] Anderson S.P., A. de Palma and J.-F. Thisse, 1993, *Discrete Choice Theory of Product Differentiation*, The MIT Press.

[3] Anderson S.P., A. de Palma and Y. Nesterov, 1996, "Oligopolistic Competition and the Optimal Provision of Products", *Econometrica*, 63, 6, 1281-1301.

[4] Arthur W.B., Y. Ermoliev and Y. Kaniovski, 1984, "Strong laws for a class of path-dependent processes with applications", in: Proceedings of International Conference on Stochastic Optimization (Kiev), 287-300.

[5] Arthur W.B., Y. Ermoliev and Y. Kaniovski, 1987, "Path-Dependent Processes and the Emergence of Macro-Structure", *European Journal of Operational Research*, 30, 1, 294-303.

[6] Arthur W.B., 1989, "Competing Technologies, Increasing Returns and Lock-In by Historical Events," *Economic Journal*, 99, 116-131.

[7] Besanko D., M.K. Perry and R.H. Spady, 1990, "The Logit Model of Monopolistic Competition: Brand Diversity," *The Journal of Industrial Economics*, 38, 4, 397-415.

[8] Chamberlin E.H., 1933, *The Theory of Monopolistic Competition* (Harvard University Press, Boston).

[9] Church Jeffrey and N. Gandal, 1992, "Network Effects, Software Provision and Standardization", *Journal of Industrial Economics*, 40, 1, 85-104.

[10] Conlisk J., 1976, "Interactive Markov Chains", *Journal of Mathematical Sociology*, 4, 157-185.

[11] David P.A., 1985, "Clio and the Economics of QWERTY", *Papers and Proceedings of the American Economic Review*, 75, 332-337.

[12] Deneckere R. and A. De Palma, 1992, "The Diffusion of Consumer Durables in a Vertically Differentiated Oligopoly", *Center for Mathematical Studies in Economics and Management Science Discussion Paper*.

[13] de Palma A. and L. Leruth, 1993, "Equilibrium in Competing Networks with Differentiated Products", *Transportation Science*, 27, 1, 73-80.

[14] de Palma A., 1995, "From Monetarization to the Adoption of a Single Currency", *Working Paper, HEC Université de Genève*.

[15] Dixit A., and J.E. Stiglitz, 1977, "Monopolistic Competition and Optimum Product Diversity", *American Economic Review*, 67, 297-308.

[16] Dosi G., Y. Ermoliev and Y. Kaniovski, 1994, "Generalized Urn Schemes and Technological Dynamics", *Journal of Mathematical Economics*, 23, 1-19.

[17] Falmagne J.-C. (1985). *Elements of Psychophysical Theory* (Oxford University Press, Oxford).

[18] Farrell J. and G. Saloner, 1985, "Standardization, Compatibility and Innovation", *Rand Journal of Economics*, 16, 70-83.

[19] Farrell J., and G. Saloner, 1986, "Standardization and Variety", *Economic Letters*, 20, 71-74.

[20] Hotelling H., 1929, "Stability in Competition", *Economic Journal*, 39, 41-57.

[21] Katz M.L., and C. Shapiro, 1985, "Network Externalities, Competition, and Compatibility", *American Economic Review*, 75, 424-440.

[22] Katz M.L., and C. Shapiro, 1994, "System Competition and Network Effects", *Journal of Economic Perspectives*, 8, 2, 93-115.

[23] Lancaster K., 1979, *Variety, Equity and Efficiency* (Columbia University Press, New York).

[24] Lehoczky J.P., 1980, "Approximations for Interactive Markov Chains in Discrete and Continuous Time", *Journal of Mathematical Sociology*, 7, 139-157.

[25] Matutes C., and P. Regibeau, 1992, "Compatibility and Bundling of Complementary Goods in a Duopoly", *Journal of Industrial Economics*, 40, 1, 37-54.

[26] McFadden D., 1981, "Econometric Models of Probabilistic Choice", In C.F. Manski and D. McFadden (eds.), *Structural Analysis of Discrete Data with Econometric Applications*. Cambridge. MIT Press. 198-272.

[27] Miyao T., and P. Shapiro, 1981, "Discrete Choice and Variable Returns to Scale", *International Economic Review*, 22, 2, 257-273.

[28] Perloff J.M. and S.C. Salop, 1985, "Equilibrium with Product Differentiation", *Review of Economic Studies*, 52, 107-120.

[29] Rao V.R., 1984, "Pricing Research in Marketing: The State of the Art", *Journal of Business*, 57, 1, S39-S60.

[30] Sattinger M., 1984, "Value of an Additional Firm in Monopolistic Competition", *Review of Economic Studies*, 51, 321-332.

[31] Spence M., 1976, "Product Selection, Fixed Costs, and Monopolistic Competition", *Review of Economic Studies*, 43, 217-235.

[32] Williams H.C.W.L., 1977, "On the Formation of Travel Demand Models and Economics Evaluation Measures of User Benefit", *Environment and Planning A*, 9, 283-344.

CHAPTER 4
ROUTINES, STRUCTURES OF GOVERNANCE AND KNOWLEDGE-CREATING PROCESSES

Patrick COHENDET, Francis KERN, Babak MEHMANPAZIR, Francis MUNIER

Introduction

In a recent article, Coriat and Dosi (1995) assume that the concept of routines, which is at the heart of the evolutionary theory of the firm, involves two main characteristics. The first, which is currently the subject of important developments in the literature on the evolutionary theory, concerns the cognitive dimension of organisational routines. It is a whole which encompasses and reproduces the knowledge of the firm in terms of problem-solving activities. On the basis of the concept of routines, the evolutionary approach is able to define the main concept of competence which highlights the strategic aspects of the firm and its relevance in relation to the external environment. In this approach, routines serves as the basis of co-ordination within the firm. Indeed, as Nelson and Winter (1982) pointed out: *"what is important for the organisational performance in the production process is co-ordination, what is important in co-ordination is that individuals know their job, interpret and respond correctly to the messages they receive"*. The second characteristic, which to date has not been investigated to any great extent, considers that routines are governance or control mechanisms. Nelson and Winter (1982) were the first to introduce this idea and suggested considering routines *"as truces among conflicting interests"*, but Coriat and Dosi (1995) should be credited for clearly underlining that routines may be considered *"as being a locus of conflict, governance, and a way of codifying micro-economic incentives and constraints"* [1].

This article aims at examining the foundations and the implications of the second vision of routines. In this context, the firm has work out an efficient co-ordination of the tension between decentralisation and centralisation of learning processes. In other words and this falls within the scope of self-organisation (Lesourne, 1991), the main issue is how to combine the autonomy of individuals, which is a source of disorder, ambiguity and organisational deliquescence. Nevertheless, at the same time, the individual is also a source of creativity, with the constraints of incentives implying order, coherence but which can likewise be source of inertia. In this respect, Nonaka's theory (1994)

---

1. The authors analyse this assumption by studying the archetypal forms of organisation such as Taylorism, Fordism and Ohnism.

of organisational knowledge creation provides a relevant conceptual framework, in particular in order to understand the strategic restructuring of large firms, through new communication and information networks, and their implications in terms of knowledge creation.

In the first part, we recall briefly the main characteristics of the evolutionary approach of the firm. The second part is devoted to the theoretical analysis of the representation of routines as mechanisms of governance. In the third part, we use Nonaka's model (1994) in order to show that the different modes of "knowledge conversion" are also subject to risks linked to incentive and control mechanisms, in particular in network phenomena. The fourth and final part is devoted to explaining the evolutionary and self-organisational aspects of the model of organisational knowledge creation developed by Nonaka (1994).

1. The evolutionary approach of the firm

To a large extent, it is premature to speak today of an evolutionary theory of the firm. A series of convergent and promising ideas, results and principles exist which might eventually allow us to draw up a coherent theoretical corpus and which will account more accurately, than others theories for the essential properties of a firm.

The evolutionary approach of the firm characterized first of all in that it relies on the use of the constituent principles of any theory of evolution. It puts great emphasis on interaction between mechanisms which generate diversity and those which promote selection. To be more specific, it considers on the one hand routines as principle of permanency or heredity, as the real biological genes of the firm. On the other hand, it accepts, as the principle of variation or mutation, the searching behaviour which is the basis of mechanisms generating diversity. Finally, it accepts, as filters of evolution, the mechanisms of selection which influence the genes/routines and/or the mutation/searching (the market being one selection mechanism amongst others. Within this framework of hypotheses, a large part of the theoretical debate is devoted to the permanent tension between exploitation mechanisms of existing routines and the exploration mechanisms of new routines.

Alongside these basic principles, the evolutionary approach of the firm is characterized by the acknowledgement of the essential role played by cognitive mechanisms. These imply the development of a collective knowledge base, the definition of a set of rules, of a code and of a common language. The important element of this approach is the set of cognitive processes by which agents create their representation of the world. The functioning of these processes (which over time constitute and change the behavioural routines of agents) occupies, within the evolutionary approach of the firm, the place of substantive rationality in the traditional theory. The creation of new knowledge and the development of new learning procedures are thus at the heart of the analysis. On this point, the evolutionary approach differentiates itself completely from those theories which see the firm as a *"processor of information"* (as Fransman interprets it, 1994) and which consider that the behaviour of a firm can be inferred from the informational signals which it detects in its environment. According to the evolutionary approach, the firm is primarily conceived as a place for organizing up, building up, selecting and keeping up knowledge; it is not so much sensitive to the distribution of information as to the sharing of knowledge; it is not so much interested in the saturation of its abilities to deal with information, as in the risk of becoming too confined by inefficient routines. And above all, the mechanisms of governance which guide the firm are not focused on information problem-solving through its transactions, but they structure the schemes for accumulating and producing new knowledge. The incentive and control mechanisms which develop in such a context aim to regulate the interactions between employees who are permanently in a situation of *"interpretive ambiguity"* (Fransman, 1994). In general, it is impossible to generate knowledge in an unambiguous manner from a set of information retained by an agent, especially if he is in a situation of incomplete information. It is also clear that different agents will infer different, even contradictory, knowledge from the same set of information.

Finally, the evolutionary approach is characterized by stress put on the concept of competencies. This concept, which relies on that of routines, refers to a view of the firm as a social institution. The main characteristic of which is to know (well) how to do certain things. These competencies correspond to a set of routines, of various skills and complementary assets *"which express the efficiency of the problem-solving procedures which the firm creates for itself"* (Guilhon, 1994). Therefore, competencies constitute compact sets of knowledge and capabilities to combine this knowledge. A company's strategic dimension comes down to building up and selecting these competencies which will provide the firm with a sustainable competitive advantage (*"core competencies"* according to Teece (1988)). This selected is based on productive knowledge gained previously in problem-solving. The way these competencies are managed, produced and combined, plays a crucial part in understanding the limits of the firm and the incentive and control mechanisms which develop between the firm and its contracting parties.

The specific features of the evolutionary approach described above show that the ambition of evolutionary theory of the firm does aim *"to explain the structure and behaviour of a firm as a emergent property of dynamic interactions, on the one hand between the constituent parts of the firm, and on the other between the firm itself and its environment"* (Cohendet, Llerena and Marengo, 1994). The organisational structure defines the rules of the game which individuals within the organisation permanently play. What is important for the evolutionary firm is that this definition does not assume that the rules of the game are given exogenously only once and for all but, on the contrary, that they emerge endogenously within the organisational structure through continuous interactive processes between individuals. As stressed by Llerena D. (1996): *"insofar as individual learning processes are strongly dependent on the context and the commitment of individuals in cognitive actions, the evolution of knowledge within the firm cannot be understood without taking into account the organisational context into which the individuals themselves fit. This particular context – in defining the circulation of information, the tasks and possibilities for interaction, hierarchical relationships and relations of authority – guides the cognitive activities of the members of the organisation and determines the various of interpretation framework"*.

2. Routines as co-ordination and governance mechanisms

The role of routines as co-ordination mechanism in the firm is one of the main orientations of the evolutionary theory. As Nelson stressed (1994) *"a firm can be understood in terms of hierarchy of practised organisational routines, which define lower order organisational skills and how these skills are co-ordinated, and higher order decision procedures for choosing what is to be done at lower level"*.

In this representation of the hierarchy of routines, the evolutionary approach pays particular attention to the tension between centralisation and decentralisation in the organisational learning process. Indeed, firms need both centralisation and decentralisation to be able to function satisfactorily in a turbulent environment. Henceforth, one of the major aims of the firm is to maintain a co-existence between these two dialogic forms. Learning processes can thus be compared to self-organisational phenomena. According to Lesourne (1991), self-organisation can be defined as *"the possibility of a system to acquire new properties while organising or changing its own organisation"*. Therefore, self-organisation requires from the firm a certain capacity to adapt and to question. But, as Walliser (1988) suggested, the process of self-organisation also confers on a system the capacity to bring about local processes in an organisational structure. Here *"the interference of levels"* (Héraud and Garrouste, 1993) is a determining factor. The emergence of new properties comes, therefore, both from individuals and from the organisation.

Decentralisation in the acquisition of knowledge is a source of variety, experimentation and learning. However, it may be that this knowledge needs to be made available to the whole organisation. When employees differ in their representation of the environment and in their cognitive capacities, a body of common knowledge must exist within the organisation, which guarantees the coherence of the learning processes in order to provide for an efficient management of competencies. In order to be able to confront a perturbed environment, the means of creating and modifying such a body of common knowledge must respect certain forms of centralisation, even if it is basically maintained by decentralised learning processes. Thus, inevitably, there is a conflict between the forces which favour decentralised learning and those which favour the setting up of a shared knowledge base. The *"balance"* between these two forces depends on the characteristics of the learning processes and those of the environment in which the firms operate. By means of simulation models, Marengo (1994) has shown that, when it is necessary to adapt in a fine and flexible way to the environment, local learning processes can be more effective provided that hierarchical levels are able to co-ordinate them globally. Real decentralisation can happen much more from extended knowledge and from *"bottom-up"* flows as from simple horizontal flows of information as stated by Aoki: *"If the correct emphasis is placed on knowledge and learning, higher degrees of decentralised learning are not necessarily conducive to higher degrees of organisational learning, but only to the extent in which they can be pulled together and made coherent with the overall organisational learning process"* (Marengo, 1994).

These results are important, they suggest that each specific method of organising production implies a specific set of routines oriented towards problem-solving. However, they also suggest that the idea of routines contains another characteristic through the implementation of mechanisms of governance and authority in the context of a collective behaviour where each employees strive towards their own interest. The establishment of a routine within an organisation, its evolution, the testing of its problem-solving capacities, its reinforcement or its rejection, require a direct link between the notion of routine and the control and incentive mechanisms. The conflict-solving mechanisms and the sharing-mechanisms of the relational quasi-rente which govern relationships between individuals whose interests are not necessarily convergent. And, as Coriat and Dosi (1995) stress, governance feature of routines is strictly dependent on the given mode of organisation of production: *"The set of 'Japanese' production routines does not only embody different channels of information processing but also distributes knowledge within the organisation in ways remarkably different from the Tayloristic/Chandlerian enterprise. And, at the same time, on the governance side, individuals' incentives to perform efficiently and learn are sustained (in the Japanese firm) by company-specific rank-hierarchies, delinked from functional assignments, while in the Taylorian approach, the specific mechanism of incentive governance is twofold: on the one hand the design of a new pay system (the so called 'differential piece rate system'), on the other hand, incentives had to be matched by direct visual control upon workpractices by foremen"*.

In this conception, the new focus which is directed towards the mechanisms of governance comes from the fact that the creation and the distribution of knowledge appear as being indissociably and principally linked to the distribution of power and of conflicts of interests. Inequalities in the distribution of information are no longer so much considered to be the origin of the mechanisms of governance, but rather the stakes which the dynamics of the creation and distribution of knowledge reveals. In this context for example, setting up incentive schemes results not so much from the need to correct asymmetries of information as from the need to control learning dynamics. In fact, the existence of shared knowledge reduces, *a priori*, the risks of moral hazard and of adverse selection as the risks of asymmetries of information become less acute. One can even put forward the hypothesis that if one considers that all agents possess cognitive capacities, the divergence of preferences may lead to other effects than those generated by the strategic use of organisational asymmetries. Cohen (1984) thus showed that diversity with regard to preferences and objectives in a disrupted environment where learning and the creation of competencies are the main elements for success, can be a source of increased performances. In this way, he stressed that where agents pursue objectives which are specific to their unit, and which might be contradictory, the resulting performances are more higher compared to the situation where a group of members concentrate on the same objective. Such a situation can be explained by the effects of cross fertilisation in the solution-seeking process. The collective advantage of this type of diversity is also mentioned by Loasby (1989) for whom the differences in interpretation by individuals of the same group are the origin of organisational learning. The same reasoning is to be found in Schelling (1978) in the prisoner dilemma with N number of players. Whereas the traditional principal-agent theory is explained in a static context, a dynamic approach of learning in a evolutionary perspective leads to a thorough reconsideration of the setting up of incentive schemes. But, how can one orientate learning towards desired directions while at the same time ensuring the "repatriation" of different experiences; how can diversity be stimulated while maintaining coherence; how can individuals be incited to launch a process of error-seeking, to implement new tasks and to evaluate their results and use them widely; and how can new incentive schemes be created which would make it possible to carry out, in the best conditions, processes for the creation and distribution of knowledge?

The origin of incentive schemes from an evolutionary perspective must therefore, according to us, aim to avoid, within the firm, a number of risks which are specific to a collective learning framework. Among these risks are the following:

– the risk of a lack of incentive to improve an existing routine by "locking oneself in" a given practise without ever seeking to change. This refers to the risk of over-exploiting existing routines and causing practises to become inflexible without questioning them in the light of new experience and new information;

– the risk of a lack of incentive to explore new routines. As Nonaka (1994) stated, incentive schemes should influence an individual's commitment to create new knowledge. This commitment, which aims to avoid the risk of too great a conservatism, relies on the deep-rooted "intention" of the individual to evolve in a learning context;

– the risk of "conflicts" between individual learning and collective learning. This type of risk of a lack of incentive to combine individual and collective learning can take on many forms. Argyris and Schön (1978) noted that a major obstacle to the evolution of learning or of common knowledge stems from the gap which may exist between what individuals say ("espoused theory") and what they actually do ("theory in use", which actually controls agents' actions).

But other risks, maybe even more important, are inherent in the procedures of the "conversion" of knowledge (Nonaka 1994). The examples given below illustrate the inherent risks in the processes of creating and distributing knowledge and attempt to identify incentive mechanisms which are linked to these.

3. Modes of knowledge conversion and incentive mechanisms

The wave of redeployment by large firms of their basic competencies is a major characteristic of the strategies of firms in a globalisation context. This redeployment focuses attention on the need to control and transfer knowledge from one centre of competence to than other within the bounds of the firm, or on the need to know how to gain access to competencies situated outside the firm. The main problem is always that of knowing how to build up sufficient common knowledge to ensure that the firm remains coherent while allowing local initiatives and diversified experiences to develop. Firms which have moved towards these strategies have had to experiment with new incentive and control schemes based on the understanding of processes of distribution of knowledge, using communication and information networks (BETA, 1996).

In the light of experiences which have been studied, it seems appropriate to refer to the representation given by Nonaka (1994) of the different modes of "knowledge conversion" to interpret on-going changes in incentive and control mechanisms.

The author puts forward two dimensions as conceptual foundations for his model. The first, called epistemological, concerns the classic distinction between tacit knowledge and codified knowledge, developed in particular by Polanyi (1966). The second dimension, called ontological, underlines the importance of the interaction between individuals.

The distinction is made between four types of conversion (knowledge creation): tacit to tacit (socialisation), codified to codified (combination), tacit to codified (externalisation) and codified to tacit (internalisation) (cf. Table 1).

Socialisation allows the acquisition of tacit knowledge, through shared experiences, trust and mutual understanding. By setting up teams, or a self-organised network of experts, the organisation endeavours to build, by these means, a base of common knowledge. This effort implies the creation of

Table 1. *Different modes of conversion of knowledge, Nonaka, 1994*

		To	
		codified	tacit
From	codified	*combination*	*internalisation*
	tacit	*externalisation*	*socialisation*

a context for social interactions where individuals are progressively brought to share their experience through continuous horizontal exchanges. These are interactive schemes in which individuals commit themselves both physically (being presence in the team and meeting with other persons) and intellectually (problem-solving with the team) in a process of mutual experience and collective learning. The incentive to cooperate remains here a key factor in the operation of such a scheme.

The combination of codified knowledge takes place between individuals. Communication networks (notably through intranet) are one of the ways of accelerating the accessibility and the transfer of this knowledge which can be centralised and shared by other individuals by promoting a dynamic process of knowledge creation through combination. It is a mode of knowledge transfer whereby experts' explicit knowledge is transformed into an explicit base of knowledge. For example, in the case of data bases (technical, commercial, etc.), we can see that electronic information and communication networks increase the speed of access to and transfer of data which may be both centralised and shared. The capacity to share and to circulate is a determining factor in the setting up of this mode of knowledge conversion which requires multi-agent interaction contexts where experts exchange and combine different types of explicit knowledge.

Externalisation starts when contradictions between individuals appear and slow down the firm's activities. The new codified knowledge then becomes a solution to these problems. This implies that an organisation is capable of devising a common knowledge base which includes explicit elements derived from parts of its experts' implicit knowledge. This makes the experts' work significantly easier in as much as access to the knowledge base can eliminate the duplication of efforts when solving problems. Externalisation is important in as much as it allows experts to have access to other experts' knowledge within the organisation. This contributes to the efficiency of co-ordination schemes, given the possibility for individuals to share knowledge in explicit forms. This is, no doubt, the transfer mode which attracts the most interest these days due to the potential offered by these new means of communication (Cohendet *et al.*, 1996). This transfer method also brings about deep changes in power relationships. Coriat and Dosi (1995) showed how the wave of externalisation, which accompanied the development of Taylorism, gave the hierarchy (here the planning department) the opportunity to "capture" or control part of the knowledge which had so far been tacit: *"Indeed, the story of 'Scientific Management' is precisely the story of the transformation of individual skills into organisational competencies codified into a hierarchy of routines"*.

Internalisation refers to a learning process linked to repetitiveness of tasks (trial and error procedures) which allows tacit knowledge to emerge. Thus new knowledge and skills linked to the firm's base of experience can originate from such a mode. It must be stressed that this conversion can be achieved when the co-ordination scheme allows for communication between individuals who share a common knowledge base (socialisation). As a result, the information and communication structure which shapes the exchange framework between individuals also influences the succession of different conversion modes.

The typology of knowledge conversion modes provides a better understanding of incentive mechanisms which develop progressively to control the distribution of knowledge. Again, the hypothesis of a strong dependence of the mechanisms adopted on the type of dominant organisation seems valid to explain current trends. Western style companies seem to prefer incentive mechanisms which correspond to an externalisation conversion mode, after having favoured the so-called "combination" type. The wave of codification of tacit knowledge linked to certification strategies (like ISO) falls within this reasoning. Several specific incentive schemes accompany this wave (longing for acknowledgment, specific training courses, etc.). Japanese style companies, on the other hand, are pursuing an incentive logic which favours more a change towards a conversion mode oriented towards "socialisation", after having favoured more "internalisation". "Peer pressure" and "reputation effect" type mechanisms further this type of knowledge conversion. However, these archetypal organisation schemes are, of course, only two extreme types of reference. Other mechanisms can be designed to facilitate the circulation of knowledge. Thus Nonaka (1994) advocated increasing circulation between tacit and codified knowledge in order to deploy learning in satisfactory conditions. At the same time, he stressed the extent to which incentive schemes themselves are part of a learning process and need progressive adjustment.

4. Modes of knowledge conversion, self-organisation and evolutionary theory

As already mentioned above, Nonaka's model of knowledge creation introduces characteristics which are both evolutionary and self-organising. We intend to clarify these points in order to underline the relevance of this model.

The other important idea put forward by Nonaka is that knowledge creation depends on the interaction between these various conversion modes in the form of a spiral. Socialisation generates the creation of tacit (sometimes contradictory) knowledge transformed into codified knowledge by the process of externalisation. This knowledge is then combined through co-ordination between individuals, which, by trial and error, develop new tacit knowledge via the process of internalisation. Thus the cycle starts at individual level and moves towards an intermediate level, that of the team, and ends at organisational, indeed interorganisational, level.

The knowledge spiral represents a sort of recursive process. Admittedly, according to the author, the spiral depicts a strong sequentiality of conversion modes. We suggest, nevertheless, that, on the one hand, the different stages of the spiral work according to the principle of recursion and that, on the other hand, sequentiality is not systematic. Indeed, different conversion modes develop new knowledge which, as far as socialisation and combination are concerned, contributes to the creation of new knowledge of the same nature. However we also think that knowledge contributes to the conversion mode without necessarily being "converted". Knowledge is not only a form in motion, it is also a support, a permanent tool which allows for a better understanding, to learn and to supplement one's knowledge base. As such, recursion does apply to the spiral and the knowledge can be compared with the "funds" in the sense used by Georgescu-Roegen (Munier, 1996). Knowledge therefore can be considered as routines which are related both to exploitation and exploration. To illustrate this, let us dwell on reflexive knowledge on action, on the knowledge of knowledge and on some generic knowledge. These express a certain degree of permanency in a firm. The permanency of some knowledge is a necessary requirement to favour the creation process. Let us take the example of company culture. It becomes part of the behaviour of individuals and is reflected in the organisation. It often stems from the personalities of those who created the company and remains a permanent reference in its activities, whether consciously or not. Finally, the principle of permanency could be verified through the hypothesis we put forward.

A fundamental trait of this model is that it is the individuals who create new knowledge, the organisation only plays a role in articulating and expanding this knowledge. Here we find the hologram-type property of self-organisation. This is the case where the whole exists in the individual parts; and the individual parts exist in the whole. In fact, the hologram-type dimension represents the basis of Nonaka's model: the knowledge created by individuals are at the root of organisational knowledge, which itself influences the creative behaviour of individuals. The dialogic nature is to be found in the multiple types of interaction between individuals. In effect, the ontologic dimension implies communication between individuals often with divergent and opportunist interests. Antagonism is obviously manifold in an organisation. But we may suggest that disorder, seen as an Ashby "required-variety", is a source of knowledge comparable to order. In an organisation, the complementary and conflicting relationship between individuals can both construct and destroy. In this respect, the hierarchical structure constitutes the order which allows the fruit of these interactions, which are sometimes divergent, to be maintained and appropriated.

The concept of commitment presented by Nonaka explains exactly this primacy of individuals in the process of knowledge creation. Three factors influence this commitment: intention, autonomy and fluctuation.

"Intention" relates to a well-defined and oriented action. The different types are obviously very varied and profitably maintained in order to preserve some flexibility in the acquisition and interpretation of information. Nonaka explained that intention is more than just a simple state of mind, it is above all the vector of a well-defined and oriented action. This action, in evolutionary terms, aims to maintain the perennity of individuals and therefore also the company. The individuals' intention is expressed in the design of cognitive models in order to understand better their surrounding environment. This process involves value criteria, methods for judging information: *"Without intention, it would be impossible to judge the value of the information or knowledge perceived or created"* [1]. Indeed, an organisation needs to focus on a given point in order to accelerate the creation of shared knowledge. This convergence requires justification which will determine the quality of the knowledge created and therefore implies criteria and/or standards [2]. The intention accorded to individuals represents the need or willingness to provide events with a meaning. Individuals do only act as programme operators but also as project initiators. As such, they allow for events to evolve.

The types of intention are obviously manifold depending on the individuals concerned. An organisation represents a certain type of variety which it is useful to maintain in order to preserve a certain flexibility in the acquisition and interpretation of information. In ensuring the "autonomy" of individuals in their beliefs and judgement, the company increases the likelihood of securing future opportunities, even, as the author explains, those which the company did not expect. Hazard and indeterminism are therefore important components in the mode of knowledge creation. This sort of self-organisation generates knowledge creation by favouring the synergy of individual varieties.

"Environmental fluctuations", more or less turbulent, give rise (or not) to a change in behaviour and a reappraisal of the representations of the world. As such, they are an incentive to knowledge creation according to the capacity of the individuals to understand and assimilate external changes, and also according to their intentions and their autonomy. In this context, the concept of rupture seems to be a determining factor. Only a certain kind of rupture, in relation to its habits, routines and beliefs, allows the firm to perpetuate itself: *"Any organisation that dynamically deals with a changing environment ought*

---

1. Nonaka (1994), p. 17.
2. Establishing these standards falls basically within the responsability of top or middle management.

not only to process information efficiently but also create information and knowledge" (Nonaka, 1994). The relation with the environment is important in the model. The firm forms relationships with the outside while maintaining a certain autonomy. As such, it erects a sort of organisational "fence" which allows it to develop a sense of self-awareness. One typically finds self-organisational forms and properties. The process of creating organisational knowledge is not limited to inside the organisation, in permanent contact with its environment. The latter is a permanent source of stimulation to knowledge creation. In this respect the author refers to the existence of a knowledge system in the shape of a network which allows the firm to understand its environment better.

The selection principle is therefore taken into consideration in the model, fluctuations representing this dimension. Admittedly, selection works implicitly. Indeed, fluctuations only represent information which could be qualified as "inoffensive", insofar as the author does not mention the consequences of selection. It is assumed simply that the fluctuations are more or less absorbed by the organisation in accordance with its capacity to keepwatch and to interpret. Nevertheless we must not forget that Nonaka's article confines itself mainly to opening the "black box" of the knowledge creation process and does not explicitly address the matter of the regime to which the company is subject. The model is basically microeconomic and does not integrate the company into a market structure; this is the reason why the organisational and strategic context of the firm is not clearly identified. Therfore, even if the issue of selection does not have an evolutionary "quality", it nonetheless remains a determining factor in the knowledge creation process as defined by Nonaka.

Conclusion

The remarks set out above plead for the existence of mechanisms of governance which are linked to the distribution of knowledge. A priori, this analysis seems to differentiate itself from Williamson for whom the analysis of forms of governance is intrinsically linked to the approach based on transaction costs. According to him, a transaction is the basic unit and a structure of governance can be assimilated itself to an institutional scheme through which the whole of a transaction is decided: "*More generally, the study of governance is concerned with the identification, explication, and mitigation of all forms of contractual hazards, and the mechanisms of governance show how and why simple contracts give way to complex contracts and internal organisation as the hazards of contracting build up*" (Williamson, 1996). However, in our opinion, far from substituting Williamson's analysis, the taking into account of mechanisms of governance linked to the distribution of knowledge supplements the construction based on these transactions. It abides by a wider perspective of governance as Williamson himself explains when he writes: "*Governance is the means by which order is accomplished into a relation in which potential conflicts threaten to undo or upset opportunities to realise mutual gains"* (Williamson, 1996). Williamson's analysis of transactions describes the mechanisms which govern a world of resource allocation where the asymmetry of information is the main bias to be corrected. Mechanisms of governance concerning the distribution of knowledge are part of a world of resource creation, where bad circulation (repartition and distribution) of knowledge is the main problem to be overcome. These two worlds are not of course disconnected. The mechanisms of governance of knowledge distribution are dependent on the mechanisms of governance of transactions and vice-versa. This conjecture leaves open a number of areas for research: for example one can put forward the hypothesis that the existence and generalisation of hybrid forms of governance in larger quantities than Williamson expects result in a need to compromise between the two contexts of governance.

A second research area consists in admitting that in terms of governance and incentives, the distribution and creation of knowledge must comply with two rules. On the one hand, the autonomy of individuals must be respected in order to favour creation and diversity (cf. notably networks like intranet through multi-media and groupware practices). On the other hand, it is necessary to maintain the principle of hierarchy in order to respect the difference between intra and inter-functional organisational levels, in order to favour common practices and reference which are often crystallised in the achievement of a project.

Thus in order that the self-organising property of the spiral of knowledge be allowed to operate, the interaction of organisational levels must be provoked by the decision-making authority (top management). If the self-organising and evolutionary dimension of Nonaka's model is explained, its transposition at an organisational level requires that new modes of governance be identified and taken into consideration. The latter should provoke or reinforce the creation of transversal authorities, of the sort project management, at inter-functional level, but also of the bottom-up sort at intra-functional level, to supplement continuously the knowledge base of the firm. Nonaka's view of the firm also implies taking into consideration the importance of sub-groups whose dynamics agrees with certain characteristics of the intrapreneurship.

REFERENCES

Argyris C. & Schön D. A. (1978), *Organisational Learning: a Theory of Action Perspective,* Addison-Wesley Publishing Company.

BETA (1996), *Firme-réseau: l'impact des NTIC dans le processus de création de compétences dans l'industrie chimique;* Rapport France télécom (P. Cohendet, F. Kern, B. Mehmanpazir).

Cohen M. D. (1984), "Conflict and Complexity: Goal Diversity and Organizational Search Effectiveness" *The American Political Science Review* n° 78.

Cohendet P., Kern F., Mehmanpazir B. & Munier F. (1996), "Organisation of Transnational Firms and Networks of Telecommunications" EMOT Workshop (European Science Fondation), *Learning and Embeddedness: Evolving Transnational Firm Strategies in Europe;* Collingwood College, University of Durham New-Castle UK, 27-29 June 1996.

Cohendet P., Llerena P., & Marengo L. (1994), "Learning and Organizational Structure in Evolutionary Models of the Firm"; EUNETIC Conference Evolutionary of Technological Change, European Parliament Strasbourg, October 1994.

Coriat B. & Dosi G. (1995), "Learning how to Govern and Learning how to Solve Problems: On the Co-evolution of Competences, Conflicts and Organizational Routines", Laxenburg. Austria IIASA, Working paper 95-06.

Fransman M. (1994), "Information, Knowledge, Vision and Theories of the Firm", *Industrial and Corporate Change*, Vol. 3 n° 3.

Guilhon B. (1994), "Le processus d'apprentissage de la firme J: contenu et limites", *Revue d'Economie Industrielle*, n° 74.

Héraud J. A. & Garrouste P. (1993), "Auto-organisation et création technologique" in Ancori B. (ed), *Apprendre, se souvenir, décider,* CNRS éditions, Paris.

Lesourne J. (1991), *Economie de l'ordre et du désordre,* Economica, Paris.

Llerena D. (1996), *Internalisation de l'environnement et apprentissage dans les organisations*, Thèse de Sciences Economiques, Université Louis Pasteur Strasbourg I.

Loasby B. J. (1989), "Organization, Competition, and the Growth of Knowledge", in Langlois R. N. (ed), *Economic as process,* Cambridge University Press.

Marengo L. (1994), "Knowledge Distribution and Coordination on Organization: On some Social Aspects of the Exploitation vs. Exploration Trade-off", *Revue Internationale de systémique,* n° 1.

Munier F. (1996), "L'entreprise évolutionniste: connaissances et performances innovatives" Colloque Université Paris 1 – CNRS-METIS à la Sorbonne, *L'évolutionnisme, fondements, perspectives et réalisations*, 19 et 20 septembre 1996.

Nelson R. (1994), "The Co-evolution of Technology Industrial Change and supporting Institutions", *Industrial and Corporate Change* vol. 3.

Nelson R. & Winter S. (1982): "An Evolutionary Theory of Economic Change", Belknap press of Harvard, Cambridge.

Nonaka I. (1994), "A Dynamic Theory of Organizational Knowledge Creation", *Organisation science*, vol 5.

Polanyi M. (1966), *The Tacit Dimension,* Doubleday & Co, Inc Garden City New York.

Schelling T. (1978), *Micromotives and Macrobehavior*, Norton.

Teece D. J. (1988), "Technological Change and the Nature of the Firm", in Dosi *et al.* (eds), *Technical Change and Economic Theory*.

Walliser B. (1988), "Systémique et économie", *Revue Internationale de Systémique,* vol. 2, n° 3, pp. 245-260 (citée par Héraud et Garrouste, 1993).

Williamson O. E. (1996), *Mechanisms of Governance,* Oxford Unversity Press.

CHAPTER 5
TECHNOLOGICAL EVOLUTION AND FIRM BEHAVIOUR

Pier Paolo SAVIOTTI

1. Introduction

This paper is an attempt to develop a model of firm behaviour based on a population approach and on replicator dynamics, a technique of biological origin. The development of this paper follows from a number of important goals. First, to incorporate the results of the research on technological innovation that has taken place in the last twenty years. Second, to develop a model which can, at least in principle, deal with the problem of qualitative change in economic development. Third, to enable us to reconstruct a higher level of aggregation starting from the lowest possible one, that of the firm. The first goal follows from the neglect of technological innovation in firm theories. Innovation, even when it is incorporated into economic theories, is treated in an implicit way, that is by emphasizing its effects on the economy and not the mechanisms that create it. This paper tries to incorporate within the model several features of technological innovation that have been discovered within the last twenty years. One of the most important effects of technological innovation is the new goods, services and activities that it creates. Thus in the course of economic development innovation gives rise to qualitative change, that is to the emergence of entities qualitatively different with respect to those that existed previously. The same phenomenon can de described as a change in the composition of the economic system. The problem which is discussed in this paper and in a number of other papers by the same author (1994, 1995, 1996) is whether changes in the composition of the economic system are only an effect of economic development or whether they can be determinants of subsequent development. The model discussed in this paper can make a contribution to the analysis of qualitative change because it contains a representation of the dynamics of development and interaction of different technological populations and of the emergence of completely new technological populations. In this paper a technological population is defined by the firms that are producing a given product technology. In turn, product technology is represented by means of two sets of characteristics, describing the internal structure of the technology and the services performed for its users respectively. Moreover, this paper contains a concept of competition which, while related to the literature on imperfect competition, integrates other concepts and intuitions developed either in biology or in organization theories (Hannan, Freeman,1989). Finally, the approach based on a population approach and on replicator dynamics, while adapted here to the analysis of a population of firms, is capable of a considerable generality, because it can be formulated in terms of processes which are in principle present in any type of population. All these points will be analysed before proceeding to the presentation of the structure of the model. Accordingly, the following part of the paper is divided into two sections, dealing with the conceptual background and with the structure of the model respectively.

2. The conceptual background of the model

2.1. A characteristics representation of product technology

Each product technology is represented by means of two sets of characteristics, describing the internal structure of the technology (technical characteristics) and the services performed for its users (service characteristics) respectively (Saviotti, Metcalfe, 1984, 1991; Saviotti, 1988, 1994, 1995, 1996). The two sets of characteristics are related by a pattern of imaging, because the purpose of technical characteristics is to provide services (fig. 1).

$$\begin{pmatrix} X_{i1} \\ X_{i2} \\ \cdot \\ \cdot \\ \cdot \\ X_{in} \end{pmatrix} \Leftrightarrow \begin{pmatrix} Y_{i1} \\ Y_{i2} \\ \cdot \\ \cdot \\ \cdot \\ Y_{im} \end{pmatrix}$$

TECHNICAL CHARACTERISTICS   SERVICE CHARACTERISTICS

Figure 1: The twin characteristics representation of technology i. The double arrow between technical and service characteristics represents the pattern of imaging

Such an approach can be considered an adaptation of Lancaster (Lancaster, 1966; Lancaster, 1971) characteristics approach to the study of technological innovation. While Lancaster needed only one set of characteristics because he was only interested in demand, studies of technological innovation need to deal also with the supply side. We can consider that Lancaster characteristics are service characteristics, representing demand, and that technical characteristics have to be added in order to represent the supply side. Moreover, the two sets of characteristics can be conceptualized as the inner structure (technical characteristics) and the interface (service characteristics) of the technological system, following Simon's (1969, 1981) distinction between the inner structure, the outer structure, and the interface or boundary of the system. The twin characteristics framework has a number of interesting applications, such as allowing us to distinguish between radical and incremental innovation, and to define elementary phenomena in technological evolution. The applications which are of primary importance in this paper are those to the analysis of technological populations and of competition.

2.2. Technological populations

A technological population is here defined as the set of all the product models of a given technology. In turn, a technology is defined on the basis of its technical characteristics/internal structure: technologies are different when they are represented by qualitatively different technical characteristics. Each product model is represented by a point in characteristics space. Since different models have different values or levels of characteristics, a population will be represented by a cloud, corresponding to the distribution of models in characteristics space (fig. 2).

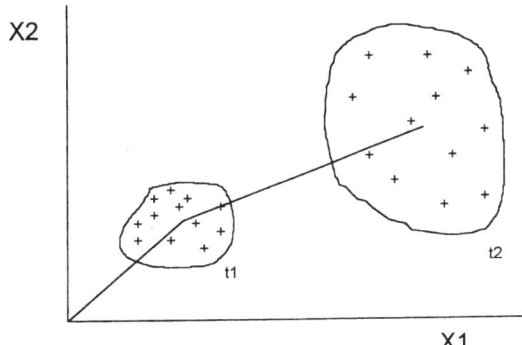

Figure 2: Between times t_1 and t_2 the position and density of the technological population change. The centre of the technological population describes a trajectory

There are three types of changes that can take place in a technological population: first, a change in the position of the population, caused by the variation in the values of the characteristics of the models constituting the population; second, a change in the density of the population; third, a change in the number of distinguishable populations. The third type of change can take place either by means of specialization, in which a technological population separates into two or more populations within the same dimensions of characteristics space (fig. 3), or by means of radical innovation, in which one or more new populations are created in new dimensions of characteristics space. To the extent that an industry is defined by its type of product, a technological population corresponds to an industry. A technological population can then be mapped onto the population of firms producing a given product.

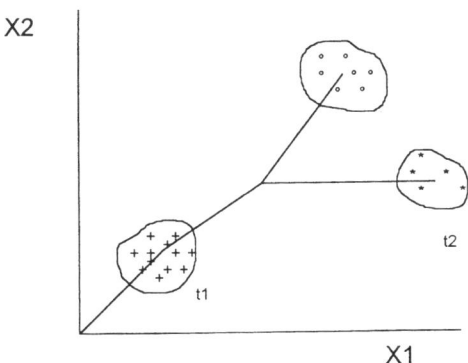

Figure 3: During the evolution of the technological population specialization/ fragmentation takes place, giving rise to a bifurcation in the trajectory

2.3. Competition

In the most traditional approach the number of competitors/participants was considered the measure of the intensity of competition. Thus in perfect competition the number of competitors is infinite, while it falls to one in monopoly, where there is no competition, and to few in oligopoly. The position taken in this paper is that the number of competitors is an important aspect of competition, but that it is not the only one. In order to obtain a complete representation of competition it is important to add a description of what happens in product space. The relevant dimensions of characteristics space are the density of the technological population and the average distance $D_y(i,j)$ between the chosen technological population (i) and possible competing populations (j) in service characteristics space. The density ρ_i of the technological population and the distance $D_y(i,j)$ represent intra- and inter- technology competition respectively. The density of the technological population is related to the similarity of the products of different producers: the greater the similarity, the lower the distance and the higher the density. If all producers were producing the same product, as it would happen in perfect competition, the technological population would collapse into a point, which would represent the analogue of perfect competition for a heterogeneous, multicharacteristics product. If now, starting from perfect competition we imagine to differentiate gradually the product models of different producers, we can foresee that their representative points will separate more and more in characteristics space. In this process the density of the technological population will gradually fall. We can see that perfect competition would correspond to an infinite population density, while product differentiation will lead to a fall in density. We can then realize that the density of a technological population is an important component of the intensity of competition which needs to be added to the number of competitors. It is in fact possible for the number of competitors to fall, while simultaneously the density in characteristics space increases. We can then define the intensity of competition as the product of the number of competitors and of the density in characteristics space:

$$IC_i = N_i \times \rho_i \qquad (1)$$

where IC_i is the intensity of competition in the ith technological population, N_i is the number of competitors, and ρ_i is the density of the ith technological population. Here it must be observed that it is the density in service characteristics space that we need to use. It is in this space that producers compete, although in order to do it they use different technical characteristics.

The concept of competition used in this paper constitutes an evolution of that contained in the literature on imperfect competition, derived mainly from the work of Chamberlin (1933), Hotelling (1929) and Lancaster (1975). However, with respect to this literature the approach used in this paper differs in two respects: first, it is aimed towards understanding the relationship between competition, qualitative change and long term economic development, as opposed to understanding the short term demand and welfare implications of product differentiation in a narrow product group; second, it draws inspiration also from a concept of competition used in the biological (Maynard Smith, 1974) and organizational (Hannan, Freeman, 1989) literature. In the latter a density based approach is used. However there density is defined as the number of participants.

The approach used in this paper gives some important advantages. First, it can represent all the possible types of competition, starting from perfect (population collapsing into one point) to monopolistic (population expanding and fragmenting in the same dimensions of characteristics space) and to schumpeterian competition (new technological populations arising in new dimensions of characteristics space); second, it allows us to distinguish between intra- and inter-technology competition, where intra-technology is the competition occurring within a given technological population, while inter-technology is the competition occurring between two different technological populations. Here we have to point out that for a sufficiently heterogeneous population (i.e. one having a large volume in characteristics-space) intra-technology competition occurs only between nearest neighbours, that is product models in very close proximity in characteristics-space. Moreover, inter-technology competition occurs between two technologies which are different because they have different technical characteristics, but provide comparable services (e.g. train and plane).

The distinction between intra- and inter-technology competition is important because the only type of competition that economists normally think about is intra-technology competition. In fact a monopolist is only free from intra- but not from inter-technology competition. Other technologies supplying similar services can threaten the monopoly, as air and road-transport do for the train, and as fax and e-mail do for the postal service. The existence of inter-technology competition contributes to market contestability: the greater inter-technology competition the more contestable the market.

Following these considerations we need to add the effect of inter-technology competition to the overall intensity of competition. We can expect a technology j different and distinguishable from the the one that we are considering (i) to compete to the extent that the output technology j provides services similar to those of i. The degree of similarity of i and j is inversely proportional to the distance $D_y(i,j)$ in service characteristics space. Consequently Eq (1) has to be modified as follows:

$$IC_i = \frac{N_i \rho_i}{D_y(i,j)} \qquad (2)$$

2.4. Knowledge bases, search activities and fitness

Search activities are a more general analogue of R& D, including all the activities aimed at exploring alternatives to existing routines, even if they are not classified formally as R& D. Search efforts represent the amount of resources allocated to search activities. Different types of search efforts can be described by means of a) the range, and, b) the probability of success. For example, we can think that a very basic type of research over an unexplored field is likely to scan over a very wide range, but to have a limited probability of success. We can imagine to represent this situation as a very flat distribution of the probability of success over a very wide range (fig. 4). On the other hand, we can imagine that a very applied and specific piece of knowledge will have a much more skewed probability distribution over a narrower range and with a higher maximum, corresponding to a greater probability of success (fig. 4). The advantage of this type of representation is that basic, applied research and development can be described by means of the same parameters, range and probabilty of success. Furthermore, we can hypothesize a life cycle which begins when basic search first uncovers the fundamental concepts required to understand the new field. subequently more applied search achieves partial, limited success (local peaks in the probability distribution of successful outcome) which lead to focusing on narrower ranges. Finally development improves on these successes by focusing on even narrower ranges, thus increasing the probability of success. In this paper both the range and the probability of success are described in characteristics space.

The main outcome of search activities considered in this paper is changes in product technology. Each product is represented by means of two sets of characteristics, one describing its internal structure (technical characteristics) and the other the services performed for their users (service characteristics) (Saviotti, Metcalfe, 1984). As a result of firms' search activities their KB grows,

98 | Consumers and firms behaviors

the characteristics of the products improve, and their fitness increases. Fitness is defined here as the capacity of a technology to adapt to its external environment (Saviotti, Mani, 1995). Such a definition has the merit of being general, but it would be easily applicable only if the external environment of a technology could be described by means of a set of characteristics. In this case the degree of correspondence between environment and service characteristics would measure fitness. Since environmental characteristics are rarely measurable, fitness can be approximately measured as the ratio of the degree of technical change undergone by a given product model to its price (Saviotti Mani, 1995).

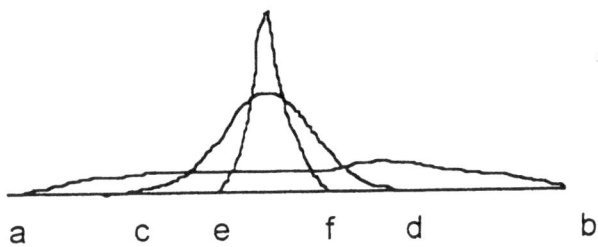

Figure 4: Range of search and probability of success for basic ($a-b$), applied ($c-d$) search and development ($e-f$)

$$F_i = \frac{\bar{Y}_i}{P_i} \tag{3}$$

Fitness, search efforts and the knolwege base are related through the following formula (Saviotti, Mani 1995b):

$$\frac{dF_i}{dSE} = \frac{dF_i}{dKB} \times \frac{dKB}{dSE} \tag{4}$$

where:

$$\frac{dF_i}{dSE} = \text{rate of return on search efforts} \tag{5}$$

$$\frac{dKB}{dSE} = \text{rate of learning due to search efforts} \tag{6}$$

$$\frac{dF_i}{dKB} = \text{technological opportunity of a given knowlege base} \tag{7}$$

According to equation (3) the rate of return from a technological search effort SE depends on the rate of learning within a given technology and on the opportunity of the technology itself. Neither fast learning in a technology with limited opportunity nor slow learning in a highly applicable technology will ensure market succes. As it was already evident to students of technological innovation in the1970s (e.g. Langrish *et al.*, 1970; Rosenberg, 1976) successful innovation requires a marriage of technological opportunity and market demand.

2.5. Variety, qualitative change and economic development

Qualitative change creates new entities, which are different and distinguishable from the pre-existing ones. If qualitative change was only an effect of economic development the need to incorporate it within economic theories would be limited. However, the situation is considerably different if qualitative change is also a determinant of subsequent economic development. In this case theories of economic development have to take the composition of the system into account as one of the important variables. The importance of qualitative change had clearly been foreseen by Schumpeter, for whom radical innovations, introducing completely new goods into the economic system, were the determinants of long term economic development. However, we have to overcome one of the limitations of Schumpeter's theories, that is we have to develop an analytical approach. In order to do this we have to define one or more variables which allow us to represent qualitative change. One variable which can be very useful in this sense is variety. We can in principle think of defining and measuring variety as the number of the distinguishable entities that are created by economic development. To be slightly more accurate, if we think of economic processes as the transformation of inputs into outputs, we can define variety as 'the number of actors, activities and objects necessary to characterise the economic system'. Such definition, while not being perfect, captures the essential features of qualitative change and can be the basis of quantitative and analytical treatments of economic development. First, such concept of variety is considerably different from the one that economists have commonly used. In the economic literature variety was used to refer to the degree of product differentiation within a product group. The problems that concerned this literature were mainly consumer welfare and imperfect competition (See for example, Lancaster, 1975). Authors working within this perspective had a static approach and were not concerned with the relationship between qualitative change and economic development. The emphasis in this paper is on the role of qualitative change in economic development. The approach used here is dynamic and focuses on a higher level of aggregation, at least the one of a national economic system. The concept of variety used here is more similar to what biologists call diversity, by which they mean the number of species living in a given habitat (e.g. Pielou, 1977). Second, variety is not necessarily an easy concept to measure. This problem is not discussed here in any detail, except for observing that measurements of variety/diversity have been proposed and used by biologists (see Pielou, 1977) and more recently by Weizmann (1992). In what follows of this paper it is assumed that the measurement of variety/diversity is possible, although difficult, and that it can be of very considerable help in characterizing the qualitative change that occurs during economic development.

We can now proceed to discuss more explicitly the role of variety in economic development in terms of two hypotheses formulated in a previous paper (Saviotti, 1994).

Hypothesis 1: The growth in variety is a necessary requirement for long-term economic development.

Hypothesis 2: variety growth, leading to new sectors, and productivity growth in pre-existing sectors, are complementary and not independent aspects of economic development.

There is both empirical evidence and theoretical support for these two hypotheses. Empirically the variety of several technologies has been observed to grow, in some cases enormously, during the last two hundred years (Saviotti, 1994). Although this phenomenon is not reflected in some economic statistics (e.g. output), the evidence for variety growth is considerable. The absence of variety from economic statistics is rather a proof that measurements are not blindly empirical, but that they reflect pre-theoretical categories. No one who is unaware or uninterested in variety will try to measure it.

The theoretical support for the two hypotheses comes from Pasinetti's models (1981, 1993) of economic development and structural change. Not by chance they are amongst the few models which can be used to support these hypotheses: Pasinetti's models contain a variable number of sectors, that is, they take into account the composition of the economic system and its relationship to economic development, a problem that is almost excluded ex-ante from traditional and new growth models. However, Romer's models (1987, 1990) include a growth in the number of capital goods amongst the consequences of innovation, and they provide a limited support for the hypothesis of variety growth. Returning now to Pasinetti's models, we can say that an economy with a constant set of activities (that is with a constant composition and constant variety), with constant productivity growth and saturation of demand in particular goods/services, would not be stable. Such an economy would generate underutilization of resources, including unemployment. It would become possible to produce the whole demanded output using smaller and smaller percentages of existing inputs/resources. However, while technological change, leading to productivity growth, would be partly responsible for this imbalance, it could also provide a form of compensation. Technological change creates new goods and services, and, therefore, new sectors, which can "re-employ" the resources made redundant by the imbalance arising in the pre-existing sectors, thus acting as a form of compensation. Of course, no actual unemployment or re-employment needs to be involved if there is sufficient coordination between productivity growth in pre-existing sectors and the emergence of new sectors caused by innovations. Thus growing variety can help overcome the bottlenecks created by the imbalance between productivity growth and demand saturation in pre-existing sectors. On the other hand new goods/services/sectors can only be created by the resources made available by productivity growth in pre-existing sectors. Such resources can be invested in search activities, the most important of which is R& D, which create new goods/services. In this sense the complementarity between variety growth and productivity growth in pre-existing sectors bears a considerable similarity to that between productivity growth in agriculture and investment in the new industries during the process of industrialization (see Kuznets, 1965).

Before concluding this section it must be stressed that the two previous hypotheses have a considerable degree of support both at the theoretical and empirical level, but that they cannot be considered as definitively proved. In particular, Pasinetti's models are not fully dynamic. While they can tell us that an economy with a constant composition, with constant productivity growth and saturation of demand would run into a bottleneck, they cannot give us any indication about the dynamics of emergence of new sectors. A more conclusive proof of the above hypothesis awaits the development of a fully dynamic evolutionary model of economic development. For the moment the two previous hypotheses can be considered strong working hypotheses in the course of articulation and development. Finally, it must be stressed that the two hypotheses are intended to be valid at a high level of aggregation and in the long run.

The hypothesis that variety growth is a necessary requirement for the long term continuation of economic development was previously justified by the bottleneck caused by the saturation of demand while productivity keeps growing. However, we can also expect demand saturation to be a further inducement for firms to exit their present technological populations.

3. The structure of the model

As pointed out at the beginning, the model presented in this paper is an example of replicator dynamics, a technique of biological origin. Here a replicator means anything that can reproduce. The model developed here can describe the evolution of interacting populations. The model can describe both quantitative change in the number of members of the population, and qualitative change, both for what concerns the nature of the members of existing populations and the emergence of completely new populations. Quantitative change is represented by the combination of the basic processes of birth and death, where any phenomenon that contributes to raise the number of members of the population is a component of birth and any phenomenon that contributes to lower the number of members of the population is a component of death.

Qualitative change in the members of existing populations can take place in a number of ways. For example, in a previously developed model of technological evolution (Saviotti, Mani, 1995) incremental innovation gave rise to changes in the characteristics of population members. On the other hand, qualitative change can be created by the emergence of completely new populations. Of course, the structure of the equations that represent the evolution of a particular system is specific to the system itself. For example, the phenomena contributing to birth and death are specific to the system. On the other hand, the model is capable of considerable generality, in the sense that we can represent the evolution of very large classes of populations in terms of birth, death, changes in the nature of the members of existing populations and emergence of completely new populations. Finally, before getting into the details of the model, we have to point out that its level of aggregation is that of technology, defined as a distinguishable population in X-space. That is, all firms in a population produce some variant of the technology. It is a micro model because it contains the composition of the system. However, the same technology can be produced all over the world. As a consequence, the population of firms can be distributed over the world economic system. Furthermore, the model can describe the evolution of several interacting populations. Therefore, its level of aggregation can be greater than that of a national economy. In principle we can use it to reconstruct aggregated features starting from the lowest possible level of aggregation, that of the firm.

3.1. Birth and death processes

The inducement for new firms to enter, leading to birth, can be split into a number of components: a) the example of existing firms (imitative behaviour); b) the possibility/capacity to enter; c) the expected growth potential of the sector. The example of existing firms can be considered to reduce uncertainty about the prospects in a new technology, to create routines which can be followed by imitating firms, and to establish legitimation (Hannan, 1989), both in terms of market acceptance and of institutions that can support the market. The possibility/capacity to enter is determined both by the knowledge and competences of the firm, that is by what we call its knowledge base (KB), and by the availability of financial capital.

$$\frac{dN_i}{dt} = k_1 N_i^\beta + k_2 FA(F_i - \bar{F}) + V(Y_i) \times \sum_{j \neq i=1}^{n} \frac{N_j \rho_j m_j(t)}{D_y(i,j) M_j} \tag{8}$$

where N_i is the number of members of the ith population, FA is a measure of financial availability, F_i is the fitness of the technology, F is the average fitness of all technologies, $V(Y_i)$ is the volume of the ith technological population in service characteristics space, and ρ_j is the density of another, pre-existing population. F_i is related to the knowledge base of firms by equations (4)-(7).

The first term on the right of the equal sign, $k_1 N_i^\beta$ represents the effect of imitation. The presence of firms already in place reduces uncertainty, creates routines, and helps to establish institutions and organizations for the new technology. Since $\beta < 0$ the imitation effect falls with the number of firms already in place. The second term represents the capacity of a firm to enter the new technology i. It is the product of FA, financial availability, and of $(F_i - F)$, the differential fitness of the new technology with respect to the average fitness of all other technologies. FA, financial availability, depends on the number and size of financial institutions and on the degree of confidence they have in the new technology i. Thus FA is likely to depend on the number of firms already present in the new technology (N_i), on $V(Y_i)$ and on $(F_i - F)$.

The term $V(Y_i) \times \sum N_j \rho_j [m_j(t)/M_j]$ altogether represents the inducement to exit pre-existing technological populations (j) and to enter a new one (i). Following the previous considerations on competition, the term $N_j \rho_j$, the product of the number of competitors and of the density of the technological population, represents the intensity of competition of a technological population that pre-existed the ith one. $N_j \rho_j$ represents the inducement to exit a pre-existing technological population to establish a niche, where there will be temporary monopoly. $m_j(t)/M_j$ represents the fraction of the population of households that has already adopted the good/service j. On the other hand, $V(Y_i)$, the volume of the ith technological population in service characteristics space, measures the scope or potential of the ith technoloy. The greater $V(Y_i)$, the greater the number of niches (Saviotti, Mani, 1995) that can be established within the technological population, and the greater the expected development potential of the technology.

The inducement of firms to exit the ith technological population, leading to death, depends on both intra- and inter-technology competition and on demand saturation. Intra-technology competition is measured by the term Nipi, the intensity of competition within the ith technological population, while inter-technology competition depends on the distance, or on the degree of similarity, between technology i and other potentially competing technologies in service characteristics space. As already pointed out, the closer two technological models are in characteristics space, the more similar they are, and the smaller their distances. Thus distances are inversely proportional to degrees of similarity. Demand saturation is, as before, represented by $m_i(t)/M_i$, the fraction of the population of households that can adopt the good/service i. Moreover, it has been observed that death rates vary considerably with firm size, large firms having a substantially lower mortality rates than smaller ones (Hannan et al., 1990). Consequently death rates are given by the expression:

$$-\frac{dN_i}{dt} = k_3 \frac{N_i \rho_i m_i(t)}{D_y(i,j) M_i} + at_i^{a-1} S_{i,t}^{-\gamma} \qquad (9)$$

where N_i is the number of competitors in technology i, ρ_i is the density of the ith technological population, $D_y(i, j)$ is the average distance between technologies i and j in service characteristics space, $S_{i,t}$ is the average size of the average size of the firms in technology i at time t, $0 < a < 1$, $0 < \gamma < 1$. Therefore, size decreses mortality at a decreasing rate.

Carroll and Hannan (1990) suggest that death rates depend also on the age of firms. While we do not want to dispute this suggestion, for the time being we leave this factor out of consideration.

The net rate of birth, that is the balance of birth and death rates, is given by:

$$\frac{dN_i}{dt} = k_1 N_i^\beta + k_2 FA(F_i - \bar{F}) + V(Y_i) \times \sum_{j \neq i=1}^{n} \frac{N_j p_j m_j(t)}{D_y(i,j) M_j}$$

$$- k_3 \frac{N_i p_i m_i(t)}{D_y(i,j) M_i} - at_i^{a-1} S_{i,t}^{-\gamma} \qquad (10)$$

3.2. Firm size

The size of a firm can vary either through internal growth or through mergers and acquisitions. internal growth will be influenced by the rate of growth of demand and by the differential fitness of firms in the technology.

$$\frac{dL_{i,l}}{dt} = k_4 \left(1 - \frac{m_i(t)}{M_i}\right) VA(F_{i,l}) L_{t-1} \exp(-\delta L_{t-1}^2) + (V_a - V_f) \quad (11)$$

where $L_{i,1}$ is the size of a firm (l) in the ith technological population measured by its total employment, $(1 - m_i(t)/M_i)$ is the rate of growth of demand for the output of the technology at time t, here considered exogenously determined; $VA(F_{i,1})$ is the variance in the fitness of the firms within the ith technological population, L_{t-1} is the average size or firms within the ith technological population at time $t-1$, V_a and V_f are the assets and financial values of the firms in the ith technological population.

We can expect that the opportunities for the growth of the best firms will be greater the larger the variance in the firms' fitness. Conversely we can expect that, when this variance falls as the less efficient firms go out of business, the rate of size growth is going to fall. This situation is similar to that described by Fisher's fundamental theorem in biology (Nelson, Winter, 1982), which says that the rate of growth of a population is proportional to the variance in the fitness of the population. Also, we can expect that beyond a minimum size level larger firms will have advantages in a number of situations, for example in obtaining loans from banks, in setting up alliances with other firms etc. Such positive influence of size on growth is represented by the term $L_{i,t-1}$, the average firm size at time $t-1$. The disadvantages of large size are instead represented by the term $\exp(-\delta L_{i,t-1}^2)$. The term $(V_a - V_f)$, the difference between the average assets and financial values of firms, represents the contribution of mergers and acquisitions.

Here it must be pointed out that the rate of size growth can also be written in terms of firm output $Q_{i,l}$. This equation can be derived from eq. (11) in the following way:

$$\frac{dQ_{i,l}}{dt} = \frac{dQ_{i,l}}{dL_{i,l}} \frac{dL_{i,l}}{dt} \qquad (12)$$

where:

$$Q_{i,l} = q_{i,l} L_{i,l} \qquad (13)$$

$q_{i,l}$ being the productivity in the production of good/service i by firm l.

We can expect to derive $dQ_{i,l}/dL_{i,l}$ from the following:

$$q_{i,l} = f(HC_{i,l}, K_{i,l}) \qquad (14)$$

where $HC_{i,l}$ is the human capital and $K_{i,l}$ is the physical capital in firm l.

3.3. Firm structure

Firms structure is represented in this model by the number of divisions or departments $n_{D,i,j}$:

$$n_{D,i,l} = k_5 L_{t,i,l} V(Y_i) V(X_i) N_x \qquad (15)$$

where $L_{t,i,l}$ is the size of firm l in the ith technological population at time t, and $V(Y_i)$ is the volume of the ith technological population in service characteristics space, $V(X_i)$ is the volume of the ith technological population in technical characteristics space, and N_x is the number of dimensions in technical characteristics space. Eq. (15) tells us that the expected number of divisions or departments in a firm is likely to increase with firm size, with the degree of product differentiation in the technology, with the differentiation of the competences required, here represented by $V(X_i) N_x$. The effect of firm size can be considered to lead to a multifunctional, or U, structure, while that of product and of competences differentiation to a multidivisional, or M, structure.

3.4. The number of distinguishable technological populations

The net number of technological populations is the result of the processes that create new technological populations and of those that eliminate existing ones. The factors that can be expected to lead to each one of these two processes are:

a) Creation of new populations

• inducements, such as increasing competition in pre-existing technological populations or as saturation of demand in pre-existing products;

• new technological opportunities, arising out of R& D or of search activities.

As a result of new technological opportunities products which give new or enhanced services begin to be produced. Such products can be assumed to have an increased fitness with respect to existing ones.

b) Elimination of existing technological populations

Every time a new product or service with improved performance is produced existing products or services may be displaced. The disappearance/extinction of the old technological population will happen with certainty only when the services supplied by the new technology/product/service are identical in type and level to those of the old one, but they are cheaper, even marginally. This corresponds to what has previously been called pure substitution (Saviotti, Metcalfe, 1984; Saviotti, 1996). If the substitution process is not pure, that is if the services supplied by the new product/service are superior to those of the old one, then the old product/service does not need to disappear. In this case the most likely outcome is a process of specialization in which the new product/service supplies a different niche or subset of the market. Thus death of a population will take place with certainty only when a perfect substitute of it appears. Otherwise the old product/service might survive even if its market share were reduced. Hence the rate of death should be proportional to the degree of sustitutability between the old and the new product/service and to the advantage of the new product/service with respect to the old one. Of course, the rate of death will also be proportional to the intensity of competition and to the saturation of demand in the old technological populations.

As a consequence of the previous considerations the equation for the net number of technological populations will contain a positive term for the birth of new populations and a negative term for the death of old ones.

$$\frac{dn}{dt} = k_6 \frac{N_j p_j m_j(t)}{D_Y(i,j) M_j} V(Y_i) \left[SE_i + \frac{k_7 \sum_{j=1}^{n} SE_j}{D_X(i,j)} \right] - \frac{N_j p_j m_j(t) F_i}{D_Y(i,j) M_j F_j} \qquad (16)$$

where n is the net number of distinguishable technological populations at time t; SE_i represents the search efforts in technology i, SE_j the search efforts in technology j, $D_x(i,j)$ is the distance between technologies i and j in technical characteristics space, $D_y(i,j)$ is the distance between technologies i and j in service characteristics space, $N_j \rho_j$ represents the intensity of competition in technology j, F_i and F_j the fitness of technologies i and j respectively, $m_j(t)/M_j$ the extent of demand saturation for good/service j.

Eq. (16) tells us that the rate of birth of new technological populations increases with the intensity of competition in pre-existing technologies j, with the saturation of demand in pre-existing technologies, with the scope or potential of the new technology i, with search efforts in technology i and in technologies j. The search efforts contributing to the birth of new technological populations are both those carried out within the new technology i and those carried out within old technologies j. The effectiveness of external search efforts (j) depends on how similar they are to the internal ones (i), as shown by the presence of the distance $D_x(i,j)$ in technical characteristics space between the new and the old technology. The inverse dependence from $D_x(i,j)$ is related both to the local character of knowledge and to the fact the absorption capacity of a firm for a given type of external knowledge increases when the firm has previously done search activities on similar types of knowledge (Cohen, Levinthal, 1989, 1990). On the other hand the rate of death of pre-existing technological populations increases with the intensity of competition, with the saturation of demand, with the degree of substitutability between the old and the new technologies, and with the advantage of the new with respect to the old, represented by the ratio of their fitnesses.

4. Some implications of the model

4.1. A competition life cycle

The model as formulated in the previous section is a representation of the conceptual background described in section 2. At this stage it can de considered a first version that needs both refinements in its structure and several applications. A first implication of this model, which consists of predicting the existence and nature of a competition life cycle, is described in this subsection.

As we have seen previously, the intensity of competition in a technological population is proportional to the product of the number of participating firms and of the density of the technological population divided by the average distance between the technological population and competing ones in service characteristics space. As we have seen, the intensity of competition in a pre-existing technological population constitutes the inducement for a firm to exit such a population and to establish a niche, where there will be a temporary monopoly. By definition in the niche the intensity of competition will be very

108 | Consumers and firms behaviors

low, at its minimum as long as in the niche there is only the original entrepreneur. To the extent that the innovation introduced by the entrepreneur who set up the niche is successful, it will induce imitation. Imitation leads to entry, and thus increases both the density and the number of participants in the niche. The intensity of competition increases gradually until it reaches values comparable to those of pre-existing technological populations. The inducement to enter a new technological population is inversely proportional to the intensity of competition in the population itself. As long as the intensity of competition is low, due to both a low N_i and a low p_i, there will be a high inducement to enter, stimulating a Schumpeterian bandwagon of imitators. As a consequence of imitation, the intensity of competition increases until the point is reached where the inducement to enter becomes first zero and then negative, that is, a inducement to exit appears. At this point there is a finite probability that a new niche will be created, starting the competition life cycle all over again. We can place this reasoning on a slightly more analytical basis by returning to the definition of competition given before:

$$IC = \frac{N_j p_j}{D_y(i,j)}$$

The evolution of IC depends on the three variables N_j, p_j and $D_y(i,j)$. We start by analyzing the simplest possible case by assuming that N_j and $D_y(i,j)$ are constant and that IC changes only due to changes in the density of the technological population j. Then:

$$p_j = \frac{R_j}{V_y(j)} \tag{17}$$

where R_j = number of distinguishable models in the technological population j and $V_y(j)$ is the volume of such a technological population in service characteristics space. Again, to start by the simplest possible case, we assume $V_y(j)$ to be constant, which means that the total range of services performed by the technology j is constant. In this case:

$$IC = \frac{N_j R_j}{V_y(j) D_y(i,j)} \tag{18}$$

where the only variable term contributing to change IC is R_j, the number of distinguishable models in the technological population j. If at this point we assume that the number of distinguishable models existing at a given time costitutes an indication of the success and of the scope of the niche, we can write:

$$\frac{dR_j}{dt} = aR_j \tag{19}$$

which leads to the expression:

$$R_j = e^{at} \tag{20}$$

In other words, the more entry there is, the more further entry will be encouraged. The formula for the intensity of competition will then become:

$$IC = \frac{N_j e^{at}}{V_y(j) D_y(i,j)} \tag{21}$$

According to this expression the intensity of competition would increase indefinitely and exponentially. The rate of increase of the intensity of competition would be even greater if entry was accomplished not just by a set number of participants introducing more models, but by the entry of new participants, which would raise N_j. Clearly, this expression can only be valid up to the upper boundary of intensity of competition tolerable to most participants is reached. At that point, exit starts taking place, reducing both N_j and ρ_j, and allowing some of the participants to survive in population j. This treatment then confirms the intuition of the competition life cycle described before. Such a competition life cycle agrees with the description of economic development we find in Schumpeter (1912, 1934). The entrepreneur creates an innovation and establishes a niche, where he/she enjoys a temporary monopoly. This leads to imitation and entry, thus reducing the degree of monopoly in the niche, until the niche becomes one more of the routine components of the economy. Further entry is then discouraged.

The competition life cycle previously described is a possible but not necessary outcome of the evolution of the populations of firms. Up to this point we have assumed that only ρ_j could vary. If we let other variables to vary, then more complex development paths are obtained. For example, we can assume that the density of the technological population j varies not only due to the number of models M_j, but also due to the change in the volume $V_y(j)$ of the technological population in service characteristics space. We make the assumption that $V_y(j)$ will increase in the course of time, due to search activities, to innovation and to process of specialization occurring within the technological population j. We can understand right away that, even if the number of models R_j keeps increasing, the density $\rho_j = R_j / V_y(j)$ might not increase or it might even fall, depending on the relative rates of change of R_j and of $V_y(j)$. If $V_y(j)$ kept increasing at a rate at least equal to that of R_j, the competition life cycle analyzed before would never take place. However, it is unlikely that the range of services provided by a technology can keep increasing indefinitely. We can expect that in the end diminishing returns will set in, leading to an upper boundary in the development of the technology. In this case we can expect $V_y(j)$ to have an upper boundary V_m. We can also expect that increases in

110 | Consumers and firms behaviors

$V_y(j)$ will be easier to achieve at the beginning, but that learning effects will accumulate gradually during the evolution of the technology. An evolution of this type is captured by the expression:

$$\frac{dV_y(j)}{dt} = \beta V_y(j)(V_m - V_y(j)) \qquad (22)$$

where β is a constant and V_m is the maximum possible volume of the technological population j. By integrating (19) we obtain:

$$V_y(j) = \frac{V_m}{1 - \exp(-\beta t)} \qquad (23)$$

This is the expression of the logistic curve. The shapes of R_j, of $V_y(j)$ and of p_j are represented in Figure 5. We have to remember that the relative position of these curves depends on the values of a and β. In the extreme case represented in Figure 5 $R_j < V_y(j)$. In this case the density of models p_j would initially fall, and then it would start increasing after the saturation of $V_y(j)$, determined by the onset of diminishing returns to the exploitation of the technology, occurred. In this case the critical level of competition preventing further entry and leading to exit would be reached after a longer time than in the previous case. In general, even if p_j were not to fall at any time, its progression would be slower than when only R_j can change. Allowing $V_y(j)$ to change can then either suppress the competition life cycle or modify its time path, the most likely outcome being a delay in the achievement of the critical level of IC which leads to exit.

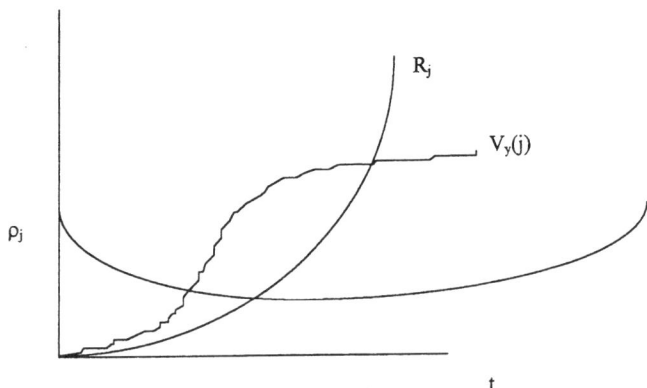

Figure 5: The time paths of p_j, $V_y(j)$ and R_j when $dV_y(j)/dt > dR_j/dt$

So far we have assumed $D_y(i,j)$ to be constant, which would correspond to a constant intensity of inter-technology competition. If $D_y(i,j)$ were to change, it would either accelerate or slow down the competition life cycle. In summary then, we can expect that a competition life cycle will be generated by the combination of firm dynamics and of technological evolution. Such a competition life cycle will have a multiplicity of possible time paths, depending on the combination of the variables R_j, $V_y(i)$, N_j, $D_y(i,j)$.

The basic Schumpeterian intuition of the role of entrepreneurs and of innovations in economic development is confirmed by this model. As in Schumpeter's theory, the innovation establishes a situation of temporary monopoly, leading to imitation. Imitation, while realizing the economic potential of the innovation, gradually erodes the temporary monopoly and reduces the niche to one more of the routine activities of the economic system. At this point the impulse of a new innovation is required to start the process all over again. This model provides an analytical structure for such a competition life cycle, and it demonstrates that its dynamics depends on a number of variables and can be fairly complex. Clearly, these are first tentative analyses of the competition life cycle and of its relationship to qualitative change. This is one of the directions in which further exploitaion of the model is required.

5. Summary and conclusions

In this paper a model of firm behaviour based on replicator dynamics and on a population approach has been developed. In the model a population of firms is based on a product technology, defined in characteristics space. A density based concept of competition is used in the model, in which the intensity of competition is given by the product of the number of participating firms N_i and of the density p_i of the technological population. In other words, the measurement of the intensity of competition is based both on the number participants and on what happens in characteristics space. The structure of the model relies on the basic processes of birth, death, changes in the nature of the population members, and the emergence of completely new populations. The details of the model depend on the system to which it is applied. However, the model is in principle applicable to a wide range of populations. Moreover, since it contains both changes in the nature of the population members, and the emergence of completely new populations, the model can be used to study the qualitative change which occurs during economic development. The first implication of the model which has been discussed is the prediction of the existence of a competition life cycle. In this life cycle the intensity of competition in a pre-existing population constitutes the inducement to exit the population and to establish a new niche. Entry creates a temporary monopoly with low intensity of competition. However, if the innovation that established the niche is successful, imitation will gradually raise the intensity of competition, until further entry will be discouraged and the inducement to exit and to establish a new niche will be created again. This paper constitutes the initial formulation of the model. The model itself is quite general and will require further analysis.

REFERENCES

Carrol G.R., Hannan M.T. (1990), "Density delay in the evolution of organizational populations: a model and some empirical tests", in *Organizational Evolution: New Directions*, Ed Singh J.V., Newbury Park: Sage, 1990.

Chamberlin E.J. (1933), *"The Theory of Monopolistic Competition"*, Cambridge, Mass: Harvard University Press, 1933.

Hannan M.T., Freeman J. (1989), *Organizational Ecology*, Cambridge, Mass: Harvard University Press, 1989.

Hannan M.T., Ranger-Moore, J. Banaszak-Holl J. (1990), "Competition and the evolution of organizational size distribution", in *Organizational Evolution: New Directions*, Ed Singh J.V. Newbury Park: Sage.

Hotelling H. (1929), "Stability in competition", *Economic Journal*, 39, 41-57.

Krugman P.R. (1979), "Increasing returns, monopolistic competition and international trade", *Journal of International Economics*, 9, 469-479.

Kuznezts S. (1965), *Economic Growth and Structure*, New York: Norton.

Lancaster K.J. (1966), "A new approach to consumer theory", *Journal of Political Economy*, 14, 133-156.

Lancaster K.J. (1971), *Consumer Demand: a New Approach*, New York: Columbia University Press.

Lancaster K.J. (1979), *Variety, Equity and Efficiency*, New York: Columbia University Press.

Maynard Smith J. (1974), *Models in Ecology*, Cambridge: Cambridge University Press.

Nelson R. and Winter S. (1982), *An Evolutionary Theory of Economic Change*, Cambridge Mass: Harvard University Press.

Pasinetti L.L. (1981). *Structural Change and Economic Growth*, Cambridge: Cambridge University Press.

Pielou C. (1977), *Mathematical Ecology*, New York: John Wiley.

Romer P. (1987), "Growth based on increasing returns due to specialization", *American Economic Review*, 77, 565-62.

Romer P. (1990), "Endogenous technical progress", *Journal of Political Economy*, 98.

Saviotti P.P. (1988), "Information, variety and entropy in technoeconomic development", *Research Policy*, 17, 89-103.

Saviotti P.P. (1991), "The role of Variety in economic and technological development", pp. 172-208 in Saviotti P.P., Metcalfe J.S. (Eds), *Evolutionary Theories of Economic and Technological Change: Present State and Future Prospects*, Reading: Harwood Publishers.

Saviotti P.P. (1994), "Variety, economic and technological development", in *Technology, Industries and Institutions: Studies in Schumpeterian Perspectives,* Eds Shionoya Y., Perlman M., Ann Arbor: the University of Michigan Press.

Saviotti P.P. (1996), *Technological Evolution, Variety and the Economy*, Aldershot: Edward Elgar.

Saviotti P.P., Mani G. (1995), "Competition, variety and technological evolution: a replicator dynamics model", *Journal of Evolutionary Economics*, 5, 369-392.

Saviotti P.P., Mani G.S., "Technological evolution, self-organization and knowledge", presented at the conference "La connaissance dans la dynamique des organisations productives" Aix-en-Provence, 14-15 September 1995.

Saviotti P.P., Metcalfe J.S. (1984), "A Theoretical Approach to the Construction of Technological Output Indicators", *Research Policy*, 13, 141-151.

Saviotti P.P., Metcalfe J.S. (1991), Eds, *Evolutionary Theories of Economic and Technological Change: Present State and Future Prospects*, Reading: Harwood Publishers.

Schumpeter J. (1934, original edition 1912), *The Theory of Economic Development*, Cambridge, Mass: Harvard University Press.

Schumpeter J. (1943), *Capitalism, Socialism and Democracy*, London: George Allen and Unwin.

Simon H.A. (1969), new edition (1981), "The natural and the artificial world", in Simon H.A. *The Sciences of the Artificial*, MIT Press: Cambridge, Mass.

Singh J.V. (Ed) (1990), *Organizational Evolution: New Directions*, Newbury Park: Sage.

Weitzman M.L. (1992), "On diversity", *Quarterly Journal of Economics*, 107, 363-405.

CHAPTER 6
PUSHING TECHNOLOGICAL PROGRESS FORWARD
A Comparison of Firm Strategies

Uwe CANTNER, Horst HANUSCH and Andreas PYKA

1. Introduction

Joseph Alois Schumpeter (1942) was among others prominent in emphasizing that innovative activities of firms are to be considered as active and intended search processes for new technological possibilities and opportunities rather than solely accidental events. Although this statement was a first attack on neoclassical general equilibrium theory, it was the neoclassical camp itself which presented an approach to formalize these ideas; the *new industrial economics* (Arrow (1962), Dasgupta/Stiglitz (1980), Reinganum (1985)) was born. Within a traditional cost-benefit framework the conditions for an optimal allocation of R& D resources are derived. For doing so, however, this approach has to rely on several strong assumptions where known technological opportunities, perfect capabilities, perfect foresight and full information combined with weak uncertainty are the most crucial ones.

This neoclassical approach, however, has been critized by modern innovation theory, which claims that the neoclassical assumptions on opportunities, information and uncertainty do neglect the very nature of the innovative process: opportunities are not known ex-ante, information is far from complete, uncertainty is strong, capabilities are heterogeneous and far from perfect. On this basis, the strategic behaviour of firms is not only to be seen as a response to other firms' actions — a play against competitors as in traditional industrial economics — but also as a device to play a *game against nature*.

Within this context, the so-called *behavioural approach* to innovation theory asks how firms behave in situations of substantive and procedural rationality (Simon (1976), Dosi/Egidi (1991)). For answering these questions this approach follows an *evolutionary modelling,* emphasizing selection in and generation of variety. With respect to the former, different behaviour or ideas coexist for some time, and by a selection process fitter alternatives come to dominate, reducing variety. Variety generation, on the other hand, has to be considered – contrary to biological evolution – not as a blind search but as a *conscious, purposeful* and often *directed* activity where actors design strategies and rules in order to survive economically. By this, they react on selective pressures, on the one hand, and, on the other, they often attempt to learn from the activities of others. This all, however, is done in a far from perfect or optimal way.

On this basis, our paper investigates how different *routines of innovative behaviour* perform. The design of those routines is derived from the technological environment a firm faces, i.e. opportunities, uncertainty and appropriability conditions, from economic factors such as profits and sales, as well as from the individual capability and willingness to cope with (technological) uncertainty. Principally, the "constructed" routines contain *fixed* and *flexible* components, where the former are labelled *strategies* and the latter *learning rules*. Three different strategies are investigated: the *absorptive strategy* where the ability to use technological spillovers plays the central role, the *conservative strategy* which acts rather in isolation and relies only on own research efforts, and the *imitative strategy* which, contrariwise, relies not on own research efforts but tries to catch up by imitating best-practice technologies.

With this routine-based modelling of innovative activities of heterogeneous actors our model is analytically not solvable, and thus, we rely on simulation experiments in the tradition of Nelson/Winter (1982). Under different conditions and different flexible routines we show that the absorptive strategy is very likely to dominate other strategies in the long-run. Moreover, we find that learning rules focussing on technological rather than economic performance accelerate the speed of technological progress considerably.

Our analysis proceeds as follows: In section 2 we discuss the theoretical foundations where we explicitly introduce and explain the different strategies and the motives behind them. Section 3 describes the simulation model. Section 4 shows the most important results of different simulation runs. We close our discussion with some concluding remarks in section 5.

2. The Design of R& D-Strategies

One of the major attempts of modern innovation theory is to provide new insights in the process of technological change by dismissing the often unrealistic assumptions of traditional economic theory. There the assumption of abundant technological opportunities, perfect capabilities, information and foresight combined with an only weak uncertainty provide that innovative activities are boiled down to an *optimal* R& D allocation game against competitors. By this, technological progress – banned into a "black-box"– is designed in a way to allow for optimal cost-benefit calculations. Dismissing with these assumptions and taking into account that technological progress is also a *game against nature,* it is not at all clear how and along which lines firms design their R& D.

In the following we investigate how different innovation strategies as found in the literature perform in a comparative analysis. For this purpose we first briefly discuss the technological environment firms are faced with. Based on this, the second step provides a characterization of different R&D-strategies.

2.1. Supply-Side Factors Influencing Innovation

The statement that innovative activities are (also) a *game against nature,* and thus against the unforseeable, suggests that firms invest resources mainly in order to acquire more information which allows for better decisions and improved performance: they learn and explore their environment which is not a "black-box", but which has its own structural and dynamic features. Since the 80's innovation theory has been mainly engaged in investigating those environments which show the following main features:

– *technological uncertainty and the endogenous generation of technological opportunities.*

The search for new technologies and even the improvement of existing technologies are risky and uncertain endeavours. This uncertainty – intrinsic to the innovation process – does not allow to exactly predict the timing, the technological features and the economic consequences of innovations: on the one hand, firms try to find new technological solutions for their production processes with *ex-ante* not anticipated consequences; on the other hand, new unforeseen and unexpected discoveries external to a firm may change the current situation. Thus, firm decisions and behaviour are to be seen as *bounded rational.*

The development space within which firms learn and which firms attempt to explore consists of a broad set of technological opportunities providing potentials for progress. Here several regularities can be observed. First, the developmental potential of a specific technology is increasingly exhausted with progress on the respective technological trajectory. So-called "intensive technological opportunities" (Coombs (1988)) are becoming depleted step by step. By this technological as well as scientific boundaries come into effect more and more making further improvements increasingly difficult and sometimes even impossible to achieve.

Second, besides intensive opportunities characterizing a specific technology there are also "extensive technological opportunities" which arise out of *cross-fertilization* among different technologies (Mokyr, (1990)). Here, new technical solutions are often actively initiated by firms which then generate new opportunities by the combination of already existing technologies. Sometimes the amalgamation of different – *ex-ante* considered as unrelated – technologies leads to totally new technological fields; mechatronic or bionic are points in case. As Dahmén (1990) states, "structural tensions" between complementary technologies may be resolved in the course of time providing for new technological opportunities.

Such interdependencies and their combining effect arise out of different sources: Besides new ideas and findings in academia the manifold effects between up- and downstream productions among firms within and between industries are potential sources of such *cross-fertilization*. These mutual influences come into effect mainly by technological spillovers.

– *Appropriability, absorptive capacities, and endogenous spillover pools*

These spillover effects arise whenever new technological know-how is not a purely private good and thus not entirely appropriable by the innovating firm. [1] Imperfect appropriability conditions are responsible for inventors realistically anticipating that they will receive less than the maximum benefits arising out of an innovation. In mainstream economics – modelling homogeneous agents and single innovation processes – this is a reason for a suboptimal level of innovative activity [2]. New innovation theory does not deny this but emphasizes the *idea-creating* features of knowledge spillovers in the context of heterogeneous agents and different complementary and substitutive innovation activities.

The main reason for imperfect appropriability conditions are the "latent public good" features of technological know-how. To a large extent this knowledge is only partly excludable and non-rival, making R&D laboratories of firms the potential source of spillovers. Accordingly, this has different impacts on a firm's incentives for R&D. On the one hand, other firms eventually can use its new knowledge, and this will have a negative effect on the incentive to undertake costly innovative endeavours. On the other hand, this leakage of own know-how is often "compensated" by the opportunity to use know-how of other firms. The latter argument underlines also the often complementary character of R&D.

The existence of spillover effects necessarily requires both heterogeneity of actors as well as their very ability to understand the respective information content. With respect to the former, the assumption of *bounded rational behaviour* of agents directly leads to technological heterogeneity resulting from local search processes with specific cumulative experiences, knowledge, and competences as well as lock-in effects. Based on heterogeneity defined in this way, firms require specific (technological) competences or *absorptive capacities* to understand the information content of (technological) spillovers. These competences may be partly given by talent etc., however, quite often they have to be acquired actively.

Local search processes – and thus heterogeneity – and spillover effects are to be seen in a mutual relationship, and thus, they are *endogenously* determined.

---

1. See e.g. Winter, S.G. (1989).
2. The fundamental reference is Arrow, K. (1962).

Keeping first spillovers aside, local search processes often lead to increasing heterogeneity allowing for a larger pool of potential spillovers. The feedback of spillovers on heterogeneity, however, can be seen twofold. First, with substitutive know-how stocks, spillovers tend to reduce heterogeneity because local search activities become more similar (*negative feedback*). Second, by cross-fertilization between complementary know-how, spillovers may lead to further heterogeneity because new local opportunities are opened up (*positive feedback*).

Within a context where innovative activities are considered as local search and exploration, one may ask which strategies do firms design in order to cope with the uncertainty envolved? We take up this issue next.

2.2. Firm Strategies to Cope with Innovation

The rate of technological progress is not God-given but determined by the specific behaviour of firms which try to improve or to introduce new technologies. The restrictions arising from technological heterogeneity, uncertainty, and rationality constraints are – as just mentioned – indeed responsible for an abandonment of the global optimization principle with a clear-cut optimal strategy derivable. This, however, does not imply that there are no longer regularities in firm behaviour. In their decisions firms do not randomly allocate R& D budgets and select certain research directions just by chance. Instead they are guided in a cumulative manner by their past experiences and the capabilities they have already built up. Consequently, the resulting behaviour is neither unique among actors nor optimal and can be described by the concept of *routines*.

– Routines

Strong regular patterns in the innovative activities of firms suggest to describe the innovative behaviour as "routinized" (Nelson, Winter (1982)). Firms operate in environments characterized by a spectrum of market and technological possibilities providing opportunities to overcome current constraints. Despite the prevalence of technological uncertainty with respect to the results of their actions, firms have expectations. Hence, within the above restrictions and constraints firms are able to design different innovation strategies (Freeman (1982)) in which they decide how to use and employ their technical skills and resources.

These strategic decisions are guided by a "procedural rationality" (Simon (1976)). Not abstract questions of how to measure the marginal productivity of R& D expenditures are on the agenda of firms, but questions on reasonable procedures for fixing these quantities are to be answered. Therefore, we simply regard R& D decision rules as behavioural patterns which cannot be explained by optimization, but by reference to historical circumstances, experiences and evolutionary development. Firms design and adjust their routines by means of learning and adapting towards changing environments. In this perspective firms are learning organizations, constrained by their cognitive capabilities (Heiner (1988)). They do not exactly know the complete set of actual and future opportunities open to them, and therefore they cannot choose the globally best alternative; they are rather constrained to local opportunities.

– *exploitation vs. exploration*

The introduction of new technologies, the improvement of existing ones, learning how to adjust behaviour, and imitation of other successful actors are the most important components for improving the firms' (technological) performance and strengthening their competitive advantage. Within this context, modern organizational theory points to a trade-off problem between the exploitation of existing, and exploration of new opportunities (Winter (1971), March (1991)). Typically included in exploration are behaviours such as search, variation, risk taking and experimentation, whereas exploitation means refinement, production, efficiency and execution. This is also reflected in the returns from exploration which are, compared to the returns from exploitation, less certain and more remote in time. In the following we introduce three general behavioural patterns and show how exploration and exploitation find a variety of expressions in different routines.

– *The conservative strategy*

The first strategy considered is the so-called *conservative strategy* [1] where all innovative efforts exclusively concentrate on own research. External technological developments are neglected as far as only investment in the refinement of own specific opportunities is undertaken. Thus, the technology and knowhow required for growth and competitiveness are generated in (technological) isolation. Innovative efforts are directed into exploitation of the existing technology, i.e. process improvements, and into exploration of new technologies, i.e. product innovation.

– *The imitative strategy*

Firms applying the *imitative strategy* [2] do not devote resources in explorative search. By introducing new technologies they attempt to only imitate the most successful methods generated elsewhere instead of innovating by themselves (Winter (1986)). Thus, by this strategy solely external knowledge and opportunities are exploited. Firms acting in this way are not willing to explore risky

---

[1]. In the literature, for this strategy the notion "go-it-alone strategy" is used alternatively. See Fusfield, H.I., Haklish, C.S. (1985).
[2]. Freeman, C. (1982) alternatively uses the notion "defensive or dependent strategy".

new opportunities. They want to avoid failure and, even more, learn from failures of competitors. Therefore, they are satisfied with not being technological leaders. According to Freeman (1982) the imitative strategy is a kind of insurance. It enables firms to react and adapt to technical change introduced by competitors.

Imitation becomes possible whenever new technological know-how is not completely appropriable by the innovating firm. In a regime of total non-appropriability of the know-how, imitative firms have the advantage of knowing and learning ex-ante that the aim of their imitative efforts is a workable solution. However, technological knowledge is typically characterized by specificity, tacitness as well as by cumulativeness. "In such cases'technology transfer'may be as expensive and time consuming as independent R& D" [1]. Therefore, it is the very nature of technological knowledge that also makes imitation a costly endeavour. Thus, the imitative strategy also requires R& D expenditures and imitative firms may also be research intensive. Moreover, in cases of limited access to the technology to be imitated, it is very unlikely that imitation yields the same technological results as the original innovative technology [2].

– *Absorptive strategy*

Firms applying the so-called *absorptive strategy* decide to run a mixture of using internal and external know-how. With respect to the former they undertake research endeavours aiming at two goals which are also targeted by conservative firms: They exploitatively improve their production processes and exploratively introduce product innovations. Additionally, they exploit external knowledge sources, but not in order to imitate but to achieve cross-fertilization effects allowing them to extend the opportunity space.

It is far-fetched, however, to believe that these spillovers can be integrated in the knowledge stock of a receiving firm without costs. Just contrary, firms with an absorptive strategy have to invest a share of their R& D budget for scanning the general (external) technological development [3]. Doing this, they expect synergistic benefits which help to overcome limited technological opportunities.

Contrary to imitative firms absorptive firms do not simply copy a successful technology but try to integrate external knowledge in order to *create* additional technological opportunities. And contrary to conservative firms, they do not spend their total R& D budget on improving their inhouse technology. Absorptive firms rather attempt to find a balance between short-term benefits of

---

1. Nelson, R.R. (1990), p. 197.
2. See Winter, S.G. (1986).
3. Cohen, W. and Levinthal, D. (1989) state in this respect: "When a firm wishes to acquire and use new knowledge that is unrelated to its ongoing activity, then the firm must dedicate exclusively to creating "absorptive capacity" (i.e. "absorptive capacity'is not a by-product)" p. 129.

exploiting own specific opportunities with a mixture of a long-ranged exploring and exploiting of external technological possibilities. In this respect, they try to avoid – at least in a dynamical perspective – that "exploitation of existing knowledge reduces the capabilities and the speed with which new alternatives can be explored" (Levinthal, March (1981)).

Following the above characterization of the innovative process, investing in absorptive capacity in technological heterogeneous environments is done in order to exploit extensive technological opportunities by understanding the content of knowledge spillovers. Therefore, investing in absorptive capacity is not immediately targeted towards a specific well described research purpose. In a way, it is done for some precautionary motives allowing to be prepared for some unforeseen technological developments. In this context Cohen and Levinthal (1994) refer to the words of Louis Pasteur *"Fortune favours the prepared mind"*.

In reality a clear distinction between these stylized strategies is obviously impossible. This applies especially to the building up of absorptive capabilities which is often to be taken as a kind of by-product of "normal" R&D activities. In these cases conservative as well as imitative firms indirectly acquire the capabilities to understand and use know-how applied in close neighbour technologies. With increasing technological distances, however, these absorptive capabilities become less effective and direct efforts to acquire complementary knowledge become necessary. Despite this, for analytical purposes we will, however, distinguish the three strategies clear-cut.

3. The Simulation Model

In this section we present a model of a dynamic oligopoly in which firms do not only compete in the market, but also may influence each other by their innovative activities. The firms under consideration belong to three "camps", each characterized by a fixed strategy: the *conservative* strategy, the *imitative* strategy, and the *absorptive strategy*.

– *Market competition in a heterogeneous oligopoly*

In order to deal with market competition, we choose a model of heterogeneous oligopoly as discussed in Kuenne (1992) [1]. Here, n firms (indexed with i, $i = \{1, ..., n\}$) differ in their production processes and in their product qualities. Despite the fact that firms are continuously confronted with uncertainty and myopically try to improve their technologies, they are assumed to be able to statically optimize their purely economic decisions. In this respect,

---

[1]. The heterogeneous oligopoly is also applied in another simulation study by Meyer, B. et al. (1996).

knowing their demand function they compute reaction functions taking into account the economic decisions of the competitors. This modelling strategy allows to focus on the technology side of behaviour, whereas the economic decisions are represented by a well understood oligopolistic setting [1]. This model of heterogeneous oligopoly is standard and is described in more detail in Cantner/Pyka (1998). The mode of competition is both price and quality competition, where a certain degree of substitutability between the different products is assumed. Regarding the production techniques, we assume constant returns to scale; consequently unit costs $c_i(t)$ are independent of output. Since each firm faces an individual demand function, there is an exogenous degree of heterogeneity among firms. Their respective innovative activities will provide for an additional endogenous effect on this heterogeneity. We discuss this aspect in the following.

– *R& D investment decisions and learning rules*

Besides mere production firm i periodically devotes investment $r_i(t)$ to research, development and imitation. Since the development of a new technology and even the improvement of an existing one is a risky and uncertain endeavour, R& D routines are guided by "procedural rationality", allowing firms to learn and adapt their routines to changed environments. The respective routines determine a share of turnover $\gamma_i(t)$ which firms invest in R& D.

In our model we distinguish two different methods of adjusting these routines. A first learning rule, the *economic learning rule*, applies as a criterion an economic indicator, the return on turnover $\beta_i(t)$.

$$\gamma_i(t) = \gamma_0 + \omega \left(\frac{\bar{\beta}_t - \beta_i(t)}{\bar{\beta}_t} \right) \tag{1a}$$

$\gamma_0 :=$ initial value; $\omega :=$ exogenous rate of adjustment;
$\beta_i(t) :=$ rate of turnover; $\bar{\beta}_t :=$ average rate of turnover;

Whenever firm i's own return on turnover is lower (higher) than the market average rate the firm rises (reduces) its share $\gamma_i(t)$. A second learning rule, the *technological learning rule*, does not look at an economic indicator but uses relative technological positions with respect to process technology $RP_i^{PC}(t)$ and product technology $RP_i^{PD}(t)$. Both indicators are restricted to]0, 1], with a value of 1 indicating the leading position. The share $\gamma_i(t)$ determining R& D

---

1. Keeping in mind our investigation goal, the market framework should not be too complicated. Of course, there are more realistic and in an evolutionary sense better suited market representations (e.g. mark-up pricing models, replicator dynamics etc.), which, however, are not in the center of interest in this paper.

efforts is increased or decreased according to the respective technological position:

$$\gamma_i(t) = \gamma_0 + \omega[1 - RP_i^{PC}(t)*RP_i^{PD}(t)]. \tag{1b}$$

In a sense both learning rules represent a kind of satisficing behaviour. When the own position – whether economical or technological – is unsatisfactory, an adjustment mechanism with respect to the periodical R&D investments should ensure the catching up. We will compare the effects of these different learning rules in the following simulations.

Firms running the *absorptive strategy* additionally have to decide on the respective share $\sigma_i(t)$ of their R&D-budget to be invested in building up absorptive capacity $ac_i(t)$. For this it is plausible to assume that firms on (below) the technological frontier cannot (can) learn from their competitors. Accordingly, absorptive firms adjust their investment in absorptive capacity due to their relative technological position:

$$\sigma_i(t) = 1 - [RP_i^{PD}(t)*RP_i^{PC}(t)] \quad \sigma^{min} \leq \sigma_i(t) \leq \sigma^{max}. \tag{2}$$

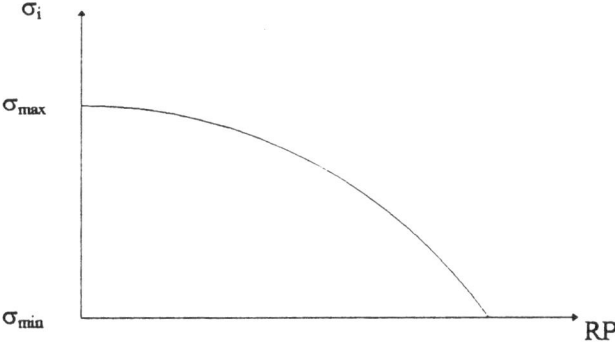

Figure 1

There are upper and lower bounds for variable $\sigma_i(t)$: a minimum share, at which firms invest in absorptive capacity due to exogenous spillovers from sciences and inter-industrial spillovers, and a maximum share, because firms do not reduce their own R&D below a certain level. Figure 1 shows this decision rule in a simplified way ($RP_i^{PC} = RP_i^{PD}$).

– *Spillover pool*

In the model absorptive firms may be able to use spillovers. For this purpose we formulate a spillover pool which is partly endogenous. First, due to the exogenously given heterogeneity of the oligopolistic firms, spillovers already arise out of these differences. Second, additional spillover effects are the result of endogenously generated cost and quality differences among the competitors. The variances of those differences serve as a measure for the spillover pool. Based on this, a certain firm i may use a spillover pool fed by its competitors – the measure is the variance in unit costs or product qualities of all firms except i. These variances are the *endogenous* part of the spillover pool.

– *Process innovation*

R& D and imitative endeavours of firms are partly directed to process innovations in order to make production techniques more efficient. The efficiency level is dependent on the know-how, and efficiency gains are represented by unit cost reductions. The know-how level of firm i at time t is given by the cumulated innovative success $ie_i(t)$ which translates with a time-lag of one period in unit cost reductions:

$$c_i(t) = c_0[1 - ie_i(t-1)] \quad \text{with } c_0 := \text{initial value of unit costs}. \quad (3)$$

To achieve a certain technological level, the preceding levels have to be passed through, because otherwise the relevant technological understanding has not been built up. To represent the cumulative feature of technological progress, the R& D capital stock – given by the accumulated periodic R& D investments $r_i(t)$ – determines the cumulated innovative success in t. Besides the level of R& D and thus the magnitude of $R_i(t)$, the rate of technological progress also depends on the degree of exhaustion of intensive technological opportunities. To model this, we assume the cumulated innovative success $ie_i(t)$ to be positive but decreasing in $R_i(t)$. To take account of technological uncertainty, the occurence of such a success is determined stochastically applying an equally distributed random number ψ_t.

Taken this, for the *conservative firms* innovative success in t is given by:

$$ie_i(t) = 1 - \text{Exp}[-a*R_i(t)] \quad \text{and} \quad (4)$$

$$ie_i(t) = \begin{cases} ie_i(t) & \text{for } f(R_i(t)) \geq \psi_t \\ ie_i(t-1) & \text{for } f(R_i(t)) < \psi_t \end{cases}$$

$a :=$ bending of the innovation success;

$$\frac{\partial f}{\partial R_i} > 0 \; ; \quad \frac{\partial f^2}{\partial^2 R_i} < 0 \; ; \quad f(R_i) = 1 - e^{-aR_i} .$$

For the *absorptive strategy* spillover effects and the ability to use them are relevant. The respective absorptive capacity $ac_i(t)$, necessary to integrate the knowledge content of spillovers, has to be accumulated like the stock of R&D-capital:

$$ac_i(t) = \sum_t \sigma_i(t) * r_i(t). \qquad (5)$$

Of course, the adoption of externally created technological know-how in the form of spillovers is also a cumulative process. This implies that the potential impact of spillovers increases with the accumulation of absorptive capacity and the increasing informational content of the spillovers already integrated [1].

Additionally, for using spillovers the technological distance $G_i^{PC}(t)$ in process technologies (PC) to the other competitors is relevant. The impact of technological spillovers on the innovative success $F[G_i^{PC}(t)]$ is given by equation (6) [2], where RMP_i^{PC} is a measure for the relative technological distance of firm i towards the mean technology of all firms except i:

$$F[G_i^{PC}(t)] = (\delta - RMP_i^{PC}(t)^2) * ac_i(t) \qquad (6)$$

$F[G_i^{PC}(t)] :=$ spillover function (process technologies); $\delta :=$ parameter limiting spillovers.

This formulation allows backward as well as leading firms to use spillovers out of a spillover pool. It also takes into account that a position technologically too far backward reduces the ability to understand the respective knowledge. Equivalently, for a position technologically too far ahead the respective know-how becomes less useful.

Using this, the innovative success for process innovations by conservative firms as given in (4) is now modified by a term containing the spillover pool $s(t)^2$ and the spillover function $F[G_i^{PC}]$. This reflects a non-linear process, which should show the threshold effect of the impact of additional information, if the necessary basis is already built-up [3]:

$$ie_i(t) = 1 - \mathrm{Exp}\left[-\alpha \frac{\xi + s(t)^2}{1 + \mathrm{Exp}\{\tau * d_i(t) - F(G_i^{PC}(t))\}} \cdot R_i(t)\right] \quad \text{and} \quad (7)$$

$$ie_i(t) = \begin{cases} ie_i(t) & \text{for } f(R_i(t)) \geq \psi_t \\ ie_i(t-1) & \text{for } f(R_i(t)) < \psi_t \end{cases}$$

$$d_i(t) = [1 - \varepsilon * ac_i(t)] * (1 + \theta)^t \qquad (8)$$

---

1. "... limited competence is caused by the imperfect ability to use information, which is to be distinguished from the usually considered case of imperfect information", Pelikan, P. (1992), p. 383.
2. If in the spillover function (6) the technological gap G_i^{PC} is substituted with the gap in product technology G_i^{PD}, we get the spillover function with respect to product innovation.
3. "Learning is a process by which repetition and experimentation enable tasks to be performed better and quicker and new production opportunities to be identified", Dosi, G., Teece, D.J., Winter, S. (1992).

$\varepsilon :=$ scaling parameter; $\tau :=$ difficulty in building-up absorptive capacity;
$\theta :=$ learning-parameter; $d_i(t) :=$ impact of absorptive capacity;
$\xi :=$ interindustry spillovers and feedbacks from the sciences.

By building up absorptive capabilities, a learning process as given in (8) will take place: On the one hand, there are experiences with respect to the richness of different spillover sources and, on the other hand, an advantage in experience with the integration of external knowledge should be expected. In the model the learning effect as well as the accumulated absorptive capacity determine the term $d_i(t)$ which describes the specific impact of absorptive capacity.

Imitative firms try to improve their production processes by imitating the most successful technologies ie_{t-1}^{max} of their competitors. Because they are already imitating applied technologies, their endeavours are not confronted in the same way with risk and uncertainty like the innovative efforts of other firms. Nevertheless, at least some degree of appropriability suggests a stochastic determination of their imitative success. The imitative success $pcimit_i(t)$ is given by:

$$pcimit_i(t) = ie_{t-1}^{max} * \mu_t^{PC} * [1 - \exp(-a * R_i(t))] \qquad (9)$$

$ie_{t-1}^{max} :=$ max of innovation success of innovative firms;
$\mu_t^{PC} :=$ equal distributed random number; $\mu_t^{PC} \in [\mu^{min}, \mu^{max}]$.

– *Product innovation*

Besides improving production processes, firms engage in product innovation which when successful is represented by quality improvement having a twofold effect: First, the mutual price dependence $h_i(t)$ of the successful oligopolist decreases with higher heterogeneity in quality levels. Second, a successful product innovation changes all prohibitive prices [1]. The innovating entrepreneur i produces a higher quality connected with an increase in consumers' assessment. Other firms j experience a decrease of their individual prohibitive price, because the innovation of i decreases the relative qualities of their products.

The uncertainty envolved in new product research is quite different from the one we assume for process innovations. Whereas the direction and impact of process innovations (and thus exploitation) along certain trajectories can be roughly expected, this does not apply to product innovations (and thus

---

1. Each firm faces an individual linear demand function $p_i(t) = a_i(t) - \eta x_i(t) + \dfrac{h_i(t)}{(n(t-1))} \sum_j p_j(t-1)$; $p_i :=$ price of firm i; $\eta =$ slope of demand function; $n :=$ number of firms; $h_i :=$ variable which expresses mutual price dependence.

exploration). In order to represent this distinction, we use a *poisson-distributed* random number for innovative success in new product research [1].

R& D efforts devoted to product innovations are again represented by the stock of R& D capital $R_i(t)$. With this stock firms accumulate success probability $pr_i(t)$ [.] which approximates asymtotically the mean value of the Poisson-distributed random number. The increase of success probability for *conservative* firms is characterized by positive, but decreasing rates:

$$pr_i(t) \, [PDI = 1] = 1 - \text{Exp}[-a*R_i(t)], \qquad (10)$$

$$PDI = \begin{cases} 1 & \text{for } pr_i(t) \geq p_t \\ 0 & \text{for } pr_i(t) < p_t, \end{cases}$$

$p_t :=$ poisson distributed random number;
$PDI :=$ binary variable, which takes the value 1 in the case of success.

Absorptive firms again take into account the idea-creating effects of spillovers. The respective success probability for a product innovation is supported by learning from product spillovers. The respective spillover pool of firm i is given by the variance $s_a(t)^2$ of the prohibitive prices $a_j(t)$ $(j \neq i)$. The stock of R& D-capital is again weighted with the spillover function $F[G_i^{PD}(t)]$ and the spillover pool. This should reflect the cross-fertilization possibility of technological spillovers in connection with product innovations:

$$pr_i(t) \, [PDI = 1] = 1 - \text{Exp}\left[-a* \frac{\xi + s_a(t)^2}{1 + \text{Exp}[\tau*d_i(t) - F[G_i^{PD}(t)]]} *R_i(t)\right] (11)$$

$F[G_i^{PD}(t)] :=$ spillover function (product technology).

Imitative firms engage in imitation only, if one of the competitors successfully introduced a new product. Then, they accumulate a success probability in the following manner:

$$pdimit_i(t) \, [PDI = 1] = [1 - \text{Exp}(-a*R_i(t))], \qquad (12)$$

$$PDI = \begin{cases} 1 & \text{for } pdimit_i(t) \geq \mu_t^{PD} \\ 0 & \text{for } pdimit_i(t) < \mu_t^{PD}, \end{cases}$$

$\mu_t^{PD} :=$ equal distributed random number; $\mu_i^{PD} \in [\mu^{min}, \mu^{max}]$.

---

[1]. This probability distribution, which in the literature is often called "the distribution of the low probability for happenings with a low probability", seems to be adequate with respect to product innovations.

– *Obsolescence*

Whenever a firm succeeds in introducing a product innovation, the knowledge of mastering the old technology is assumed to become irrelevant. Therefore, the old stock of R& D capital will be totally depreciated every time a product innovation occurs. The new technology shows full technological opportunities and, consequently, a large potential for new process innovations.

For a firm deciding to invest in absorptive capacity, a product innovation bears two additional consequences: The absorptive capacity like the stock of R& D capital becomes obsolete and will be depreciated. Also the learning variable $d_i(t)$ will be set back to the initial value.

4. Simulation Results

For all simulations we run the respective programs 500 periods. We assume that all firms start with identical unit production costs and product qualities. Our simulation experiments are performed in two steps. In step 1 we investigate each strategy in isolation where we assume an oligopoly with 5 firms following the respective innovation strategy. The simulation results here show the principle influence of the firms' behaviour on the development of the sector. By this one gets a feeling for the economic and technological interdependencies working.

In step 2 a comparative analysis between the three different principle strategies is performed. We then deal with an oligopoly of 15 firms [1]. According to the three different strategies these enterprises are subdivided into three "camps". Since we want to derive results on the comparative performance of strategies and to avoid distortions due to the several stochastic elements, we run all simulations 30 times and calculate the respective averages. Additionally, we only present average results of the different groups. Moreover, we investigate whether the two different learning rules introduced have a distinctive impact [2].

4.1. Strategies in isolation

In order to investigate the three different strategies in isolation we show the results concerning the development of profits and unit costs as well as the

---

1. The different parameter values are listed in the appendix.
2. The robustness of the different simulation results was tested in Cantner/Pyka (1998). There, two additional scenarios were investigated. The first scenario is a regime of high appropriability and therefore low spillover pools. In the second scenario we lower the oligopolistic interdependence. This scenario comes close to a situation where the firms can be considered as different industries technologically connected by inter-industry spillovers. Our basic results hold under these changed settings. The sensitivity analysis in the setting of this paper can be found in the appendix. Additionally, the range of the profit variable, due to numerous simulation runs, is shown there.

degree of technological heterogeneity with respect to production processes and product quality.

– *Conservative strategy*

For the conservative strategy Figures 2a-d show the respective developments, when a constant R& D budget is invested in each period. With respect to profits (fig 2a), in the beginning differential profits are due to the respective success in improving the production process as given by the development of unit costs (fig. 2b). As technological opportunities become depleted, all five firms tend to perform rather equally. Whenever the first firm succeeds in launching a new product, the profit structure becomes quite heterogeneous, where an innovator first experiences a sharp drop because of initially high unit production costs. This development is also reflected in the development of heterogeneity with respect to process technologies (fig. 2c) and product qualities (fig. 2d). As for profits, here one observes a tendency of increasing heterogeneity. This is due to a *first-mover-advantage* of the first innovator which allows him to accumulate earlier a R& D capital stock for the next product innovation.

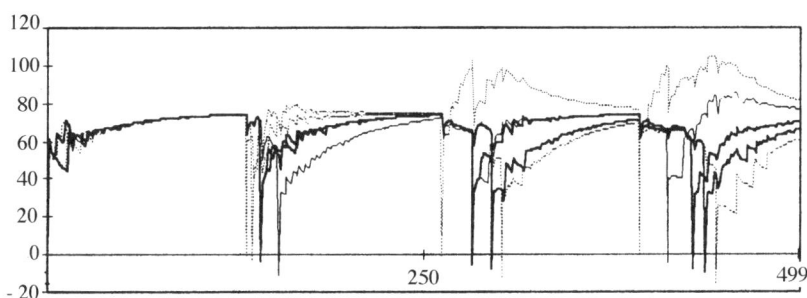

Figure 2a: conservative strategy I - profits

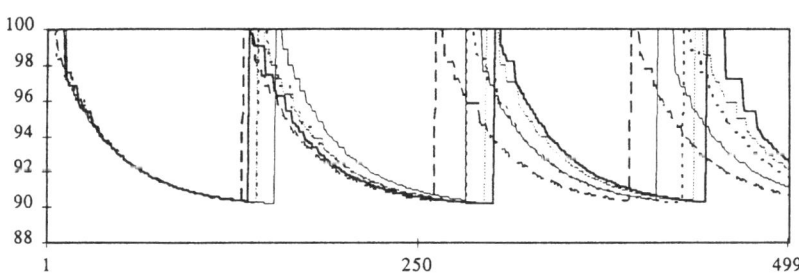

Figure 2b: conservative strategy I - unit costs

Modifying the R& D investment strategy by assuming a dependence of R& D on sales or profits changes the respective development considerably.

130 | Consumers and firms behaviors

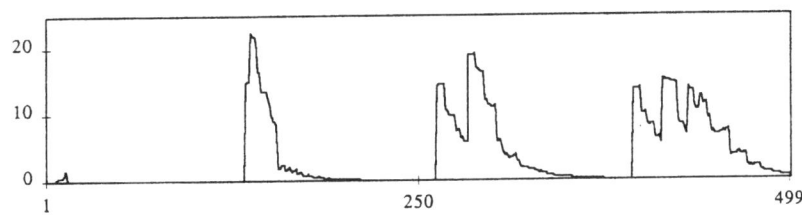

Figure 2c: conservative strategy I - process heterogeneity

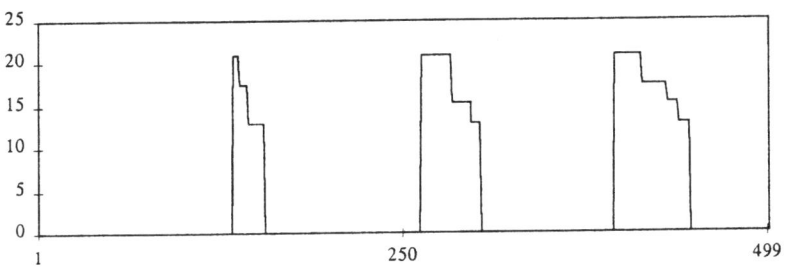

Figure 2d: conservative strategy I - product heterogeneity

Figures 3a-d show the results. First the rate of technological progress increases – within the 500 periods we have now 4 instead of three product innovations and the opportunities for process improvements also exhaust earlier (fig. 3b). This result is due to increased R& D budgets of technology leaders which leads to *success-breeds-success*. Obviously, the heterogeneity with respect to process technology (fig. 3c) and product quality (fig. 3d) increases. Concerning profits, this increased heterogeneity is reflected in comparably higher profit differentials. This development is due to the economic interdependence among the competitors with a *virtuos circle* for the technology leaders and a *vicious circle* for the backward firms.

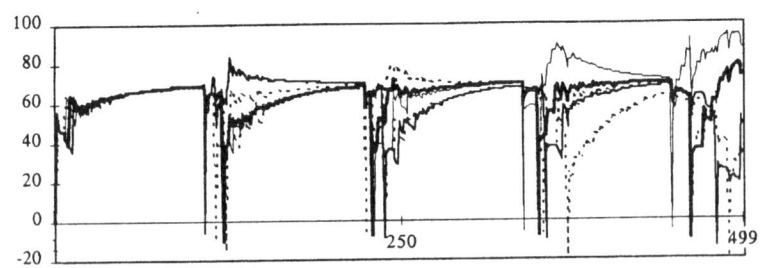

Figure 3a: conservative strategy II - profits

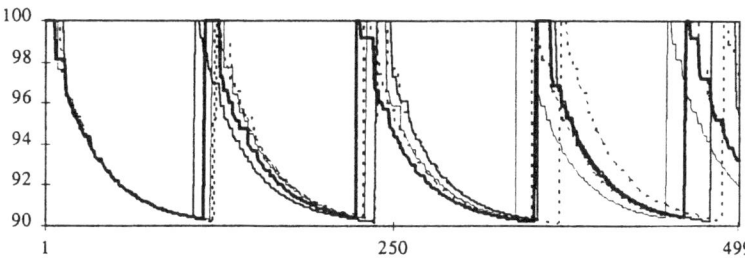
Figure 3b: conservative strategy II - unit costs

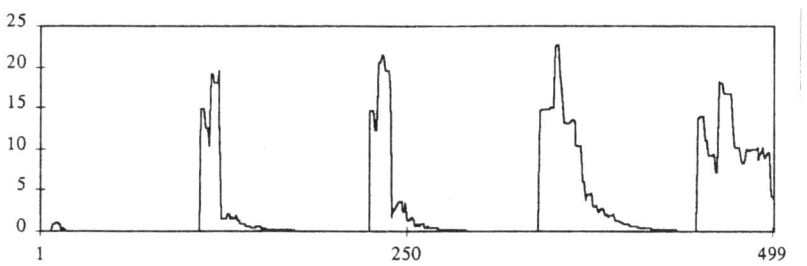
Figure 3c: conservative strategy II - process heterogeneity

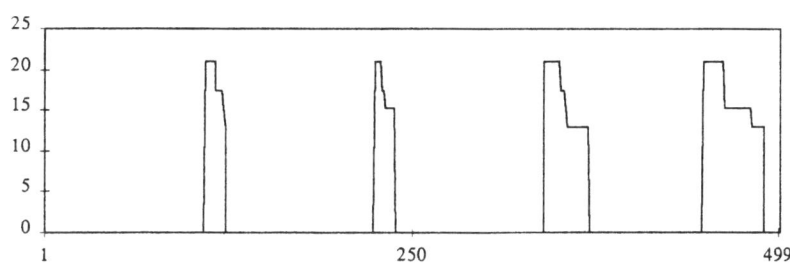
Figure 3d: conservative strategy II - product heterogeneity

– *Imitative strategy*

Introducing the imitative strategy shifts our attention to *technological relationships between competitors*. This is done by allowing firms to innovate just as conservative firms did before. Whenever one firm is successful, backward firms imitate the technologies of the leading firm.

Figures 4a-d show the respective results. First, there is no significant difference in the rate of technological progress compared to the conservative strategy (fig 4b). Second, however, technological heterogeneity is lower here – we find a catch-up result, where imitators are closer behind the frontier. This result is evident with respect to process technology (fig. 4c) as well as product quality (fig. 4d). The comparatively lower degree of profit differentials also reflects this result (fig. 4a).

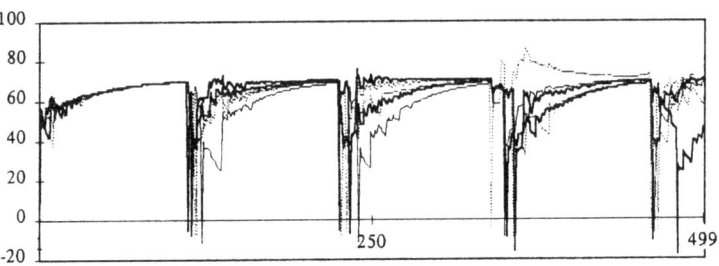

Figure 4a: imitative strategy - profit

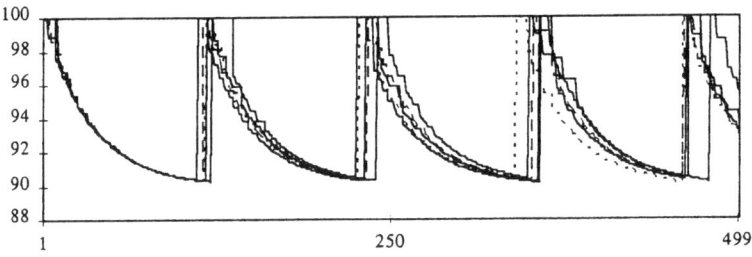

Figure 4b: imitative strategy - unit costs

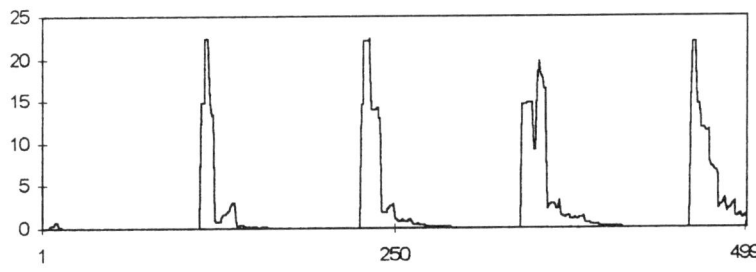

Figure 4c: imitative strategy - process heterogeneity

– *Absorptive strategy*

The absorptive strategy explicitly aims at the *cross-fertilization effects* of technological spillovers. Technological interdependence among competitors is thus enhanced. Figures 5a-e clearly show a significant change in the respective developments. First, the rate of technological progress is again enhanced - the success-dependent R&D budget as well as the cross-fertilization effects for the technology leaders accelerate the speed of progress with now 5 product innovations (fig. 5a and 5b). The observed higher heterogeneity (fig. 5c and 5d)

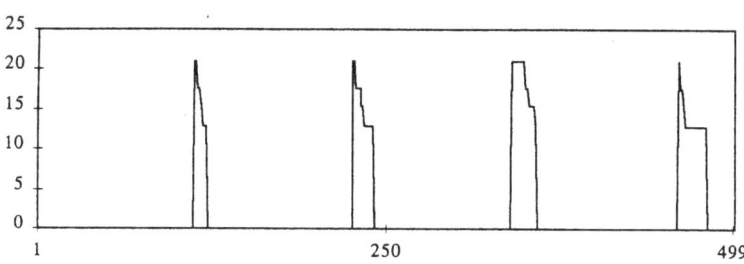

Figure 4d: imitative strategy - product heterogeneity

is the result of the interplay between absorptive capacity and relative technological position towards the competitors. Since here all firms are identical in the beginning, it is only by chance that a specific firm gains the lead, whereas the others are backward. As such a lead is enhanced, some firms will slip back to a constantly worse position. Whenever the technological distance to the leaders becomes to large, cross-fertilization effects come to cease which aggrevates the lagging position. The sector splits up as the development of profits and unit costs of two firms clearly show (fig. 5a and 5b). In this respect figure 5e explicitly shows the degree of access to the common spillover pool. Access is maximum whenever a firms has a distance of 0, any deviation shows technological backwardness (−) or lower technological usefulness (+). For two firms backwardness increases, whereas for the leading firms the usefulness declines.

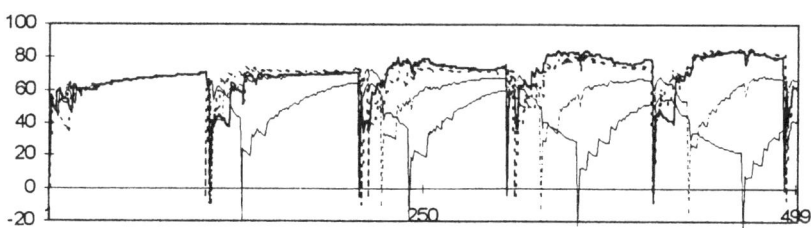

Figure 5a: absorptive strategy - profits

4.2. Comparative Performance of Strategies

Having investigated the different strategies in isolation, the following simulations are addressed to their comparative performance. For this purpose we run a sector consisting of 15 firms, 5 of which always follow the same strategy. To compare these strategies economically, we use the criterion profit.

134 | Consumers and firms behaviors

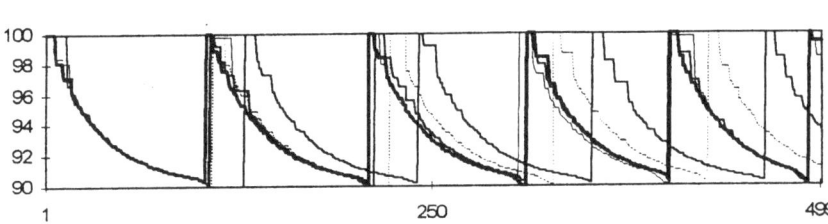

Figure 5b: absorptive strategy - unit costs

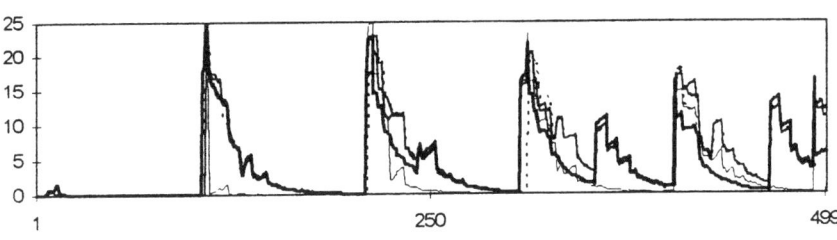

Figure 5c: absorptive strategy - process heterogeneity

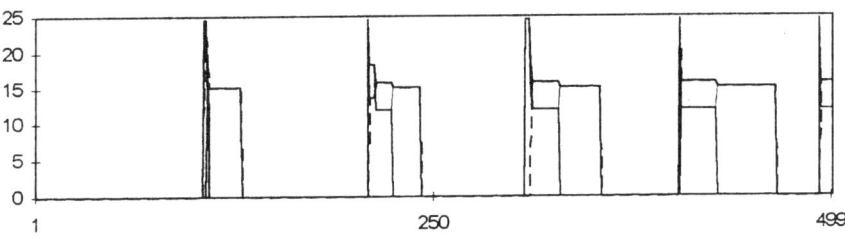

Figure 5d: absorptive strategy - product heterogeneity

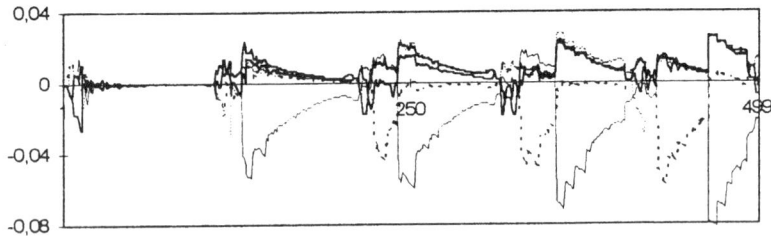

Figure 5e: absorptive strategy - access to spillover pool

– *Strategies' performances*

The following figures show the development of profits for the different strategies [1]. In Figures 6a and 6b firms behave according to the technological learning rule (1a) and the economical learning rule (1b) respectively.

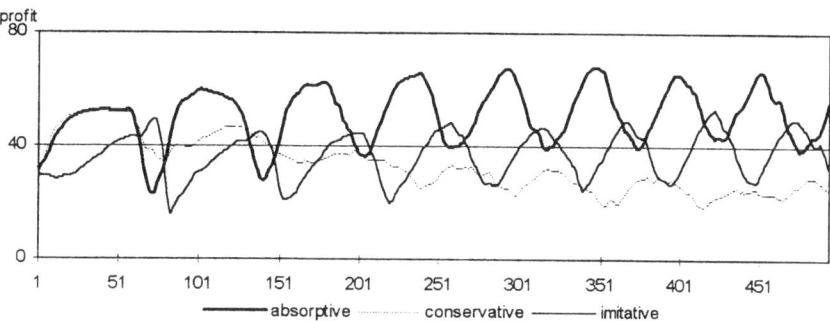

Figure 6a: technological learning rule

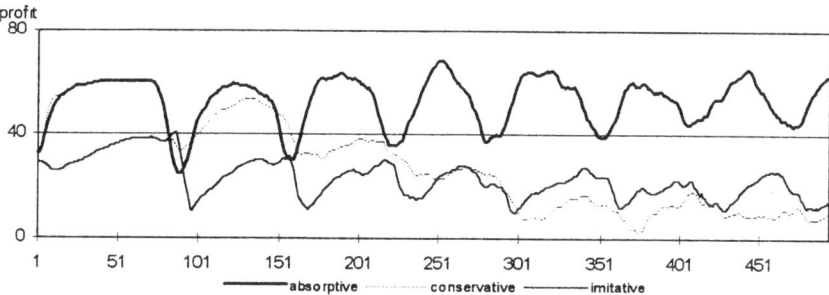

Figure 6b: economic learning rule

In the beginning, the periodic profits of the absorptive and the imitative firms are below the ones of the conservative camp. Conservative firms are able to exploit the intensive technological opportunities faster, because they do not invest in absorptive capacity. By the ongoing exhaustion of intensive opportunities the absorptive firms are technologically catching up which soon leads to a narrowing of profits between these two strategies. Contrary to conservative competitors struggling with nearly depleted opportunities, absorptive firms finally are able to explore new technological potentials with the help of know-how created outside their own laboratories and transferred by technological spillovers. Technologically, this effect is depicted in the additional sharp

---

1. We show 5-periods moving averages to make the respective curves somewhat smoother because they represent an aggregation over different firms and 30 simulation runs.

136 | Consumers and firms behaviors

decrease of the best-practice unit cost frontier (I) at about period 75 shown in Figure 7 for the technological learning rule and the first 250 periods.

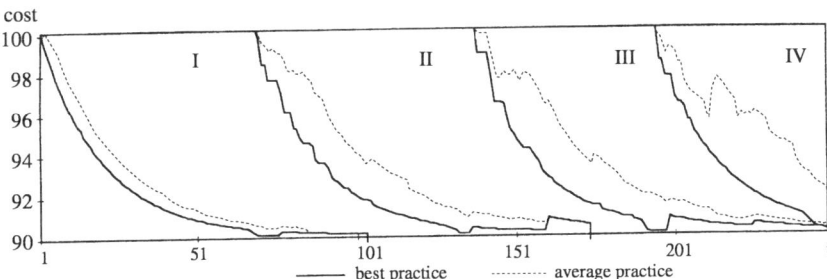

Figure 7: best-practice and average-practice unit cost frontier

With respect to periodic profits, absorptive firms leapfrog their conservative competitors and are now in the leading profit position. During this period imitative firms are on the last profit position. They imitate the technological improvements of their competitors and therefore technologically lag behind. Nevertheless, due to imitation they are able to continuously increase their periodic profits.

Obviously, the ability of absorptive firms to exploit external knowledge also supports innovative endeavours aiming at product innovation [1]. Because of their capability to integrate know-how of technological spillovers, these firms are the first to introduce a product innovation. On the new technological trajectory they are confronted with high unit costs, depicted by the best-practice unit cost frontier (II) in Figure 7. This product innovation and the corresponding jump onto a new trajectory leads to an initial profit erosion which, however, does not last long. Despite the higher quality and the higher consumers' assessment of product II, in the beginning of that product cycle conservative and imitative firms are able to attract some demand of the absorptive firms, because of high unit costs there. But with relatively fast cost reductions – due to new technological possibilities –, absorptive firms are able to gain the leading profit-position again just some periods later. The technological gap of imitative and conservative firms on the second trajectory increases, because they are still lagging behind in introducing product II. These increasing technological advantages finally provide for higher profit margins of the absorptive firms. Despite introducing a third technology later on, they keep their leading profit position over the remaining periods.

On the second trajectory the imitative firms technologically lag behind the self-sufficient conservative firms who introduce the new technology II earlier.

---

1. The effects of absorptive capacity on product innovations are described in detail in Cantner/Pyka (1998).

This technological disadvantage of the imitative strategy also translates into an economic one. This holds until the fifth product innovation. Here, they leapfrog their conservative competitors. The latter then show a continuously declining profit. These results are independent of whether the economic or the technological learning rule is followed.

Another possibility to compare the different strategies is to investigate the respective "R& D effectiveness". Here, one has to distinguish between success in process and product innovation. Concerning the latter, firms following the absorptive strategy are always the first to introduce a new product. With respect to process innovations the following Figure 8 shows for the three strategies the relationship between the periodic R& D-budgets and the resulting cost-reductions. The learning rule applied here is the technological one. However, the results by and large also apply to the scenario with economic learning. To interpret these figures, observations are represented by "sun-flowers". The number of petals to each sun-flower gives an account of the number of observations falling in a certain intervall.

The following results are interesting: First, the average R& D-budgets are higher for the absorptive group, because on the average they are more profitable and have higher market shares. Second, the R& D-success is higher for the absorptive firms than for the firms of the other groups. This is caused mainly by three effects:

(1) Higher R& D-budgets allow for higher R& D-stocks and consequently for higher R& D-success probability.

(2) A considerable share of the R& D-budgets is spent on absorptive capacity, which allows to exploit externally generated know-how (with equivalent effects on R& D-success probability).

(3) Finally, since these firms open up a new product cycle more often, they do not exploit depleted intensive opportunities very long, but they can "enjoy" the refreshed opportunities on the new trajectory.

– *Comparing the different learning rules*

Considering the development of profits in Figures 6a and 6b a significant difference arises when the imitative and the absorptive strategies are compared. With the economic learning rule the dominance of absorptive firms is evident, whereas in the case of the technological learning rule imitative firms can catch-up in profits, at least partially. It is also observable that there seems to be a regular catch-up and falling behind of the imitative firms with respect to the leading absorptive firms. The main reason for this finding is the different rate of technological progress in the two scenarios. A closer look at the introduction rate of new products shows this.

After the introduction of the first product innovation, in the scenario of the technological learning rule, the share of the old technology decreases relatively

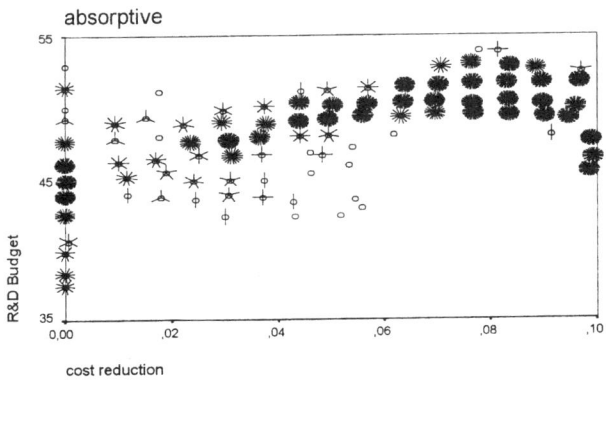

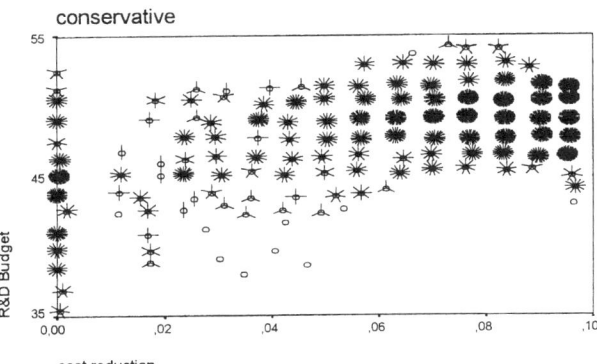

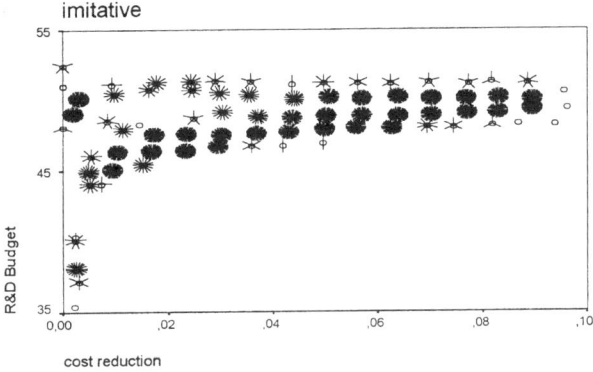

Figure 8: R& D effectivness

fast. This is shown in Figure 9a, illustrating the product cycles for the first half of the simulation. Firms lagging behind the technological leaders increase their R& D expenditures to catch up technologically. Consequently, some periods later one firm after the other rather quickly introduces a new technology.

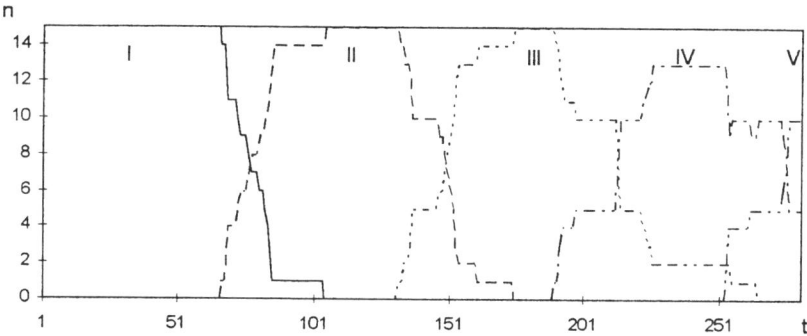

Figure 9a: technological learning rule - product cycles

Contrary, in the scenario of the economical learning rule firms lagging behind in jumping on the new trajectory can temporarily increase their periodic profits, due to the switching problems of the successful innovators. Doing this, they are able to increase their rate on turnover with a negative effect on their R& D endeavours. This is illustrated in Figure 9b showing the respective product cycles for this scenario. One can observe a lower speed of diffusion and, consequently, a lower number of product innovations.

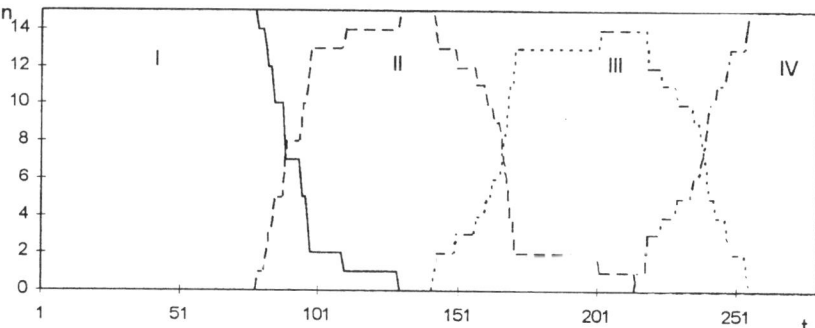

Figure 9b: economic learning rule - product cycles

Therefore, firms applying the economical adjustment mechanism of R& D budgets exploit their technological opportunities on a trajectory more intensely and take advantage of the short-term problems of the innovating firms.

Contrariwise, firms applying the technological learning rule accelerate the speed of innovation, because they attempt to close their technological gaps to the leaders as soon as they become aware of them. They introduce new products faster and, by this, they allow competitors to charge higher prices and earn higher profits. The comparatively higher economic success of imitative firms by applying the technological learning rule underlines this.

5. Conclusions

In this paper we investigate the technological and economic implications of different strategies and learning rules firms apply in pushing forward technological progress. These strategies are not optimal decisions, they are more or less rules-of-thumb which have been successful in the past. This modelling takes account of the inherent technological uncertainty, the technological constraints and the bounded and procedural rationality of agents.

Within this framework three different strategies are investigated: the absorptive, the conservative and the imitative strategy. Additionally, we distinguish between learning rules for adapting R&D-budgets, which on the one hand are oriented along the economic success, and on the other hand, along the technological success of the different strategies.

In a first step we analyse the three strategies in isolation which lead to insights concerning the development of the sector with respect to economic and technological success. In a second step the different strategies compete which each other. It is a quite solid result that in the medium and long run the absorptive strategy dominates with respect to the technological as well as economic performance. As to the different learning rules a clear result is that with technological learning the rate of technological progress is comparatively higher. Applying the economic learning rule, oligopolistic competition quite often allows for sufficient economic success, so that the necessity to intensify R&D-activities is relatively low.

These latter results *in some way* reflect the discussion between neoclassical and new innovation theory. In the former it is the computable economic efficiency of R&D-budgets and, in some sense, it is static efficiency that counts. To a certain degree the economic learning rule is designed in this way, although this is not to be taken literally. In the latter, however, it is the experimental character of innovative behaviour and its focus on – an even only assumed – dynamic efficiency. Here, it is not present profitability but the relative technological performance which drives R&D activities, the main feature of the technological learning rule.

Appendix

a) Parameter values:

bending of the innovation success	a	0.001
exogeneous rate of adjustment	ω	0.01
difficulty in building-up absorptive capacity	τ	15
interindustry spillovers	ξ	1
parameter limiting spillovers	δ	0.3
absorptive capacity max	σ^{max}	0.2
absorptive capacity min	σ^{min}	0.05
upper bound of μ	μ^{max}	1
lower bound of μ	μ^{min}	0.8
scaling parameter	ε	0.0001
learning-parameter	θ	0.001

b) Initial values:

price	$p_i(0)$	110
share of turnover for R&D	γ_0	0.025
costs	c_0	100
impact of absorptive capacity	d_0	1
prohibitive price	a_0	25
output	$x_i(0)$	10
number of firms	$n(0)$	15

c) Sensitivity analysis

Parameter	Reference value	Range
a (bending of the innovation probability)	0.001	$0.0001 \leq a \leq 0.01$
a (prohibitive price)	25	$20 \leq a$
τ (slope of the R&D-weighting function)	15	$5 \leq \tau$
θ (learning parameter)	0.01	$\theta \geq 0.001$
ε (scaling parameter)	0.0001	$\varepsilon \geq 0.00001$
ξ (interindustry and science spillovers)	1	$\xi \geq 0.1$

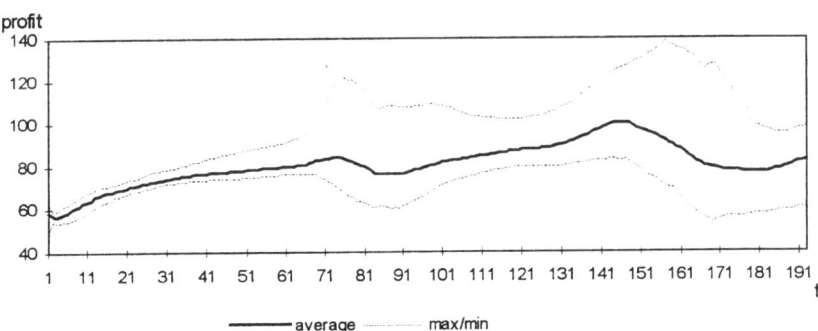

Range of profit variable of the absorptive camp (economic learning rule, moving average, average standard deviation 9,04)

In the sensitivity analysis we test the robustness of our model (only for the case of the economic learning rule) due to several parameter variations. Thereby, always only one parameter is varied, keeping the others on their value of the reference case. The aim of this exercise is to draw attention to the ranges of parameter values for which the basic results of our investigation hold. The respective workable ranges are listed in the above table.

- If the a parameter, which represents the bending of the innovation success function takes values smaller 0.0001, no product innovation occurs in the observed time-interval. Despite staying on the first trajectory, after 35 iterations absorptive firms are head to head with the conservative firms. And after 110 iterations these absorptive firms are clearly ahead. Imitative firms are not able to hold their intermediate position. Because there is less to copy they are on the last position during the 200 iterations. For a-values bigger than 0.01 (which means an increase by factor 10) there are no bottlenecks with respect to the own opportunities, and therefore the firms very often introduce new products. Building up of absorptive capacity leads more or less to the same success than spending all the R& D budget in the way the conservative firm does. In this scenario sometimes the absorptive camp, sometimes the conservative camp is in the leading profit position. Imitative firms behave quite well in this case, they do not introduce as much new products as the other camps and therefore they are able to intensively exploit the opportunities of a single trajectory. Under this setting the long-term advantage of absorptive firms is not as decisive as in the reference case due tue the votality of profits.

- The next parameter varied is the prohibitive price a. Values lower than 25 support the absorptive firms to some degree. Demand constraints are responsible for large gains resulting from early cost-reduction. With respect to quality improvement only these firms introduce new products. But quality improvement is connected with increasing unit-costs. Under this setting increasing costs together with demand constraints are responsible for the problems absorptive firms are confronted with after their successful product innovation. Imitative firms are able to copy improvements of their absorptive competitors, so that they even threaten the position of the conservative camp. If the prohibitive price *a* is higher than 25, larger profits due to the increased demand make higher R&D-budgets available. Therefore, heterogeneity between agents and also spillovers increase. This development clearly supports absorptive firms, who now have no severe problems to keep their market position when introducing new products, which arised due to demand constraints in our reference scenario. Conservative firms cannot exploit absorptive firms during their weak position after introducing new products because of the strong competition with imitative firms. Under this setting there is always leapfrogging between the conservative and the imitative camp.

- The slope of the R&D-weighting function τ does not significantly influence the basic results. Nevertheless, one has to mention some implausible results which occur for likewise low values ($\tau \leq 5$). Here, the impact of absorptive capacity already comes into action in the beginning of the learning process.

- If the learning parameter θ is set at a value of 0.0001 (which means a decrease by factor 10) absorptive strategies need more time to introduce their product-innovation. Nevertheless, they are still the first firms to introduce new products. Conservative and imitative firms behave more or less in the same way. For even further decreases of θ the conservative firms will be the first to introduce new products.

- If the scaling parameter ε is decreased by factor 10 ($\varepsilon = 0.00001$) also the conservative firms are the first to introduce a new product. But the absorptive camp is able to catch-up and even to leapfrog on the second trajectory due to the increased spillover pool.

- Finally, we investigate the impact of the interindustry and science spillover parameter ξ. Our results hold for values larger than 0.1. But even if we assume that there are no external feedbacks ($\xi = 0$) we find a long-run dominance of absorptive firms when we broaden the investigation period. In this setting dominant absorptive firms are already found in the first 200 periods, if appropriability in the model is reduced and larger endogenous spillover pools are established this way.

REFERENCES

Arrow K.J. (1962), "Economic Welfare and the Allocation of Resources for Invention", in: Nelson, R.R. (ed.) (1962), *The Rate and Direction of Inventive Activity*, Princeton, Princeton University Press.

Cantner U., Pyka A. (1998), Absorbing Technological Spillovers - Simulations in an Evolutionary Framework, *Industrial and Corporate Change*, vol. 7, 1998, forthcoming.

Cohen W.M., Levinthal D.A. (1989), "Innovation and Learning: The two Faces of R& D", *The Economic Journal*, 1989, Vol. 99, pp. 569-596.

Cohen, W.M., Levinthal, D.A. (1994), Fortune Favours the Prepared Firm, *Management Science*, 40(2), 1994, pp. 227-251.

Coombs, R. (1988), Technological Opportunities and Industrial Organization, in: DOSI, G. *et al.* (eds.), pp. 295-397.

Dahmèn E. (1990), "Development Blocs in Industrial Development", in: Carlsson, B. (ed.), *Industrial Dynamics*, Kluwer Academic Publishers, Dordrecht, 1990.

Dasgupta P., Stiglitz J.E. (1980), Industrial Structure and the Nature of Innovative Activity, *The Economic Journal* 90, 1980, pp. 266-293.

Dosi G. *et al.* (1988) (eds.), *Technical Change and Economic Theory*, Pinter Publisher, London 1988.

Dosi G., Egidi M. (1991), "Substantive and Procedural Rationality", *Journal of Evolutionary Economics*, Vol. 1, pp. 145-168.

Dosi G., Teece D.J., Winter S. (1992), "Towards a Theory of Corporate Competence: Preliminary Remarks", in: Dosi G., Giannetti R., Toninelli P.A. (eds.), *Technology and Enterprise in a Historical Perspective*.

Freeman C. (1982), *The Economics of Industrial Innovation*, 2nd edition, Pinter Publishers, London, 1982.

Fusfield H.I., Haklish C.S. (1985), Cooperative R& D for Competitors, *Harvard Business Review*, Vol. 6, 1985.

Heiner R. (1988), "Imperfect Decisions and Routinized Production: Implications for Evolutionary Modelling and Inertial Technical Change", in: Dosi G. *et al.* (eds.), pp. 147-169.

Kuenne R.E. (1992), *The Economics of Oligopolistic Competition*, Blackwell Publishers, Cambridge, Mass., 1992.

Levinthal, D.A., March J.G. (1981), "A Model of Adaptive Organizational Change", *Journal of Economic Behaviour and Organization*, 2, 1981, pp. 307-333.

March J.G. (1991), Exploration and Exploitation in Organizational Learning, *Organization Science*, Vol. 2(1), 1991, pp. 71-87.

Meyer B., Vogt C, Vosskamp R. (1996), "Schumpeterian Competition in Heterogeneous Oligopolies", *Journal of Evolutionary Economics*, 1996, Vol. 6, pp. 411-424.

Mokyr J. (1990), *The Lever of Riches: Technolological Creativity and Economic Progress*, Oxford, Oxford University Press, 1990.

Nelson, R.R. (1990), What is Public and what is Private about Technology?, CCC Working Paper #90-9, University of California at Berkeley, 1990.

Nelson R.R., Winter S. (1982), *An Evolutionary Theory of Economic Change*, Cambridge, Massachusetts, 1982.

Pelikan, P. (1992), "Can the Innovation System of Capitalism be Outperformed", in: Dosi G. *et al.* (eds.) (1992).

Reinganum J.E. (1985), "Innovation and Industry Evolution", *Quarterly Journal of Economics* 100, 1985, pp. 81-99.

Schumpeter J.A. (1942), *Capitalism, Socialism and Democracy*, 5th. edition, Allen & Unwin, 1976

Simon H.A. (1976), From Substantive to Procedural Rationality, in: Latsis S.J. (ed.), Method and Appraisal in Economics, Cambridge, London *et al.*, 1976.

Winter S.G. (1971), "Satisficing, Selection, and the Innovating Remnant", *Quarterly Journal of Economics* 85(2), 1971, 237-261.

Winter S.G. (1986), "Schumpeterian Competition in Alternative Technological Regimes", in: Day R., Eliasson G. (eds.), *The Dynamics of Market Economics*, Elsevier, North-Holland, 1986, pp. 199-232.

Winter S.G. (1989), "Patents in Complex Contents: Incentives and Effectiveness", in: Weil V. *et al.* (eds.), *Owning Scientific and Technical Information*, Rutgers, University Press, 1989.

PART 2

Markets' Self-Organization

CHAPTER 7
A FORMAL APPROACH TO MARKET ORGANIZATION: CHOICE FUNCTIONS, MEAN FIELD APPROXIMATION AND MAXIMUM ENTROPY PRINCIPLE

Jean-Pierre NADAL, Gerard WEISBUCH, Olivier CHENEVEZ, and Alan KIRMAN

1. Introduction

In the bounded rationality approach to agents behaviour, individuals are not supposed to have a perfect knowledge of the economic system in which they participate. The simplest view is that their economic choices are based on very rudimentary rules. Of course the question arises as to the origin of the chosen rules. Obviously, these rules reflect some "knowledge" about the world, whether innate or learned. Learning involves using past or present information, but in most cases agents have a lot of available information and a first step in learning is simply coding this information by some set of variables. In a neural net approach for instance, coding is achieved by architecture and synaptic weights, in time series analysis by the linear coefficients of an ARMA model etc. As we show here and as proposed in other economic models such as the discrete choice theory of product differentiation [1], coding can be very direct and simple, such as a list of weighted profits or utility functions. The second step of a choice theory is the definition of a choice function which describes the choice of the agents based on the coded available information. Discrete choice theory for instance uses probabilistic choice among possible actions, such as purchasing a given product or visiting a given shop, where the probability is a fraction of a function of the coded information divided by the sum of such functions corresponding to the all available choices. The simplest possible function is the linear function, but we will show here that behavior of agents based on such a linear function is rather peculiar.

In this paper we address the question of the role and interpretation of choice functions. We limit the discussion to the case where agents only use past private information and have no access to public information, concerning for instance the behavior of other agents. After defining the general framework in section 2, in section 3, we make use of the *mean field approximation* [7] in order to compare the qualitative behaviour obtained from different choice functions. We show that for some of them, such as the so-called logit function [1, 5, 10], *phase transitions* can be observed. Next, in section 4, we show that the logit choice function can be derived from an optimization principle, analogous to the maximum entropy principle used in physics and inference theory. We discuss the possible meanings of such an optimization scheme. Possible avenues for future research are given in the Conclusion.

2. A general framework for the study of buyer's dynamics

We are interested in the modeling of buyers' behaviour. In this paper we consider that each buyer makes use of previous experience to select a seller. Since we want to emphasise the role of the individual buyers' choice functions, we assume that there is *no direct interaction between buyers*. We also assume that information on a seller is only obtained on the occasion of a transaction with him (there are no "posted" prices; see [11] for a real instance of such a condition). The general framework, illustrated in Figure 1, is thus the following. Each time a buyer makes a transaction with a seller, he acquires some information about what he can expect from this particular seller (quality of goods, profit,...). This information will be encoded in some way which updates the previously acquired information about sellers. This stored information is the input to the (possibly probabilistic) choice (or decision) rule used by the buyer in order to select a seller for the next transaction.

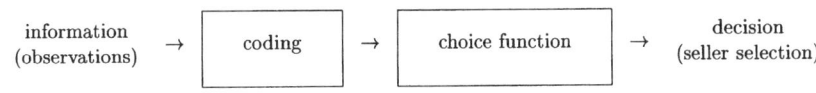

Figure 1: The general model

Let us illustrate this general model with simple specific examples. Considering one given buyer, we will denote by $\mathbf{J} = \{J_j, j = 1, ..., N\}$ the stored information, J_j being the information concerning the jth seller. In the simplest case, J_j is a scalar. For instance, J_j may be the profit obtained the last time the buyer dealt with the jth seller; or it may be some moving average value of past profits from seller j, e.g.,

$$J_j(t) = \gamma J_j(t-1) + (1-\gamma)\pi_j(t) \qquad (1)$$

where $\pi_j(t)$ is the actual profit at time t if j is the seller visited at time t, and $\pi_j(t) = 0$ otherwise. The parameter γ is smaller than 1: events far in the past are progressively forgotten. The normalization in (1) is such that for a time independent profit $\pi_j(t) = \pi$, if j is always chosen, one has at each time $J_j = \pi$. An updating rule such as (1) is an example of a coding scheme. One may consider more involved rules, taking into account not only the mean profit obtained from each seller, but also some information on the frequency of visits to each seller. In the following, we will only consider the case of a single variable J_j stored for each seller. We note, however, that our approach can be easily generalised to more complicated situations.

The choice rule, to be denoted by $P(j|\mathbf{J})$, is the probability that the buyer choose the jth seller based on his knowledge of the stored information $\mathbf{J}$. A large class of model encountered in the literature corresponds to a decision rule defined by

$$P(j|\mathbf{J}) = \frac{f(J_j)}{\sum_{k=1}^{N} f(J_k)} \quad (2)$$

where $f(\,.\,) \geq 0$ is some a priori chosen function – to be called below the *choice function*. If, as above, J_j is a scalar, f is a real valued function of a single variable. Typical choices for f are, a linear or affine function [9], or an exponential function [1, 5], in which case the choice rule is called the *logit* rule.

3. Choice functions and phase transition

3.1. Mean field approximation

In this section we consider, for a general choice function, the mean field approximation as used in [11] for the logit case (the mean field approach has been also applied to other economic problems, see e.g. [2, 6]). We consider a buyer whose choice rule is as defined in (2), and the coding rule as in (1) (the discussion can be easily generalised to other coding rules). Moreover, we assume for simplicity a constant, seller independent, profit π from each transaction (this imply in particular that the transaction is always possible and realized between the buyer and the chosen seller). Hence we have:

$$\pi_j(t) = \pi \text{ if } j \text{ is chosen,}$$
$$= 0. \text{ otherwise} \quad (3)$$

The Mean Field Approach [7] consists in replacing randomly fluctuating quantities by their expectation, thus neglecting fluctuations. Averaging (1), one gets

$$J_j(t) = \gamma J_j(t-1) + (1-\gamma)\pi P(j|\mathbf{J}(t-1)) \quad (4)$$

In the large time limit, one gets the fixed point (mean field) equations:

$$J_j = \pi \frac{f(J_j)}{\sum_k f(J_k)} \quad (5)$$

In the above equation we have replaced $P(j\,|\mathbf{J})$ by its expression (2).

Let us study now the solutions of the mean field equations. More precisely, the equations (5) are fixed point equations of a dynamical process: among the solutions, only the stable ones are meaningful, so that we will have to study the stability of the solutions.

As a preliminary remark, summing over j the fixed point equations (5) one sees that any solution $\mathbf{J}$ satisfies

$$\sum_j J_j = \pi. \tag{6}$$

Obviously,

$$J_j = \frac{\pi}{N} \quad j = 1, ..., N \tag{7}$$

is always a solution. Developing (5) at the vicinity of this symmetric fixed point (7), one finds that it is stable if the quantity a defined by

$$a \equiv \left(\frac{d \ln f(x)}{d \ln x}\right)_{x = \frac{\pi}{N}} \tag{8}$$

is smaller than 1. Otherwise, that is if

$$a \geq 1 \tag{9}$$

the symmetric solution (7) is unstable: there must exist other, stable, solutions.

To simplify the discussion, let us consider the simplest case of two sellers, $N = 2$. In that case, we can work with the single variable J_1, since according to (6) the other one J_2 is equal to $\pi - J_1$. Then the mean field equations becomes simply

$$J_1 = \pi \frac{f(J_1)}{f(J_1) + f(\pi - J_1)} \equiv g(J_1) \tag{10}$$

In fact it is clear that if J_1 is a solution, then $\pi - J_1$ is also a solution. Hence we have at least two stable solutions. Since we have $J_2 = \pi - J_1$, each pair of solutions can be written $\{J_1, J_2\}$. To keep the discussion simple, we will restrict the discussion below to the simplest case of a unique stable pair of solutions (hence one unstable and two stable solutions). Geometrically, a solutions J_1 of (10) is given, in the plane $\{x, y\}$ by the intersection of the straight line $y = x$ with the curve $y = g(x)$. One can show that the parameter a defined above is here equal to the slope of g at that value $\frac{\pi}{2}$ of J_1. Hence the condition for having the symmetric point unstable is

$$a = \left(\frac{\mathrm{d}g(x)}{\mathrm{d}x}\right)_{x=\frac{\pi}{2}} \geq 1. \tag{11}$$

Remark: if $f(0) = 0$, it is easily seen that there are always (at least) three solutions, the symmetric point (7), and the pair $\{0, \pi\}$. Performing the stability analysis one finds that the non symmetric solutions $\{0, \pi\}$ are stable if

$$\frac{\pi f'(0)}{f(\pi)} < 1. \tag{12}$$

3.2. Interpretation

If the only stable solution of the equilibrium equations is $J_j = \frac{\pi}{N}$, the frequencies of visits to any seller are equal. The probabilities of visiting any seller simply fluctuate without any stable preference for one seller emerging.

If there are other stable solutions $J_j \neq \pi/N$, one frequency of visit is larger than the others. The buyer has a stable preference for one seller. According to the above discussion, the qualitative behaviour of the buyer depends on the choice function $f(\ .\ )$, the number of sellers N and the profit π only through the quantity a defined in equation (8). If the buyer modifies his choice strategy, or if his profit varies, in such a way that his a changes, an abrupt change of behaviour will be observed if a crosses the critical value 1. This is analogous to a second order phase transition in physical systems, where the parameter a has the meaning of the inverse of the temperature. If one starts with a small value of a, the stable solution $\left\{J_j = \frac{\pi}{N}, j = 1, ..., N\right\}$ remains valid until a reaches 1. Just above the transition, $\mathbf{J}$ starts to depart from the symmetric solution, with

$$\left|J_j - \frac{\pi}{N}\right| \sim \sqrt{a-1} \tag{13}$$

Now it is reasonable to assume that the buyers of a market have different choice strategies, or/and make different profits, so that they have different values of a. When there exists a wide range of a values, distributed around the critical value 1, one will observe two categories of buyers: the ones who choose randomly the seller they will visit and the other who have strong preferences. We say that the distribution is bimodal.

3.3. Specific choice functions

The linear and affine cases

Let us consider the simplest case, that is an affine choice function. As can be seen from the definition (2) of the choice rule, $f(x)$ and $af(x)$, for any

$a > 0$, give the same choice rule. Without loss of generality, an affine choice function can thus be defined by

$$f(J_j) = \beta J_j + 1 \tag{14}$$

with $\beta \geq 0$. For that case the quantity a is

$$a = \frac{1}{1 + \frac{N}{\beta \pi}} \tag{15}$$

The purely linear case, $f(J_j) = J_j$ (studied in [9]), is obtained for $\beta \to \infty$. For that case $\frac{1}{\beta} = 0$, the number of solutions is infinite: every $\mathbf{J} = \{J_j, j = 1, ..., N\}$ such that $\sum_j J_j = \pi$ is a stable solution. This is analogous to what happens in the classical model of Blackwell's urns. If $\beta < \infty$, this degeneracy does not subsist. There is only one solution, the symmetric one, $\{J_j = \frac{\pi}{N}, j = 1,...,N\}$ (which is indeed stable: $a < 1$). In any case, that is whatever β, there will exist no transition.

The power law case

Let us consider the power law case, a simple generalization of the affine case:

$$f(J_j) = (\beta J_j)^n + 1 \tag{16}$$

with $n > 0$ and $\beta \geq 0$. For this choice function a is given by

$$a = \frac{n}{1 + \left(\frac{N}{\beta \pi}\right)^n} \tag{17}$$

For $n = 1$ one recovers the results for the linear and affine cases: a is always smaller than 1 for $\beta < \infty$, and equal to 1 if $\frac{1}{\beta} = 0$. For $n < 1$, a is always smaller than 1, there is no transition as found in [9].

For $n > 1$, there exists the possibility of observing a transition, hence a bimodal situation: a is larger than 1 for $\frac{\beta \pi}{N} > (n-1)^{-\frac{1}{n}}$.

Remark: in the particular case $\beta \to \infty$, that is for $f(J_j) = (J_j)^n$, one has $f(0) = 0$. Since $n > 1$, $f'(0) = 0$, so that, according to (12), the non symmetric solutions $\{0, \pi\}$ are stable.

To conclude, in this case (16), the convexity of f is a necessary condition for observing a bimodal behaviour.

The exponential case

The standard logit case corresponds to an exponential choice function:

$$f(J_j) = \exp(\beta J_j). \qquad (18)$$

In that case a is simply given by

$$a = \frac{\beta \pi}{N} \qquad (19)$$

The symmetric point is unstable if $a = \frac{\beta \pi}{N} > 1$.

A last remark concerning the possible occurrence of bimodality. In all the case considered a is an increasing function of $\frac{\beta \pi}{N}$, where β parametrises the buyer's choice function. Let us assume that the distribution of β values among buyers is not (or only weakly) dependent on their profits. It follows that buyers making large profit are more likely to have $a > 1$ than buyers making small profits. This is in agreement with what is observed in the fish market of Marseille, where big buyers develop fidelity to one particular seller, whereas small buyers do not. A more detailed discussion of this market is presented in ref. [11].

4. Derivation of the logit function from an optimization principle

4.1. An exploration-exploitation compromise

In the previous section we studied the qualitative behaviour that we can expect for a general choice function. The next question is then: in what sense a given choice function is efficient? One attractive feature of a choice function is that it may represent some sort of "best behaviour" with respect to some criterion. Here we will show that the logit function can be derived from an optimization strategy. In particular we argue below that, for modeling the buyer's strategy, one can define a maximization principle, formally identical to the so call *maximum entropy principle* [3] considered in statistical physics – and to be shortly presented later on for comparison.

Let us assume that the buyer wants to find a compromise between getting the best profit at the next transaction, and keeping the best possible knowledge of a market in order to be able to make good choices in the future: the market can vary in time because of external events or because the sellers strategies moves. This requires that he will visit every seller as frequently as possible (he can only get information about a seller by making transactions with this seller). If p_j is the probability of visiting seller j, $p_j = p_j^0 \equiv 1/N$ would correspond to maximum information. A proper measure of the similarity between this uniform distribution $\{p_j^0\}_{j=1}^N$ and the actual distribution $\{p_j\}_{j=1}^N$ is the entropy S,

$$S = - \sum_j p_j \ln p_j. \quad (20)$$

The entropy is a measure of uncertainty in the occurrence of the events $j = 1, ..., N$. In the context of Information Theory [4], it is the minimal *amount of information* (measured in bits if the logarithm in (20) is taken in base 2) required in order to code the set of events.

One may thus want to choose the p_js from a compromise between the maximization of the entropy and a maximization of the immediate profit. Taking the (moving) average J_j as an estimate of the profit to be obtained from seller j, we thus maximise

$$C \equiv S + \beta \sum_j p_j J_j \quad (21)$$

over all possible p_j's. The quantity $\frac{\ln 2}{\beta}$ is equal to the amount of profit considered to be equivalent to one bit of information.

Introducing a Lagrangian multiplier λ in order to impose the normalization constraint $\sum_j p_j = 1$, one finally maximises

$$C = S + \beta \sum_j p_j J_j - \lambda \left(\sum_j p_j - 1 \right) \quad (22)$$

Taking the derivative of C with respect to one p_j, one gets

$$-1 - \ln p_j + \beta J_j - \lambda = 0 \quad (23)$$

which gives precisely

$$p_j = \frac{1}{Z} \exp \beta J_j \quad (24)$$

with $Z = \sum_j \exp \beta J_j$.

The logit strategy is thus obtained as a consequence of the optimization of a cost function which expresses the compromise between short term profit and preservation of information for long term profits.

4.2. Link with physics and inference theory

The exponential family of probability distributions plays a central role in statistical physics, where it is derived from the *maximum entropy principle* [3]. The maximum entropy principle is more generally a tool for making inferences. In fact, it has already been used in economics in order to justify the choice of an exponential distribution (see e.g. [10, 12]).

For completeness we restate here this inference principle. One constructs a probability distribution $\{p_j, j = 1, ..., N\}$, based on some prior knowledge, in such a way that the resulting probability law does not contain more information than what can be gained from this prior knowledge. The measure of uncertainty in the occurrence of the events is given by the entropy S of the probability distribution, as defined in (20). If we know some mean value E of an observable quantity E_j, we estimate the p_js by maximizing the entropy S under the constraint that E is given. This leads to

$$p_j = \frac{1}{Z}\exp - \beta E_j \qquad (25)$$

where Z is the normalization constant (the "partition function"). For a physical system, $T \equiv \frac{1}{\beta}$ is the temperature, and E is the energy. If one works at a given value of β (instead of a given value of E), one sees that as T goes to zero (β goes to ∞) the system will choose the states with the smallest possible values of the energy. In our model of buyer's strategy, the quantity which play the role of the energy is thus *minus* the mean profit (since the profit has to be maximised). With the maximum entropy principle one predicts the probability distribution without making any hypothesis on the dynamics. The resulting probability distribution is the best guess based on the knowledge we have about the system: the logit function can be understood as the best description of the buyer's strategy based on the knowledge of the mean profit he obtains.

The specificity of Statistical Physics is that the application of this *inference* principle leads precisely to the correct *physical* description – the law of thermodynamics. Clearly, there is no reason *a priori* for expecting such a success in the context of economics. Nevertheless, there are several approaches tending to show that the exponential family may play also a fundamental role in economy, as discussed in particular in [10]. What we have shown in this paper is that the maximum entropy principle has an appealing "physical" interpretation in the context of the search for an exploitation/exploration compromise.

A last remark is in order. One should note that to derive a choice function from an optimization principle does *not* imply that one assumes the buyer to be aware of optimizing some criterion. An analogy can be made with living systems evolving according to past experiences. One of the main approach to the modeling of Evolution in nature assumes the optimization of some cost function, the survival fitness. Clearly, no genetic system is aware of what is really going on, and only mutation rules can be observed at the level of individuals. Similarly, it is commonly believed that the brain organization is *optimally* fitted to the tasks it has to solve, through evolution and adaptation. It is not unreasonable to expect that a buyer follows some empirical rule, the rule itself being chosen according to some kind of cultural knowledge, based on past experiences possibly including those of previous generations, in such a way that, implicitly, the rule implements the optimization of some cost function.

5. Conclusion

In this paper, we have focussed on two aspects of the modeling of a buyer's choice of seller in a market. We have been concerned with the case in which buyers only learn from their own private experience. We have used the mean field approach to show that a phase transition may occur in individual behaviour – even in the extremely simple case where he gets the same profit from any seller. Previous work [11] provides empirical evidence from the Marseille wholesale fish market for the behaviour predicted by the present formal model.

Then, we have shown that the logit function (which generates phase transitions) can be obtained from maximizing a cost function which expresses a compromise between exploration – keeping information about the market – and exploitation – making the largest profit at the next transaction. We have discussed the possible meanings of such an optimization process.

Our results can be easily extended or adapted to other situations: models with other coding schemes, with interactions between buyers, etc. In particular one can consider models in which individuals also receive information about the experience of others (see [8]), and can thus be related to standard models of evolutionary games in which, for example, players know the frequencies of choices for the whole population. In such a case where an agent has access to information about other agents'choices, phase transitions will exist as well, although the related market dynamics might be different.

Another application is the case in which buyers have access to public information that they code by some utility function, see for instance [9], such as the utilities of different brands, or different strategies. The transition which will be observed in such case will be a transition between coexistence of different brands in the market in the case of low a, and supremacy of one brand which sells better than the others for large values of a.

REFERENCES

[1] Anderson S.P., de Palma A. and Thisse J.F. (1993), *Discrete Choice Theory of Product Differentiation*, MIT Press, Cambridge MA.

[2] Aoki M. (1996), *A New Approach to Macroeconomic Modelling*, Cambridge University Press, New York.

[3] Balian R. (1992), *From Microphysics to Macrophysics*, Springer.

[4] Blahut R.E. (1988), *Principles and Practice of Information Theory*. Addison-Wesley, Cambridge MA.

[5] Blume L. (1993), "The Statistical Mechanics of Social Interaction", *Games and Economic Behaviour*, 5, pp. 387-424.

[6] Brock W.A. and Durlauf S.N. (1996), "Discrete choice with social interactions I: Theory", Santa Fe Institute working paper, April 1996

[7] Derrida B. (1986), "Phase transitions in random networks of automata", in *Chance and Matter*, Ed. by Souletie J. Vannimenus J. and Stora R., North-Holland.

[8] Follmer H. (1974), "Random economies with many interacting agents", *Journal of Mathematical Economics*, vol. 1, 1, March, pp. 51-62.

[9] Kilani K. and Lesourne J. (1995), "Endogenous preferences, Self-organizing systems and Consumer theory", Mimeo 95-6, Laboratoire d'Econométrie, Conservatoire National des Arts et Métiers, Paris.

[10] de Palma A., Kilani K. and Lesourne J. (1996), "Network externalities and the Polya-Logit model", This workshop, and Preprint of the Laboratoire d'Econométrie, Conservatoire National des Arts et Métiers, Paris.

[11] Weisbuch G., Kirman A. and Herreiner D. (1998), "Market organization". This volume.

[12] Williams H.C.W.L. (1977), "On the formation of travel demand models and economics evaluation measures of user benefit", *Environment and Planning* A # 9, 283-344.

CHAPTER 8
MARKET ORGANIZATION

**Gerard WEISBUCH, Alan KIRMAN
and Dorothea HERREINER**

1. Introduction

Markets can have very different structures. They may be based on an auction mechanism, on a system of sellers who post prices or on bilateral trading and bargaining. Within each of these structures a considerable amount of organisation may develop. In particular certain trading relationships will be established. Some individuals in a market will systematically deal with certain others and this gives rise to a graph of trading or communication links. In most economic models this feature is ignored and, for example, in the standard Walrasian model, an equilibrium is considered to be attained if aggregate excess supply is zero at certain prices. How the exchanges necessary to equilibrate the market actually take place, that is who trades with whom, is not analysed. In other models such as the standard "search models" (see, for example Diamond (1989) agents visit sellers and buy from the cheapest according to some rule. While this is a step towards realism the idea that buyers will become attached to certain stores is, in general, not taken into consideration. All sellers are anonymous and are searched with equal probability. While such models may be plausible for transactions which take place infrequently they do not seem adequate for transactions that are made often and on a repeated basis.

A networks of preferential links between sellers and buyers is especially appropriate to markets of perishable goods as opposed to durable goods. When goods are perishable, sellers have to calculate with care the amount they wish to bring to the market since no surplus can be kept as inventory. For this they try to obtain an accurate estimate of how many customers they expect to attract. Buyers are aware also that sellers are trying to minimize excess supply and will therefore prefer stores at which their demand will be satisfied. From their experience they may learn that these will not necessarily be those which offer the lowest prices.

Thus what interests us is how agents may learn to develop certain links with each other rather than simply match at random.

There are several models in which there is a network of links between agents but where the trading structure represented by these links is fixed and given. A typical example is a model in which economic agents "live" on a lattice and only interact with their neighbours. This can be thought of as representing some sort of spatial organisation (see Follmer [1974], Durlauf [1990], Benabou

[1992], Blume [1993] and Ellison [1993]). In this case one is interested to know whether pockets or clusters with certain behaviour or characteristics may form. The spatial connotation is by no means necessary however and alternative structures of links can be considered (see Kirman, Oddou and Weber [1986], Ioannides [1990], and Gilles *et al.* (1994)). Indeed in many problems in economics, links are created as a result of community of interest or relationship between characteristics rather than mere geographical proximity. It may also be the case that although agents react only to their neighbours the consequence of their choices may have more widespread effects (see Weisbuch *et al.* (1994)). Yet, in all of these contributions the communication or trading links are taken as given exogenously. Our aim, in this paper, is to try to bridge the gap between the two extremes, on the one hand random matching and on the other, fixed exogenous links between individuals.

We wish to examine how links between agents develop and are reinforced. A market which has strong links which persist over time can be thought of as one which has organised itself whereas one in which agents simply search at random might be thought of one which is lacking in any organisation. A small number of authors have examined the problem of this sort of self organisation in markets although from a rather different point of view. Durlauf [1990] introduces something of this sort when he considers not the network itself as changing but rather that agents may choose when to place themselves in the network, and this recalls an older model of neighbourhood preferences due to Schelling. Another example is that of Stanley *et al.* (1994). They develop an evolutionary model of the repeated prisoners dilemma in which, as agents learn from experience, they may refuse to play with certain others and one can examine the distribution and local concentration of communication links and of strategies that develop. Lesourne (1992) discusses at length the self-organisation of markets and looks at the emergence of privileged relations between certain buyers and sellers. A lot of his emphasis is, however, on self organisation through prices something which will not feature directly in our model.

Aoki (1995a) examines a situation in which agents are faced with a binary decision set and where their behaviour can be modelled through their interaction with a "field variable". In his case this is the proportion of agents choosing the first of the two possible alternatives. In our model, however, we have to keep track of the results of the binary interactions between all of the pairs of agents and this cannot be aggregated into some representative variable with which the agents interact. Even though what interests us is, in part, the number of buyers at each store, we also wish to know how faithful the individuals are. Thus a situation in which individuals move from store to store but in which the number at each store remains constant is, for us, different from one in which the same individuals always return to the same store. In another paper, motivated by the idea of a group of agents making choices between various alternatives, Aoki (1995b) treats the division of these agents as a random partition and examines its evolution over time. Although this model is more closely related to our market model Aoki, is concerned as before with the evolution of the partition. Agents do not interact through a field variable but they move from one store to another with a probability which depends on the current choice and not on their personal history.

More directly related to the present paper is Vriend's [1994] contribution which presents a first step to simulating a model in which either the individual links themselves or the probability that they will be used over time evolve. He constructs a model of a market in which buyers learn when to shop and firms learn, from experience, when to buy. The term "learn" has a very particular meaning here. What agents do is to select between rules on the basis of the profitability, in the past, of having used those rules. Thus learning in Vriend's context does not involve updating within a parametric model as it will in this paper. In his model firms sell indivisible units of a homogeneous good, the price of this good is fixed and agents demand at most one unit. Nevertheless it is particularly interesting to note the development and persistence of a non degenerate size distribution of firms even though all firms are identical to start with. Furthermore some buyers always return to the same store whilst others continue to search. Thus both loyalty and searching behaviour coexist. The approach adopted by Vriend and pursued in Kirman and Vriend (1995) is to look at a market in which agents have no knowledge of the market structure and they can only learn by observing the payoffs from the actions they take. In such a model which is in the spirit of the "artificial life" approach agents know and calculate nothing a priori and one observes to see what sort of organisation emerges. The advantage of this approach is that very little structure is imposed, a priori. The difficulty is that one has to rely essentially on simulations since such a model is not analytically tractable and furthermore it is difficult to attribute emergent features to any one particular feature of the model.

Here we adopt a rather different approach. We analyse several simple models of a market for a perishable good, in which buyers, (retailers), meet sellers, (wholesalers) once or several times in a day and buy quantities of the homogeneous good to resell on their own local market. However, unlike the models of Vriend and Kirman and Vriend, we build quite a lot of calculating ability for the agents into the model in that prices are chosen as a result of specific calculations about the amount buyers, behaving in an intelligent way will be prepared to purchase. Learning here involves updating by agents within a parametric model and we are able to examine analytically the consequences of changes in the values of the parameters of the model. We concentrate our analysis on the problem of whether links will be established between particular buyers and sellers and what is the nature of these links: are they permanent, "marriage", do buyers occasionally have "affairs" with other sellers while remaining basically "faithful" to their regular partners, do buyers "divorce" their sellers and then remarry or do they continually "shop around"? The important parameter in this is the sensitivity of buyers to past profits from sellers when making their choice as to whom to visit in the next period. This will depend on two factors, the extent to which the buyer is positively influenced by obtaining profit from a seller and the rate at which he "forgets" his experience. Thus it is the extent to which profits from a particular seller "reinforce" the probability that a buyer will visit that seller that is important (for discussions of the role of reinforcement learning in economics see Marimon(1995) and Erev and Roth (1995)).

We find that the change from order, settled marriage patterns to disorder is surprisingly abrupt as a function of the learning parameter particularly for the simplest one session model. We show analytically why this is so using the "mean field" approach (for other applications to economics see, for example, Aoki (1996)), and then do simulations of more complex models. These show that the same patterns of behavior persist. We finally compare our theoretical predictions with empirical data from the wholesale fishmarket in Marseille.

Our model is a springboard for future research in which many other features can be the subject of learning but by starting in this way we are able to obtain simple and clear characterisations of the basic relationships between aggregate structure and the parameters of the individual learning process.

2. The simplest Model

Let us consider a set of buyers and a set of sellers.

2.1. Prices and quantities

The buyers will wish to buy a quantity from sellers given the price per unit p which is proposed and are able to resell in their own local market where they face a demand function $p(q)$, which determines the relationship between the price they obtain and the quantity q that they bring to the local market. Let us suppose in order to simplify matters that $p(q)$ is known by the buyers, is the same for all buyers and that it is a simple function of q such as:

$$p(q) = \frac{b}{q+c} \qquad (1)$$

The particular choice of the function $p(q)$ is of no importance and is made to facilitate calculations and to provide clear benchmarks. For the model any monotonic decreasing function would suffice. The buyer's profit is then:

$$\pi_b = q\left(\frac{b}{q+c} - p\right) \qquad (2)$$

We suppose then that the buyer knows the demand curve he faces and is thus able to compute the quantity that will maximise his profit for a given price proposed by the seller. This quantity is:

$$q = \sqrt{\frac{bc}{p}} - c \qquad (3)$$

We make similar assumptions for the sellers, in particular that they know the behavior of buyers described by the three equations above, and they can therefore maximize their own profit per transaction:

$$\pi_s = q(p - p_a) = \left(\sqrt{\frac{bc}{p}} - c\right)(p - p_a) \qquad (4)$$

with respect to the price p that they charge to the buyers, where p_a is the price at which the sellers themselves purchase the fish. (Since the price p which maximises equation 4 is the solution of a third degree equation, its expression is rather complicated and not given here).

In order to simplify assumptions as much as possible, let us suppose that:

- All sellers propose a single price to all their customers.

- Customers choose one shop everyday. As long as the shop has supplies, they are offered goods at price p; customers then purchase q given by equation 3. Whether they do get supplies when they visit the shop depends upon the time they visit the shop, which is randomly chosen in the simulations. It also depends on how much the sellers bring each day to the market.

- Each day sellers bring a fish quantity Q in relation to n_b, the expected number of customers for that day. In the simplest version of the model, this fish quantity is $(n_b + a)q$, where n_b is the number of customers who visited yesterday and a a constant extra fraction brought to attract for the future extra customers that could show up.

2.2. Preference coefficients, learning and choice probabilities

Now that we have specified how quantities and prices are determined, what happens in the market depends on the actual visits of buyers to sellers: sellers are chosen by buyers according to certain probabilities. The latter are derived from "preference coefficients" which are built upon the history of each buyer's past profits with each seller. The learning and probabilistic choice processes to be described in this section are the "invariant core" of the model. They are largely inspired from the formal neural networks approach to reinforcement learning as described for instance in Weisbuch (1990). They will not be modified in any of the subsequent versions of the model (which is not the case for the simple rules for choosing price and quantities described above).

Let first specify the learning process of the buyers. By assumption the only information available to them come from previous transactions. We first propose to map that information into preference coefficients J_{ij} of buyer i for seller j. These are constructed by recording the profits that buyer made i from his previous transaction with seller j. At the same time these previous profits are discounted at a constant rate γ. Since we use discrete time for transactions, preferences are updated at each time step according to:

$$J_{ij}(t) = (1-\gamma) J_{ij}(t-1) + \pi_b(t) \quad (5)$$

In other words, at each time step, all preferences coefficients are discounted at a constant rate, while the preference coefficient for the shop with which a transaction occurs is increased by the profit made in that shop. Discounting previous profits at a constant rate is important in ensuring that information is relevant to the current situation: in general, shops do not have stationary characteristics in terms of the profits that they offer because of changes in prices or the level of their supply with respect to the number of customers they have to serve. Preference coefficents thus appear as the sum of discounted past profits.

Buyers then use these preference coefficents to choose a shop. One way to do so is to choose the shop with the best record, that is the shop with the highest J_{ij}. However, by always doing this, the buyer will become a captive of the selected shop which would then be in a position to increase its prices, thus diminishing the buyer's profit. The shop can do this until the buyer's profit becomes negative before running any risk of losing that buyer. It is therefore in the buyer's interest to search from time to time among other sellers to check whether he could get a better profit elsewhere. In other words, a good strategy for the buyers would be a balance between the deterministic choice in favor of those shops which gave the best profits in the past and random search among other sellers. This raises the well known issue of the trade-off between exploitation of old knowledge and exploration to acquire new knowledge. We suppose here that a buyer chooses a shop j with a probability P_j which is proportional to the exponential of the preference coefficient for that shop. That is:

$$P_j = \frac{\exp(\beta J_{ij})}{\Sigma_j \exp(\beta J_{ij})} \quad (6)$$

where β measures the non-linearity of the relationship between the probability P_j and the preference coefficient J_{ij}.

The exponential rule has been widely used in economics and elsewhere. In particular, several justifications for its use are given in the discrete choice literature, see e.g. Anderson *et al.* (1992). For a direct derivation of the exponential rule see Nadal *et al.* (1997).

3. Mean Field Approach

The simple model can be formally analysed within the framework of the Mean Field approach. This consists in replacing randomly fluctuating quantities by their average, thus neglecting fluctuations. It is only an approximation, but is often convenient to obtain at least a qualitative understanding of the behavior of the system.

3.1. The order/disorder transition

A generalization of this approach to our problem is to write a differential equation describing the time evolution of one J_{ij}:

$$\frac{dJ_j}{dt} = -\gamma J_j + \langle \pi_j \rangle \tag{7}$$

where $\langle \pi \rangle$ is the average profit, related to π the profit obtained from one actual transaction as follows:

$$\langle \pi_j \rangle = \pi P(j) \frac{\exp(\beta J_j)}{\sum'_j \exp(\beta J_{j'})} \tag{8}$$

where the fraction represent the probability of that buyer i visits seller j and $P(j)$ is the probability that the shop still has goods to sell when he comes. We suppress here the i index corresponding to the buyer. In other words, the above set of equations couples the evolution of all the J_j. Equilibrium values are obtained by equating the derivatives to zero.

Let us consider the simplest case of two shops and to further simplify computation, let us suppose, for the moment, that $P(j) = 1$, which happens when buyers always find what they require at the seller they visit. The equilibrium relations are in this case:

$$\gamma J_1 = \pi \frac{\exp(\beta J_1)}{\exp(\beta J_1) + \exp(\beta J_2)} \tag{9}$$

$$\gamma J_2 = \pi \frac{\exp(\beta J_2)}{\exp(\beta J_1) + \exp(\beta J_2)} \tag{10}$$

Subtracting equation 10 from equation 9, we see that the difference between the two fidelities, $\Delta = J_1 - J_2$, obeys the following implicit equation:

$$\gamma \Delta = \pi \frac{\exp(\beta \Delta) - 1}{\exp(\beta \Delta) + 1} \tag{11}$$

The right hand side of the equation is in fact the hyperbolic tangent of $\beta \Delta/2$. The above equation has either one or three solutions according to the slope of the hyperbolic tangent at the origin.

By developing the hyperbolic tangent in series for small values of $\beta \Delta/2$, it is easily seen that for:

$$\beta < \beta_c = \frac{2\gamma}{\pi} \qquad (12)$$

there is only one solution $\Delta = 0$ and $J_1 = J_2 = \frac{\pi}{2\gamma}$. Since in this case the average J_j are small and equal, the probabilities of visiting either shop simply fluctuate. No order is observed.

In the opposite situation, when β is above β_c, the zero solution is unstable and one obtains two symmetrical solutions where one fidelity is larger than the other one by a factor which is exponential in $\frac{\beta\pi}{\gamma}$. The transition between the two regimes is abrupt. A development in series of the hyperbolic tangent around 0 shows that the larger fidelity increases in β as the square root of the distance to the transition:

$$\Delta = \sqrt{\frac{12(\beta - \beta_c)}{\beta^3}} \qquad (13)$$

Fidelities are then continuous across the transition, but they rise (or decrease) with an infinite slope at the transition. Expression (14) can be generalized to any number n of shops:

$$\beta_c = \frac{n\gamma}{\pi} \qquad (14)$$

The above analysis shows that as long as the mean field approximation remains valid, the qualitative behavior of the dynamics, ordered or disordered, only depends on one parameter, namely the ratio between β and β_c. All other parameters simply change the scale of profits, prices, numbers of shops and customers. The time scale of learning depends on γ: order, when achieved, is reached faster for larger values of γ.

The three parameters π, β and γ control the transition. Sellers set prices and thus determine π, the buyers' profit. The buyers characteristics determine β and γ. We might reasonably assume that agents are not all identical and that their characteristic parameters vary. Prices may not vary widely since there is competition between sellers. On the other hand, memory (characterised by γ) and discrimination rate (characterised by β) might differ between buyers. If these variations are large enough, we might expect to observe two distinct

168 | Markets' self-organization

classes of buyers: faithful buyers, who most of the time visit the same shop, would be those whose parameters are such that $\beta > \beta_c$, while searchers with parameters such that $\beta < \beta_c$ would wander from shop to shop. Indeed precisely this sort of "division of labour" is observed on the Marseille fish market which was the empirical starting point for this paper.

Let us also note that the predicted nonhomogeneous distribution of behavior is a dynamical feature which is very different from the phase transitions observed when agents use information from the behavior of other agents through social interactions (Follmer 1974, Arthur and Lane 1993, Brock and Durlauf 1995, Orlean 1995, Kilani and Lesourne 1995), rather than from their past experience as in this model. In the case of social interactions, order or disorder is a characteristic of the market, and all agents share the same behavior, either ordered or disordered depending upon average values of the parameters.

3.2. Hysteresis

Another important qualitative result of the mean field approach is the existence of hysteresis effects: buyers might still have a strong preference for one shop that offered good deals in the past, even though the current deals they offer are less interesting than those now offered by other shops.

Let us come back once more to the case of two shops 1 and 2, and now suppose that they offer different prices and hence different profits π_1 and π_2. Replacing profit π in equations 9 and 10 by respectively π_1 and π_2, equation 11 becomes:

$$2\gamma\Delta - (\pi_1 - \pi_2) = (\pi_1 + \pi_2) \frac{\exp(\beta\Delta) - 1}{\exp(\beta\Delta) + 1} \quad (15)$$

When β is above β_c, the three intersections remain as long as the difference in profits is not too large. Which of the two extreme intersections is actually reached by the learning dynamics depends on initial conditions.

Thus, as illustrated on figure 1, buyers can remain faithful to a shop asking for a higher price (which results in a lower profit for the buyer), provided that they became attached to this shop when it practiced a lower price. When the most often frequented shop changes its prices, the fidelity to that shop describes the upper branch of the fidelity versus profit curve (fig. 1). The fidelity remains on the upper branch as long as it exists, i.e. until the point where the slope is vertical. When profit decreases beyond that level, a sudden and discontinuous transition to the lower branch occurs. This is the point when customers change their policy and visit the other shop. But, if the first shop reverses its high price/low buyer profit policy when fidelity is on the lower branch, the transition to the higher branch only occurs when the slope of the lower branch becomes vertical, i.e at a higher profit than for the downward transition.

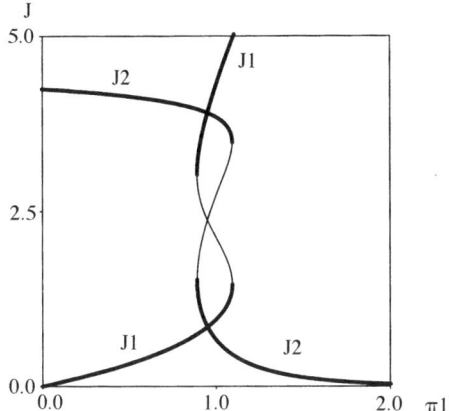

Figure 1: Hysteresis of fidelities. Plot of both fidelities versus π_1, the profit to be obtained from shop number 1 when π_2 the profit to be obtained from shop number 2 isheld equal to 1. ($\beta = 0.5$ and $\gamma = 0.2$). The thick lines correspond to stable equilibria for both fidelities, J_1 and J_2, and the thin lines, existing when π_1 is around $\pi_2 = 1$, to unstable equilibria. In the three solutions region, the larger value of J_1 is reached from initial conditions when J_1 is already large. Thus if π_1 is decreased from above one, J_1 is kept large (and J_2 is kept small) even when π_1 becomes less than π_2. The stability of this metastable attractor is lost when $\pi_1 = 0.89$. In a symmetrical manner, the high J_2 attractor existing at low π_1 can be maintained up to $\pi_1 = 1.095$ (the figure was drawn using GRIND software, De Boer 1983).

A consequence of this phenomenon, is that in order to attract customers who are faithful to another shop, a challenger has to offer a profit significantly greater than the profit offered by the well established shop: when preference coefficients have reached equilibrium in the ordered regime, customers switch only for differences in profits corresponding to those where the slopes of the curves $J(\pi)$ in Figure 1 are vertical (i.e. not when profits are equalised!!). In other words, economic rationality (i.e. choosing the shop offering the best deal) is not ensured in the region where hysteresis occurs.

4. Multi-agents simulation results

4.1. Indicators of order

Simulations generate a large number of data about individual transactions such as which shop was visited, purchased quantities, and agents' profits. The organization process itself, involving the dynamics of vectors of buyers J_{ij}'s is harder to monitor. We used two methods to do this.

Firstly, adapting a measure used in (Derrida [1986]) for instance, we defined an order parameter y by

$$y_i = \frac{\sum_j J_{ij}^2}{\left(\sum_j J_{ij}\right)^2} \qquad (16)$$

In the organized regime, when the customer is faithful to only one shop, y_i gets close to 1(all J_{ij} except one being close to zero). On the other hand, when a buyer visits shops with equal probability, y_i is of order $1/n$. More generally, can be interpreted as the inverse number of shops visited. We usually monitor y, the average of y_i over all buyers.

Secondly, when the number of shops is small, 2 or 3, a simplex plot can be used to monitor on line the fidelity of every single buyer. Figures 2a and 3a, for instance, display simplex plots at different steps of a simulation. Each agent is represented by a small circle whose colour or shade is specific to the agent. The circle's position is the barycenter of the triangle for a choice of weights proportional to the fidelity of the agent to the 3 shops each of which corresponds to one of the 3 apexes of the triangle. Proximity to one corner is an indication of fidelity to the shop corresponding to that corner. Agents represented by circles which are close to the center are undecided.

4.2. The simplest model

The simplest model, with fixed price, was run with 3 sellers and 30 buyers, for a large variety of parameter configurations and initial conditions. The following parameter configuration was chosen to give simple time charts for shop performance and to highlight differences in buyers behavior. Price parameters b, c, and p_a where respectively 1, 1, and 0.3, which corresponds to a price of $p = 0.579$ for a purchased quantity per transaction $q = 0.314$ (according to equation 3), a profit per transaction for the buyer $\pi_b = 0.0572$ (equ. 2), a critical non-linear parameter $\beta_c = 5.2$ (equ. 16) and a profit per transaction for the seller $\pi_s = 0.0877$ (equ. 4). Our choice of the memory constant of equation (7) is $\gamma = 0.1$. Initial J_{ij} were all 0.

Depending on the value of the non-linear parameter, the two predicted behaviours are observed.

4.2.1. Disorganized behavior

For low values of the non-linear parameter β buyers never build-up any fidelity. This is observed in Figure 2, which describes the dynamics obtained

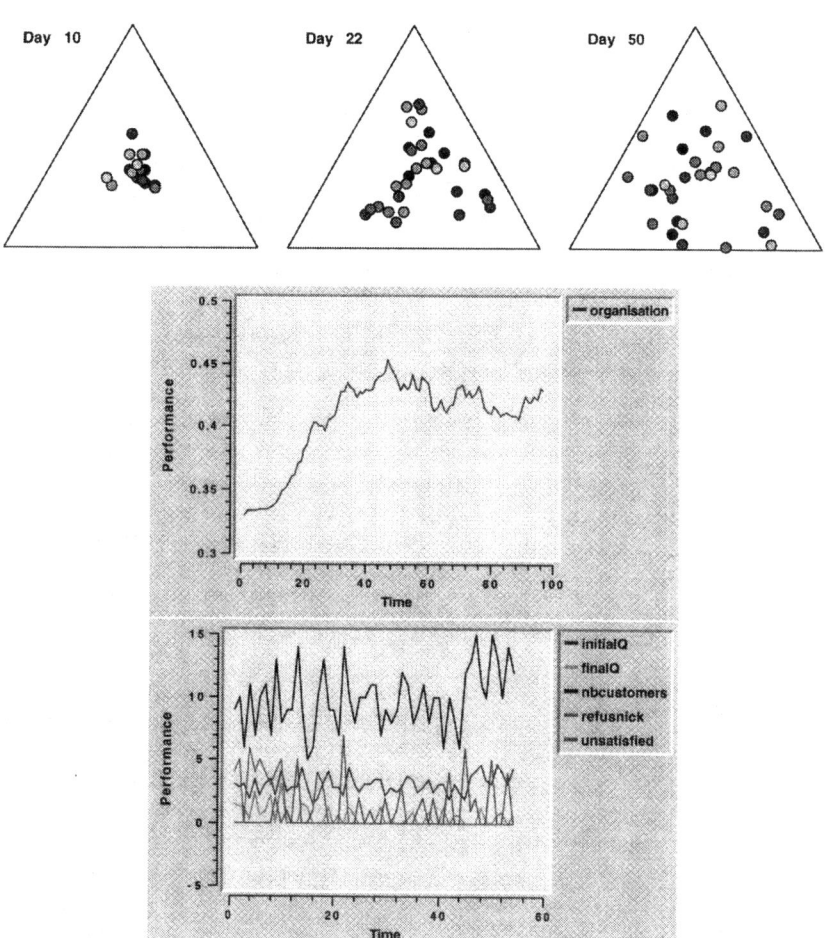

Figure 2: Charts for the disorganized regime (30 agents visiting 3 shops, when the learning parameter $\gamma = 0.1$ and $\beta = 0.15\,\beta_c$). a The organization process is monitored by simplex plots taken at times 10, 22 and 50. Even at time 50, agents are still scattered around the barycenter of the triangle, an indication of a disordered regime without preference of any agent for any of the shops. b Time plot of the order parameter y. c Performance log of morning transactions in shop number 1. The time charts display the initial quantity of goods to be sold every morning, the remaining unsold goods by the end of the morning, the number of customers, of those customers refusing the proposed price (which soon falls to zero for the present choice of a, b and p_a), and of those unsatisfied customers who did not manage to buy anything.

172 | Markets' self-organization

with $\beta = 0.8$. The daily profit of buyers averaged over all buyers and over 100 days after a transition period of 100 days, is 0.0502. This result is lower than the average profit per transaction for the buyer $\pi_b = 0.0572$. This is due to all those occasions on which a buyer visited an empty shop. The daily profit of sellers averaged over all sellers and over 100 days after a transition period of 100 days, is 0.6532. This result is lower than 10 times the average profit per transaction for the seller $\pi_s = 0.877$ (the factor 10 corresponds to the average number of buyers per shop). This difference was also generated indirectly by buyers who visited empty shops since, at the same time, some shops with supplies were not visited, and this resulted in losses for their owner.

The order parameter, y fluctuates well below 0.50 and thus corresponds to randomly distributed J_{ij}. This feature is also clear from the simplex plots of the J_{ij}. Figure 2 shows that the performance of shop number 1 exhibits large fluctuations. The same is true for the two other shops.

4.2.2. Organized behavior

In sharp contrast, the same analysis performed with $\beta = 10$ shows a great deal of organisation (see fig. 3).

The order parameter, y, steadily increases to 1 in 200 time steps. As seen on the simplex plot at time 50, each customer has built-up fidelity to one shop. Performance of shop number one also stabilizes in time, and variations from stationarity are not observed after 20 time steps.

The daily profit of buyers averaged over all buyers and over 100 days after a transition period of 100 days, is 0.0572, exactly the average profit per transaction for the buyer. Because buyers have not changed shops during the last 100 days, sellers learned to purchase the exact exact quantity needed to satisfy all their buyers, and they had no losses themselves: their daily average profit of sellers is 0.877.

By avoiding daily fluctuations in the number of customers visiting a shop, the ordered regime is beneficial to both customers and sellers, that is both obtain higher profits than in the disorganised situation.

4.3. Beyond the mean field approximation

The results of the mean field approach were obtained from a differential equation modeling a discrete time algorithm. They are valid when the changes at each step of the algorithm can be considered as small. Variables y and π thus have to be small, which is true for the simulation results given in Figures 2 and 3. One of the features noticed by observing on-line the motion of individual buyers on the simplex plots is that agents sometimes move "backward" towards shops which are not the shops that they prefer in the ordered regime. But since for most of the time they move towards preferred shops, these "infidelities"

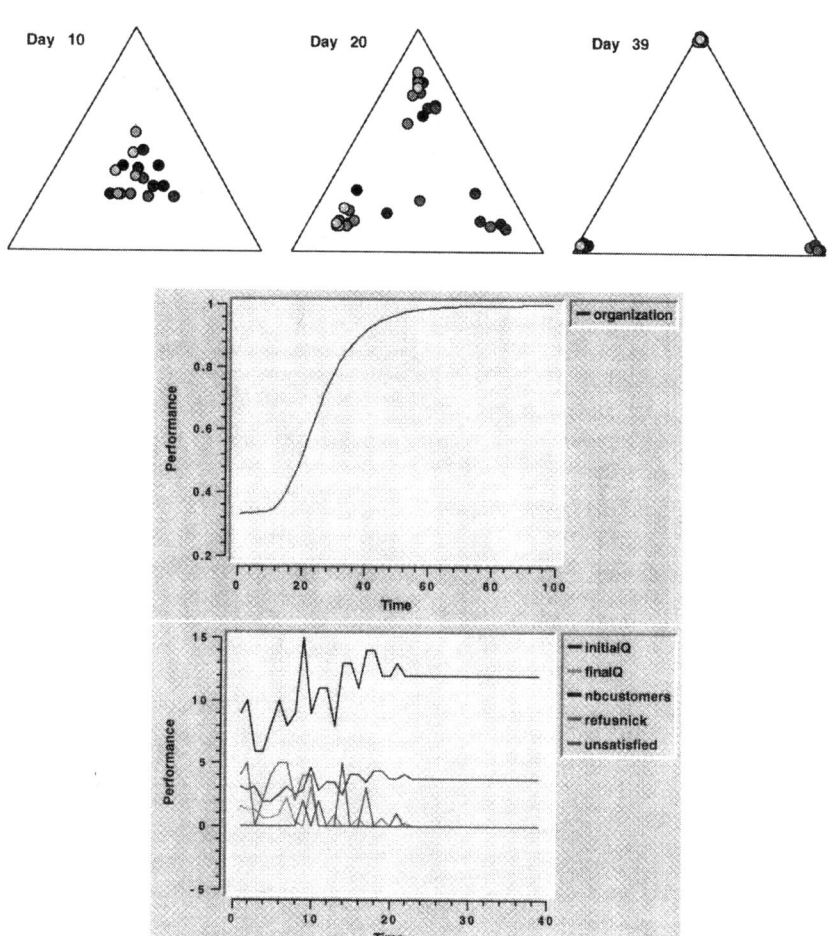

Figure 3: Charts for the organized regime (30 agents visiting 3 shops, when the learning parameter $\gamma = 0.1$ and $\beta \simeq 2\beta_c$). All charts and notation are the same as for Figure 2, except for the scale of the order parameter plot (y). a Starting from all J_{ij} equal to 1, all representative circles move to the triangle corners representing the preferred shops. b y, the order parameter, varies from 0.33 (equal interest for all shops) to nearly 1 (strong preference for only one shop). c Due to organization, fluctuations of performance attenuate in time.

never make them change shops and preferences permanently. They commit "adultery", but do not "divorce".

When variables γ and π are increased, infidelities have more important consequences, and customer might change fidelity: they may "divorce" one shop for another one. Indeed increasing π results in larger steps taken by customers on the simplex, which might make them go from one corner neighborhood to another one in a few time steps. In fact the probability of a given path on the simplex varies as the product of probabilities of individual time steps: when fewer steps are needed the probability that the process will generate such changes becomes higher. Because of the exponential growth of time of the "divorce" process with respect to π, a small change in relevant parameters, π or γ results in a switch from a no-divorce regime to a divorce regime. Divorces are observable on-line on the simplex plots and also by examining the evolution of the number of customers as a function of time.

5. More complicated models and results

We will discuss, in this section, further refinements of the simple model and see what influence they have on the behaviour of the agents. All the variants to be discussed share the same fundamental mechanism by which buyers choose sellers and the same way of updating preference coefficients as defined in section 2.2. The difference comes from the fact that sellers may choose the prices and quantities taking into account the fact that they can make further transactions.

These more realistic variants of the model are no longer analytically tractable and we are therefore obliged to resort to computer simulations to compare their dynamical properties with those of the simple soluble model and with empirical data.

It is important at this stage to specify the type of comparison that we intend to make between the variants of the model and empirical evidence. We certainly expect some changes to occur at the global level when modifications are introduced in the way in which individual agents make their decisions. Nevertheless, the main point here is to check whether the *generic properties* of the dynamics are still preserved after these changes. The existence of two distinct, ordered and disordered regimes, separated by a transition, is for instance such a generic property. On the other hand, we consider as non-generic the values of the parameters at the transition and the values of variables in the ordered or disordered regime. Since even the more elaborate versions of our model are so simplified in comparison with a very complex reality, a direct numerical fit of our model with empirical data would not be very satisfactory. This is because so many parameters which are not directly observable are involved. But the search for genericity is based on the conjecture that the large set of models which share the same generic properties also includes the real system itself. This conjecture, which is basic in the dynamical modeling of complex systems, rests on the notion of classes of universality in physics or of structural stability in mathematics.

5.1. Morning and afternoon

The one-session model described in section 2 is a considerable simplification of the way buyers search for sellers. As is commonly observed in several markets with the sort of structure we are modelling here, customers that refuse a deal with one seller, usually shop around to find other offers. Indeed this is generally regarded as the principle motivation for refusal in standard search models. An alternative explanation is that customers refuse now in order to induce better offers in the future. In either case, to take this into account, we have to consider a model in which customers are given at least two occasions to purchase goods.

One further assumption to relax particularly in the case of perishable goods is the idea of a constant price for all sessions. In fact p is the price sellers would charge at each transaction if they were sure to sell exactly all the quantity they bring to the market. If they were able to predict precisely how many customers would visit their shop and accept this price, they would know exactly how much to supply. But, when their forecasts are not perfect they may not have the appropriate quantity, given the number of possible buyers they actually face at the close of the market. It might therefore, in this case, be better for them to sell at a lower price rather than to keep goods that they are not, by assumption, able to sell the next day. We ran the simulations with a constant afternoon price which is the morning price lowered by a factor $1 - \epsilon$. A more intelligent choice for the sellers would be to monitor previous fluctuations of the number of buyers and to decrease afternoon price in proportion.

To summarise then, we divide the day into two periods:

- During the morning, sellers maximize their profit and sell at a price p_{am} close to p. Buyers visit one shop in the morning.

- During the afternoon they sell at a lower price $p_{pm} = (1 - \epsilon) \cdot p$ which reduces losses from unsold quantities. Buyers visit one shop in the afternoon.

Sellers arrive in the morning with a quantity Q of the good corresponding to the number of customers they expect times q, plus some extra quantity of that good in case they have more customers than expected. The profit they expect from this additional amount is that obtained by satisfying new customers or unexpected former customers who might appear.

Buyers have to decide every morning whether to buy at the morning price or to wait for a better price in the afternoon. Of course waiting has a trade-off: they might not find anything to buy in the afternoon and thus make no profit. They choose an action according to their expectations of the average afternoon profit with respect to what they would get by buying in the morning, which they know from equation 2. Average afternoon profit is estimated from their past history of afternoon profits. We used in the simulations a simple quadratic fit of the afternoon profit as a function of morning prices. But for all reasonable choices of afternoon prices and extra supply by the sellers, expected afternoon profits for buyers are much smaller than morning profits, essentially because their chances of finding goods in the afternoon were smaller than in the morning. We discovered that even with their primitive prediction abilities, buyers soon (say after 50 time steps) realised that they would do better to accept the morning offers. For the present, we have not investigated further the issue of refusals by buyers.

Numerical simulations show that the introduction of a second session does not change the qualitative behaviour of the system: a low β disordered regime and a high β ordered regime still exist with the same characteristics as in the one session model. But the time to eventually reach the ordered regime and the width of the transition are increased. Estimated β_c is 20 percent lower with two sessions than with one.

A change induced by the introduction of an afternoon session is that divorces are observed in the ordered regime for a much wider range of the learning parameter γ, for instance as soon as γ is larger than 0.1. This is because on the occasion of an infidelity, since a buyer has a much better chance of making a higher afternoon profit with a new shop that has extra supplies, she then runs faster across the simplex.

5.2. Quantities brought by the seller

We previously mentionned that the sellers should adjust the quantities brought to the market every morning to take into account the expected number of customers, including eventually fluctuations. In order to optimise the next day's profit, a seller with a perfect knowledge of $f(n_b)$, the probability distribution of the number of visitors, would bring to the market a quantity n'q where n' is given by the following equation:

$$1 - \int_0^{n'} f(n_b) \, dn_b = \frac{p_a}{p} \qquad (17)$$

The above expression is optimal for one day, but does not take into account future gains that could be obtained by systematically bringing extras to make unexpected customers loyal.

Anyway, we did not suppose for the simulations that sellers have a perfect knowledge of the probability distribution of visitors, but that they use a simple routine to add extra whenever they observe fluctuations in the number of visits. The extra at time is computed according to

$$a(t) = (1 - \epsilon) \cdot a(t-1) + \epsilon \cdot \text{var}(n_b) \qquad (18)$$

where ϵ is small and var (n_b) is the variance of the number of buyers computed from the beginning of the simulation. The initial value of a is non zero at the beginning of the simulation. We checked by several numerical simulations with different choices of initial a and of ϵ that the only observable changes were variations of β_c, the critical threshold for order, in the ten percent range. The existence of two dynamical regimes persists.

Another possible refinement would consist in improving the predictive ability of the seller with respect to the number of customers. We tried a moving average prediction rather than the prediction based only on the preceeding day but this only downgraded performance (β_c increases). A multi-agents approach to seller strategy is developed in Vriend 1994.

5.3. Price fluctuations

The idea of a market with a uniform price is not realistic and we wanted to check the influence of price variations on the agents' behavior. In fact, the above section 3.2 on hysteresis already gives us a clue as to the possible results of price changes: price differences resulting in profit differences for the buyer lower than the width of the hysteresis curve do not change fidelity and then should not distroy order. Figure 1 shows that this width in profits is around 20% (and hence 40% in prices) when β is 25% above the theshold for order.

We made simulations with morning price $p(t)$ fluctuating in each shop with an auto-regressive trend towards the morning price computed to maximize profits p. Price is also decreased when potential buyers refuse the offer, a situation seldom encountered by the end of the simulations as mentioned earlier. The morning price of each shop is then varied in the simulations according to the following expression:

$$p(t+1) = \eta(t)\left[p(t) - \lambda(p(t)-p) - \mu\frac{r_n}{n}\right] \quad (19)$$

$\eta(t)$ is a stochastic multiplier with average 1, n and r_n are respectively the number of customers of the shop and the number of customers having refused the previous price during the last session.

The simulation results are remarkably close to the results obtained with constant morning price for both sessions: the transition is sharpened and order is obtained for slightly lower values of β.

6. Empirical Evidence

In order to see whether there was any empirical evidence of ordered or disordered behavior of buyers in a market, we started from a data base of the 237162 transactions that took place on the wholesale fish market in Marseille from 1/2/1988 to 6/29/1991 inclusive. On this market over 700 buyers meet over 40 sellers, to trade different types of fish. The market is organised as in our model, that is, no prices are posted, sellers start with a stock of fish which has to be disposed of rapidly because of its perishable nature. Buyers are either retailers or restaurant owners. Deals are made on a bilateral basis and the market closes at a fixed time. Of course the model is a caricature of the real situation since the alternative for a buyer to purchasing his optimal good is, in fact, to purchase, in his view, some inferior alternative.

The direct examination of the 16 Mb transactions file with the help of standard sorting facilities reveals a lot of organisation in terms of prices and buyers preferences for sellers. In particular, one immediately observes that most frequent buyers, those who visit the market more than once per week, with very few exceptions visit only one seller, while less frequent buyers would visit several sellers, which is consistent with our model. The transactions data will be sumarized in this section in terms that only address the organisation issue. But since they data were collected, Marseilles GREQAM research teams have devoted a lot of effort to classifying and interpreting the data, and especially to investigate the price dynamics which, for instance, show price dispersion, and smaller prices by the end of the selling session (see Kirman and Vignes (1991) and Hardle and Kirman (1995)).

A first step in comparing our theory with empirical data is to check whether individual buyers display ordered or disordered behaviour during those three years. Since the classical approach to agent behaviour predicts search for the best price, and hence what we call the searching behaviour implying visiting different shops, any manifestation of order would tend to support our theoretical prediction. If we find evidence of ordered behaviour for certain participants, a second step is then to relate the difference in the observed behaviours of these traders to some difference between their characteristics and those of other buyers.

For the first step, the existence of faithful buyers, we consider statistics of cod, whiting and sole transactions in 1989. About 23 sellers offer cod, but the quantities that they sell are very different: the three biggest sellers respectively offer 43, 14 and 12% of the fish sold on the market. Since we were interested in fidelity issues we only processed the data concerning the transactions of those 178 buyers that were present for more than 8 months on the market. A striking fact is that 86 of these buyers made a yearly average of more than 95% of their monthly purchase with one seller! In other word, we would say that nearly half of the buyers were very faithful.

In the case of whiting and sole, faithful behaviour was slightly less frequent. For whiting, where the fractions sold by the 3 biggest sellers were 27, 8 and 8%, 55 buyers out of 229 purchased more than 95% of their monthly purchase with one seller, but still 124 sellers purchased above 80% with one seller. The corresponding figures for sole were respectively 15, 14 and 14 for the largest fractions, 91 out of 280 buyers purchased more than 95% of their monthly purchase with one seller, and 154 sellers purchased more than 80% with one seller.

To look at the second step, let us recall that in its crudest version, the theory that we propose relates fidelity to parameters β (discrimination rate) and π/γ (cumulated profit). β, the discrimination parameter probably varies a lot for different buyers, but we have a priori no direct way to test it. On the other hand π/γ is strongly and positively related to the total purchases of buyers, which is empirically measured for all buyers. We used standard statistical tests to check the idea that the population of buyers should exhibit two types of behaviour. We divided the buyers of cod into two groups. We choose as our dividing criterion a total purchase of two tons of cod over 36 monthes. We calculated the fraction of transactions with the most often visited seller and found 0.85 for the big buyers and 0.56 for the small buyers. If we consider, as in the model, that the two populations consist of individuals drawing their "favorite seller" with probability $P1$ in one population and $P2$ in the other one, we can test the hypothesis $P1 = P2$. Given the two values for the tested data set, both the standard Maximum Likelihood test and Fisher's Exact test rejected the hypothesis $P1 = P2$ at all levels of confidence.

7. Conclusions

We have examined a simple model of a market in order to see how the "order" that is observed on many markets for perishable goods develops. "Order" here means the establishment of stable trading relationships over the many periods during which the market is open.

In the simplest model, we have shown analytically that an ordered regime appears whenever the agents discrimination rate among shops divided by the number of shops is larger than the reciprocal of the discounted sum of their profit. When an individual parameters put him into the organized regime, a buyer has strong preferences for one shop over all others. On the other hand, in the disordered regime, agents do not show any preference.

Since individual properties of buyers govern the ratio of their discrimination rate β to the threshold rate $\beta_c = n\gamma/\pi$, a bimodal distribution of buyers, some with an ordered behavior some not, is to be expected in real markets. A comparison with empirical data from Marseille fishmarket indeed shows the existence of a bimodal distribution of searchers and faithful buyers, and the positive correlation of the faithful behavior with the frequency of transactions.

When more realistic assumptions are introduced, such as adaptive behavior of sellers, fluctuations in prices, and later sessions with lower prices to clear the market, simulations show that the critical value of the transition parameter is increased and the transition becomes somewhat less abrupt. However both regimes can still be observed. The simple model is thus robust with respect to changes that can be made to improve realism: its main qualitative property, namely the existence of two regimes of dynamical behavior is maintained.

Stable trading relationships can be interpreted as an institution which is mutually profitable to both kind of partners. In the case described here, memory of previous profits rather than kinship is the basis for the emergence of the institution. In most cases the combined effects of several such mechanisms result in the emergence and stabilisation of social or political organisation.

Acknowledgment

We thank Derek Smith for help with the Tk/Tcl interactive display of simulation results, Rob Deboer for the use of his GRIND software, Paul Pezanis for his help in the analysis of Marseille fishmarket data, Nick Vriend for helpful comments, and Olivier Chenevez, Bernard Derrida, Jean Pierre Nadal and Jean Vannimenus for helpful discussions and important suggestions. The Laboratoire de Physique Statistique of ENS is associated with the CNRS (UA 1306). This work was started during a visit by GW and AK to the Santa Fe Institute which we thank for its hospitality.

REFERENCES

Anderson S.P., A. de Palma and J.F. Thisse (1993), *Discrete Choice Theory of Product Differentiation*, MIT Press, Cambridge MA.

Aoki M. (1995a), "Economic Fluctuations with Interactive Agents: Dynamic and Stochastic Externalities", *The Japanese Economic Review*, Vol. 46, pp. 148-165.

Aoki M. (1995b), "Statistical Description of Market Shares in Emergent Market", Working Paper no. 26, Center for Computable Economics, University of California, Los Angeles, CA.

Aoki M. (1996), *A New Approach to Macroeconomic Modelling*, Cambridge University Press, New York.

Arthur, Brian W. and Lane, David A., (1993), "Information contagion", *Structural Changes and Economic Dynamics,* 4, 81-104.

Benabou R. (1992), "Heterogeneity, Stratification and Growth", mimeo MIT, Cambridge, MASS.

Blume L. (1993), "The statistical mechanics of strategic interaction", *Games and Economic Behaviour*, 5, pp. 387-424.

Blume L. (1995), "Population Games". Mimeo, Dept.of Economics, Cornell University.

Brock W.A. and Durlauf S.N. (1995), "Discrete choices with social interactions I: Theory", Working Paper 95-10-084, Santa Fe Institute, Santa Fe, NM.

Chwe M, (1996), "Structure and strategy in collective action: communication and coordination in social networks", Mimeo, Department of economics, University of Chicago.

De Boer, R.J. (1983), "GRIND: Great Integrator Differential Equations", Bioinformatics Group, University of Utrecht, The Nederlands.

Derrida B. (1986), "Phase transitions in random networks of automata" in *Chance and Matter*, Ed. by Souletie J. Vannimenus J. and Stora R. North-Holland.

Diamond P. (1989), "Search theory", in The New Palgrave: *A Dictionary of Economics*, (J. Eatwell, M. Milgate and P. Newman eds.), Macmillan, London, pp. 273-79.

Durlauf S. (1990), "Locally Interacting Systems, Coordination Failure and the Behaviour of Aggregate Activity", mimeo, Stanford University, Stanford, CA.

Ellison G. (1993), "Learning, Local Interaction and Coordination", *Econometrica*, Vol. 61, pp. 1047-1072.

Erev I. and A. Roth (1995), "On the Need for Low Rationality, Cognitive Game Theory: Reinforcement Learning in Experimental Games with Unique Mixed Strategy Equilibria", Mimeo, Department of Economics, University of Pittsburgh, Pittsburgh, PA.

Follmer H. (1974), "Random economies with many interacting agents", *Journal of Mathematical Economics*, vol. 1, 1, March, pp. 51-62.

Gilles R.P. and P.H.M. Ruys (1989), "Relational constraints in coalition formation", Department of Economics Research Memorandum, FEW 371, Tilburg University.

Hardle W. and A. Kirman, (1995), "Non classical demand: a model-free examination of price-quantity relation in the Marseilles fish market", *Journal of Econometrics*, vol. 67.

Ioannides Y.M. (1990), "Trading uncertainty and market form", *International Economic Review*, vol. 31, 3, August, pp. 619-38.

Kirman Alan P., C. Oddou and S. Weber (1986), "Stochastic communication and coalition formation",Econometrica, vol. 54, January, pp. 129-138.

Kirman Alan P. and A. Vignes, (1991), "Price dispersion. Theoretical considerations and empirical evidence from the Marseilles fish market", in *Issues in contemporary economics*, ed. K.G. Arrow, Macmillan, London.

Kirman, Alan P. and N. Vriend (1995), "Evolving Market Structure: A Model of Price Dispersion and Loyalty" Mimeo, Department of Economics, Virginia Polytechnic Institute and State University, Blacksburg, VA.

Lesourne Jacques (1992), *The Economics of Order and Disorder*, Clarendon Press, Oxford.

Luce R. Duncan (1959), *Individual choice behaviour*, Wesley, New York.

Marimon R. (1995), "Learning from Learning In Economics", Mimeo, European University Institute, Florence, Italy.

Nadal J.-P., Chenevez O. and Weisbuch G. and Kirman A. (1998), "A formal approach to market organization", this volume.

Orlean A. (1995), "Bayesian interactions and collective dynamics of opinions: herd behavior and mimetic contagion", *JEBO*, 28, pp. 257-274.

Stanley E.A., D. Ashlock and L. Tesfatsion (1994), "Iterated prisoner's dilemma with choice and refusal of partners" in Artificial Life III, C.G. Langton (ed.), Santa Fe Institute Studies in the Sciences of Complexity, proc. vol. XVII, Addison-Wesley.

Vriend N. (1994), "Self-organized markets in a decentralized economy", Working Paper 94-03-013, Santa Fe Institute, Santa Fe, NM.

Weisbuch G., Gutowitz H. and Duchateau-Nguyen G. (1994), "Dynamics of economic choices involving pollution", *JEBO*, 29, pp. 389-407.

CHAPITRE 9
RISK AVERSION AND EMERGENCE OF A WHOLESALE MARKET*

Gilbert LAFFOND and Jacques LESOURNE

1. Introduction

Economists have always been interested in the reasons that lead individuals to organise themselves in productive teams. The benefits of such organisations may result from (1) increasing returns (productivity gains resulting from division of labor), (2) comparative advantages (induced by diversified individual skills), (3) large entry cost sharing, (4) risk sharing (the propensity to share the risks in order to diminish the likelihood of bankrupcy)... The role of these factors have mostly been modelized in the framework of game theory, without any reference to the market in which the firm operates.

In this paper, our approach will be different and, sticking to the line of previous research of the team of the "Laboratoire d'Econométrie du CNAM" (Lesourne 1992), we shall study the dynamics of self-organizing markets. In the basic version of our models, producers and sellers meet on a potential market. During a single period, the producers appear successively and randomly on the market, and discover a random set of buyers. A producer sells the production of that period to one of the meeted buyers if an acceptable bilateral agreement is obtained. From one period to another, each agent does modify its claim as a function of his situation at the end of the preeceding period. We have shown that, in the simplest cases, and under some specific assumptions, the market converges towards a situation where (1) all the transaction prices are equal (2) the set of producers and the set of buyers are each partitioned in two subsets: the first one contains active agents (they always make transactions) and the second one passive agents. We observe in this model self-organisation since there is no exogeneous intervention.

If one accepts this conceptual framework, is it possible to observe the birth of firms as a result of the association of producers during the market evolution dynamic process? Two ways have already been explored by the team of the "Laboratoire d'EconomËtrie du CNAM": the first one have considered a model on which workers may operate individually or in a firm and in this case as managers or wage-earners. Assuming that individuals differ in their professional abilities when they operate as craftsmen or managers, but are identical as

---

* The authors would like to thank the Laboratoire Informatique of CNAM for useful help in the simulations.

wage-earners, it was shown that the market progressively determined the roles of the various individuals and the firms which were created.

Alternatively, Laslier and Lesourne (1989) have supposed that on a labor market, the entrepreneur (who acts as a consumer on a good market) may employ zero, one or two workers. The returns may be increasing or decreasing. It is shown that firms may appear, the number and the size of those firms being path dependent. Increasing returns may lock the market in situations that prevent the development of potentially efficient firms.

In this paper, we want to explore a different situation, in which producers have diverse risk aversions and may consider therefore to sell to other producers (or to buy from them) in order to avoid uncertainties (or to increase their probable profit). Hence, in parallel with the retail market, a wholesale market will appear creating links between producers. Under the assumptions which will be described, the retail market will always converge to the same price, while the wholesale market will generate a unique price depending on history.

In a stable state the relations between an individual operating in the retail market and an individual operating on the wholesale market are permanent. Therefore one can consider this process as a process of firm's birth. The price on the wholesale market is in fact a wage paid to the workers by the agents who have emerged as entrepreneurs. But, *in contrast with other situations, this wage is not predetermined.* It is a function of the level of the different risks that agent have really beared during the historical process.

The paper is divided into five sections devoted to the presentation of the general framework, the description of the operations on the two markets, the revision of the consumers'and the producers'requests, the analysis of the results.

2. The general framework

Let us consider an economy on which exist producers and consumers of a commodity which cannot be stocked and the production of which is instantaneous.

A consumer $i(1 \leq i \leq n)$ is characterized by the limit price $\bar{v}_i$ at which he is willing to buy a unit of the commodity and the consumers are ordered in the decreasing order of their limit prices which are supposed to be integers and different.

A producer $k(1 \leq k \leq m)$ is characterized by its production cost $\underline{w}_k$ of one unit of the commodity and the producers are ordered in the increasing order of their production costs which are supposed to be integers and different.

It is assumed that there exists an integer K such that $\bar{v}_K = \underline{w}_K$. Any economist will immediately recognise that this common value is the price that would prevail on a perfect market implying those producers and consumers.

Risk aversion and emergence of a wholesale market | 185

Time t is an integer which denotes instant t and the time interval between instants t and $(t+1)$, i.e. period t. Period t is decomposed into two subperiods:

– during the first subperiod, the market between producers is opened: some producers may buy the production of other producers. However to simplify modeling the following assumption is made:

H1. On the market between producers, a producer can only sell the unit he has himself produced and cannot buy from other producers more than one unit.

– during the second subperiod, the market between consumers and producers is opened. On this market a producer may have to sell 0 unit, 1 unit (his own or the one he has bought in the preceding subperiod) or 2 units. In this last case, he will try to sell at the best possible price the unit bought and, if he can do it profitably, his own production [remember that he produces only if the unit is sold.

On the two markets, the agents have only partial information. Hence, they separate their counterparts into two groups:

– those with whom they have made a transaction during the last period (one or two per agent) and who will be called *internal partners*; in such a case, the agents remember the transaction price(s) and the identity of the buyer(s);

– the other counterparts, who will be called *external partners*; in such a case, the agents only remember the last price they have eventually proposed.

The variables corresponding to internal partners will bear one star and those corresponding to external partners two stars.

Let us now consider the consumers, the producers on the retail market, the producers as sellers on the wholesale market, the producers as buyers on the wholesale market.

N and M will be respectively the set of consumers and the set of producers.

2.1. A consumer $i \in N$

$k_t(i) \in M \cup \{0\}$ is the internal partner of i, i.e. the producer which has sold to i a unit on period $(t-1)$. If i has not bought during that period $k_t(i) = 0$.

$v_t^*(i) \in \mathbb{N}$ is the price proposed by i in period t to his internal partner (if $k_t(i) = 0$ one assumes $(v_t^*(i) = 0)$.

$v_t^{**}(i) \in \mathbb{N}$ is the price proposed by i in period t to an external partner.

Of course:

$$v_t^*(i) \leq \bar{v}_i \quad v_t^{**}(i) \leq \bar{v}_i$$

2.2. A producer $k \in M$ on the retail market

If producer k has one unit to sell, his own, he accepts any offer superior or equal to $\underline{w}_k$. It he has one unit to sell, a unit bought from another producer, he accepts any price. If he has two units to sell, he will try to sell the unit bought at any price then his own at a price superior or equal to $\underline{w}_k$.

2.3. A producer $k \in M$ selling on the wholesale market

$k'_t(k) \in M \cup \{0\}$ is the internal partner of k, i.e. the producer who has bought k's production in period $(t-1)$.

$x^*_k \in \mathbb{N}$ is the price which k accepts from his internal partner in period t.

$x^{**}_k \in \mathbb{N}$ is the price accepted by k from an external partner in period t.

Of course:

$$x^*_t(k) \geq \underline{w}_k \quad x^{**}_t(k) \geq \underline{w}_k$$

2.4. A producer $k \in M$ buying on the wholesale market

$k''_t(k) \in M \cup \{0\}$ is the internal partner of k, i.e. the producer who, in period $(t-1)$ has sold his production to k.

$y^*_t(k) \in \mathbb{N}$ is the price which, in period t, k accepts from his internal partner.

$y^{**}_t(k) \in \mathbb{N}$ is the price which, in period t, k accepts from an external partner.

Two more notations have to be introduced:

– Each producer is characterized by the minimum level of risk he is ready to accept at any time $\underline{b}_k$; in period t, this level is:

$$b_t(k) \geq \underline{b}_k$$

We shall see later the precise meaning of the parameters $b_t(k)$ and $\underline{b}_k$.

– At time t, each producer "estimates" the average level of the transaction prices on the retail market. We denote $\pi_t(k)$ and call k's price index this estimation.

The set of prices accepted or proposed, of risk aversion parameters and of price estimates by producers will be called *a state of the economy*.

3. The operations on the wholesale market

To avoid negotiations between several buyers and several sellers, we introduce the following assumption:

Risk aversion and emergence of a wholesale market | 187

H2. *On the wholesale market, during period t, all the individuals appear on the market once and only once in a random order. When an individual is active on the market, he behaves as a buyer.*

In addition, we suppose:

H3. *A contract between producers is immediately enforced.*

This assumption means that the unit is instantaneously produced by the seller and transfered to the buyer.

Let us consider then the τth individual present on the market at period t. This individual, denoted k_τ, tries to buy a unit from another producer at the smallest possible price. The following assumption describes his search behaviour:

H4. *When a producer appears on the wholesale market, he draws at random a sample of producers (his internal partner being excluded) in such a way that any producer has a positive probability to be drawn.*

The set of producers drawn constitute the external partners of k_τ.

Two cases have to be distinguished:

$$y_t^{**}(k_\tau) = y_t^{*}(k_\tau) \qquad (1)$$

In this case, individual k_τ considers first his internal partner. If his offer is refused, he turns his attention to external partners and select the first (if any) who accepts the offer.

$$y_t^{**}(k_\tau) < y_t^{*}(k_\tau) \qquad (2)$$

In this case, k_τ examines first the external partners and if all refuse, he turns to the internal partner. Otherwise he accepts any of the partners accepting the offer.

4. The operations on the retail market

The functioning of this market is similar. Assumption 2 is replaced by:

H5. *On the retail market, during period t, all the sellers appear on the market once and only once in a random order.*

and assumption 4 by:

H6. *When a seller appears on a retail market, he draws at random a sample (excluding his internal partner(s)) in such a way that any buyer has a positive probability to be drawn.*

188 | Markets' self-organization

The set of buyers drawn constitute the external partners of producer k present on the market.

Then, each partner of k makes an offer: it may be 0 if the consumer has already bought, or the internal offer or the external offer.

Producer k orders all the offers in a decreasing order giving priority to the internal partner when an external partner makes a similar offer.

He sells first at the highest possible price the unit that he has bought (if any) and thereafter his own unit if the best possible price is superior or equal to $\underline{w}_k$.

In addition, he registers the maximum offer he has received.

5. The revisions of consumers' requests

At the end of period t, consumer i modifies $v_t^*(i)$, $v_t^{**}(i)$ and $k_t(i)$. Two cases are possible:

− the consumer has not bought anything during period t. He has no longer an internal partner:

$k_{t+1}(i) = 0$ and, without any loss of generality: $v_{t+1}^*(i) = 0$. The consumer increases if possible his offer to external partners:

$$v_{t+1}^{**}(i) = \min\{\bar{v}(i), v_t^{**}(i) + 1\}$$

− The consumer has bought a unit during period t at price $v_t(i)$ from seller $k_t^s(i)$. In this case:

$$k_{t+1}(i) = k_t^s(i)$$
$$v_{t+1}^*(i) = v_t(i)$$

Simultaneously, the buyer tries to get a better offer from a future external partner:

$$v_{t+1}^{**}(i) = v_t(i) - 1$$

6. The revision of producers' requests

Since the producers operate on two markets, they may experience during period t a lot of different situations. To describe their behaviour as simply as possible we shall start from the market between consumers and producers.

6.1. Retail market

In this model, the behaviour of the producers on the retail market is similar from one period to the next. Therefore, no revision of requests has to be considered.

6.2. Wholesale market

We shall proceed in two steps, first excluding the existence of risk aversion and then introducing it.

Let us stard without introducing risk aversion. In period t, producer k may have sold, bought or done nothing. If he has sold, his buyer becomes his internal partner and the price of the transaction $x_t(k)$ his new request. Therefore:

$$x^*_{t+1}(k) = x_t(k)$$

Simultaneously, as a seller, he will try to get a better price from his external partners:

$$x^{**}_{t+1}(k) = x_t(k) + 1$$

If he has not found a buyer, he has no longer an internal partner and he will try to get from external partners:

$$x^{**}_{t+1}(k) = \max \{x^{**}_t(k) - 1, \underline{w}_k\}$$

If k has bought, his seller becomes his internal partner and the price of the transaction $y_t(k)$ his new request. Therefore:

$$y^*_{t+1}(k) = y_t(k) \quad (1)$$

Simultaneously, as a buyer, he will try to get from external partners a reduced price:

$$y^{**}_{t+1}(k) = y_t(k) - 1 \quad (2)$$

If he has not found a seller, he has no longer an internal partner and he will accept to pay a higher price to external partners:

$$y^{**}_{t+1}(k) = y_t(k) + 1 \quad (3)$$

Let us now introduce risk aversion. During period t, producer k may have taken a risk in buying a unit from a colleague and in selling it on the retail market. As a conséquence he may have made a profit or a loss. This should normally have an influence on the level of risks he is willing to take in the next period. Here come into play, the parameters $b_k(t)$ and $\underline{b}_k$, the introduction of which has already been mentioned.

In case of a profit, producer k decreases his risk aversion coefficient:

$$b_{t+1}(k) = \max\{b_t(k) - 1, \underline{b}_k\}$$

In case of a loss, he increases this coefficient:

$$b_{t+1}(k) = b_t(k) + 1$$

But to take a decision, producer k has also to estimate the price at which he may expect to sell a unit he has bought. For that purposes he will use his price index $\pi_t(k)$.

The evolution of this price index is assumed to be the following:

– k has not received an offer from any consumer:

$$\pi_{t+1}(k) = \pi_t(k)$$

– The highest offer received from a consumer is lower than $\pi_t(k)$:

$$\pi_{t+1}(k) = \pi_t(k) - 1$$

– The highest offer received from a consumer is higher than $\pi_t(k)$:

$$\pi_{t+1}(k) = \pi_t(k) + 1$$

Then, when he considers to buy a unit from a colleague, producer k expects that he will be able to sell on the retail market at $\pi_{t+1}(k)$, but to take into account the risk, he considers necessary to have a margin equal to the risk aversion coefficient. Therefore:

$$y^*_{t+1}(k) = \min\{y_t(k), \pi_{t+1}(k) - b_{t+1}(k)\}$$

this expression replacing (1). As for the new request from external partners, it is given by:

$$y^{**}_{t+1}(k) = \min\{y^{**}_t(k), \pi_{t+1}(k) - b_{t+1}(k)\}$$

$y^{**}_t(k)$ being defined by (2) or (3).

Finally, as a seller on the wholesale market, producer k may be afraid of selling it at too low a price. Therefore, to define his new requests he adds a new lower bound equal to:

$$\pi_{t+1}(k) - b_{t+1}(k) + b'_k$$

For simplicity, b'_k is assumed to be a personal and constant coefficient.

This completes the description of the model.

One of the major feature of this model, is, at evidence, that individuals do have different behaviours under risk. These differences are twofolds: the invariant individual parameters (**bk and b'k**) and the timing of losses and gains encountered by individuals.

7. The results

We shall successively present theoretical results, simulations and comments on the lessons of this model.

7.1. Theoretical results

If we define a stable state as a state of the economy in which no agent is able to find a move he is willing to make, the following theorem may be proved:

Theorem: In a stable state, a unique price equal to $\underline{w}_K$ prevails on the retail market.

The proof is a variant of similar proofs on models without wholesale trade. As is usual in such models, a unique price p means a price in the bracket $[p-1, p+1]$.

The second theoretical result is a conjecture confirmed by many simulations.

7.2. Conjecture

The model converges in probability, as t increases, towards a stable state such that:

– price $\underline{w}_K$ prevails on the retail market,

– a unique price inferior to $\underline{w}_K$ prevails on the wholesale market, but this price depends on history.

In the final stable state, the consumers buying on the retail market are always the first K ones (for which $\bar{v}(i) \geq \underline{w}_K$). On the contrary, from an history to

192 | Markets' self-organization

another, the producers selling on the retail market differ. They may not belong to the subset of producers for which $\underline{w}_k \leq \underline{w}_K$.

Simulations will help us to better understand this result.

7.3. Simulations

Among many simulations made, with the same M, N, $\bar{v}'_i$s, w'_ks, $\underline{b}'_k$s, $b'_k s' \pi_0(k)'s$, ... i.e. with the same sets of consumers and producers and the same constant parameters and the same initial state of the economy, we shall present two.

In the stable state, the price on the retail market is 3000 and the number of consumers buying (for whom $(\bar{v}(i) \geq 3\,000)$ equal to 24.

In simulation 1, the price prevailing on the wholesale market in the stable state is 2792. Six producers buy on this market. Among them, 5 for whom $\underline{w}_k \leq \underline{w}_K$ (they will be called efficient) and one for whom $\underline{w}_k > \underline{w}_K$.

On the retail market, the 24 transactions may be decomposed in the following way:

– 18 imply efficient producers who sell the unit they produce and are not active on the wholesale market,

– 5 imply efficient producers who sell two units, one being bought on the wholesale market,

– 1 implies an inefficient producer who produces nothing and sells a unit he has bought on the wholesale market.

In simulation 2, the price prevailing on the wholesale market in the stable state is 2883. 12 producers (inefficient) buy on this market.

On the retail market the 24 transactions are decomposed in this way:

– 12 imply efficient producers selling the unit they produce,

– 12 imply inefficient producers selling a unit bought on the wholesale market.

7.4. Lessons from the model

What does this model tell us? That efficient producers who have a high risk aversion prefer to sell immediately at an intermediary rather than to wait and possibly, get a better price on the retail market. Such producers are not determined from the start since their risk aversion may be the consequence of random bad experiences during the first phases of the operation of the wholesale market. Simultaneously, other producers, efficient or not, may discover that they take a "reasonable risk" in buying from colleagues. For inefficient producers, that may be the cause of the "comparative advantage" which enables them to be present on the retail market.

Under these conditions, two types of firms will emerge. The first one correspond to the team "maitre-compagnon". The "maitre" always orders work from the "compagnon". He bears the risk of gain or loss when trying to sell this production. The "maitre" can decide to sell his own production if he finds an interesting buyer. The second type of firm is constituted by a "seller-worker" team. The seller is inefficient as a producer, but exploits his propensity to bear high risk levels.

Furthermore, the path dependency is not the same on the two markets.

While history has no impact on the final state of the retail market (as far as the consumers are concerned), it may modify deeply the final situation on the wholesale market (number of units sold and price prevailing).

In other words, the wages of "compagnon" or workers depend on history, but the retail price is predetermined. The paradoxical feature is obvious: Even if the risk plays a major role in the market evolution, there is no risk anymore in the final stable state. Then the question is: Why don't "compagnons" or workers leave the firms and enter the retail market? In this case, they break the market stability and allow for a new dynamics. To prevent this risk, "maitre" and sellers can seek to obtain the exclusive right of selling in the retail market. They can also sign contracts with "compagnon" and workers or offer them loans which they will have difficulties to reimburse. Such customs have frequently been observed during the preindustrial period.

REFERENCES

Laffond, G. (1989), "La révélation de la qualité par les prix sur un marché en auto-organisation", *Economie Appliquée*.

Laffond, G. and Lesourne, J. (1981), "Market dynamics and search processes with information costs", *Communication to the European Meeting of the Econometric Society*, Amsterdam.

Laffond, G. and Lesourne, J. (1985), « Un exemple d'auto-organisation : la création de capacités professionnelles par le marché du travail », *Economie Appliquée*.

Laslier, J.F. and Lesourne, J. (1989), « Rendements croissants et dynamique d'un marché », *Economie Appliquée*.

Lesourne, J. (1992), "The economics of order and disorder", Clarendon Press Oxford.

PART 3

Dynamics of Technological Systems

CHAPTER 10
SURVIVAL AND EXIT IN MARKETS: ASSESSING THE RESPECTIVE ROLE OF SUPPLY AND DEMAND EFFECTS

Emmanuelle FAUCHART

Identifying the dynamics of firm populations is a crucial issue for understanding the process through which some firms survive and grow while some others decline and exit.

An immediate explanation which comes to mind is that firms which are able to survive are those which are the more efficient in providing good products and services at a reasonable price to customers. In fact, this very immediate explanation is consistent with most theoretical approaches of economic survival.

In the famous debate which took place in the fifties about the theoretical status of "natural selection" in economics, divergences came out on whether the surviving firms were adopting the right behaviour by chance (A. Alchian, 1950) or rather as a result of some maximizing attitude (E. Penrose, 1952). The fundamental stake in this debate was to decide whether "natural selection" was a relevant mechanism for capturing the process driving to survival and exit respectively if survival resulted from the selection among existing behaviours of the most efficient ones, then market dynamics was well described as deriving from the operation of a function independent from the behaviour of the firms themselves. The idea of natural selection as used in Biology was then preserved. But if survival was attributed to deliberate actions of firms, willing to build and manipulate their economic environment, then the idea of natural selection was useless, Penrose concluded.

We know that M. Friedman (1953) tried to synthesize the divergent arguments by assessing that in any case the surviving firms could only be the one who were maximizing, no matter if they were conscious of it or not. The intuition that selection as a *collective function* had to do with market dynamics was thus eliminated.

It was only thirty years later with the seminal book by R. Nelson and S. Winter (1982) that the idea came back in the foreground. Nelson and Winter propose that firms are selected according to their differential competitiveness. Differential competitiveness translates into variations in market shares. Firms can react to their economic results by innovating.

This framework uses the intuition of Alchian that *relative* performance rather than maximization explains survival or exit. But Nelson and Winter have made the major step of providing a modelling of the dynamics of firm populations, showing how interactions drive to aggregate structures in terms of market shares, productivity level or else wage levels. Microfoundations are organized on the basis of a selection function which operates according to some criteria (like relative prices for instance). In other words, selection orients the market dynamics, but firms have their own strategies and react to the results of selection.

In fact the most immediate explanation for market dynamics may prove only one type in a set of possible dynamics. Two series of arguments have driven us to think of market dynamics in different terms.

First, some economists have recently suggested that the way customers make their choices may possess specific properties under some conditions. More specifically, the process of adoption may exhibit increasing returns because positive feedbacks are associated to some crucial variables which influence the choice (Arthur *et al.*, 1983; P. David, 1985). In this context, some specific choices are able to durably orient the adoption process and then firms may be powerless at some point in managing their position in their market.

Second, most sectors are concerned with activities in which the production of physical entities and the supplying of services are indissociable. But industrial and service activities respectively have different market properties in terms of both interactions between producers and customers and production processing. For instance, the production of physical entities is concerned with economies of scale and minimization of unit costs. On the other side, service activities have some specific properties in terms of proximity between providers and customers. We can notice that this form of interaction may well be changing in the recent period: while spatial proximity is crucial in most service activities, new information technologies allow for substituting software interfaces to personal connections between providers and customers.

Then the coexistence of such different and evolving properties make market dynamics more complex to grasp and in any case non reducible to an *industrial* dynamics only. Whether this situation is recent or historically verified is hard to strongly assess. But if we extend the analysis of most industries to their complementary products and services, we immediately realize that *first*, they have always existed and *second* that they may have historically played a role that has been neglected by most studies focused on industrial dynamics.

These two arguments drive to two conclusions. *First*, the theoretical framework for analyzing market dynamics should not be exclusively adapted to the production of physical entities, in other words to industrial activities as differenciated from service activities. And *second*, the differential strategies and abilities of firms in supplying the market should not be considered as the exclusive engine able to define and reorient the trajectory followed by a market dynamics. The demand side of any market may acquire an active role in many circumstances – that we will identify more precisely further on – each time the collective process of customer choices is able to modify the utility and performances of the competing goods and services for other customers. In this context, the demand side of market interactions does not only consist in selecting among competing products on the basis of some criteria (relative prices, relative quality etc.) but is also able to orient and modify the trajectory followed by the market dynamics.

In order to suggest a generic framework able to take these elements into account, we propose to come back to the crucial moment *when* the ability of firms to survive is "evaluated", that is to say to the ***interaction between supply and demand***. Interactions give rise to ***logics of selection***, which depend upon the way the evaluation of the respective products or services is generated. This evaluation of the differential competitiveness of the products or services offered by firms can follow *either* a logic based upon the differential abilities and strategies of firms in providing good and innovative products and services *or/and* a logic based upon the interdependence of customer choices in valuing the utility and performance of the competing options. These two logics of selection introduce two types of market dynamics: a ***supply-oriented dynamics***, where the supply side continuously gives the impulsion to the dynamics in terms of differential attributes (price, quality, security, reliability etc..) and introduction of novelty (innovations) which customers then evaluate. And a ***demand-oriented dynamics*** where the process of choice by customers possesses some specific properties in terms of interdependence, which makes evaluation an evolving function. Yet in most cases, market evolutions are rather fuelled by a mixed dynamics which possesses aspects of both a supply-oriented and a demand-oriented dynamics. We will discuss the conditions under which one or another dynamics is likely to take place. Each sector is not strictly associated to one dynamics all over its life span. In fact different types of dynamics may take place over time in a same activity.

We think that such an approach of population dynamics is important for understanding some current issues about evolutions in, for instance, network industries under deregulation, or sectors which experience discontinuities such as some areas of the computer industry in the recent period. Then this framework may prove useful for considering public policies in modern economies.

1. A supply-oriented dynamics

1.1. Differential abilities, innovation and survival

An industry is fuelled by a supply-oriented dynamics when the capacity of a firm to capture the demand is solely due to her differential efforts and ability and when the competing products remain substitute all along. This means that even if the path followed by each firm exhibits some *micro path-dependence* –

implying a reinforcing mechanism in the internal dynamics – this does not alter the fundamental substitutability of the different products. Some products become more competitive than their competitors because the increasing number of units produced makes possible both economies of scale and learning by doing driving to higher quality and reliability. And this increased attractiveness translates into increases in market shares. But an innovation can allow a firm to catch up in terms of market share if this innovation gives an advantage valued by customers. In other words, innovating is a viable strategy all along, even if it is likely that some firms won't be able to be competitive at all and some others won't be able to sustain their advantages.

These characteristics are likely to concern products which don't imply any sunk cost for customers and which are regularly replaced or renewed. This is for instance the case of most consumption goods.

Thus the respective trajectories of differential competitiveness can be perturbated by innovations introduced by a competitor or by the entry of new firms challenging the incumbents. Yet empirical analysis show that the firms which are already the most competitive are likely to devote resources to R & D or other learning activities and then to innovate and reinforce their initial advantage. In fact this may depend on the technological regime (S. Winter, 1984; F. Malerba & L. Orsenigo, 1994), and more particularly on the degree of cumulativeness of technological knowledge. According to Malerba and Orsenigo, in a Schumpeter Mark I regime, innovations generally come from new entrants because they consist in disruption in the knowledge base whereas in a Schumpeter Mark II regime, innovations are more likely initiated by incumbents because they rely on a cumulative knowledge base. In the first case, the demography of firms is narrowly associated to the rate of innovations. Whereas in the second case, market shares vary more as a result of shifts in differential competitiveness of incumbents rather than as a result of entries and exits.

This type of dynamics is far the more familiar to economic analysis. The textile industry and most consumption goods industries can certainly be considered as archetypes of a supply-oriented dynamics. Firms gain and loose market shares as a result of their relative ability to capture the demand through time. These industries are particularly competitive because firms compete harshly and consumers have strong requirements in terms of quality and price. Loyalty to brand names can be high in some niches but potential and effective competitors are fierce challengers. In both kinds of industries some firms are able to benefit from some micro path dependence in building market shares. For instance, firms making profits can invest funds in promoting their brand. Then they gain some new customers and provoke loyalty among users. Incremental innovations are generally important and frequent in these markets.

1.2. Substitutability and micro path-dependence

A supply-oriented dynamics applies when the impulsion of the dynamics at each moment results from the differential ability and efforts of the respective firms. Competitiveness is affected by efficiency in production, quality management, innovation and organization. Each buyer chooses a product according to his/her criteria. As preferences and revenues differ, several products may be viable. As competitiveness varies and evolves differently for each firm, as innovations arise, as new firms enter, firms experience some particular trajectories either allowing for durable survival or driven to failure.

Thus the dynamics relies on two principles:

– An *evaluation* based upon the respective abilities of the firms in providing products and services, as valued by customers.

– A *micro path-dependence* due to economies of scale, learning by doing and reinvestment of profits. The degree of micro path-dependence attached to firms in an industry depends in a large part on the technological regime (degree of cumulativeness of technological knowledge and then degree of cumulativeness of learning and ability to take advantage of previous productive and marketing experiences). Yet the long term impact of some micro path-dependence mainly depends on the behaviour of the firm in reinvesting her profits for consolidating her advantages and for promoting long term growth.

Some formal representations of this type of dynamics are provided by models following the basic models proposed by R. Nelson and S. Winter (1982). In those models, micro interactions make possible the emergence of some aggregate structures. A selection function screens the differential competitiveness of the products according to some criteria valued by customers (price and/or quality etc.) and translates them into variations in respective market shares. A central dimension of this dynamics is that there exists a relationship between the scope of diversity in performances and the scope and speed of changes in the characteristics of the population of firms (Nelson and Winter, 1982, S. Metcalfe, 1995). Those models are based on a Replicator equation which defines selection in terms of comparison of individual performances with the average performance.

Market dynamics follow a Markov process: "what the industry condition of a particular period really determines is the probability distribution of its conditions in the following period. If we add the important proviso that the condition of the industry in periods prior to period t has no influence on the transition probabilities between t and $t + 1$ we have assumed precisely that the variation over time of the industry's condition state is a Markov process" (Nelson and Winter, 1982, p. 19). This process is based on Simple Markov Chains in the sense that transition probabilities (summarized in a transition matrix to which the market state in terms of distribution of market shares is multiplied at each period of time) from a state of the market to the next one are fixed.

This representation of market dynamics is tested with simulation methods which allow for incorporating a multiplicity of behaviours in the model as well

202 | Dynamics of technological systems

as stochastic processes of entry and innovation. We shall give a few examples. Silverberg, Dosi and Orsenigo (1988) show that the timing in adopting a new production technology is likely to imply different trajectories in terms of relative performance. Depending on whether there are some learning externalities between firms or not, it is better to adopt the new technology either late or early as compared to competitors. Dosi *et al.* (1995) show what are the trajectories followed by new entrants and incumbents respectively in different technological regimes. In a Schumpeter I regime where technological and learning opportunities are high for new entrants compared to what they are for incumbents, the market dynamics is fuelled by the entry of new firms which renew the set of products offered to customers. On the opposite, in a Schumpeter II regime, opportunities are much higher for incumbents than for potential entrants. Then the market dynamics is fuelled by the differential abilities of incumbent firms and by their innovative capacities and their involvement in R & D.

2. A demand-oriented dynamics

2.1. Ex ante uncertainties, sunk costs and externalities

An industry is fuelled by a demand-oriented dynamics when the utility or quality of the competing products emerge endogenously as a consequence of the adoption process. Thus there is some *uncertainty ex ante* concerning the utility or quality of the respective products. This uncertainty takes place in a context where buying implies some sunk costs (in the form of irreversible tangible and intangible investments).

The reduction of uncertainty is associated with the fact that some *externalities* become effective. In that context, the utility of a product increases with the exploitation of *network externalities*. And the quality of a product increases with *learning externalities*.

Network externalities exist when the utility of a product depends on the number of agents using it. If this utility increases as the number of users rises, it is better to buy the product that most people have already chosen. Those who have bought a product of which the producer will disappear in the end could become "angry orphans", if the cost of changing is too high.

Learning externalities arise when the technological characteristics and performances of the competing products are not stable when launched. They evolve with the adoption process. As some users feed back the innovation and learning processes of the producers with their remarks, specific requirements and technical problems, the products tend to converge towards a more stable set of characteristics and performances. Thus flaws and information asymmetries decrease. These learning externalities clearly differentiate from the learning by doing which is concomitant with economies of scale. Externalities are arising from interactions and may be qualified as "learning by using".

These situations are far from marginal.

Network externalities especially arise when technological systems are involved. Technological systems consist in complementary products or services which are used together and which must then be compatible. For instance, computers work with disks or CD Rom. Also they can be bought into components and assembled. VCR work with tapes. And people like to rent pre-enregistered tapes to watch movies at home. With these two examples we immediately see that network externalities raise the issue of the *compatibility* between the different pieces of the system. In the VCR example, the kind of tape format that their closer renting shop is offering is then of crucial importance in influencing the format that people will buy. In fact, after a certain point, the information on the global market is also of importance in the sense that anticipations about the future are part of the decision function. If there is only one shop in the country which rents a specific format of pre-enregistered tapes, this won't be enough for people living close to it to buy this type of format. They may prefer to buy the format that most people have in the country rather than the format that their local environment provides. In fact, the case of the battle between VHS and Betamax in the VCR industry has shown how important are the strategies of firms in terms of gathering relevant partners for providing compatible complementary products and services.

In the computer example, the case is as straightforward. The decision to buy a Apple Macintosh or a PC embeds as much anticipation as consideration of the current situation. What one's close environment (family, friends, work, university...) already possesses in majority is very important but what the global market seems to indicate also implies some anticipation of what the future will be, including for this local environment – which may switch when the product has to be renewed. In other words, increasing returns can either be global or local.

Learning externalities are especially significant when new technologies are introduced. At the beginning, any new technology is likely to be pretty different from what it will become once the learning process has taken place (N. Rosenberg, 1982). Imperfections and flaws are numerous, the characteristics and performances are evolving, the scope of uses is not well defined. Only adoption can lead to the revelation of well defined set of characteristics and performances. Here we could call the entire history of technologies for examples. Once the adoption process has started, huge markets emerge for producers of those technologies. And also fierce battles for gain and, ultimately, survival. In fact, firms offering those new technologies may have to fight as much against producers of old technologies as with new competitors (N. Rosenberg, 1972). Those who soon benefit from learning externalities will be able to lock-in the market because customers will more benefit from buying a better known technology, which performances and potential are revealed and which price is likely to be lower as a result of economies of scale.

2.2. Interdependent demand and macro path-dependence

A demand-oriented dynamics applies when the probability to buy a product rather than another is influenced by the *collective* structure of adoption, that is to say by what the others are buying. Thus the dynamics relies on two principles:

– an evaluation based upon an *interdependence* between choices made by customers;

– a *macro path-dependence* associated with the emergence of collective effects affecting the process of choice.

The interdependence between choices comes from the existence of some externalities. At some point these externalities tend to reinforce the trend followed by the structure of adoption probabilities. In other words, the product which has been the most chosen until then tends to have an increasing probability of being further chosen. Then the process is called non-ergodic and the *collective* system of adoption is path-dependent.

Positive externalities tend to benefit to a small number of products which are then able to lock the market. Under some specific conditions, one out of the set of products may be able to corner the market. One famous example is the victory of VHS as a standard for VCR in its battle with Betamax. One explanation is that the impact of externalities is self-reinforcing. This property derives from the fact that externalities take place through some formal connections. Thus the density of connections (the size of the network of potential users) and the receptivity of producers to informations sent by users (interactive learning) are positively correlated to the level of externalities. And then to the ability to lock-in the market.

This dynamics may drive to a more or less diversified structure of adoptions. In other words, it can allow for the survival of only one product out of the set of competing options or rather to the survival of several of them. This may happen if the collective process of adoption possesses some specific properties in terms of either preferences expressed in the sequence of adoption (B. Arthur *et al.*, 1987) or connections between users (P. David & D. Foray, 1993, Dalle, 1996). In that respect the demand side of interactions between demand and supply acquires a crucial role in a context where the relative performance of the respective products depends either on the *sequence of adoptions* or on the *structure of connections* between buyers. In the first case, the heterogeneity in preferences and the structure of adoption consist in a global information available for each new adopter. In the second case, customers are more sensible to their local environment and then the information that they care for is a local one rather than an information on the global structure of adoption. When the relevant information is local, the user is influenced by its network of connections, that is to say by the spatial structure he is embedded in. Spatial proximity can be as much social as geographical.

Both the characteristics of the sequence of adoptions and/or of the structure of connections explain that several producers in a market may be economically viable or rather that only one firm may be able to survive. The emergent structure is also very dependent on the nature of the increasing returns of adoption. If they are limited, a diversified structure is likely to emerge whereas if they are unlimited, the structure is likely to be uniform, provided that adopters with different preferences don't make their own choice in a regular interval of time – in which case each option will develop in parallel and will durably conquer a part of the market- and provided that potential users are sufficiently connected together for a dominant choice to propagate – or percolate – across the network. These results are summarized in table 1.

Table 1

	emergent structure	
nature of returns	*uniformity*	*diversity*
unlimited or limited	unlimited	limited
global *or* **local**	the different types of adopters arrive irregularly and alternance is not frequent	the different types of adopters arrive regularly and alternance is frequent
	probability of percolation > s^*	probability of percolation < s^*

The sunk costs associated with adoption explain that the agent has to assume his/her choice, at least for a certain period of time. In fact the market dynamics is likely to differ if choices are made once for all or if they can be revised. In the first case, the *stable proportions* towards which the probability of adopting each product converges is the interesting result. And the number of adopters of each product at one time does not reflect the current probabilities of adoption but the history of the system. In the second case, the relevant result is provided by the *final structure of adoptions* since transition probabilities are instrumental as compared with the final structure towards which they are driving the process. Thanks to choice revisions, this structure is likely to be progressively relieved from former choices. These results are summarized in table 2.

The empirical literature suggests that a significant number of situations consist in agents revising their choice time to time rather than in agents making just one choice. In this context, local connections between agents are recognized as influencing choices. The case of computers is probably a good one.

Table 2

	spatial structure		
	yes	*no*	
finite population	Markov random fields David & Foray (1993) Gibbs fields Dalle (1996)	pure percolation	**revocable choice**
infinite population	New developments in Polya Urns Dosi & Kaniovsky (1993)	Polya Urns Arthur, Ermoliev & Kaniovski (1987)	**non revocable choice**

One may be more sensible to the choices made in his/her local environment (friends, work...) than to the structure of the global market. This attitude may as well result in a uniform structure of adoption as in the survival of several products. In fact the notion of local environment may be fuzzy in most cases. If connectivity and receptivity are high, a unique choice may percolate through the entire network.

The different types of models we have referred to above drive to divergent kinds of convergence. Arthur *et al.* (1987) shows that with Polya urns, the system converges with probability one towards stable proportions. If there are two products, the market may lock in into one of the product or may rather split equally. David & Foray (1993) show convergence towards complete uniformity with probability equals to one (thanks to revocable choices, everybody ends up adopting the same option). Dalle (1996) shows that the presence of some deviant attitudes (each choice is not totally dependent upon the choices of connected neighbours) is likely to maintain some diversity in uses. Kirman (1992) challenges the tendency to describe convergence towards stable shares (either uniformity or diversity). He proposes some way to represent convergence towards unstable shares. Yet, for products implying some sunk costs, changes can theoretically be credible only if they imply some durability afterwards. In other words, they should not be frequent. Then, if unstability is to take place it is likely to be due to regular waves of new adopters. But each wave of identical choices must not be able to drive the system towards lock-in. Clear conditions remain to be established. They are a good introduction to the third type of dynamics that we want to describe.

3. A mixed dynamics

In fact, in many cases, specific aspects of each of the two former dynamics are likely to co-exist. In these cases the following characteristics are significant:

– Differential abilities and efforts (investments, innovations) of firms continuously matter.

– There are some externalities which affect individual choices but they don't drive to durable lock-in effects.

These aspects may qualify situations where:

1. *despite of the presence of externalities, substitution between competing products is preserved or regularly regenerated.* This may happen in two cases. First, there exists a gateway or a compatibility standard which makes possible the connection between competing products. For instance, the recent strategy of Apple of making its Macintosh computers able to read PC files is changing the nature of the market dynamics. A competition based on differential prices, quality and characteristics in a context where network and learning externalities remain important is substituting for a competition between exclusive standards.

Second, there are some opportunities for offering substantially superior products, which superiority is able to compensate for the effect of externalities. For instance, in the computer industry, the firm AMD may be able to challenge the total lock-in that have benefited to Intel until now thanks to network externalities and huge economies of scale. The strategy of AMD is to make its chips compatible to former generations of Pentium. Its chip K6 is considered by certain observers as much more competitive than the new generation of Pentium. But will it be able to gain some market shares?

2. *Despite of differential abilities of firms as a fuel for market dynamics, there is a certain degree of interdependence between choices* thus creating some externalities. In this case, some networks are likely to compete. For instance, in the Airline industry, network externalities imply that the most successful companies possess the highest number of lines and as a consequence are able to attract the highest number of customers. In this case, profitability allows to enlarge the network of connections offered to customers. Yet some smaller companies survive and are profitable in some niches. They offer things that the big companies are not providing. For instance, they serve small lines which do not depart nor arrive to any big hub or they propose cheap prices.

As these qualifications suggest, many situations in industrial and service activities are likely to be characterized by a mixed dynamics. We shall now turn to a few examples.

The computer industry is as suggested a good example of the first situation. Despite of the presence of both learning and network externalities, fierce competition is going on. The industry is differentiated because there is a high degree of heterogeneity in customer preferences due to different needs and requirements. According to Bresnahan, Stern and Trajtenberg (1996), the computer industry can be clustered along two dimensions: "brand name" and "technological frontier". In fact we can roughly associate these two dimensions with two types of externalities. A brand name is associated with some network externalities consisting in the providing of good complementary products and services whereas being positioned at the technological frontier is associated with learning externalities along the adoption process. Clusters differ in terms of the respective influence of both brand name and technological frontier. Thus, different clusters differentiate the influence of differential abilities and externalities respectively. In one cluster, brand name producers compete on reputation. In another one, clone producers compete on differential price. And so on. This would suggest that IBM has more suffered from the competition coming from other brand name firms like Compaq than from clones.

Thus the heterogeneity in consumer preferences and needs consist in a different impact of differential abilities and externalities on their choices. The study conducted by Bresnahan *et al.* (1996) suggests that brand name is able to shift the demand function (the willingness to pay) whereas being early on at the technological frontier is not. This means that for gaining market shares, learning externalities encouraging adoption of products embedding frontier technology are effective after a longer period and are less decisive than network externalities associated with a brand name. In fact a paradox may well be that in the computer industry network externalities are more easily circumvented by competitors than learning externalities and then may allow to gain market shares more quickly. This is because the huge investments and the strategy adopted by firms willing to acquire a reputation can allow to challenge an established network. Whereas learning externalities associated with specific investments made by users (in acquiring specific competences or physical support) are more difficult to devaluate, both past and new required investments have some importance in the sense that new investments should not necessitate to modify all the learning and competences already accumulated. The switching costs that the organization must undertake in order to be able to absorb the new technology have then to be considered. This explains that the diffusion of radically new technologies is slow. According to Bresnahan and Greenstein (1996), co-invention by users is the bottleneck in the diffusion of new technologies because learning and further innovations are involved. Then a firm willing to challenge a well established competitor may pay attention to the competences that adopters have prealably accumulated when they had to absorb former technologies.

The Automobile industry and the Fast-Food sector are two examples of the second type of situation. In the case of automobiles, firms compete harshly on price, quality, security and performances. Yet, there are some network externalities in terms of physical presence of the brands in space. The existence of a large network of car dealers is of crucial importance in the buying decision since cars may need spare parts and repairing competences. Thus, the positive relationship between the number of customers for a car brand and the size of the network of dealers of that brand imply some path-dependence in the adoption process. Then firms may likely be conscious of the importance of this externality deriving from the need for complementary products and services. Thus it can be crucial for a new firm to have an aggressive strategy in terms of putting dealers in many places. This can be costly but lately beneficial.

In the Fast-Food sector, network externalities are important in terms of spatial location of restaurants. The more the number of restaurants of a brand the more people are likely to choose this brand as compared to other brands. Yet if two firms have made the same investments in locations, differential abilities in terms of price and quality will matter. There is a positive relationship between the number of restaurants and the number of customers in the sense that benefits may be reinvested in opening restaurants in new places. We see here that this positive relationship heavily depends on the strategy adopted by the firms. In fact, a firm which initially realizes high profits but which does not take advantage of those profits to invest can be outstripped by a firm initially not so profitable but which uses credit to finance an aggressive investment strategy both opening new locations and improving the attractiveness of its products and services.

4. Some specific and neglected issues

Demand-oriented and mixed dynamics raise very specific problems. While most of public policy concerns rely on a vision of market dynamics as driven by a supply-oriented dynamics, these specific problems are generally neglected or not fully understood. In fact, demand-oriented and mixed dynamics raise some particular questions in terms of both efficiency and collective welfare. Whereas in supply-oriented dynamics, efficiency and welfare consist in maintaining prices consistent with maximizing the consumer surplus, in the two other dynamics issues of welfare and efficiency are considerably more complex. For instance, the welfare problem arising from the elimination of a standard – resulting from a battle between standards – poses the question of the efficiency of the selection process as soon as some "angry orphans" are left on the side. In the same way, ex ante selection of standards either in committees or in public agencies raises the question of the welfare gains and losses that such selection processes generate as compared with pure market selection.

4.1. Identifying welfare gains and losses

In sectors concerned with a demand-oriented or a mixed dynamics, welfare gains and losses can be estimated by three indicators:

1. The *price* proposed to customers.

2. The *ability to use* the purchased product *effectively*. For instance, this ability is altered for orphans and users of a small network.

3. *Technological evolution* : technological progress rapidly depreciates the performances of current products as compared with the performances of new products or new generations of existing products.

210 | Dynamics of technological systems

In fact, in most sectors fuelled by a demand-oriented or a mixed dynamics, decreases in price are almost always a condition for creating a mass market. Then huge decreases in prices are likely to be the rule. Competition is fierce in those activities and prices benefit from potential and effective competition because dominant firms are challenged. Then the two other issues may be the most difficult when it comes to questions of welfare.

These elements of welfare are affected by the operation of the selection process resulting from both choices (demand-side) and strategies and decisions of firms (supply-side). Then the following issues become important:

1) The temporality of market experimentation

It can be too long or too short. In the first case, customers don't take full advantage of network externalities and bear an *avoidable cost*. In the second case, a *potential regret* may emerge as a consequence of an excess of alignment in choices thus driving to premature lock-in. This regret comes from the fact that a technology has been eliminated too quickly although its potentialities had not been sufficiently explored. It can then be suspected that this technology could have provided better performances in the long run than its victorious competitor had it received as much attention and commitment.

2) Excessive inertia in the structure of adoption

The emergence of a competing option challenging a dominant firm and its standard may not be given a chance if the cost of switching standard is high and the installed base is already huge. This new option can only succeed in the market whether its performances and its price are very attractive or whether bandwagons of new customers are expected. Yet, making its product compatible with the current standard is likely to be an extra condition for the new standard to get into the market.

3) Market selection (demand) versus centralized choice (command): which institutional mechanism is the most appropriate in terms of welfare? Public authorities have sometimes been tempted to centrally organize the selection of alternative technologies in order to cope with the risks associated with an excessive pace in market experimentation or with the emergence of a potential regret. For instance, in the US, the selection of a technology for High Definition TV has resulted from an organized competition between several producers. Firms had then the opportunity to develop their own technology under cover of the pressure of a market adoption process. This process may improve the efficiency of the selection process by allowing to choose the technology presenting the highest potential but it may also drive to wastes in resources. In fact, firms which have allocated huge amounts of resources to develop a technology have probably built a complex network of co-operation in the industry and are less likely to be in a position of exit once public authorities are deciding which technology to preserve. So this kind of process may encourage the preservation of an excessive diversity.

To these characteristics of the selection process, strategies of firms add some complexity in the thinking about efficiency and welfare in the context of complex dynamics. We shall give some examples (C. Shapiro, 1996).

4) A compatibility standard promoted by a competitor may lower the rate of technological progress by moving competition toward prices.

5) Ex Ante standards established in committees may decrease technological exploration and diversity.

6) Mergers between former standard sponsors may imply higher prices.

7) A false pre-announcement by a dominant firm may prevent an innovative start-up from getting a credible chance.

All these issues concern both the properties of the collective process of choice and the actions that can modify the value associated to former, current and future choices. These specific properties and actions determine welfare gains and losses in sectors fuelled by a demand-oriented or a mixed dynamics. Then they set the context into which the opportunity for public action must be evaluated. We shall now discuss more precisely some issues in antitrust and industrial policies in the context of these dynamics.

4.2. Antitrust and industrial policy issues

As some of the examples given in the previous point suggest (in particular examples 6 and 7) some of the issues are already dealt with by existing rules implicitly inspired by supply-oriented types of dynamics. In fact, some economists pretend that there is no need for new antitrust rules since existing rules can solve some of the problems raised in what they call network industries while economic analysis does not provide any useful guidance for improving the relevance of antitrust policy in a network context (R. Schmalensee, 1995). We think that this opinion should be moderated in two respects. *First*, demand-oriented and mixed dynamics raise extra issues in terms of welfare and economic efficiency. Then they diversify the set of problems and dimensions that public policy has to deal with. And *second*, the issues that seem traditional (abuse of a dominant position, mergers which may affect consumers welfare etc.) have now to be examined with consideration of three welfare measures instead of just one (the price).

A consequence is that issues in antitrust and industrial policy are more intricate in contexts of demand-oriented and mixed dynamics than in a traditional context of supply-oriented dynamics. The conditions into which competition takes place are associated which questions of welfare which have partly to do with industrial policy issues. We shall now discuss some of them.

a) Antitrust policy in context of demand-oriented and mixed dynamics should be concerned with two problems. *First*, what may promote welfare can call for strategies which are by now considered as anti-competitive by antitrust policies. For instance, in most network industries co-operation is the norm (C. Shapiro, 1996). In fact, horizontal co-operation can enhance competition in the market if it takes place between challengers trying to compete with well established products. The ability to challenge may be profitable for consumers in terms of both price and technological progress.

And *second*, some attitudes and effects which may hinder welfare are neglected by traditional antitrust policy because its frame of reference is supply-oriented dynamics. For instance, the elimination by a pure market process of all competing standards but one may left some orphans and may then generate some welfare losses. Yet welfare gains may be much higher than welfare losses. Whether or not this should be a relevant argument for neglecting those welfare losses is a difficult question.

b) Industrial policy. While it is more and more accepted that national policies have greatly promoted competitive advantages – for instance allowing some laggard nations to catch up – the theoretical foundations for justifying industrial policies remain very weak. The issues that we have precedently pointed out allow to provide a few elements. In particular, the typology of market dynamics that we propose suggest that in demand-oriented and mixed dynamics, antitrust and industrial issues are partly intricate.

In fact issues related to the properties and temporality of selection processes suggest that industrial policies have a role to play in improving welfare but at the same time recommend great caution in those public interventions. In other words, the difficulty to theoretically found industrial policy is shifted towards a question of temporality, that we will now illustrate.

Decentralized choices may exhibit excessive alignment and drive to too rapid lock-in towards a unique solution (R. Cowan, 1990). To deal with the loss of welfare which may occur as a consequence of this rapid pace, a public intervention can extend the period of experimentation and guarantee a better collective structure of choice. Industrial policy may subsidy the option which has taken the worst start by bad luck, in order to give it a chance of improving its performances and of revealing its potential (P. David, 1995). Then evaluation of the competing options could take place on a more efficient basis. Yet public policy should know *when* the moment has come to let the market decide.

On the opposite, insufficient alignment of choices driving to the co-existence of several standards can be partly solve by a public policy encouraging or funding the emergence of a gateway allowing to fully exploit network externalities. The resulting shift of the competition process towards the resurgence of some supply effects may then solve the problem of an excessive diversity.

Then the temporality of selection processes must not be ignored by national strategies aiming at promoting competitive advantages in some industries. The french strategy which has consisted in helping the firm Bull to promote its own standard in computers is a good example of a failure. This failure can be attributed to the fact that externalities had already focused on other standards. Then developing specific competences in computer was not a viable strategy since the supply side was not the only engine of the market dynamics. Some demand effects were operating which should not have been ignored. A better strategy would probably have been to encourage Bull to be part of the bandwagon of PC producers. Bull could have produced either cheap clones or brand name computers.

This example teaches that industrial policies concerned with national independence in critical technologies should not be obsessed with the promotion of a specific and proprietary technology. Relative national independence can be obtained by producing a technology which embeds a widely accepted standard. This option is likely to be both less risky and less costly in most circumstances.

Some aspects of industrial policies may well be confronted to a great difficulty: when uncertainties are high ex ante and when the exploration of diversity is a great engine of economic progress, evoking some failures of market processes in managing the reduction of uncertainty and the tension between exploration of diversity and exploitation of economies of scale and positive externalities may provoke some debates. In particular, the role of industrial policy in subsidizing and promoting a standard for an industrial battle may be accused of suffering the same uncertainties as private agents making decentralized choices. In fact, what should be evaluated here is the balance between the risks and sunk costs associated with defending a specific standard which could fail and the benefits of adopting a well accepted standard. In other words, the uncertainties and costs of an ex ante commitment must be confronted with both the loss of potential profits following a wait-and-see attitude and the secure gains provided by a bandwagon strategy. Those costs and gains can only be anticipated, which means that industrial policy may be in most cases a question of bets when it consists in sponsoring a technological option in a context of ex ante uncertainty.

A crucial point is that public authorities are concerned with what national firms are doing. When national firms are not undertaking the sponsoring of new technologies, public intervention is more likely to be motivated. Then depending on national economic structures, the State can either undertake this sponsoring in public firms or fund some private firms and public research institutions. Firm deficiencies may justify industrial policy under the goal of preserving national independence in some generic technologies.

Conclusion

This analysis gives great importance to the ***temporality and properties of processes producing feedbacks and externalities***. There may be "opportunity windows" for specific actions and public intervention. But there may also be necessity for a retreat in some cases. In particular, demand effects susceptible to drive to some uniform structure of adoptions may only be weakened during a short opportunity window by a public policy aimed at preserving diversity for promoting experimentation and evaluation. In the same vein, when network effects or learning externalities are definitively orienting the process of adoption towards a few surviving options, it is illusory for a firm which has not benefited from these externalities to stay in the market. It is time for a retreat.

Yet temporality does not matter in the same place when supply effects and demand effects respectively dominate. Demand effects imply some *path-dependence at the system level*. Each choice of adoption has an impact on the performance or utility of the respective options and then modifies the respective probabilities that each option will be chosen by the next customer. Thus path-dependence qualifies the whole distribution of market shares while each customer has only an impact on this structure when he/she makes a choice. On the opposite, in a supply-oriented dynamics, the evolution in the distribution of market shares is rather *past*-dependent while the trajectory followed by each firm is *path*-dependent. In short the dynamics of the aggregate structure is well represented by a state matrix multiplied by a fixed transition matrix. Each firm is continuously affected by feedbacks and those feedbacks imply a micro path-dependence in its performance trajectory. Of course, the strength of the feedbacks partly depend on the behaviour of firms in terms of investments and strategic choices.

The complexity of mixed dynamics relies in the fact that both micro and macro path-dependence operate as decisive processes. The tension between those processes relies on both the properties of the selection process and the strategies of firms.

The typology of market dynamics that we have presented in this paper is relevant in several respects. *First,* it is adapted for grasping market dynamics as well in production activities as in service activities. *Second,* this framework considers both the abilities and strategies of firms and the existence of some demand effects in order to identify the properties of market dynamics. In particular, this typology of market dynamics suggests that specific forms of interaction between firms and customers are associated with each type of dynamics. For instance, in a supply-oriented dynamics, this interaction likely possesses the property of allowing most attractive firms to exploit economies of scale and most innovative firms to renew the set of products available. In a demand-oriented dynamics, interactions drive to an increase in the number of spatial locations – that is to say the enlargement of a physical network – or an increase in the number and performance of complementary products and services. And in the presence of learning externalities, interactions drive to improvements in the performances of both firms and users. This focus on the results of interactions – of which we have just given a few illustrations – for both firms and customers allow to consider both the abilities and strategies of firms and the choices made by customers. *Third,* this typology is a useful guide for thinking about public policies in modern economies. And *fourth,* it points out the crucial empirical and theoretical importance of *collective effects* in economic dynamics. These effects derive from interdependences between agents (either customers or/and firms). They consist in externalities and complementary products or services.

REFERENCES

ALCHIAN A. (1950), Uncertainty, Evolution and Economic Theory, *Journal of Political Economy,* vol. 58, n° 3.

ARTHUR B., ERMOLIEV Y. M. and KANIOVSKY Y. M. (1987), Path-dependent processes and the emergence of macro structure, *European Journal of Operational Research,* vol. 30, n° 3, June.

ARTHUR B., ERMOLIEV Y. M. and KANIOVSKY Y. M. (1983), On generalized urn schemes of the Polya kind, *Cybernetics,* n°19.

BRESNAHAN T. and GREENSTEIN S. (1996), *Technical Progress and Co-Invention in Computing and in the Uses of Computers,* Working Paper, NBER, July.

BRESNAHAN T, STERN S. and TRAJTENBERG M. (1996), *Market Segmentation and the Sources of Rents from Innovation: Personal Computers in the late 1980's,* Working Paper, NBER, July.

COWAN R. (1990), *Technological variety and competition issues of diffusion and intervention,* Working Paper, New York University.

DALLE J. M. (1996*), Heterogeneity, interaction structures and the diffusion of technological innovations,* Working Paper, September.

DAVID P. (1995), Standardization policies for network technologies: the flux between freedom and order revisited, in HAWKINS, MANSELL and SKEA eds. (1995), *Standards, Innovation and Competitiveness,* Edward Elgar.

DAVID P. (1985), Clio and the economics of Qwerty, *American Economic Review, Papers and Proceedings,* vol. 75.

DAVID P. and FORAY D. (1993), *Percolation structures, Markov random fields and the economics of EDI standards diffusion,* Discussion Paper Series, n° 326, CEPR, Standford University.

DOSI G. and KANIOVSKY Y. M. (1993), *The method of generalized urn scheme in the analysis of technological and economic dynamics,* Working Paper, IIASA, n° 93-17.

FRIEDMAN M. (1953), *Essays in Positive Economics,* The University of Chicago Press.

KIRMAN A. (1992), Variety: the coexistence of techniques, *Revue d'Economie Industrielle,* n°59.

MALERBA F. and ORSENIGO L. (1995), Schumpeterian Patterns of Innovation, *Cambridge Journal of Economics,* n° 19.

METCALFE S. (1995), The design of order: notes on evolutionary principles and the dynamics of innovation, *Revue Economique,* n° 6, November.

NELSON R. R. and WINTER S. (1982), *An Evolutionary Theory of Economic Change,* Cambridge, MA, The Belknap Press of Harvard University Press.

PENROSE E. (1952), Biological Analogies in the Theory of the Firm, *American Economic Review,* vol. 42.

ROSENBERG N. (1982), *Inside the black box,* Cambridge University Press.

ROSENBERG N. (1972), Factors affecting the diffusion of technology, in *Explorations in Economic History,* Fall, vol. 10, n° 1.

SCHMALENSEE R. (1995), *Antitrust issues related to networks,* NERA, December.

SHAPIRO C. (1996), *Antitrust in Network Industries,* Address before the American Law Institute and American Bar Association, San Francisco, January 25th.

SILVERBERG G., DOSI G. and ORSENIGO L. (1988), Innovation, diversity and diffusion: a self-organization model, *The Economic Journal,* n° 393, vol. 98.

WINTER S. (1984), Schumpeterian competition in alternative technological regimes, *Journal of Economic Behaviour and Organization,* vol. 5, n° 3-4.

CHAPTER 11
ERRORS AND MISTAKES IN TECHNOLOGICAL SYSTEMS: FROM POTENTIAL REGRET TO PATH DEPENDENT INEFFICIENCY *

Dominique FORAY

In his communication to the Stockholm Seminar on Evolutionary Economics, P. Bowler (1997) – an historian for biology thought – claimed that at whatever we look for variation in the economic sphere, it is difficult to imagine anything precisely equivalent to random copying errors. People are usually fairly rational, and if they change something, they usually hope to achieve a meaningful goal as a result. Technological innovation is almost by definition purposeful.

This paper is precisely on errors and mistakes in technological systems. However, the kind of errors that we want to deal with is not that of directly proceeding from individual failures and ignorance. Our goal is to analyse errors and mistakes, that appear as emergent properties of "systems of interactions" among individuals. While people are doing deliberate actions, having preferences, pursuing goals, minimizing efforts or maximizing comfort, the aggregate (or emerging collective structure) is not intentional, and perhaps inefficient. To clarify this differentiation between the level of the individual units (either an individual agent or a firm) exhibiting "purposive behaviours" and the level of the aggregate characterized by undeliberate outcomes, we can refer to the framework proposed by Tom Schelling. In a famous example, Schelling (1978) described the occurrence of an accident in one of the lanes of the highway. Why is it the traffic jams up? Drivers have reduced their speed to get a glimpse of the wreckage on the other side of the divider. Eventually, large numbers of commuters spend an extra 10 minutes driving, for a ten-second look. It costs each driver ten minutes to get his look. But he pays ten seconds for his own look and nine minutes, fifty seconds for the curiosity of the drivers ahead of him. In this exemple, individual actions are purposive (they are the result of a simple trade-off between looking at the accident and reducing the speed). But the complex process of interactions transform those deliberate individual actions

---

* I thank Robin Cowan, Emmanuelle Fauchart, James Foreman-Peck and Stan Metcalfe for extensive comments on an earlier draft. Comments provided by the participants to the "path-dependent workshop", held at IIASA (Laxenburg, Austria) in August 1995 – especially from Giovanni Dosi, Arnulf Gruebler, Youri Kaniovski and Gerry Silverberg – were very helpful. Finally, Paul A. David has been responsible for shaping my view about most of the issues treated here, in the course of many conversations. I am grateful to all the aforementioned.

into a collective mistake. Such a complex transformation does not permit any simple summation or extrapolation from individual actions to the aggregates.

In some cases, it is possible to extrapolate the collective result from the individual actions and, in this case, any collective failure is the simple and straightforward consequence from individual failure. For example, Schelling showed, if we know that every driver, on his own, turns his lights on at sundown, we can expect the illumination of local area considered. In this case the collective result is as intentional as the individual actions.

In some other cases, however, the nature of interactions among agents is more complex and the system of interactions does not permit any simple summation or extrapolation to the aggregates. In those cases, errors and mistakes must be analyzed as "system failures" rather than as a straightforward consequence of individual failures. The complex system of interactions generates a risk of "random copying errors".

This paper is on technology because the history of technological systems provide a domain of inquiries in which system's failures are important.

1. A technological prelude

Gasoline now dominates as the power source for automobiles. It may well be the superior alternative, but certainly in the early twentieth century, great uncertainties characterized the respective qualities of the three alternatives: steam, internal combustion and electric-powered vehicle. Internal combustion engine had many defects and it was held to be the least promising option. Gasoline was hard to obtain in the right grade; it was dangerous; and the internal combustion engine required more numerous and more sophisticated moving parts than steam. It is important, Mokyr argued (1990, p. 131), not to underestimate the steam engine, as providing initially a competitive alternative to gasoline-powered vehicle. The steam-powered automobile in the early twentieth century was technically and economically on a par with the gasoline engine. Throughout the period 1890 to 1920, developers, with predilections depending on their previous engineering experience, produced constantly-improving versions of the steam, gasoline and electric automobiles. *"Local economies rose and fell, firms prospered and failed, and personal fortunes were made and squandered in search of an answer to the question, "What type of engine will power the automobile?"* (Kirsch, 1994, p. 4).

A series of circumstances, as well as the existence of some historical bias favouring gasoline (for example, in the US, electric cars were handicapped by the absence of rural electric grids early in the twentieth century, while steam-powered automobiles were handicapped by the public ordinances prohibiting waters troughs on the road side) gave gasoline enough of a lead that it subsequently proved unassailable. At the end of the first decade, gas-powered cars outsold electric and steam powered cars by several orders of magnitude [1].

To this point, there is no economic issue. The above argument is nothing other than the story of a technological choice with many historical details. In order to transform this history into an economic metaphor demonstrating how failure in dynamic co-ordination games can conduce to long term inefficiency, it is necessary to develop a counterfactual argument. In other words, to make the case that this story has significant welfare implications, one needs to establish that there is an outcome that would have been better. As suggested by R. Cowan [2], two things are important in this last sentence: the tense "would have been" which implies a conditional, and therefore counterfactual claim; and "better" which is an *ex post* notion involving the entire sequence of technological choices. The claim is not "combustion engines, as they now exist, are better than steam engines" but rather that "had they been adopted to the same extent as combustion engines have in fact been adopted steam engines would be better than combustion engines". This is perfectly compatible, Cowan claimed, with the statement that today, anyone building a car should use combustion engine.

Of interest in this regard is the argument of historians of technologies: *"theoretically the steam engine could have presented an attractive alternative to the combustion engine had quantities of ingenuity and capital been spent upon it comparable to those spent, from the automobile's inception, in making the combustion engine the technological marvel it is today"* (Payen, 1990) [3]. In other words, the historical process described above becomes an important welfare economic issue if we can prove that under some different minor conditions around the beginning of the twentieth century, perhaps today's cars would not be powered by internal combustion engines (Arthur, 1983). The path-dependent selection approach to technological choice favours the view that there is no *ex ante* "fittest-technology". It is only the sequence of choices – driven by chance and trivial circumstances – that will eventually give to one technology the attributes of the fittest.

This paper addresses the issue of path-dependent selection and inefficiency, counterfactual methods and the empirical evidence employed in this research trajectory. The general message is basically that the theoretical argument to prove path-dependent inefficiency is relatively straightforward, while empirical demonstrations, as well as the analysis of welfare implications are much more difficult. The paper is structured as follows: in the next section, we briefly state

---

1. See Foreman-Peck (1996) for the history of power source options at the turn of the century, based on data set of about 2800 car manufacturers in 4 countries before 1963.
2. Communication at the "path dependence" Forum held at IIASA (Laxenburg) in August 1995.
3. On this point I would like to cite the subtitle of an article in the French newspaper *Le Monde*, reporting on recurrent experimentations on steam engines within large car companies :*"The steam engine could have supplanted the combustion engine but the whims of history decided otherwise"*.

the basic argument explaining how localized learning leads to an incomplete exploration of the variety distribution of a technology. We then synthetize the most interesting historical studies, which get "potential regret" results and ask whether these suggest a large welfare loss. To answer to this question, we start from the critical arguments of Liebowitz and Margolis to discuss the theoretical and empirical difficulties of establishing path-dependent inefficiency.

2. An introduction to path-dependence and potential regret

If you have increasing returns, especially through learning by doing, learning by using or some other similar dynamics, if you start down one path, you are likely to find it easier to continue to move down that path rather than changing to another. The theoretical meaning of this proposition is that technological learning is essentially localized: technical change does not correspond to a complete shift of the productive function but consists rather in the shifting of one point in this function. The works by Atkinson and Stiglitz (1969), David (1975), Stiglitz (1987) and Antonelli (1995) shaped this theoretical evolution. Learning is associated with a specific process (a point in the production function for actual output or for knowledge), so that in allocating resources a firm must not lose sight of the possibility that any subsequent technological change (to $t + 1$) will wipe out the accrued gains from localized learning associated with the technology chosen at t. The firm cannot opt for a "transitional" change of technology in the belief that by doing so it will be able to keep up with all the successive changes in relative price structure, since localized learning makes it likely that it will have to carry on with the "transitional" technology after the re-establishment at $t + 1$ of the price structure that characterized $t - 1$.

2.1. From localized learning to positive feedbacks: up to macro-behaviours

However, the concept of localized learning represents only one element of path-dependence. Localized learning, when analysed in a 2-period choice problem of an individual agent, is not path-dependence and actually can be formalized with (first-order Markovian) state dependent probability transitions.

Localized learning is an agent of irreversibility, which generates path-dependent dynamics in systems of interdependent agents; each having to make the same choice. Instrumental to this particular class of dynamics is the mechanism of increasing return to adoption: the value of adopting a particular technology rises with the degree of adoption of that technology. There are various mechanisms which are at the origin of this phenomenon. Different kinds of learning as well as the simple process of reduction of uncertainty operate as positive feedbacks, making technologies more valuable as the number of experimentations increases. Systems that operate under positive feedbacks of this type are path-dependent, in the sense that the long run equilibrium can be changed by historical events along the path to it (sensitive dependence on initial conditions or early circumstances).

A technical definition is provided in David (1993): A process whose outcomes are path-dependent does not possess a limiting, invariant probability distribution that is continuous over all the states that are compatible with the energy of the system; the state space of the system is thus "disconnected"; if its structure is undisturbed, such a system never "shakes loose" from the influence of events in the past. (See papers by Antonelli (1996) and by David and Foray (1995) for surveys and applications of the techniques developed for modelling path-dependent processes).

2.2. Positive feedbacks and the incomplete exploration of the variety distribution of a technology

In presence of positive feedbacks, the collective behaviour of a process of technological choice leads to the incomplete exploration of the distribution of variety for a particular technology (i.e. of the "morphological space" of the technology (Foray and Gruebler, 1990)). One can readily visualize the development of a technology as an evolutionary tree (including many types and variants and potentially evolving towards different directions), some parts of the tree will be actually explored while some others will be largely ignored (David, 1988). The existence of positive feedbacks causes regions of the state space to become effectively disconnected from the rest: having got itself onto one of the lower branches of the tree, the system might be able to move around freely among all the higher branches emanating from that one, while being unable to escape to visit other parts of the tree. Thus, the property of localized learning implies that technological learning is a process with two faces: exploration and (at the same time) selection. In this sense, the mode of development of a technology (including many potential routes) is strongly influenced by initial decisions. Initial (or transitory) actions do put a system on a path that cannot be left without some costs. And because the context of these initial decisions is one of great uncertainty and ignorance about the respective qualities and properties of the various options (Rosenberg, 1992, Cowan, 1991), the collective dynamics of localized learning can lead to inefficiency. Taking decisions and (at the same time) eliminating options in a context of ignorance entail the risk of missing the best route of development. Technological variants having unique properties may be lost and never properly explored. The long run effect is that the scope for future developments will be narrowed. Technological advances that depend on the prior developement of these unique, and now lost, properties are put in jeopardy. The short run effect is the diffusion of an inferior technology. Now what is unfortunately very difficult to evaluate deals with the welfare implications of such a process. As questioned by Arrow (1995, p. 27): *"is this a big factor? The difficulty is that none of these* (the empirical studies frequently quoted in the literature, see below) *suggest a large welfare loss: it may be that in the long run you didn't get to the best solution. It is hard to believe that you are losing a great deal"*.

2.3. Potential regret in economic history

In this section, I want to discuss the property of potential regret. This property refers to the possibility of locking in to a technology that does not provide maximal payoffs.

It is a constant feature of the empirical literature on path-dependent to get "potential regret" results: *"Given equal developement"*, technology B could have presented a superior alternative to A. A first simple question is whether such a condition automatically implies outcomes will be inefficient. In this section, I will present very brief sketchs of the main "inefficiency stories" presented in the literature. All these cases are based on the argument that in the domain of increasing returns it is history, the details of timing and circumstances (rather than an exogenous pre-ordered technological classification) that decide that one technology is more efficient than another.

Power source for the motor car: This is perhaps the most spectacular study, leading to the provocative conclusion that the steam engine could have presented an attractive alternative to the internal combustion engine. Careful and deep studies on the circumstances and details of the first and the second battle between engine technologies have been carried out by economists and historians (see Foreman Peck, 1996 and Kirsch, 1995 for further references). Of great interest in this regard is the shortness of the period during which some balance was maintained between the three options (roughly from 1899 to 1904); which leads to appreciate the decisive and pervasive impact of some ponctual and trivial events (car races) occurring during this period; as well as of some individual decisions to switch from one technology to another. A property clearly drawn from those stories is the time sensivity of the outcome of the process. As demonstrated by Kirsch (1995), at the time when the competition started between gasoline, steam and electric alternatives, the electric had no chance: the absence of a rural electric grid in the early twentieth century clearly decreased the appeal of electric vehicles. Had the first automobiles been introduced twenty years later, the outcome might have been different. Thus, the position of the present on the axis of historical time matters. The specific timing of the technological competition shape the battle and help define winning and losing. Results in terms of potential regret are, however, ambiguous. Some parallel developments of electric car (such as the milk delivery vehicles in the 30s in UK, or the Californian programmes for electric road vehicle development in the 60s) suggest that this option is intrinsically inferior: electric cars still lack range and power [1]. The question, however, remains opened in the steam engine case.

QWERTY: David (1985) showed how the interaction of uncoordinated decisions by early typists and their employers, typing schools and typewriter

---

1. I am grateful to J. Foreman-Peck who drew my attention on the interest of these "parallel developments", as valuable experiments in real time to assess the outcome of the selection process

manufacturers, resulted in the adoption of the QWERTY keyboard layout. Now, this keyboard arrangement is thought to be ergonomically and in other ways inferior to several alternatives that have been available for some time. The Dvorak Simplified Keyboard is probably best known among these, but to date it has not been successful in inducing a switch from the QWERTY standard. Of interest in this regard is that the QWERTY arrangement is still used on computer. This fact reveals the persistence of intentions which are no longer relevant. Indeed, the QWERTY keyboard was designed with a clear intention caused by mechanical problems raised by the first generations of design. The objective was to slow down the typists in order to keep the keys from getting stucks. The persistence of this design clearly illustrates the gap between a primitive intention, which persists over time, and the new conditions of use of the keyboard (no mechanical problem arises from typing on a computer).

Alternating current: David and Bunn (1988) have documented the historical emergence of polyphase alternating current (AC) as the standard for electrical supply systems in the US at the end of the last century. Here again, the technological superiority of the selected variant is a matter of discussion. The direct current (DC) variant had many advantages as well as an initial lead in installed base. In such a context of a competition between initially incompatible technical options, central was the role of some particular extraneous and transient factors. According to the authors, the conception and diffusion of an AC-DC converter technology, as well as the personal inclinations and financial situations of key industry leaders were the decisive factors which have pushed the selection of AC as the technological standard.

Nuclear power: Robin Cowan (1990) has identified the event which rapidly and definitively led the nuclear technology system to a "lock in" situation (to the so called "American" technology based on pressurized-water reactors). This technology, specialists today agree, is "inferior" to certain others. This historical accident resulted from the post-war military purchase order addressed to Westingshouse and General Electric for the construction of a submarine reactor. Subsequently, when it became necessary (after the first Soviet nuclear detonation in 1949) rapidly to develop a civil nuclear programme, it was the familiar technology that was chosen, even though its suitability for military applications could not in any way guarantee a successful transfer to other areas (Canada is the only country to have followed a trajectory not selected via military purposes, the "natural uranium and heavy water" technology was initially chosen independently of military constraints and has higher probability to be more pertinent for civilian applications). Indeed, much of the engineering literature contends that, given equal development, the gas-cooled reactor would have been superior. This example provides another illustration of the persistence of obsolete intention. Light water reactors were originally designed to propel nuclear submarines. Thus engineering intentions addressed the problem of designing highly compact unit adapted to "confined atmosphere"; intentions which are no longer relevant in the case of civilian nuclear plants.

224 | Dynamics of technological systems

Ferrous casting: According to Foray and Gruebler (1990), the history of ferrous casting can be treated as a case of competing technologies. Two technologies can be used to realize ferrous metal products by a casting process: sand molding process technology and the gasifiable pattern process technology. The latter is the most recent technology. It entails an extreme simplification of the operating methods, as well as a higher degree of flexibility. It is again a case of technological superiority, collectively acknowledged but which did not lead to a switch from the old to the new technology. Data collected in France and Germany show that this intrinsically superior technology is impeded from supplanting the older one. The main factors of excess of inertia include technical interrelatedness, learning by using and uncertainty.

Pest control strategies: In a recent empirical study, Cowan and Gunby (1996) explain why chemical control of agricultural pests remains the dominant technology in spite of many claims that it is inferior to its main competitor, Integrated Pest Management. Chemical control consists in covering a crop with insecticide or herbicide in order to kill offending weeds, insects, and diseases. Integrated Pest Management, by contrast, is largely a set of responses to current conditions. It might involve biological control such as predator or sterile insects, and cultural controls like crop rotation, as well as focused pesticide application. According to the authors, Integrated Pest Management has several inherent advantages over conventional controls. However, the authors identify a situation of excess of inertia in which the presence of increasing returns and technological uncertainty entailed by novelty make it difficult for a market or group of users to switch from an entrenched technology to a new one.

Video cassette recorder: Cushmano *et al.* study (1990) on the development of VCR standards has shown that the technical superiority of the more compact Sony Betamax format notwithstanding, the eventual dominance of the VHS format as the industry standard emerged from the interplay of adventitious and seemingly unrelated background conditions and events. Prominent among these were the incidental ability of the VHS cassette initially to carry a tape with a longer playing time, and the unanticipated introduction of pre-recorded movies on videocassettes. The case of VCR standard is a good example to illustrate the role of the dynamic complementarities (here the pre-recorded tapes) as generating path-dependence in a selection process. There are two periods in this story. The first one goes on before the conception and diffusion of the pre-recorded tape. At the end of the first period, the market exhibited an advantage for VHS, which benefited from 2/3 of the market demand. This advantage was related to many important and *not accidental* reasons, including in particular the success of the strategic maneuvering of JVC and Matsushita against Sony. That strategic behaviour of non-anonymous agents played a great role in the selection of the outcome of the initial period is not disputable. However, this fact does not deny the validity of a path-dependent interpretation of the process of selection in this particular case. Of interest in this regard is that, at the end of this period, the system was remarkably stationary (in terms of market shares), leading to a stable situation of technological co-existence and multiple standards: the market-share of Beta (the technology with a lower market share) was sufficiently large to permit significant scale economies while the existence of switching costs hampered large migration of users from one technology to the other [1]. As a result, this gap in terms of market shares did not create any tendency towards market elimination of Beta. It is then the creation of the complementary product (the pre-recorded tape) which introduced positive feedbacks (indirect effects giving rise to consumption externalities) and de-stabilized the system. Because the quantity and variety of pre-recorded tapes that are supplied for use with a given VCR is an increasing function of the number of VCR units that have been sold, the stable VHS superiority in terms of market-share became a dynamic, self-reinforcing mechanism: *"the greater abundance of VHS program material gave buyers greater incentive to choose VHS players, which then led tape distributors to stock more VHS tapes, in a reinforcing pattern"* (Cusumano, et al., 1990, p. 86). Since this moment, the macro-behaviour of the system exhibited path-dependent properties: positive feedbacks amplified the distribution of choices produced during the first period.

All processes described above include a first period – perhaps very short, perhaps very long – in which the dynamics of choice exhibits constant or very low increasing returns. It is typically the case at the time of the very early process of adoption, which do not yet generate a time series long enough for the agent involved to be able to use it to form consistent probability estimates about future possible states of the world. In this situation, individual agents make choices according to their natural preferences and "mentality", which are shaped by a particular historical context. The process is thus driven by specific historical intentions, without any (or very low) mechanism of positive feedbacks This initial period leads to a distribution of choices that reflects preferences and which is not influenced by any local or global "precedents".

A second period starts with the appearance of dynamic complementarities. Some positive feedbacks are introduced into the system: the need for and the availability of a complementary good, the accumulation of localized knowledge, the constitution of technical or institutional interelatedness; all those complementarities introduce positive feedbacks, magnifying the outcome (choice distribution) of the first period, and hence, making persistent the primitive intentions as reflected through the choices made in the initial period. The system now exhibits path-dependent properties. The outcome of the sequence of interdependent additive choices is shaped by the intentions that were prevailing at the very beginning of the history.

It is important to note that the initial period can be very short in terms of event time (as opposed to calender time); such as in the case of nuclear power

---

1. See David, Foray and Dalle (1996) who address the problem of the maintenance of technological diversity, on markets in presence of switching costs, and positive local externalities.

where it included only a single choice. It can be very long; such as for VCR technology selection where it involved a very large number of choices. But whatever the length of this period, the process leads to a distribution of choices (1,0, 0), in the case of nuclear power, or (2/3, 1/3) in the case of VCRs, which reflects historical intentions; that is to say intentions produced by certain historical circumstances [1].

3. Recent insights on path-dependence inefficiency

Does potential regret automatically imply outcomes will be inefficient? The theoretical conditions of path-dependent inefficiency must be clarified. This issue was addressed in a series of papers by Liebowitz and Margolis (1990, 1995), who discussed the welfare analysis of the historical outcomes of path-dependence process.

3.1. Three classes of path-dependence

According to these authors, there are three important features which must be proved to get path-dependence inefficiency:

(a) sensivity to initial conditions (intertemporal relations)

(b) inferiority exists (but appears only in retrospect)

(c) inferiority exists and the outcome is remediable.

In this set of conditions, (a) means that intertemporal relationships propagate initial actions; (b) intertemporal relationships propagate errors; and (c) intertemporal relationships propagate errors which were avoidable

---

1. From a modeling point of view, we should be able to formalize some preliminary processes, generating an initial, possibly jumbled, configuration of users of incompatible options. See David (1992) for some suggestions in the framework of the "voter model" (a model of spatial stochastic interactions with local positive feedbacks within a finite population of agents). In this model, individual revision policies, which are driven by stochastic reassessments of the local situation (the local distribution of choices) by each agent, operate as the mechanism pushing the system towards an extreme correlation of choices. David (1992) suggests that in such a model, one could add a first phase at the outset, during which new agents take up positions randomly in the graph – each of whom come with an initial policy assignment reflecting his inherent preferences. During this first period, the population will be tending to increase without limit and correspondingly, the proportion of both ensembles of agents in the growing total would tending towards random fluctuations between the extreme. This first process leads thus to a distribution of choices, that reflects preferences and which is not influenced by any local or global "precedents". The second period starts then when the entry rate becomes sufficiently slow, so that only the stochastic replacement process (based on positive feedbacks) is driving further changes in the share of the total assignement. The system now exhibits path-dependent properties, magnifying the accidental events which have generated the "final" distribution of choices of the first random period.

* It is easy to find allocation processes, exhibiting a) only. In this case, the sensivity to initial conditions exists but has no implied inefficiency. It does not harm. The structure of the allocation process exhibits intertemporal relations (positive feedbacks): action a_0 from the set A_0 taken at t_0 affects the set of choices A_n at t_n.

All situations conforming only to (a) can be refered to some kinds of pure co-ordination game problems, which means that the alternatives are not clearly Pareto rankable in terms of their intrinsic economic efficiencies. The right and left hand sides of the road story (Arthur, 1983) offers a good metaphor for this kind of process. Consider an island in which cars are introduced, all at more or less the same time. Drivers are free to choose between the right- and left-hand sides of the road and have no in-built bias toward either. Each side possesses increasing returns: as a higher proportion of drivers chooses one side, the very real returns to choosing that side rapidly rise. In this context, the two options (right side or left side driving) are not rankable in terms of their intrinsic efficiencies. They will gradually take on their property, as they recruit or forfeit new agents. This explains why the initial decisions are random and the system is unstable. The individual selection of an option leads to positive feedbacks in the sense that it heightens the "performance" of this option from the viewpoint of those who have already chosen it and increases the likelihood of the same choice recurring. There are two states of equilibrium which make up the two absorbing states of the system. Once one of these states has been achieved, any further change is completely ruled out (On this example, see also Adams, 1990, and Young, 1996). Therefore, the complex behaviour of this system of interactions throws up properties of a persistent nature in the influence of initial or transient conditions, possibilities of multiple equilibria, but no sub-optimality.

* Processes exhibiting (a) + (b) features are processes characterized by sensivity to initial conditions and inferiority of one (or some) competing options. But inferiority can only be seen *ex post*. At the time of the choice the inferiority of the selected path was unknowable. In this case, there is no inefficiency property given the state of knowledge (imperfect). Demonstrating *ex post* inefficiency requires counterfactual methods and hypothetical arguments ("*the steam engine could have supplanted...if*"). The structure of the allocation process exhibits intertemporal relations and *ex post* inefficiency: action a_0 is *ex ante* efficient if at t_0 there is no known alternative action a_1 that would provide better benefits.

* Processes exhibiting (a) + (c) are processes characterized by sensivity to initial conditions and inferiority existing *ex ante*: some better options were available and some agents have or would obtained the information required to make a correct choice. It is a "remediable lock in" situation; i.e. the error was avoidable. To get this strong form of inefficiency, the system needs two classes of agents: some have the right information, know enough to make the correct choice but fail to take advantages of the implied profit opportunities; and agents who know nothing more than the payoff going to the next adopter. The structure of the allocation process is the following: at t_0 there is an alternative action $a_1 \in A_0$ such that the discounted present value of the social benefit of selecting a_1 instead of a_0 are known to be greater yet the action a_0 is taken nonetheless. "*Remediable efficiency, if it occurred, would be a significant lapse and a demonstrated instance would be an interesting finding worthy of analysis*" (Liebowitz and Margolis, 1995, p. 224).

In summary, Liebowitz and Margolis claimed that, while process of path-dependence *mark 1* are easy to find in the real world (the selection between the right and the left sides for driving is probably the best example); path-dependence *mark 2* and *mark 3* (*ex post* and *ex ante* inefficiency) are difficult to demonstrate. *Ex post* inefficiency can only be obtained with counterfactual constructions. The literature, so they claimed, cannot provide examples nor can it be disproved. *Ex ante* inefficiency requires demonstration that a feasible alternative exists at the time of the choice and that some agents have the knowledge. This third form, which does imply irremediable error, is based on highly restrictive assumptions.

3.2. Discussing the notion of remediability

The remediability condition, which is at the core of the theoretical of the argument of Liebowitz and Margolis, is a questionable condition as applied to any kind of evolutionary problem. This condition, dealing with the state of knowledge among the agent implies that "*if no one in the economy is aware of the potential returns to a technology – it cannot be argued that the technology has been discovered in any meaningful sense*" (Liebowitz and Margolis, 1995). It is of course a very strong implication, if we look at one crucial postulate of the path-dependent literature. Fulfilling the remediability condition would mean eliminating technological uncertainty, which is the basic principle of the models considered: any study on path-dependent technological choices premises that new inventions are typically very primitive at the time of their birth. Their performance is usually poor compared to existing (alternative) technologies and to their future performance. The functions and services which will be efficiently performed by the technology are not well understood; the appropriate technological and institutional environment may not exist yet, and, an important point in this discussion, the criteria selected in order to evaluate the technology (to compare it with the existing one) may be not appropriate. It is then the role of learning of different kinds to allow the technology to be improved, better understood, better integrated into large systems, better evaluated and assessed, as this technology progressively diffuses within the economy. This means that it is the very nature of those models to have initially high uncertainty about the potential returns of the competing technologies. And it is because of this uncertainty that localized experimentations will be carried out, acting as positive feedbacks within the system of choices. "Remediable lock-in" is, thus, a self-contradictory proposition.

4. On path-dependence inefficiency

We must now go further to investigate the nature of path-dependent inefficiency. We should note, before proceeding to our own investigation, that Liebowitz and Margolis do not clearly distinguish between the theoretical and the empirical issues. In the following discussion, we will try to keep this distinction in order to clarify the arguments.

4.1. The theoretical problem

Persistence of obsolete intention as a first source of inefficiency

Let start by proposing that path-dependence economics is obviously a theory of selection with positive feedbacks and, consequently, involves a general principle of "irremediability", persistence and durability of technological, institutional or pure economic structure. This inertia phenomenon is generated by two factors: the level of (technological and organizational) investments in the old technology, entailing high transition costs; and the difficulty of co-ordinating decisions of migration in presence of agent's uncertainty about the behaviours of others (if only one agent migrates, he will support all the costs of transitory incompatibility). These two factors generate persistent structures. Whether these structures are the outcome of a deliberate (rational) choice or of an accidental sequence of events does not really matter. What really matters is that this property of persistence will automatically introduce, sooner or later, some gaps between the intentions under which the structure was selected and the new circumstances and environment.

As shown above, the exemple of QWERTY (David, 1986) perfectly illustrates this particular source of inefficiency. It is not surprising that this particular keyboard arrangement is slower than some other possible solutions, because it was precisely the initial design intention to slow-down typing (with the old mechanical equipment embodying type-bars, typing too quickly increased the risk of type-bars clashes; so that it was better to have a slower but regular type speed than a quicker but with frequent interruptions). However, the conception and the diffusion of new equipments, which are relieved from the type-bar constraint (such as computers), make the initial intention (slowing the speed) obsolete and should induce a switch from QWERTY to new arrangements. QWERTY, however, still dominates the market. It is, thus, the persistence of intentions, which are no longer relevant with regard to the new environment, that represents the main source of path-dependent inefficiency.

This example helps us to understand that the exogenous initial or transient events, which strongly influence the outcomes, need not to be irrational in order to generate inefficiency. They are "accidental" in the sense that the decisions taken initially did not take into account the possible persistence and durability of the choices made before the introduction of some dynamic complementarities into the system. It is the reason why these particular events are only "accidental" in the case where their consequences are persisting over time. Thus, the term "historical accident" seems to be unwarranted. The decisions made by the US navy to select the "light-water" technology (Cowan, 1990) were certainly consistent in the light of history and reconstructing them is a task best left to historians. If there are indeed accidental events inherent in the models, these derive from the behaviour of the dynamic system. It is the persistence of intentions over time which is accidental, while the intentions themselves always reflect consistent behaviour with respect to the historical circumstances prevalent during the early choices. The theoretical problem raised by this coincidence between individual rationality and collective inefficiency is connected to the definition of "a better technology" [1]. As an *ex post* definition, it says nothing about the rationality of the agents – to be at a worse outcome need not imply that any agent pursued an individually worse action. Indeed in most path dependent analyses agents are economically rational in that they use all the available information, and in the light of it take the actions that will maximize their utilities.

Premature standardization and excess of diversity as a second source of inefficiency

Having claimed the importance of persistence, as entailing necessarily a gap between the primitive intention and some new circumstances, it is then necessary to qualify the structure which may acquire a certain degree of durability, through positive feedbacks. Here, there are obviously two cases.

First, the structure can be characterized by an extreme correlation of choices, leading to market elimination of many but one (or very few) option and ultimately achieving complete uniformity. The existence of positive feedbacks, which entails for example virtuous circles between unit costs levels declining and market shares increasing, makes this case as the general one (Metcalfe 1994). The exemple of the VCRs battle perfectly illustrates the concomitance of those two attributes.

When the path-dependent outcome is associated with both characteristics of persistence and uniformity, inefficiency not only derives from the persistence of obsolete intentions (from t_0 to t_n), but can also be generated by the fact that there is no guarantee that the intrinsically better technology is selected (at t_0) and the absence of diversity does not provide the system with any "second chance", if it fails once to select the best technology.

Second, there are particular cases where the persistent structure involves the co-existence of various alternatives. To get such a configuration of stable diversity, the system needs very particular conditions:

---

[1]. R. Cowan, communication at the "path dependence" Forum held at IIASA (Laxenburg) in August 1995.

– First, the system needs a condition of strong regularity and symmetry in the entry (and replacement) process among the agents having opposite preferences; so that the performances of competing technologies (or of the complementary goods or institutions respectively assigned to each technology) can increase in the same way.

– Second, the system needs high switching costs, which are the result of a certain initial heterogeneity, leading to the development of installed bases, during the initial period.

– Three, the system needs some particular structures of percolation (of connection between agents) which does not allow it to get extreme correlation of choices. Some subset of agents are sufficiently isolated to be protected from any propagation of a given choice through the local networks.

(Note that these conditions matter for different kinds of models; the first one allows a system to maintain diversity in the framework of a Polya urns model, while condition 3 allows a system to maintain diversity in the framework of a percolation model (see Antonelli, 1996).)

Under one of those conditions, a system can tolerate diversity or (better say) multiple standards, even in presence of positive feedbacks.

What can be say regarding path-dependent inefficiency at this second level (the level of the structure – standardization or diversity – which is analyzed as persisting over time)? Both structures have a specific economic value [1]. Regarding diversity, it is the value of increasing the probability to select (or at least to maintain) the best variant. We refer here to a particular kind of learning, called "learning from diversity". This process involves experiments with a variety of options, and through the results of the experimentation, leads to the elimination of certain avenues of development. In this phase the objective is to gain broad knowledge of many possible avenues by which the problem at hand can be attacked. Regarding standardization, the economic value deals with static efficiency gains through economies of scale, and accumulation of learning on a particular option. We refer here to a second type of learning, called "learning by standardization", in which attention is concentrated on one technological variant, making it easier to identify empirical irregularities, anomalies and problem areas deserving further investigation, correction and elaboration.

This means that we cannot once and for all ascribe a given economic value respectively to diversity and standardization. The economic values of diversity and standardization must not be considered as invariable dimensions. They change along the technological life cycle: in general the economic value of

---

1. This section draws upon my work with R. Cowan on standardization and diversity (Cowan and Foray, 1995a and b), as well as on David and Rothwell, 1994.

diversity is very high at the beginning of the technological life cycle and then is decreasing as uncertainty about qualities and properties of its variants reduces. It can even be negative if diversity is maintained too long, beyond the critical point where enough information has been gained. Symmetrically the economic value of standardization is high at the end of the cycle, while it is negative if too early a selection prematurely stops experiments.

This suggests a need for policies to maintain diversity, but with the foresight that at some point in time diversity can decrease benefits by preventing economies of scale, a reduction in costs through intensive learning about a technical option, and the potential for network externalities. Thus, we must not underestimate the inverse risk of a selection delayed too long, that conduces to irreversible situation of excess of diversity. Late introduction may result in the formation of wrong expectations about the chances of competing technologies – there will be users who adopt technologies which will not be selected as the future standard.

The possibility of eventually reaching a situation where a unique technology survives, preferable as regards welfare to a final situation where many technologies co-exist, is dependent upon various conditions, dealing with the problem of choosing the right technology (which in any case will become wrong in the future): i) conditions in which agents do not have *ex ante* preferences regarding the identity of the standard that would emerge as the collective choice, other than the preferences that they maximise at the time of their selection, and ii) conditions concerning the discount rate and the possibility of experimentation with the various alternatives in order eventually to select the most efficient design (David and Foray, 1994).

Summary on path-dependence inefficiency

We have discussed two sets of sources of inefficiency: the problem of persistence, on the one hand; and the problem of diversity versus uniformity on the other hand. This gives us four possibilities, as suggested in table 1.

The best policy flux should proceed from the north-east quadrant (learning from diversity) towards selection and standardization, after having carried out enough experiments to gain better information on the distribution of variety and to be able to select the best option. However, even in following this trajectory (from north-east to south-west), sooner or later, the persistence of the structure will generate some gaps between the standard and the new environment.

4.2. The empirical problem [1]

As already suggested, one of the most frequently cited method for providing empirical foundations on path-dependent inefficiency is the counterfactual

---

1. This section draws upon my work with R. Cowan on the counterfactual method (Cowan and Foray, 1997).

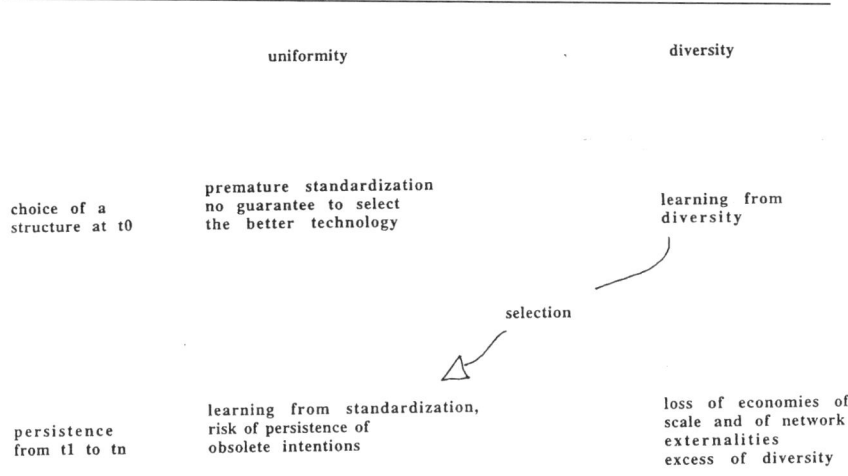

Table 1. Two sources of inefficiency

method. The purpose is to carry out the evaluation of potential alternatives, which were not actually exploited, in order to compare in welfare terms those deserted ways with the way actually explored.

It is clear that generating relevant and robust results from a counterfactual argument would make the life of evolutionary economists easier, challenging in particular the perception that if the theory is pretty good, empirical evidence is frequently weak. Such an exercize is, however, impeded, by severe difficulties that Cowan and Foray (1997) have surveyed in a recent paper. The principal source of difficulty is that the very feature that makes counterfactual history necessary – increasing returns and positive feedbacks through which an entirely different world could derived from minor initial differences – makes counterfactual history difficult to carry out. In fact, the counterfactual method consists in vitalizing (reviving) something that never happened. Therefore, without severe theoretical constraints on what history can produce, the analysis runs the risk of being far from compelling.

It is thus required: i) to place restrictions on what can be postulated (constraining the world of potential developments); and ii) to construct relevant sequences of events (linking antecedents with consequences).

Predisposing structural conditions: when is your system susceptible to counterfactual

Condition i) is relatively easy to understand: The antecedent must be feasible in a static sense; that is, it must describe a state that is internally consistent. The antecedent must be "insertable"; there must be some feasible historical path, from a real historical state, that would produce the state described in the counterfactual antecedent. Thus, a strong argument pre-requires the identification of a finite set of options or potential trajectories, which in their initial state, must be consistent with the historical context of the development process. For example, if we can ex post identify (a, b, c, and d) as alternative solutions to assume a given function; (a) being finally selected; the strong argument could be developed for (b, and c) but not for (d) if this potential solution did not exist (even as project) at the period of initial decisions. If a, b, and c all existed at some point in the past, then we can ask, what would have happened had b been chosen at that point. We cannot ask the same question about d. To ask what would have happened had d been chose at that point, we have to go further back in history, and construct a path that includes d being available at that point. Option d is not insertable at that point in time. But this can be source of strength for the analysis. A small set of options at the branching point chosen by the analyst will have the effect of circumscribing the future. One of the difficulties faced by practitioners of evolutionary economics is that the future is not circumscribed nearly to the extent it is in neo-classical analysis. Branching points with few branches make this circumscription stronger, which makes the analysis easier and more compelling.

The second condition ii) – the consequent must be linked to the antecedent by a dynamic theory – is more difficult to clarify. A counterfactual argument needs a strong law to have an accurate representation or construction of the links between antecedents and consequences in order to avoid getting an uncompelling result through uncontrolled construction of chains of events. This law must be strong in two senses: it must be general (robust) and important. The dimension of generality is quite straightforward: this law must cope with a variety of (spatial and temporal) contexts. Many macro- and micro-economic laws are strong in that particular sense (even if some limits of their generalization can always be found) [1].

The dimension of importance is less simple. We need a law "important enough" to cause our counterfactual construction based on this law to be, in effect, isolated from the influence of other laws. That is, other effects must be secondary in magnitude. It becomes immediately clear that such a dimension implies that "strong" is an attribute which cannot be dissociated from the object under consideration: for example, while the network externality effect is a strong law for studying various counterfactual constructions in the field of telecommunication technologies; it is not by itself a strong law for creating hypothetical situations in the field of regional polarisation (because in the latter case, the dynamics generated by network externalities cannot be isolated from the dynamic effects of transportation costs, infrastructure externalities, innovation capabilities, local labour markets and so on). "Importance" means that the association between the law and the object has a particular attribute which is to make "ceteris paribus conditions" plausible; and that implies a restriction of the use of strong counterfactual argument to a particular class of problems.

---

1. On the question of the robustness of economic laws see Kindleberger (1989).

This discussion implies severe restriction to the potential use of the strong counterfactual arguments.

Many macroeconomic laws are strong in the sense of robustness and generalization (see Kindleberger, 1989). These laws however do not meet the condition of importance in the sense this attribute acquires here (or better say the association of these laws with macroeconomic object such as growth and development make them unable to produce "ceteris paribus conditions"). Contrasting with that, some microeconomic laws as used for studying particular and discrete objects are strong in both senses: it is the case for example of the learning curve when used for estimating and extrapolating efficiency improvements of a particular technology. Such a law is robust and important. It appears immediately from this discussion that the feasibility and relevance of the counterfactual method are strongly dependent upon the object of analysis. Whether you want to create counterfactuals on a "never adopted technology" or on a "never developed world" changes completely the nature of the problem in hand and will strongly influence your method and ambitions in terms of counterfactual analysis.

Considering that the structural conditions are highly restrictive, it is also possible to build a weaker counterfactual argument.

The purpose of the weak counterfactual argument is to identify important events, decisions, and accidents which have eliminated options and branches; that is to say which have dramatically altered the probability distribution for the system to get its possible final state. In a sense, weak counterfactual history is an application of appreciative theory. The point is to understand what has happened, why it happened and what was important in bringing about the current state. The point of this exercise is to understand the world as we see it, rather than to make claims about either what will happen, or how good such a world is. That is, there is little attempt at prediction, or at normative statements in this exercise.

We have qualified this approach as weak because it does not claim to generate knowledge on the respective properties, qualities and efficiency of the deserted branches. Constructing counterfacts in this weaker sense does not require us to know what the deserted branches would have looked like. The claim is restricted to the understanding of the major events and chains of decisions, which, coupled with the process that magnified rather than damped those decisions, can be considered as having played a role in disconnecting some sub-regions of the tree from the branches actually explored.

Advantages of a weak counterfactual argument are clear. It makes the two conditions listed above not necessary and thus allows economists to treat a large range of problems in those terms. Drawbacks, however, seem also clear. Weak counterfactual arguments do not give welfare results and in a sense give no more than the classical "potential regret" argument (as used for example in path-dependent economics). This statement should, however, deserve more attention. Weak counterfactuals, certainly, give more. Potential regret only recognises our ignorance regarding the social benefits of costs of actually being in one given world without saying anything about the underlying structure of events having produced this situation; while weak counterfactuals is undertaken in order to express this underlying structure. Potential regret is in fact a very weak claim, namely that there were other possible paths, and that one of them may have been better in some sense than the one we actually took. Weak counterfactual analysis is consistent with this point of view, in that it identifies points at which other paths would have diverged from the actual path. Weak counterfactual argument does not demonstrate actual regret, nor does it demonstrate actual happiness, but it does indicate the points at which actual regret may have begun to be created (and identifies potential culprits). Thus while the potential regret result claim is that multiple, non-welfare-equivalent equilibria exist, weak counterfactual history argues that there are moments at which history could have taken us to a different one. To argue that that different one could have been better, or more aggressively, probably was better, strong counterfactual history must be employed.

It is thus important to adjust the method of constructing counterfactual (weak or strong) to the object of analysis. The possibility of constraining potential developments and of using a strong law (in both senses) must be carefully checked before deciding what kind of counterfacts can be constructed.

5. Agenda for future research

In this paper, we have shown that the theoretical conditions of path-dependent inefficiency are relatively straightforward. They deal on the one hand with the problem of persistence; and on the other with the problem of the tension between diversity and standardization. We agree, however, that the empirical side of this subject is much more difficult. Arrow (1995) writes: *"The theory is pretty good, the empirical evidence may be by definition hard to come by, not just as a practical question"*. It is the reason why future research in path-dependence economics of technological choices should focus strongly on the empirical part of the programme. While many stimulating works providing the details of timing and circumstance (narrative history) have been done to illuminate the pervasive role of transient situations and events leaving a persistent influence, statistical work on time series have been largely neglected. In this sense, the recent work from Foreman-Peck (1996) is promising. Using a new data set of about 2800 car manufacturers in four countries before 1963, the author proposed a test of both lock-in and natural selection hypotheses. This data set provides some quantitative insights into the timing and survival of power source types. The data distinguishes the power source which producers chose for their vehicles, and their dates of industry entry and exit. Of great interest in this regard is the result that similar outcomes (the emergence of combustion engine as the standard) were obtained virtually independently of each other in different environments [1]. Over the long run, Foreman-Peck claimed, the emergence of the internal combustion engine car was not sensitive to small changes in initial conditions. However, the transition paths from the initial situations of technological diversity to the emergence of the standard were very different among the four countries. They were highly sensitive to initial conditions. This study provides a good example of the type of future research we need, in order to test the path-dependent selection hypothesis: working on time series and identifying path-dependent properties with statistical methods.

REFERENCES

Adams M. (1990), Norms, standards, rights, Invited Lecture Seventh Annual Conference of the European Association of Law and Economics, Rome, September.

Antonelli C. (1995), *The Economics of Localized Technological Change and Industrial Dynamics,* Kluwer.

Antonelli C. (1996), "The economics of path-dependence in industrial organization", draft, Dipartimento di Economia, Universita di Torino.

Arrow K. (1995), "Economic as it is and as it is developing: a very rapid survey", in Albach and Rosenkranz eds., *Intellectual Property Rights and Global Competition,* Berlin: edition Sigma, 11-32.

Arthur B. (1983), On Competing Technologies and Historical Small Events: the Dynamic of Choice under Increasing Returns, Working Paper, 83-90, IIASA, Austria.

Atkinson B. and J. Stiglitz (1969), "A New View of Technical Change", *The Economic Journal,* 573-578.

Bowler P. (1997), The transfer of metaphors between evolutionary biology and economics, Stocholm International Seminar of Evolutionary Economics, Stockholm Business School.

Cowan R. (1990), "Nuclear Power reactors: a study in technological lock-in", *The Journal of Economic History*, 5(3), 541-567.

Cowan R. (1991), "Tortoises and hares: choice among technologies of unknown merit", *The Economic Journal,* 101, 801-814.

---

1. But the assertion that the four systems were "virtually independent" should deserve more discussion. One should claim that after one or two decades, there was enough trade to support the existence of some intersecting networks of local relationships which transmit and communicate their effects. See David and Foray (1994) for an exploration of the role of those intersecting networks in the generation of a perfect correlation of standards choices throughout a global population.

Cowan R. and D. Foray (1995a), "Quandaries in the economics of dual technologies and spillovers from military to civilian research and development", *Research Policy*, vol. 24, n° 6, 851-868.

Cowan R. and D. Foray (1995b), The changing economics of technological learning, IIASA Working Paper, 95-39.

Cowan R. and Foray D. (1997), Counterfactual history and evolutionary economics, Stockolm International Seminar of Evolutionary Economics, Stockholm Business School.

Cowan R. and P. Gunby (1996), "Spread to death: pest control strategies and technological lock" in, *Economic Journal*, May, vol. 106, 521-542.

Cusumano M., Y. Mylonadis and R. Rosenbloom (1992), "Strategic maneuvering and mass-market dynamics: the triumph of VHS over Beta", *Business History Review*, 66, 51-94.

David P. A. (1975), *Technical Choice, Innovation and Economic Growth*, London: Cambridge University Press.

David P. A. (1986), "Understanding the economics of QWERTY: the necessity of history", in Parker ed., *Economic History and the Modern Economist*, Oxford: Basil Blackwell, 30-49.

David P. A. (1987), "New Standards for the Economics of Standardization", in Dasgupta and Stoneman, eds., *Economic Policy and Technological Performance*, London: Cambridge University Press, 206-239.

David P. A. (1988), *Path dependence: putting the past in the future of economics*, Stanford University, Institute for Mathematical Studies for the Social Science.

David P. A. (1992), "Path-dependence and predictability in dynamic systems with local network externalities: a paradigm for historical economics", in Foray and Freeman eds., *Technology and the Wealth of Nations*, London, Pinter, 208-231.

David P. A. (1993), "Historical economics in the long run: some implications of path dependence", in Snooks ed., *Historical Analysis in Economics*, London, Routledge, 29-40.

David P. A. and J. Bunn (1988), "The economics of gateway technologies and network evolution: lessons from electricity supply history", *Information Economics and Policy*, 3, 165-202.

David P. A. and G. Rothwell (1996), "Standardization, diversity and learning: strategies for the coevolution of technology and industrial capacity", *International Journal of Industrial Organization*, 14, 181-201.

David P. A. and D. Foray (1994), "Percolation Structures, Markov Random Fields and the Economics of EDI Standard Diffusion", in Pogorel ed., *Global Telecommunications Strategies and Technological Changes*, North-Holland, 135-170.

David P. A. and D. Foray (1995), "Dépendance du sentier et économie de l'innovation: un rapide tour d'horizon", *Revue d'Economie Industrielle*, Hors série, numéro exceptionnel, 27-52.

David P. A., D. Foray and J. M. Dalle (1996), Marshallian externalities and the emergence and spatial stability of technological enclaves, Economics of Innovation and New Technology (forthcoming).

Foray D. (1994), "Users, standards and the economics of coalitions and committees", *Information Economic and Policy*, 6.

Foray D. and A. Grübler (1990), "Morphological analysis, diffusion and lock-out of technologies: Ferrous casting in France and the FRG", *Research Policy*, vol. 19, 6, 535-550.

Foreman-Peck J. (1996), "Technological Lock-in" and the Power Source for the Motor Car, Discussion Papers in Economic and Social History, University of Oxford, 7.

Kirsch D. (1995), Flexibility and Stabilization of Technological Systems: The Case of the Second Battle of the Automobile Engine, Program in History of Science and Technology, Depatment of History Stanford University.

Lesourne J. (1991), *Economie de l'ordre et du désordre*, Economica

Liebowitz S. and S. Margolis (1990), "The fable of the keys", *Journal of Law and Economics*, 22, 1-25.

Liebowitz S. and S. Margolis (1995), "Path dependence, lock in and history", *The Journal of Law, Economics and Organization*, V11 N1, 205-226.

Metcalfe J. S. (1994), "Competition, Fischer's principle and increasing returns in the selection process", *Journal of Evolutionary Economics*, 4, 327-346.

Mokyr J. (1990), *The Lever of Riches*, Oxford University Press.

Payen M. (1990), *L'aventure scientifique et technique de la vapeur*, Paris: ed. du CNRS.

Rosenberg N. (1992), "Economic Experiments", *Industrial and Corporate Change*, vol. 1, n° 1, 181-203.

Schelling T. (1978), *Micromotives and Macrobehaviors* (Norton).

Stiglitz J. (1987), "Learning to learn, localized learning and technological progress", in Dasgupta, P. and P. Stoneman eds., *Economic Policy and Technological Performance*, London: Cambridge University Press, 125-153.

CHAPTER 12
LOCAL INTERACTION STRUCTURES, HETEROGENEITY AND THE DIFFUSION OF TECHNOLOGICAL INNOVATIONS *

Jean-Michel DALLE

1. Introduction

The diffusion of technological innovations is, notably since the works of Griliches (1957) and Mansfield (1960), and after Schumpeter, an essential question in economics, even if we were only to consider all the repercussions which readily come to mind between the speed and the extent of the diffusion of at least some new technologies and the competitiveness of a national industry. It has therefore been studied not only in an empirical way, but also with the help of various explicative models, the aim of all these works obviously being to understand better the factors which are likely to influence the diffusion processes. In fact, the essentially dynamic nature of these processes, as well as the fact that they clearly involve many different agents, have certainly led the economists to take up very early on a particularly innovative and original approach: besides the essential importance of the empirical approach, and its close links with modeling, the models employed are not classical and the parameters which they indicate as being important are not the most traditional ones either. Amongst these [1], two in particular seem to us to merit considerable attention: they relate to the heterogeneity of agents and to the occurrence of interactions between agents. These two factors are actually invoked in order to explain on the one hand the fact that the diffusion curves, which represent the market share of a new technology as a function of time, regularly display a logistic character [2], and on the other hand the variations in these curves in the context of this general model, notably in terms of diffusion speed.

---

* This article has benefited from several discussions with Benoît Simon. I also wish to thank those who participated in a seminar organized by the Centre de Recherche en Epistémologie Appliquée (CREA), France, as well as those who took part in the conferences titled "Self-Organization and Evolutionary Economics: New Developments" in Paris, September 1996, and "3e Ecole-Chercheurs d'Economie des Institutions" at Dourdan, France, December 1996, and especially Dominique Foray, Jacques Lesourne, André Orléan, Robert Salais, Richard Topol & Bernard Walliser.
1. Concerning these points, we can notably consult the recent surveys by Metcalfe (1988) and Lissoni & Metcalfe (1994).
2. The diffusion curve of a technology, also characterized as a "S curve", actually nearly always reveals three successive phases: the market share of the technology firstly grows slowly, followed by a very rapid growth phase during which the technology nearly completely "floods" its market, and finally a new slow growth phase during which the extent of its diffusion becomes almost total.

The heterogeneity is without doubt one of the main ideas invoked by several models in order to explain the fact that the decisions to adopt taken by firms are not all simultaneous and that the diffusion of a technology is a dynamic process. Consequently the general idea is to assume that a characteristic parameter changes with time – the firms' turnover, the performances of the technology –, leading to gradual decisions to adopt, according to the heterogeneous microeconomic characteristics of the firms. At a given moment in time, all the firms which should have rationally adopted have done so, but the evolution of this parameter then makes the decision to adopt rational for new firms. In this way explanations are provided for the logistic character of the diffusion curve: their main weakness is due to the fact that they are specific to each situation, while a general explanation is needed for a property which appears in empirical works as a structural regularity. Another weakness is that the governing parameter is nearly always exogenous. Moreover, it is clear that these models consider the firms to be perfectly and identically informed, in a continuous manner, on the characteristics of technologies: this obviously is not the case, as the study of technological subjects implies that an essential role should be accorded to uncertainty, not only for emerging technologies whose characteristics are very uncertain, but also because the adoption of a technology is always a precarious decision for a firm, even when this technology is already quite well known, due to all the changes it implies to the very structure of a firm and possibly to its markets. If the main advantage of these models, often called equilibrium models, comes from the role they accord to the heterogeneity of the firms in the explanation of technological diffusion phenomena, as is widely and clearly established by the empirical literature (Lissoni & Metcalfe, 1994), they completely neglect on the other hand the role played by the diffusion of technological information.

This last point is in fact the essential argument for another category of models which were actually developed prior to the equilibrium ones: that is, the so called "epidemic" models, which attempt to explain the logistic character of the diffusion curve by the diffusion of technological information. Actually it is quite easy to establish the occurrence of logistic diffusion curves in this type of approach, which considers for example that the probability a firm is informed of the availability of a profitable technology depends on the number of firms having adopted it earlier. The underlying idea is that found in an encounter model, i.e. the idea of a technological information diffusion process depending on encounters which explains the logistic shape of the diffusion curve. However, the hypothesis of information diffusion seems to be very unlikely as soon as, inevitably, information on the characteristics and performances of technologies is widely available, via external information sources, as it will at least be disseminated by the producers of the innovations, if not by specialized or professional reviews. What these models in fact neglect, besides inaccuracies concerning the level of rationality credited to actors condemned to epidemic behaviors, is the essentially local character of any technological adoption. Actually, these models seem to assume that as soon as a firm has information on the profitability of a technology, it adopts it. However it's not evident that the acquisition of the type of information considered by these models should systematically lead to a decision to adopt: the fact that the firms hold information does not eliminate the specific risks associated with an adoption, and above all does not reduce the adoption costs. The particular characteristics of a firm make the adaptation of this technology necessary, and this adaptation implies important switching and conversion costs notably due to the complementarity of the different elements which constitute a firm's production system: in all cases, the adoption risks and costs cannot be disregarded. In other words, the acquisition of pertinent technological information is expensive, not instantaneous and never perfect insofar as it depends amongst others on characteristics specific to each firm; in the same way, information available identically to all firms does not resolve their individual dilemma.

In fact these works don't take into account the occurrence of local externalities and local interaction structures between the potential adopters, such as they have since been established and insisted upon (David, 1988; David & Foray, 1994; Dalle, 1995), and even when the neutrality of such factors to the economic analysis is not at all evident (Dalle, 1997b), not only in the sense where these interaction structures correspond to the existence of informational interactions between the firms – the local transmission of then truly pertinent technological information –, but also in the sense of *the taking into account of all the other factors which lead to the modification of individual optimization programs according to the adoption decisions of the other agents,* such as the competition mechanisms or furthermore the technological complementarity with sub-contractors or technological partners, etc. In this way, local interaction modeling frameworks are perfectly compatible with the hypothesis of the rationality of the individual actors and also take into account their heterogeneity.

The approaches in terms of equilibria attach an important role to the heterogeneity, but neglect the role of interaction structures at the price of unrealistic hypotheses regarding the information available to the agents, while the epidemic approaches perceive the existence of interaction structures, but then limit themselves to the global diffusion of information on the technologies, avoiding what is implied by the existence of local ones, and at the same time avoiding the question of the micro-economic fundamentals and that of the heterogeneity. At the same time, we have been prompted, in previous works, to show that a modeling category can be defined – stochastic interaction models – taking into account the existence of local interaction structures, compatible with the rationality hypothesis, and for which the heterogeneity of the actors indeed has an essential influence on the very nature of the dynamics (Dalle, 1995, 1997a, b). As a typical conclusion, and in the case of competition between technological standards, the heterogeneity of the actors as compared with local externalities plays the role of a state parameter leading to the appearance of a phase transition: when heterogeneity is weak and less than, even if only slightly, a certain critical parameter, spontaneous standardization is inevitable; when it is strong and above this parameter, again even if only slightly, spontaneous standardization will never take place. In this context, the aim of this article is to prove that we can also study the diffusion of technological innovations with the help of stochastic interaction models: it implies, as we will have realized, an attempt to reconcile the two approaches mentioned above in a framework which takes into account simultaneously the heterogeneity of the actors and the existence of interactions between them. The regular logistic shape of the diffusion curves, observed with the help of simulations, is thus provided with a very general explanation, based on the existence of local interaction structures between heterogeneous actors. We will also demonstrate that the heterogeneity has an important influence on the diffusion speed of technologies, as, once again, several empirical studies have already shown.

Beyond these validations, this approach can also lend its full meaning to another empirical observation considered less often in the literature – the formation of niches and the survival of technological enclaves –, and consequently leads us to suggest a new way to analyze diffusion processes of technological innovations, whose inception is strictly dependent on an approach taking into account the existence of local interaction structures and the heterogeneity of the actors in a dynamic context [1]. In this framework, these technological niches and enclaves, whose appearance are due to the existence of local interactions between heterogeneous actors, clearly seem to be essential elements which indeed determine the technological diffusion processes as *the diffusion paths followed by the technological innovations indeed appear to be marked and influenced by the appearance and disappearance of successive technological niches*. Such an analysis, if is was to be confirmed, would evidently have significant consequences notably for the strategies of both public and private actors.

2. Heterogeneity and local interaction structures

To define the framework for an economic analysis of technological innovation diffusion processes, let us first of all consider a population of firms which are likely to adopt a new technology: these firms are more often than not "naturally" heterogeneous, at least when we are concerned with process

---

[1]. From this point of view, a reference should be made to the works which have gradually led to the emergence of such approaches in the last few years: the revival of the aggregation question (Schelling, 1971, 1978) and the criticism of the representative agent (Kirman, 1992); the emergence of a truly dynamic approach to economic phenomena where the notions of path-dependence and trajectories are essential (David, 1985; Arthur, 1989; Dosi, 1988); the recognition of the role that falls to local interactions (David, 1988; Kirman, 1983; David & Foray, 1994; Dalle, 1995); and the progressive development of models well suited to taking into account all these questions (Schelling, 1971; Föllmer, 1974; David, 1988; Arthur, 1989; Orléan, 1990, 1992; Kirman, 1993; Durlauf, 1993; David & Foray, 1994; Dalle, 1995, 1997a, b).

innovations, as they are distinguished by their products and markets, and therefore by their structure, size, organization... For example digital control of machine tools, the diffusion of which was supported by the French state in the 1970's and 80's, appeals to firms whose products are different and which are themselves different: in the same way as today information technology appeals to firms which are fundamentally heterogeneous in both their structures and products.

Further more, and even within the same industry, it indeed seems that firms are permanently heterogeneous, as demonstrated by many recent empirical works. This observation in fact finds a justification as soon as we consider the historicity of economic processes. It's evident that the knowledge bases firms possess differ, as the firms differentiate with time due to the learning process itself, that is to say learning by doing: this was illustrated by Atkinson & Stiglitz (1969), through the notion of localized technical change, which have since been followed up by other authors (David, 1975; Stiglitz, 1987; Antonelli, 1995). The main idea involves recalling that the production function represents all of the possible technologies to produce a given asset: the learning process, and knowledge, and through them the improvements made to a technique consequently modify a firm's production function, but they only modify it locally. With time, the firms learn, and this learning process therefore induces a dynamic disposition towards differentiation, which tends to maintain or even reinforce their heterogeneity. The potential adopters of a given technology are therefore mainly heterogeneous, naturally when their products and markets are different, but even when they belong to the same industry insofar as the intertemporal cumulativity of their productive investments tends to differentiate them.

Consequently this heterogeneity finds itself at the very heart of decisions to adopt technologies: actually, for a given firm, adopting a technology obviously leads to costs and risks, and a firm will adopt a new technology when, *in its case*, the expected costs will be less than the expected profits. These costs and risks should neither be under-estimated, nor reduced to the simple price of the technology: it involves the so called switching costs (David, 1975), where the costs for the firm to adapt to the new technology, and vice versa, are often very important, without even considering the risks related to the adoption of any new technology (Hélioui & Simon, 1997), due to the uncertainly associated with the performances of new technologies and due to the very existence of a process to adapt the technology to the firm and the firm to the technology. In this context, adoption costs and risks will be particularly specific to each firm, that is to say different for firms having different production functions. To put it another way, it is expensive and risky for a firm to modify its production function, and these costs and risks are specific to the firm's initial production function. Each firm therefore has a rational behavior, which can be described in the form of an optimal decision, *but the parameters for this decision are specific to each firm.* In other words, the firms' optimization programs are different due to their heterogeneity.

If the heterogeneity renders the optimization programs of the potential adopters different, the presence of an interaction structure makes them interdependent. The adoption costs and risks for a specific firm are actually significantly modified as soon as other adopters declare themselves in the neighborhood of this firm. When one of the "neighbors" of a firm adopts the technology, this contributes to reducing the adoption costs and risks for this firm, or indeed increases the costs and risks associated with the decision not to adopt. There are many reasons for this (Arthur, 1989), notably related to problems of technological compatibility and accessibility to knowledge and specific information acquired by others, which therefore reduce adoption costs and risks. Technological adoptions are therefore locally cumulative: the adoption decision of each agent is rational, but these decisions take into account the decisions of a certain number of other agents, i.e. his "relevant neighbors" (David, 1988) with whom he is interacting. We can therefore attribute to each of these agents a neighborhood, that is to say a group of agents with whom he is interacting: if we then assume that these neighborhoods are interconnected (David & Foray, 1994), we obtain what we propose to call a connected *local interaction structure*. Obviously this notion of neighborhood should be seen in a non-geographical way: if we find in the geographical case the notion of marshallian externalities, the adoption of a technology by sub-contractors, competitors and technological partners will have the same type of influence in the absence of geographical proximity. Furthermore, this notion of neighborhood makes no reference to the idea of distance, as it simply involves associating with each potential adopter the others whose adoption decisions are relevant to him: we are actually satisfied with just considering sets or at best graphs, but in no way do we enter into the notion of distance or metrics.

The adoption by one or several neighbors of a firm modifies the adoption costs and risks for the latter. The optimization programs of firms themselves evolve with time, and successive adoptions induce, in a sense, certain subsequent adoptions, by making the technology available with reduced the costs and risks. The diffusion processes are therefore mainly dynamic and without doubt path-dependent (David, 1985), with all the implied consequences (Foray, 1997), in the sense that the cumulative nature of individual adoption decisions makes itself evident in a dynamic context. Due to the presence of local interaction structures, the diffusion process itself modifies in an endogenous way the actors individual optimization programs, without it being necessary to call upon exogenous parameters. At this stage, it therefore appears logical to us to propose, in order to study technological diffusion processes, the use of models which take into account the factors whose importance we have just demonstrated, that is to say the heterogeneity of potential adopters and the existence between them of interaction structures, both in a dynamic context: such a model, which would anyway belong to the "order-disorder" class (Lesourne, 1992), and would constitute what we have elsewhere (Dalle, 1997b) suggested to call a "stochastic interaction model", should also allow, in spite of the apparent complexity of these parameters, sound conclusions to be obtained.

3. A stochastic aggregation model and some preliminary results

Let us therefore consider again a population of potential interacting heterogeneous adopters. For each adopter a, we designate its neighborhood by $V(a)$, that is to say all of the other potential adopters whose decisions influence its own, i.e. those whose decisions it takes into account for its own adoption decision. In other words, the decision to adopt or not the technology in question implies that a resolves an optimization program with the form

$$O(a, V(a)) = Ca < RaPa$$

which depends on the idiosyncratic characteristics specific to a – the adoption costs Ca and risks Ra, and the profit anticipated by the firm a, Pa – and the neighborhood of a, which can in itself, in a certain way, be considered as one of the idiosyncratic characteristics of a. Then

$$S = \{V(a)\}$$

then represents the local interaction structure of the population, which can also be described by:

$$\{(b, c) \text{ where } c \text{ belongs to } V(b)\}$$

If we now assume all that matters in $V(a)$ is the number of adopters in $V(a)$ who have already adopted, which we designate by $n(V(a))$, then the optimization programs reduce to:

$$O(a, n(V(a))) = Ca(nV(a)) < Ra(n(V(a))) Pa(n(V(a)))$$

Let us also assume that we know all the actors' characteristics perfectly: we should therefore know the number of adopters who would adopt when

$$n(V(a)) = k$$

and therefore the statistical probability $F(k)$ that an a selected randomly from the population adopts when $n(a) = k$. In fact, this should simply be derived from the solution, for each actor, of his optimization programs, i.e.:

$$F(k) = P[O(a, k) \text{ holds in the population of potential adopters}]$$

and therefore:

$$F(k) = P[Ca(k) < Ra(k) Pa(k) \text{ in the population}]$$

for all values of k. We therefore define the *statistical behavioral function* of the population, $F(\ .\ )$, for all possible values of k.

This model now implies obtaining results for the probable diffusion trajectories: for this, and insofar as this model cannot obviously be solved analytically except for a few exceptional cases, and in a quasi-static context associated with altered interaction structures [1], our *simulation protocol* involves simulating trajectories obtained by drawing randomly, at each time step, one agent from the population whose adoption probability as a function of his neighborhood is then given by F [2]. As a consequence to the fact that the agents are heterogeneous and in interaction, we have therefore been led towards a stochastic model: the model is stochastic, but empirically grounded on a statistical behavioral function.

This protocol corresponds precisely, as it happens, to the approach of Schelling (1971), as we intend simply to obtain results relating to the probable qualitative properties of trajectories. Insofar as the studied phenomena reveal non-linearities, it is absolutely essential to employ this type of methodology: extreme trajectories will certainly nearly always be possible, but often very improbable. The presence of "chaotic" phenomena in a non-linear system should not lead us to conclude the complete unpredictability of the trajectories: on the contrary, these trajectories are subject to the occurrence of "attractors" which we can in fact study at least by the simulation of many different trajectories, in order to determine which properties do not change from one trajectory to the next; such is our method here. Finally, as we just said, this protocol also offers another advantage, as it provides access to empirical results through the statistical behavioral function: the properties of these actually depend on the characteristics of the agents who make up a given population, such as they can be studied empirically, with if necessary the identification of different behaviors for different types of actors.

---

1. We can notably consult the works of Föllmer (1974), Allen (1982a, 1982b), Orléan (1990), Durlauf (1993), Dalle (1995), David, Foray & Dalle (1997) to ascertain that the properties which can be demonstrated analytically are mainly, in this context, related to the existence of a phase transition. This property is itself only obtained at the price of a traditional hypothesis in physics, the mean-field hypothesis, the validity of which in economics is not evident (Dalle, 1997a). In fact, the weakness in the obtained analytical results sometimes appears to be extreme: Allen (1982a, b), in her attempt – the only one to our knowledge – to use a local interaction model in order to study the diffusion of technologies, and besides other economically dubious hypotheses such as the neglect of technological information, is a classic example where the conclusions are either very inadequate, or obtained at the price of replacing local interactions by a random encounter model therefore accompanied by the loss of major properties, such as the role of niches (see below), and with no real control on the validity of the results.

2. To refer to the introduction, and in a synthetic way, we could say that this model is neither an equilibrium model, as it calls upon a process, nor a dis-equilibrium model, as each action involves returning locally to an "individual" optimum calculated according to the optimization program of a given agent: it rather involves sequential cumulative actions. The stochastic interaction models as we present them here can therefore also be characterized as sequential cumulative action models.

248 | Dynamics of technological systems

To obtain results, obviously only very preliminary in this context, we will neglect the different possible versions of the technology which diffuse, as well as eventual global externalities which will be considered to be constant throughout the diffusion process, which notably corresponds to the hypothesis adopted here of an already well established profitability provided by the technology [1]: as a matter of fact, and as we will see further on, some of the results obtained with the help of simple local interactions tend to lead to the conjecture according to which local interaction structures might often predominate over global externalities. In the following, we will also specify more accurately the interaction structure, S, between the agents and clarify the properties of F. As for S, the agents are assumed to be located at the intersections of a 2-dimensional toric square lattice connecting them with their nearest neighbors: each agent therefore has 4 relevant neighbors. Such a structure has the advantage of simplicity, and above all that of providing for the moment the same number of neighbors to all of the agents which from this point of view avoids introducing supplementary hypotheses at this stage: to summarize, its essential advantage is its uniformity, but other works must be carried out with alternative structures to see if the properties revealed here remain valid, or indeed depend on certain features of the interaction structures. Turning our attention to F, the statistical behavioral function of the population of potential adopters, it is therefore characterized for S by providing 5 possible probabilities, i.e. $F(0)$, $F(1)$, $F(2)$, $F(3)$, $F(4)$ with the form $F(i)$, where $F(i)$ is the probability that an agent adopts the diffusing technology when i of his 4 neighbors have already adopted it. Some properties of F can therefore be deduced from the economic problem considered, in this case the diffusion of technological innovations: first of all, $F(i)$ is a probability, which implies for all i between 0 and 4:

$$0 <= F(i) <= 1$$

Obviously F is moreover an increasing function, as the adoption of the technology by an agent is all the more probable if it has already been widely adopted in the neighborhood of this agent, as the adoptions in the neighborhood create positive externalities in costs and risks. In the same way, we will assume:

$$F(0) \neq 0 \quad \text{and} \quad F(4) \neq 1$$

in order to take into account the heterogeneity of the population: even when nobody in the neighborhood of an agent has adopted the technology, it is possible that he may do so; in the same way, even when all the neighbors of an

---

1. Other simulations, currently in progress, might allow us if the first results were to be confirmed to extend the results presented here to the case where the profitability of a technology increases with its diffusion.

Local interaction structures, heterogeneity and the diffusion | 249

agent have adopted a technology, it is possible that he does not. We therefore have in total:

$$0 < F(0) <= F(1) <= F(2) <= F(3) <= F(4) < 1$$

In order to interpret the profitability of the technology, we will also assume:

$$F(2) > 1/2$$

When at least half the neighbors of a potential adopter have adopted the diffusing technology, the probability that this potential adopter decides to adopt it when he makes his decision is at least one in two. Or, which amounts to the same thing, this is the case as soon as the majority of firms in the neighborhood of an agent have decided to adopt the technology. As a result, $F(3)$ and $F(4)$ are greater than ½, while $F(0)$ and $F(1)$ are less than ½, as F increases with i. We finally assume that $F(3)$ and $F(4)$ are very close to 1: the adoption costs and risks are greatly reduced for nearly all of the potential adopters as soon as nearly all of their relevant neighbors have already adopted.

Knowing that other simulations not presented in this article have corroborated the results obtained here for other values, we will assume here:

$$F(2) = 0.6; \quad F(3) = 0.95; \quad F(4) = 0.98$$

For different pairs of values of $P(0)$ and $P(1)$, such as $P(0) <= P(1)$, which according to the preceding hypotheses fully determine the model, simulations are accomplished with the software EXCEL and macro-commands developed by ourselves. They are implemented on a 30×30 torus, i.e. comprising 900 firms [1], and the basic algorithm involves selecting a firm randomly and simulating its decision to adopt a technology with the help of the statistical behavioral function F. As a result we can observe the shape of the diffusion curve, and in particular determine if the technology floods or not the market.

In this context, the diffusion curve seems to have a logistic appearance whatever the values of $P(0)$ and $P(1)$ – cf. for example Figure 1 for the case $P(0) = 0.05$ and $P(1) = 0.10$ –. In other words, the market share of the technology tends to 100 % with time in an approximately constantly increasing manner: the diffusion curve displays only one inflection point, i.e. the diffusion is rather slow to start with, then quite quick afterwards before slowing down when the market share approaches 100%. These two properties qualitatively characterize a curve with a "logistic appearance", and seem to be observed for

---

[1]. According to other simulations, this simulation parameter does not seem to have an influence on the qualitative results obtained.

all values of $P(0)$ and $P(1)$. In other words, the hypotheses that we advanced – heterogeneity, sequentiality and local interaction structures – are sufficient, once they have been incorporated into the language of a stochastic interaction model, to qualitatively explain the "logistic" shape of diffusion curves. This result obviously tends first of all to support the very non-neutrality of these hypotheses for the economic analysis. To put it yet in another way, the shape of the diffusion curves appears to be structural and can be explained by the heterogeneity of the agents and the existence between them of local interaction structures: it originates neither from epidemic phenomena concerning the spread of information, nor from an exogenous dynamic parameter specified in an ad hoc manner. It is the heterogeneity which is responsible for the stochastic nature of the model and thus for part of its dynamics (Dalle, 1997a). The heterogeneity, common in equilibrium models, combined with the existence of an interaction structure, implicit in epidemic models, provides an explanation for the logistic character of the diffusion curves based on rational behaviors and local adoption decisions. *It is the diffusion process itself which generates a succession of rational adoption decisions.*

Furthermore, when $P(0)$ and $P(1)$ vary, it seems that only the diffusion speed varies: the diffusion appears to be more or less rapid, and in certain cases extremely slow – cf. Figure 2 for a few different diffusion curves –. More analyses are obviously required from this point of view: as an indication, it seems however that we can relate this result to various analyses (Lissoni & Metcalfe, 1995) which tend to credit the size of the firms with an important role in explaining the diffusion speed of a technology. Actually, if the firms which constitute the population have on average an important size, the adoption costs and risks will certainly be reduced by the presence of well developed technical services, or even internal R& D, and similarly by the possibility of testing the technology internally, on only one production line for example: as a result, *the probabilities $P(0)$ and $P(1)$ will be higher in such a population,* i.e. the propensity of firms to adopt alone or when only a few number of previous adopters exist in their neighborhood will be rather high, thus influencing, according to our modeling framework, the diffusion speed. We will have realized, this opens the way to analyses which would tend to fit empirical observations on the probable behaviors of adopters, according to their characteristics, with the overall diffusion characteristics, notably the speed [1].

But, more generally, we are prompted at this stage to propose a dynamic interpretation of diffusion processes, which credits the heterogeneity and the existence of interaction structures with an essential role. Actually this analysis is made possible insofar as the stochastic interaction model that we proposed allows the observation of not only the diffusion curve but also of the evolution of the firms' choices on the interaction structure which we assumed to exist

---

[1]. And for example starting with the idea of the value of the "wait and see" option, as suggested by Hélioui & Simon (1997).

Local interaction structures, heterogeneity and the diffusion | 251

between them, that is to say the particular history of the diffusion process: Figure 3 presents an evolution in the diffusion process corresponding to the diffusion curve in Figure 1. The demonstration of the presence of an interaction structure which renders possible this analysis, which would be almost impossible in its absence.

4. Local interactions, technological niches and enclaves

At the start of the process, we therefore observe a few isolated adopters whose adoption behavior can be explained by their situation: because they are faced with reduced adoption risks due for example to their size, or else because they anticipate an enhanced profitability or lower adoption and adaptation costs due to their idiosyncratic characteristics, or else because they are encouraged by a special market environment, for example very competitive – negative profits in case of non-adoption, for instance –: all these explanations of course play a role in the heterogeneity of the firms. To put it another way, we might say that, due to their specific knowledge and history and production functions, a few agents will have optimization programs which will render the adoption of a new technology profitable very early on, even in the absence of other adoptions in their neighborhood: here we allocate not only all the cases where the particular characteristics of a new technology correspond extremely well with the product of a given firm and with its specific needs, but also all the firms which have, due to their background, the skills or a production facility which renders particularly cheap or safe the adoption of a new technology.

Afterwards, the existence of local externalities essentially tends to provoke the appearance of *technological niches*. These niches should not be interpreted in a simply geographical manner, alongside quite the same line of reasoning as the one we presented above about the notion of neighborhood: simply, the first adoptions render locally more probable subsequent adoptions by the nearest neighbors, as the adoption risks and costs are consequently reduced for the latter – technological information or expertise having become available –. The taking into account of local interactions therefore provides an explanation for the formation of technological niches and enclaves (Dalle, 1995, 1997a; David, Foray & Dalle, 1997) and corroborates after all several empirical works (Foray & Grübler, 1990, for example) whose theoretical importance, we believe, may well have been under-estimated up to now.

The first niches to appear initially grow slowly, or even fail to survive, because the technology which is gradually being abandoned is itself still subject to strong local externalities which incite its users to continue to exploit it: the switching costs are still statistically high, and all the more so if the firm is dealing with others who exploit the same technology. This growth then becomes much more rapid: due to the growth of one or more of the niches, the remaining potential adopters have statistically an ever increasing number of neighbors

252 | Dynamics of technological systems

who have already adopted it, which renders their own adoption more and more likely. Finally the diffusion gradually becomes complete as the number of adopters still not having adopted slowly decreases: it actually tends to zero as the probability that an adopter of the new technology returns to the former becomes extremely weak when the quasi-totality of his neighbors have also adopted the new technology.

Before it is so, we can observe, after simulating several diffusion processes in this way, the more or less durable *survival of technological enclaves*: actually, the users of the former technology will continue to exploit it all the more so, even if its performances are inferior and it has been widely adapted, if they still have neighbors who in the great majority also continue to exploit it. Enclaves of the gradually abandoned technology can survive for a certain time thanks once again to the existence of local externalities which increase the probability that an agent keeps the former technology if all or nearly all of his relevant neighbors do the same, as in this case the adoption costs and risks for the new technology are not yet reduced. The disappearance of these enclaves, if it appears at this stage to be highly inevitable, seems to be rather slow, or at least slower than we would have been perhaps anticipated, which again tends to confirm many empirical observations (David, Foray & Dalle, 1997).

From this point of view, the underlying dynamics in diffusion processes are significantly different from those in models which base the diffusion or more precisely the competition-and-standardization dynamics on global externalities (Arthur, 1989): it thus seems possible for us to hypothesize and to affirm henceforth that it is not necessary for each new adopter to have access to increasing global externalities for the diffusion of the technology to occur and for the diffusion curve to adopt its recognized shape. On the very contrary, the taking into account of the heterogeneity of the agents and the existence of a local interaction structure provides a more complete explanation for the diffusion processes. The heterogeneity of the agents is seen to be absolutely essential at the start of the diffusion process as the first adoptions are made by "isolated" adopters for whom the adoption proves itself to be profitable in a precocious way due to their idiosyncratic characteristics. The presence of these first adopters is essential for the formation of the first technological niches, *and are indeed allowed in this context by the existence of local externalities*. These niches then appear as essential for the diffusion process itself: it is from them that the diffusion spreads out to the whole of the population considered. The technology spreads because after a few adoptions, sometimes with no connections between them, initiated by a few potential adopters for whom the characteristics of the technology are very well adapted for one reason or another, technological niches form related to local externalities, from which the technology can then flood the market. The technology diffuses step by step, and this diffusion is "transmitted" by the formation of coherent technological niches. As a result, it seems that a convincing explanation for the formation of technological niches can only be provided by taking into account local interaction structures: this therefore leads us, reciprocally, to hypothesize that the local interactions are often more pertinent than the global interactions to study diffusion phenomena, or just as important, insofar as the formation of such niches or enclaves seems to be frequent [1].

This last point is all the more important as the niches no longer appear to be epiphenomena, but seem to play an absolutely crucial role, even critical, for the diffusion of technologies. As a matter of fact, the diffusion processes for technologies indeed appear to be above all influenced, even marked, by the appearance, disappearance, development and survival of successive technological niches and enclaves. The spread of Internet use, for example, seems well suited to analysis in this way. Inaugurated in the military sector, because the network structure of decision centers provided protection vis-à-vis an atomic attack for example – the first, precocious adopters –, it developed in the research community because the very nature of research work implies frequent debates with geographically distant partners, and notably the exchange of texts – the first important niche –: today it has reached part of the general public – diffusion is indeed gaining momentum –, and its future development today seems to be particularly influenced by the spread of commercial practices, currently still limited to a few special niches.

5. Some consequences

According to this, we are also provided with some quite straightforward interpretation of some of the strategies of firms producing such technology: actually, if it was to be confirmed that technological diffusion processes very often start with the appearance of technological niches, it would become essential for the producers to identify, as soon as possible, the potential niches offering the most growth, i.e. the target center. The characteristics of certain potential adopters render their adoption more likely right from the start of the process: it is therefore to these potential clients that a firm must initially pay the more attention, not only because it wants to sell, but also, so it seems, because the future success of its technology will often depend greatly on its success in these niches, as the future adopters will actually be greatly influenced by these first ones. In the same way, as the diffusion processes reveal niches and enclaves, certain firms might also decide to produce only and specifically for these niches and enclaves: they may therefore propose to a certain number of special clients a product suitable to their needs by becoming "niche players"

We can certainly interpret in this context certain elements in the present strategy of the firm Apple: its technology is actually today completely minor,

---

1. We have also suggested elsewhere (Dalle, 1997a) that at least sometimes global interactions may be considered as a special case of local ones: actually in certain cases everything happens as if all the agents had in their neighborhoods the same "global agent". We also hypothesized, still based on simulations, that the circumstances of the appearance and survival of technological niches and enclaves would be different in the presence and absence of such an agent.

and subsists mainly within niches, which depend on the heterogeneity of the agents' preferences attributed to the greater adaptability of this technology to certain types of needs due to its inherent characteristics – its user-friendliness, its power for image processing – which lead to the survival of stable and profitable niches *thanks to the existence of local interaction structures and externalities* – file exchange between users, specialized software producers for example –. Among these niches, we can for instance mention the Macintosh "faithful", never mind if this fidelity is irrational and affective or that it represents the extent of the investments made and therefore the eventual switching costs, but also and above all the image processing and DTP professionals or furthermore the educational institutions. In a certain way, what the analysts today reproach Apple for, is its failure to recognize the opportunity to establish itself in the niche which still constitutes the Internet users, while its exploitation system seemed to be very well adapted to this purpose: while the predictions tend to indicate that this niche should in the near future spread to the whole of the population, it was an occasion for an innovation and a change in the technological dynamics which has perhaps been missed.

Such "niche" strategies, which obviously tend to maintain technological diversity, are not necessarily detrimental from a collective point of view: if the benefits from a total standardization are not completely exploited, the presence of a technology within a niche or an enclave, where it is used and therefore may be improved by its users or by its producers, preserves a form of *option value* which can result in the possibility that innovations are made to it which render it for example superior to another, indeed dominant, technology (Foray & Grübler, 1990). An innovation made to an abandoned technology can render it sufficiently profitable for it to flood the market again. Could the "Apple" technology have been better than the "Microsoft" technology? It had in any case an important advance, and its maintenance in a few specific niches may have led to its improvement, consequently allowing it to demonstrate all of its potential, notably in the context of Internet. An opportunity may have been missed here, which may have led not only to a significant increase in the market share of Apple, supported by the success of Internet, but also to a possible improvement in the general social welfare...

The appearance of niches and survival of technological enclaves are indeed also pertinent from a collective point of view, and hence for the public actors: this applies especially when it involves accelerating the diffusion of a technology. In this context, the emergence of technological niches offers the possibility of other pertinent strategies distinct from those which simply involve creating incentives to adopt by subsidizing technologies through appropriate encouragements. We could also imagine that the public actors contribute to the formation and development of a certain number of technological niches by promoting for example the adoption by a certain number of potential adopters that they control, distributed across the interaction structure and likely to induce the adoption by a certain number of their neighbors who would then form a coherent technological niche. The existence of this niche, and the growth in its size, could then provoke a more widespread diffusion process.

As for the survival of technological enclaves, it may be important to the State as soon as it appears necessary to keep alive or to maintain a reserve of technologies for future needs due to their option value: it may be that an obsolete technology in a given industrial sector tomorrow becomes the panacea in another sector, subject to a few innovations of course. Two examples of this type of evolution are the conversion of a large part of the china industry in Limousin, France, to ceramics, or furthermore that of the clock and watch-making industry in the Jura, both in France and Swiss, in full recession due to the competition from the economies of the developing world, to micro-mechanics, a sector in full expansion, and which requires more or less the same precision mechanic skills and tools. An apparently obsolete technology can tomorrow lead to, subject to a certain number of innovations and restructurings, and above all often subject to a change in product, a booming industrial sector with consequent employment opportunities. The Limousin and Jura examples illustrate to the State the important option value that certain technologies may represent, or more precisely certain industries which continue to exploit an old technology: consequently they can lead to evolutions which appear to be a clear form of product differentiation logic and which can therefore be classified as a diversification to new high-growth markets, due to the specific characteristics of the technologies exploited. If the survival of technological enclaves actually offers opportunities for product differentiation to the firms producing technology, it represents to the State a value option which is difficult to estimate but which a priori is just as difficult to neglect. Consequently there may be an economic value in keeping "alive" certain industrial sectors while of course also defining which diversifications may be recommended to exploit to the maximum the possibilities offered by the technology already used.

6. Conclusion

It goes without saying that the results presented in this paper are only very preliminary: it seems however that henceforth we can envisage explaining the logistic character of diffusion curves and the formation of technological niches with no further hypotheses besides that of the presence of local interaction structures between rational heterogeneous agents. With the help of a stochastic interaction model, we can in this way provide an explanation for the appearance of certain collective "aggregated" properties which result from many individual rational actions [1]: the resulting method consequently seems to provide the opportunity to study dynamic economic processes whose fundamental units are

---

1. Concerning the more methodological aspects as far as "stochastic interaction models" are concerned, we can also refer to Dalle (1997b).

individual actors' actions, rather than pre-determined macro-economic aggregates. This approach to economic analysis does not therefore pretend to specify the determinants for the decisions of each actor, but only considers statistically the parameters which can influence the distribution of these determinants and therefore the variety of actions, all rational but heterogeneous, in order to deduce properties from them likely to provide explanations for some empirically observed economic patterns. Indeed, the essence of such dynamics depends on the fact that economic agents make rational decisions in order to adapt in the best possible way to their situation. In this context, and in the absence of analytical results, simulation appears to be a useful tool, but which must be exploited with care and with clear protocols: the results presented here in fact just lead us to conjectures, whose eventual validity must then notably be supported by the analysis of empirically confirmed stylized facts.

In this context, our principal conclusion here, besides the verification of the logistic character of diffusion curves and variations in the diffusion speed, lies in providing an explanation for the appearance of technological niches and enclaves and to suggest *that the diffusion processes should be analyzed as essentially marked by the appearance of successive niches*. Such an approach clearly calls for local interaction structures to be taken into account, and is only allowed insofar as this parameter is taken into account in a dynamic context and with heterogeneous agents. The heterogeneity actually explains the isolated adoptions which will then lead to the appearance of niches, and it is *from niche to niche* that the technology will spread, or rather by the growth of certain niches and the appearance of a few others.

Finally, as we have emphasized, and still in a completely preliminary way, the formation of niches and the survival of technological enclaves are also not neutral, neither for the public actors, nor for certain private actors. But it should also be clear that such an analysis of collective processes would also lead to quite fundamental theoretical questions, among which notably the one which tries to get some measure of the influence that individual actions might have on collective phenomena (David, 1987; Dalle & Foray, 1995, 1997): indeed, if we can explain using the notions of heterogeneity and interaction structure the fact that the collective dynamics sometimes present regularities, economists should then question the possible influence that the individual actions of private actors, or perhaps public actors, may have on such phenomena. As a conclusion, we would easily be inclined to suggest here that the preliminary aspect of the results is perhaps tantamount to the amplitude of the research agenda.

REFERENCES

Allen B. (1982a), A stochastic interactive model for the diffusion of information, *Journal of Mathematical Sociology*, 8: 265-281.

Allen B. (1982b), Some stochastic processes of interdependent demand and technological diffusion of an innovation exhibiting externalities among adopters, *International Economic Review*, 23: 595-608.

Antonelli C. (1995), *The economics of localized technological change*, Kluwer, London.

Arthur W.B. (1989), Competing technologies, increasing returns and lock-in by historical events, *Economic Journal*, 99: 116-131.

Atkinson B. & Stiglitz J. (1969), A new view of technical change, *Economic Journal*, 79: 573-578.

Dalle J.-M. (1995), Dynamiques d'adoption, coordination et diversité, *Revue Economique*, 46: 1081-1098.

Dalle J.-M. (1997a), Heterogeneity vs. externalities: a tale of possible technological landscapes, *Journal of Evolutionary Economics*, 7: 395-413.

Dalle J.-M. (1997b), Rationality and heterogeneity in stochastic agregation models, forthcoming in Cohendet P. & Stahn H. Eds, *Local interactions and global phenomena*, Springer Verlag.

Dalle J.-M. & Foray D. (1995), Des fourmis et des hommes: modèles stochastiques d'interactions et rationalité individuelle active, *Cahiers d'Economie et de Sociologie Rurale*, 37: 70-92.

Dalle J.-M. & Foray D. (1997), When are agents negligible (or decisive)? An approach through stochastic interaction models, paper presented to the Workshop *Economic Evolution, Learning, and Complexity*, Augsburg, May.

David P.A. (1975), *Technical choice, Innovation and Economic Growth*, Cambridge UP.

David P.A. (1985), Clio and the economics of QWERTY, *American Economic Review*, 75: 332-337.

David P.A. (1987), The hero and the herd in technological history: reflections on Thomas Edison and the "Battle of the Systems", *CEPR Publication* n° 100, Stanford University.

David P.A. (1988), *Putting the past into the future of economics*, Institute for Mathematical Studies in the Social Sciences Technical Report 533, Stanford University.

David P.A. & Foray D. (1994), *Markov random fields, percolation structures, and the economic of EDI standard diffusion*, in Pogorel ed., Global Telecommunication Strategies and Technological Changes, Amsterdam: North-Holland, 135-170.

David P.A., Foray D. & Dalle J.-M. (1997), Marshallian externalities and the emergence and spatial stability of technological enclaves, *Economics of Innovation and New Technology*, Vol 5 n° 1, forthcoming.

Durlauf S.N. (1993), Nonergodic economic growth, *Review of Economic Studies*, 60: 349-366.

Dosi G. (1988), Sources, procedures, and microeconomic effects of innovation, *Journal of Economic Literature*, 26: 1120-1171.

Föllmer H (1974), Random economies with many interacting agents, *Journal of Mathematical Economics*, 1: 51-62.

Foray D. & Grübler A. (1990), Morphological analysis, diffusion and lock-out of technologies, *Research Policy*, 19: 535-550.

Foray D. (1997), The dynamic implications of increasing returns: technological change and path-dependent inefficiency, *International Journal of Industrial Organization*, 15: 733-752.

Griliches Z. (1957), Hybrid corn: an exploration into the economics of technical change, Econometrica 25: 501-522.

Hélioui & Simon (1997), Information expectations and the efficiency gap paradox: the shoe press case in the paper industry, paper presented to the *1997 ECEEE Summer Study*, June.

Kirman A.P. (1983), Communication in markets, *Economics Letters*, 12: 101-108.

Kirman A.P. (1992), Whom or what does the representative individual represent?, *Journal of Economic Perspectives*, 6: 117-136.

Kirman A.P. (1993), Ants, rationality and recruitment, *Quarterly Journal of Economics*, 108: 136-156.

Kirman A.P. (1994), Economies with interacting agents, *Working Paper* SFI 94-05-030.

Lesourne J. (1992), *L'Economie de l'Ordre et du Désordre*, Economica, Paris.

Lissoni F. & Metcalfe J.S. (1994), Diffusion of innovation ancient and modern: review of the main themes, in Dodgson M. & Rothwell R. eds, *The Handbook of Industrial Innovation*, Edward Elgar, 106-141.

Mansfield E. (1961), Technical change and the rate of imitation, *Econometrica*, 29: 41-66.

Metcalfe J.S. (1988), The diffusion of innovation: an interpretative survey, in Dosi G. & al. eds, *Technical Change and Economic Theory*, Frances Pinter, London.

Orléan A. (1990), Le rôle des influences interpersonnelles dans le fonctionnement des marchés financiers, *Revue Economique*, 41: 839-868.

Orléan A. (1992), Contagion des opinions et fonctionnement des marchés financiers, *Revue Economique*, 43:4, 685-698.

Schelling T.C. (1971), Dynamic models of segregation, *Journal of Mathematical Sociology*, 1: 143-186.

Schelling T.C. (1978), Micromotives and macrobehavior, Norton, NY.

Stiglitz J. (1987), Learning to learn: localized learning and technological progress, in Dasgupta & Stoneman Eds, Technology policy and economic performance, Cambridge UP.

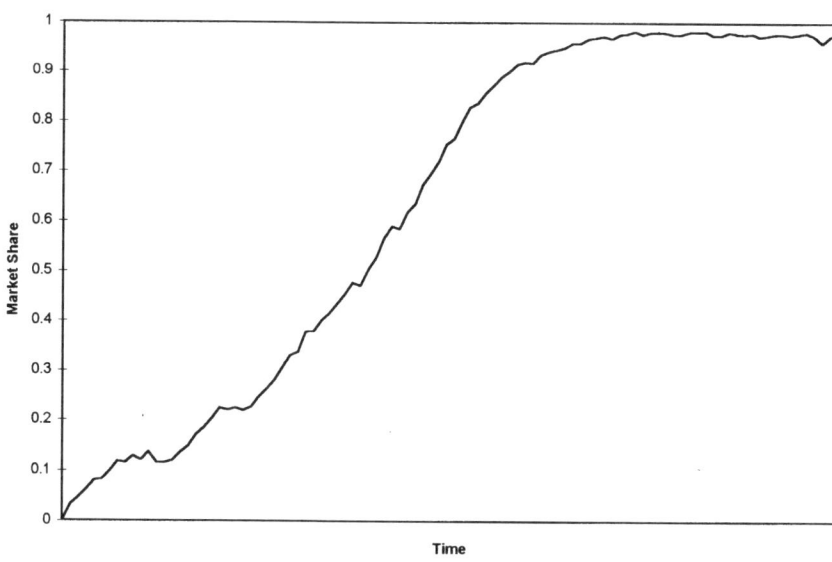

Figure 1: a typical diffusion path

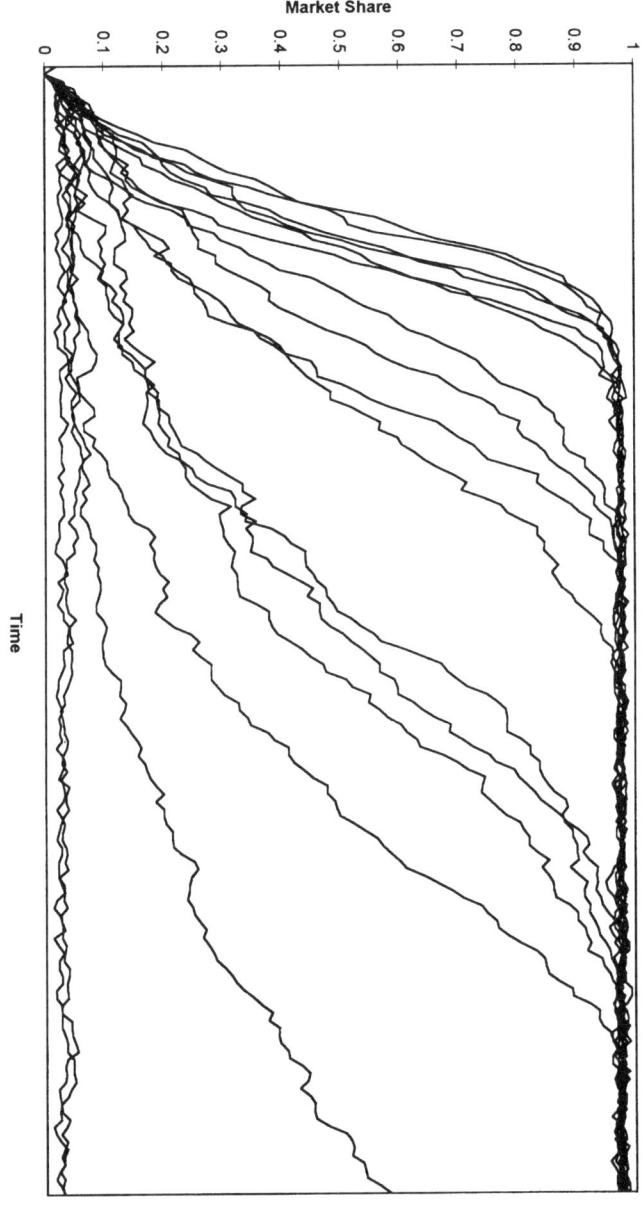

Figure 2: a few other diffusion paths

Local interaction structures, heterogeneity and the diffusion | 261

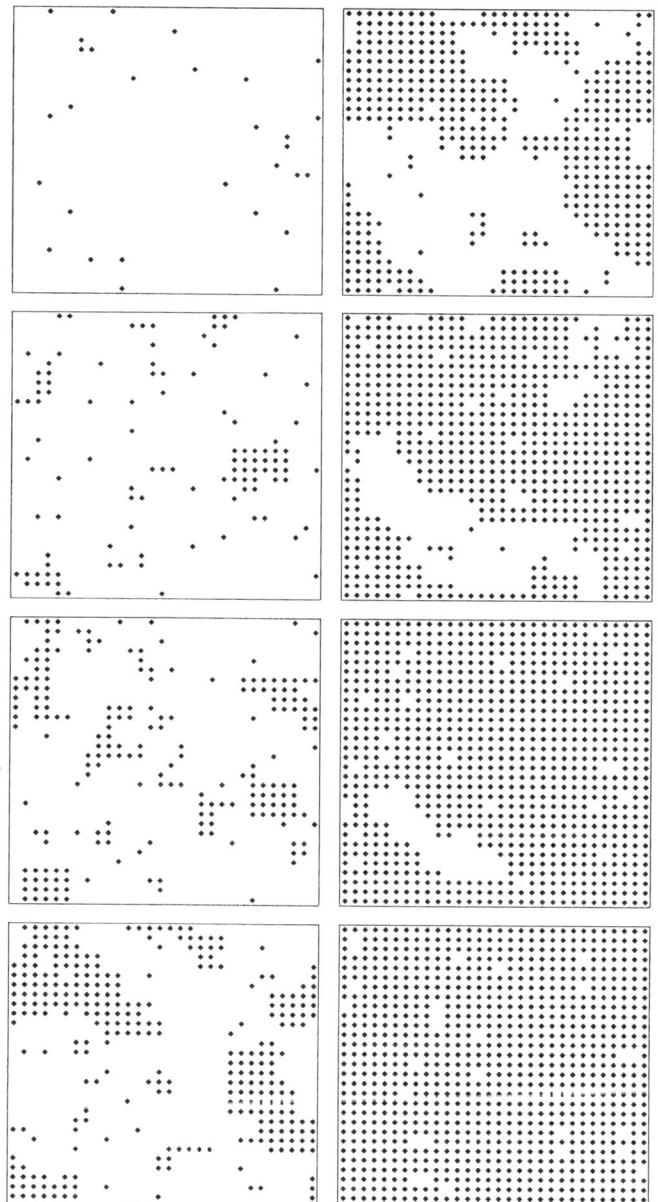

Figure 3: another way to look at a typical diffusion path

PART 4

Evolutionary Approaches to Economic Growth

CHAPTER 13

ECONOMIC GROWTH AS AN EVOLUTIONARY PROCESS *

Gerald SILVERBERG and Bart VERSPAGEN

1. Introduction

Evolutionary thinking and economic growth would seem to be two subjects with a natural affinity. Yet historically, nothing could be further from the case. Formal growth theory of the Harrod-Domar sort arose as an attempt to dynamize the Keynesian model, while the Solovian full-employment alternative succeeded in making factor substitution a saving grace. Until the recent advent of endogenous growth theory, these early approaches have dominated all later thinking on the matter. But none of them, including endogenous growth theory in its various forms, bears the least resemblance to an evolutionary process.

While an evolutionary perspective has been urged upon economists since at least Marshall 1890 (see Hodgson 1993 for a recent reiteration), what has been lacking until recently, at least for a large portion of the economics profession, has been a body of formal theory and quantitative analysis on an explicitly evolutionary basis. This has changed since the work of Nelson and Winter in the 1960s and 1970s (summarized in Nelson and Winter 1982), which operationalized and extended many of the concepts going back to Schumpeter (1919), Schumpeter (1947), Alchian (1951), Downie (1955), Steindl (1952), and others. Since then a number of authors have been enlarging on this foundation and systematically extending the evolutionary economics paradigm in a number of directions. A survey of some of these can be found in Nelson (1995).

There are essentially two reasons for believing that an evolutionary approach is applicable to economics. One is based on analogy and an appeal to the type of explanation common in biology: that forms of competition, innovation, variation and selection have analogues in the two subjects and thus that similar reasoning can profitably be applied in the nonbiological domain. Here most authors stress that the analogy should not be taken too seriously, so that it is useless to search for whatever corresponds exactly to genes, sexual reproduction, crossover or mutation in the economic sphere. Moreover, discredited forms of evolution such as Lamarckianism, the inheritance of acquired characteristics, may be perfectly conceivable in the socioeconomic realm.

---

* The research of Bart Verspagen has been made possible by a fellowship of the Royal Netherlands Academy of Arts and Sciences.

The second takes a more universalist perspective. It argues that, just as biological evolution has passed through distinct stages (prokaryotic and eukaryotic life, asexual and sexual reproduction, as well as a prebiotic stage), so modern industrial society is just a distinct stage of this single process, subject to the same underlying laws if constrained by specific features of its current realization. Thus economic evolution would be an intrinsic component of a larger evolutionary process, and not merely something accidentally amenable to certain forms of reasoning by analogy.

What reasons might we have to believe this? Lotka (1924) proposed the concept of 'energy transformers' to capture the common thermodynamic features of all life forms. This is quite similar to what later was termed dissipative systems (Nicolis and Prigogine 1977), i.e., thermodynamically open systems, far from equilibrium, which maintain a high state of internal organization by importing free energy from their environment, consuming it for purposes of self-repair and self-reproduction, and exporting the resulting waste as high entropy back to the environment. Thus the apparent paradox of life, already pointed out by Henry Adams (1919), of complex structure emergence in the face of the Second Law of Thermodynamics (that in thermodynamically closed systems entropy, i.e., disorder, must increase) is transcended [1]. Life (or at least carbon-based life as we know it until the industrial revolution) can be seen as a sea of such 'converters' living off the waterfall of free energy flowing between the sun and the low-value infrared radiation reflected by the earth into deep space [2].

From this perspective human civilization is distinguished from earlier forms of biological evolution by the fact that the information carriers of the selforganizing structures, rather than being encoded in a form like DNA internal to the organism, now have attained an *exosomatic* [3] (Lotka 1945) form. Information is encoded both in an intangible sphere existing between human minds known as culture, and a more tangible sphere consisting of writing and

---

1. The observation that open systems (in particular, organisms) can seemingly circumvent the second law of thermodynamics by exporting entropy to the environment (or equivalently, importing 'negentropy' or free energy, i.e., energy of a higher 'quality' than the ambient heat, which can be converted to mechanical work) goes back at least to Bertalanffy (1932) and Schrödinger (1945).
2. "Summarizing we may say that selforganization is necessarily connected with the possibility to export entropy to the external world. In other words, selforganizing systems need an input of high-valued energy and at the same time an output of low-valued energy. In the interior of selforganizing systems a depot of high-valued energy of another form is observed. The evolution processes on our planet are mainly pumped by the 'photon mill' with the three levels sun-earth-background radiation (let us mention however that the geological processes are pumped by the temperature gradients between the centre of the earth and the surface). On the cosmic scale the general strategy of evolution is the formations of islands of order on a sea of disorder represented by the background radiation." (Feistel and Ebeling 1989, p. 91)
3. There is of course another level of *endosomatic* information processing based on the neuronal system of animals, which Edelman (1987) hypothesizes to function according to neuronal group selection. This allows organisms to learn from experience during their lifetimes, i.e., is a type of acquired characteristic with clear survival value. However, until the advent of language and culture,

other forms of representation, and cultural and industrial artifacts. But the fact remains that, within the constraints imposed by the various physical substrates of information storage and transmission, evolution still must proceed along the basic Darwinian lines of (random) variation and selection. The complication associated with modern socioeconomic evolution is that we now have to deal with a mosaic of simultaneous biological (DNA), culturally tacit (existing in the human pyschomotoric systems of individuals and groups) and culturally codifiable (existing in exosomatic artifacts) information transmission and variation mechanisms, the latter category being increasing machine based.

The task of an evolutionary theory of economic growth, then, might be to formulate a population dynamics of this multilevel evolutionary process, taking account both of the human components and of the increasingly sophisticated forms of artifactual energy and information transformers collectively referred to by economists in a rather undifferentiated manner as capital [1]. But even if we agree that this more fundamental perspective on economics as an integral part of the evolutionary process has a certain validity, the 'genetic code' of the various non-DNA-based levels still remains to be discovered. Even in biology, in fact, where a firm understanding of the molecular basis of genetics has emerged since the 1950s, many extreme simplifications of a phenomenological sort still have to be made in formal models of population genetics and evolution [2]. Thus from a practical point of view it may not make much difference whether we apply evolutionary thinking to economics as an exercise in restrained analogizing or regard the economics of human societies as a specific stage in a universal evolutionary process, until such time as canonical descriptions of the "genetic deep structure" of socioindustrial processes can be agreed upon [3]. For the time being we will have to make do with more or less plausible and heroic assumptions about the entities and variation and transmission mechanisms implicated in economic evolution, and judge them on the basis of a limited range of micro and macroeconomic 'stylized facts'.

---

which permit *intergenerational* transmission, the neuronal system in itself cannot serve as a basis for long-term evolution but must still rely on the DNA substrate to generate further development.
1. This is the theme of Boulding (1978) and Boulding (1981), without the author proceeding very far down the road of formal modeling, however.
2. Thus one often assumes asexual rather than sexual reproduction to simplify the mathematics.
3. One difference, however, is the central importance placed upon energetic and environmental constraints associated with the latter perspective. These, for better or worse, will not play any explicit role in the following discussion.

2. Behavioral foundations and formal evolutionary modelling in the economics of growth and Schumpeterian competition: selection

Formalization of evolutionary thinking in biology began with Fisher (1930), who introduced what are now called *replicator equations* [1] to capture Darwin's notion of the survival of the fittest. If we consider a population to be composed of n distinct competing "varieties" with associated, possibly frequency-dependent fitnesses $f_i(x)$, where x is the vector of relative frequencies of the varieties $(x_1, x_2, ..., x_n)$, then their evolution might be described by the following equations:

$$\dot{x}_i = x_i(f_i(x) - \bar{f}(x)), \quad i = 1...n, \quad \text{with} \quad \bar{f}(x) = \sum_{i=1}^{n} x_i f_i(x).$$

The intuition is simple: varieties with above-average fitness will expand in relative importance, those with below-average fitness will contract, while the average fitness $\bar{f}(x)$ in turn changes with the relative population weights. If the fitness functions f_i are simple constants, then it can be shown that the variety with the highest fitness will displace all the others and that average fitness will increase monotonically until uniformity is achieved according to

$$\frac{d\bar{f}}{dt} = \text{var}(f) \geq 0,$$

where var (f) is the frequency-weighted variance of population fitness. Thus average fitness is dynamically maximized by the evolutionary process (mathematically, it is referred to as a Lyapunov function). This is known as Fisher's Fundamental Theorem of Natural Selection, but it should be noted that it is only valid for *constant* fitness functions. In the event of frequency-dependent selection, where fitness depends on population shares, including a variety's own share, and increasing and decreasing "returns" may intermingle, multiple equilibria are possible and no quantity is *a priori* necessarily being maximized (see Ebeling and Feistel 1982 for an extensive discussion of maximal principles). The replicator equation only describes the relative share dynamics and thus takes place on the unit simplex S^n (where $\sum_{i=1}^{n} x_i = 1$), an $n-1$ dimensional space. To derive the absolute populations it is necessary to introduce an additional equation for the total population level. An alternative

---

[1]. See Sigmund (1986) and Hofbauer and Sigmund (1988, pp.145-6) for a discussion of their basic form and various applications.

description due to Lotka and Volterra, which will be used in the model described below, is based on growth equations for the population levels y_i (with the frequently used log-linear version on the right hand side):

$$\dot{y}_i = A_i(y) = r_i y_i + \sum_{j=1}^{n} a_{ij} y_i y_j$$

A theorem due to Hofbauer asserts that Lotka-Volterra and replicator systems are equivalent (see Hofbauer and Sigmund 1988, p. 135).

Most evolutionary economics models to a considerable extent consist of giving the functions f_i or g_i economic meaning in terms of market competition or differential profit rate driven selection mechanisms. The former usually defines a variable representing *product competitiveness*, which may be a combination of price, quality, deliver delay, advertising and other variables (for examples see Silverberg, Dosi and Orsenigo 1988 or Kwasnicki and Kwasnicka 1992). The latter assumes that product quality and price are homogeneous between producers (or subject to fast equilibrating dynamics compared to the evolutionary processes of interest) but unit costs of production differ, so that firms realize differential profit rates. If their growth rates are related to profits, as seems reasonable, then their market shares or production levels (corresponding to x_i and y_i in the biological models) can be described by replicator or Lotka-Volterra equations, respectively.

The model presented below, as most other growth models in the evolutionary tradition, focuses primarily on technical change as the central driving element of the evolutionary processes with which they are concerned. A major distinguishing characteristic is whether technology is *capital embodied* or *disembodied*, i.e., whether changes in technological performance are primarily (though not necessarily exclusively) related to investment in new equipment or not. In the former case technical change is highly constrained by investment in physical capital (as well as possible complementary factors); in the latter case it is not and can be almost costless. Yet even on the assumption of embodied technical change, there can be important differences in formal treatments. The classical approach to embodied technical change uses the *vintage* concept going back to Salter (1960), Solow (1960) and Kaldor and Mirrlees (1962), as in essence do national statistical offices with the perpetual inventory approach to the measurement of the capital stock. One assumes that at any given time there is a single best-practice technology in which investment is made. The capital stock consists then of the vintages of past investment going back in time until the scrapping margin, i.e., that oldest vintage on the verge of being discarded due to technological obsolescence and/or wear and tear. This defines a technological lifetime of capital equipment [1]. The aggregate capital stock is a sum or integral (in the discrete and continuous time cases, respectively) over the vintages during this lifetime, and average technical coefficients (labour productivity, capital/output ratios) are the corresponding vintage-weighted sum or integrals. Vintage capital stock may be easy to compute from data, but they have two disadvantages which detract from their realism and tractability. First is the assumption of a single best-practice technology, which rules out multiple competing technologies at the investment frontier, a topic dear to the hearts of most evolutionary economists and students of innovation diffusion. This can be overcome to some extent by assuming multiple, parallel vintage structures of distinct technologies, as in Silverberg, Dosi and Orsenigo (1988). The second is that, although particularly discrete-time vintage capital stocks can be easily calculated from data, when they are embedded in a dynamic framework with endogenous scrapping they can lead to awkward mathematical complications. Delay difference or differential equations and even age-structured population dynamics become involved whose mathematical properties, except under extremely simple assumptions, are still poorly understood compared to systems of ordinary difference or differential equations.

An alternative implicitly exploited in the model below, as well as in models by Metcalfe (1988), Iwai (1984a,b), Henkin and Polterovich (1991), Silverberg and Lehnert (1993, 1994), might be termed a *quasi-vintage* framework. Capital 'vintages' are labelled by their type instead of their date of acquisition, so that the service age no longer plays a role, only the technical characteristics (although decay by type independently of age is still possible). Thus several qualitatively distinct technologies can diffuse simultaneously into and out of the capital stock. Furthermore, only ordinary differential (or difference) equations are needed to handle the quasi-vintage structure, a considerable mathematical simplification. This gain in realism and tractability is compensated for by an inability to track the vintages by chronological age, however. But quasi-vintages lend themselves more naturally to the kind of multiple replacement dynamics investigated by Marchetti and Nakicenovic (1979), Nakicenovic (1987), and Grübler (1990). And one view on evolution holds that its essence resides exactly in the sequence of such replacements (Montroll 1978), whether related to technologies, behavioral patterns, or social structures.

The disembodied side of technical change (disembodied at least in the sense that it is not representable by tangible equipment) is still even more of a black box than the embodied side. It can reside in (tacit) human skills or organizational and societal capabilities, but little is known of a very fundamental nature about how it is accumulated, stored, and refreshed. *Learning by doing* (Arrow 1962) is a standard phenomenological approach finding expression in power

---

1. Except in the case in which capital is assumed to decay exponentially according to some presumed depreciation rate, in which case its lifetime is infinite, although older vintages rapidly become insignificant.

laws for the relationship between productivity and cumulative investment or production. Recently, it has also become central to much of the neoclassical endogenous growth literature. The effects of *technological spillovers* between competitors have also received considerable attention. One possible way of combining learning by doing and spillovers in a dynamic framework is Silverberg, Dosi and Orsenigo (1988), but nothing along these lines has been attempted in an evolutionary growth model, to our knowledge. The net effect of both of these phenomena is usually one form or another of increasing returns, such as increasing returns to adoption or agglomeration, network externalities, etc. (see Arthur 1988, 1994). Within the replicator framework this means that the fitness functions $f_i(x)$ truly depend on the frequencies x, resulting in multiple equilibria, threshold phenomena, lock-in, etc. [1].

3. Behavioral foundations and formal evolutionary modelling in the economics of growth and Schumpeterian competition: innovation and learning

Evolution would soon come to an end were it not for the continual creation of new variety on which selection (as well as drift) can act. This is especially crucial for growth models, where the ongoing nature of the technical change process is at the fore, although other aspects may well converge to stable stationary patterns. Thus considerable attention has to be devoted to how innovation is realized by firms, individually and collectively. In principle most scholars agree that innovation should be modelled stochastically, to reflect the uncertainty in the link between effort and outcome. The details on how this is done may very considerably, however. The classical formulation is due to Nelson and Winter, who lump technologies and behavioral rules/strategies together under the concept of *routines*. Since technical change is disembodied in their model, this equivalence is perhaps admissible, since a change in technique for a firm's entire capital stock requires only the expenditure necessary to undertake innovative or imitative search, not investment or training per se. While there is technological learning at the economy-wide level, firms themselves are completely unintelligent, since they operate according to given search and investment rules that cannot be modified as a result of experience. Instead, the firm is subject to selection as a consequence of the technologies it has stumbled upon. A somewhat peculiar aspect is the very

---

[1]. The increasing returns phenomenon was studied by Arthur, Ermoliev and Kaniovski using the Polya urn stochastic tool, which assumes an indefinitely increasing population to establish asymptotic results. The alternative case of a fixed population size with stochastic effects can be studied using Master equation methods (see Feistel and Ebeling 1989 and Bruckner, Ebeling, Jiménez Montaño and Scharnhorst 1994, and especially Jiménez Montaño and Ebeling 1980 for a stochastic formulation of the Nelson and Winter model). We will only make limited use of stochastic tools in the following, so that the deterministic replicator equation will serve our purposes.

literal application of Simon's notion of satisficing to mean that firms only undertake innovative search if their performance is unsatisfactory.

While learning based on selection/mutation dynamics has begun to play a major role in the evolutionary games literature (e.g., Kandori, Mailath and Rob 1993, Young 1993), very little has found entrance into evolutionary models of a general economic orientation. The game-theoretic learning literature has a few peculiar features. First, it has concentrated almost exclusively until now on 2×2 repeated games with multiple Nash equilibria, and its implicit intent has been to resolve the equilibrium selection problem. Second, it has generally employed best-practice reaction dynamics instead of a boundedly rational approach to imitation and interaction. And third, mutations have been introduced to represent experimentation or error in a highly specific way. There is a uniform probability ε of a transition from any strategy to *any* other strategy in the space of all strategies, and the resulting limiting distributions of the associated Markov process are examined in the limit $\varepsilon \to 0$. This is not as innocent an assumption as it might appear, as has been pointed out by Bergin and Lipman (1996). For if ε is not assumed to go uniformly to zero from all states, then *any* equilibrium can be obtained in the limit, and the equilibrium selection problem remains unresolved. They argue that in fact these transition problems may well have a particular structure imposed by the specific problem at hand, and no general *a priori* assumptions such as uniformity may be valid. Indeed, it is rather far reaching to assume a transition between arbitrary strategies, since learning seems to imply that states may not be directly accessible from each other but may require variable numbers of intermediate steps (of course in the 2×2 case this would not apply). Instead it seems reasonable that account must be taken of the *topology* of strategy space in terms of the realistic transitions agents can perform in elemental steps, and the structure of associated probabilities.

In the model presented here, mutations are *local* around the current strategy, and the probability of imitation is an increasing function of dissatisfaction with current performance and the size of the imitated firm. In contrast to the Nelson and Winter tradition, strategies and technologies are treated separately. The learning algorithm applies only to the firms' R&D expenditure strategies; their technological performance then follows in a somewhat complex manner from these decisions and market feedbacks. In this way it is possible to implement simple boundedly rational decision rules gleaned from actual business practice, such as targeted R&D/total investment or R&D/sales ratios, or a combination of the two.

Genetic algorithms and classifier systems have also been gaining favour in recent years as mechanisms for operationalizing learning with artificial agents [1]. Although these appeal even more directly to a discrete genetic mechanism of inheritance à la biological DNA than social scientists may feel comfortable with, they may also be employed agnostically simply as algorithmic tools to allow learning to happen, if not as models of how learning actually happens. The goal of an *artificial economics* modelling philosophy as espoused by Lane (1993) is to put together a basic web of economic interactions between artificial agents endowed with a *tabula rasa* knowledge of their environment, but fairly sophisticated abilities to learn, and see what sorts of markets, institutions and technologies develop, with the modeller prejudicing the developmental possibilities as little as possible. Something along these lines has already been implemented to a certain extent in the "sugarscape" model of Axtell and Epstein (1996), paralleling the artificial worlds movement in the biology domain (cf. Langton 1989 and Langton, Taylor, Farmer and Rasmussen 1992). While this direction of research has generated much excitement, it has not avoided the fate of many over hyped scientific trends in the form of a sceptical backlash (see Horgan 1995).

3. The model

In the following, we will present the basic structure of a model which takes into account the elements of an evolutionary perspective on economic growth. Thus, the central elements of our model will be the formalization of selection, technical change and behavioral learning. To deal with these different aspects of the problem, we have constructed the model around three basic blocks. The first block describes how the artificial economy evolves with a given set of technologies and firms, with selection taking place at both levels. This block consists of equations for the rate of capital accumulation, the diffusion of new technologies in the total capital stock of the firms, and the real wage rate. The second block describes a set of rules that is used to introduce new technologies and firms into the economy. This block takes the behaviour of firms as given, and then describes the probability that individual firms will make an innovation, as well as how innovations are introduced. The third block describes how innovative behaviour changes under the influence of the evolution of the economy and firm learning. This block, in other words, describes a feedback from performance to innovative behaviour and thus a form of collective learning. The parameters of the model and the values used in the simulations are summarized in the Appendix.

---

1. See Booker, Goldberg and Holland (1989), and Goldberg (1989) for basic theory and methodology and Holland and Miller (1991), Kwasnicki and Kwasnicka (1992) and Lane (1993) for some economic applications.

a. Selection in the artificial economy

The basic framework for selection in the model is a set of Lotka-Volterra equations, as in Silverberg and Lehnert (1993), which in turn draws on Silverberg (1984) and Goodwin (1967). Let hats above variables denote proportional growth rates, w be the (real) wage rate, v the employment rate (persons employed as a fraction of the labour force), and m and n parameters (both positive). Then the wage rate is determined by the following differential equation:

$$\hat{w} = -m + nv.$$

It is assumed that there is a fixed number q of firms in the economy, while each of these firms has a variable number p_q of different types of capital goods that it utilizes to produce a homogeneous product. New capital arises from the accumulation of profits, a process described by the following equation:

$$\hat{k}_{ij} = (1 - \gamma_{1i}) r_{ij} - \frac{\gamma_{2i}}{c} + a(r_{ij} - r_i) - \sigma.$$

The capital stock is denoted by k, r stands for the profit rate, and σ is the exogenous rate of *physical* depreciation of capital (technological obsolescence is an endogenous component of the model itself). The subscript $i(1...q)$ denotes the firm, and $j(1...p_q)$ the type of capital (the absence of any these indices indicates an aggregation over this particular dimension). Eq. (2) assumes that the principal source for type ij-capital accumulation is profits generated by ij-capital. This is modelled by the first term on the rhs of (2), i.e., $(1 - (\gamma_{1i}) r_{ij})$. A firm-specific portion of profits (denoted by (γ_{1i})) plus a firm-specific portion of total output (sales) (denoted by (γ_{2i})) is used for the development of knowledge (R&D) (when $r_i < 0$, $(\gamma_{1i}$ is set to zero).

However, profits may also be redistributed in such a way that more profitable types of capital accumulate even faster, less profitable even slower, than would otherwise be the case. The mechanism used to model this was first proposed by Soete and Turner (1984), and is represented by the second term on the rhs of eq. (2). By changing the value of α, redistribution of profits takes place faster (larger α) or slower (smaller α).

It is assumed that each type of capital is characterized by fixed technical coefficients, c and a (for capital coefficient and labour productivity, respectively). The capital coefficient is assumed to be fixed throughout the economy (and time), while labour productivity is assumed to change under the influence of technical progress. The profit rate of ij-capital is then given by $(1 - w/a_{ij})/c$.

The principal variable used to describe firm dynamics is the share of the labour force employed on each capital stock. Production is assumed to be always equal to production capacity (the influence of effective demand is absent), so that the amount of labour employed by each capital stock is equal to $k_{ij}/(a_{ij}c)$. Dividing this by the labour force (assumed to grow at a fixed rate β) gives the share of labour employed, v_{ij} (called the employment share hereafter). The expression for the growth rate of this variable is

$$\hat{v}_{ij} = \hat{k}_{ij} - \beta = (1 - \gamma_i) r_{ij} - \frac{\gamma_{2i}}{c} + a(r_{ij} - r_i) - (\beta + \sigma)$$

R&D also has an employment effect. We assume that the ratio between R&D expenditures and R&D labour input is equal to a fraction δ of the economy-wide labour productivity. The employment rate v_q resulting from production is then found by summing v_{ij} over i and j. Under these assumptions, it can then be shown that the overall employment rate v is equal to $(1 + \delta(\gamma_1 rc + \gamma_2)) v_q$.

Eqs. (1) and (3) together form a Lotka-Volterra system, and thus create a selection mechanism in our artificial economy. Eq. (3) describes how more profitable (i.e., with above-average labour productivity) technologies tend to increase their employment share, whereas more backward (below-average) technologies tend to vanish. The real Phillips curve eq. (1) ensures that real wages tend to track labour productivity in the long run. In a situation in which new technologies are continually being introduced, this implies that all technologies, after an initial phase of market penetration and diffusion, will eventually vanish from the production system.

However, for a given set of technologies, long-run per capita growth is no longer possible once all firms converge to exclusive employment of the highest productivity technology (because the fitness of the vintages is fixed and does not depend on individual employment shares, Fisher's Fundamental Theorem applies). The next section outlines how new technologies can enter the system and thereby open up the possibility of long-run growth.

b. *Introducing technological change*

It is assumed that in each time period, firms devote resources (R&D) to the systematic search for new production possibilities (i.e., new types of capital). The outcome of this search process is assumed to be stochastic. The structure of the *technological space* is assumed to be a simple directed graph (fig. 1). More complicated graphs could well be imagined with branching and even merging nodes; this remains a subject for future research.

Each time an innovation occurs, the firm creates a new type of capital. The labour productivity of this type of capital is given by the following process:

$$a^*_{i,t} = (1 + \tau) a^*_{i,t-1}$$

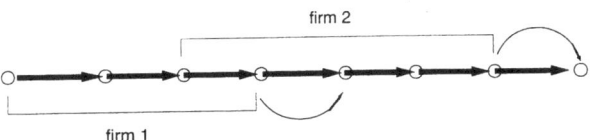

Figure 1: The technology space is a simple directed graph. Firms' current capital stocks are bracketed, and their next innovations are shown by the circular arrows.

where τ is the fixed proportional increase in labour productivity between innovations and $a^*_{i,t}$ is the firm-specific best practice labour productivity. The new type of capital is seeded with a small employment share (say 0.0001). In order to keep the total employment rate constant, this seed value is (proportionally) removed from the other types of capital of the innovating firm. The number of technologies employed by any given firm may vary in time.

As real wages rise over time, every technology will generate negative profits at some stage (because of its fixed labour productivity). It is assumed that these losses are financed by an equivalent decrease of the capital stock. In other words, losses imply that capital will be scrapped, and scrapped capital can be 'consumed' to cover the losses. Note that for individual capital stocks, the point at which scrapping occurs lies *prior* to the point where profits are negative, due to the α-related diffusion term in eq. (2). When a technology's employment share falls below a specified (very small) value E, it is scrapped completely.

A firm's R&D activities as well as possibly those of its rivals enter an innovation potential function T_i. This in turn determines the firm's probability of making an innovation according to a Poisson process with arrival rate p_i. The simplest relation is simply linear:

$$p_i = AT_i + p_{min},$$

where p_{min} is the (small) autonomous probability of making a fortuitous innovation without doing formal R&D, and A is the innovation function slope. One can also posit a nonlinear relationship with both increasing and decreasing returns to R&D, such as a logistic:

$$p_i = \frac{p_{min} \, p_{max}}{p_{min} + (p_{max} - p_{min}) \, e^{-AT_i}}.$$

This logistic function has intercept p_{min} and (asymptotic) saturation level p_{max}. In this case, the parameter A determines the speed at which the saturation level is approached.

T_i, the innovation potential, is determined both by the firm's own R&D level (h_i, to be defined below) and its ability to profit from other firms' R&D (technological spillovers):

$$T_i = h_i + \phi_1 h + \phi_2 h h_i$$

These spillovers can take two forms. First, there is a term related to the economy-wide value of h (written without subscript). The economy-wide R&D level h is defined to be the market share weighted average of firm-specific R&D levels. Second, there is a term related to the product of the economy-wide and the firm-specific value h_i. This latter term takes into account the argument that in order to assimilate spillovers, a firm has to have some technology-generating proficiency itself (see Cohen and Levinthal 1989, Nelson 1990). The parameters ϕ_1 and ϕ_2 determine the importance of each spillover mode [1].

The firm-specific R&D level h_i is defined to be the ratio of a moving average of firm R&D investment to its total physical capital stock. A ratio is used to normalize for firm size, since otherwise such a strong positive feedback between R&D and firm growth exists that monopoly becomes inevitable. While *a priori* it is by no means clear why the size of individual R&D effort should not directly relate to innovative success, a pure scale effect must be ruled out by the continuing existence of competition and the ability of small countries to remain or even advance in the technology race. The exponential moving average RD_i on R&D for a lag of L (or a depreciation rate of $1/L$) is given by the following differential equation:

$$\frac{d}{dt} RD_i = ((\gamma_1 r_i + \gamma_2 /c) k_i - RD_i)/L.$$

Hence the firm-specific R&D level is

$$h_i = RD_i / k_i.$$

An innovation can be defined in a narrow or a wide sense. In the wide sense, the adoption of any technology not yet employed by a firm (or a country) is an innovation to that unit. In the narrow sense, only technologies that have never been employed before anywhere are considered innovations at their time of introduction. If firms innovate according to the above Poisson arrival rates in the narrow sense, however, a very considerable intertemporal externality is created, because firms' innovations always build on each other. Thus there can be no duplication of effort and, as long as firms maintain a minimal level of R&D, no cumulative falling behind. On the other hand, once an innovation has

---

1. Spillovers will not be dealt with in this paper. They are examined within the context of one-parameter strategies in Silverberg and Verspagen (1994a, b).

been introduced somewhere into the economy, it should be progressively easier for other firms to imitate or duplicate it; it should not be necessary to reinvent the wheel. We capture this by introducing a catching-up effect. Let the labour productivity of the economy-wide best practice technology be a^*, and the best practice technology of firm i a_i^*. Then firm i's innovation potential T_i will be augmented by a measure of its distance from the best practice frontier:

$$T_i' = T_i(1 + \kappa \ln(a^*/a_i^*)).$$

Thus, adopting an old innovation is facilitated for backward firms, but they are still required to invest in their technological capacity to reap these catchup benefits. Here, however, R&D efforts should be interpreted in the larger sense of technological training and licensing, reverse engineering, or even industrial espionage (all costly activities, if not as costly as doing state-of-the-art R&D).

We have also experimented with innovations in the narrow sense, but the results on strategic selection are rather ambiguous. This is not surprising, since the import of the intertemporal externality is indeed quite large. We consider the Ansatz in eq. 10 therefore to be a justifiable first formulation, since technology adoption decisions are never passive, but rather require technological efforts of the adopting firm. However, it does place too much of the burden of catching up onto R&D.

In the artificial economy modelled here, entry of a new firm occurs only as a result of exit of an incumbent firm. Exit occurs whenever a firm's employment share (excluding its R&D employment) falls below a fixed level E. While exit of incumbent firms is completely endogenous, entry only occurs in case of exit, so that the total number of firms is constant. Naturally, this feature of the model is not very realistic, as in reality entry may be independent of exit and the total population of firms may vary. However, it is not the aim of this model to describe the phenomena of entry and exit as such. Instead, the main function of entry and exit is to maintain potential variety in the population of firms while providing for firm elimination.

Whenever entry occurs, the entrant is assigned a single technology with an amount of capital corresponding to an employment share of $2E$ (the remaining employment is proportionally removed from other firms so that total employment remains constant). The labour productivity of this technology is drawn uniformly from the range $[(1-b)A, (1+b)A]$, where A is the unweighted mean value of labour productivity of all the firms in the economy, and b is a parameter. The values for h and γ are (uniformly) drawn from the range existing in the economy at the time of entry.

c. Behaviour and learning

In Sections (a) and (b) we have outlined the system whereby innovating firms generate technical change and undergo selection in a closed economy model as

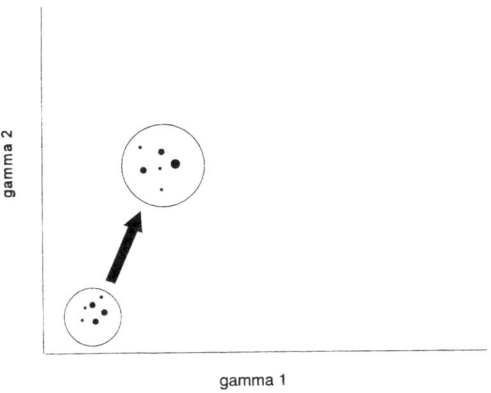

Figure 2: The space of behavioral evolution. A firm's strategy is represented as a point in a two-dimensional space whose diameter corresponds to the firm's market size. In the course of time the economy 'cloud' shifts through this space.

a function of their R&D strategy parameters γ. Learning now enters the picture in the form of two 'genetic' operators, mutation and imitation. Thus *behavioral evolution* takes place in a two-dimensional continuous space, where the economy at any given point in time is represented by a cloud of points (fig. 2). With probability Π each decision period, which is set exogenously and is equal for all firms, a firm will draw from a normal distribution and alter one or both of its strategy-parameters γ within the admissible range [0, 1] (mutation). Given that mutation occurs, each possibility (change either one or both parameters) occurs with equal probability:

$$\gamma_{1it} = \text{Min}(1, \text{Max}(\gamma_{1it-1} + \varepsilon, 0)), \quad \varepsilon \sim N(0, s), \vee$$
$$\gamma_{2it} = \text{Min}(1, \text{Max}(\gamma_{2it-1} + \varepsilon, 0)), \quad \varepsilon \sim N(0, s), \vee$$
$$\gamma_{lit} = \text{Min}(1, \text{Max}(\gamma_{lit-1} + \varepsilon_l, 0)), \quad \varepsilon_l \sim N(0, s), \quad l = 1, 2.$$

With variable probability Π_i^c the firm simply imitates the strategy of another firm. Again, given that imitation occurs, each possibility (imitate either one or both parameters) occurs with equal probability:

$$\gamma_{1it} = \gamma_{1jt-1}, \quad j(\neq i) \in [1...q]_i, \vee$$
$$\gamma_{2it} = \gamma_{2jt-1}, \quad j(\neq i) \in [1...q]_i, \vee$$
$$\gamma_{lit} = \gamma_{ljt-1}, \quad j(\neq i) \in [1...q]_i, \quad l = 1, 2.$$

The imitation probability is partly endogenous to reflect satisficing behaviour. Only firms with unsatisfactory rates of profit with respect to economy leaders will choose or be forced (for example by their stockholders or by hostile takeovers) to adopt the strategy of a competitor:

$$\Pi_i^c = \mu \left(1 - \frac{y_i - y_{\min}}{y_{\max} - y_{\min}} \right).$$

y_i is the firm's rate of expansion of physical capital (defined as min $(r_i - (\gamma_{2i}/c, \sigma)(1 - \gamma_{1i}) r_i - (\gamma_{2i}/c))$, $y_{\max}$ and $y_{\min}$ are the maximum and minimum values of y in the sample, and μ is the (exogenously determined) maximum imitation probability. Thus, the more profitable a firm is, the less likely it will change its strategy by imitating another firm. The most profitable firm has an imitation probability equal to zero; the least profitable the maximum probability. Once a firm has decided to imitate, it selects a firm to imitate randomly from the industry with weight equal to the target firm's market share in output. If neither imitation nor mutation occur, the firm simply retains its strategy from the previous period.

4. Identification of steady states by random and spontaneous generation

The model has been implemented to run on both MS-DOS and Unix computers. To make the solution as time-step invariant as possible, the selection mechanism, which is basically a system of differential equations, is solved using a fixed-step, fourth-order Runge-Kutta algorithm. The innovation decisions are executed during each computational step (using Poisson arrival rates scaled by the computation time step), and when an innovation is made, the corresponding changes in initial conditions, number of equations, and coefficients are made for the next step. Mutation and imitation are only performed at fixed intervals of one 'year', which may be many times the step employed in the Runge-Kutta algorithm.

In investigating the model, rather than simply presenting one or several simulation outcomes, we wish to focus on the question which outcomes are robust features of the model. In other words, which outcomes are due to systematic underlying relationships in the model, and which are simply due to contingencies and random factors in the simulation? [1]. To this end, we will perform multiple simulation experiments, with different randomizations for identical parameter sets, in order to explore the impact of stochastic factors, as well as 'step through' the key parameters to explore the impact of parameter variations. The results of these simulation experiments will be presented in the form of observed distributions of the relevant variables in the model.

---

1. See Silverberg and Verspagen (1995b) for a more detailed discussion of the dual role of "chance" and "necessity" in economic evolution.

The main feature of the model we will investigate in this way is the existence and nature of an "evolutionary attractor" in the dynamics, i.e., whether a "stable" configuration of firm R&D strategies exists to which our artificial economy will converge from particular classes of initial conditions. We have initialized the system in two ways: first in a 'grapeshot' mode we term random generation in which the initial γ's are drawn from a uniform distribution over [0, 1] and [0, 0.2] (respectively for γ_1 and γ_2); and second, in a 'spontaneous generation' mode in which all initial γ's are set to zero. We present the results of these experiments by means of density plots made on the basis of 3-dimensional histograms of the two γ's. On the horizontal axis we plot the experimental parameter that is being varied through different simulation runs (A or μ). The (market share weighted) mean value of the strategy parameter over the firms in each run is shown on the vertical axis. The data are pooled from the last 1 000 years of five simulation runs for each value of the experimental parameter, each generated with a different random seed. Darker shading indicates higher frequencies.

In Figure 3, we plot the results for the runs initialized by random generation. The figure shows clearly that the converging behaviour of the two strategy parameters is quite different. Parameter 1 (the targeted R&D to profits ratio) does not converge very clearly, except for higher values of the innovation slope, when relatively high frequencies are found at values near zero. Parameter 2 targeting R&D to sales shows a more tight convergence, although there are still high frequencies near zero (the white band between the horizontal axis and the attractor is quite narrow). Thus, firms show a tendency to select a relatively tight range of values for parameter 2, while parameter 1 tends to drift or, if anything, go to zero. Summarizing, firms seem to display a tendency to select tightly defined strategies based upon parameter 2 and indifference to parameter 1.

Figure 4 shows corresponding results for the case of spontaneous generation, i.e., a situation in which firms have to discover R&D as an activity. In this case, the economy starts out in a stagnant phase, with no intentional technical progress. As firms explore the strategy space by mutation and imitation, they may (or may not) find R&D a useful activity. The density plots show that in this case, the evolutionary attractor is much more clearly defined. The type 1 strategy parameter remains at values near zero (in our interpretation, the positive values found are largely attributable to random 'evolutionary' noise). The type 2 strategy parameter, however, shows a well-defined peak significantly distant from zero, as indicated by the white space bordering it from below.

This behaviour of the system can be interpreted as a particular form of lock-in or path dependency. When the system is started 'clean', without any form of 'commitment' to any type of R&D-strategy, it will select a much more unambiguous evolutionary attractor than in the random generation case. This is not the case when only the type 1 strategy parameter is employed (compare Silverberg and Verspagen 1994a, b). There the asymptotic steady states of the two initializations are identical.

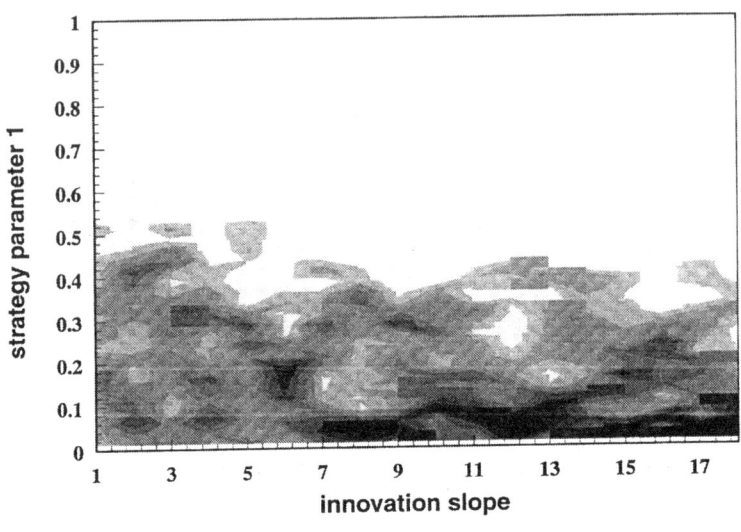

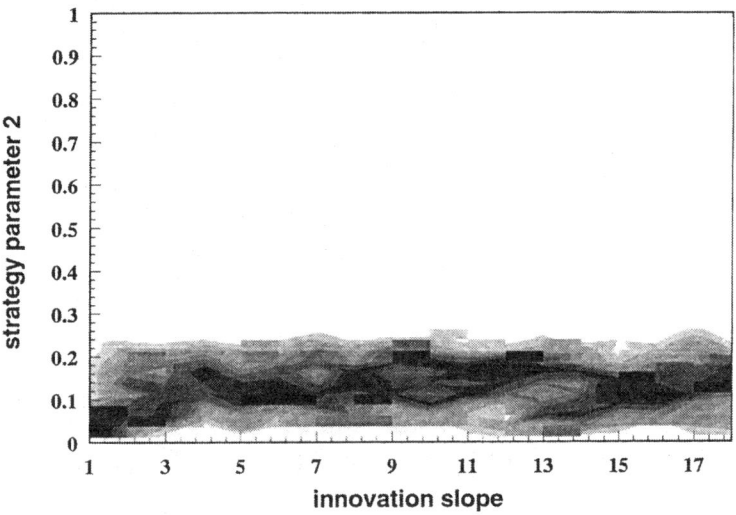

Figure 3: Histograms of strategy parameters from pooled data of five runs per value, last 1 000 years of 8 000 years runs (random generation), for a linear innovation function.

For a logistic innovation function (eq. 6) we obtain similar patterns from the histograms over innovation opportunity (fig. 5). In contrast to the linear case, however, the steady-state value of parameter 2 does seem to decline somewhat with increasing technological opportunity. What is also remarkable is the sudden collapse of the technological regime below values of A of about 40. The

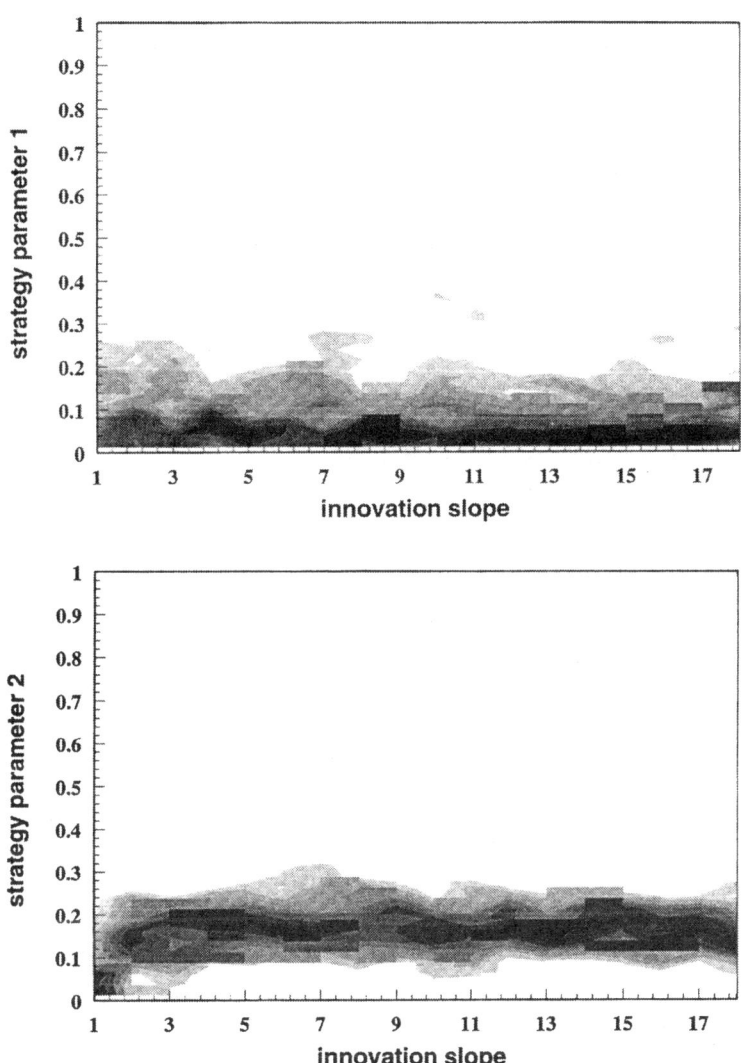

Figure 4: Histograms of strategy parameters from pooled data of five runs per value, last 1 000 years of 8 000 years runs (spontaneous generation), for a linear innovation function.

steady-state values of parameter 2, in the range 20-30%, are also higher than in the linear case.

Why is strategy parameter 2 subject to positive selection, while parameter 1 displays either drift or is constrained to zero? Our interpretation is that R&D comes to be regarded as a 'core' business activity in the model, for, due to the

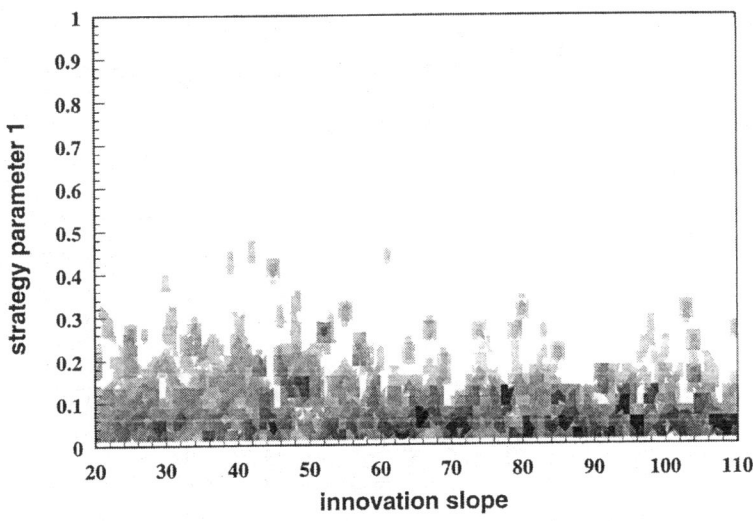

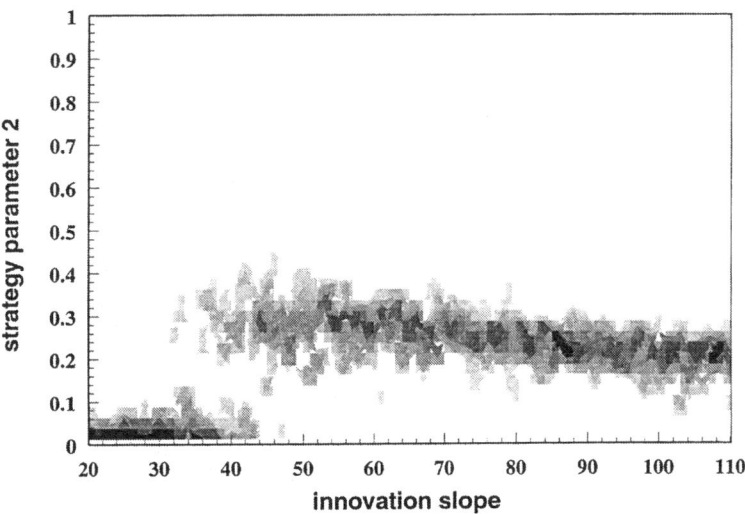

Figure 5: Histograms of strategy parameters from pooled data of five runs per value, last 1 000 years of 8 000 year runs (spontaneous generation), for a logistic innovation function.

'Goodwin' business cycles of the underlying economy, profits are more variable than sales. Thus, firms which base their R&D expenditures upon profits will have more fluctuating R&D stocks than firms which base their R&D on sales.

The selection environment seems to favour the latter firms because, in the long run, their R&D behaviour provides a more reliable stream of innovations.

Whereas the steady-state values of the strategy parameters do not appear to depend on technological opportunity, as represented by the value of A [1], the rate of technical change is a simple linearly increasing function of it (fig. 6). The transient time paths in the spontaneous generation case on the way to a growth steady-state are also of interest in themselves. Figure 7 displays the market-share-weighted values of the two strategy parameters for a single run over 8 000 years. Convergence is relatively rapid in comparison with the single parameter case. Figure 8 shows the time paths of the rate of technical change and the Herfindahl concentration index [2]. Viewed as a process in historical time and not just as out-of-equilibrium transient, this figure recapitulates a piece of virtual economic history. The economy starts off with no R&D and an essentially vanishing rate of technical change. Within this regime the rate of market concentration is quite high, although the identity of the near monopolist changes at almost regular intervals, as indicated by the breaks in the level of concentration. As the γ's rise with time and with them the overall rate of technical change, this market regime breaks down. It is replaced by low levels of concentration and considerable market turnover.

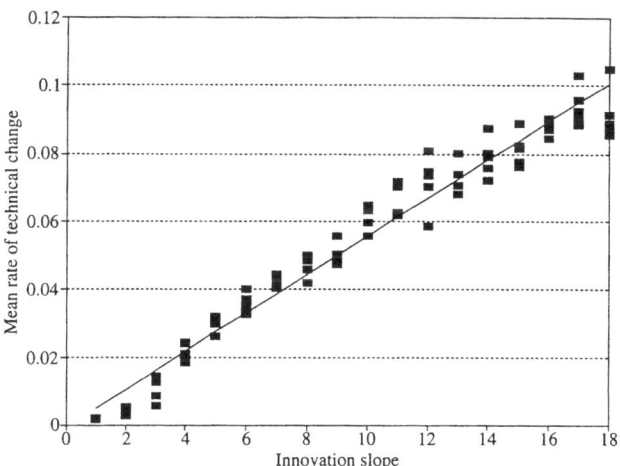

Figure 6: The rate of technical change is an increasing function of the innovation slope ($A = 10$, 50 firms, spontaneous generation).

---

1. This is not true when only parameter 1 is used. In this case, the value gradually *falls* with increasing A.
2. This is defined as $H = \Sigma f_i^2$, where f_i is the market share of the ith firm. It ranges from $1/n$, for n equally sized firms, to 1, for complete monopoly.

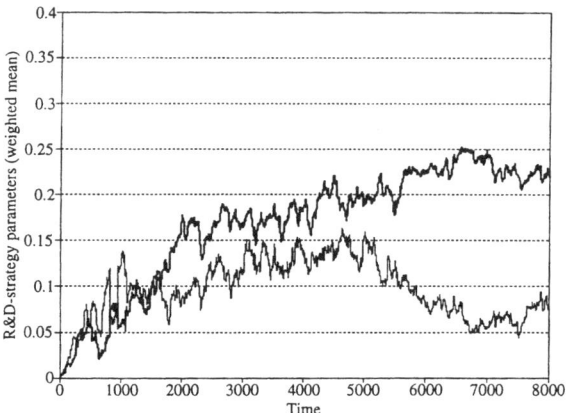

Figure 7: Time paths of market share-weighted-strategy parameters in a spontaneous generation run (50 firms, $\tau = 0.04$). The light line is γ_1, the heavy line is γ_2.

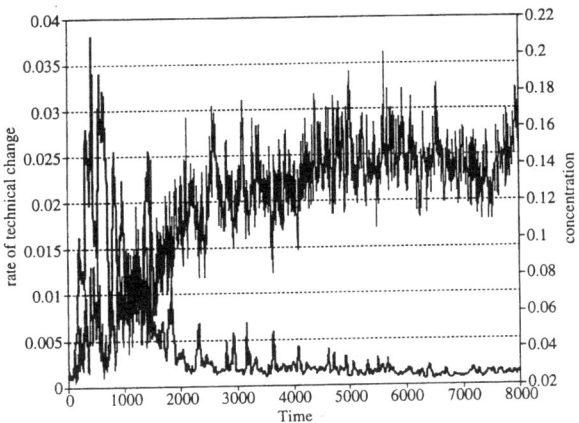

Figure 8: Time paths of rate of technical change (light line) and Herfindahl index of concentration (heavy line) for the same run as in Figure 5.

We have also begun to investigate how the structure of the evolutionary learning process affects the outcomes of these experiments. Recall that the variables Π and μ, representing the probability of mutation and imitation, are exogenously imposed. We have compiled histograms for the two strategy parameters by varying each of these rates separately. Figure 9 shows the results for mutation, Figure 10 for imitation, for runs with $A = 10$ and random generation initial conditions. Varying the mutation probability does not change the picture in any essential way. In contrast, increasing the ceiling on the imitation probability leads to a progressive collapse of γ_2 selection. If firms imitate each other too strongly, they become involved in an evolutionary game of musical chairs, and no nontrivial strategy is able to establish itself.

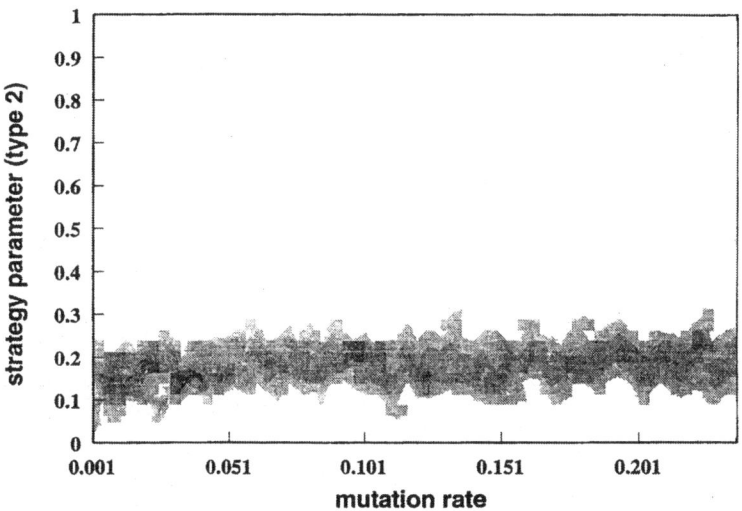

Figure 9: Histograms of strategy parameters for varying rates of the mutation probability ($A = 10$).

5. Discussion and conclusions

In this paper we have developed an evolutionary model describing the relation between endogenous technological change and economic growth along the lines of an evolutionary modelling philosophy. By this we mean that the economy is disaggregated into diverse individual behavioral subunits (instead of the representative agent so prevalent in most macroeconomic modelling) connected by nontrivial nonlinear dynamic interactions based on plausible notions of disequilibrium competition and investment. Rather than search for a strategic equilibrium based on a concept of rationality, we have assumed that these agents use boundedly rational behavioral procedures. In the present case this is an extremely simple rule for the R&D/profits (or gross investment) and R&D/sales ratios, which is parameterized by two real numbers between 0 and 1. Learning is modelled by allowing for mutation and imitation rules operating on the agents' strategy parameters. An element of behavioral realism is injected into the model by insisting that mutations are local in the strategic 'genotype' space, and that imitation is only prompted by less than satisfactory performance.

Using both a linear and a logistic innovation function we were able to show that evolutionary steady states exist that are attractive in the behavioral space,

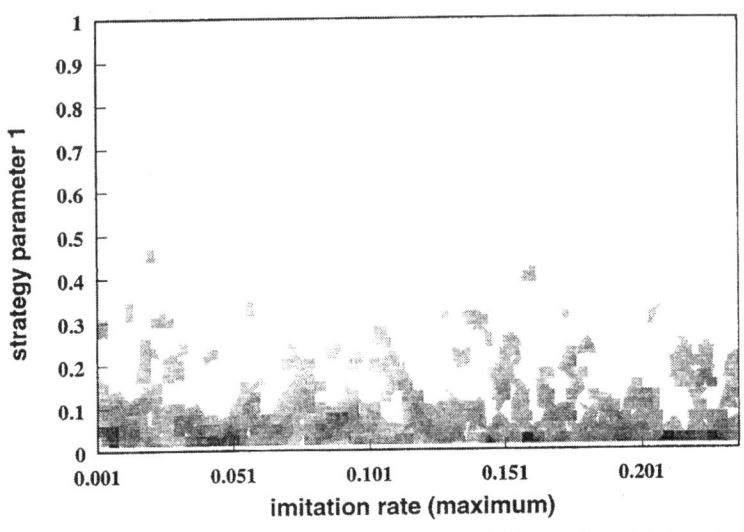

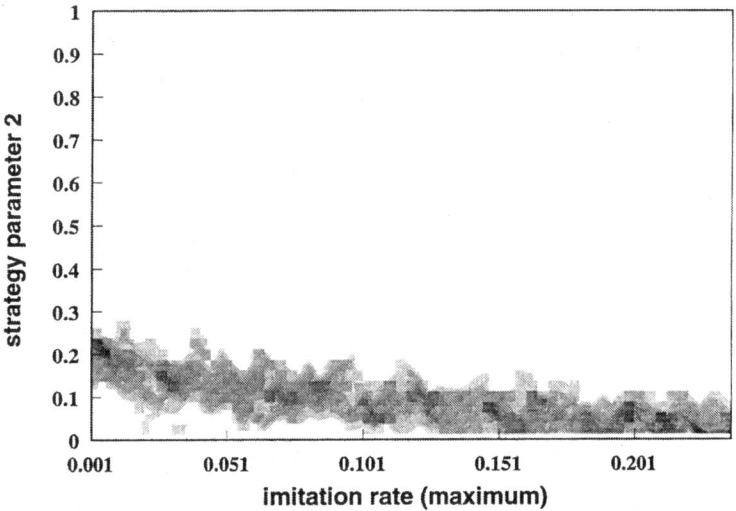

Figure 10: Histogram of strategy parameter for varying rates of the maximum imitation parameter ($A = 10$).

but may differ depending on 'history'. Thus the model does establish a case for endogenous growth in the sense of demonstrating that economic competition, even with very relaxed assumptions about individual goal-seeking behaviour and profit maximization, leads to an approximately steady-state growth path with a positive rate of technical change and R&D investment.

However, the spontaneous generation experiments underline the fact that the mere existence of such a steady state does not mean that history does not matter. Quite the contrary. A society starting with no or low rates of R&D will pass through a phase of very high market concentration, but with periodic upheavals or 'palace revolts' of market leadership on a time scale of centuries. Eventually such an economy will 'bootstrap' itself to higher rates of R&D and technical change [1].

In many evolutionary growth models found in the literature one implication of modelling technological change stochastically is that a wide range of 'economic histories' is possible, some of which seem to be compatible with the 'stylized facts' of actual empirical observations. While these results are often used to justify a 'minimalist' position that an evolutionary theory can explain the phenomena explained by mainstream theory but with a more realistic (Nelson 1995, p. 67) microeconomic foundation, we wish to argue that evolutionary theory would have to be more precise on the possible range of outcomes it predicts. For example, in the model outlined in this paper, we asked the question under what circumstances a fairly 'narrow' band of outcomes exists in the sense of a small range of values for our 'strategy parameters'.

Such an approach admittedly does not help us much in understanding specific events in economic history. It does not give us an answer to the question why a 'takeoff' of the strategy parameters (or its possible counterpart in reality, the industrial revolution) takes place at a given point of time. However, given the argument of evolutionary theory that clearcut monocausal mechanisms explaining phenomena like these do not exist, the further development of methods like the one applied here could provide a powerful analytical tool, which would take the field a step further than currently available results. In order to stimulate other contributors to the evolutionary debate to take a similar perspective in the future, further work on methodological issues, such as the status of simulation experiments relative to analytical results, or the statistical evaluation of results generated by computer simulations, is obviously required.

Although we do not wish to overburden our simple model with historical interpretations, it would be unfortunate to restrict the concept of endogenous growth to steady-state growth paths with no real structural development, social learning, and historical contingency. For this reason an evolutionary approach like the one proposed here appears to offer an attractive alternative explanation of how an economy can 'bootstrap' itself in historical time through a succession of growth phases and market structures. The concepts of growth or development stages, takeoffs and changes of regime were prominent in a classical line of thought associated with Marx, Schumpeter and later Rostow. The criticism that these theories smacked of rigid mechanistic determinism is overcome by the

---

1. This should be compared with the one-parameter strategy case, where the evolution is slower and passes through at least three distinct historical phases.

artificial worlds methodology, which demonstrates that reversions, variable delays, and path dependence resulting from underlying stochasticity and nonlinearity cannot be excluded. Needless to say, such a broad and differentiated perspective on economic growth has mostly fallen by the wayside in the postwar literature on growth and development (cf. Rostow 1990).

Our model also demonstrates that a bounded rationality approach to the theory of the firm, coupled with an evolutionary framework for analyzing market selection and collective learning, does yield dividends both in terms of explaining how identifiable patterns of behaviour emerge from *profit-seeking* rather than completely rational *profit-maximizing* assumptions, and how market structures and growth regimes may be simultaneously endogenized. In contrast to much of the recent evolutionary literature, both game-theoretic and computer-based, however, we argue that attention has to be paid to realism of the mutation and imitation mechanisms in order to extract historically meaningful implications about collective learning in genuine economic contexts.

Appendix

A summary of the parameters and the values employed in the runs analyzed in the paper is presented below.

$q = 10$	number of firms
$m = 0.9$	parameters of the Phillips curve eq. 1
$n = 1$	
$a = 1$	Soete-Turner coefficient eq. 2
γ (endogenous)	R&D/investment ratio in eq. 2
$c = 3$	capital-output ratio
$\sigma = 0$	rate of physical depreciation in eqs. 2 and 3
$\beta = 0.01$	rate of growth of labour force eq. 3
$\delta = 1$	ratio of productivity in goods and R&D sectors
$\tau = 0.06$	proportional jump in labour productivity eq. 4
A (variable)	innovation slope in eq. 5
$\rho_{min} = 0.01$	autonomous rate of innovation eq. 5
ϕ_1 (variable)	type 1 spillover coefficient in eq. 7
ϕ_2 (variable)	type 2 spillover coefficient in eq. 7
$L = 5$	lag for R&D moving average eq. 8
$\kappa = 4$	catch-up parameter eq. 10
$\Pi = 0.02$	mutation probability eq. 11
$s = 0.02$	standard deviation of mutation step size eq. 11
$\mu = 0.02$	maximum imitation probability eq. 12
$E = 0.005$	exit level in employment share
$b = 0.1$	labour productivity bandwidth for entrants

REFERENCES

Adams, H., 1919/1969, *The Degradation of the Democratic Dogma*, New York: Harper & Row.

Aghion, P. and Howitt, P., 1992, "A Model of Growth through Creative Destruction", *Econometrica*, **60**: 323-351.

Alchian, A.A., 1951, "Uncertainty, Evolution, and Economic Theory", *Journal of Political Economy*, **58**: 211-222.

Arrow, K., 1962, "The Economic Implications of Learning by Doing", *Review of Economic Studies*, **29**: 155-73.

Arthur, W.B., 1988, "Self-Reinforcing Mechanisms in Economics", in P.W. Anderson, K.J. Arrow and D. Pines, (eds), *The Economy as an Evolving Complex System*, Reading, Mass.: Addison-Wesley.

Arthur, W.B., 1991, "Designing Economic Agents that Act Like Human Agents: A Behavioral Approach to Bounded Rationality", *American Economic Review. Papers and Proceedings*, **81**: 353-359.

Arthur, W.B., 1994, *Increasing Returns and Path Dependence in the Economy*, Ann Arbor, MI: University of Michigan Press.

Axtell, R. and Epstein, J., 1996, *Growing Artificial Societies. Social Science from the Bottom Up*, Washington, DC: Brookings Institution.

Bergin, J. and Lipman, B.L., 1996, "Evolution with State-Dependent Mutations", *Econometrica*, **64**: 943-956.

Bertalanffy, L.v., 1932, *Theoretische Biologie, 1,* Berlin: Borntraeger.

Booker, L., Goldberg, D. and Holland, J., 1989, "Classifier Systems and Genetic Algorithms", in J. Carbonell, (ed.), *Machine Learning: Paradigms and Methods,* Cambridge, MA: MIT Press.

Boulding, K.E., 1978, *Ecodynamics: A New Theory of Societal Evolution,* Beverly Hills and London: Sage.

Boulding, K.E., 1981, *Evolutionary Economics,* Beverly Hills and London: Sage.

Bruckner, E., Ebeling, W., Jiménez Montaño, M.A. and Scharnhorst, A., 1994, "Hyperselection and Innovation Described by a Stochastic Model of Technological Evolution", in L. Leydesdorff and P. van den Besselaar, (eds), *Evolutionary Economics and Chaos Theory,* London: Pinter.

Cohen, W.M. and Levinthal, D.A., 1989, "Innovation and Learning: The Two Faces of R&D", *Economic Journal*, **99**: 569-596.

Downie, J., 1955, *The Competitive Process,* London: Duckworth.

Ebeling, W. and Feistel, R., 1982, *Physik der Selbstorganisation und Evolution,* Berlin: Akademie Verlag.

Edelman, G.M., 1987, *Neural Darwinism: The Theory of Neuronal Group Selection,* New York: Basic Books.

Feistel, R. and Ebeling, W., 1989, *Evolution of Complex Systems,* Berlin: VEB Deutscher Verlag der Wissenschaften.

Fisher, R.A., 1930, *The Genetical Theory of Natural Selection*, Oxford: Clarendon Press.

Goldberg, D., 1989, *Genetic Algorithms in Search, Optimization, and Machine Learning*, Reading MA: Addison-Wesley.

Goodwin, R.M., 1967, "A Growth Cycle", in C.H. Feinstein, (ed.), *Socialism, Capitalism and Economic Growth*, London: Macmillan.

Grübler, A., 1990, *The Rise and Decline of Infrastructures. Dynamics of Evolution and Technological Change in Transport*, Heidelberg: Physica-Verlag.

Helpman, E., 1992, "Endogenous Macroeconomic Growth Theory", *European Economic Review*, **36**: 237-267.

Henkin, G.M. and Polterovich, V.M., 1991, "Schumpeterian Dynamics as a Non-linear Wave Theory", *Journal of Mathematical Economics*, **20**: 551-590.

Hodgson, G., 1993, *Economics and Evolution: Bringing Back Life into Economics*, Ann Arbor, MI: University of Michigan Press.

Hofbauer, J. and Sigmund, K., 1988, *The Theory of Evolution and Dynamical Systems*, Cambridge: Cambridge University Press.

Holland, J.H. and Miller, J.H., 1991, "Artifical Adaptive Agents in Economic Theory", *American Economic Review Papers and Proceedings*, **8**: 363-370.

Horgan, J., 1995, "From Complexity to Perplexity", *Scientific American*, **June 1995**: 74-79.

Iwai, K., 1984a, "Schumpeterian Dynamics. I: An Evolutionary Model of Innovation and Imitation", *Journal of Economic Behavior and Organization*, **5**: 159-90.

Iwai, K., 1984b, "Schumpeterian Dynamics. II: Technological Progress, Firm Growth and 'Economic Selection'", *Journal of Economic Behavior and Organization*, **5**: 321-51.

Jiménez Montaño, M.A. and Ebeling, W., 1980, "A Stochastic Evolutionary Model of Technological Change", *Collective Phenomena*, **3**: 107-114.

Kaldor, N. and Mirrlees, J.A., 1962, "A New Model of Economic Growth", *Review of Economic Studies*, **29**: 174-92.

Kamien, M.I. and Schwartz, N.L., 1982, *Market Structure and Innovation*, Cambridge: Cambridge University Press.

Kandori, M., Mailath, G.J. and Rob, R., 1993, "Learning, Mutations, and Long Run Equilibrium in Games", *Econometrica*, **61(1)**: 29-56.

Kwasnicki, W. and Kwasnicka, H., 1992, "Market, Innovation, Competition: An Evolutionary Model of Industrial Dynamics", *Journal of Economic Behavior and Organization*, **19**: 343-368.

Lane, D.A., 1993, "Artificial Worlds and Economics. Parts 1 and 2", *Journal of Evolutionary Economics,* 3(2& 3): 89-108, 177-197.

Langton (ed.), C.G., 1989, *Artificial Life,* Redwood City, CA: Addison-Wesley.

Langton, C.G., Taylor, C.,Farmer, J.D. and Rasmussen, S. (eds), 1992, *Artificial Life II,* Redwood City, CA: Addison-Wesley.

Lotka, A.J., 1924/1956, *Elements of Mathematical Biology,* New York: Dover.

Lotka, A.J., 1945, "The Law of Evolution as a Maximal Principle", *Human Biology,* **17**: 167-194.

Marchetti, C. and Nakicenovic, N., *The Dynamics of Energy Systems and the Logistic Substitution Model,* Research Report RR-79-13, Laxenburg, Austria: IIASA.

Marshall, A., 1890, *Principles of Economics,* London: Macmillan.

Metcalfe, J.S., 1988, "Trade, Technology and Evolutionary Change", University of Manchester, mimeo.

Montroll, E.W., 1978, "Social Dynamics and the Quantifying of Social Forces", *Proceeding of the National Academy of Sciences, USA,* **75**: 4633-4637.

Nakicenovic, N., 1987, "Technological Substitution and Long Waves in the USA", in T. Vasko, (ed.), *The Long-Wave Debate,* Berlin: Springer-Verlag.

Nelson, R.R., 1990, "What is Public and What is Private about Technology?", Berkeley: CCC Working Paper No. 90-9.

Nelson, R.R., 1995, "Recent Evolutionary Theorizing About Economic Change", *Journal of Economic Literature,* **33**: 48-90.

Nelson, R.R. and Winter, S.G., 1982, *An Evolutionary Theory of Economic Change,* Cambridge MA: The Belknap Press of Harvard University Press.

Nicolis, G. and Prigogine, I., 1977, *Self-Organization in Non-Equilibrium Systems,* New York: Wiley-Interscience.

Rostow, W.W., 1990, *Theorists of Economic Growth,* Oxford: Oxford University Press.

Salter, W., 1960, *Productivity and Technical Change,* Cambridge: Cambridge University Press.

Schrödinger, E., 1945, *What is Life? The Physical Aspect of the Living Cell,* Cambridge: Cambridge University Press.

Schumpeter, J., 1919/1934, *Theorie der wirtschaftlichen Entwicklung,* English translation: *The Theory of Economic Development,* Cambridge, MA: Harvard University Press.

Schumpeter, J., 1947, *Capitalism, Socialism, and Democracy,* New York: Harper.

Schwefel, H.P., 1995, *Evolution and Optimum Seeking,* New York: Wiley.

Selten, R., 1989, "Evolution, Learning, and Economic Behaviour", *Games and Economic Behaviour,* **3**: 3-24.

Sigmund, K., 1986, "A Survey of Replicator Equations", in J.L. Casti and A. Karlqvist (eds), *Complexity, Language and Life: Mathematical Approaches*, Berlin, Heidelberg, New York and Tokyo: Springer-Verlag.

Silverberg, G., 1984, "Embodied Technical Progress in a Dynamic Economic Model: the Self-Organization Paradigm", in *Nonlinear Models of Fluctuating Growth*, ed. R. Goodwin, M. Krüger, and A. Vercelli, Berlin, Heidelberg, New York: Springer Verlag.

Silverberg, G., Dosi, G. and Orsenigo, L., 1988, "Innovation, Diversity and Diffusion: A Self-Organisation Model", *Economic Journal*, **98**: 1032-54.

Silverberg, G. and Lehnert, D., 1993, "Long Waves and 'Evolutionary Chaos' in a Simple Schumpeterian Model of Embodied Technical Change", *Structural Change and Economic Dynamics*, **4**: 9-37.

Silverberg, G. and Lehnert, D., 1994, "Growth Fluctuations in an Evolutionary Model of Creative Destruction", in G. Silverberg and L. Soete (eds), *The Economics of Growth and Technical Change: Technologies, Nations, Agents*, Aldershot: Edward Elgar.

Silverberg, G. and Verspagen, B., 1994a, "Learning, Innovation and Economic Growth: A Long-Run Model of Industrial Dynamics", *Industrial and Corporate Change*, **3**: 199-223.

Silverberg, G. and Verspagen, B., 1994b, "Collective Learning, Innovation and Growth in a Boundedly Rational, Evolutionary World", *Journal of Evolutionary Economics*, **4**: 207-226.

Silverberg, G. and Verspagen, B., 1995a, "An Evolutionary Model of Long Term Cyclical Variations of Catching Up and Falling Behind", *Journal of Evolutionary Economics*, **4**: 209-227.

Silverberg, G. and Verspagen, B., 1995b (in press), "Evolutionary Theorizing on Economic Growth", in K. Dopfer (ed.), *The Evolutionary Principles of Economics*, Cambridge: Cambridge University Press.

Silverberg, G. and Verspagen, B., 1996, "From the Artificial to the Endogenous: Modelling Evolutionary Adaptation and Economic Growth", in E. Helmstädter and M. Perlman, (eds), *Behavioral Norms, Technological Progress and Economic Dynamics: Studies in Schumpeterian Economics*, Ann Arbor, MI: University of Michigan Press.

Soete, L. and Turner, R., 1984, "Technology Diffusion and the Rate of Technical Change", *Economic Journal*, **94**: 612-623.

Solow, R.M., 1957, "Technical Change and the Aggregate Production Function", *Review of Economics and Statistics*, **39**: 312-320.

Solow, R., 1960, "Investment and Technical Progress", in K.J. Arrow, S. Karlin, and P. Suppes (eds), *Mathematical Methods in the Social Sciences 1959*, Stanford: Stanford University Press.

Steindl, J., 1952, *Maturity and Stagnation in American Capitalism*, New York: Monthly Review Press.

Winter, S.G., 1984, "Schumpeterian Competition in Alternative Technological Regimes", *Journal of Economic Behavior and Organization,* **5:** 137-158.

Young, H.P., 1993, "The Evolution of Conventions", *Econometrica,* **61:** 57-4.

CHAPTER 14
ON THE MICRO FOUNDATIONS OF ECONOMIC GROWTH
Human capital, firm organization and competitive selection

by Gunnar ELIASSON

1. The brave new world of limited understanding, reduced policy ambitions and a more adventurous economic life

The bulk of resource use in a business organization is devoted to various forms of competence intensive information processing (Eliasson 1990b) like R & D, product development, marketing, management etc. These are the transactions costs incurred to innovate and co-ordinate production in markets and hierarchies [1]. Their relative size determines the relative division of production in markets and hierarchies (Coase 1937). Above all, such transactions costs determine the "equilibrium" properties of the economic system by making them dependent on the factor allocation processes in markets and hierarchies. Heterogeneity of factors of production and output is what explains the large transactions costs, making for instance the value and volume of labor input dependent on a more or less efficient labor market process (Eliasson 1994). To understand firm behaviour this information use and the building of requisite competencies have to become an explicit part of economic theory. This is not a matter of marginal and almost costless exchanges of asymmetrically distributed information, as bounded rationality is commonly interpreted in I/O theory. The tacit human-embodied knowledge that figures dominantly in production is allocated over internal (firm) and external labor markets and in the form of team-based competence in the mergers and acquisitions (M & A) markets. The firm itself should most appropriately be represented as a team of tacit, human embodied competencies (Eliasson 1990a) and the creation of that team is more than the hiring and firing of people in the market; it requires entrepreneurial talent to compose a competent business team.

Addressing the problem of firm behaviour in the *knowledge-based information economy* (Eliasson 1990b), hence, means addressing the fundamentals of economic dynamics. And there is no better way of misunderstanding the dynamics of an economy populated with live firms and human beings

---

1. Transactions costs is a term conventionally reserved for costs incurred in market transactions. I use it more generally to cover all information and communications costs needed to innovate and coordinate production in markets and in hierarchies.

embodying radically different endowments of knowledge capital, than beginning with the assumptions of received neowalrasian [1] economic theory. It is in fact rather embarrassing for the profession that the young students of such problems are referred to an intellectual construct that hardly even recognizes the existence of behaving firms.

This paper addresses the role of knowledge in firm formation and performance and in economic growth and hence has to make theoretical room for live and recognizable firms. Is this firm still the minuscule computing and planning entity of received theory or the dynamic hierarchies of teams of competent people that we see?

The small transparent state space upon which the entire neowalrasian construction rests, and which is necessary to impose its static equilibrium properties is utterly at variance with the dynamics of markets for competence. A small and reasonable modification of this state space into a large, heterogeneous and non transparent *investment opportunity set* is sufficient to push our analysis outside that theory. In the new dimensions of the vastly expanded state space rational firms set up *business experiments* based on scant and biased information. Economic growth occurs through innovative entry, reorganization and rationalization among incumbent firms, and exit of low performers. In this non-linear environment of the *experimentally organized economy (EOE)* dominated by selection mechanisms (Eliasson 1991a, 1996b) there is no way of obtaining a complete overview of the economy from any centralized position. The Walrasian auctioneer, if he tried, would never be able to perform his text book role. Firms constantly commit errors and business failure becomes a standard cost for economic learning and development. Contrary to the advice of the static neowalrasian model business mistakes should not be minimized. Contrary to the static neowalrasian model a distinction has to be made between *uncertainty* and *risk* in the earlier tradition of Frank Knight (1921). Firms are seen as experts in organizing themselves to convert uncertainty into subjectively calculable risks.

The paper discusses the nature of firm knowledge creation and allocation in this theoretically new world, arrived at through modifying one fundamental assumption of the neowalrasian model. And one fundamental conclusion from this analysis is that growth theory, to warrant the name, has to be based on an explicit foundation of firm behaviour in dynamic markets.

In the brave new world of economics that I open by slightly modifying one critical assumption of the neowalrasian model, there is a much smaller role for the economist than we have been used to think, and for the economic advisor in particular. The new "problem" is the new awareness of the limits of our understanding of matters economics when we leave the worlds of keynesian and

---

1. I use Clower's (1996) terminology to refer to the Walras, Arrow-Debreu model (1954).

neowalrasian economics and as a logical consequence a reduction in our perceived ambition to control the economy through policy making.

2. Modifying one fundamental assumption slightly

The economic environment of each actor is composed of nature and the perceived and combined action of all other actors. This set of *opportunities* can be thought of as defined for all relevant futures. Since it is perceived by a large number of actors it is extremely multidimensional and as a whole entirely non transparent. It can be defined in principle, but not be operationally determined at any point in time and from any location. This last distinction, and its ramifications, are what my essay is all about.

In facing this opportunity set each actor forms a prior view of its characteristics as they are expected to impinge on its opportunities. The degree to which this view is limited and modified by the particular intelligence characteristics of the actor I take to constitute what Simon (1955 etc.) termed *bounded rationality* [1]. This interpretation of the term makes it close to the concept of competence, and to the extent that the particular competence characteristics of individuals differ such competence becomes an intrinsically *tacit* form of knowledge capital, embodied in human beings. It is tacit because of limited communicability, due to lacking *receiver competence*. Receiver competence is just another element of human embodied knowledge capital, namely (Eliasson 1986, 1990a) the ability to *recognize, intelligently absorb* and *competently use externally available knowledge*. It is both tacit and subjective because of indeterminacy. Each actor has to form a comprehensive and strategic view of the strategic positions of all other actors vis-à-vis each other.

Complexity is the characteristic of the opportunity set that limits the view and introduces bounded rationality in individuals and groups of individuals. Any degree of heterogeneity in the composition of that bounded rationality is sufficient to limit communication and hence necessary and sufficient to establish the existence of tacit knowledge (Eliasson 1990a) [2]. Tacitness furthermore may not be enough. There may not be anything stable to learn about. Information, communication and learning (read transactions) costs constitute the dominant resource use. Hence, it is only natural that *the opportunity set changes character as you learn about it*. This particular manifestation of the Heisenberg principle is typical of pronouncedly non-linear systems. In this particular setting it becomes synonymous to a positive sum game. The deeper into the opportunity space you probe the larger it grows. You might even

---

[1]. Simon (1959) suggests that "the economic actor" acts on and responds to "the subjective environment that he perceives".
[2]. Tacit knowledge so defined is conceptually different from asymmetric information in the sense that some knowledge will remain private even after infinite learning costs have been expended.

become relatively less knowledgeable about the whole the more you learn (Eliasson 1990b, p. 46 f.) and the faster the economy grows as a result of learning. It is like the Scandinavian Viking pig Särimner (Eliasson 1987, p. 29) that was eaten for supper but returned to life next morning. In economics it might even grow in the process. Again, the character of the opportunity set will determine what we should say about bounded rationality and tacit knowledge.

Each agent can be more or less free to enter and operate (behave) within the opportunity set. *Institutions* restrict access to and regulate operations within the opportunity set. Such institutions can be based in law or convention or be vested in the power (economic or in other ways) of competing agents and other bodies. The three items with sub categories listed in Table 1 characterize in full a national economy (Eliasson 1987, 1990a and 1991a).

Table 1. The three fundamental categories of economics

1. Opportunity set
2. Agent competence and behaviour
 - bounded rationality
 - tacitness
 - intuition
3. Access

Source: Eliasson (1996a, p. 24).

The prior assumptions we make about these categories set the limits of the analytical game we are now going to pursue. Prior assumptions about state space are part of the implicit understanding of a scientific shop, but the consequences for scientific discourse and understanding of these implicit assumptions tend soon to be forgotten. Neowalrasian mainstream economics as exhibited in static general equilibrium theory and all its accompanying superstructures imposes *convexity, differentiability and market clearing* at all times to achieve an interior point solution for each exogenously given set of prices. This amounts to assuming that the opportunity set is sufficiently small and for all practical purposes transparent such that all its interior characteristics can be communicated between agents [1]. Each agent, or his adviser (the auctioneer) can see all of it, or most of it from any point. If agents are less than fully informed, this lack of information is a small part of the total information base of the economy. All missing information, furthermore, can be communicated to all other agents at a predeterminable small (transactions) cost. Hence, there is no tacit knowledge and intuition plays no role. Bounded rationality now

---

1. Barring, possibly, a stochastic element.

means being asymmetrically informed [1]. Agents can thus engage in optimizing behaviour under conditions of full information, or lack of costly information that the agent has rationally decided not to acquire. As a consequence behaviour carries no economic meaning. You can compute ahead of time where you will end up and stay. Central planning is possible.

Since agents not yet "born" are in exactly the same information situation as incumbents, access to the opportunity set has no economic meaning, and for decades economists did not find entry and exit phenomena worth investigating (Eliasson 1991b).

In the alternative representation of a national economy, the *Experimentally Organized Economy* (EOE, Eliasson 1987, 1990a, 1991a, 1996a) exactly contrary conditions rule. The properties of the EOE are thus radically different from those of the mainstream economic model and the distinctive assumptional feature is a slight, reasonable and entirely empirical modification of the character of the opportunity set.

Agents are now informed of a small part of what is relevant for them and a negligible part of the whole opportunity set that is known to exist, but about which nobody and/or no central institution is fully informed or can be fully informed. With grossly uninformed agents the Walrasian auctioneer can no longer do his job. In general, what little each agent knows is quite different from what little other agents know. Heterogeneity rules and the conditions for a dominant, incommunicable tacit knowledge base are in place. Under these conditions the game has no traditional equilibrium solution, since each actor has always reason to believe that it can improve its position by acting on its particular expectations. So what does this mean for the nature of firm knowledge, firm behaviour and macroeconomic growth?

One implication follows directly. Understanding, macro requires that you take a look at the dynamics of micro behaviour. Not because it has to be that important, but because it is likely to be, considering what we have just said. Let us, therefore, proceed as if internal aggregation dynamics matter for aggregate behaviour (Lucas 1983) and ask what it means for understanding macroeconomics.

3. Business mistakes

First, agents in the EOE are only fractionally aware of their environment. Their information is normally grossly biased and unreliable when it comes to the future behaviour of other competing agents. It is normally not possible to set

---

1. Financial theorists makes no distinction between risk and uncertainty and between knowledge and information, beyond accepting that moral hazard and adverse selection may be a problem. If you have read the instruction book, you are both informed and competent.

up realistic competition games in which actors learn to find mutually consistent and, above all, unique equilibria. As a rule each actor soon learns that it has been more or less, and sometimes grossly in error, and has to factor that experience into its assessment as a standard cost for learning. An important additional conclusion is that such errors are not statistically well behaved as assumed in rational expectations, efficient market and statistical learning theory. If (systematic) errors originate in the underlying non-linear structure of the EOE, that in turn changes as a consequence of competitive selection that moves economic growth (see below), systematic statistical analysis of the data generated by the evolving system won't tell anything reliable about the structural characteristics of the system. Each business agent now has to act on the presumption that his business intuition is vaguely right, but also be aware that he may be entirely wrong. Human beings normally have difficulties combining such faculties in one person, and to act decisively under such circumstances. The solution is to organize many individuals in a *competent team*, or a firm.

4. The competence specification of an actor

Since antiquity human knowledge acquisition has been seen as monotonically cumulative, You add knowledge to an existing non depreciable knowledge base. This prior understanding is found in religious thinking and exists in derived form in academia. Perhaps it reflects a human craving for something stable to hold on to. Such belief in a for ever valid knowledge base is, however, utterly at variance with the environment of the business firm. The destruction of the intellectual foundation of a discipline (a shift of paradigm) may not come naturally to the armchair thinker but for the business man it is an all too obvious part of reality.

In business life the current conceptualization of reality is constantly disrupted and disregarding that fact soon spells disaster. Not only does the basis for a technology or a product change radically from time to time. It is dangerous to wait for it to happen. With many competitors freely accessing the opportunity set some competitors may already be on the right new track. If you believe that you have a good idea the most natural thing to expect in the market is that you cannot be alone having such a good idea.

This means that the business man has to be more than a learner. He or she has to be both innovative to create new ideas, capable of recognizing new ideas (discovery) early and of seizing the commercial initiative on what he or she sees. To be successful on this score the business person has to be both a leader of repetitive production and an entrepreneur in new activities. While repetitive production is built on focus, well defined information structures and effective coordination, innovation and entrepreneurship require variety and the intellectual capacity to recognize the commercial value of something you have not seen

Table 2. Competence specification of a business

ORIENTATION

1. Sense of direction (intuition)
2. Risk willing

SELECTION

3. Efficient identification of business mistakes
4. Effective correction of mistakes

OPERATION

5. Efficient coordination
6. Efficient feed back to (1)

before. How to *combine focus and variety within the same organization* has always been **the** management problem.

Several conclusions follow from this observation. First, the two tasks are usually kept organizationally apart. Second, to maximize the probability of the right match of competence and decision making in a very diversified technological environment the matching process has to be taken down to the micro level for an efficient exploitation of the knowledge base of society to be achieved; efficiency in the sense of achieving faster macroeconomic growth.

Firms to succeed have to have an intuitive business idea (item 1 in Table 2). In the neowalrasian model they drew up a plan based on research and information. Firm managers in the EOE act as if they are risk willing. They believe in their intuition and consider their risks low and under control, while the outsider does not understand what they are doing, a problem not unfamiliar to the innovator, entrepreneur in search of financing (Eliasson, and Eliasson 1996). Once firm management has decided, organized finance and set the business in motion it has to be aware of the possibility that it may be in error and – if so – correct the course (items 3 and 4). This schizophrenic outlook on life (to believe strongly, but consider seriously to be all wrong) is at variance with the normal intellectual constitution of human beings. The problem is normally solved through appropriately composing and organizing the top competent team of the organization (Eliasson 1976, 1990a).

When top management has ticked off the check list of Table 2 and is down at item 5 the standard job as a routine manager of a repetitive business of economic theory begins.

This competence specification of the firm, the special nature of uncertainty, as distinct from risk, the non-stochastic character of business mistakes and the special characteristics of business competencies all have their origin in the assumptions implicitly made of the opportunity set or state space. If we reduce it to full transparency uncertainty and risk become synonymous, ex ante equals ex post, barring a random error, and the firm (to the extent it exists) becomes a planning machine.

The firm competence set is then reduced (in Table 2) to operations, i.e. item 5 and possibly 6.

5. Non-linear growth through competitive selection

5.1. A dynamic Salter curve analysis

The dynamics of a growing economy and the mechanisms through which individual autonomous actors contribute to macroeconomic growth can be illustrated by the Salter (1960) curve in Figure 1. The Salter curve for a market gives a snapshot of the relative ex post performance rankings of individual firms (a column). Each firm faces superior performers to the left and inferior to the right. It has to work on improving itself in order not to lose resources to the better firms. But it also has to worry about the fact that the firms to the right have to do the same things, and may leapfrog them in their attempts to counter competition through innovation.

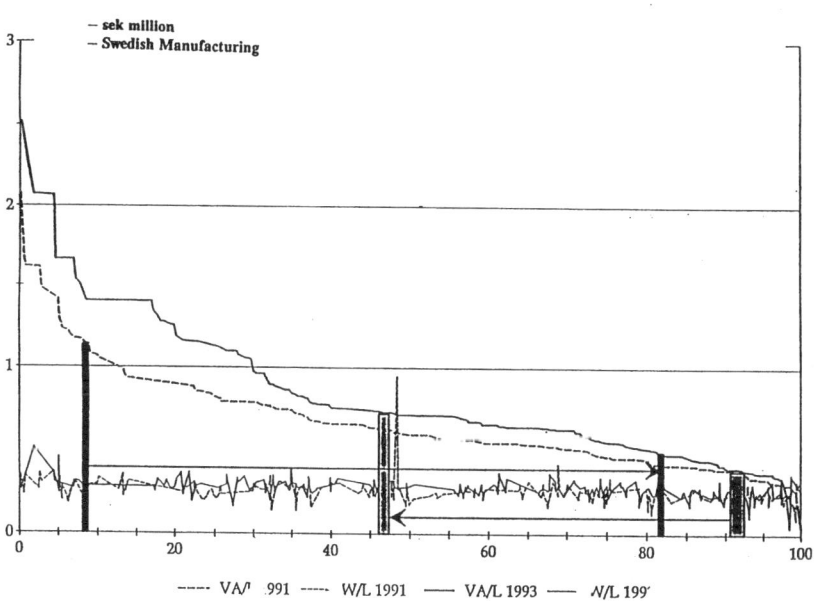

Figure 1. Labor productivity and wage cost per full-time employee, 1991 and 1993

Each incumbent firm, furthermore, has to worry about unexpected entrants to be expected from the left. The slope of the ex ante Salter curve incorporating incumbents and potential entrants thus reflects the competitive situation in the market. The realization of competition and entry forces relative prices to change (violating the price taking assumption of the neowalrasian model), some firms to fail and exit to the right and the Salter curve to shift outward. Macroeconomic growth is realized in the process through competitive selection. Macroeconomic growth, thus, can be exhaustively represented by the four investment growth mechanisms of Table 3, i.e. by entry, reorganization, rationalization and exit (Eliasson 1996a, b).

The economic system, as described, can thus be kept expanding through a more intense exploration of the opportunity set. The system is moved through *competition* creating a situation of constant insecurity for every actor. Challenged actors innovate, reorganize and rationalize to stay ahead. They are forced to do that, because not doing anything to safeguard their position eventually means sure failure.

This competitive enforcement of positive change would, however, soon cease, when the market is populated by one, or a few surviving actors only. To ensure that none of the incumbent actors of today can be sure of being the only long-run survivors *incentives* have to be sufficient to ensure significant *competitive entry*.

Such incentives can be there for two reasons: (1) *increasing returns* to exploring the investment opportunity set and (2) *entrepreneurial optimism*. If increasing returns exist, the presumption is that this will soon be learned in the market. One reason for the existence, or creation of such an increasing returns situation may be the existence of a synergistic *competence bloc* [1], suggesting a number of policy implications. A competence bloc will eventually give rise to a successful industrial development.

Entrepreneurial optimism is a sociological explanation based on attitudes, more like opening a pizza restaurant. People start firms to realize ambitions. There does not have to be an industrial (increasing returns) opportunity and growth does not have to be created.

Table 3 can be interpreted in terms of well defined units of behaviour (read firms) that perform either of the four functions. More realistically, however, the firm and the market (all other actors) are not well defined in Coasian (1937) terms. Firms steadily reorganize to cope with competition. They sometimes do it internally, but often through recombinations in the market for mergers &

---

1. See Eliasson, and Eliasson (1996). The way I have formulated it here, it is very similar to Marshall's (1919) idea of industrial districts. The industrial district functioned as an externality that exhibited economies of scale as a whole, very much as postulated in the so-called "new growth theory". Each firm in the district, however, featured diminishing returns, which made the system as a whole consistent with the walrasian model.

acquisitions (M & A), thereby interacting with both 1, 3 and 4. This does not really change the nature of the analysis but it makes modelling growth in terms of Table 3 more complicated.

The Swedish micro-to-macro model MOSES (Eliasson 1977, 1991a) currently does not allow for such reorganization through the M & A markets. Otherwise it operates more or less as the EOE has been presented above.

Table 3. The four investment growth mechanisms

1. Entry
2. Reorganization
3. Rationalization
4. Exit

Source: Eliasson (1996a, p. 45).

6. The reduced controllability of the economic system

6.1. Policy implications

Expanding state space and allowing for significant heterogeneity and tacit knowledge are synonymous to introducing immense complexity into the economy, creating disorderly non-linear behaviour (Day 1986, Lesourne 1991). This is in turn synonymous to forcing economic actors to set up subjectively risky business experiments with uncertain outcomes.

One among many such adventurous actors is Government, only that the scale of its operation can turn otherwise normal business mistakes into national long-run disasters, and hence should prevent it from acting adventurously.

Government operates under the same kind of uncertainty as all other actors facing an uncertain environment and runs the risk of committing significant systematic errors. The neowalrasian model removed such errors on the part of Government due to its assumed ability to control the economy through informed policies. In the EOE this illusion of being in control is intellectually removed. Being able to exert significant policy leverage rather aggravates the risk of policy mistakes by requiring (Eliasson 1990a) that the Government not only understands its influence on an external, exogenous environment, but also how all actors in that environment react to Government policy making [1]. The economics profession is not intellectually prepared for giving advice in such complicated situations. The ambitions policy maker entering the economy to

---

[1]. To arrive so far we don't have to be more specific about the objective function of firms and the feed back of demand through income generation. To see how this is handled in MOSES, see Eliasson (1985).

correct what he perceives to be a *market failure* in fact is more litely to create a more serious *government failure*. This conclusion, however, rests on a different theory than the conventional neowalrasian story. The logical conclusion is that policy control of the EOE diminishes compared to policy control of the neowalrasian economy, and that policy ambitions consequently should be reduced.

The economic systems analysis presented offers a feasible alternative to the unrealistic policy fine tuning to specific targets in the Tinbergen (1952) tradition, namely to create an institutional environment that induces (and makes possible) a more efficient exploitation of the opportunity set in such a way that increasing returns to exploration and growth can be realized. The support of the institutions of competence blocs and the creation of incentives that induce such positive game exploration is a viable possibility, only that the final composition of the explorative growth process cannot be determined in advance.

REFERENCES

Arrow Kenneth J. and Gérard Debreu (1954), Existence of an Equilibrium for a Competitive Economy, *Econometrica*, 22 (July), 265-290.

Clower R. W. (1996), New Microfoundations for the Theory of Economic Growth? Paper prepared for The 6th international conference of the International Joseph A. Schumpeter Society, Stockholm, June 2-5, 1996. To be published in Eliasson-Green (1998).

Coase R. H. (1937), The Nature of the Firm, *Economica*, New Series, IV (13-16), 386-405.

Day R. H. (1986), *Disequilibrium Economic Dynamics: A post-Schumpeterian Contribution;* in R. H. Day and G. Eliasson (eds.), *The Dynamics of Market Economies*. Amsterdam: North-Holland.

Eliasson Gunnar (1976), *Business Economic Planning – Theory, Practice and Comparison*, London etc., John Wiley & Sons.

– (1985), *The Firm and Financial Markets in The Swedish Micro-to-Macro Model,* Stockholm: IUI.

– (1986), Kompetens, kommunikation och kunskapsuppbyggnad – sammanfattning och arbetshypoteser för industripolitiken; in G. Eliasson, B. Carlsson et al., *Kunskap, information och tjänster; en studie av svenska industriföretag* (The manufacturing firm as an information processor and service producer). Stockholm: IUI and Liber.

– (1987), *Technological Competition and Trade in the Experimentally Organized Economy,* Research Report No. 32. Stockholm: IUI.

– (1990a), *The Firm as a Competent Team, JEBO* 13 (3) 175-298.

– (1990b), *The Knowledge Based Information Economy*, Stockholm: IUI and Teldok.

- (1991a),Modeling The Experimentally Organized Economy, *JEBO* 16 (1-2), 153-182.
- (1991b), Deregulation, Innovative Entry and Structural Diversity as a Source of Stable Rapid Economic Growth, *Journal of Evolutionary Economics* (1) 49-63.
- (1994), Educational Efficiency and the Market for Competence, *European Journal for Vocational Training*, 2/94, pp. 11 ff.
- (1996a), *Firm Objectives, Controls and Organization – the use of information and the transfer of knowledge within the firm*, Dordrecht/Boston/London: Kluwer Academic Publishers.
- (1996b), Endogenous Economic Growth through Selection; in Harding (ed), *Microsimulation and Public Policy*, Amsterdam: North-Holland.

Eliasson Gunnar, and Åsa Eliasson (1996), The Biotechnological Competence Bloc, *Revue d'Economie Industrielle. Numero Exceptionel.*

Eliasson Gunnar and Chris Green (eds.) (1998), *The Micro Foundations of Economic Growth*, Ann Arbor: University of Michigan Press.

Knight Frank (1921), *Risk, Uncertainty and Profit*, Boston: Houghton-Mifflin.

Lesourne J. (1991), *Economie de l'ordre et du désordre, Economica*, Paris.

Lucas R. E., Jr. (1983), Econometric Policy Evaluation: A Critique; in K. Brunner, and A. Meltzer (eds.), (1983), *Theory, Policy, Institutions*, Papers from the Carnegie-Rochester Conference Series on Public Policy, Amsterdam: North-Holland.

Marshall Alfred (1919), *Industry and Trade*, London.

Salter, W. E. G. (1960), *Productivity and Technical Change*, Cambridge, MA: Cambridge University Press.

Simon H. A. (1955), A Behavioural Model of Rational Choice, *Quarterly Journal of Economics* 69, 99-118.

Simon H. A. (1959), Theories of Decision Making in Economics and Behavioural Sciences, *American Economic Review* 49 (3), 253-283.

Tinbergen J. (1952), *On the Theory of Economic Policy*, Amsterdam: North-Holland.

Varian H. (1992), *Microeconomic Analysis*, New York, Norton.

CHAPITRE 15
EXPLORING THE UNKNOWN. ON ENTREPRENEURSHIP, COORDINATION AND INNOVATION-DRIVEN GROWTH *

Giovanni DOSI and Giorgio FAGIOLO

1. Introduction

The determinants of economic growth in general, and the possibility of a self-sustained process fueled by technological advances, have recently brought back the attention of the economic discipline, with respect to both formal theorizing and historical analysis. Concerning the former, "Endogenous Growth" models (broadly in the spirit of Romer (1986, 1990) and Grossman and Helpman (1991a, 1991b)) and "Schumpeterian" and "Evolutionary" models (mainly building on Nelson and Winter (1982)) have been all trying – in different perspectives – to tell stories where per-capita incomes grow (also) as the outcome of positive feedbacks in knowledge accumulation. At the same time, a rapidly expanding empirically grounded literature on the economics of technological change has been exploring the drivers of innovation and diffusion; the mechanism through which they occur; and their effects – at the levels of firms, sectors and whole countries [1].

Notwithstanding all that, we largely share the assessment spelled out in much more detail by Nelson (1997) of an enormous gap still remaining between what we historically know about technical change and its economic exploitation, on the one hand, and the ways we represent them in formal growth models, on the other [2].

While some tensions between "appreciative" (empirically drawn) generalizations and much more "reduced forms" models is likely to always appear, our departing diagnostics is somewhat more pessimistic than that. In fact, a few general properties of the empirical patterns of innovation and diffusion seem to

---

* Support to this research by the Italian National Research Council (CNR), the Italian Ministry of Research (MURST) and IIASA, Laxenburg, Austria is gratefully acknowledged. An early sketch of some ideas behind the model which follows is in Dosi and Orsenigo (1994). Comments by several participants to the Conference of CNAM, Paris, October 1996 helped a lot in sharpening the arguments. Usual caveats apply.
1. See, among others, Freeman (1982) and (1994), Rosenberg (1982) and (1994), David (1975), Dosi (1988), Nelson (1993), Lundvall (1993), Grandstrand (1994), Stoneman (1995), and fair parts of Dosi *et al.* (1988) and Foray and Freeman (1992).
2. Cf. also Dosi, Freeman and Fabiani (1994), where one tries to outline a series of historical "stylized facts" which the theory should ideally account for.

Exploring the unknown. On entrepreneurship | 309

be neglected in a good deal of contemporary (formal) growth literature. Among them, and strictly related to the model presented here, in our view, there are the following.

First, aggregate formal accounts (in most of both the "old" and "new" growth models) tend to neglect the systematic heterogeneity in microeconomic technological competencies highlighted in the empirical literature. Relatedly, note that any "representative agent" reduction might be highly misleading whenever the aggregate dynamics depends not only on the mean characteristics of any population but also on the distributions themselves and on the details of the interaction mechanisms among microentities [1].

Second, there appear to be a striking conflict between the incredibly sophisticated forward-looking rationality one typically imputes to agents in aggregate formal stories and the messy experimentation which empirical students of innovation and business history usually find – full of stubborn mistakes, "animal spirits" and unexpected discoveries [2].

Third, partly as a consequence, it seems quite hard to interpret macrodynamics as equilibrium paths isomorphic to some underlying "representative" behavioral pattern.

Fourth, economic change appears to be driven at least as much by time-consuming diffusion as from innovation [3].

Here, we shall present a model of growth that builds on the foregoing properties, together with few other "stylized facts" stemming from empirical analyses of technological change but often neglected in formal aggregate endeavors. In section 2, we shall outline the building blocks and theoretical conjectures supporting the model presented in section 3. Next, we discuss some simulations results (section 4), and, finally, flag some research developments ahead (section 5).

2. Decentralized Knowledge Accumulation and Collective Outcomes: Some Preliminaries

Technological advances, to a significant extent, are generated, *endogenously*, through resource-expensive search undertaken by a multiplicity of profit-motivated agents. Search itself is generally uncertain and innovative entrepreneurs (or, for that matter, incumbent firms undertaking innovative activities) are

---

1. For highly pertinent considerations on this point cf. Kirman (1989) and (1992) and Allen (1988).
2. For example, on entry dynamics of new firms cf. the evidence discussed in Dosi and Lovallo (1997).
3. This point has indeed been emphasized within otherwise rather orthodox models by Jovanovic and Rob (1989), Jovanovic (1995), and, of course, is near the concerns of evolutionary modelers (cf. Nelson and Winter (1982), Silverberg *et al.* (1988), Metcalfe (1988) and (1996)).

driven by the beliefs that "there might be something profitable out there", but are generally unable to form probability distributions on the outcomes of their search efforts.

Innovations are not entirely appropriable: knowledge progressively diffuses to other agents who might well catch-up by investing in imitation – most likely, with a lag proportional to some measure of the distance between the knowledge which they master and that which they want to acquire.

Knowledge accumulation generally entails dynamic increasing returns both at the levels of individual agents (typically, business firms) and collection of them (i.e. industries), grounded upon collectively shared "learning paradigms". However, radically new technologies involve, to different degrees, ruptures and "mismatchings", so that only part of the old knowledge might be useful to the exploitation of future technologies [1].

On the grounds of these basic building blocks, the model that follows addresses three major issues.

First, under what circumstances processes of innovation and diffusion with the above characteristics can *self-organize* and yield aggregate outcomes with the properties corresponding to the empirically observed patterns of growth? Since the model does not rest on any *a priori* commitment to individual rationality and collective equilibria, the question involves an issue which could be called of *Schumpeterian coordination,* namely: can "boundedly rational" agents, heterogeneous in their beliefs and technological competences, (imperfectly) coordinate their efforts of search for novel opportunities and of exploitation of what they already know such as to yield relatively ordered patterns of self-sustained aggregate growth? [2]

Second, we shall undertake some experiments of comparative dynamics and map different conditions of generation and diffusion of knowledge into the resulting growth patterns. For example, what happens to the mean (and higher moments) of the distribution of growth rates across independent sample paths as technological parameters change (including the richness of innovative

---

1. On these points, see in particular Rosenberg (1982) and Freeman (1982) regarding technological uncertainty; Freeman (1982), Levin *et al.* (1987), Nelson and Winter (1982) and the remarks in Dosi (1997) and Nelson (1997) on appropriability; Arrow (1962a), Arthur *et al.* (1987), David (1975) and (1988), Romer (1990); Atkinson and Stiglitz (1969), Nelson and Winter (1982), Dosi (1988), Malerba and Orsenigo (1993) on different – theoretical and empirical – appreciations of dynamic increasing returns; Nelson and Winter (1977), Dosi (1982), Freeman and Perez (1988) on somewhat complementary notions of "technological paradigms" and relatively ordered "trajectories" in learning patterns.

2. For a thorough discussion on the exploitation-exploration trade-off arising in adaptive learning systems see March (1991), Schumpeter (1934), Holland (1975), Allen and McGlade (1986) and Kuran (1988). See also Levinthal and March (1981) and Levitt and March (1988) on the trade-off between the refinement of an existing technology and invention of a new one.

opportunities, the easiness of imitation/diffusion, and the degree of path-dependence in learning processes)?

Third, the model highlights a few sources of potential conflict between individual and collective rationality. It is an established result that in presence of externalities and dynamic increasing returns of some kind, one should not in general expect the dynamics generated by self-seeking agents to correspond with the socially optimal one. Abandoning "representative agents" compression of the microeconomics of innovation makes the point even more vividly clear: there is no reason to expect that a decentralized economy would handle the dilemma between "exploration" of novelty and "exploitation" of incumbent knowledge the same way as an omniscient (and benign) planner would [1]. Moreover, by relaxing the assumption of hyper-rational agents with correct *technological* expectations, one is also able to consider those circumstances where collective growth finds its *necessary* condition in the presence of a number of "irrational" entrepreneurs; that is, the vindication of innovative "animal spirits" as public virtue, even when "irrational acts" of private *hubris*...

In this work, we explicitly take on board four out of the five "facts" that Paul Romer (1994) identifies as underlying New Growth Theories, namely: (i) multiplicity of agents; (ii) non-rivalry in the use of knowledge; (iii) replicability of physical production activities; (iv) endogeneity of discovery efforts. The fifth one – i.e. the rents associated with successful discoveries – is implicitly there but plays no role. On purpose, we mean to partly de-link the expectations on these rents from their actual average values (which is implied by the abandonment of any rational technological expectation hypothesis). Hence, while acknowledging that agents search for innovations because they can *sometimes* earn a rent on them, we don not assume any monotonic relation between the "true" expected value of those rents and the propensity to innovate. As a first approximation, we prefer to study the ways the patterns of knowledge accumulation, together with institutionally nested "animal spirits", affect growth – with rent-related incentives just as permissive conditions, above a minimum threshold [2].

Moreover, well in the spirit of an evolutionary perspective, we assume: (i) heterogeneity among agents in their technological and behavioral features – e.g. their problem-solving knowledge and their propensity to search and to quickly

---

1. But any actual planner, too, would fall well short of that standard, being equally ignorant of long-run learning opportunities.
2. In fact, this is quite in tune with the empirical evidence. While it is obviously true that with zero appropriability of innovation no private actor has any incentive to undertake expensive search (e.g. for a long time agricultural research on new varieties of seeds, etc.), on the other side, to our knowledge, there is non convincing evidence, either cross-country or over time, that innovative efforts respond smoothly to the fine tuning of appropriability conditions.

312 | Evolutionary approaches to economic growth

imitate [1] –; (ii) diversity in the knowledge-bases upon which agents are able to draw; (iii) path-dependency in learning achievements; (iv) bounded rationality in both decisions to allocate resources to search and choices on the directions of search efforts (hence, unlike stochastic New Growth models of "creative destruction" – such as Cheng and Dinopoulos (1991) and Aghion and Howitt (1992) – or "hybrids" between "old" and "new" ones – such as Jovanovic and Rob (1990) and Jones and Newman (1994) – we shall not confine the analysis to those rather special cases whereby decentralized agents on average "get it right"...) [2]; (v) "open-ended" dynamics in the technology space (so that learning opportunities are notionally unlimited, but what each agent can achieve at any one time is constrained by what one has learned in the past).

However, unlike full-fledged evolutionary models [3], we do not account for any selection dynamics through which individual agents (*in primis*, firms) grow, shrink on die according to their revealed technological and market success. Hence, the following could be regarded as a reduced form "toy model" of evolutionary growth, focusing upon the collective outcomes of decentralized patterns of knowledge accumulation, while suppressing – alike most traditional growth models – any explicit competitive interaction.

3. The model

Think of a *knowledge base* (i.e. a technological paradigm) as a metaphorical "island" on a stochastic n-dimensional lattice (in the following, 2-dimensional for simplicity). Each island is characterized by dynamic increasing returns, associated to knowledge-accumulation, which drive the exploitation of any knowledge base.

However, notionally unlimited opportunities exist – so that, as time goes to infinity, whatever economic performance measure may go to infinity, too.

Relatedly, conflicts between "exploration" of known technologies and "exploration" of potentially superior ones might emerge (cf. March (1991) for

---

1. Parts of the overwhelming evidence on this point are surveyed in Nelson (1981), Freeman (1982), Dosi (1988).
2. On this point, the empirical evidence indeed matches quite solid theoretical reasons on the impossibility of forming unbiased expectations on future technological advances. After all, innovation is about solving problems that one has been unable to solve so far. But if one could know, even in probability, how to solve them, that would mean that the solution algorithm has already been found! The issue bears on problem-solving complexity and, more generally, on the predictability of discovery. More on this is in Dosi and Egidi (1991) and Dosi, Marengo and Fagiolo (1996), within a vast literature.
3. See, among others, Nelson and Winter (1982), Winter (1984), Chiaromonte and Dosi (1993), Silverberg and Verspagen (1994), Dosi *et al.* (1994), Silverberg and Lehnert (1993), Conlisk (1989) and Metcalfe (1988).

an illuminating illustration of the dilemma) [1]. Moreover, we assume that individual efforts of "exploration" slowly yield a collective externality, via, first, diffusion of knowledge, and, second, incremental improvements upon specific knowledge bases [2].

Search (i.e. exploration of new islands), as well as imitation, require a resource investment, which we assume to be proportional to the average current per capita output of the economy. Labor is the only formally accounted input – although one can easily think of a much higher dimensionality of the actual search and production input spaces as ultimately projected into labor productivity dynamics.

In this spirit, the economy is represented as a set of production activities, "spatially" distributed on the 2-dimensional integer lattice $\mathbb{N}^2$ and it is composed of a fixed population of agents $I = \{1, 2, ..., N\}$, $N \ll \infty$, and a countable infinite number of islands, indexed by $j \in \mathbb{N}$. There is only one good, which can be "extracted" from every island. Time is discrete and the generic time-period is denoted by $t \in \mathbb{N} \cup \{0\}$.

The lattice, i.e. the sea, is endowed by the "Manhattan" metric d_1. Each node $(x, y) \in \mathbb{N}^2$ can be either an island or not, while each island has a size of one node. Let $\pi(x, y)$ be the probability that the node $(x, y) \in \mathbb{N}^2$ is an island. We will assume throughout that $\pi(x, y) = \pi$, all $(x, y) \in \mathbb{N}^2$, where $\pi \in (0, 1)$ [3].

Each island $j \in \mathbb{N}$ (is completely characterized by its coordinates (x_j, y_j) in the lattice [4] together with an initial (or intrinsic) "productivity" coefficient $s_j = s(x_j, y_j) \in \mathbb{R}_+$.

Without loss of generality, we suppose that, at time $t = 0$, the population is randomly distributed on a (small) set of islands $L_0 = \{1, 2, ..., \ell_0\} \subset \mathbb{N}$. More precisely, assume that $d_1[(x_j, y_j)] \leq d_1[(x_{\ell_0}, y_{\ell_0})]$, for all $j \in L_0$, and that each

---

1. The distinction between "incremental" and "radical" technical progress (i.e. between paradigm changes and within-paradigm improvements) is increasingly accepted also in other modeling perspectives: cf. for example Cheng and Dinopoulos (1992), Jovanovic and Rob (1990), Jovanovic and McDonald (1994), Amable (1995).
2. Again, the issue of a time-consuming (and/or resource-consuming) adaptation and diffusion is beginning to make inroads also into equilibrium growth models: cf. Jovanovic and McDonald (1994), Jovanovic (1995) and Jones and Newman (1994). In the model below we especially emphasize "creative destruction" aspects of technological discontinuities, with relatively lower attention to the possible complementarities among them (on this point, in the formal growth literature, cf. A. Young (1993)). However, note that the complementarity aspect is implicit in the possibility that we allow in our model for agents to "carry over", so to speak, part of their previous production skills to new knowledge bases.
3. As Silverberg and Verspagen (1995) point out, following Nelson and Winter (1982), "innovation should be modeled stochastically, to reflect the uncertainty in the link between effort and outcome".
4. Notice that there is a one-to-one mapping between the index $j \in \mathbb{N}$ (and the pair $(x_j, y_j) \in \mathbb{N}^2, j \in \mathbb{N}$.

agent $i \in I$ has an initial location $(x_{i,0}, y_{i,0})$ such that, for all $i \in I$, there exists a $j \in L_0$: $(x_{i,0}, y_{i,0}) = (x_j, y_j)$. Furthermore, let initial productivity coefficients s_j to be uniformly distributed with mean $d_1[j] = d_1[(x_j, y_j)] = x_j + y_j, j \in L_0$, and variance σ_s, so that, on average, the performance of a "mine" (i.e. an "island") increases with its distance from the origin of the lattice.

All agents are thus initially mining inside the smallest box containing islands in L_0, i.e. $B_0 = \{(x, y) \in \mathbb{N}^2: x \leq x_0^* \text{ and } y \leq y_0^*\}$, where $x_0^* = \max\{x_j, j \in L_0\}$ and $y_0^* = \max\{y_j, j \in L_0\}$ [1]. In Figure 1 a very simple example of a conceivable initial configuration of the economy is depicted in order to make clearer the above assumptions.

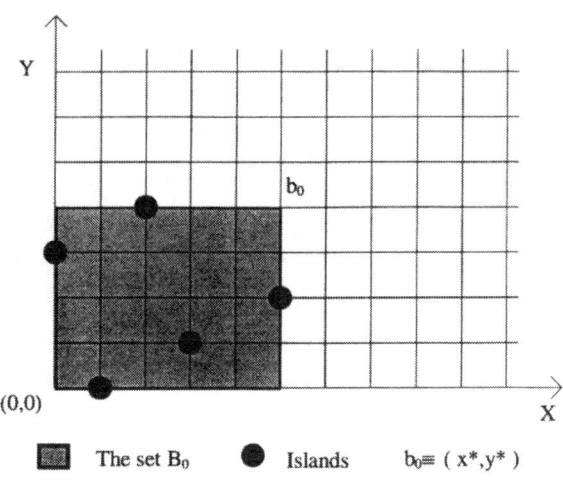

Figure 1: A simple example of initial distribution of islands ($\ell_0 = 5$)

Finally, assume that each agent $i \in I$ has an exogenously determined *willingness to explore* defined by the number $\varepsilon_i \in [0, 1]$ [1].

3.1. Dynamics and Endogenous Novelty

Let us turn now to the description of how the economy evolves. At time $t = 1, 2, ...$ each agent can be in one of three different states, namely be a "miner", an "explorer" or an "imitator". Let $a_{i,t}$ the state of agent $i \in I$ at time t, where $a_{i,t} \in \{mi, ex, im\}$, i.e. it can be a miner, an explorer or an imitator, and denote by $j \in \mathbb{N}$ the island currently occupied by the "miner" $i \in I$, i.e. the agent $i \in I$ such that $a_{i,t} = mi$.

---

1. As we will see below, in each time period the "miner" $i \in I$ decides to leave its island and explore around it with probability ε_i.

Agents are allowed (with a certain probability) to leave the island they are working on, gradually explore the lattice around and, possibly, discover previously unexploited (and possibly more productive) islands. In order to illustrate how this is formalized, we need some additional notation.

Denote by $n_t(x_j, y_j)$ the number of miners working on island $j \in \mathbb{N}$ at time t. Then, define an island $j \in \mathbb{N}$ to be "known" at time t if $n_\tau(x_j, y_j) > 0$ for at least a $0 \leq \tau \leq t$, i.e. if it currently has some people on it or if it was so at least some finite time in the past. Accordingly, let the set of currently "known" islands be given by:

$$L_t = \{j \in N : \exists 0 \leq \tau \leq t : n_\tau(x_j, y_j) > 0\} \qquad (1)$$

Among all known islands, let us call "colonized" those currently exploited, i.e. all $j \in L_t$: $n_t(x_j, y_j) > 0$. Conversely, all islands in $\mathbb{N} \backslash L_t$ will be called "unknown", since no agent has previously exploited them. Furthermore, denote the cardinality of L_t by ℓ_t and the current location in the lattice of agent $i \in I$ by the pair $(x_{i,t}, y_{i,t})$ [1]. Finally, as we did for L_0, consider the smallest box containing all islands in L_t, i.e. let

$$B_t = \{(x, y) \in \mathbb{N}^2 : x \leq x_t^* \text{ and } y \leq y_t^*\} \qquad (2)$$

where $x_t^* = \max\{x_j, j \in L_t\}$ and $y_t^* = \max\{y_j, j \in L_t\}$. Since the node $b_t^* \equiv (x_t^*, y_t^*)$ will only coincide by chance with a "known" island, we can think of b_t^* just as a "proxy" of the most efficient island (i.e. the best practice) currently exploited by the agents [2].

The model allows for an endogenous dynamics on the set L_t and, consequently, on the box B_t, in the sense that the set L_t changes in time because of the actions of agents in I. A crucial distinction has to be made here between what we will call the "currently realized" economy and the economy *tout court*. As the box B_t contains all exploited technologies up to time t, it therefore represents a proxy of what is actually at disposal of the economy, i.e. the current set of "fundamentals" or the "realized economy".

However, outside B_t there is a whole – eventually better – world waiting to be discovered. The model depicts precisely the process of the gradual endogenous discover of the economy by economic agents themselves.

---

1. Notice that the location of an agent at time t will correspond to that of an island, say j, if and only if currently there is at least one "miner" on j, i.e.: for $t > 1$, $(x_{i,t}, y_{i,t}) = (x_j, y_j)$, some $j \in L_t$ if and only if $a_{i,t} = $ "mi".
2. Notice that here, at any given moment in time there is no a single best-practice technique, but many competing technologies located near the frontier of the box B_t (see also Silverberg et al., 1988).

Hence, given the endogenous nature of innovation/imitation activities, it is crucial to account for the process by which agents in different states make "crucial decisions", i.e. irreversible choices that change forever the economic environment [1]. Let us consider the "mining" process, first.

3.2. Mining

A "miner" $i \in I$ currently located on island $j \in L_t$ with coordinates (x_j, y_j), will necessarily get, at no cost, a gross output $q_{i,t}$ according to the simple production function:

$$q_{i,t} = s(x_j, y_j) [n_t(x_j, y_j)]^{a-1} \tag{3}$$

where $s(x_j, y_j)$ is the initial "productivity" coefficient defined above, $n_t(x_j, y_j)$ is the number of "miners" currently working on island j and $a > 1$. Returns to scale are thus increasing at the islands' level, since the current total gross output of island $j \in L_t$ is:

$$Q_t(x_j, y_j) = s(x_j, y_j) [n_t(x_j, y_j)]^a \tag{4}$$

The economy total gross output (GDP) will then be:

$$Q = \sum_{j \in L_t} Q_t(x_j, y_j) \tag{5}$$

As all agents are "miners" at $t = 0$, then, for all $i \in I$:

$$q_{i,0} = s(x_{i,0}, y_{i,0}) [n_0(x_{i,0}, y_{i,0})]^{a-1} \tag{6}$$

so that, aggregating, one obtains: $Q_0(x_j, y_j) = s(x_j, y_j) [n_0(x_j, y_j)]^a$ for all $j \in L_0$ and $Q_0 = \sum_{j=1}^{\ell_0} Q_0(x_j, y_j)$.

3.3. Exploring

At time t, each miner has the opportunity to become "explorer". For sake of simplicity, we will assume here that this happens with probability $\varepsilon_i = \varepsilon$, for all $i \in I$ which are in the state of "miner". As soon as a "miner" currently working on island $j \in L_t$ decides to become "explorer" (i.e. $a_{i,t+1}$ = "ex"), it leaves its island, "sailing" until it finds another one – possibly not known. Notice that up

---

1. See also Shackle (1955) and Davidson (1996) for some hints in a similar spirit.

to now we have not endowed agents with any "forecasting" skill. However, when a "miner" leaves its island at time t, we let it to carry the memory of the last output which the agent was able to get in the state of "miner" (i.e. its past knowledge and skills). We denote the memory of explorer $i \in I$ leaving island j at time τ by $q_{i,\tau}$. During the search, it does not extract any output but rather it pays a per-period "transportation" cost equal to a given share $\beta \in [0, 1)$ of the last-period per-capita GDP, raised to $\delta \geq 0$ [1], i.e. if $a_{i,t} =$ "ex" then individual transportation cost in period t will be: $c_{i,t} = \beta \cdot [Q_{t-1}/N]^{\delta}$. From time $t+1$ on, it moves on the lattice following the "naïve" stochastic rule:

$$\text{Prob}\{(x_{i,t+1}, y_{i,t+1})\} = \begin{cases} 1/4 & \text{if } |x - x_{i,t}| + |y - y_{i,t}| = 1 \\ 0 & \text{otherwise} \end{cases}, \text{ all } (x,y) \in \mathbb{N}^2 \quad (7)$$

That is, at each time period the "explorer" moves from its current node $(x_{i,t}, y_{i,t})$ by randomly selecting one out of the four adjacent nodes. Notice that we are assuming that agents are not aware of the fact that islands are (on average) more and more productive the further away one goes from the origin of the lattice.

The new location of the explorer $(x_{i,t+1}, y_{i,t+1})$ might obviously be: (i) the "sea"; (ii) a "known" island $j \in L_t$; (iii) a "new" island $j \in \mathbb{N}\setminus L_t$. In the first case, i.e. $(x_{i,t+1}, y_{i,t+1}) \neq (x_j, y_j)$ for all $j \in \mathbb{N}$, we still have $a_{i,t+1} =$ "ex" and the exploration goes on. In the second case, there will be a $j \in L_t$ such that $(x_{i,t+1}, y_{i,t+1}) = (x_j, y_j)$ and hence the explorer $i \in I$ becomes miner on $j \in L_t$, i.e. $a_{i,t+1} =$ "ex". The third case is the most important. Suppose, for simplicity, that at time t each explorer is allowed to find new islands only outside the box B_t [2]. As stated above, the node occupied by the "explorer" $i \in I$ at time $t+1$ could be a "new" island with probability π. In case of discovery, the new island j^* with co-ordinates $(x_{j^*}, y_{j^*}) = (x_{i,t+1}, y_{i,t+1})$ is added to the set of "known" islands, i.e. $L_{t+1} = L_t \cup \{j^*\}$ and $\ell_{t+1} = \ell_t + 1$. Moreover, both the set $B_{(.)}$ and the "best practice" proxy $(x^*_{(.)}, y^*_{(.)})$ are accordingly updated.

3.4. Path-Dependence and "Ordinary" vs. "Extraordinary" Discoveries

In the model we allow discoveries to be either "ordinary" or, to different extents, "extraordinary". In order to capture the distinction from the innovation

---

[1]. This form of cost has been assumed for sake of normalization. However, since in this version of the model the willingness of explore is assumed to be independent of transportation costs, the latter have no effects on the dynamics of the model, but only on the magnitude of the total net output: see also section 4.4.
[2]. This is not a necessary assumption, however. As we will see below, the economy is naturally driven, although only on average, toward more efficient islands by the process of diffusion of information, so that the event of finding a new island inside L_t does not change the thrust of the model.

literature between innovations within existing knowledge bases and the introduction of radically new "technological paradigms" (Dosi, 1982), the "initial" productivity coefficient of a "new" island j^* discovered by the "explorer" $i \in I$ carrying the output memory $q_{i,\tau}$, will be given by:

$$s_{j^*} = s(x_{j^*}, y_{j^*}) = (1 + W) \cdot \{d_1[x_{j^*}, y_{j^*}] + \varphi q_{i,\tau} + \xi\} \tag{8}$$

where $d_1[(x_{j^*}, y_{j^*})] = x_{j^*} + y_{j^*}$ is, as usual, the distance of j^* from $(0, 0)$; W is a random variable distributed as a Poisson with mean $\lambda > 0$; ξ is a uniformly distributed random variable, independent of W, with mean zero and variance σ_ξ and, finally, $\varphi \in [0, 1]$. The interpretation of Eq. (8) is straightforward. The initial productivity of a "new" island depends on four factors, namely: (i) its distance from the origin (as for initial islands); (ii) a cumulative learning effect directly linked to the past "skills" of the discoverer, i.e. $\varphi q_{i,\tau}$; (iii) a random variable W which allows low probability "jumps", that is, changes in technological paradigms; (iv) a stochastic i.i.d. zero-mean noise ξ.

Two considerations are in order. First, the mechanism through which innovations are introduced in the economy is both path-dependent (Arthur, 1988 and 1994) and influenced by random (small) events (Arthur, 1989; David, 1992). On one hand, a large implies that more skilled "explorers" (i.e. more efficient past "miners") are likely to discover more productive islands and to produce more in the future, thanks to a sort of "learning-to-learn" mechanism (Stiglitz, 1987). Moreover, the stochastic nature of innovation, together with increasing returns associated with learning by doing (as in Arrow (1962b) and Parente (1994)), allow even "ordinary" discoveries to drive the process of growth. Second, notice that, as by independence:

$$Es(x_{j^*}, y_{j^*}) = (1 + \lambda) [(x_{j^*} + y_{j^*}) + \varphi q_{i,\tau}] \tag{9}$$

then, on average, a larger λ lets "extraordinary" discoveries to be more likely in the economy. The parameter λ, together with π, are measures of the degree of notional "opportunities". Indeed, a large λ lets, in expectation, the productivity of a newly discovered island to be sensibly larger than those associated to the currently "known" islands; likewise, a larger π implies a larger average number of per-period discoveries.

3.5. Diffusion of Knowledge and Imitation

Due to the uncertainty of the exploration process and to within-island dynamic increasing returns, there is an incentive for both "miners" and "explorers" to imitate the most productive islands existing in the "currently realized" economy. In the model we formalize a process of diffusion of knowledge which tries to capture some basic features of empirically observed patterns of imitation and diffusion (Nelson and Winter, 1982; David, 1975;

Dosi, 1988 and 1992; Freeman, 1994; see also Jovanovic and Rob, 1989; Jovanovic and McDonald, 1994).

Let m_t be the number of "miners" currently present in the economy. At time t, from each "colonized" island $j \in L_t$ a signal is delivered and instantaneously [1] spread all around. Signals are characterized by an *intrinsic intensity* proportional to the share of miners present on $j \in L_t$ – i.e. $n_t(x_j, y_j)/m_t$ – and a *content* given by the actual productivity of the island – i.e. $Q_t(x_j, y_j)/n_t(x_j, y_j)$. Moreover, they decay exponentially with the distance from the source, so that the *actual intensity* with which a signal delivered from (x_j, y_j) reaches an agent currently located at (x, y) is given by:

$$w_t(x_j, y_j; x, y) = \frac{n_t(x_j, y_j)}{m_t} \exp\{-\rho[|x - x_j| + |y - y_j|]\}, \quad \rho \geq 0 \quad (10)$$

Agent i will then collect the "contents" of all *received* signals (i.e. those coming from islands $j_{h_1}, ..., j_{h_M}$, where $M \leq \ell_t$ is a random variable) and contrast them with *its own performance*. The latter is simply agent i's current productivity if it is a "miner" (say on island j), or the "memory" on the productivity of its island of origin, if it is an "explorer". Hence, it will choose among the $M + 1$ available options by drawing from the set $\{j, j_{h_1}, ..., j_{h_M}\} \subseteq L_t$, with probabilities proportional to the associate productivities. If the choice is j, then it will decide not to imitate any island but rather to remain in the current state. Otherwise, it will become an "imitator" – i.e. $a_{i, t+1} =$ "im"– and it will move toward the imitated island, say (x', y'), reaching it after $k = d_1[(x', y'); (x, y)] = |x - x'| + |y - y'|$ time periods – i.e. making one step at each period and following the shortest path. During this lapse of time, an "imitator" behaves as an "explorer" for what concerns both production and transportation costs [2]. Finally, once the imitated island is reached, it will turn again its state into "miner", i.e. $a_{i, t+k+1} =$ "mi".

3.6. Interactions

Interactions in our economy are basically "local" [3]. Indeed, agents locally interact both deterministically through increasing returns in the mining process and stochastically through the process of knowledge diffusion. In the latter, the parameter $\rho \geq 0$ tunes the "degree of locality" of the interactions: the larger ρ, the more the process of diffusion of knowledge is local, in the sense that signals tend to reach, in probability, only the nearest neighbors. Two extreme

---

1. In an alternative version of the model, not discussed here, to every signal is also associated a "speed" which measures how quickly the signal is spread around the economy.
2. For the sake of simplicity, notice that an imitator cannot be reached by any other signal while committed to a particular destination.
3. A more detailed discussion of local interaction models in Fagiolo (1997a).

cases are: (i) $p = 0$, i.e. interactions are global, in that they do not depend on the distance between source and receiver; and (ii) $p = \infty$, i.e. no signal is spread, i.e. there is no diffusion of information.

3.7. Micro and Macro System Variables

At each time period $t = 0, 1, 2, ...$, the economy will be completely characterized by the following *micro variables*. Concerning *islands*: (a) the set of "known" islands L_t; (b) the co-ordinates set: $Z_t = \{(x_j, y_j), j \in L_t\}$; (c) the initial productivity coefficients $S_t = \{s_j, j \in L_t\}$. Concerning *agents*, one might consider the mappings $A_t: I \to \{\text{"mi"}, \text{"ex"}, \text{"im"}\}$, $C_t: I \to \mathbb{N}^2$ and $\Theta_t: I \to \mathbb{R}$, recording current states, coordinates and individual gross outputs.

The *macro variables* of interest are: (i) the triple $(m_t, e_t, i_t) \in \mathbb{N}^3$, $m_t + e_t + i_t = N$, i.e. the current number of "miners", "explorers" and "imitators" in the economy; (ii) the pair $(\ell_t, \ell_t^C) \in \mathbb{N}^2$ (where ℓ_t is the number of currently *known* islands and $\ell_t^C \leq \ell_t$ is the number of the *colonized* ones), together with their coordinates and their initial productivity; (iii) the log of GDP, namely $q_t = \log Q_t$; (v) the growth rate of GDP, denoted by g_t.

4. Some results

Let us start with some qualitative results focusing on the different patterns of growth the model is able to generate. To begin, note that the model is an example of "artificial economies", that one is bound to study mainly via computer simulations. Analytical solutions – at least as long as one looks at the model in its full-fledged form – are indeed not achievable because of the underlying complexity of the stochastic processes which update micro – and accordingly macro – variables [1].

Some other considerations are in order. First, we will mainly focus on the aggregate properties of simulated time series of (log of) GDP and growth rates. The main goal is to analyze how the model behaves in some "benchmark" parametrizations, in order to assess the roles played by knowledge-specific increasing returns, imitation and exploration in the dynamics of the economy. In particular, we will address the question whether the model is able to display self-organizing patterns of persistent growth [2] and – if so – under which behavioral and system parametrizations (especially concerning innovation and diffusion rates). Second, let us emphasize the preliminary nature of the results which follow. In order to get a deeper understanding of the behavior of the model, one should actually perform even more systematic searches of the

---
1. For a thorough discussion of "artificial economies" models, see Lane (1993).
2. More on the notion of self-organization is in Lesourne (1991). See also Silverberg (1988) and the remarks in Coriat and Dosi (1995).

parameter space and try to accurately map different regions of that space into (statistically) different behaviors of the variables of interest [1].

4.1. A closed economy without exploration

Let us analyze a very simple "stationary" case. Assume exploration is not allowed, i.e. let $\varepsilon_i = \varepsilon = 0$, $\forall i \in I$. In this set-up, the economy is "closed", since agents can only exchange information about the initial set of islands and exploit them (i.e. act on the ground of *given* fundamentals), but are not supposed to endogenously introduce innovations. Without loss of generality, we can assume $\ell_0 = 2$ and $s_1 \leq s_2$. In this case, given the initial productivities, the system is completely characterized by a stochastic process on $\underline{m} = (m_1, m_2)$, with $m_1 + m_2 = N$ (i.e. on the number of miners on island $j = 1, 2$), which is a Markov chain with two absorbing states, namely $\underline{m}^{1*} = (N, 0)$ and $\underline{m}^{2*} = (0, N)$. Accordingly, the GDP will converge with probability one to the attractor set $\Theta = \{s_1 N^a, s_2 N^a\}$. However, the process on $\underline{m}$ is not *ergodic*, implying also potential inefficiency of the economy [2]. Indeed, path-dependency entailed by increasing returns will tend to drive all agents, through waves of imitation, toward the island with the *actual* (not *initial*) best productivity. Hence both initial conditions $\{s_1, s_2\}$ and $\{(m_{10}, m_{20})\}$ – i.e. productivity coefficients and the initial distribution of miners on islands $j = 1, 2$ – and "small stochastic events" – i.e. stochastic imitation decisions – could lead agents to converge on the inefficient island $j = 1$ [3].

However, the probability that the system will be absorbed by the "efficient" limit state, i.e. $p^* = \text{Prob}\left\{\lim_{t \to \infty} Q_t = s_2 N^a\right\}$, will be increasing in both $\Delta s_0 = s_2 - s_1$ and $\Delta m_0 = m_{20} - m_{10}$ [4]. For what concerns GDP and growth rates one usually observes simulated time series as that in Figure 2. Hence, in this simple setting, growth is a transitory phenomenon because, once the lock-in on an island is achieved, no further dynamics is allowed in the system and no fluctuations will arise thereafter.

4.2. A closed economy with exploration

Suppose now that exploration is allowed, i.e. let $\varepsilon_i = \varepsilon > 0$, $\forall i \in I$, but only *inside* the initial "realized economy", i.e. inside an unchanged set of "knowl-

---

1. As shown below, we did indeed begin this type of analysis.
2. For a more detailed discussion of these properties of path-dependency cf. Arthur (1994) and David (1988).
3. The behavior of the model in this simple set-up is close to those obtained in different frameworks by David (1992), Arthur et al. (1987).
4. A Montecarlo study of the frequencies of absorption as functions of Δs_0 and Δm_0, not reported here, gives support to intuition.

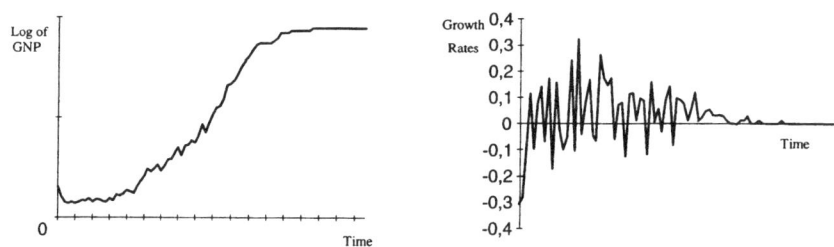

Figure 2: GDP (left) and Growth Rates in a Closed Economy without Exploration ($N = 100$, $\pi = 0.1$, $\sigma_s = 0.1$, $\rho = 0.1$, $a = 1.5$, $\beta = 0.1$)

edge bases". This means that "miners" can become "explorers" but they can "sail" only inside the box B_0. Hence, they are still not able to "innovate" (i.e. to discover islands other than the already "known" ones) and must necessarily exploit the existing technologies. However, unlike the previous case, they can always decide to leave the island they are working on, even though all agents are mining on it. All that introduces a potential source of "exploration", or, more extremely, of "irrationality" and "idiosyncrasy" in individual behaviors. Although the decision to become explorer is not linked – in this version of the model – to any system variable, we are tempted to define this behavior as a "nonconformist" one, as in a few models of "social interaction" and "herd behavior" [1]. Indeed, when exploration is allowed, the lock-in of the system will not generally occur, since there is always a positive probability that "non conformist" decisions will induce phase transitions in the system.

In this setting, the economy can be described as before by a Markov process over the **m** states which the system can attain. However, unlike the previous case, the transition probabilities are not only influenced by the propensities to imitate technologies with a higher (revealed) efficiencies, but also involve a certain probability of "exploring". Islands represent here "basins of attraction" among which the system persistently oscillates exhibiting the mentioned phenomena of phase transitions [2]. The stochastic process of exploration/imitation yields persistent output fluctuations. Indeed, as depicted in Fig.3, the simulated time-series of GDP display an autoregressive stationary pattern - as econometric analyses (not reported) usually show. Note that, in this setting, over finite time periods, the number of miners working on each island obviously depends on earlier states of the system, as Figures 4(a) and 4(b) show for the two cases $s_1 = s_2$ and $s_1 < s_2$. Increasing returns and knowledge diffusion induces agents – on average – to move toward currently more efficient islands.

---

1. See Brock and Durlauf (1995), Hirshleifer (1993), Bikchandani *et al.* (1992), Scharfstein and Stein (1990), Kirman (1993).
2. These properties are quite similar to those displayed by models based on Fokker-Planck equations. Cf. also Kirman (1993) and Orléan (1992).

However, exploration allows with positive probability "de-locking" bursts, also toward notionally less efficient islands. In a sense, persistent fluctuations are in this case generated by a problem of *imperfect Schumpeterian coordination* in presence of dynamic increasing returns to learning [1].

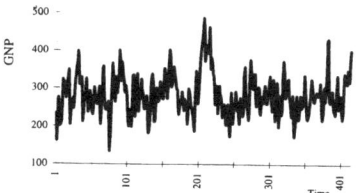

Figure 3: GDP in a Closed Economy with Exploration ($N = 100$, $\pi = 0.1$, $\sigma_s = 0.1$, $\rho = 0.1$, $a = 1.5$, $\beta = 0$, $\varepsilon = 0.1$)

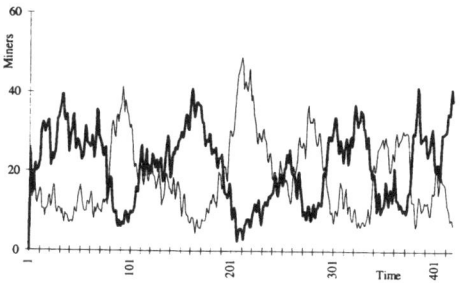

Figure 4(a): Number of miners on islands $j = 1, 2$ when $s_1 = s_2$ (thick line: Island 2) ($N = 100$, $\pi = 0.1$, $\sigma_s = 0.1$, $\rho = 0.1$, $a = 1.5$, $\beta = 0$)

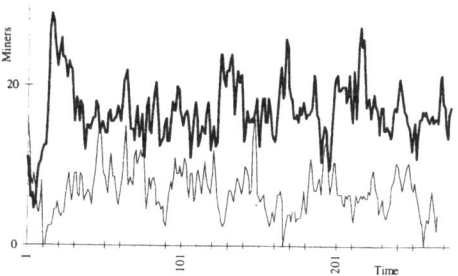

Figure 4(b): Number of miners on islands $j = 1, 2$ when $s_1 < s_2$ (thick line: Island 2) ($N = 100$, $\pi = 0.1$, $\sigma_s = 0.1$, $\rho = 0.1$, $a = 1.5$, $\beta = 0$, $\varepsilon = 0.1$)

---

1. Notice here the loose analogy with the coordination-related dynamics treated by Cooper and John (1988) and Durlauf (1994).

324 | Evolutionary approaches to economic growth

Moreover, here – as in the closed-economy / no exploration case – as long as one does not allow for the possibility of endogenous novelty, self-sustaining growth could emerge only if one superimposes an exogenous Solow-like drift on the best-practice production function.

4.3. Exploring in an open-ended economy: the emergence of self-sustaining growth

Consider now the more general case of exploration in an *open-ended* economy. In this set-up the economy displays, for a wide range of parameters, patterns of self-sustaining growth [1].

Typically, the simulated time-series of GDP are exponentially shaped (so that its logarithm displays a linear trend, as in Figure 5). More precisely, what one usually find in the case of self-sustaining growth is that the time-series of the (log of) GDP seem to be "difference stationary", according to standard ADF test [2] (see Table 1). Indeed, irrespective of whether the constant and/or the trend terms are included in the ADF regression, one is unable to reject at 5% the null of a unit root, which is on the contrary not accepted for both first differences Δq_t and growth rates $g_t = (q_t - q_{t-1})/q_{t-1}$ [3].

---

[1]. In the following, a Montecarlo analysis giving a more precise meaning to this statement is presented.

[2]. The lag order $k = 5$ in the standard ADF regression $\Delta q_t = \mu + \gamma t + \theta_0 q_{t-1} + \theta_1 \Delta q_{t-1} + \cdots + \theta_{k-1} \Delta q_{t-k+1} + \zeta_t$ has been suggested by both Akaike and Schwarz criteria. All econometric analyses reported here refer, as an example, to a single time-series (i.e. that plotted in fig. 5). Nevertheless, the same conclusions appear to hold in all simulations displaying self-sustaining growth. However, in order to give more rigorous bases to the above outcomes, a Montecarlo study of the percentage of rejection of the null of a unit-root (for different parametrizations) has been undertaken.

[3]. The above results seem to match those obtained for GDP time-series for the U.S. by Nelson and Plosser (1982) and Stock and Watson (1986). However, it is a well-known result that standard ADF tests for "stochastic trend" (against "deterministic trend" alternatives) suffer from very low power. In particular, many authors have recently shown that unit-root tests are unlikely to discriminate between difference- and trend-stationarity, (see Christiano and Eichenbaum (1989) and Rudebusch (1993)), giving birth to the so-called "we don't know" literature. Conversely, many other contributions have recently appeared suggesting that unit-root tests can be nonetheless informative, at least over long spans (DeJong and Whiteman, 1991 and 1994). In this connection, Cochrane (1988) has pointed out that the use of longer GDP samples (as in our case) may produce sharper unit-root inference. Yet, evidence stemming from this strand of literature seems to conclude that U.S. aggregate output is *not* likely to be difference stationary (Diebold and Senhadji, 1996; Bernd, 1994). Hence, the question of deterministic vs. stochastic trend in real economic aggregates remains open.Notice also that whenever the permanent component is interpreted as the outcome of productivity shocks – as thoroughly argued by Lippi and Reichlin (1994) – "the random walk identification assumption is not appropriate because it does not take into account well-known features of the way in which technological change is absorbed by different firms throughout the economy. In fact, the random walk carries several implausible implicit assumptions, about the technical change process; e.g. it excludes any learning at the firm-level; it implies simultaneous adoption of technical innovation by all firms, so that even the co-existence of different capital vintages is ruled out" (Lippi and Reichliu (1994), p. 19). Many of these drawbacks are indeed

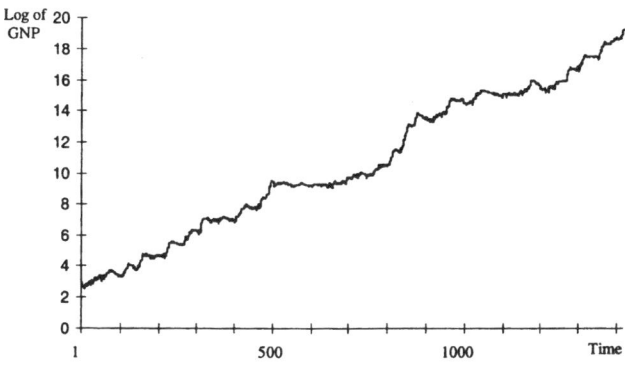

Figure 5: Exponential Growth in an Open-Ended Economy with Exploration (Log of GDP) ($N = 100$, $\pi = 0.1$, $\sigma_s = \sigma_\xi = 0.1$, $\rho = 0.1$, $a = 1.5$, $\beta = 0$, $\varepsilon = 0.1$, $\lambda = 1$, $\varphi = 0.5$)

In the Appendix, some further results about persistence of output fluctuations are reported. In analogy with Campbell and Mankiw (1987, 1989), we address the question of whether fluctuations in GDP are characterized by a permanent component and how big such a component might be. They consider two different measures of persistence [1] based on sample estimates of auto-correlations of changes in the log of GDP, finding that in "six out of seven countries a 1% shock to output should change the long-run univariate forecast of output by well over 1%". We computed the same statistics for both time-series of change in the log of GDP (i.e. Δq_t) and growth rates (i.e. ($g_t = (q_t - q_{t-1})/q_{t-1}$), getting similar results. As table 4 in the Appendix shows, all estimated measures of persistence generally exceed unity, suggesting that our simulated GDP is characterized by non transitory fluctuations [2].

However, exponential growth is not the sole regularity one can get from the simulated time-series of GDP. Indeed, for different parametrizations, the model is able to generate "no growth" economies – see Figure 6(a) – or "low growth" ones [3], as depicted in Figure 6(b).

---

overcome in our model, where – absent capital vintages – there is however a time-consuming process of diffusion of heterogenous pieces of knowledge.
1. See the Appendix. For details, cf. also Cochrane (1988).
2. Notice, incidentally, that our estimates are very close to those of the U.S. (log of) real GDP obtained by Campbell and Mankiw (1989). Again, there is no consensus in the literature about the size of the long-run response of actual real GDPs to an innovation. Christiano and Eichenbaum (1989), for instance, show that Campbell and Mankiw's results are very sensitive to the choice of the ARMA representation of the data.
3. By a "low growth" economy we mean a situation where the GDP time-series fluctuates around a linear (stochastic) trend, while its log follows a "s-shaped" pattern, so that in the long run growth rates tend to become stationary around zero.

Table 1
ADF Tests on simulated series of log of GDP $[q_t]$, first differences of log of GDP $[\Delta q_t]$ and growth rates $[g_t = (q_t - q_{t-1})/q_{t-1}]^*$

(a) 1 500 Obs., Critical values: 5% = − 2.864, 1% = − 3.438; Constant included

Variable	Lag	ADF *t*-Test	σ	*t* Lag	*t*-Probability
Log of GDP q_t	5	0.1169	0.072001	1.3317	0.1832
	4	0.14585	0.072021	2.8253	0.0048
	3	0.20439	0.072199	1.1937	0.2328
	2	0.22725	0.07221	− 1.2462	0.2129
	1	0.20157	0.072225	0.49482	0.6208
	0	0.21226	0.072205		
First Diff. Δq_t	5	− 13.397**	0.071939	− 1.707	0.088
	4	− 15.086**	0.071988	− 1.2748	0.2026
	3	− 17.190**	0.072004	− 2.7825	0.0055
	2	− 21.328**	0.072176	− 1.1552	0.2482
	1	− 27.255**	0.072185	1.2672	0.2053
	0	− 37.052**	0.072201		
Growth Rates g_t	5	− 15.046**	0.010963	− 2.7796	0.0055
	4	− 17.329**	0.010989	1.1188	0.2634
	3	− 18.595**	0.01099	− 0.81087	0.4176
	2	− 21.829**	0.010989	− 4.8012	0
	1	− 32.801**	0.011075	7.3257	0
	0	− 38.851**	0.01128		

(b) 1500 Obs., Critical values: 5% = − 3.415; 1% = − 3.97; Constant and Trend included

Variable	Lag	ADF *t*-Test	σ	*t* Lag	*t*-Probability
Log of GDP q_t	5	− 2.4513	0.071869	1.4905	0.1363
	4	− 2.3567	0.0719	2.9716	0.003
	3	− 2.1664	0.0721	1.3261	0.185
	2	− 2.0876	0.072119	− 1.1085	0.2678
	1	− 2.1655	0.072125	0.6366	0.5245
	0	− 2.1283	0.07211		
First Diff. Δq_t	5	− 13.398**	0.071961	− 1.7014	0.0891
	4	− 15.086**	0.07201	− 1.2704	0.2042
	3	− 17.190**	0.072025	− 2.7771	0.0056
	2	− 21.326**	0.072197	− 1.1506	0.2501
	1	− 27.251**	0.072206	1.2718	0.2036
	0	− 37.044**	0.072221		
Growth Rates g_t	5	− 15.313**	0.010939	− 2.6601	0.0079
	4	− 17.595**	0.010962	1.2743	0.2028
	3	− 18.837**	0.010965	− 0.6385	0.5233
	2	− 22.057**	0.010963	− 4.5807	0
	1	− 33.052**	0.01104	7.5376	0
	0	− 39.016**	0.011257		

* Econometric analyses refer to the following parametrization: $N = 100$, $\pi = 0.1$, $\sigma_s = \sigma_\zeta = 0.1$, $\rho = 0.1$, $a = 1.5$, $\beta = 0$, $\varepsilon = 0.1$, $\lambda = 1$, $\varphi = 0.5$.

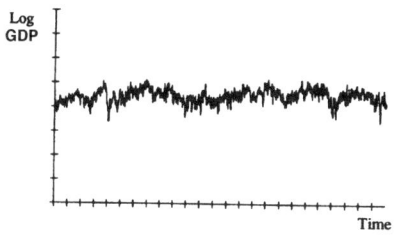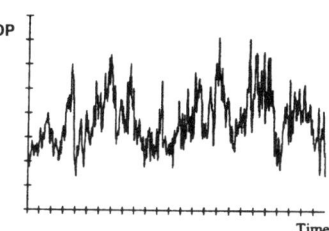

Figure 6(a): No Growth in an Open-Ended Economy with Exploration ($N = 100$, $\pi = 0.1$, $\sigma_s = \sigma_\xi = 0.1$, $\rho = 0.1$, $a = 1.5$, $\beta = 0$, $\varepsilon = 0.1$, $\lambda = 1$, $\varphi = 0.1$)

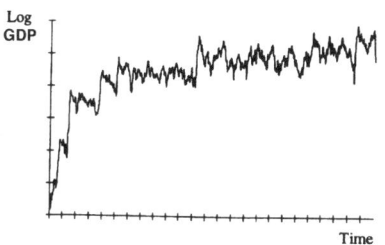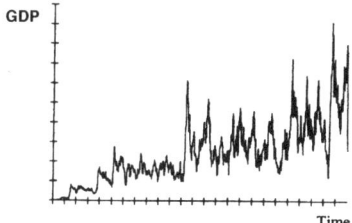

Figure 6(b): "Linear" Growth in an Open-Ended Economy with Exploration ($N = 100$, $\pi = 0.1$, $\sigma_s = \sigma_\xi = 0.1$, $\rho = 0.1$, $a = 1.5$, $\beta = 0$, $\varepsilon = 0.1$, $\lambda = 1$, $\varphi = 0.2$)

Our conjecture is that necessary condition for the model to exhibit exponential growth is, of course, the presence of increasing returns, but, moreover, the following further conditions – or a suitable mix of them – ought to apply, namely: (i) both the level of opportunities and the average number of current "explorers" have to be sufficiently large; (ii) knowledge diffusion is not too "local"; (iii) there is some path-dependency in innovation. Putting in another way, one should expect self-sustaining growth to emerge for large values of φ, π and λ and for small values of ρ.

In the following, some support to this conjecture will be shown.

The sources of self-sustaining growth: Some "Qualitative" Evidence

A basic insight stemming from a qualitative analysis of the behavior of the model is that self-sustaining growth seems to be generated in the system – above certain thresholds – by non-linear interactions among innovation, path-dependency, increasing returns and diffusion of knowledge and *not* by any of these forces taken in isolation. In order to illustrate this point, assume to start from a fairly uniform distribution of the N agents on the initial "known" islands L_0. On the one hand, diffusion of knowledge is likely to drive agents to concentrate on a relatively small cluster of "known" islands – generally close to the frontier of the "realized economy" – which, by dynamic increasing returns, might be, often but not always, the most efficient ones. On the other hand, some "lucky" explorers – which have decided not to imitate one out of the cluster of colonized islands – will sometimes find intrinsically superior islands outside the "realized economy". Although they might not be able to adequately exploit the opportunities of the "new" island by themselves, the "extraordinary" character of their discovery might nevertheless induce other agents to move there in the future and, consequently, increase its actual productivities. Hence, a "rare event" (i.e. the exceptional discovery), feeding path-dependently upon diffusion and incremental innovations thereafter, might be able to trigger a self-reinforcing process whose ultimate outcome might be a pattern of exponential growth.

The above intuition can be further supported by looking at some other pieces of qualitative evidence on the dynamics of the model. Indeed, given a set-up yielding exponential growth [1], the story that simulated time-series tell us might be rephrased as follows.

First, time series of the number of "miners", "explorers" and "imitators" typically follows a stationary pattern, see Figure 7.

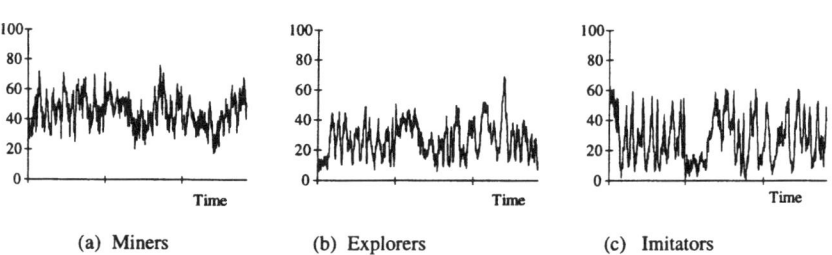

Figure 7: Number of Miners, Explorers and Imitators in an Open-Ended Economy displaying self-sustaining growth ($N = 100$, $\pi = 0.1$, $\sigma_s = \sigma_\xi = 0.1$, $\rho = 0.1$, $a = 1.5$, $\beta = 0$, $\varepsilon = 0.1$, $\lambda = 1$, $\varphi = 0.5$)

Second, although the number of currently "known" islands (at any τ) displays a linear trend, both the ratio "colonized"/ "known" islands and the number of "colonized" ones – Figure 8(a) and 8(b) respectively – fall quickly and then follow a stationary process. Hence, imitation leads agents to exploit (i.e. to "colonize") a small subset of islands (out of the "known" ones).

---

1. Unless differently stated, we refer throughout, as an example, to the basic parametrization: $N = 100$, $\sigma_s = \sigma_\xi = 0.1$, $\beta = 0$, $a = 1.5$. All results reported in this sub-section refer to: $\pi = 0.1$, $\rho = 0.1$, $\varepsilon = 0.1$, $\lambda = 1$, $\varphi = 0.5$.

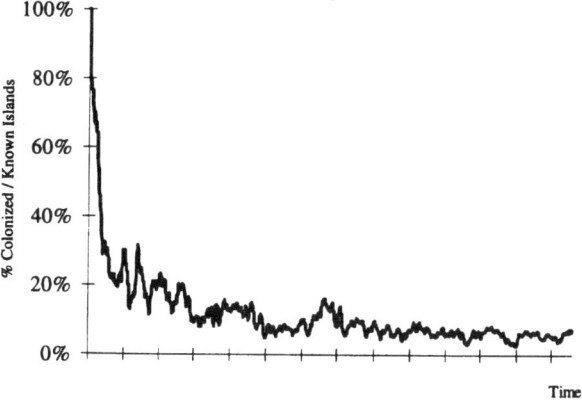

Figure 8(a): % of Colonized Islands in an Open-Ended Economy displaying self-sustaining growth ($N = 100$, $\pi = 0.1$, $\sigma_s = \sigma_\xi = 0.1$, $\rho = 0.1$, $\alpha = 1.5$, $\beta = 0$, $\varepsilon = 0.1$, $\lambda = 1$, $\varphi = 0.5$)

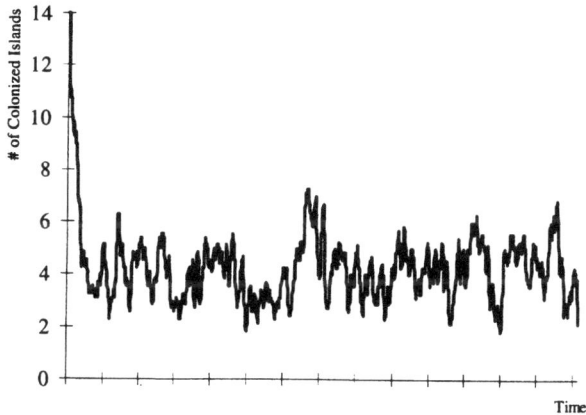

Figure 8(b): Number of Colonized Islands in an Open-Ended Economy displaying self-sustaining growth ($N = 100$, $\pi = 0.1$, $\sigma_s = \sigma_\xi = 0.1$, $\rho = 0.1$, $\alpha = 1.5$, $\beta = 0$, $\varepsilon = 0.1$, $\lambda = 1$, $\varphi = 0.5$)

Third, since the number of "explorers" is a stationary process, the average per-period number of "discoveries" keeps constant. Moreover, as the uniform nature of the "exploration" rule should suggest – cf. Eq. (7) – the distance from the origin of a new island increases linearly with the number of discovered islands (see fig. 9(a)). However, the path-dependent nature of innovation implies that the initial productivity of a new island (i.e. the coefficient s_j.) is generally greater than the average current productivity over all "known" islands (see fig. 10) while the one-time push irregularly caused by the introduction of "new paradigms" keeps the order of magnitude of initial productivity of new islands constantly above that level predictable from their distance from the origin (see fig. 9(b)).

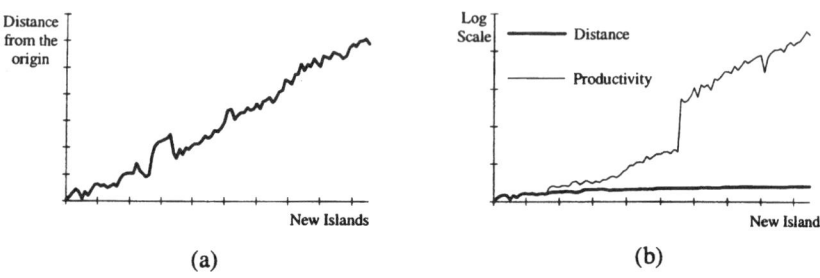

(a)   (b)

Figure 9: Distance from the origin and actual productivities of new islands (Number of new islands on x-axis) in an economy displaying self-sustaining growth ($N = 100$, $\pi = 0.1$, $\sigma_s = \sigma_\xi = 0.1$, $\rho = 0.1$, $a = 1.5$, $\beta = 0$, $\varepsilon = 0.1$, $\lambda = 1$, $\varphi = 0.5$)

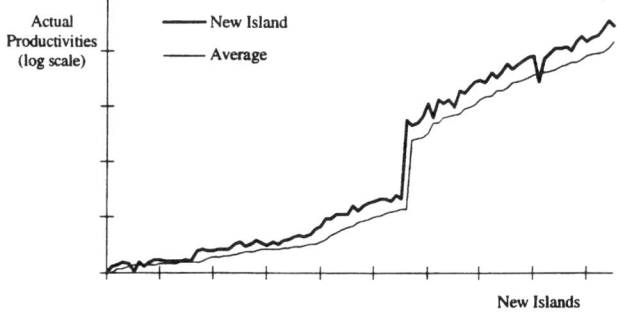

Figure 10: Actual productivity of new islands vs. average current productivity of "known" islands in an economy displaying self-sustaining growth ($N = 100$, $\pi = 0.1$, $\sigma_s = \sigma_\xi = 0.1$, $\rho = 0.1$, $a = 1.5$, $\beta = 0$, $\varepsilon = 0.1$, $\lambda = 1$, $\varphi = 0.5$)

Finally, relatively ordered spatial patterns of colonized islands are likely to emerge, due to the local nature of both the exploration and imitation processes. In Figure 11 the path of expansion of the "best practice" proxy b_t^* is plotted together with four "snapshots" showing the locations of currently "colonized" islands for different time periods $t = 0, 500, 1\,000, 1\,500$. While in the early time periods of the simulation small (stochastic) events select the region of the lattice where the exploration is going to take place, the path-dependent nature of the overall process tends to keep the economy inside that region. At each time period, only few islands are exploited and the economy is seldom producing under the notionally most efficient conditions.

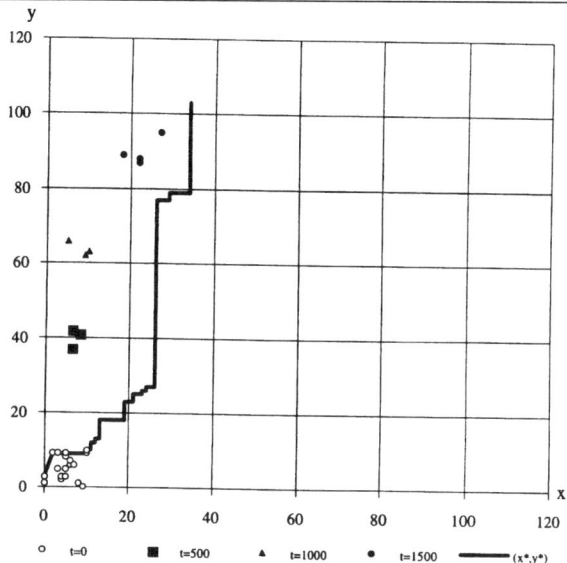

Figure 11: Spatial Diffusion Patterns of Colonized Islands and "Best Practice" proxy $b_t^* = (x_t^*, y_t^*)$ in an economy displaying self-sustaining growth ($N = 100$, $\pi = 0.1$, $\sigma_s = \sigma_\xi = 0.1$, $\rho = 0.1$, $a = 1.5$, $\beta = 0$, $\varepsilon = 0.1$, $\lambda = 1$, $\varphi = 0.5$)

A Montecarlo Analysis

In order to give strength to the above interpretation, we have performed some Montecarlo (MC) studies with the goal of investigating (i) how behavioral and system parameters affect average growth rates (AGRs); and (ii) the robustness of the results across different sample paths, holding the parametrization constant [1].

First, we have considered the role played by opportunities, path-dependency and locality of knowledge diffusion in the emergence of "self-sustained" growth.

For a given level of "willingness to explore" ($\varepsilon = 0.1$), two benchmark cases, namely a "low opportunities" set-up (i.e. $\pi = 0.1$ and $\lambda = 1$) and a "high opportunities" one (i.e. $\pi = 0.4$ and $\lambda = 5$), have been analyzed. For different

---

1. For a given parametrization, let $\{g_m, m = 1, 2, ..., M\}$ be the Montecarlo sample of average growth rates, where, for a given simulated time series $\{q_t = \log Q_t, t = 0, ..., T\}_m$, we simply define $g_m = 100 \cdot [(q_T/q_0)^{1/T} - 1]$. In the following, $T = 2\,500$ and $M = 1\,000$.

combinations of "path dependency" and "locality of knowledge diffusion" [1], a sufficiently large number of independent simulations have been run, yielding correspondent distributions of AGRs [2]. In Figure 12a (low opportunities setup) and 12b (high opportunities), MC mean values and variances of the distributions of AGRs are plotted. The histograms for mean values seem to confirm the above intuition. Mean values of AGRs are increasing in both path-dependency (φ) and globality of knowledge diffusion (ρ) [3] for a given level of opportunities, while high-opportunity AGRs are larger than low-opportunity ones for a given combination of path-dependency and globality of knowledge diffusion. Moreover, histograms of MC variances suggest an interesting emergent property of the model. Indeed, as a general result, one observes a strong positive correlation between high AGRs and larger variances in the MC distributions (see also below) [4]. Finally, a recursive analysis of the first four moments of AGRs MC distributions (not reported here) has been undertaken. For each combination in the above parameter grid, moments of *MC* distribution over the first M^* simulations – where $M^* = M_0, M_0 + 1, ..., M$ – have been computed and plotted against M^*. In all cases one can observe convergence of the first four moments after a number of simulations well below $M = 1\,000$.

Second, the net effect of "willingness to explore" on AGRs (i.e. the effect of a change in ε, everything else being constant) has been investigated. For a given parametrization yielding as a usual outcome a pattern of self-sustaining growth [5], we have performed several simulations for varying ε, under the two above opportunities setups. An interesting emergent property is that MC means of AGRs seem to be small whenever the "willingness to explore" is either very low or very large – see Figure 13(a) and 13(b). Furthermore, the system appears to be characterized – in both opportunities setups – by "optimal" levels of "willingness to explore", somehow increasing in the notional level of opportunities. The intuition here corresponds to that suggested in March (1991, p. 71). As he points out, systems that engage in exploration to the exclusion of exploitation "exhibit too many undeveloped new ideas and too little distinctive competences", while, conversely, systems at the opposite extreme "are likely to find themselves trapped in sub-optimal stable equilibria". Hence, also in our model the losses stemming from the exploration-exploitation trade-off seem to be minimized by an appropriate balance between the two forces (March, 1991; Allen and McGlade, 1986), which, however, agents are generally unable to correctly evaluate ex-ante.

---

1. In each case, a grid for ρ and φ has been prepared, namely: $\rho \in \{0, 0.1, 0.5, \infty\}$ and $\varphi \in \{0.1, 0.2, 0.3, 0.5\}$. Notice that if $\rho = 0$ the knowledge diffusion is"global", while if $\rho = \infty$ it is absent.
2. The null of normality is accepted at 5% for all AGR Montecarlo distributions (χ^2 test).
3. Notice that, as a "rule of thumb", only mean values of AGR above 0.06 imply "self-sustained growth", or, put it differently, a $I(1)$ process for the log of GDP.
4. For a similar property of actual time series in a cross-section of countries, cf. Fatas (1995).
5. The parametrization is $\rho = 0.1$ and $\varphi = 0.5$. For each value of $\varepsilon\{0.01, 0.03, 0.07, 0.10, 0.20, 0.30, 0.40, 0.50, 0.60, 0.70, 0.80, 0.90\}$, $M = 1\,000$ simulations have been run.

Figure 12: Montecarlo Means and Variances of the Distributions of Average Rates of Growth (1000 Sim., $N = 100$, $\sigma_s = \sigma_\xi = 0.1$, $a = 1.5$, $\beta = 0$, $\varepsilon = 0.1$)

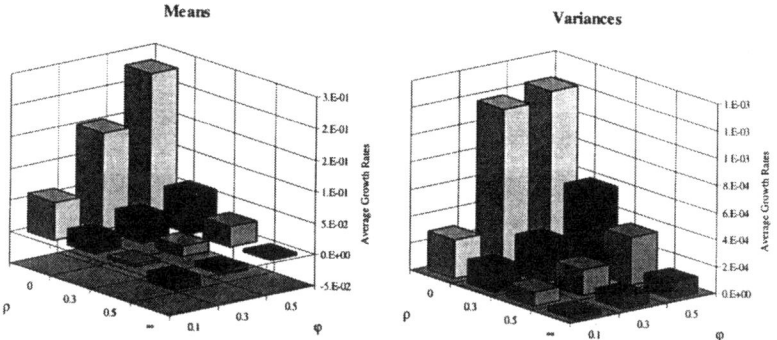

Figure 12 (a): Low Opportunities ($\pi = 0.1$; $\lambda = 1$)

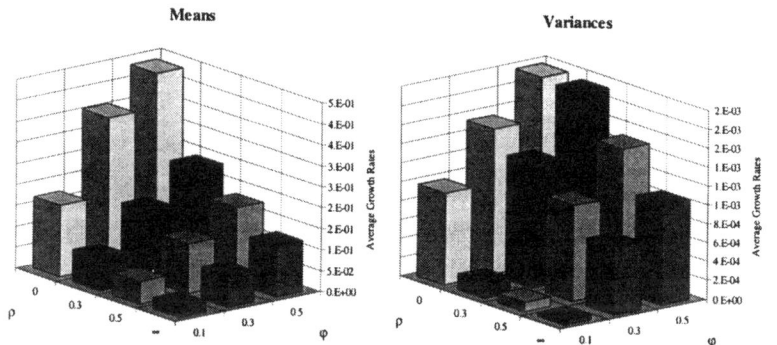

Figure 12 (b): High Opportunities ($\pi = 0.4$; $\lambda = 5$)

Third, in order to further investigate the emergence of some positive correlation between higher AGRs and larger variances in growth rates, we have computed, for different parametrizations, MC estimates of the frequency distribution of the simulated time-series of growth rates. This has been done by averaging, over $M = 100$ simulations, the frequency distributions of the time-series $\{h_t = (Q_t - Q_{t-1})/Q_{t-1},\ t = 1, ..., 2\,500\}$. The results about the mean of those distributions (Table 2), together with those obtained before, suggest that "self-sustaining" growth seems to be strongly related to a larger variability in the distributions of growth rates both *across* independent simulations and *within* a single sample path. The interpretation of this emergent property is strongly related to both the non-linear and self-reinforcing nature of the mechanisms involved. Indeed, what one usually get by gradually increasing the strength of the sources of growth in the model is that the self-reinforcing mechanisms of exploration, innovation and production become somewhat explosive.

Figure 13: Montecarlo Means of Average Growth Rates vs. Willingness to Explore (1 000 Simulations; $N = 100$, $\sigma_s = \sigma_\xi = 0.1$, $\beta = 0$, $a = 1.5$, $\rho = 0.1$, $\varphi = 0.5$)

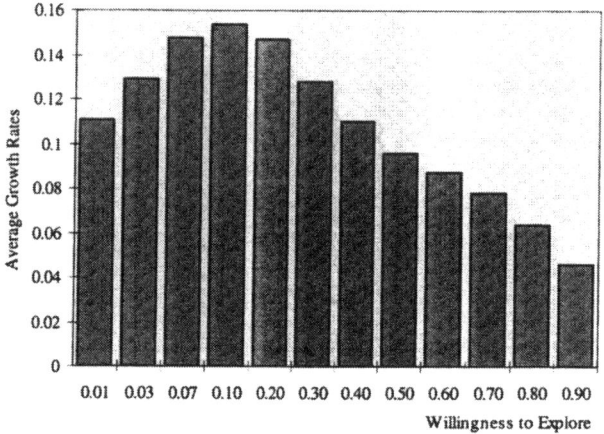

(a) Low Opportunities ($\lambda = 1; \pi = 0.1$)

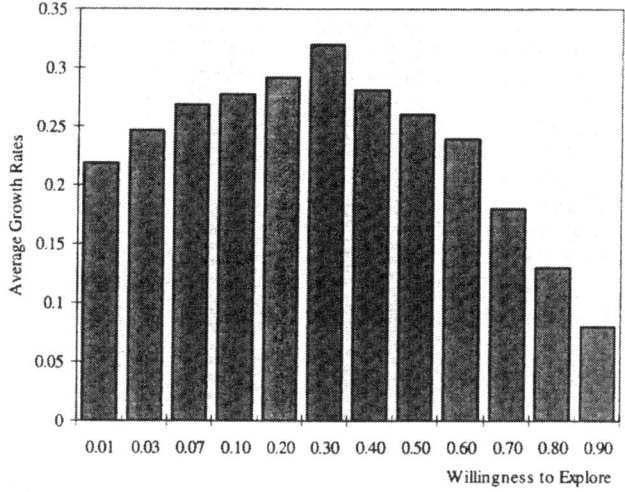

(b) High Opportunities ($\lambda = 1; \pi = 0.1$)

Self-sustaining growth appears to *imply* the co-existence of periods of moderate growth intertwined by "jumps" caused by radical innovations (i.e. the arrival of new "paradigms") which however diffuse through the economy thanks to a time-consuming process of adjustment of all agents to the new knowledge base. Hence, the model, despite it simplicity, is able to account for some of those "retardation factors" emphasized by Abramovitz (1989, 1993)

Table 2
Means of Montecarlo Estimates of Frequency Distributions of Growth Rates within a Simulation
(100 Simulations; $N = 100$, $\sigma_s = \sigma_\xi = 0.1$, $\beta = 0$, $\varepsilon = 0.1$, $a = 1.5$)

Path-Dependency and Globality of Diffusion		Low Opportunities ($\lambda = 1; \pi = 0.1$)		High Opportunities ($\lambda = 5; \pi = 0.4$)	
φ	ρ	Means	Variance	Means	Variances
∞	0	0.4678	115.4997	0.4618	97.0392
0.7	0.1	0.4779	115.0756	0.4771	95.8557
0.6	0.2	0.4838	113.6873	0.5085	97.3178
0.5	0.3	0.4961	112.6352	0.5518	98.0393
0.4	0.4	0.5157	111.9287	0.5946	95.7192
0.3	0.5	0.5440	112.1560	0.6801	94.3299
0.2	0.6	0.6230	113.9795	1.3825	188.0971
0.1	0.7	0.7124	112.7626	1.5167	187.7883
0	0.8	0.7905	113.0802	1.8653	229.5539

and David (1991), and, relatedly, for the appearance over finite time periods of distinct patterns (or "phases") of development.

Moreover, higher average rates of growth entail *higher within-simulation variability* in the rates themselves and *also a higher cross-simulations variability* of AGRs [1]. The latter property seems to suggest a sort of path-dependency in growth patterns which becomes more marked the more one "fuels" the economy with learning opportunities.

Size of the economy and growth

A well-known drawback of many models of endogenous growth based on some forms of increasing returns - involving dependence of a *flow* variable upon a *stock* variable, e.g. arrivals of technological"blueprints" as a function of their levels - is that sheer size effects influence growth rates [2]. For instance, many one-factor models, such as Aghion and Howitt (1990) predict that growth rates are increasing, other things being equal, in the size of the population.

---
1. On the point, see also Aghion and Howitt (1992).
2. We refer here to R& D-based models of endogenous growth, such as Aghion and Howitt (1992), Romer (1990), Grossman and Helpman, (1991a, 1991b). Conversely, in many models in which growth is endogenously generated by the accumulation of human and physical *rival* capital, any increase in the scale of the economy might not have impact on growth rates (cf., Jones and Manuelli (1990) and Rebelo (1991)). Furthermore, cf. Young (1995) and Jones (1995a) for recent examples of R& D-based models of endogenous growth *without* scale-effects.

Furthermore, when one considers extensions of these basic models – such as multi-factors models (Aghion and Howitt, 1992; Grossman and Helpman, 1991a; Romer, 1990) and with international trade (Grossman and Helpman, 1991b) – the standard result is that growth rates are increasing in the factor used intensively in the "innovative" activity (e.g. skilled labor)[1].

The present model, notwithstanding increasing returns to learning, *does not* display that unreasonable property. To see this, we have computed MC mean values of AGRs across $M = 100$ simulations holding all parameters constant [2] but just increasing the size of the economy N, i.e. the number of agents. Moreover, in order to ascertain whether the time-length of observed histories affects our results, we have reported MC mean values of AGRs computed at different time-periods (i.e. for different econometric sample periods T). As Table 3 shows, there is a weak evidence on falling AGRs the larger the economy is *for a given time-length*, while AGRs do not display any monotone pattern even if one compares AGRs for N and T both increasing.

Table 3

Montecarlo Mean Values of Average Growth Rates (AGRs*) as a function of the Size of the Economy (N) and the Econometric Sample Size (T) (100 Simulations, $\pi = 0.4$, $\lambda = 5$, $\sigma_s = \sigma_\xi = 0.1$, $\beta = 0$, $a = 1.5$, $\rho = 0.1$, $\varepsilon = 0.1$, and $\varphi = 0.5$.)

	Size of the Economy				
Sample Size	$N = 50$	$N = 100$	$N = 200$	$N = 500$	$N = 1000$
$T = 250$	0.2526	0.2402	0.2454	0.2196	0.1275
$T = 500$	0.2879	0.2104	0.2278	0.1602	0.1563
$T = 1\,000$	0.2300	0.2262	0.1901	0.1889	0.1485
$T = 1\,500$	0.2448	0.2536	0.2287	0.2044	0.1895
$T = 2\,500$	0.2529	0.2048	0.2102	0.1707	0.1912
$T = 5\,000$	0.2347	0.2141	0.2163	0.2267	0.2156

* Note: AGRs are defined as $g_m = 100 \cdot [(q_T/q_0)^{1/T} - 1]$, where: $q_t = \log Q_t$ is the log of the GDP at time $t = 0, ..., T$; $m = 1, 2, ..., M$ where M is the Montecarlo sample size; T is the econometric sample size.

---

1. Taken literally, they would predict India growing faster than, say, Singapore. Cf. Jones (1995b) for a detailed discussion on empirical evidence on these points.
2. In what follows (cf. Table 3), we report as an example the results obtained considering a "high-opportunity" set-up yielding "exponential growth" (we set $\pi = 0.4$, $\lambda = 5$, $\sigma_s = \sigma_\xi = 0.1$, $\beta = 0$, $a = 1.5$, $\rho = 0.1$, $\varepsilon = 0.1$, and $\varphi = 0.5$.) However, the same pattern holds also for other opportunity setups and different parametrizations of knowledge diffusion, path-dependency and dynamic increasing returns.

Exploring the unknown. On entrepreneurship | 337

The intuition behind this is that, while *ceteris paribus* larger economies face potentially higher returns to knowledge exploitation, it is also true that they must cope, in probability, with higher "adjustment lags" to new knowledge bases (as proxied in our model by the time it takes to move a certain fraction of the N agents to the notionally superior islands). Hence, larger economies which are potentially able to fuller exploit increasing returns to any one knowledge base need also a relative longer time to achieve persistently higher growth rates.

4.4. Individual vs. Collective rationality: A Simple Example

As conjectured above, the model highlights a few sources of potential conflict between individual and collective rationality. In order to illustrate this point, consider the following simple example. Assume an economy characterized by: (i) constant returns to scale (i.e. $\alpha = 1$); (ii) no knowledge diffusion (i.e. $\rho = \infty$); (iii) no path-dependency in innovation (i.e. $\varphi = 0$); (iv) all N agents working at time $t = 0$ on a single island ($\ell_0 = 1$) with co-ordinates (x^*, y^*) and initial productivity $s^* = x^* + y^*$ [1]; (v) a constant positive transportation cost β (i.e. $\delta = 0, \beta \in [0, 1)$, see section 3.2).

Given the above parametrization, we will consider two different settings for what concerns behavioral assumptions.

In the first one, the population is composed of N agents behaving according to the behavioral rules defined in section 3.

In the second one, we will introduce a "representative individual" (*RI*) endowed by "rational expectations". More precisely, assume that the latter has unbounded computational skills and complete information, so that it knows: (i) the co-ordinates (x^*, y^*); (ii) the system parameters; (iii) the model of the economy. Although it knows that, on average, the initial productivity of a new island is increasing in its distance from the origin, he does not know where new islands are actually located. Hence, starting from the node (x, y), it will make use of an exploration rule which gives equal probability to the nodes $(x + 1, y)$ and $(x, y + 1)$. Finally, assume for simplicity that the intertemporal discount rate is zero [2].

At time $t = 1$, the problem for the *RI* is to decide whether to continue to extract the good at time $t = 2$ or start to explore. In the first case, it will get a per-period net output from mining equal to $\theta_M = s^*$. In the second case, the expected per-period net output from exploration will be:

---

[1]. Notice that with constant returns to scale the output of the agent working on island (x^*, y^*) is equal to its initial productivity s^*, irrespective of the number of agents that are working on the island.
[2]. Our conjecture is that the following results will hold *a fortiori* for a strictly positive discount rate.

$\theta_E = [(1 + \lambda)(s^* + \tau) - \beta\tau]/\tau$, where $\tau = 1/\pi$ is the expected length of exploration [1]. Then, the *RI* will decide to remain on island (x^*, y^*) if and only if $\theta_M > \theta_E$, i.e. iff:

$$\pi < \frac{1}{1+\lambda} - \frac{1}{s^*} + \frac{\beta}{(1+\lambda) \cdot s^*} = \pi^*(\beta, \lambda, s^*) \tag{11}$$

As one can easily check, $\pi^*(\beta, \lambda, s^*)$ is decreasing in λ and increasing in s^* and β, as expected [2]. More generally, one could single out – for given values of s^* – a correspondent region in the space spanned by feasible values of (β, λ) satisfying (7) for some $\pi \in (0, 1)$.

For instance, assume for simplicity $\beta = 0$. Then, the pair $\pi = 0.15$ and $\lambda = 5$ satisfies Eq. 11 for $s^* = 100$. In this setup, the *RI* will decide to continue to work as a "miner". Hence, such an economy will get a net per-capita output $\theta^* = 100$. On the contrary, consider an economy characterized by the same parametrization [3], composed of $N = 100$ agents, all starting as "miners" on the island (x^*, y^*), $x^* + y^* = 100$, and behaving as described in section 3. Notice that agents live here in a rather "poor" environment, in which there is *neither* knowledge diffusion, *nor* path-dependency in innovation, *nor* increasing returns to scale. Furthermore, assume that agents are characterized by a very low "willingness to explore" (i.e. $\varepsilon = 0.05$). Notwithstanding all that, simulations show (fig 14) that the economy is able to get, as a general outcome, a per-capita net output persistently greater than $\theta^* = 100$.

Thus, even in this very simple setting, collective growth finds its necessary condition in the presence of a number of "irrational" individuals.

Even more so, this potential conflict between individual rationality and collective welfare emerges in the general setting with unlimited notional opportunities of exploration and transportation costs born up front by the "explorers" themselves.

Note that, as mentioned earlier, this property significantly expands upon the common result from e.g. New Growth literature that in presence of externalities or dynamic increasing returns a systematic divergence between endogenously generated growth rates and socially optimal ones (whatever the latter means...) is likely to emerge. Here, one may require indeed the presence of straightforwardly *irrational* agents in order to have endogenous growth at all.

---

1. Notice that τ is also the expected distance between (x^*, y^*) and a new island.
2. If we allow β to be greater than the unity, then $\pi^*(\beta, \lambda, s^*)$ is increasing in s^* only if $\lambda > \beta - 1$, i.e. if opportunities are large enough. Notice that if $s^* \to \infty$ the *RI* will always stay on (x^*, y^*) while if $\lambda^* \to \infty$ it will always leave.
3. That is $\beta = 0$, $\delta = 0$, $\varphi = 0$, $\lambda = 5$, $\pi = 0.15$, $\rho = \infty$, $\sigma_s = \sigma_\xi = 0.1$, $a = 1$.

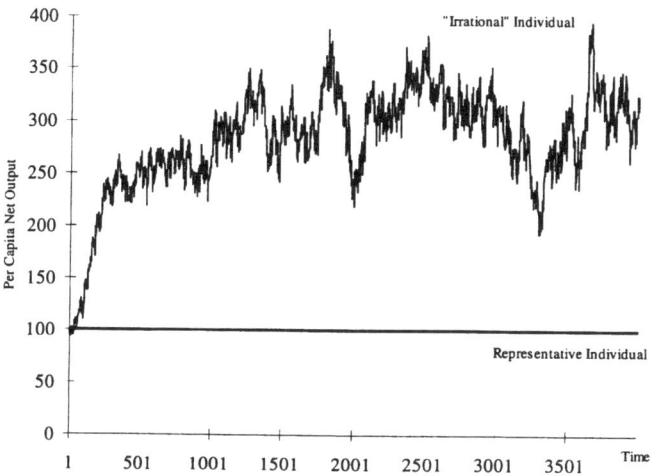

Figure 14: Individual vs. Collective Rationality: A simple example ($s^* = 100$, $N = 100$, $\varepsilon = 0.05$, $\beta = 0$, $\delta = 0$, $\varphi = 0$, $\lambda = 5$, $\pi = 0.15$, $\rho = \infty$, $\sigma_s = \sigma_\xi = 0.1$, $a = 1$)

5. Conclusions

The foregoing model presents a rather simple dynamics through which "incremental" knowledge accumulation, diffusion and random discoveries of new technologies interact as to yield persistent – and persistently fluctuating — growth.

As mentioned, it could be considered as a sort of "reduced form" evolutionary model, with an almost exclusive emphasis upon the learning/diffusion aspects of economic evolution, while repressing the competition/selection features of market interactions.

While the limitations of this reduced form are quite obvious (for example, the "microeconomics" is bound to be rather poor), on the upside, it still allows predictions on the dynamics of aggregate variables (and first of all growth rates of the economy), mapping them into system- and behavioral parameters capturing the conditions of generations and diffusion of knowledge.

In particular, the model is able to study the effects upon the patterns of growth of: a) *technological opportunities* (as captured by both the density of "islands" and the probability of Poisson jumps to radically new paradigms); b) *cumulativeness of learning* and *path-dependency* (i.e. the increasing return coefficient a, for each island, and the fraction of idiosyncratic knowledge, φ, that agents are able to carry over to newly discovered technologies); c) *locality of learning* (i.e. an indirect inverse proxy for appropriability), captured by the diffusion parameter ρ; and, finally, on the behavioral side, d) the *propensity to explore*, ε.

Note also, that, in principle, the above variables and parameters can find empirical (although inevitably rough) proxies. Therefore, one might not dispair to test the qualitative properties generated by the model against actual data.

As simple as it is, the model is comparable with New Growth ones, with some overlappings and some major differences. It is similar to the former in that it identifies in knowledge diffusion *cum* dynamic increasing returns the primary sources of self-sustained growth. However, it departs from them in a few important respects.

First, knowledge is neither treated as entirely appropriable or a pure externality: rather, its benefits partly accrue to those who embody it and partly leak out as a sort of spillover.

Second, dynamic increasing returns to learning are, at least to some extent, technology-specific.

Third, diffusion takes time rather than being instantaneous (and indeed is a major source of growth).

Fourth, problems of "Schumpeterian coordination" always emerge out of microeconomic heterogeneity in both technical knowledge and innovative decisions.

Finally, the radical uncertainty intrinsic in the innovation process involves the possibility that agents make *systematic* mistakes in innovative search and adoption.

Among other properties, our model shows how a decentralized economy with heterogeneous interacting agents, under certain technological and behavioral conditions, can *self-organize* into exponential growth, without appealing to the forecasting powers of any far-sighted "representative agent". In fact the result is stronger than that, since the economy might require *non-average* (and individually irrational) behaviors in order to achieve such a self-sustained path [1]. Hence the permanent dilemma between *exploitation* of what one knows and *exploration* of the unknown (March, 1991) and, consequently, also the crucial collective role of entrepreneurial "animal spirits", even when ill-grounded in the "true" probability distributions of gains and losses stemming from innovative search.

As it stands, the model seems quite well suited to account for some generic properties of knowledge-driven growth. Nevertheless, further developments come easily to mind.

First, one could try to see how this basic story about growth is modified by the introduction also of a "Keynesian" coordination problem affecting interdependent demand generation mechanisms.

---

[1]. A similar point on non-average behaviors inducing symmetry breaking in the distribution of particular features or performances of a population of agents is in Allen (1988).

Second, one might likewise study the relevance of adding explicit selection processes affecting the frequency in the population (and the size) of different agents which are "carriers" of different technologies.

And, on a methodological side, together with computer simulation, it might not be out of reach to study some analytical properties, at least in some special cases, of the Markovian process plausibly underlying the model presented here.

However, even before all that come, it seems to us that the foregoing work might contribute to the understanding of how endogenous learning processes, with imperfect collective adaptation and heterogeneous agents, drive growth notwithstanding (or rather *because of*) the absence of fantastically rational agents and equilibria fulfilled throughout.

Parameters of the Model

N = Number of agents

ε = Willingness to Explore

π = Probability that a node is an island

λ = Expected Value of Jumps in Innovation

ρ = Globality of Knowledge Diffusion

φ = Path Dependency in Innovation

a = Returns to Scale

β = "Transportation" Cost parameter

δ = "Transportation" Cost parameter (hence. $c_{i,t} = \beta \cdot [Q_{t-1}/N]^\delta$)

σ_s = Variance of the distribution of initial productivity coefficients for islands inside L_0

σ_ξ = Variance of the noise in the initial productivity coefficients for islands outside L_0

Appendix

Some results on persistence of output fluctuations

Assume that the change in the log of GDP follows a stationary process with moving average representation: $\Delta q_t = A(L) v_t$, where $A(L) = \sum_{j=0}^{\infty} A_j L^j$, $A_0 = 1$ and v_t is a white noise. Following Campbell and Mankiw (1987, 1989) and Cochrane (1988), we computed estimates of the following persistence measures: (i) $V \equiv \lim_{k \to \infty} V^k$, where $V^k = \left[1 + 2 \sum_{j=1}^{k} \left(1 - \frac{j}{k+1} \right) \rho_j \right]$ and ρ_j is the jth autocorrelation coefficient of Δq_t; (ii) $A(1) = \sum_{j=0}^{\infty} A_j$. An estimate of V^k (which consistently estimates V for large k) is found simply by replacing population auto-correlations with sample counterparts, while $A(1)$ must be estimated non-parametrically (for large k) by $\hat{A}^k(1) = \sqrt{\frac{\hat{V}^k}{1 - \hat{\rho}_1^2}}$. Since both $\hat{V}^k$ and $\hat{A}^k(1)$ are downward biased, they have been multiplied by the correction factor $T/(T-k)$. For a random walk $A(1)$ and V^k equal one, while for any series stationary around a deterministic trend $A(1)$ is zero and V^k approaches zero for large k. Thus, if both measures are above unity the output exhibits fluctuations with high persistence. Campbell and Mankiw (1987, 1989) and Cochrane (1988) provide Montecarlo studies on 90% critical values of $\hat{V}^k$ and $\hat{A}^k(1)$ for different data generation processes and $k = 20, 40, 60$.

Table 4
Estimates of persistence in simulated series of log GDP

k	g_t	Δq_t
	Bias Corrected $\hat{V}^k$	
20	1.35	1.46
40	1.30	1.65
60	1.46	1.89
	Bias Corrected $\hat{A}^k(1)$	
20	1.18	1.22
40	1.17	1.32
60	1.26	1.43

Sample autocorrelation functions for the change in log of GDP [Δq_t] and for growth rates [$g_t = (q_t - q_{t-1})/q_{t-1}$] are reported in Figure 15 [1]. In Table 4 both statistics $\hat{V}^k$ and $\hat{A}^k(1)$ are computed for Δq_t and g_t and $k = 20, 40, 60$. Autocorrelation coefficients are quite small (in particular for Δq_t) but similar to those obtained in reality (see Campbell and Mankiw, 1989). Moreover, all estimates of persistence are greater than unity and quite similar to those obtained for empirical data. Comparing them with the corresponding 90%

---

[1]. As done in Table 1, econometric analyses refer to a simulation generated by the following parametrization: $N = 100$, $\pi = 0.1$, $\sigma_s = \sigma_\xi = 0.1$, $\rho = 0.1$, $a = 1.5$, $\beta = 0$, $\varepsilon = 0.1$, $\lambda = 1$, $\varphi = 0.5$.

percentiles, one is able to reject all stationary processes with smaller roots less or equal to 0.9. In particular, the values of $\hat{V}^*$ for Δq_t fit quite well the case where q_t is generated by an $AR(2)$ process with roots $(1, 0.25)$.

Figure 15: Sample Auto-correlations

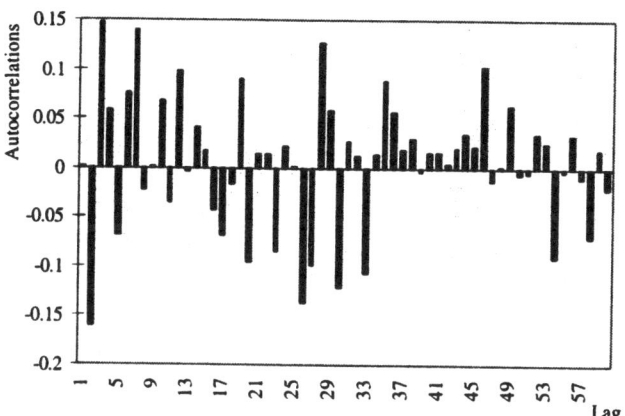

(a) Growth Rates $[g_t = (q_t - q_{t-1})/q_{t-1}]$

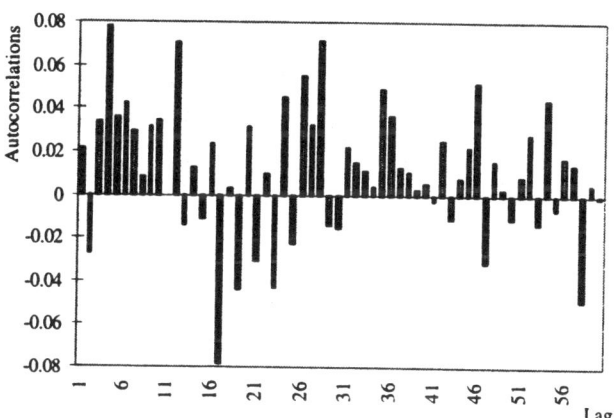

(b) Change in log of GDP $[\Delta q_t]$

REFERENCES

Abramovitz, M. (1989), *Thinking about Growth*, Cambridge, Cambridge University Press.

Abramovitz, M. (1993), "The search for the sources of growth", *Journal of Economic History*, 53, 2.

Aghion, P., Howitt, P. (1992), "A model of growth through creative destruction", *Econometrica*, 60, 2.

Allen, P.M. (1988), "Evolution, innovation and economics", in Dosi, G. *et al.* (1988).

Allen, P.M., McGlade, J.M. (1986), "Dynamics of discovery and exploitation: the case of the Scotian shelf groundfish fisheries", *Canadian Journal of Fishery and Aquatic Sciences*, 43.

Amable, B. (1995), "Endogenous growth and cycles through radical and incremental innovation", CEPREMAP Discussion Paper, 9504.

Arrow, K. (1962a), "Economic welfare and the allocation of resources to invention", in Nelson, R. *et al.* (Eds.), *The Rate and Direction of Inventive Activity*, National Bureau of Economic Research, Princeton.

Arrow, K. (1962b), "The economic implications of learning by doing", *Review of Economic Studies*, 29, 155-173.

Arthur, W.B. (1988), "Self-reinforcing mechanisms in economics", in Anderson P.W. *et al.* (Eds.), *The economy as an evolving complex system*, Addison-Wesley.

Arthur, W.B. (1989), "Competing technologies, increasing returns and lock-in by historical small events: the dynamics of allocation under increasing returns to scale", *Economic Journal*, 99.

Arthur, W.B. (1994), *Increasing returns and path-dependency in economics*, Ann Arbor, Univ. of Michigan Press.

Arthur, W.B., Ermoliev, Yu.M., Kaniovski, Yu.M. (1987), "Path-dependent processes and the emergence of macro-structure", *European Journal of Operational Research*, 30.

Atkinson, A., Stigliz, J. (1969), "A new view of technical change", *Economic Journal*, 79, 573-578.

Bernd, L. (1994), "Testing for unit-roots with income distribution data", *Empirical Economics*, 19, 4, 555-573.

Bikhchandani, S. *et al.* (1992), "A theory of fads, fashion, custom and cultural change as informational cascade", *Journal of Political Economy*, 100, 5.

Brock, W.A., Durlauf, S.N. (1995), "Discrete choice with social interactions: (I) Theory", Working Paper, University of Wisconsin at Madison.

Campbell, J.Y., Mankiw, N.G. (1987), "Are output fluctuations transitory?", *Quarterly Journal of Economics*, 102, 857-880.

Campbell, J.Y., Mankiw, N.G. (1989), "International evidences on the persistence of economic fluctuations", *Journal of Monetary Economics*, 23, 319-333.

Cheng, L.K. and Dinopoulos, E. (1991), "Stochastic Schumpeterian economic fluctuations", mimeo, University of Florida.

Cheng, L.K. and Dinopoulos, E. (1992), "Schumpeterian growth and international business cycles", *American Economic Review Papers and Proceedings*, 82, 2, 409-414.

Chiaromonte F., Dosi, G. (1993), "Heterogeneity, competition and macroeconomic dynamics", *Structural Change and Economic Dynamics*, 4, 39-63.

Christiano, L.J., Eichenbaum, M. (1989), "Unit roots in real GDP: do we know and do we care?", Natioanl Bureau of Economic Research, Working Paper #3130.

Cochrane, J.H. (1988), "How big is the random walk in GDP?", *Journal of Political Economy*, 96, 893-920.

Conlisk, J. (1989), "An aggregate model of technical change", *Quarterly Journal of Economics*, 104, 787-821.

Cooper, R., John, A. (1988), "Coordinating coordination failures in Keynesian models", *Quarterly Journal of Economics*, 103.

David, P.A. (1975), *Technical choice, Innovation and Economic Growth*, Cambridge, Cambridge Univ. Press.

David, P.A. (1988), "Path-dependence: putting the past into the future of economics", Stanford, Institute for Mathematical Studies in Social Sciences, Technical Report 533.

David, P.A. (1991), "Computer and dynamo: the modern productivity paradox in a not-too-distant mirror", in OECD, *Technology and Productivity*, Paris, OECD.

David, P.A. (1992), "Path-dependence and predictability in dynamic systems with local externalities: a paradigm for historical economics", in Foray D., Freeman C. (1992).

Davidson, P. (1996), "Reality and economic theory", *Journal of Post-Keynesian Economics*, 18, 4.

DeJong, D.N., Whiteman, C.H. (1991), "The case for trend-stationarity is stronger than we thought", *Journal of Applied Econometrics*, 6, 4, 413-421.

DeJong, D.N., Whiteman, C.H. (1994), "The forecasting attributes of trend- and difference-stationary representations for macroeconomic time-series", *Journal of Forecasting*, 13, 279-297.

Diebold, F.X., Senhadji, A.S. (1996), "The uncertain unit root in real GDP: Comment", *American Economic Review*, 86, 5, 1291-1298.

Dosi, G. (1982), "Technological paradigms and technological trajectories", *Research Policy*, 11(2), 147-162.

Dosi, G. (1988), "Sources, procedures and microeconomic effects of innovation", *Journal of Economic Literature*, 26, 126-171.

Dosi, G. (1992), "Research on innovation diffusion: an assessment", in Grubler, A., Nakicenovic, N. (Eds.), *Innovation Diffusion and Social Behaviors*, Heidelberg-Berlin-New York, Springer Verlag.

Dosi, G. (1997), "Opportunities, incentives and the collectives patterns of economic change", *Economic Journal*.

Dosi, G., Egidi M. (1991), Substantive and procedural uncertainty, *Journal of Evolutionary Economics*, 1.

Dosi, G., Fabiani, S., Aversi, R., Meacci, M. (1994), "The dynamics of international differentiation: a multi-country evolutionary model", *Industrial and Corporate Change*, 3, 1, 225-242.

Dosi, G., Freeman C., Fabiani S. (1994), "The process of economic development", *Industrial and Corporate Change*, 3, 1.

Dosi, G., Freeman, C., Nelson R., Silverberg, G., Soete, L. (Eds.) (1988), *Technical change and economic theory*, London, Pinter.

Dosi, G., Lovallo D. (1997), "Rational entrepreneurs or optimistic martyrs? Some considerations on technological regimes", in Garud, R., Nayyar P., Shapiro, Z. (Eds), *Foresights and Oversights in Technological Change*, Cambridge University Press.

Dosi, G., Orsenigo, L. (1994), "Macrodynamics and microfoundations: an evolutionary perspective", in Granstrand, O. (1994)

Durlauf, S.N. (1994), "Path-dependence in aggregate output", *Industrial and Corporate Change*, 3,1.

Fagiolo G. (1997a), "Spatial interactions in dynamic decentralized economies: a review", European University Institute, mimeo.

Fagiolo G. (1997b), "An artificial model of coordination and innovation-driven growth in decentralized economies with heterogeneous interacting agents", European University Institute, mimeo.

Fatas, A. (1995), "Endogenous growth and stochastic trends", Paris, INSEAD, Working Papers 95/85/EPS.

Foray, D., Freeman, C. (Eds.) (1992), *"Technology and the wealth of nations"*, Paris, OECD.

Freeman, C. (1982), *"The economics of industrial innovation"*, London, Pinter.

Freeman, C. (1994), "The economics of technical change", *Cambridge Journal of Economics*, 18, 463-514.

Freeman, C., Perez, C. (1988), "Structural crises of adjustment: business cycles and investment behavior", in Dosi, G. *et al.* (1988).

Grandstrand, O. (1994) (Ed.), *The economics of technology*, North Holland, Amsterdam.

Grossman, G.M., Helpman, E. (1991a), *Innovation and growth in the global economy*, Cambridge: MIT Press.

Grossman, G.M., Helpman, E. (1991b), "Quality ladders and product cycles", *Review of Economic Studies*, 106, 557-586.

Hirshleifer, D., (1993), "The blind leading the blind: social influence, fads and informational cascades", The J.Anderson Graduate School of Management, UCLA, Working Paper 24-93.

Holland, J.H. (1975), *Adaptation in natural and artificial systems*, Ann Arbor, Univ. of Michigan Press.

Jones, C.I. (1995a), "R& D-based models of economic growth", *Journal of Political Economy*, 103, 4, 759-784.

Jones, C.I. (1995b), "Time series tests of endogenous growth models", *Quarterly Journal of Economics*, 110, 495-525.

Jones, L.E., Manuelli, R. (1990), "A convex model of equilibrium growth", *Journal of Political Economy*, 98, 1008-1038.

Jones, R., Newman, G. (1994), "Economic growth as a coordination problem", Working Paper, University of British Columbia, 94/11.

Jovanovic, B. (1995), "Learning and growth", National Bureau of Economic Research, Working Paper #5383.

Jovanovic, B., McDonald, G.M. (1994), "Competitive diffusion", *Journal of Political Economy*, 102, 1.

Jovanovic, B., Rob, R. (1989), "The growth and diffusion of knowledge", *Review of Economic Studies*, 56.

Jovanovic, B., Rob, R. (1990), "Long waves and short waves: growth through intensive and extensive search", *Econometrica*, 58, 6.

Kaldor, N., Mirrlees, J.A. (1962), "A new model of economic growth", *Review of Economic Studies*, 29, 174-192.

Kirman, A.P. (1989), "The intrinsic limits of modern economic theory: the emperor has no clothes", *Economic Journal*, 99 (Conference 1989), 126-139.

Kirman, A.P. (1992), "Whom or what does the representative individual represent?", *Journal of Economic Perspectives*, 6, 2.

Kirman, A.P. (1993), "Ants, rationality and recruitment", *Quarterly Journal of Economics*, 108.

Kuran, T. (1988), "The tenacious past: theories of personal and collective conservatism", *Journal of Economic Behavior and Organization*, 10, 143-171.

Lane, D.A. (1993), "Artificial worlds and economics, parts I and II", *Journal of Evolutionary Economics*, 3 (2 and 3), 89-108 and 177-197.

Lesourne, J. (1991), *"Economie de l"ordre et du désordre"*, Economica, Paris.

Levin, R.C., Klerovich A., Nelson R., Winter, S. (1987), "Appropriating the returns from industrial research and development", *Brookings Paper on Economic Activity*, Special Issue in Microeconomics, 783-820.

Levinthal, D.A., March J.G. (1981), "A model of adaptive organizational search", *Journal of Economic Behavior and Organization*, 2, 307-333.

Levitt, B., March J.G. (1988), "Organizational learning", *Annual Review of Sociology*, 14, 319-340.

Lippi, M., Reichlin, L. (1994), "Diffusion of technical change and the decomposition of output into trend and cycle", *Review of Economic Studies*, 61, 19-30.

Lucas, R.E. (1988), "On the mechanics of economic development", *Journal of Monetary Economics*, 22, 3-42.

Lundvall, B.A. (Ed.) (1993), *National systems of innovation*, London, Francis Pinter.

Malerba, F., Orsenigo, L. (1993), "Technological regimes and firm behaviors", *Industrial and Corporate Change*, 2 (1), 54-71.

March, J.G. (1991), "Exploration and exploitation in organizational learning", *Organization Science*, 2, 1.

Metcalfe, J.S. (1988), "Trade, technology and evolutionary change", University of Manchester, Mimeo.

Metcalfe, J.S. (1996), *Lectures on evolutionary theory*, Manchester, Manchester University, Mimeo.

Nelson, C.R., Plosser, C.I. (1982), "Trends and random walks in macroeconomic time series", *Journal of Monetary Economics*, 10, 139-162.

Nelson, R. (1981), "Research on productivity growth and productivity differences", *Journal of Economic Literature*, 19, 1029-1064.

Nelson, R. (1994), "What has been the matter with Neoclassical Growth Theory?", in Silverberg, G., Soete, L. (Eds.), *The economics of growth and technical change*, Edward Elgar.

Nelson, R. (1997), "The agenda for growth theory: a different point of view", forthcoming in *Cambridge Journal of Economics*.

Nelson, R. (Ed.) (1993), *National innovation systems: a comparative analysis*, New York, Oxford University Press.

Nelson, R., Winter, S. (1977), "In search of a useful theory of innovation", *Research Policy*, 6, 36-76.

Nelson, R., Winter, S. (1982), *An evolutionary theory of economic change*, Cambridge, MA, Belknap Press of Harvard Univ. Press.

Orléan, A. (1992), "Contagion des opinions et fonctionnement des marchés financiers", *Revue Économique*, 4.

Parente, S.L. (1994), "Technology adoption, learning by doing and economic growth", *Journal of Economic Theory*, 63, 2.

Rebelo, S. (1991), "Long run policy analysis and long run growth", *Journal of Political Economy*, 99, 500-521.

Romer, P.M. (1986), "Increasing returns and long-run growth", *Journal of Political Economy*, 94.

Romer, P.M. (1990), "Endogenous technological change", *Journal of Political economy*, 98.

Romer, P.M. (1994), "The origins of endogenous growth", *Journal of Economic Perspectives*, 8, 1, 3-22.

Rosenberg, N. (1982), *Inside the black-box*, Cambridge, Cambridge Univ. Press.

Rosenberg, N. (1994), *Exploring the black-box: technology, economics and history,* Cambridge, Cambridge University Press.

Rudebusch, G.D. (1993), "The uncertain unit root in real GDP", *American Economic Review*, 83, 1, 264-272.

Scharfstein, D.S., Stein, J.C. (1990), "Herd behaviour and investment", *American Economic Review*, 80, 3.

Schumpeter, J.A. (1934), *The theory of economic development*, Cambridge MA, Harvard Univ. Press.

Shackle, G.L.S. (1955), *Uncertainty in economics*, Cambridge, Cambridge Univ. Press.

Silverberg, G., Dosi, G., Orsenigo L. (1988), "Innovation, diversity and diffusion: a self-organization model", *Economic Journal*, 98, 1032-1054.

Silverberg, G., Lehnert, D. (1993), "Long waves and evolutionary chaos in a simple Schumpeterian model of embodied technical change", *Structural Change and Economic Dynamics*, 4, 9-37.

Silverberg, G., Verspagen, B. (1994), "Collective learning, innovation and growth in a boundedly rational, evolutionary world", *Journal of Evolutionary Economics*, 4.

Silverberg, G., Verspagen, B. (1995), "Evolutionary theorizing on economic growth", IIASA Working Paper, WP-95-78.

Solow, R. (1960), "Investment and technical progress", in Arrow K. *et al.* (Eds.), *Mathematical methods in social sciences*, Stanford, Stanford Univ. Press.

Stiglitz, J.E. (1987), "Learning to learn, localized learning and technological progress", in Dagupta, P., Stoneman, P. (Eds.), *Economic policy and technological performance*, Centre for Economic Policy Research, Cambridge Cambridge University Press.

Stock, J.H., Watson, M.W. (1986), "Does GDP have a unit root", *Economic Letters*, 22, 147-151.

Stoneman, P. (Ed.) (1995), *Handbook of the economics of innovation*, Oxford, Basic Blackwell.

Winter, S. (1984), "Schumpeterian competition in alternative technological regimes", *Journal of Economic Behavior and Organization*, 5, 287-320.

Young, A. (1993), "Substitution and complementarity in endogenous innovation", *Quarterky Journal of Economics*, 108, 3, 775-807.

Young, A. (1995), "Growth without scale effects", National Bureau of Economic Research, Working Paper #5211.

Part 5

Evolutionary Game Theory

CHAPTER 16
DISCRETE EVOLUTIONARY PROCESSES:
Stationary probabilities, strategic asymmetries and learning schemes

Gisèle UMBHAUER

Journal of Economic Literature classification numbers: C70, C72

1. Introduction

The paper builds upon the now growing literature that investigates the connection between evolutionary processes and Nash refinements. It deals with an intricate phenomenon. On the one hand, one observes that traditional Nash refinements rest on special, sometimes seemingly ad hoc, learning schemes. But on the other hand, one also observes that these special learning schemes, even in general learning contexts, express dynamic properties that have an impact on the values of the probabilities in the stationary distributions. In addition, they even shed some light on the notion of progressive change in economic and management problems.

For example, the backward induction principle requires an order of learning with the property that the last players in a game are the first ones to learn. Yet this way of learning, even if seemingly ad hoc, puts into light the asymmetric strategic content of different actions (for example credible threats versus incredible ones); in turn, these asymmetries can result in dynamic asymmetries that are in favor of backward induction outcomes even in a general learning context. If mutations sequentially perturb the system, then this special order of learning also explains a possible progressive behavior adjustment toward the perfect outcome states, even if the players learn in any general random way.

In this paper we restrict attention to discrete learning mutation processes, pioneered, among others, by Kandori, Mailath & Rob(1993), Nöldeke & Samuelson(1993), Samuelson(1994) and Young(1993). We mainly focus on games in which these processes lead to a limit distribution with large support, which includes both states that satisfy Nash refinements and states that do not.

The paper is organized as follows: Section 2 sets the basic framework for our study. It recalls the main features of the discrete processes we focus on. It underlines why these processes, in an economic context, often lead to limit stationary distributions with large support. Hence, in order to differentiate the states in the support, we turn to the values of the probabilities in the limit stationary distribution, we compute by means of what we refer to as the limit Markov graph. Sections 3 and 4 focus on backward induction. Nöldeke &

Samuelson (NS hereafter) (1993) established that for extensive form games of perfect information, the support of the limit stationary distribution includes the perfect outcome states but may not restrict to them. We aim to go beyond this result as follows. In a first time, we illustrate that NS's result follows from the special, restrictive, learning scheme underlying backward induction criteria. But in a second time, we show that this special learning scheme, in a general learning context, expresses a dynamic asymmetry, called *first asymmetry*. This asymmetry can influence the values of the probabilities in the limit stationary distribution, by leading to higher probabilities for perfect outcome states. In section 4, we put into light why this order of learning can in addition throw some light on the notion of progressive evolution in some economic or management contexts. Section 4 also provides some limits of our results. Sections 5 and 6 deal with equilibria in weakly dominated strategies. Samuelson(1994), among others, established that these equilibria do not necessarily vanish in the long run. We go beyond this result by looking for the probabilities assigned to the different strategies in the long run. The obtained results are contrasted. On the one hand, we establish that the difference between weakly and non weakly dominated strategies gives rise to a dynamic asymmetry, we call *second asymmetry*. For a given game, we calculate the impact of this asymmetry on the probabilities in the limit stationary distribution. Thereby we put into light, on the other hand, that other factors may strengthen or moderate the impact of the second asymmetry. Section 7 concludes the paper by shedding light on the special learning speeds which underly some forward induction criteria.

2. Discrete learning mutation processes and limit Markov graph

We mainly focus in this paper on *NS*'s learning-mutation process, developed for finite N player extensive form games.

According to this process, each player becomes a finite population of Δ identical agents, where Δ is a finite integer. Time is divided into an infinite number of discrete periods. In each period t, each agent is randomly matched against $N-1$ agents in the $N-1$ opposing populations. To put it more precisely, all happens as if each agent plays against the $N-1$ representative agents of the $N-1$ opposing populations. An agent, in period t, is described by a characteristic, which consists of his (pure) strategy, coupled with a conjecture which specifies his beliefs (at each of his information sets) about the actions taken by the other players. The state of the system in period t, denoted by θ_t, is the description of how many agents in each population have each possible characteristic. Θ is the set of all possible states of the system.

In *NS*, each agent, in each period t, when called on to play, *learns* with probability μ, $0 < \mu < 1$, in which case he observes all the actions that were played in the current period, updates his beliefs to match with the observed

Discrete evolutionary processes | 355

actions and plays accordingly [1]. If he does not learn (with probability $1 - \mu$), his actions and beliefs are the preceding period ones. The learning mechanism gives rise to a Markov process on the state space.

Besides having the possibility to learn, each agent may *mutate*. To put it more precisely, he mutates with probability λ, $0 < \lambda < 1$, in which case he switches to any possible characteristic with strictly positive probability. Hence the mutation mechanism, coupled with the learning process, gives rise to a new Markov process, whose transition matrix is irreducible and aperiodic. It follows that there exists a unique stationary probability distribution for each λ.

NS are interested in the limit of the stationary distribution, called *limit distribution*, when λ goes to 0. This limit exists and does not depend on the value of μ nor on the values of the probabilities assigned to the different characteristics in case of mutation [2]. Very roughly, the states that appear in the limit distribution are the absorbing states which are the easiest to reach in terms of mutations. This immediately derives from the fact that the probability of a transition goes exponentially to 0 with the number of required mutations. To put it more precisely, a state θ is in the support of the limit distribution only if it is contained in a locally stable component. Moreover, if θ is in the limit distribution, so are all states which are in the *locally stable component* containing θ. The definition of a locally stable component is recalled below.

Definitions (out of NS):

Two states θ and θ' are adjacent if one mutation can change the state from θ to θ'. The single-mutation neighborhood $M(Q)$ of an absorbing set [3] Q is the set of all θ' adjacent at some θ of Q. A collection of absorbing sets Φ is a cycle if for all $Q, Q' \in \Phi$, there exists absorbing sets $Q_1, ..., Q_n \in \Phi$, such that $Q = Q_1$, $Q' = Q_n$ and for $i = 1, ..., n-1$: $M(Q_i) \cap B(Q_{i+1}) \neq \emptyset$ ($B(Q_{i+1})$ being the basin of attraction of Q_{i+1}). A cycle Φ is a component if there exists no cycle $\Phi' \neq \Phi$ containing Φ.

A component Φ is locally stable if there exists no pair of absorbing sets $Q \in \Phi$ and $Q' \notin \Phi$ such that $M(Q) \cap B(Q') \neq \emptyset$.

A salient feature of many economic games is their huge number of adjacent states. For example, when the equilibrium path of a game does not reach all the

---

1. To put it more precisely, the agent repeats his past action whenever it is a best response to the updated conjectures. In the other case, he switches to a best response, chosen according to a probability distribution, which puts positive weight on all best responses.
2. This fact contrasts with the less general results obtained with continuous processes, where the possibility of large jumps (many simultaneous mutations) is precluded (see Foster & Young(1990), Fudenberg & Harris(1992)). For the proof of the result see NS.
3. An absorbing set is a minimal set of states with the property that the learning process can not take the system out of this set. The basin of attraction of an absorbing set Q is the set of states from which there is a positive probability that the learning process drives to Q in a finite number of periods.

information sets, then it generally gives rise to a large set of adjacent states with the same payoff. Hence all these states belong to a same cycle. It follows that, if one of these states is observed over the long run, then all the states in the cycle are observed too. It derives that the presence of the cycle in the limit distribution depends on the behavior of the system at *each* of its elements.

This fact results in two often observed phenomena.

Firstly, the fragility (against mutations) of one state in the cycle is enough to provoke the *fragility of the whole cycle*. In other terms, if the system, with the aid of one mutation, can switch away from one state in the cycle to a state out of the cycle, then it can leave the whole cycle with one mutation.

For one, this can explain that a whole cycle does not appear in the limit distribution because of the fragility against mutations of just one of its states. This fact is stylized in figure 1a. Suppose that the game leads to only two cycles E_1 and E_2. One mutation is enough to transform the system from the state s_1 in the cycle E_1 to the state s_2 in the cycle E_2; given that more than one mutation are required to switch from each state in E_2 to any state in E_1, only E_2 will be observed over the long run. This fact namely explains that the tit for tat strategy in Young & Foster's (1991) approach of the prisoner's dilemma is not observed over the long run.

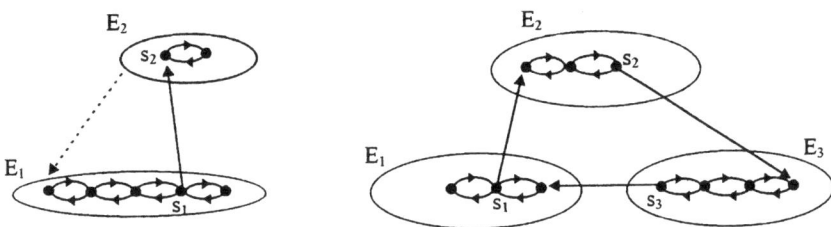

Figure 1a and Figure 1b: Each point in the Venn diagrams symbolizes an absorbing state. The arrows represent moves that require only one mutation. The dotted arrow means that more than 1 mutation are necessary to reach E_1 when starting from any state in E_2.

For another, this fragility can explain that many payoffs are observed in the long run, as is illustrated in figure 1b. The three Venn diagrams, E_1, E_2 and E_3, are the sets of adjacent states corresponding to three different equilibrium payoffs. One mutation allows to transform the system from s_1 in E_1 to a state in E_2; one mutation allows to reach E_3 when starting from s_2 and one mutation allows to reach E_1 when starting from s_3. It follows that either all or none of the three sets of states are in the support of the limit distribution. In particular, if the game has no other cycle, the three sets appear in the support of the limit distribution. This fact explains that *NS*'s process often leads to a limit distribution which assigns positive weight to all the equilibria of the game; this is namely true for the problem of revelation of quality through prices (see Nöldeke & Samuelson(1994), Umbhauer(1995, 1997)). For an illustration, see the game in section 3.

In this paper we mainly focus on games with the above property, i.e. games that lead to a limit distribution with large support. To put it more precisely, we mainly work with games with a unique locally stable component which contains many absorbing states. Hence, in order to differentiate the states, we have to tackle the probabilities assigned to them. So we work with the concept of *limit Markov graph* we developed in Umbhauer(1996). We define hereafter the limit Markov graph for games with only one locally stable component.

Definition 1: When a game has a unique locally stable component, the limit Markov graph is the oriented graph defined by:
– the set of nodes in the graph is the set of absorbing states of the absorbing sets which belong to the locally stable component;
– for any two different absorbing states θ and θ' in the graph, there is an arrow from θ to θ' if and only if zero or one mutation is enough to change the system from θ to θ'. Each arrow, from θ to θ', is endowed with the probability to switch from θ to θ'.

This definition calls for comments.

The key point is that the limit Markov graph is *sufficient* to compute the stationary probabilities. In fact, on grounds that a mutation occurs with a probability which goes to 0, *a switch from an absorbing state to another occurs with significant probability only if it requires only one mutation*. In other terms the stationary equations satisfy the property that all the moves which require 2 or more mutations vanish. Hence all happens as if the system stays in an absorbing state with probability 1 minus the probability to switch to the states which lie zero or one mutation away from them. One can add an arrow which goes from each absorbing state to itself, to symbolize this "inertia", but these arrows can be omitted in that they have no impact on the stationary equations.

At the same time it is necessary to stress that the limit Markov graph explicitly makes use of *NS*'s assumption according to which *the probability of learning, μ, is a given constant, bounded away from 0, whereas λ goes to 0* [1]. More generally the limit Markov graph requires that λ/μ goes to 0. It is this difference between λ and μ that allows to only focus on the mutations to get the arrows in the limit Markov graph. If the learning process is defined differently, so that, for example, μ can go to 0 (and λ/μ does not go to 0), then the limit Markov graph is no longer the appropriate tool to get the limit distribution probabilities. So, on the one hand, the limit Markov graph has the flaw to be inadequate in a context where λ/μ does not go to 0. On the other hand, as long

---
1. I am thankful to Larry Samuelson for this remark.

as μ and λ are not one the same level, it is a rather easy tool to get the limit distribution probabilities.

Let us discuss the property $\lambda/\mu \to 0$. This property means that learning is the main driving force of the system. Of course, paradoxically, it also gives a crucial role to the mutations, in that the presence of a state in the limit distribution only depends on the number of mutations required to reach it.

This fact partly explains that many authors introduce learning processes where the probability of learning can also go to 0 (and λ/μ does not go to 0). They namely suppose that the probability of learning goes to 0 in a state close to a best response (Nash) state. The idea behind this assumption is that the incentive to adjust behavior is increasing in the distance between the current payoff and the best response one.

Given the complexity of real behavior, this assumption is of course not necessarily true to the facts. As a matter of fact, it may be that a player whose strategy is close to a best response better uncovers it (and hence plays it) than a player whose behavior is far away. Moreover, many learning processes with the above learning assumption are deterministic (like the replicator equations). It follows that they preclude a whole range of strategic behaviors, because, for example, they do not allow people to react quickly in any situation. Yet we share the point of view that, even if the system is close to a Nash equilibrium, all agents should have the possibility to quickly and simultaneously switch to their best response, even if such a behavior will not change their payoffs in a large degree. Nevertheless, in order to allow for the possibility that μ goes to 0, we also partly study, in the examples we develop in the paper, the impact of learning schemes that differ from *NS*'s one (see especially section 6).

3. Backward induction and first asymmetry

In this section we work with finite generic [1] extensive form games of perfect information, with each player moving at most once along each path. We intend to go beyond NS's result, according to which, for this class of games, there exists a unique locally stable component which contains, *sometimes not only*, the subgame perfect equilibrium.

Let us first turn to the game, depicted in figure 2, they use to illustrate their result.

In this game adjacent perfect outcome states are defined by: the agents 1 (2) play R_1 (R_2), the agents 3 play any strategy, and the agents 2 believe that less than 1/3 of the agents 3 play L_3. Call E_1 this set of states; each state in E_1 yields

---

1. A *generic* game is defined by the fact that each player i, i from 1 to N, has a different payoff at each endnote of the game.

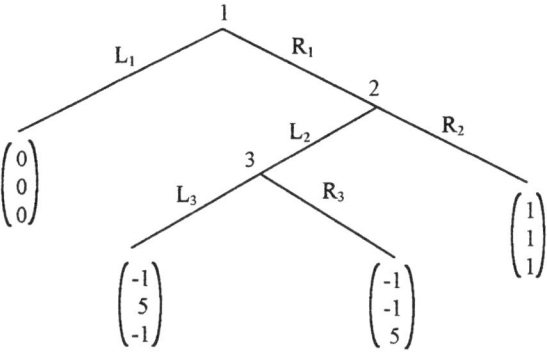

Figure 2: The ith coordinate of each column vector is the payoff of player i. The same convention holds for later games.

the perfect payoff $(1, 1, 1)$. All the states in which the agents 1 play L_1 and expect that more than ½ of the agents 2 play L_2 are also adjacent absorbing states. Call E_2 this set of states; each state in E_2 yields the payoff $(0, 0, 0)$. Both E_1 and E_2 appear in the long run because the system can reach with one mutation a state in E_1 (respectively E_2) when starting from E_2 (respectively E_1).

Namely, if one starts with a perfect outcome state where the agents 1 and 2 play R_1 and R_2, the agents 3 play L_3, whereas the agents 2 believe that the agents 3 play R_3, a mutation from an agent 2 to L_2 can set off a learning behavior which drives the system to the outcome $(0, 0, 0)$. In fact, the agents 2 may learn [1] and switch to L_2; thereafter the agents 1 may learn and switch to L_1.

In other terms, this game has a unique locally stable component that includes all the states of E_1 and E_2.

What matters in the learning behavior that drives the system from E_1 to E_2 is the *order in which the agents learn*. It is *crucial*, for the system to find its way to an E_2 state, that the agents 1 learn *before* the agents 2 learn (and hence switch back to R_2). One immediately observes that this order is not the order of learning behind backward induction (see Selten (1975) for the definition of backward induction criteria). Actually, the backward induction principle

---

1. One can observe that beliefs, when updated, are updated in a drastic way. As a matter of fact, when an agent 2 is called on to learn, and observes the response by the (representative) agent 3 playing after the mutant agent 2, he expects all the agents 3 to play L_3, despite of his beliefs in the previous period (all the agents 3 play R_3). This fact highlights that beliefs, whenever possible (i.e. each time the information sets are reached), have to match with *actions* if an agent learns (it also stresses the one period memory context). In other terms, the possible smooth adjustment of the behaviors does not follow from a smooth adjustment of the beliefs but rather from the fact that not everybody learns at a given time.

amounts to requiring that *the agents 3 learn before the agents 2, who in turn learn before the agents 1*. One immediately observes that such an order of learning prevents the system from switching to an E_2 state. In fact, the same mutation as above implies the following behavior: the agents 3 learn and switch to R_3; thereafter the mutant agent 2 switches back to R_2, which leaves the system in an E_1 state. Hence all happens as if backward induction only allows a special learning scheme in which each agent learns in turn, the first agents to learn being the last agents in the game. In contrast, *NS*'s random learning process, and more generally true to life learning processes, do not impose this order of learning; it results that they give rise to much more behavior evolution possibilities. That is why *NS*'s support of the limit distribution in the above game does not restrict to the perfect outcome states.

It follows, at first sight, that the special order of learning behind backward induction stresses a flaw of this principle, in that it puts into light a seemingly ad hoc way to learn in a game. Yet this special order has an interesting property. Even in general learning contexts, the strategic asymmetry it allows to put into light, results in a dynamic asymmetry that can have an effect on the probabilities in the limit distribution.

We first illustrate this asymmetry in the game of figure 2.

Proposition 1: One mutation is enough to drive the system from each E_2 state to an E_1 state, but the reverse proposition does not hold: one has to start from special E_1 states for the system to move to an E_2 state thanks to only one mutation.

Proof: To prove the second part of proposition 1, it is enough to observe that, if the system starts from the perfect equilibrium state in which the agents 1, 2 and 3 play *R*, then more than one mutation are required to leave this state because at least 1/3 of the agents 3 have to switch to L_3 and one agent 2 has to mutate to L_2.

To prove the first part of the proposition, first suppose that in the starting state, each agent 2 plays R_2. It immediately follows that a mutation from an agent 1 to R_1 is enough for the system to find its way to an E_1 state, as the agents 1 may learn and switch to R_1. Now suppose that at least some agents 2 play L_2 in the starting state. Suppose again that an agent 1 mutates to R_1. This mutation can set off the following learning behavior. The agents 3 switch to R_3 (unless they already play this action), causing in turn the agents 2 who play L_2 to switch to R_2, which finally leads the agents 1 to switch to R_1. ■

This asymmetry is symbolized in figure 3.

It is immediate, due to the construction of the limit Markov graph, that *this asymmetry can have an effect on the values of the limit distribution probabilities*, in that it leads to an asymmetry in the number of (one-mutation) flows in and out of the two sets E_1 and E_2. We refer to this asymmetry as *first asymmetry*.

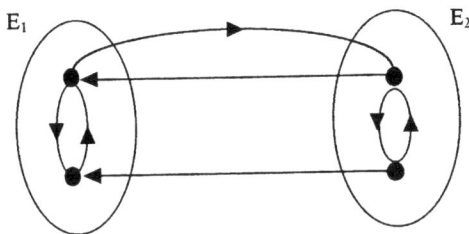

Figure 3: Each point of the E_1 (E_2) Venn diagram is an absorbing state of E_1 (E_2). Each arrow symbolizes a move that only requires one mutation.

For more general games, one mutation is no longer necessarily sufficient to switch from each non perfect outcome state to a perfect one. The game in figure 4 is meant to illustrate this point.

The perfect outcome is (5, 4, 1, 3) and corresponds to the path (L_1, R_2, r_3). Let us start in the Nash non perfect outcome state e where the agents 1 play R_1, the agents 2 play L_2, the agents 3 play (r_3, L_3), the agents 4 play L_4, and beliefs match actions. For the system to reach a perfect outcome state, 2 mutations are necessary. One agent 1 has to mutate to L_1, otherwise no agent is incited to change actions or beliefs. But this mutation is not sufficient, because it does not induce the agents 2 to switch to R_2. In fact, L_2 offers a payoff 5 which is higher than the expected payoff after R_2, i.e. 4. Moreover, neither the agents 3 nor 4 will change their action. The agents 4 are not called on to play. The agents 3 get 4 by staying on L_3, whereas they expect a payoff 3 by switching to R_3. Hence, for the system to move to a perfect outcome state, a second mutation is necessary. One can check that a mutation from an agent 3 from L_3 to R_3 is sufficient. These two introduced mutations can actually set off the following learning behavior: the agents 4 learn and play R_4, the agents 3 learn and play R_3, the agents 2 learn and play R_2 and finally the agents 1 learn and switch to L_1.

However, *two* mutations are still a few number of mutations. This fact can be generalized as follows:

Proposition 2: Let G be a finite generic extensive form game of perfect information. The number of mutations necessary to switch from a non perfect outcome state to a perfect outcome state is bounded by a number which depends on the cardinal of the strategy sets. To put it more precisely, a sufficient number of mutations is the number of information sets of the game minus the number of last level information sets. By contrast, the number of mutations required to go from some perfect outcome states to a non perfect one also depends on the size of the populations.

Proof: Given the genericity of the payoffs, the system does not leave the perfect equilibrium state unless a fraction of at least one population switches to

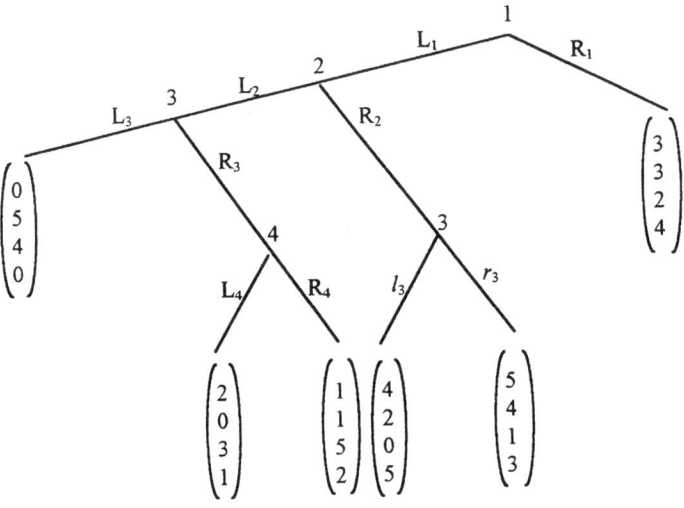

Figure 4

a non perfect equilibrium action. This immediately follows from the definition of the perfect equilibrium concept and proves the second part of the proposition.

Let us now prove the first part of the proposition by induction on T, the number of levels of the game. The introduced mutations are the following ones: at each information set, except for the last level ones, we introduce a mutation toward the perfect equilibrium action (unless somebody is already playing this action).

Call t the agents playing at level t. If the agents T, at a given information set, are called on to play, they *may* learn, which leads them to switch (if not already there) to the perfect action.

Suppose that if the agents $t + i$, at the information sets of level $t + i$ (with i from 1 to $T - t$) are called on to play, they play the perfect actions. Now consider the agents t. If the agents t, at a given information set of level t, are called on to play, they *may* learn and hence switch to the perfect action. As a matter of fact, first suppose that only a mutant t agent plays the perfect action, A, and that other agents play different actions B. If the agents t are called on to play, the agents $t + i$, with i from 1 to $T - t$, are called on to play at the reached information sets after A and B. By assumption, the agents play the perfect actions at these sets. It follows, by definition of perfection, that A yields a higher payoff than B. Yet it may be that all the agents t first switch to an action C, if C yields a higher payoff than A; yet, if the agents t switch to C, they activate the information sets after C, causing, by assumption, every agent to switch to the perfect action at the subsequent levels. Hence, at the end, by definition of perfection, C yields a lower payoff, and the agents t switch to A.

Consider now the agents *1* at level *1*. They are called on to play. By induction on *t*, they play the perfect action.

This reasoning ensures that the introduced mutations are enough to reach the perfect equilibrium path. ∎

Proposition 2 gives rise to three comments.

Firstly, the proof entirely rests on the backward induction reasoning. As a matter of fact, we introduced a way of learning (from the agents *T* to the agents *1*), which is such that the activated agents learn in the backward induction order. It follows that the dynamic asymmetry underlined in proposition 2 is entirely linked to the special learning order of the backward induction (perfect equilibrium) reasoning. This fact stresses, perhaps paradoxically, the importance of this way of learning.

To understand the reason for the dynamic impact of backward induction, let us come back to the origins of the backward induction reasoning in games. The aim of the perfect (and Nash perfect) equilibrium concept is to prevent the players, at each level of the game, from threatening to play actions they would not play when called on to play *(incredible threats)*. To this aim, Selten(1975) introduces small but *systematic errors* at each information set, causing the agents to play each available action with small but strictly positive probability. It follows that all the information sets are reached with strictly positive probability. Hence each payoff maximizing agent has to play optimally at any of his information sets, knowing that he is at all these sets. This is especially true for the last level (*T*) agents, who therefore play their best response. It is also true for the $T-1$ level agents who know that the *T* level agents are incited to play their best response, and so on; the backward induction reasoning automatically follows.

It is easy to observe that the *mutations* introduced in the proof *(which are possible because NS's mutation process is a binomial process) play a role* which is *similar to the role of Selten's(1975) systematic errors.* Their aim is to call on the agents to play. And, given that learning *may* proceed in the backward induction order *(because NS's learning process is a random binomial process)*, it automatically follows that the system can evolve, thanks to the introduced mutations, to the perfect outcome state.

Secondly, proposition 2 establishes that if we focus on the moves that require a number of mutations lower or equal to *M* (= the number of information sets minus the number of last levels information sets), then we get for each game, provided that Δ is much higher than *M*, a figure similar to figure 3, except that an arrow now symbolizes a move that requires *M* mutations or less. In other terms, proposition 2 underlines a strong asymmetry: the number of mutations necessary to reach the perfect outcome depends on the *size of the game (number of branches)*, whereas the number of mutations necessary to leave, for example, the perfect equilibrium, depends, among others, on the *size of the populations*.

This *structural asymmetry* may of course have an *impact on the values of the probabilities in the limit distribution,* which should be in favor of the perfect outcome, *as long as Δ is large enough.*

Δ has to be large for the number of agents corresponding to a fraction of the population to be much higher than M. In fact, if Δ is small relative to the size of the game, proposition 2 is no longer in support of possible higher probabilities for perfect equilibrium outcome states. Moreover, if the game is not generic, in that some players get the same payoff for different actions at a same information set, then the fraction of population having to switch action for the system to leave the perfect outcome may go to 0, which again prevents from concluding that evolution should favor the perfect outcome.

4. Sequential mutations, progressive behavior evolution and limits of the first asymmetry

The proof of proposition 2, and therefore the special learning scheme underlying backward induction, also implicitly allows to yield some first insights into the notion of *progressive evolution* in an economic or management context.

For this purpose, let us turn, in this paragraph, to the game in figure 2 and to a mutation process that differs from *NS*'s one in the fact that mutations are *isolated*, so that a new mutation can perturb the system only after the preceding one has no more effect.

Within this framework, me mean by *progressive evolution* from a first equilibrium state to a second equilibrium state, a process which requires more than one mutation, each mutation driving to a state which comes closer to the second equilibrium state.

Proposition 3: When starting from any non perfect outcome state, the system can always progressively evolve to a perfect outcome. By contrast, a progressive evolution to a non perfect outcome is generically impossible.

Proof: Suppose that the system starts from a non perfect outcome state e_2, in which all the agents 2 play L_2 and all the agents 3 play L_3 (the proof immediately generalizes to any other E_2 state). If an agent 1 mutates to R_1, he may switch back to L_1 before the agents 2 and 3 learned and respectively switched to R_2 and R_3. Yet, in *any* context in which the order of learning is random, some agents 3, with strictly positive probability, may learn before the mutant agent 1 learns; hence some agents 3 switch to R_3 before the mutant agent 1 plays again L_1. Therefore, even if the system is back in an E_2 state, it is in a *new state e'_2*, which is characterized by the fact that more agents 3 (than in e_2) play R_3. If, starting from this new state, an agent 1 mutates again to R_1, some additional agents 3 may learn and switch to R_3 before the mutant agent 1 switches back to L_1. It follows that the system, albeit still in an E_2 state, is again in a new state e_2'', where more agents 3 play R_3. The repetition of this procedure ensures that the system progressively reaches a state in which more than 2/3 agents 3 play R_3. Starting from this state, a new mutation from an agent 1 to R_1 can lead some agents 2 to R_2 before the mutant agent 1 goes back to L_1. And so on, till at least half of the agents 2 play R_2, in which case an additional mutation from an agent 1 to R_1 leads the system to an E_1 state.

Let us now start from a perfect E_1 outcome state. If one mutation is not enough to lead from this state to an E_2 state, then *an additional mutation has no impact*. In fact, if one mutation is not sufficient, then, in the new state, the agents 1 still play R_1, which means that at least half of the agents 2 still play R_2. And the actions of the agents 2 mean that at least 2/3 of the agents 3 play R_3. Hence, in the general case (i.e. unless exactly 2/3 agents 3 play R_3 or exactly half of the agents 2 play L_2), a new mutation, starting from this state, can not lead the system to a state closer to an E_2 state. In fact, it can only induce the learning of some agents, and hence lead some additional agents 2 or 3 to switch to the perfect actions R_2 and R_3. ■

The result obtained in proposition 3 is not a chance event, in that the reasoning behind the first part of the proof is a smooth backward induction reasoning. *Each additional mutation leads to a new state that is closer to a perfect outcome state* than the preceding state, in that more agents 3 and more agents 2 switch to R_3 and R_2. And what matters is that this progressive evolution is obtained *without resorting to the ad hoc backward induction learning scheme*. The only required property for the learning process is that the *order of learning is random. In fact, the role of the repetitive introduction of mutations is to bypass the ad hoc learning scheme of backward induction:* mutations are repeated *till* the agents 3 learn, *which allows to not suppose that they are necessarily the first agents to learn.*

Apart from stressing that progressive evolution may favor evolution to perfect outcome states without resorting to the ad hoc backward induction order of learning, the sequential introduction of mutations and its consequences may be worthy of interest in economic and management problems. In fact, it sheds some light on some conditions required for successive mutations to actually provoke an evolution of an economic context, provided these contexts can be compared to a game of perfect information.

It is easy to check, by looking at the starting state e in the game in figure 4, that the reasoning in the proof of proposition 3 again applies, provided that we replace the successive introduction of *one* mutation with a *successive introduction of 2 simultaneous mutations*, a mutation from an agent 1 to L_1 and a mutation from an agent 3 to R_3. The reasoning again rests on the backward induction principle without resorting to the ad hoc learning scheme behind it, and hence puts again into light the possible progressive evolution to a perfect outcome state.

366 | Evolutionary game theory

This result is again worthy of interest in economic and management sciences. As above, it sheds light on sufficient and necessary conditions for a context to change. In addition it highlights that a possible *coordination* among some agents may be necessary to provoke a progressive change in a given context.

Let us finally conclude our study on backward induction by observing that, unfortunately, proposition 2 does not easily generalize to games with imperfect information.

To see why, consider the game out of Selten(1975), depicted in figure 5.

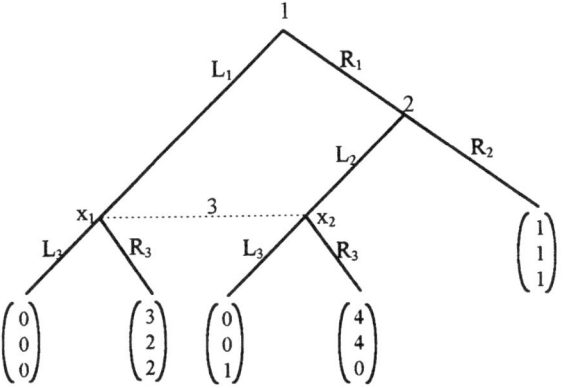

Figure 5: The dotted line figures the information set of player 3, who does not distinguish the node x_1 from the node x_2.

The unique locally stable component of this game both includes the E_1 Perfect outcome states (payoff (1, 1, 1)) and the E_2 non Perfect outcome states (payoff (3, 2, 2)). One mutation is enough to switch from any E_2 state to an E_1 state (it is enough for one agent 1 to mutate to R_1).

The point is that, regardless of the starting E_1 state, one mutation is enough to switch from this state to an E_2 state. In other terms, proposition 2 does not hold. To see why, suppose that one agent 1 mutates to L_1. This mutation can set off the following learning behavior: the agents 3 switch (if not already there) to R_3, inducing all the agents 1 to switch to L_1.

The reason for this fact is that player 3's optimal response at his non singleton information set *is not uniquely determined, even for generic payoffs*, as his best response is R_3 at x_1 and L_3 at x_2. It follows that a single mutation can drastically modify his behavior, even when starting from the perfect equilibrium state, which explains that the number of required mutations to switch from a perfect state to a non perfect one is no longer dependent on the size of the population.

5. Weakly dominated strategies and second asymmetry

We now turn to weakly dominated strategies. Samuelson (1994) established that equilibria in weakly dominated strategies do not necessarily vanish in the long run. In this section we are interested in whether they appear, in the limit distribution, with a lower probability than the equilibria in non weakly dominated strategies. We establish that weakly and non weakly dominated strategies generate asymmetric driving forces, which can result in different limit stationary probabilities.

To this end we study the game in figure 6, out of Samuelson(1994).

This game has many absorbing states, each corresponding to a particular Nash equilibrium. $E_{A/3}$, $E_{(A/3)-1}$, ..., E_i, ..., E_1, are the states characterized by: in E_i, i from 1 to $A/3$, the agents 2 play L, and all the agents 1 play M, apart from i agents who play T. E_0 is the state which corresponds to the only perfect equilibrium of the game. It is defined by: the agents 1 play M and the agents 2 play L. Finally E_A is the state in which the agents 1 play B and the agents 2 play R.

All states, except for E_A, appear in the support of the limit distribution [1]. Yet only E_0 contains no weakly dominated strategy, because T is weakly dominated by M.

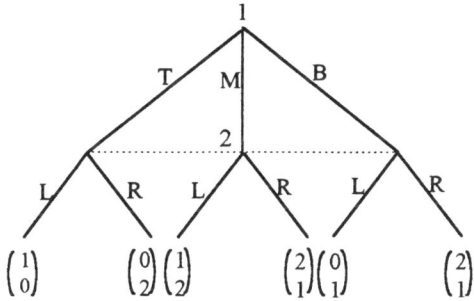

Figure 6: The dotted line means that player 2 does not observe player 1's actions.

The large support again stems from the fact that all states $E_{A/3}$ ... E_0 belong to a same cycle of adjacent states. In fact, switching an M playing agent 1 to T is

---

1. In Samuelson's(1994) paper, as long as a best response state is not reached, the agents can switch to alternative best responses, even if they already play a best response. It follows that E_A is also in the Samuelson's limit distribution support. In fact, E_A can be reached from $E_{A/3}$ by switching an M playing agent 1 to T. This switch can induce all the agents 2 to learn and play R, causing all the agents 1 to switch to B.

enough to transform the system from E_i to E_{i+1}, with i from 0 to $(\Delta/3) - 1$; conversely, switching a T playing agent 1 to M is enough to transform the system from E_i to E_{i-1}, with i from $\Delta/3$ to 1. In addition, switching an agent 1 from B to M is enough for the system to find its way from E_Δ to E_0. Finally, given that the M playing agents 1 do never change their action by learning, more than one mutation are necessary to switch from any state E_i to the state E_Δ, regardless of i (from 0 to $\Delta/3$).

Yet, though the support of the distribution is large, weakly dominated states and non weakly dominated ones lead to a dynamic asymmetry, we call *second asymmetry* and summarize in proposition 4 below.

Proposition 4: There are more ways out from and less ways into a weakly dominated state than ways out from and into a non weakly dominated one.

Proof: For a start, let us compare the states $E_{\Delta/3}$ and E_0. There is only one possibility to stray away from E_0 with the aid of only one mutation. A player 1 agent has to switch from M to T, which drives the system from E_0 to E_1. By contrast, it is possible, with only one mutation, to switch from $E_{\Delta/3}$ to *any* other state E_i, with i from 0 to $\Delta/3 - 1$. It is for example enough that an agent 2 mutates from L to R for 1, 2, ..., $\Delta/3$ agents 1 to possibly move from T to M.

What is more, there exist several one-mutation moves from $E_{\Delta/3}$ to the other states. For example, there are three possibilities to switch from $E_{\Delta/3}$ to $E_{\Delta/3-1}$ by way of one mutation. The first mutation switches a T playing agent 1 to M. The second leads an M playing agent 1 to switch to T; this switch can set off the following learning behavior: some agents 2 switch to R, causing two agents 1 to switch from T to M, which finally leads the agents 2 back to L. The last mutation causes an agent 2 to switch to R; this mutation can lead an agent 1 to switch from T to M, causing the mutant agent 2 to go back to L.

This asymmetry, called second asymmetry, is depicted in figure 7a.

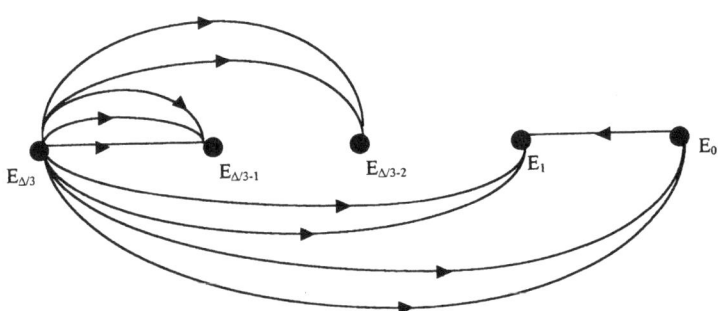

Figure 7a: In figure 7a, $\Delta = 12$, but the generalization to any value of Δ is immediate. This remark also holds for the games in figures 7b and 8. Each arrow represents a one-mutation move. Attention is restricted to $E_{\Delta/3}$ and E_0.

Discrete evolutionary processes | 369

The study restricted to $E_{\Delta/3}$ and E_0 easily generalizes to all the states between these two extremes, which completes the proof. ∎

The asymmetries are depicted in figure 7b. The number on each arrow from E_i to E_j, with $i \neq j$, i, j from 0 to $\Delta/3$, indicates the number of one-mutation moves from E_i to E_j.

What matters is that the asymmetries entirely result from the difference between a weakly and a non weakly dominated strategy. To see why, consider for example the fact that one mutation is enough to reach E_j from any state E_i, with $i > j$, whereas the reverse move requires more than one mutation, unless $j = i - 1$. The first switch occurs if an agent 2 switches from L to R; this mutation causes the weakly dominated strategy T to yield a *strictly lower payoff* than the weakly dominating strategy M. This explains that, in response to this mutation, some T playing agents 1 adjust their behavior by switching to M. The reverse move is not possible (unless the two states are adjacent) because M is not weakly dominated. Hence, for example, the same mutation as above tempts no agent 1 away from M.

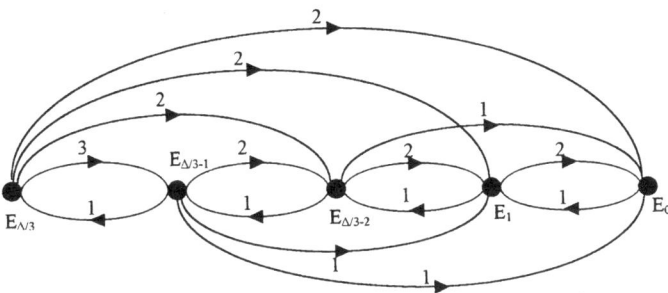

Figure 7b.

6. Second asymmetry, limit probabilities and further developments

The asymmetry established in proposition 4 has an impact on the probabilities in the limit distribution. We now calculate this impact more precisely, in order to highlight that some other parameters like *the size of the populations and the value of µ may strengthen or moderate the impact of this second asymmetry.*

To this end, we compute the limit Markov graph (figure 8) which immediately derives from figure 7b. The number on each arrow from E_i to E_j, with $i \neq j$, i, j from 0 to $\Delta/3$, indicates the probability to switch from E_i to E_j with at most one mutation.

The probability a, for example, is the probability to switch from $E_{\Delta/3 - 1}$ to $E_{\Delta/3}$ by means of one mutation. This switch happens if and only if an agent 1

370 | Evolutionary game theory

switches from M to T. In that no learning is necessary, this switch only requires that an agent 1, from a population of $2\Delta/3 + 1$ agents, mutates and, due to the mutation, switches to T. If each agent, when he mutates, switches to all of his available actions with the same probability (i.e. 1/3 for an agent 1, ½ for an agent 2), the probability a becomes: $C^1_{2\Delta/3+1} \lambda(1-\lambda)^{2\Delta-1} 1/3$. The probabilities e (for e, e', e'') of the switches from E_i to E_{i-1}, with $0 < i < \Delta/3$, are the sum of the probabilities of the two following one-mutation moves. Either an agent 2 mutates to R (followed by the successive or simultaneous learning of one T playing agent 1 and (then) the learning of the mutant agent 2), either a T playing agent 1 mutates to M. b denotes the probability to move from $E_{\Delta/3}$ to $E_{\Delta/3-1}$ by way of one mutation. We already know that there are three possibilities. The first mutation switches an agent 1 from T to M. The second causes an M playing agent 1 to switch to T (followed by the adequate learning behavior). The last causes an agent 2 to switch to R (followed by the adequate learning behavior). b is the sum of the probabilities of these three events. Computing more precisely the probabilities gives rise to the following result, we state in form of a proposition.

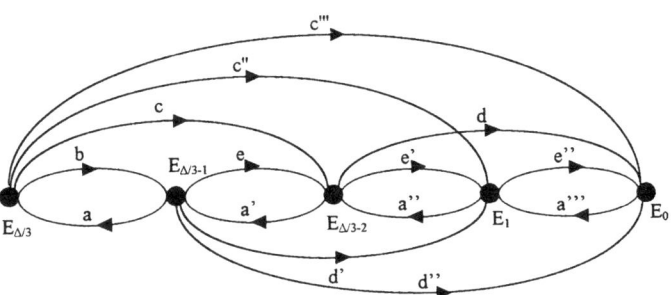

Figure 8: Limit Markov graph.

Proposition 5. If each player, when mutating, moves to each of his possible strategy with the same probability, and if μ is higher than 1/2, then the states E_i, i from 0 to $\Delta/3$, are observed with a probability decreasing in i.

Proof: Denote p_{Ei} the probability of the state E_i in the limit distribution, with i from 0 to $\Delta/3$.

We start with the states E_0 and E_1.

The vertical line in figure 9a cuts the graph and leads to the stationary equation:

$$p_{E0} a''' = p_{E1} e'' + k$$

A switch from E_1 to E_0 happens if the T playing agent 1 mutates to M, or if an agent 2 mutates to R and does not learn before the T playing agent 1 learns.

Discrete evolutionary processes | 371

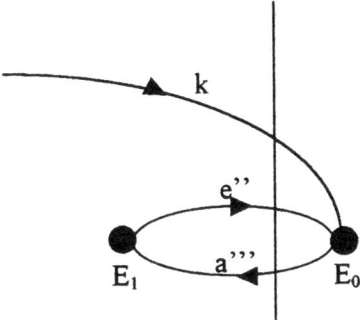

Figure 9a: The arrow indexed by k symbolizes all the one-mutation moves that reach E_0 starting from any other state E_i, i from $\Delta/3$ to 2. k is therefore the sum of all the probabilities on the arrows from E_i to E_0, with i from $\Delta/3$ to 2, weighted by the probability of the starting state.

The probability that the mutant agent 2 learns before the T playing agent 1 is:

$$\mu(1-\mu) + (1-\mu)^2 \mu(1-\mu) + (1-\mu)^4 \mu(1-\mu) + \cdots = (1-\mu)/(2-\mu)$$

It follows that the probability that the mutant agent 2 does not learn before the T playing agent 1 is equal to: $1 - (1-\mu)/(2-\mu) = 1/(2-\mu)$.

It ensues: $e'' = \lambda(1-\lambda)^{2\Delta-1}(1/3) + C_\Delta^1 \lambda(1-\lambda)^{2\Delta-1}(1/2) \cdot 1/(2-\mu)$.

a''' is the probability that an M playing agent 1 mutates to T, i.e.:

$$a''' = C_\Delta^1 \lambda(1-\lambda)^{2\Delta-1}(1/3).$$

$\mu \geq 1/2$ is a sufficient condition for e'' to be higher than a'''. It derives from the stationary equation, $p_{E0} a''' = p_{E1} e'' + k$, that $\mu \geq 1/2$ is a sufficient condition for p_{E1} to be lower than p_{E0}.

We now turn to E_2 and E_1.

The vertical cut in figure 9b leads to the stationary equation:

$$p_{E2}(d + e') + k' + k'' = p_{E1} a''$$

We have: $e' + d > e''$ and $a'' < a'''$. This result follows from the meaning of $e' + d$ and a''. a'' is the probability that an agent 1, among the ($\Delta - 1$) agents 1 who play M, mutates to T; it follows immediately that $a'' < a'''$. $e' + d$ is the probability that either an agent 1 among the two T playing agents 1 mutates to M, or one agent 2 mutates to R, and at least one of the two T playing agents 1

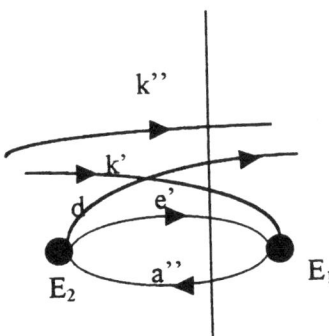

Figure 9b: The arrow indexed by k' (respectively k'') symbolizes all the one-mutation moves that reach E_1 (respectively E_0), starting from any state E_i, i from $\Delta/3$ to 3. $k' + k''$ is therefore the sum of all the probabilities on the arrows from E_i to E_1 or E_0, with i from $\Delta/3$ to 3, weighted by the probability of the starting state. $e' + d$ denotes the probability to leave E_2 with one mutation, toward E_1 or E_0.

learns before the mutant agent 2 (this last probability, equal to $[1 - \mu(1-\mu)^2/(1-(1-\mu)^3)]$, is necessarily higher than $2/(1-\mu)$).

It follows that $\mu \geq 1/2$ is a sufficient condition for $e' + d$ to be higher than a''.

It derives from the stationary equation that it is a sufficient condition for p_{E2} to be lower than p_{E1}.

The generalization of the result $p_{E_{i+1}} < p_{Ei}$, with i from 2 to $\Delta/3 - 2$ is immediate by induction on i. It is enough to observe that, for one, the probability $\tilde{e}$ (to switch from E_{i+1} to the states E_j, with $j < i + 1$) increases with i because the number of agents playing T which are susceptible to mutate to M (or to learn after a mutation from an agent 2) is increasing in i. For another, the probability $\tilde{a}$ to switch from E_i to E_{i+1} is decreasing in i, in that the number of M playing agents 1 decreases in i. The stationary equation, that follows from the cut of the limit Markov graph between E_i and E_{i+1}, completes the proof.

Let us finally establish that $p_{E\Delta/3} < p_{E\Delta/3 - 1}$.

$b + g$ is the probability that either a T playing agent 1 mutates to M, either an M playing agent 1 mutates to T, either an agent 2 mutates to R. All these mutations automatically ensure that the system goes to a state E_i, with $i < \Delta/3$. For example, if an M playing agent mutates to T, some agents 2 will learn and switch to R; given that these agents switch back to L only after at least two T playing agents 1 learn and switch to M, the rest point that the system reaches is necessarily, with probability one, a state E_i, with $i < \Delta/3$. If an agent 2 mutates to R, he does not switch back before at least one T playing agent 1

Discrete evolutionary processes | 373

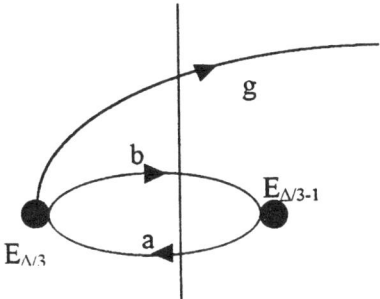

Figure 9c: b, respectively g, is the probability to reach $p_{E_{\Delta/3-1}}$, respectively any state E_i, with $i < \Delta/3 - 1$, with the aid of one mutation, when starting from $E_{\Delta/3}$.

learns and plays M; hence the rest point to which leads this mutation is, with probability 1, a state E_i, with $i < \Delta/3$.

Hence $b + g = C^1_{\Delta/3} \lambda(1-\lambda)^{2\Delta-1}(1/3) + C^1_{2\Delta/3} \lambda(1-\lambda)^{2\Delta-1}(1/3) + C^1_\Delta \lambda(1-\lambda)^{2\Delta-1}(1/2)$.

a is the probability that an M playing agent 1 mutates to T.

Hence $a = C^1_{2\Delta/3+1} \lambda(1-\lambda)^{2\Delta-1}(1/3)$, which ensures that $b + g > a$. By the stationary equation corresponding to the vertical line in figure 9c, i.e. $p_{E_{\Delta/3}}(b + g) = p_{E_{\Delta/3-1}} \cdot a$, it results that $p_{E_{\Delta/3}} < p_{E_{\Delta/3-1}}$. ∎

The proof of proposition 5 underlines the following facts.

Firstly it clearly stresses the impact of the second asymmetry.

A salient feature is that this asymmetry particularly works for the extreme state $E_{\Delta/3}$. The probability of this state, *regardless of the value of the learning probability* μ, is much lower than $p_{E_{\Delta/3-1}}$, given that $p_{E_{\Delta/3}}/p_{E_{\Delta/3-1}} = (\Delta/3 + \Delta/2)/(2\Delta/9 + 1/3)$, which is about 15/4 if Δ is large. If player 2 had 3 instead of 2 possible strategies, $p_{E_{\Delta/3}}/p_{E_{\Delta/3-1}}$ would be about 3 for large values of Δ. These probabilities clearly highlight the impact of the second asymmetry, i.e. the fact that *three* one-mutation moves allow to switch from $E_{\Delta/3}$ to $E_{\Delta/3-1}$, whereas only one one-mutation move allows to switch from $E_{\Delta/3-1}$ to $E_{\Delta/3}$. Furthermore, it is easy to check that $p_{E_{\Delta/3}}$ is strictly lower than $p_{E_{\Delta/3-1}}$ *for a very large range of probabilities assigned to the different actions in case of mutation*, which stresses the generality of this result.

Secondly, the proof makes heavy use of the fact that an agent switches to each of his available actions with the same probability in case of mutation. If an agent 1 mutates more easily to M than to L, or if an agent 2 mutates more easily to R than to L, then the proof is strengthened; but, in the reverse case, namely if an agent 1 mutates more often to L than to M, then it may no longer be appropriate.

Thirdly, we suppose that the probability of learning μ is higher or equal to 1/2. A more precise sufficient condition would be $\mu > (1/2 - 3/(2\Delta - 2))$. Even if this condition is only sufficient, it highlights the possible impact of the number of agents that can mutate, and, consequently, the impact of the *size of the populations*. *This impact can limit the impact of the second asymmetry.* For example, the asymmetry according to which there are two one-mutation moves from E_1 to E_0 and only one one-mutation move from E_0 to E_1, can be outweighed by the following fact. In E_1, there is only one agent who can mutate to M, whereas in E_0 there are Δ agents that can mutate to T. It follows that the probability on the only arrow from E_0 to E_1 may be higher than the sum of the probabilities of the two arrows from E_1 to E_0. Of course this observation has to be moderated by the fact that there is a strictly positive probability to switch from all the other states to E_0, a probability we did not calculate (and which may be high), but it has to be allowed for. It follows that, for the second asymmetry to not be outweighed, small Δ are preferable.

Let us finally stress another point. The result we get depends on the chosen learning process. To show why, we turn, in this paragraph, to a learning process, which differs from NS's one in the fact that the agents who learn first are the agents who's payoff is the most distant from the best response payoff. To put it more precisely, an agent learns with probability μ if and only if the difference between his payoff and the best response payoff is the largest one. The idea behind this process is that the incentive to learn is growing in the difference between the obtained payoff and the best response one.

Firstly, this new process has no impact on the result $p_{E\Delta/3} < p_{E\Delta/3 - 1}$, because the three one-mutation moves that led away from $E_{\Delta/3}$ in NS's process still stray the system away from this state. This results from the fact that the learning phase after each of these three mutations is *not dependent on the nature of the learning process* introduced. So, for example, when an agent 2 switches to R, the only agents who are not playing a best response are the T playing agents 1. It follows that only these agents can learn, which ensures that the system strays away from $E_{\Delta/3}$. In a similar way, if an M playing agent 1 mutates to T, the only agents who are not playing a best response are the agents 2. It derives that some of them switch to R. And the agents 2 keep on switching to R, till at least two T playing agents 1, due to learning, late or early, switch to M. Finally, a mutation from an T playing agent 1 to M induces no learning and automatically leads to $E_{\Delta/3 - 1}$. In other terms the only *very loose condition* on the learning process, necessary for $p_{E\Delta/3}$ to be lower than $p_{E\Delta/3 - 1}$, is that agents who do not play a best response have a possibility, late or early, to adjust their strategy.

This result strengthens proposition 5 when Δ is low.

But when Δ is higher than 3, the order of the probabilities given in proposition 4, except for $p_{E\Delta/3} < p_{E\Delta/3 - 1}$, is no longer sure, because the mutation

Discrete evolutionary processes | 375

that leads an agent 2 to R when starting from any state E_i, with $i < \Delta/3$, has no impact. In fact, the mutant agent 2 gets an expected payoff equal to $(2i + \Delta - i)/\Delta$ instead of $(2\Delta - 2i)/\Delta$, and hence incurs an absolute loss of $(\Delta - 3i)/\Delta$, which is between $3/\Delta$ and 1. By contrast, the absolute loss incurred by a T playing agent 1 induced by this mutation is constant and equal to $(\Delta - 1 + 2)/\Delta - (\Delta - 1)/\Delta$, i.e. $2/\Delta$. Given that $2/\Delta < 3/\Delta$ regardless of the value of Δ, it follows that the mutant agent 2 switches back to L before any T playing agent 1 learns and switches to M. As a result, the asymmetry in figure 7b loses its force: the new graph of asymmetries is depicted in figure 10.

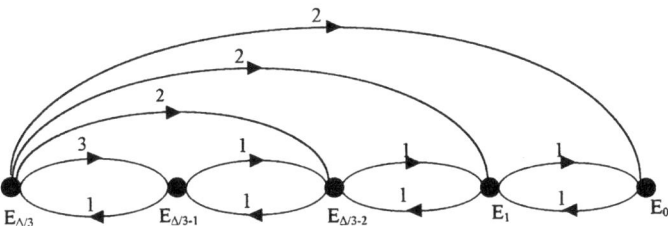

Figure 10: The number on the arrows is the number of one-mutation moves from the source to the arrival.

It follows that the limit Markov graph does no longer necessarily assign the highest weight to E_0, all the more that the switch from $E_{\Delta/3}$ to E_0 requires that many agents learn simultaneously, which happens with a probability decreasing in Δ.

Same remarks hold if we care about relative losses instead of absolute losses. In fact the relative loss incurred by the mutant agent 2 is $(\Delta - 3i)(2\Delta - 2i)$; this loss is higher than the relative loss induced for a T playing agent 1, i.e. $2/(\Delta + 1)$, when $i < (\Delta^2 - 3\Delta)/(3\Delta - 1)$. It can be checked that $i < (\Delta^2 - 3\Delta)/(3\Delta - 1)$ holds for each i lower or equal to $\Delta/3 - 1$, as soon as $\Delta > 3$.

Hence the result obtained in proposition 5 may not generalize to other learning processes. The only robust result is that the state, in which the maximal number of agents 1 play the weakly dominated strategy, is less observed than the state in which one additional agent plays the non weakly dominated strategy.

7. Conclusion: a look at forward induction

It derives from the above sections that Nash refinements like backward induction criteria and admissible equilibria are not ad hoc dynamically, in that they capture asymmetries which have an impact on the values of the stationary probabilities. Yet these asymmetries may be outweighed by other factors like

376 | Evolutionary game theory

the size of the populations and asymmetries in the probabilities assigned to the different available strategies in case of mutation.

Section 4 illustrates that, when isolated mutations sequentially perturb the system, agents can progressively adjust their behavior toward the perfect actions, without resorting to a special order of learning. We keep on in this section talking about special evolutionary processes, by turning, very briefly, to forward induction refinements.

We do not aim, in this conclusion, to develop a complete analysis of the evolutionary processes underlying the forward induction criteria. The game in figure 11 is only meant to draw attention to a special feature of some forward induction criteria.

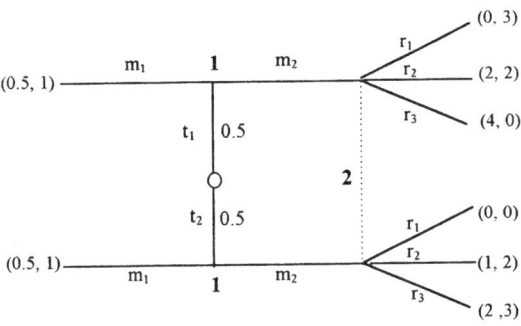

Figure 11: The player 1 can be of two types, t_1 and t_2, which occur according to a probability distribution that assigns the same weight to both types. Player 1 knows his type before playing, whereas player 2 only observes player 1's action.

In this game the outcome (0.5, 1), which corresponds to the equilibrium path E_1, in which m_1 is played by player 1 regardless of type, resists to many forward induction criteria for the following reason: t_1 is always better off with m_2 whenever t_2 is indifferent between m_1 and m_2. It follows that m_2 is an inferior strategy [1] for t_2 and should be assigned to t_1; hence it should be followed by r_1, which deters the first player from deviating to m_2. This reasoning namely underlies the criteria of Banks & Sobel (1987) and Kohlberg & Mertens(1986).

Yet the path E_1 is eliminated by other forward induction criteria (see for example Mailath, Okuno-Fujiwara & Postlewaite(1993) and Umbhauer (1991)), on grounds that assigning m_2 to both types with the a priori beliefs, for one induces these two types to deviate, for another is a consistent way to interpret m_2 given the implied actions. These criteria only select the equilibrium path E_2, defined by: player 1 plays m_2 regardless of type, followed by r_2.

---

1. see Kohlberg & Mertens(1986) for a precise definition of an inferior strategy.

In the game of figure 11, the only path observed over the long run, according to *NS*'s process, is also E_2. As a matter of fact, it takes fewer mutations to transform the system from E_1 to E_2 than from E_2 to E_1. E_2 can be reached from any E_1 state by switching an agent 1 of type t_2 to m_2. This switch can set off the following learning behavior: many agents 2 learn and play r_3, causing the agents 1 of type t_1 and t_2 to learn and play m_2, which finally leads the agents 2 to learn and play r_2. Switching from any E_2 state to an E_1 state requires more mutations.

The salient feature of the above behavior adjustment is that *many* agents 2 learn after the agent 1's deviation. In fact, let us suppose in this paragraph that *only few agents can learn at a same moment*. Stated informally, we turn to a *smooth learning process*. Let us consider an E_1 equilibrium state (beliefs are consistent with actions). In such a state, at least 3/4 of the agents 2 play r_1 after m_2. Let us again introduce a mutation from an agent 1 of type t_2 to m_2. This mutation now leads the agents 2 to smoothly switch to r_3. What matters is that this smooth learning can *only* (smoothly) lead *the t_1 agents* to switch to m_2, *because m_2 is an inferior strategy for t_2*, which ensures that the t_1 agents are incited to deviate to m_2 before the t_2 ones. But the deviation of these types causes the agents 2 to smoothly turn back to r_1, which finally leads the agents 1 of type t_1 to turn back to m_1.

The idea behind this illustration is that the notion of inferior strategy implicitly refers to a smooth, hence special, perhaps ad hoc, learning process. Future work can cope with the question of whether this seemingly ad hoc learning process expresses dynamic asymmetries that may have an impact on the stationary probabilities. Some insights into this question are given in Umbhauer (1996, 1997).

REFERENCES

J.S. Banks and J. Sobel, Equilibrium selection in signaling games, *Econometrica* **55** (1987), 647-661.

K. Binmore and L. Samuelson, Evolutionary drift and equilibrium selection, Social Systems Research Institute, University of Wisconsin Madison, Working paper 9529, 1995.

D. Foster and P. Young, Cooperation in the short and in the long run, *Games and Economic Behavior*, **3** (1991), 145-156.

D. Foster and P. Young, Stochastic evolutionary game dynamics, *Theoretical Population Biology* **38** (1990), 219-232.

D. Fudenberg and C. Harris, Evolutionary dynamics with aggregate shocks, *Journal of Economic Theory* **57** (1992), 420-441.

M. Kandori, G.J. Mailath and R. Rob, Learning, mutation, and long run equilibria in games, *Econometrica* **61** (1993), 29-56.

E. Kohlberg and J.F. Mertens, On the strategic stability of equilibria, *Econometrica* **54** (1986), 1003-1038.

G.J. Mailath, M. Okuno-Fujiwara and A. Postlewaite, On belief-based refinements in signaling games, *Journal of Economic Theory* **60** (1993), 241-276.

G. Nöldeke and L. Samuelson, An evolutionary analysis of backward and forward induction, *Games and Economic Behavior* **5** (1993), 425-454.

G. Nöldeke and L. Samuelson, Learning to signal in markets, Working Paper 9409, University of Wisconsin Madison, 1994.

L. Samuelson, Stochastic stability in games with alternative best replies, *Journal of Economic Theory* **64** (1994), 35-65.

R. Selten, Reexamination of the perfectness concept for equilibrium points in extensive games, *International Journal of Game Theory* **4** (1975), 25-55.

G. Umbhauer, Forward induction, consistency, and rationality of ϵ perturbations, Working paper BETA n° 9104, Université Louis Pasteur Strasbourg, France, 1991.

G. Umbhauer, Experience goods: an evolutionary approach, Working Paper BETA n° 9508, Université Louis Pasteur Strasbourg, France, 1995.

G. Umbhauer, Stationary probabilities in discrete evolutionary processes, Working paper BETA n° 9604, 1996.

G. Umbhauer, Induction projective et processus évolutionnaires discrets, *Revue Economique* **48** (1997), 697-706.

P. Young, The evolution of conventions, *Econometrica* **61** (1993), 57-84.

CHAPTER 17
BEHAVIORAL LEARNING

Jean-François LASLIER, Richard TOPOL
and Bernard WALLISER

Introduction

A behavioral learning process is an empirical description of the successive choices made by an individual in a repeated situation, when he only observes the results of his past actions. Study of these processes are part of the growing literature on learning, in individual decision-making and game situations. In a first part, we discuss this concept from the point of view of the history and the epistemology of Game Theory. In a second part, we review the literature on the proposed learning rules. In a third part, we compare a rule which is typical of this kind of models (the "Relative Reinforcement Randomized" rule) with the "Fictitious Play" rule.

1. The methodological relevance of behavioral learning

1.1. Classical Game Theory as a normative theory

After the initial period characterized by the work of John Von Neumann and Oskar Morgenstern, many developments of Game Theory, associated with the work of John Nash, tended to separate the problem of the choice of a strategy by an individual under risk from the problem of describing the combination of strategies chosen by several individuals in strategic situations. Modern presentation of Game Theory uses Desision Theory as a background which essentially provides the concept of utility maximization, and nothing more. The rationality of an individual is identified with the optimality of his behavior, a concept which is well-defined in Decision Theory. A central question of Game Theory is to extrapolate this identification to interactive situations.

The starting question of Game Theory is not like in most sciences the problem of finding regularities of the real world. Instead of aiming at a description of what actually happens in empirical game situations, the theory is designed to describe what *should* happen if rational players were in these situations. This point is perfectly explicit in Von Neumann and Morgenstern's *Theory of Games and Economic Behavior (1944)*. For instance (page 30):

> "... we wish to find the mathematicaly complete principles which define "rational behavior" for the participants in a social

economy, and to derive them from the general characteristics of that behavior."

Non-cooperative Game Theory here appears as a normative theory rather than a positive one; this term is for instance used by Van Damme (1987) and refers to the use of individual rationality as a norm (and not to collective rationality norms such as the ones used in Social Welfare Analysis). Assertions are not derived from observations but from the so called *general characteristics of rational behavior*. It should be pointed out that the very idea of a normative scientific theory looks puzzling for most scientists. Of course it is not, as the many sucesses of Game Theory are likely to prove. But it is true that one would like to have a positive theory of interactive human behavior, a theory of games explicitely conceived for predictive use, and testable.

One can define "Classical Game Theory" as the study of equilibrium situations under the rationality principle; this theory is the one which spreads over the whole economic field. An equilibrium is a fixed point of the best response correspondence. It is thus defined as a particular combination of joint actions for the various players. Each individual action which compounds an equilibrium does not necessarily result, at the level of an individual, of an autonomous maximization process. This reflects a holistic view violating methodological individualism. Consider for instance the very simple two-player game of coordination described by the payoff bi-matrix:

	A	B
A	(1, 1)	(0, 0)
B	(0, 0)	(1, 1)

According to Von Neumann, one should say that this game has no solution (in pure strategies); this is because, in the vocabulary of Von Neumann and Morgenstern, no player has an unambiguous rational strategy, and a "solution" is a combination of rational strategies. To quote again Von Neumann and Morgenstern (page 32):

> "The rules of rational behavior must provide definitely for the possibility of irrational conduct on the side of the others."

Consider the Nash equilibrium (A, A). Can we say that "rationality justifies the outcome (A, A)"? Suppose that it is rational for the second player to play A. From this it does not follow that it is rational for the first player to play A. Indeed, the rules of rational behavior for the first player must provide for the case where the second player does not play according to his rational action A and indeed plays B. Hence the answer to the previous question is no. Notice that, since the two equilibria (A, A) and (B, B) are not interchangeable, Nash himself would say that this game is not "solvable" (Nash, 1951).

Even taking the individual rationality norm as a behavioral hypothesis, the equilibria have little predictive power in this one-shot game: equilibrium "could" happen. Because they are interested in individual behavior, Von Neumann and Morgenstern clearly do not consider the Nash equilibria of such a game as admissible "solutions" and stick to the quest of individually optimal strategies (by enlarging the set of possibles strategies to mixed actions). One can describe the project of Von Neumann and Morgenstern as the quest for the meeting of two objectives (see Bacharach, 1989). The first objective is to find a decision process (called "rationality principles") which would be autonomous for each agent. The second objective is to study the interactions of several agents using the process. A game has a solution if and only if these two objectives meet. Most games have no solutions.

1.2. The quest for a positive Game Theory

Game theorists generally mention that there should be some trouble in taking too seriously the idea that actual games will be played at equilibria. For instance:

> "When asked why player in a game should behave as in some Nash equilibrium, my favorite response is to ask 'Why not?'" (Myerson, 1991, p. 106).

But in the applications, less care is taken and Nash equilibrium looks like the definitive tool for "solving games". Confidence in this concept can go quite far:

> "Fortunately, game theory provides a definition: two objectives are equivalent if they yield identical equilibria and thus identical predictions about outcomes." (Ordeshook, 1986, p. 159).

In many parts of Economics, including for instance Imperfect Competition, Auction Theory or Industrial Organization, the evolution of the theory has been to rely more and more on the Nash concept of equilibrium.

Obviously, equilibrium theory is not predictive when no equilibrium exists. When one exists, turning the normative theory into a positive one is always possible since equilibrium joint actions are observable. Real-world as well as laboratory data often show systematic deviations from equilibrium. If there were no such deviations, the normative theory would not only be a positive one but a confirmed positive one. Since the test is negative, it is difficult to interpret the deviations because of the ambiguous link between the two notions of rationality and equilibrium. Equilibrium without rationality is not even defined and individual rationality out of equilibrium has to be given a precise definition. For instance, one may add to the model a structure of errors and/or beliefs. It is possible to keep the idea of mutual best response if random errors are considered, either at the level of the payoffs or at the level of the chosen strategies. Such is the root of some refinements of the Nash equilibrium concept (Selten, 1975, Myerson, 1978; see Van Damme, 1987, for a survey on these refinements). The need for a positive and testable theory has led McKelvey and

Palfrey (1996) to provide an equilibrium model suitable for econometric treatment. This model is based on the idea that low-cost errors in the choice of the strategy are more likely to happen than high-cost ones. Of course, the specification of the statistical form of these deviations must be exogenously given.

1.3. Learning

In modern Game Theory, much work has been devoted to the question of learning. The fact that Nash equilibrium is not an individual concept but a collective one may lead to great difficulties in the treatment of the learning process: learning to play a Nash equilibrium can only be a collective process. But, by introducing a temporal dimension, learning allows for the breaking of the equilibrium "best responses loop". Unlike the so-called "mathematical theory of learning" (cf. Suppes, 1995), the first economic and game-theoretical literature on individual learning usually considers (more or less boundedly) rational individuals who know from the beginning how to solve maximization problems in a deterministic or probabilized environment (Fudenberg-Levine, 1993; Kalai-Lehrer, 1994). Hence the problem tackled by this literature is to understand how rational individuals learn how to play, rather than to understand how playing individuals come to act as if rational (if they do). In doing so, the theory is faithfull to its original formulation, a study of the behavior of *a priori* rational individuals. Methodological individualism is restored in the study of collective learning because of the individual decision process. Collective action is replaced by individual action together with interaction concepts like common knowledge, shared information or simply memory of a common history.

Research has later on tried to weaken the strength of the perfect information hypothesis as well as of the rationality hypothesis itself. Following Harsanyi (1967), incomplete information is already well taken into account by the standard theory, at least if one accepts systematic use of probabilistic priors for the lacking pieces of information. But the notion of bounded rationality (see Conlisk, 1996) has, for the moment, received no clear-cut and commonly accepted definition. And this despite the fact that the need for such a notion was early recognized (Simon, 1982).

Learning needs repetition, and the learning theories consider repeated games. Therefore, these theories naturally meet the other theories which are explicitely dynamic, and in particular the biological theories of Population Dynamics and Evolutionary Processes (see Sigmund and Young, 1995). But the analogies between Biology and Economics should not lead to forget that the postulates are rather different. First, an individual is not a population. Second, persons may be optimizing machines, but flowers are not rational in the same sense: as generally understood in Social Sciences, rationality of an individual embodies a notion of more or less concious cognitive process which has no place in the study of (say) flowers. On one hand, Evolutionary Game Theory can hardly be seen as another offspring of the theory designed by Von Neumann, John Nash and their many followers because it is definitely a positive theory. On the other hand, Evolutionary Game Theory cannot be considered as a theory of individual behavior because it essentially rests on group mechanisms. Some equations (such as the replicator rule) and formal results borrowed from Population Dynamics may well receive a different interpretation in terms of individual behavior, but such formal transfers should not mask that these theories investigate different objects.

1.4. Behavioral learning

With respect to the preceding discussion, learning has the following characteristics:

1. Individuals (rather than populations) are considered, and a rule of behavior is given at the individual level.

2. It defines which strategy a player is supposed to choose as a function of what that player observed in the past.

3. To be applied, the rule requires low levels of information, knowledge, computational skills, etc. In particular, in order to apply the rule, it is not needed to know which rules the opponents are using.

4. This rule may be random, meaning that a strategy is played with some probability.

5. The rule can apply in a variety of situations, including situations which are not "equilibrium" situations.

Several rules which have been introduced in the litterature satisfy these requirements. The simplest one is perhaps Cournot dynamics (playing today a best response to the opponents' move of yesterday), and another well known instance is fictitious play (which will be studied in the next sections of this article). An important distinction must be introduced (Waliser, 1998). One can consider that the individual observes the actions of the other players and responds. One can also consider that the individual simply observes the results of his own past actions. The first kind of rules describe epistemic learning while the second describe behavioral learning. Among behavioral learning rules, we shall consider the case where the player knows the strategies she choosed and what she then won, and nothing else. It is hard to imagine a poorer information set.

2. A survey of behavioral learning rules

2.1. General principles

One considers a repeated 2×2 game where each player plays an action at each period, knowing only her implemented past actions and the utility she got with each of them. For such a behavioral learning process, there is no known optimal learning rule, since each player faces endogenous uncertainty due to the fact that both players learn simultaneously. Such a rule could only be obtained as an equilibrium taken in a general class of rules, each rule for a player being the optimal one when her opponent plays his optimal rule. In contrast, when the game reduces to choice against risk, the player has an optimal rule given by the Gittins indexes, at least when knowing some prior probability on the states of nature (Gittins, 1989).

Hence, only heuristic rules can be proposed, a specific class studied below being grounded on two related principles. A utility index summarizes the past results of each action and a probability distribution deduces the probability of playing each action. Such rules have to satisfy further conditions, especially simplicity since bounded rationality is assumed for the players. They are eventually justified convergence conditions, especially towards maximizing actions in decision-making under risk.

Especially, the rule has to simulate the three – more or less continuous – successive phases that can be experimentally observed in a behavioral learning process:

– Pure exploration, where the player plays at random all actions, in order to get a first experience of the utility she can get with it.

– Sophisticated testing, where the player achieves a trade-off between exploration in order to make the utility of each action more precise and exploitation in order to maximize the expected utility she can get.

– Pure exploitation, where the player has made her mind about her best (eventually mixed) action and plays it systematically.

2.2. Utility index

At period t, if a given player plays action i, this is formalized by a Kronecker symbol such that $\delta_i(t) = 1$ and $\delta_j(t) = 0$ for the other action j; moreover, if the utility obtained at time t is denoted $u(t)$, the utility affected to action i can be written $\delta_i(t) u(t)$. The utility index $G_i(t)$ associated to the action i only depends on the preceding variables and on its initial value at period one:

$$G_i(t+1) = A((\delta_i(\tau))_{1 \leq \tau \leq t}, (u(\tau))_{1 \leq \tau \leq t}, G_i(1))$$

This index reflects the past utility obtained by each action and, by a conservation principle, the future expected utility used for exploitation of a given action. But it may also include some exploration component, giving a positive weight to the actions unsufficiently tested until now.

The most usual index AD_i is the adaptative index which is linearly updated at each period:

$$AD_i(t+1) = \lambda AD_i(t) + (1-\lambda) u(t) \delta_i(t), \quad 0 < \lambda < 1$$

It is proportional to a discounted sum of past utilities, with discount rate λ:

$$AD_i(t+1) = (1-\lambda) \sum_{1 \leq \tau \leq t} \lambda^{t-\tau} u(\tau) \delta_i(\tau) + \lambda^t AD_i(1)$$

When λ goes to one, it can be linked simultaneously to the cumulative past utility CPU_i and to the average past utility APU_i. Writing Π_i for the past frequency of action i:

$$AD_i(t+1) - AD_i(1) = (1-\lambda) CPU_i(t+1) = (1-\lambda) t\Pi_i(t) APU_i(t+1)$$

with:

$$CPU_i(t+1) = \sum_{1 \leq \tau \leq t} u(\tau) \delta_i(\tau)$$

$$APU_i(t+1) = \left(\sum_{1 \leq \tau \leq t} u(\tau) \delta_i(\tau) \right) \bigg/ \left(\sum_{1 \leq \tau \leq t} \delta_i(\tau) \right)$$

$$\Pi_i(t) = (1/t) \sum_{1 \leq \tau \leq t} \delta_i(\tau)$$

In addition to considering a utility index conditional on each action, it is possible to consider a global index associated to both actions, generally a combination of the individual ones:

$$G(t) = h(G_i(t), G_j(t))$$

Such an index is a summary of the utility obtained jointly by both actions and is sometimes interpreted as an "aspiration level" in the sense of Simon's dynamical satisficing model.

However, in this last model, a player tries at each period successive actions (in some order) until finding one above the aspiration level; if she succeeds rapidly, she increases the aspiration level for the next period and conversely. With the ungoing learning model, one action is directly chosen at each period and the global index acts rather as a "reference level" since it is increased if the present utility is above it and conversely.

The most usual global index AD is again the adaptive index which appears as the discounted sum of all past utilities:

$$AD(t+1) = AD_i(t+1) + AD_j(t+1)$$
$$= \lambda AD(t) + (1-\lambda) u(t)$$
$$= (1-\lambda) \sum_{1 \leq \tau \leq t} \lambda^{t-\tau} u(t) + \lambda^t AD(1)$$

It satisfies the following relation showing how it adjusts to the last observation of utility:

$$\Delta AD(t) = AD(t+1) - AD(t)$$
$$= (1-\lambda)(u(t) - AD(t)) = ((1-\lambda)/\lambda)(u(t) - AD(t+1))$$

A similar relation is satisfied by the average utility index, but not the cumulative utility index:

$$\Delta APU(t) = APU(t+1) - APU(t)$$
$$= (1/t)(u(t) - APU(t)) = (1/(t-1))(u(t) - APU(t+1))$$
$$\Delta CPU(t) = CPU(t+1) - CPU(t)$$
$$= u(t)$$

A more sophisticated individual index is suggested by the Q-learning method and writes (β being a discount rate):

$$Q_i(t+1) = Q_i(t) + \left[\delta_i(t) / \left(\sum_{1 \leq \tau \leq t} \delta_i(\tau)\right)\right] \left(u(t) - Q_i(t) + \beta \max_k Q_k(t)\right)$$

Such a relation stems in fact from the Bellman principle in dynamic programming since, when converging to a stationary state, the process obeys the classical induction relation:

$$Q_i(t) = \delta_i(t) u(t) + \beta \max_k Q_k(t+1)$$

During the learning process, the index obeys in fact the following rule:

$$\left(\sum_{1\leq\tau\leq t} \delta_i(\tau)\right) Q_i(t+1) = \left(\sum_{1\leq\tau\leq t-1} \delta_i(\tau)\right) Q_i(t)$$
$$+ \delta_i(t) u(t)$$
$$+ \beta\delta_i(t) \left(\sum_{1\leq\tau\leq t} \delta_i(\tau)\right) \max_k Q_k(t+1)$$

Hence, the first term (when $\beta = 0$) characterizes the average utility index $APU_i(t)$ while the second term (weighted by β) reflects the exploration value of each action.

2.3. Mixed action

At period t, each player adopts a "mixed action", the probability $p_i(t)$ of taking action i depending positively on index $G_i(t)$ and negatively on index $G_j(t)$:

$$p_i(t) = p(G_i(t), G_j(t))$$

More specifically, probability $p_i(t)$ is an increasing function r of the corresponding index $G_i(t)$ and is normalized:

$$p_i(t) = r(G_i(t))/(r(G_i(t)) + r(G_j(t)))$$

More specifically again, probability $p_i(t)$ is obtained by a power function with parameter a:

$$p_i(t) = G_i(t)^a/(G_i(t)^a + G_j(t)^a)$$

When $a = \infty$, the index-maximizing action is choosen with certainty, and reflects pure exploitation since it is a best response to the utility index:

$$p_i(t) = 1 \quad \text{iff } G_i(t) = \arg\max_k G_k(t)$$

When $a = 0$, any action is choosen with equiprobability, and reflects pure exploration since the utility index is not used:

$$p_i(t) = 1/2$$

When $a = 1$, each action is choosen proportionally to its index, and reflects a trade-off between exploration and exploitation since both actions may be played, but with differenciated probabilities:

$$p_i(t) = G_i(t)/G(t), \quad \text{with} \quad G(t) = G_i(t) + G_j(t)$$

In the last case, the variation of the probability can be easily computed:

$$\Delta p_i(t) = p_i(t+1) - p_i(t) = p_j(t) \Delta G_i(t)/G(t+1) - p_i(t) \Delta G_j(t)/G(t+1)$$

When applying the proportional probability to the adaptive index, one gets a probability evolution rule which can be written in an adaptive form:

$$\Delta p_i(t) = (1 - \lambda)(p_j(t) \delta_i(t) - p_i(t) \delta_j(t)) u(t)/AD(t+1)$$

$$= (1 - \lambda)(\delta_i(t) - p_i(t)) u(t)/AD(t+1)$$

$$p_i(t+1) = p_i(t)(1 - (1 - \lambda) u(t)/AD(t+1))$$

$$+ \delta_i(t)((1 - \lambda) u(t)/AD(t+1))$$

When applying the proportional probability to the cumulative index, one gets a similar evolution rule:

$$\Delta p_i(t) = (p_j(t) \delta_i(t) - p_i(t) \delta_j(t)) u(t)/CPU(t+1)$$

$$= (\delta_i(t) - p_i(t)) u(t)/CPU(t+1)$$

$$p_i(t+1) = p_i(t)(1 - u(t)/CPU(t+1))$$

$$+ \delta_i(t)(u(t)/CPU(t+1))$$

With either index, the deterministic associated process may converge towards a stationary mixed action:

$$E[\Delta p_i(t)] = 0 \Rightarrow E[\delta_i(t)] = p_i(t)$$

But with the cumulative index, the convergence is faster than with the adaptive index since $CPU(t)$ is always increasing while $AD(t)$ becomes constant.

Another probability evolution rule was proposed by Cross (1973) in a direct adaptive form (utility being normalized between zero and one):

$$p_i(t+1) = (1 - u(t))p_i(t) + u(t)\delta_i(t)$$

$$\Delta p_i(t) = (\delta_i(t) - p_i(t))u(t)$$

But this form, although proportional to the preceding expressions, is not reducible to them; it sounds strange because it is not homogenous in utility since the utility is not normalized by some utility index. A generalization of the Cross rule is proposed by Börgers-Sarin (1995) but it suffers from the same drawback and looks rather arbitrary:

$$\text{if } u(t) \geq AD(t) \text{ then } \Delta p_i(t) = (\delta_i(t) - p_i(t))AD(t+1)$$

$$\text{if } u(t) < AD(t) \text{ then } \Delta p_i(t) = -(\delta_i(t) - p_i(t))AD(t+1)$$

A different evolution rule is given by Karandikar et alii (1995) where the updated probability depends on the last action implemented, but not on the last probability:

$$\text{if } \delta_i(t) = 1 \text{ then } p_i(t+1) = s(u(t) - AD(t)) \text{ and } p_j(t+1) = 1 - p_i(t+1)$$

where s is an increasing function such that $s(x) \in [0, 1]$ and $s(x) = 1$ if $x \geq 0$. It can be written:

$$p_i(t+1) = \delta_i(t)s(u(t) - AD(t)) + \delta_j(t)(1 - s(u(t) - AD(t)))$$

3. A comparison between RRR and fictitious play

3.1. Presentation of the two rules

Among the classes of learning models, one sub-class consists in behavioral learning processes, a representative of which is the RRR rule (Lasher et alii, 1996). Another sub-class concerns the epistemic learning processes, among which the fictitious play rule (Brown, 1949) has been widely considered and discussed.

The comparison between the RRR and the fictitious play rules is here made within the framework of a repeated 2×2 game. Recall that such games generically exhibit three cases, as to their Nash equilibria: (i) one pure equilibrium, (ii) one mixed equilibrium or (iii) two pure and one mixed equilibria.

390 | Evolutionary game theory

Consider two players having to play repeatedly the same one-stage game with two actions (strategies) i and j for player 1 and h and k for player 2, and the following normal form bi-matrix. (with positive integer payoffs for each player):

	h	k
i	(g_{ih}, l_{ih})	(g_{ik}, l_{ik})
j	(g_{jh}, l_{jh})	(g_{jk}, l_{jk})

The RRR rule

In the RRR rule, the player's information is the simplest one: she observes her past actions and corresponding utilities. Then, at each period, she computes a "cumulative utility index" for each action. Finally, she chooses a "mixed action" the probability of playing a pure action being proportional to his cumulative index. For player 1, the probability of action i reads:

$$p_i(t) = G_i(t)/(G_i(t) + G_j(t))$$

where G_i is a cumulative utility index with null initial value :

$$G_i(1) = 0 \quad \text{and} \quad G_i(t+1) = G_i(t) + \delta_i(t) u(t)$$

Although the first player does not compute it this way because she is not aware of what her opponent played in the past, this cumulative utility can be written:

$$G_i(t) = (t-1)[g_{ih}x_{ih}(t) + g_{ik}x_{ik}(t)]$$

where $x_{ih}(t)$ is the proportion of times actions i and h have been simultaneously played by players 1 and 2 in the $(t-1)$ previous periods (similar expression holds for player 2).

Let us recall that this choice procedure is not a maximizing one. It relies on a probabilistic choice of actions which allows exploration to know utility distributions, as well as exploitation to obtain best results from them.

The fictitious play rule

In the fictitious play rule (Brown, 1949), player 1 observes at each period the actions h or k played by player 2. Let $(x_h(t), x_k(t))$ be the vector of the empirical marginal frequencies of the past actions of the opponent at time $(t-1)$. This frequence becomes the conjecture of player 1 about her opponent's future play: she believes that player 2's action will be chosen at random, with probabilities equal to the past frequencies. Knowing her utility matrix, she computes the expected utilities of her own actions:

$$v_i(t) = g_{ih} x_h(t) + g_{ik} x_k(t)$$
$$v_j(t) = g_{jh} x_h(t) + g_{jk} x_k(t)$$

Notice that $v_i(t)$ is generally not proportional to $G_i(t)$, indeed such is the case if and only if $x_{ih}/x_{ik} = x_{jh}/x_{jk} = x_h/x_k$. Finally, player 1 chooses a best reply to $(x_h(t), x_k(t))$: a pure strategy is played against a supposed mixed strategy. This can be written:

$$p_i(t) = 1 \quad \text{if} \quad v_i(t) > v_j(t)$$
$$p_i(t) = 1/2 \quad \text{if} \quad v_i(t) = v_j(t)$$
$$p_i(t) = 0 \quad \text{if} \quad v_i(t) < v_j(t)$$

This is a myopic choice of the best response to the beliefs because player 1 does not take into account the effect of his choice on the opponent's beliefs.

More recently, stochastic versions of the fictitious play have been developed. The stochastic aspect is introduced by Fudenberg and Kreps (1993) by assuming the payoffs are slightly perturbed. Kaniovski and Young (1994) proposed an extension where randomness relies on incomplete information of the players which is either due to the lack of information about what the other player has done, or to the variability of the players' payoffs, or to unexplained trembles.

To sum up, in both the RRR and fictitious play rules, the player's choice relies on some empirical frequencies which act as states variables, i. e. the ones deduced from his own past results in RRR rule, the ones observed from the opponent's past actions in the fictitious play rule. Finally, there are two questions related to both models:

(i) The arbitrariness and importance of initial conditions.

(ii) The equal weight given to each period. (This point can be avoided by a damped memory.)

3.2. Dynamics of the processes

The dynamics of the RRR and fictitious play rules are formalized by Polya urn processes which highlight their formal differences.

The RRR rule

The dynamics of the RRR rule is efficiently symbolized by a unique "referee urn", i.e. a non linear Polya urn containing four types of balls corresponding to the four possible combinations of the player's actions. At each period, one ball is selected by the modeller according to some "transition urn function" and one ball of the same type is then added to the urn. Formally, at time t, if $G_i(t)$ and $L_h(t)$ are the cumulated utilities obtained respectively by players 1 and 2 when playing actions i and h, the probability of playing the couple (i, h) at time $(t + 1)$ is:

$$r_{ih}(t) = p_i(t) q_h(t)$$

with:

$$p_i(t) = G_i(t)/(G_i(t) + G_j(t)) \quad \text{and}$$

$$q_h(t) = L_h(t)/(L_h(t) + L_k(t))$$

Notice that $r_{ih}(t)$ is indeed a function of the four variables $x_{ih}(t)$, $x_{jh}(t)$, $x_{ik}(t)$ and $x_{jk}(t)$. Similar expressions hold for the three other coordinates.

Remark: The dynamical process can physically be implemented by a couple of "player urns", i.e. linear Polya urns each containing two types of balls relative to the two actions of the corresponding player. At each period, a player chooses an action by selecting at random one ball in his own urn, and adds to the urn a number of balls of the same type, equal to the payoff he got. Of course, the evolution of the two urns are coupled since the payoff one player gets depends on the content of the other player's urn.

The fictitious play rule

The dynamics of the deterministic Fictitious Play rule can be symbolized by a couple of urns, one urn for each player. Each urn contains two types of balls corresponding to the two possible actions the player can play. At each period, player 1 knows the content of player 2's urn. She assumes (wrongly) that player 2 chooses randomly in his urn the action he will play. Player 1 then plays her best response to the mixed action defined by player 2's urn. Finally, player 1 puts another ball in her own urn, according to the action she took. Player 2 behaves in the same way.

A stochastic version of this model have been proposed by Kaniovski and Young (1994). The only difference is the following. At each period, player 1 draws at random a sample of s balls from player 2's urn and supposes that player 2 plays accordingly to this sample. This stochastic version of the fictitious play rule has two polar cases. If a sufficient sample is drawn, then the frequencies are those of the deterministic case and the standard fictitious play model is obtained; there will be no experimentation. As the size of the sample is fixed, its representativity is asymptotically weakened. If the sample consists of only one ball, then player 1, facing player 2's urn with proportions (π_h, π_k), chooses the action to play according to:

$$\underset{\{i,j\}}{\text{Arg max}} \{g_{ih}, g_{jh}\} \text{ with probability } \pi_h$$

$$\underset{\{i,j\}}{\text{Arg max}} \{g_{ik}, g_{jk}\} \text{ with probability } \pi_k$$

In this last case (as well as for the RRR rule), experimentation is active but may asymptotically disappear.

3.3. Results

Convergence results can be scrutinized both for empirical past frequencies, and for instantaneous probabilities of choice.

The RRR rule

In the RRR model, convergence of the past frequencies is equivalent to the convergence of the mixed actions. The convergence of past frequencies towards either pure or mixed equilibrium is studied in Laslier *et al*. (1996). The main results are:

(i) If the stage game has a pure strict Nash equilibrium, then the process will converge with positive probability towards it; nevertheless, even if the Nash equilibrium is unique, it has not been possible to prove that the convergence is with probability one.

(ii) If the stage game has a mixed Nash equilibrium, then two cases have to be considered. If the mixed equilibrium is accompanied by two pure equilibria, convergence towards the mixed equilibrium is with probability zero. If the mixed equilibrium is the unique equilibrium, then no result is available; however, in a slightly different model, Posch (1997) shows that if the system admits an invariant motion, then it will exhibit a cycling behavior with positive probability, but may as well converge to the mixed equilibrium or even to vertex fixed points.

The fictitious play rule

The first convergence studies were concerned by the convergence of the empirical frequencies. Nevertheless, in the recent past, some authors have been concerned by convergence of the continuation path (Nachbar, 1997).

The convergence behavior of the deterministic version of the fictitious play rule was proved in the case of a two person zero-sum game (Robinson, 1951). But Shapley (1964) shows on a specific game (with two players and three strategies for each of them) that the empirical marginal frequencies do not converge. This is due to the fact that the players play a sequence of couples of strategies inside a cycle and that each couple is played for a time interval which increases with the duration of the game. Shapley's counter-example being robust, there is no generic convergence for games with more than two strategies for each player. For generic 2×2 games, a proof of convergence was first proposed by Miyawasa (1961) but not published. Monderer and Shapley (1996) provide another proof. For particular games, convergence may not occur (Monderer and Sela, 1996).

The convergence behavior of the stochastic fictitious play rule is as follows.

(i) If the stage game has only one Nash equilibrium, either pure or mixed, Fudenberg and Kreps (1993) have shown that the empirical marginal frequencies converge with probability one to a neighborhood of the Nash equilibrium. Note that the empirical joint frequencies may not be consistent with the Nash equilibrium (Nachbar, 1997).

(ii) If the stage game is non degenerated, has two pure and one mixed Nash equilibria, Kaniovski and Young (1994) have shown that the empirical frequencies converge almost surely to a neighborhood of the stable Nash equilibria whatever pure or mixed.

The previous results are gathered in Table 1.

Table 1

The convergence of past empirical frequencies in the case of fictitious play and RRR rules, in generic 2×2 games

Types of Nash equilibrium	Deterministic fictitious play	Stochastic fictitious play	RRR model
One pure	yes	a.-s. convergence in a neighborhood	convergence with positive probability
One mixed	yes	a.-s. convergence in a neighborhood	no clear-cut result
Two pure One mixed	yes	a.-s. convergence in a neighborhood of the stable	convergence with $p > 0$ to each of the pure, with $p = 0$ to the mixed

REFERENCES

Bacharach, M. (1989), "Zero-sum games" in *The New Palgrave: A Dictionary of Economics*, J. Eatwell, M. Milgate and P. Newman (eds.) New York: Macmillan, Norton.

Börgers, T. and R. Sarin (1995), "Learning through reinforcement and replicator dynamics", mimeo.

Brown, G.W. (1949), "Some notes on computation of Games Solutions", Rand Report P-78, The Rand Corporation, Santa Monica, California.

Conlisk, J. (1996), "Why bounded rationality", *Journal of Economic Litterature* 34: 669-700.

Cross, J.G. (1973), "A stochastic learning model of economic behavior", *Quarterly Journal of Economics* 87: 239-266.

Fudenberg, D. and Kreps, D.M. (1993), "Learning Mixed Equilibria", *Games and Economic Behavior*, vol. 5, 320-67.

Fudenberg, D. and D. Levine (1993), "Steady state learning and Nash equilibrium" *Econometrica*, 61: 547-573.

Gittins, J.C. (1989), *Multi-armed Bandits Allocation Indices*, New York: Wiley.

Harsanyi, J.C. (1967), "Games with incomplete information played by "Bayesian players"", parts I, II and III, *Management Science* 14: 159-182, 320-332 and 468-502.

Kalai, E. and E. Lehrer (1994), "Rational learning leads to Nash equilibria" *Econometrica*, 61: 1019-1045.

Kaniovski, Y.M. and H.P. Young (1994), "Learning Dynamics in Games with Stochastic Perturbations", IIASA WP-94-30.

Karandikar, R., D. Mookhergee, D. Ray and F. Vega-Redondo (1995), "Evolving aspirations and cooperation", mimeo.

Laslier J.-F., R. Topol and B. Walliser (1996), "A behavioral learning process in games", ENPC Working Paper.

McKelvey, R.D. and T.R. Palfrey (1994), "Quantal response equilibria for normal form games" *Games and Economic Behavior*, 10: 6-38.

Myerson, R.B. (1978), "Refinements of the Nash equilibrium concept", *International Journal of Game Theory*, 7: 73-80

Myerson, R.B. (1991), *Game Theory, Analysis of Conflict*, Cambridge: Harvard University Press.

Nachbar (1997), "Prediction, Optimization, and Learning in Repeated Games", *Econometrica*, vol. 65, 2: 275-309.

Nash, J. (1951), "Non-cooperative games" *Annals of Mathematics*, 54: 286-295.

Ordeshook, P.C. (1986), *Game Theory and Political Theory*, Cambridge: Cambridge University Press.

Posch, M. (1997), "Cycling in a stochastic learning algorithm for normal form games", *Journal of Evolution Economics,* 193-207.

Robinson, J. (1951), "An Iterative Method of solving a Game", *Annals of Mathematics*, vol. 54, no. 2, 296-301.

Selten, R. (1975), "Reexamination of the perfectness concept for equilibrium points in extensive games" *International Journal of Game Theory*, 4: 25-55.

Shapley, L.S. (1964), "Some Topics in Two Person Games", *Advances in Game Theory*, vol. 26, 1-28.

Sigmund, K. and Young, H.P. (1995), Special issue: Evolutionary Game Theory in Biology and Economics, Guest editors; K. Sigmund and H.P. Young, *Games and Economic Behavior*, 11(2).

Simon, H.A. (1982), *Models of Bounded Rationality*, Cambridge: MIT Press.

Suppes, P. (1995), "Current directions in the mathematical learning theory" in E.E. Rosten (Ed.) *Mathematical Psychology in Progress.* Berlin, Heidelberg: Springer-Verlag, 3-28.

Van Damme, E. (1987), *Stability and Perfection of Nash Equilibria*, Berlin, Heidelberg: Springer-Verlag.

Von Neumann, J. and O. Morgenstern (1944), *Theory of Games and Economic Behavior,* Princeton: Princeton University Press (Sixth edition, 1990).

Walliser, B. (1998), A spectrum of equilibration processes in game theory, *Journal of Evolutionary Economics,* to appear.

CHAPTER 18
THE COMPROMISE BETWEEN EXPLORATION AND EXPLOITATION: FROM DECISION THEORY TO GAME THEORY

Paul BOURGINE

The compromise between exploration and exploitation is a key issue for learning processes as well as for evolutionary processes. All evolutionist processes have to deal with such a compromise between exploiting already found good solutions and exploring new possibilities.

In learning processes, this compromise has to deal with uncertainties of second order, that is: uncertainty about distribution of probabilities, of rewards, of stochastic dynamics, i.e. of all the constituents of a model for a specific decision process. Exploring allows a still poorly known model for a decision process to become more precise: the distributions quoted above become probabilistically better known. When exploring too little, one runs the risk of loosing a very good solution; the latter may be badly known but, for this very reason, it may have many potentialities that have not been enough explored. When exploring too much, one runs the risk is of incurring high costs of exploration while failing to exploit the best known solution. This is the meaning of the exploration/exploitation compromise: explore action in order to have more information or exploit best known action in order to have immediately more rewards. Thus the best trade-off between exploration and exploitation is also a feature of optimal experimentation.

Second order uncertainties are generally very difficult issues; it is not the aim of this article to deal with them in their global generality. We will only consider an abstract class of models, which is useful to illustrate the main features of the compromise exploration/exploitation; this class is known as the multi-armed bandit problem and constitutes the paradigmatic case of this compromise.

A k-armed bandit problem consists in k statistically independent arms which may be pulled in any order and one at a time. Each pull results in a random reward; the objective is to find a strategy that maximizes the expected present values of rewards over an infinite horizon. Gittins solved the multi-armed bandit problem, for independent rewards evolving in a Markovian way, by associating to each arm an index. His main result is that the optimal strategy consists in choosing at each decision time the arm with the best Gittins index.

The first part of this paper specifies the multi-armed bandit problem for decision theory. It is shown that it can be rational to experiment with a "bad" arm if it is not well known. It is also shown, if the Gittins indices converge, that it is rational to cease pratically to explore by exploiting the "best" known arm: but there is never any certainty that the "best" known arm is in fact the best.

The second part is an attempt to generalize the multi-armed bandit problem to game theory. Because of the learning process, the framework is a repeated game in a strategic form. The rewards are not well known; therefore it is a game with incomplete information. A direct generalization of the folk theorem is not easy and the important concepts of game theory have to be revisited in the case of incomplete information: (i) the concept of a penal code which is essential for the characterization of the subgame perfect equilibrium for the exploration/exploitation compromise: a backward induction procedure is provided to define an optimal penal code; it is conjectured that an optimal (or quasi-optimal) penal code can be obtained by minimaxing the index of a punished player. (ii) the concept of efficient strategy: the difficulty is that the Pareto frontier is moving with the information process; nevertheless, under the same condition of independence between the information processes related to actions, it is proved that efficient strategies are also index strategies. As in decision theory, when the indices converge, it is rational to explore a "bad" action combination and finally to stop exploring by exploiting the "best" action combination. But as is the case in decision theory, there is no certainty of converging to the Nash-equilibrium of the corresponding game with complete information, as already noted by [Kalai & Lehrer, 93].

There are some main features common to exploration/exploitation compromises: (i) they are open-ended processes; there is always uncertainty on whether they converge because of their stochastic nature; another reason reinforces this open-ended feature: when new arms or actions are found during the exploration/exploitation process, no convergence can possibly arise (ii) it is path-dependent, i.e. the continuation path is strictly dependent on the information accumulated; even in the case of a convergent exploration/exploitation process, there is no guarantee that two parallel paths of agents confronted with exactly the same reward processes converge to the same strategy; (iii) as a consequence, the convergence, if it arises, does not necessarily provide the Nash-equilibrium of the corresponding process with complete information.

1. Exploration/Exploitation compromise in decision theory

It is a very common situation to have to choose between exploiting a well known process or exploring new ones. Each process provides a sequence of rewards. If this sequence can be considered as a sequence of independent and identically distributed random variables, the process is a reward process.

Let us consider the two normal reward processes which yield sequences of independent and identically distributed normal variables (fig. 1.1): the first is a well known process while the second has only been very little investigated. The question is to decide which process one should rather presently go along with,

The compromise between exploration and exploitation | 399

given the current information described in the commentaries of the figure. With a discount rate of 0.95, for example, the theory indicates that the less investigated is better, despite its lower mean.

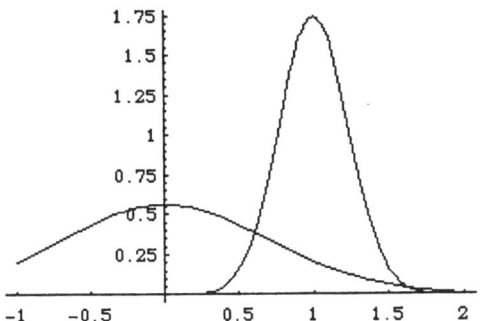

Figure 1.1: The distributions of two normal processes are represented on the figure. The first normal process has been experimented 20 times. Its empirical mean and standard deviation are (1, 1). The second one is much less experimented: only 3 times with empirical mean and standard deviation (0, 1). The theory indicates that the index of the less experimented (1.16) is better than the more experimented (1.11).

Because normal reward processes are a special case of bandit processes, the general case will be examined first.

1.1. The multi-armed bandit problem and the index theorem

A d-armed bandit problem consists of d statistically independent arms which may be pulled in any order and one at a time. Each pull results in a random reward and the objective is to find a strategy which maximizes the expected present values of rewards over an infinite horizon.

For rewards which evolve in a Markovian fashion, the problem was solved by reducing it to k independent stopping problems involving only one arm [Gittins, 75, 89]. Another Markovian solution is described in [Whittle, 81], which is both very elegant and efficient for computation. A more general setting relaxing the Markovian structure was then proposed by [Varaiya et al., 85] and [Mandelbaum, 86]. This more general setting is followed in the present article.

A d-armed bandit process is a collection of d pairs $\{(X_i, F_i), i = 1, ..., d\}$ where $X_i = \{X_i(t), t = 1, ..., \infty\}$, the reward process associated with the arm i, is a bounded real valued stochastic process and $F_i = \{F_i(t), t = 1, ..., \infty\}$, the information process associated with the arm i, is a non-decreasing family of σ-fields $F_i(0) \subseteq ... \subseteq F_i(t) \subseteq ... \subseteq F_i(\infty)$. $X_i(t)$ models the reward from the t'th pull of the arm and $F_i(t)$ models how the information accumulates through t pulls of that arm. Without loss of generality [1], X_i is supposed to be adapted to F_i. We assume that the arms are statistically independent:

Assumption 1.A: $F_i(\infty)$ are independent

A strategy is well defined as $T(t) = (T_i(t), i = 1, ..., d)$ i.e. as a function from time to N^d representing the number of pulls of each arm before time t. This function has to be measurable with respect to the information avalaible at time t, i.e. has to be adapted to the s-field:

$$F(T(t)) = \bigcup_{i=1}^{d} F_i(T_i(t))$$

Only one arm can be pulled at any time. The effect of a pull is not only to provide a reward but also to increase the information. This discussion about strategies can be summerized in the following definition.

Definition 1.1: A strategy is a function $T: N \to N^d$ such that:

(i) $T(0) = 0$

(ii) $T(t+1) = T(t) + e_i$ with one $e_i = 1$ and $e_{j \neq i} = 0$

(iii) $T(t)$ is adapted to $F(T(t))$

The present value $R(T)$ of future rewards associated with a strategy T is defined as:

$$R(T) = \sum_{t=0}^{\infty} a^t X(t) \quad \text{with} \quad X(t) = \sum_{i=1}^{d} X_i(T_i(t))[T_i(t+1) - T_i(t)]$$

The multi-armed problem consists in finding a strategy that maximizes the expectation of this present value. The solution of the multi-armed problem was first provided by Gittins for the Markovian case. The following theorem generalises his solution [Varaiya et al., 85] and [Mandelbaum, 86].

---

1. As remarqued by [Varaiya et al.], if X_i is not adapted to F_i, it is convenient to replace $F_i(t)$ by
$$F_i(t) = F'_i(t) \cup \bigcup_{s=1}^{t} \sigma(X_i(t))$$ the union with the σ-fields generated by the random process X_i. And by construction, X_i is adapted to F'_i.

Theorem 1.1. [Index theorem]:

The class of optimal strategies of the multi-armed problem satisfying assumption 1.A. coincides with the class of index strategies, i.e. always pull arms with the highest index $v_i(T_i(t))$ where the index field of a arm is defined as:

$$v_i(T_i) = \sup_{\tau \geq T_i + 1} \frac{E^{F_i(T_i)} \sum_{s=T_i}^{T_i + \tau} a^s X_i(s)}{E^{F_i(T_i)} \sum_{s=T_i}^{T_i + \tau} a^s} \quad (1.1)$$

This supremum [1] is over all the F_i-stopping times τ which are strictly later than T_i and are not necessarily finite. This supremum is attained by the following optimal stopping time [Mandelbaum, 86].

Theorem 1.2. [optimal stopping]: The supremum in (1.1) is attained by the F_i-stopping time

$$\tau_i(T_i) = \inf\{\tau > T_i | v_i(\tau) \leq v_i(T_i)\}$$

With the Index theorem, the d-armed problem as a d-dimensional problem is solved by considering d one-armed problems which are 1-dimensional. By the optimal stopping theorem, an optimal strategy is a forward strategy:

(i) at time 0, compute the indices of all arms;

(ii) pull a arm with highest index until its optimal stopping time is attained and return to (ii);

Under the condition that the indices are well estimated, index strategies are easily tractable because there is no need of a backward induction procedure to define the next optimal pull: the task of the decision maker is only to revise the index of the arm she is pulling, to keep constant the indices of the arms which remain inactive and to choose the arm with the best index; index strategies are a kind of forward induction strategies.

The last important point concerns the present optimal value. Its expression needs first the definition of the lower envelop of the index field and coincides with the present value of this lower envelope [Mandelbaum, 86].

---

1. More precisely, this maximum is an "essential supremum", i.e. an almost surely maximum [cf. Neveu, 75, p. 121].

402 | Evolutionary game theory

Definition: The lower envelope of the index field of an 1-arm and of the multi-arm bandit are respectively:

$$\underline{v}_i(T_i) = \inf_{0 \leq t \leq T_i} v_i(T_i) \quad \text{and} \quad \underline{v}(T) = \inf_{0 \leq S \leq T} \underline{v}(S) = \max_{1 \leq i \leq d} \underline{v}_i(T_i) \quad (1.2)$$

Theorem 1.3. [Optimal Present value]: Let $\hat{T}$ be an optimal strategy. Its present value is also the present value of its lower envelope

$$ER(\hat{T}) = \sum_{t=0}^{\infty} a^t \underline{v}(T(t)) \quad (1.3)$$

1.2. Markovian multi-armed problems

The general solution can now be specified for the Markovian d-armed problem. Let us consider a collection $\{(Y_i, S_i, \Pi_i, F_i), i = 1, ..., d\}$ of independent homogeneous Markov chains: the random process $Y_i(t)$ takes values in the measurable space S_i, moves according to the transition operator Π_i and has the Markov property with respect to F_i. Furthermore, when the chain is pulled in state $Y_i(t) = y$, it provides a reward $X_i(t) = h_i(y)$.

In the Markovian case, the expression of the index is simpler and becomes a function of the state in the space S_i.

$$v_i(y_i) = \sup_{\tau \geq 1} \frac{E^{y_i} \sum_{s=0}^{\tau} a^s h_i(Y_i(s))}{E^{y_i} \sum_{s=0}^{\tau} a^s}$$

If the arms has been pulled $T_i(t)$ times, the optimal strategy would proceed with the arm for which $v_i(Y_i(T_i(t)))$ is maximal.

We can now specify the Markovian case for a collection of independent normal reward processes. Each arm provides a sequence of independent identically distributed (i.i.d.) random variables: the distribution is normal with an unknown mean and standard deviation. Thus the states of the unknow process, which are the sufficient statistics $(m_i(T_i), s_i(T_i))$ of the empirical mean and the empirical standard deviation, moves randomly in R^2, according to a Markovian transition operator which is the Bayesian revision. Thus an index can be associated with each independent normal reward process.

The compromise between exploration and exploitation | 403

In the case of a normal variable, the distribution presents a location parameter and a scale parameter. It is proved in this case [cf. Gittins, 89] that the expression of the index with respect to the sufficient statistics $\{[V]FF[V]\}$ has the following elegant form:

$$v_i(m_i, s_i, T_i, a) = m_i + s_i\, v_N(0, 1, T_i, a) \tag{1.2}$$

where the index v_N has the asymptotic behavior:

$$\lim_{a \to 1,\, n(1-a) \to \infty} v_N(0, 1, n, a)\, n\, \sqrt{(1-a)} \to \frac{1}{\sqrt{2}} \tag{1.3}$$

The two terms in the index (1.2) express precisely the compromise between exploration and exploitation in the case of i.i.d. normal arm: the first term, i.e. the mean, represents the classical exploitation value, and the second the exploration value in the state (m_i, s_i, T_i). Let us note that the asymptotic decrement in (1.3.) of the exploration value with respect to n is quicker ($1/n$) than the decrement of the standard deviation ($\sqrt{n}$).

Definition: Let us consider a reward process which produces a sequence of independent identical distributed random variables, its Gittins index v and its empirical mean m. The exploration value is the difference $v - m$.

The case of i.i.d. normal arm is very important, because of the Central Limit Theorem: every i.i.d. random arm has asymptotically the behavior of an i.i.d. normal arm with the same mean and standard deviation. Thus, under some restrictive conditions [cf. Gittins, 89, p. 155], the exploration value has the same asymptotic behavior as in (1.2) and (1.3).

1.3. The exploration/exploitation compromise and its asymptotic properties

Let us return to the general case. First it is possible to introduce a kind of unicity of the optimal solution by slightly modifying the hypothesis. Suppose, following again Mandelbaum, that there is an extra lexical order between the arms, i.e. even very small extra preferences of any kind between the arms. Thus, in the case of equality of two indices (such a case is not generical), the lexical order leads to choose the arm with the best order, without changing the optimal present value. By introducing the slight modification of lexical order, the optimal solution is then unique.

Let us consider now what happens asymptotically in the case in which indices converge asymptotically when an arm is used infinitely often, as is the case of arm producing an infinite sequence of i.i.d. random variables. Then the only possibility for two arms to be chosen infinitely often, is having the same asymptotic indices: in the contrary case, the arm with the lower asymptotic index would have been already abandoned. Thus we have showed rather informally, that the convergence towards two (or more) arms (whose indices converge) happens only if their asymptotic indices coincide. Such a case is also non generic, and in general only one arm will be exploited asymptotically.

It is not necessary and even false to contrast two phases: an exploration phase where different arms are explored and an exploitation phase where it becomes certain that a particular arm will be chosen until the end. In fact the indices are path-dependent, and no certainty exists that an arm will be chosen the rest of the time, even in the simple cases of i.i.d variables. The exploration/exploitation compromise is a path-dependent and open-ended process.

In the same line of reasoning, there is no necessity that the decision process converges to the best "ideal" arm, i.e. the arm with the best asymptotic index (if it exists!). The final selected arm comes from the particular history of the decision maker: the final result is also path-dependent. By maximizing her present expected value in incomplete information situation, there is, as a consequence, no guarantee for the decision process to converge towards the best "ideal" arm. If she wants a guarantee for choosing the best arm, she has to perform more exploration between arms, which would fail to be globally optimal because of the cost of exploration.

The exploration/exploitation compromise is essentially the permanent compromise between exploring more to have more information and exploiting more to have more immediate rewards. Its most remarkable property in the case of independent arms is that the optimal strategy can be characterized by forward induction from the past history. Thus as an index strategy is optimal even if the future is not well known. It is not necessary to suppose that the list of arms is closed: it is even possible that new arms appear in the decision process.

2. The compromise exploration vs. exploitation and game theory

We will now introduce in game theory agents with incomplete information about their payoffs (cf. fig. 2.1). It is easily understable that new difficulties arise in contrast with the classical framework, where it is generally assumed that the players know the payoffs, at least their own payoffs: When one looks at Figure 2.1., what is the meaning of (i) efficient strategies and the Pareto frontier (ii) the subgame perfect equilibrium of the exploration/exploitation compromise in the presence of second order uncertainty; (iii) the penal code, very useful to define punishment strategies against a player, in case he deviates from an equilibrium of the game. Even the true structure of the game is unknown: it is impossible to say, for example, that the game is a prisoner's dilemma. This part is a first step to responding to such questions in the noncooperative game framework.

Because there is a learning process, we need a repeated game. For the objective of generalizing the multi-armed problem, we need that the game is in

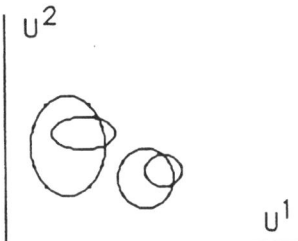

Figure 2.1: Let G be a two players repeated game in strategic form where each player has two possible actions at each stage of the game. The payoff processes are assumed to be badly known normal processes. As materialized by the confidence areas, an uncertainty remains on the precise positions of the four points corresponding to the average payoffs of pure action combinations.

a normal form. Thus an information process has to be attached to each action combination. The first task (§ 2.1) is to model the whole information process, and the relation of visibility of the information of the players *vis-à-vis* the others. But whatever the relation of visibility is, the learning processes of the players are coupled and the global process is thus a colearning game. Thus the class of noncooperative game with incomplete information will be named colearning games.

The axioms of rationality of the agents remain unchanged with respect to the classical theory. They are maximizing their Bayesian expected utility and know that the others do the same.

Two extremal directions of investigation exist according to whether the relation of visibility is only reflexive or complete. The minimal case is left outside the scope of this article; the rest of the paper is devoted to the maximal case of complete visibility. In this maximal case, the players have to search for the subgame perfect equilibrium (§ 2.2). But subgame perfect equilibrium is inseparable from punishment and penal code in the case of a deviation. We restrain this search to the set of pure strategies, because deviation is observable only in the case of pure strategies (ii) secondary they have to search for the more stable subgame perfect equilibrium which are the efficient strategies (§ 2.3). It will be proved that efficient strategies are index strategies with the same kind of hypotheses as in decision theory.

2.1. Repeated noncooperative games with incomplete information in strategic form

Let us consider a colearning game in strategic form with incomplete information between N players. For the one play game, the space of pure action combinations is $S = \Pi S^n$ where S^n denotes the finite space of actions of the nth player: a combination action is denoted by a crossed indice **i** in bold character. The payoff matrices $\{P^n, n = 1, ..., N\}$ are no longer well known reward processes but random reward processes with their associated information processes for each player and each combination action. We take the same notations as in the first part, except that the reward and information processes have a crossed indice **i** in bold character and an indice for each players:

$$P^n(T) = \{(X_i^n(T_i), F_i^n(T_i))\}$$

with $T = (T_i)$ the number of trials of the action combination **i**

The random character of each reward process expresses the role of Nature (often named the player 0) and represents for example the random effects of the player's (internal and external) environment. The associated information process expresses the incomplete information of the players; it models the information accumulated through the T_i trials and is an non-decreasing family of σ-fields; we add the non restrictive hypothesis that the reward process is adapted to the information process:

Assumption 2.1.A: $F_i^n(0) \subseteq ... \subseteq F_i^n(T_i) \subseteq ... \subseteq F_i^n(\infty)$ and $X_i^n(T_i)$ adapted to $F_i^n(T_i)$

In all cases, we assume at least that each player knows its private information processes $\vee_i F_i^n(T_i(t))$ and that the players are fully informed about the realized past action combinations: this past history $h(t)$ generates a σ-algebra $\sigma(h(t))$.

Assumption 2.1.B: each player knows $F^n(T(t)) = \vee_i F_i^n(T_i(t)) \vee \sigma(h(t))$

Finally, we have to describe how each player is informed about the information processes of the others. Let $I_n(T(t))$ denote this information process. The minimal hypothesis for a player is that she has no information about the information processes of the others: $I^n(T(t)) = F^n(T(t))$. The maximal hypothesis is that she has information related to all other players: $I^n(T(t)) = \vee_{n' \in N} F^{n'}(T(t))$. The general case consists in introducing the graph Γ of visibility by each player of the information processes of the others: $I^n(T(t)) = \vee_{n' \in \Gamma(n)} F^{n'}(T(t))$. The minimal case corresponds to a visibility restricted to private information.

A strategy for the player n is a function of the state of her information process inside the set $\Delta(S^n)$ of probability distribution on her space of actions S^n, i.e. a function adapted to her information process $I^n(T(t))$. The following generalizes the classical definition of a strategy which only takes into account the past history of action combinations (which is included in the process of information of each player by assumption 2.1.B).

The compromise between exploration and exploitation | 407

Definitions: a mixed (resp. pure) strategy of the player n is any function $t \to \sigma_n(t) \in \Delta(S^n)$ (resp. $(t \to \sigma_n(t) \in S^n)$ which is adapted to her information process $G^n(T(t))$. The set of such adapted strategies is $\bar{\Sigma}_n$ (resp. Σ_n) and the set of strategies is $\bar{\Sigma} = \prod_n \bar{\Sigma}_n$ (resp. $\Sigma = \prod_n \Sigma_n$). The utilities associated with a strategy is:

$$U_n(\sigma) = E^{I_n(0)} \sum_{t=0}^{\infty} a_n^t X_{\sigma(t)}^n(T_{\sigma(t)}(t)) \qquad (2.1.1)$$

Whatever is the crossed information of players about the information processes of the others, the global process is a coupled set of learning processes for each player, i.e. a colearning process.

Definitions: **G** = (N, S, P, A, Γ) is a colearning noncooperative game where N is the set of players, S is the set of action combinations of the repeated game, P represents the reward processes with their associated incomplete information processes satisfying assumption 2.1.A, $A = (a_1, ..., a_N)$ is the discount rate of the players, and Γ is the visibility graph of each player about the information processes of the others: the available information of each player at time t is $I^n(T(t)) = \vee_{n' \in \Gamma(n)} F^{n'}(T(t))$. Its space of strategies is $\bar{\Sigma}$ and the utilities associated with the strategies are $U(\sigma) = (U_n(\sigma), n = 1, ..., N)$.

Definition: The subgames $\mathbf{G}^{I^n(T(t))}$ are associated with each possible state $I(T(t)) = (I^n(T(t)), n = 1, ..., N)$ of the whole information process. $\hat{\sigma} \in \bar{\Sigma}^*$ is a subgame perfect equilibrium point of **G** if $\hat{\sigma}$ is an equilibrium point of each subgames $\mathbf{G}^{I^n(T(t))}$.

Such a definition extends the classical definition of subgame perfect equilibrium, which depends only on the action combinations history, to the whole information process history.

The important fact now is the following: for each player, there is a permanent compromise between exploiting well-known reward processes and exploring less known ones in order to obtain more information. Furthermore each player has to deal with the strategies of other players who are themselves dealing with the same kind of exploration/exploitation compromises. Thus we have the adequate framework for treating the exploration/exploitation compromises in a game with incomplete information.

A game with complete information can be considered as a very special case of a colearning game. Suppose that, for each player, each reward process is identically distributed (i.i.d) and very well known with mean (m_i). Then we can consider that the information processes are completed, i.e. $F^n(T(t)) = F^n(\infty)$ for each player in assumption 2.1.B. Thus the payoffs matrices are known and we have a game with complete information. In the same spirit, it is possible to associate conceptually to each colearning game its corresponding complete information game, by substituting $F^n(\infty)$ to $F^n(T(t))$ in the information processes of the players:

Definition: the complete information game associated with a colearning game $G = (N, S, P, A, \Gamma)$ consists in replacing $F^n(T(t))$ by $F^n(\infty)$, i.e. in assuming that all the reward processes are perfectly known.

As already observed in the first part for multi-armed problem, there is no hope that an optimal (or even a quasi-optimal) exploration in a colearning game leads to a subgame perfect equilibrium of its complete information associated game [cf also Kalai and Lehrer, 93].

2.2. Colearning noncooperative games with complete visibility of the information processes

There are now two extremal possible directions to investigate: the first one corresponds to the minimal visibility hypothesis for all players and the second one to the maximal visibility hypothesis. In the first one, the available information of each player on the others is contained in the past history of action combinations. In this case, we have to postulate that the players can only revise their beliefs about the strategies of the others by looking at this past history. The investigation concerns a framework which extends the framework of Kalai and Lehrer [Kalai and Lehrer, 93] to games with imperfect monitoring. In the second direction, there is a complete visibility for each player about the information accumulated by all the others. All the rest of the paper is concerned with colearning games with complete visibility.

Definition: the colearning noncooperative game $\mathbf{G} = (N, S, P, A, \Gamma)$ is with complete visibility (of the information processes) if the graph Γ is completely connected and there is common knowledge about the past information process.

We have now to discuss the concept of a subgame perfect equilibrium in the context of complete visibility. In this context, each player can, at least in principle, evaluate the utilities of the strategies for all players and find the subgame perfect equilibrium. But, in this context, the concept of a subgame perfect equilibrium is inseparable from punishment strategies for the case where a player deviates from the path of the equilibrium. But such deviation is not observable if the strategies are mixed: if actions are randomly chosen, there is no evidence for the other players that they are chosen with the optimal probability; the latter is furthermore changing with time and accumulated information. Only deviations from pure strategies can be observed. Thus, in order to have a concept of a subgame perfect equilibrium adapted to the information process, we have to restrict the strategy space to pure strategies:

Principle: in a colearning game with complete visibility, the subgame perfect equilibrium adapted to the whole information process is restricted to pure

The compromise between exploration and exploitation | 409

strategies. Thus the set of adapted subgame perfect equilibria Σ^* is included in the set of pure strategies Σ.

The most severe punishment against a particular player is a minimax strategy: such a strategy minimizes the expected discounted utility of this player and defines the minimal expected utility this player can earn in the game. We only consider pure strategies $\sigma = (\sigma_1, ..., \sigma_N) \in \Sigma$. We note classicaly $\sigma\backslash\sigma_n$ the strategy σ where σ_n has been substituted at the nth place.

Definition: a minimax strategy $\tilde{\sigma}^n\backslash\tilde{\sigma}_n$ against the nth player minimizes the maximal expected discounted utility of this player:

$$\tilde{U}_n(\tilde{\sigma}^n\backslash\tilde{\sigma}_n) = \min_{\sigma^n \in \Sigma} \max_{\sigma_n \in \Sigma_n} U_n(\tilde{\sigma}^n\backslash\tilde{\sigma}_n)$$

But a minimax strategy is not necessarily a subgame perfect equilibrium: some punishing players can have interest to deviate (and thus run the risk of being in turn minimaxed) because their minimax is better than their expected utility when they are punishing.

In order to avoid noncredible threats, a punishment for each player must be also a subgame perfect equilibrium in Σ^* (thus nobody can deviate): a penal code is a collection of N punishments, one for each player. But in order to be the most efficient, it also has to minimize in Σ^* the utility of the punished player.

Definition: an optimal penal code is a set of strategies $\{\tilde{\sigma}^n\backslash\tilde{\sigma}_n, n = 1, ..., N\}$ such that

$$\tilde{U}_n(\tilde{\sigma}^n\backslash\tilde{\sigma}_n) = \min_{\sigma^n \in \Sigma^*} \max_{\sigma_n \in \Sigma_n} U_n(\tilde{\sigma}^n\backslash\tilde{\sigma}_n) \qquad (2.2.1)$$

The following theorem is a simple generalisation of a classical result in game theory [e.g. lemma 4.2 in Friedman, 91]. Given an optimal penal code, it claims that no deviation can occur because of the penalties.

Theorem 2.2.2: Let $\mathbf{G} = (N, S, P, A, \Gamma)$ a colearning noncooperative game with complete visibility and $\{\tilde{\sigma}_n^{I(T(t))}, n = 1, ..., N\}$ an optimal penal code. Let $\mathbf{G}^{I(T(t))}$ its subgames, $\{\tilde{\sigma}_n^{I(T(t))}, n = 1, ..., N\}$ the restriction of the optimal code to $\mathbf{G}^{I(T(t))}$ and $\tilde{U}^{I(T(t))}$ the minimal utilities in this subgames. Let $\hat{\sigma}$ a subgame perfect strategy with its restrictions $\hat{\sigma}^{I(T(t))}$ to $\mathbf{G}^{I(T(t))}$ and the associated utilities $\hat{U}^{I(T(t))}$. Then:

$$\hat{\sigma}(t) \in S^{I(T(t))}(\hat{\sigma}^{I(T(t))}) \text{ where} \qquad (2.2.2)$$

$$S^{I(T(t))}(\hat{\sigma}^{I(T(t))}) = \{s \in S | \hat{U}_n^{I(T(t))} \geq \overline{U}_n^{I(T(t))}(s)\}$$

$$\overline{U}_n^{I(T(t))}(s) = \max_{s_n \in S_n} E^{I(T(t))}[X_{s\backslash s_n}^n(T_{s\backslash s_n}(t)) + a_n \tilde{U}_n^{I(T(t) + s\backslash s_n)}]$$

The above theorem can be used for the optimal code which is also composed with subgame perfect strategies. We obtain a backward induction procedure to determine the optimal code.

Theorem 2.2.3: Let $\mathbf{G} = (N, S, P, A, \Gamma)$ a colearning noncooperative game with the same notations as in theorem 2.2.2. Furthermore one sets $S_n^{I(T(t))} = S^{I(T(t))}(\sigma_n^{I(T(t))})$. The optimal penal code is defined by backward induction:

$$\hat{\sigma}_n^{I(T(t))}(t) = \hat{s}^n \backslash \hat{s}_n \text{ of } \min_{s^n \in S_n^{I(T(t))}} \max_{s_n \in S_n} E^{I(T(t))}[X_{s\backslash s}^n(T_{s\backslash s}(t)) + a_n \bar{U}_n^{I(T(t)) + s\backslash s_n}]$$

(2.2.3)

The proof can be found in appendice 1. It can be conjectured that optimal penal code or at least quasi-optimal penal code are index strategies: it is sufficient to minimax the index of a player to punish him the most severely. This conjecture is also discussed in the appendix.

2.2.3. Efficient strategies

The study of efficient strategies illustrates well the kind of difficulties arising in games with incomplete information. The underlying Pareto frontier (of the associated game with complete information) is not known: there is no certainty on the precise evaluation of expected discounted utilities (cf. fig. 2.1). Furthermore the frontier evolves in time even if the reward processes are assumed to be stationary over time: indeed the knowledge about the Pareto frontier changes through the experiments, and it can't become absolutely precise through the exploration/exploitation compromise.

It is difficult to start directly with the classical definition of an efficient strategy, because of the moving nature of the Pareto frontier. We start with a definition of an efficient strategy coming from the duality theory: for the concave parts of a Pareto frontier, an efficient strategy is associated with a vector of weights of the utilities of the players.

Definition: an efficient strategy $\hat{\sigma} = (\hat{\sigma}_n, n = 1, ..., N)$ associated with the vector $\Lambda = (\lambda_n, n = 1, ..., N)$ is a strategy which maximizes the weighted sum of the expected discounted utilities of the players

$$\bar{U}_\Lambda(\hat{\sigma}) = \max_{\sigma \in \Sigma} \sum_{n=1}^{N} \lambda_n U_n(\sigma)$$

(2.3.1)

The meaning of the vector has here to be interpreted as exogeneous, for example as coming from exogeneous different coalition structures in which the players participate. Under two restrictive assumptions, the optimal strategies are

The compromise between exploration and exploitation | 411

index strategies: (i) the information process associated with an action combination is supposed to be independent from those relative to the other action combinations (ii) the discount rates are the same for all players.

Assumption 2.3.A: the $F_i(\infty) = F_i^1(\infty) \vee ... \vee F_i^N(\infty)$ are independent

Assumption 2.3.B: $a_n = a$ for all players

Theorem 2.3.1: Let a colearning game $G = (N, S, P, A, \Gamma)$ with complete visibility satisfying assumptions 2.3.A and 2.3.B. The efficient strategy associated with the vector $\Lambda = (\lambda_n, n = 1, ..., N)$ is the index strategy corresponding to the weighted sum of the reward processes:

$$X_i = \sum_{n=1}^{N} \lambda_n X_i^n \qquad (2.3.2)$$

The proof is given in full in appendix 2. The additional assumptions are sufficient for the set of players to be in the same cognitive situation as a unique player. Thus the players are acting as a single player (the coalition of the players) and the compromise between exploration and exploitation providing the best strategy is the same as the compromise in the case of a single player facing Nature.

The above theorem defines a point of the Pareto frontier corresponding to the weighted vector Λ through an optimal compromise between exploration and exploitation. By changing Λ, this point draws the Pareto frontier.

Let us suppose first that the weights between the players remain constant over time. The index strategy is well defined but brings new pieces of information which modify the Pareto frontier. Suppose furthermore than the indices converge; then, as in the case of a single player facing Nature, the strategy of the players converges to a pure action combination.

If the weights between the players are changing over time, a more complex dynamics of deformation of the Pareto frontier arises. But the same procedure as above can be used to determine index strategies. And if the indices and the weights converge, the strategies of the players converge to a pure action combination.

Finally, it is also possible that the set of actions increases over time. As for a single player, optimal strategies still are index strategies.

As an example, let us consider the case where each reward process is known to be a normal reward process. Because the sum of normal processes is also normal, the reward processes (2.3.2) are characterized by the sufficient statistics (m_i, s_i, T_i) after T_i trials where m_i is the observed mean and s_i is the observed standard deviation. Because the indices are convergent, the strategy of the players converge (generically) to a pure action combination. The same holds in the more general case where all rewards processes are i.i.d. sequences of random variables.

In the same way as in decision theory, the asymptotic selection of a pure action combination is path-dependent: there is no certainty that the selected action combination corresponds to a Nash-equilibrium of the complete information associated game. The compromise exploration/exploitation presents its own subgame perfect equilibrium as discussed in part 2.2. An efficient strategy is not necessary a subgame perfect equilibrium: in order to be subgame perfect, it has to meet the conditions 2.2.2.

3. Conclusion and perspectives

A first step in the extension of the compromise exploration vs. exploitation from decision theory to game theory has been offered. The next most important step is to prove that optimal (or quasi-optimal) penal codes also are index strategies.

Index strategies are very useful for players with bounded rationality. They proceed forward from the past history and need only a limited backward induction procedure to evaluate: furthermore, if only ε-optimal strategies are searched, the approximation by the asymptotic form of the normal processes asymptotically equivalent to reward processes is very convenient. With such an approximation, the computation of index strategies has the same complexity as the myopic strategies which take into account only the empirical mean of each reward process.

Another essential feature of index strategies arises from their forward nature: they remain optimal in the case of new possible actions. Thus we know what is the optimal strategy for the remaining future, even though we don't know the main qualitative features of the future, like the exact list of possible actions!

Index strategies are cognitively very sophisticated because they take into account all the futures compatible with the accumulated information from the history of the players. True, they are only optimal in the case of independent information processes for the arm or the action combination. An other direction of research is to investigate how index strategies are quasi-optimal if there is dependence and to estimate the discrepancy with optimal strategies.

In game theory as in decision theory, it is rational to explore action even if this action is meanly less good than another one. The reason is the presence of values of exploration that are higher for less experimented strategies. It is also rational to stop exploring some actions. There is an exploration cost during the exploration phase. In the case of a convergence of indices, this cost leads to a convergent action which will be exploited for the rest of the future. But when

The compromise between exploration and exploitation | 413

one stops exploring, it is impossible to be sure of having reached the best action. This is the deep meaning of the compromise exploration vs. exploitation in (co)learning processes.

Appendix 1: optimal penal code

The theorem 2.2.3 expresses a backward induction procedure to construct an optimal penal code as a collection of N punishments strategies. We assume that the optimal penal code $\{\tilde{\sigma}_n, n = 1, ..., N\}$ and the related utilities $\{\tilde{U}_n, n = 1, ..., N\}$ are already constructed for a structure of information more precise than $I(T(t))$. We construct in this state $I(T(t))$ all the optimal action combinations $\{\tilde{\sigma}_n(t), n = 1, ..., N\}$ and their related utilities.

Without loss of generality, let us consider the optimal penal strategy against the player 1. This penal strategy $\tilde{\sigma}_1$ is subgame perfect and thus fulfills condition 2.2.2, which has to be slightly rewritten, because we are using 2.2.2 to search in this particular case an optimal action combination $\tilde{\sigma}_t(t) \in S_1^{I(T(t))}$ where:

$$S_1^{I(T(t))} = \{s \in S | \tilde{U}_{1,n}^{I(T(t))}(s) \geq \tilde{U}_n^{I(T(t))}(s)\} \text{ where}$$

$$\tilde{U}_s^{I(T(t))}(s) = \max_{s_n \in S_n} E^{I(T(t))}[X_{s\backslash s_n}^n(T_{s\backslash s_n}(t)) + a_n \tilde{U}_{n,n}^{I(T(t)) + s\backslash s_n}] \quad (A.1.1)$$

$$\tilde{U}_{1,n}^{I(T(t))}(s) = E^{I(T(t))}[X_s^n(T_s(t)) + a_n \tilde{U}_{1,n}^{I(T(t)) + s}] \quad (A.1.2)$$

As assumed in the backward induction argument, in A.1.1 and A.1.2 the utilities $\tilde{U}_{n,m}^{I(T(t)) + s)}$ related to the optimal penal code are already known for a structure of information $I(T(t) + s)$ more precise than $I(T(t))$: thus $S_1^{I(T(t))}$ is well defined. We now consider the expected discounted utility of the player 1, which chooses in $I(T(t))$ the best reply against the action combination s of the other players.

$$\tilde{U}_{1,1}^{I(T(t))}(s\backslash \hat{s}_1(s)) = \max_{s_1 \in S_1} E^{I(T(t))}[X_{s\backslash s_1}^n(T_{s\backslash s_1}(t)) + a_1 \tilde{U}_{1,1}^{I(T(t)) + s\backslash s_1}] (A.1.3)$$

Finally the other players want to punish as severely as possible without punishing themselves, in virtue of the definition of an optimal penal strategy. Thus they search a combination action $s \in S_1^{I(T(t))}$ (the strategy is locally subgame perfect) which minimizes $\tilde{U}_{1,1}^{I(T(t))}(s\backslash\hat{s}_1(s))$ (the penal code is optimal, taking into account the best reply of the player 1): let $\hat{s}^1$ be this strategy and $\hat{s}_1 = \hat{s}_1(\hat{s}^1)$ its best reply from the player 1. $\tilde{\sigma}_1^{I(T(t))}(t) = \hat{s}^1 \backslash \hat{s}_1$ as stated in the theorem.

414 | Evolutionary game theory

The same procedure can be applied to all the other players, providing all the optimal action combinations $\{\bar{\sigma}_n(t), n = 1, ..., N\}$ and their related utilities $\tilde{U}_{n,m}^{I(T(t))}$. The backward induction can continue. Theorem 2.2.3 is proved.

Remark 1: the optimal penal code is composed of subgame perfect strategies which are codefined through the same backward induction procedure.

Remark 2: if the punishing players have only one action combination, the most severe punishment is an index strategy. If there are more than one action combination, the same can be conjectured: the most severe punishment consists in minimaxing the index of the punished player, who is trying to maximize his index. Let us recall theorem 1.3 which provides the exact expected value in the case of an index strategy for the multi-armed problem:

$$ER(\hat{T}) = \sum_{t=0}^{\infty} a^t \underline{v}(T(t))$$

A remaining question is how to switch from one to another of a set of multi-armed problems. There is no easy argument to solve this switching problem, even if it is quite intuitive in the above expression that index strategies are optimal or quasi optimal.

Appendix 2: efficient strategies

We now prove theorem 2.3.1. Under assumptions 2.3.A and 2.3.B, efficient strategies are index strategies:

By using 2.1.1 and 2.3.1:

$$\ddot{U}_A(\hat{\sigma}) = \max_{\sigma \in \Sigma} \sum_{n=1}^{N} \lambda_n U_n(\sigma) \quad \text{with} \quad U_n(\sigma) = E^{I_n(0)} \sum_{t=0}^{\infty} a_n^t X_{\sigma(t)}^n(T_{\sigma(t)}(t))$$

Thus:

$$\ddot{U}_A(\hat{\sigma}) = \max_{\sigma \in \Sigma} \sum_{n=1}^{N} \lambda_n E^{I_n(0)} \sum_{t=0}^{\infty} a_n^t X_{\sigma(t)}^n(T_{\sigma(t)}(t))$$

by exchanging the Σ operator and the expectation operator E:

$$\ddot{U}_A(\hat{\sigma}) = \max_{\sigma \in \Sigma} E^{I_n(0)} \sum_{n=1}^{\infty} \lambda_n \sum_{t=0}^{\infty} a_n^t X_{\sigma(t)}^n(T_{\sigma(t)}(t))$$

by exchanging the two Σ operator:

$$\ddot{U}_A(\hat{\sigma}) = \max_{\sigma \in \Sigma} E^{I_n(0)} \sum_{t=0}^{\infty} \sum_{n=1}^{N} \lambda_n a_n^t X_{\sigma(t)}^n(T_{\sigma(t)}(t))$$

By using assumption 2.3.B, all the discount rates are the same:

$$\ddot{U}_A(\hat{\sigma}) = \max_{\sigma \in \Sigma} E^{I_n(0)} \sum_{t=0}^{\infty} a^t \sum_{n=1}^{N} \lambda_n X_{\sigma(t)}^n(T_{\sigma(t)}(t))$$

By introducing the weighted information process $X_i = \sum_{n=1}^{N} \lambda_n X_i^n$ related to each action combination **i**,

$$\ddot{U}_A(\hat{\sigma}) = \max_{\sigma \in \Sigma} E^{I_n(0)} \sum_{t=0}^{\infty} a^t X_{\sigma(t)}(T_{\sigma(t)}(t))$$

Assumption 2.3.A provides the independence between all the information processes related to the action combinations. Thus the theorem 1.1 can be applied and the theorem is proved whatever the information processes are, if they are independent.

REFERENCES

Friedman J.W. (1991), *Game Theory with Applications to Economics*, Second Edition, Oxford, Oxford University Press.

Harsanyi J.C. (1988), *Rational Behavior and Bargaining Equilibrium in Games and Social Situations*, Cambridge, Cambridge University Press.

Holland J.H. (1975), *Adaptation in natural and artificial systems*. Ann Arbor, University of Michigan Press.

Gittins J.C. (1975), The two-armed bandit problem: variation on a conjecture by H. Chernoff, *Sankya A*, 37, 287-291.

Gittins J.C. (1989), *Multi-armed Bandit: Allocation Indices*, John Wiley & Sons.

Kalai E. and E. Lehrer (1993), Rational Learning Leads to Nash Equilibrium, *Econometrica*, Vol. 61, No. 5, p. 1019-1045, September, 1993.

Kreps D. M. (1990), *A Course in Microeconomic Theory*, Harvester Wheatsheaf.

Mandelbaum A. (1986), Discrete Multi-armed Bandits and Multi-parameter Processes, *Probability Theory & Related Fields*, No. 71, p. 127-145, 1986.

Varaiya P.P., J.C. Walrand and C. Buyukkoc (1985), Extensions of the Multi-armed Problem: the Discounted Case. *IEEE Transactions on Automatic Control*, Vol. AC-30, No. 5, May 1985.

Whittle P. (1981), Multi-armed bandits and the Gittins index, *J. Roy. Statist. Soc. Ser. B.*, 42, 143-149.

Whittle P. (1982), *Optimization Over Time*, vols. I, II, John Wiley & Sons.

Imprimé en France. – JOUVE, 18, rue Saint-Denis, 75001 PARIS
N° 252604E. Dépôt légal : Août 1998